SETTLING SASKATCHEWAN

© 2013 University of Regina Press.

All rights reserved. No part of this work covered by the copyrights hereon may be reproduced or used in any form or by any means—graphic, electronic, or mechanical—without the prior written permission of the publisher. Any request for photocopying, recording, taping or placement in information storage and retrieval systems of any sort shall be directed in writing to Access Copyright.

Printed and bound in Canada at Friesens.

The text of this book is printed on 100% post-consumer recycled paper with earth-friendly vegetable-based inks.

COVER AND TEXT DESIGN:
Duncan Campbell, University of Regina Press.

COPY EDITOR:
Dallas Harrison.

EDITOR FOR THE PRESS:
David McLennan, University of Regina Press.

INDEX PREPARED BY:
Judy Dunlop.

Cover photo: Archives of Manitoba, Foote 466 (N2066).

Library and Archives Canada Cataloguing in Publication
Cataloguing in Publication (cip) data available
at the Library and Archives Canada web site: *www.collectionscanada.gc.ca*
and at www.uofrpress.ca/publications/Settling-Saskatchewan

10 9 8 7 6 5 4 3 2 1

University of Regina Press, University of Regina
Regina, Saskatchewan, Canada, S4S 0A2
TEL: (306) 585-4758 FAX: (306) 585-4699
WEB: www.uofrpress.ca

The University of Regina Press received a grant for research and development of this publication from the Creative Enterprise Entrepreneurship Fund of the Saskatchewan Arts Board.

The University of Regina Press acknowledges the support of the Creative Industry Growth and Sustainability program, made possible through funding provided to the Saskatchewan Arts Board by the Government of Saskatchewan through the Ministry of Parks, Culture, and Sport.

We also acknowledge the financial support of the Government of Canada through the Canada Book Fund for our publishing activities.

SETTLING SASKATCHEWAN

ALAN B. ANDERSON

University of Regina Press

CONTENTS

Preface—**VII**

List of Abbreviations—**IX**

Chapter 1
Introduction—**1**

Chapter 2
Aboriginal Reserves and Settlements—**22**

Chapter 3
British Settlements—**43**

Chapter 4
Germanic Settlements—**77**

Chapter 5
Ukrainian and Polish Settlements—**155**

Chapter 6
The Settlements of Other Eastern European Groups—**207**

Chapter 7
French Settlements—**238**

Chapter 8
Nordic Settlements—**309**

Chapter 9
Other Settlements and Urban Minorities—**350**

Chapter 10
Conclusion: Changing Times—**373**

Notes—**411**

Selected Bibliography—**436**

Index—**444**

About the Author—**485**

PREFACE

This book is the culmination of many years, even decades, of studying and writing about ethnic settlements in Saskatchewan. It represents an attempt to bring together in a single volume a comprehensive historical, geographical, and sociological overview of these settlements. It is a synthesis of three types of my personal work. First, I have made much use of my original doctoral research on ethnic identity change in the bloc settlements of a particular region of Saskatchewan, some four decades ago, back in 1968–72. That detailed study—which involved personally interviewing a thousand respondents in twenty bloc settlements and colonies—in turn led to many publications (mostly journal articles and chapters in edited books) as well as academic conference presentations pertaining to various specific topics. Second, this book draws substantially on my studies of particular ethnic groups in Saskatchewan—mainly French, Germans and Mennonites, Ukrainians, Scandinavians and Finns—found in research monographs, chapters, and conference proceedings. Third, the book utilizes my recent work for the *Atlas of Saskatchewan* (1999) and the *Encyclopedia of Saskatchewan* (2005), which updated my earlier writing and added commentaries on the settlements of many other ethnic groups; as a member of the editorial board for the encyclopedia, I was privileged to be responsible for coordinating writing by many contributors on population, immigration, and ethnic group settlements and communities. I am most grateful for the enthusiastic support of this project consistently shown by the Canadian Plains Research Center at the University of Regina.

It is perhaps surprising that historians and social scientists have devoted relatively limited attention to the development, character, and duration of ethnic settlements in Saskatchewan. Indeed, some of the best work has been recent and current. This is a story that should be told. The selected bibliographical sources accompanying each chapter might seem to reveal an expansive and continuously growing literature on immigration and settlement history in Saskatchewan. However, on the one hand, general histories of the province have tended not to devote as much attention as one might expect to this subject; on the other hand, most of the literature seems to have been on details of particular ethnic communities rather than on any analysis of demographic and social trends.

So this book aims at an overview, providing a framework that can link the general aspects of Saskatchewan history with details on particular ethnic settlements and communities while analyzing socio-demographic changes. My intention has been to produce an informative volume that will stimulate readers' interest in and appreciation of the vast ethnocultural diversity that has come to characterize the people of Saskatchewan.

LIST OF ABBREVIATIONS

AANDC	Aboriginal Affairs and Northern Development Canada
ACF	Assemblée communautaire fransaskoise
ACFC	Association catholique franco-canadienne
AHEPA	American Hellenic Educational Progressive Association
ALC	American Lutheran Church
AMNSIS	Association of Métis and Non-Status Indians of Saskatchewan
CCA	Canada Colonization Association
CCF	Cooperative Commonwealth Federation
CMA	Census Metropolitan Area
CMS	Church Missionary Society
CNLSA	Canadian National Land Settlement Association
CNR	Canadian National Railway
CPR	Canadian Pacific Railway
CSF	Conseil scolaire fransaskois
DCANR	Department of Colonization, Agriculture and Natural Resources
ELCC	Evangelical Lutheran Church of Canada
ELCIC	Evangelical Lutheran Church in Canada
EMB	Evangelical Mennonite Brethren
EMMC	Evangelical Mennonite Mission Conference
HBC	Hudson's Bay Company
JCA	Jewish Colonization Association
KMB	Krimmer Mennonite Brethren
LCA	Lutheran Church of America
LCC	Lutheran Church Canada
LICO	Low-Income Cut-Off
MCC	Mennonite Church Canada
MLA	Member of the Legislative Assembly
MNS	Métis Nation of Saskatchewan
NDP	New Democratic Party
NWC	North West Company
NWMP	North-West Mounted Police
OCA	Orthodox Church in America
PO	post office
RCAF	Royal Canadian Air Force
RM	rural municipality
SARM	Saskatchewan Association of Rural Municipalities
SGC	Saskatchewan German Council
SIA	Saskatchewan Intercultural Association
SMC	Saskatoon Multicultural Council
SODS	Saskatoon Open Door Society
SSTA	Saskatchewan School Trustees Association
UOCC	Ukrainian Orthodox Church of Canada

Chapter 1
INTRODUCTION

Vast areas of the Canadian prairies have been settled by particular ethnic or ethno-religious groups. In fact, most of the southern half of Saskatchewan, the grassland and parkland, was settled by people of specific ethnic origins and traditional religious affiliations. They established numerous bloc or group settlements within which most people were of the same ethnic and often religious identity. While rapidly an incredible ethnic and religious diversity came to characterize the rural prairies, almost all of these settlers were ultimately of European ethnic origins. Yet in a sense, prior to the establishment of bloc settlements, Aboriginal people had already contributed substantially to ethnic diversity in the prairies.

After commenting briefly on Aboriginal reserves and settlements as representing the first group settlements in Saskatchewan, this introductory chapter will proceed to describe how homesteading related to the bloc settlement process. Yet defining ethnic bloc settlements with any precision can be problematic, so we need to consider sociodemographic factors such as the size and extent of settlements as well as their relative ethnic and religious homogeneity/heterogeneity. Then historical periods of settlement will be discussed: following the consolidation of Aboriginal territoriality, settlement primarily by people of diverse European origins, the survival of ethnic settlements during the 1930s (the "dirty thirties"), and finally the process of "delocalization," which involved the closure of small country schoolhouses, the disappearance of community halls, rural depopulation, urbanization, and out-migration. Finally, the organization of the book will be explained and how ethnic group settlements can be categorized.

ABORIGINAL RESERVES: THE FIRST GROUP SETTLEMENTS
As we will see in more detail in the second chapter, in a certain sense Aboriginal reserves and settlements constituted the first group settlements within what is today the

Province of Saskatchewan. Before people of European ethnic origins began settling on the prairies, First Nations viewed all of Saskatchewan (and beyond) as their legitimate territory; however, with contact with non-Aboriginal people, these First Nations were eventually obliged—or reluctantly agreed—to consolidate their traditional territories into specific reserves. Thus, Indian reserves were essentially legally defined ethnic bloc settlements within specific boundaries. However, not all Aboriginal people were contained within reserves. In due course, most "Non-Status Indian" people either became concentrated in communities where they predominated or settled close to Indian reserves. Moreover, the Métis population, of mixed Aboriginal and European (usually French or Scottish) descent, emerged since the first contact between fur traders and the Native population. Gradually, many Métis formed their own named settlements or eventually merged into a larger francophone population.

Yet there was an important distinction between Aboriginal reserves and settlements and ethnic bloc settlements established by non-Aboriginal peoples. Aboriginal people—be they First Nations (Registered Indians), Non-Status Indians, or Métis—did not originally form settlements as such; rather, their later settlement process, which established legal reserves or non-legal settlements and communities, represented a consolidation of their territoriality instead of a completely new claim to territory, as was often the case of non-Aboriginal ethnic groups. The result, following the establishment of Indian reserves and other Aboriginal settlements primarily during the 1870s, was that these widespread pieces of Aboriginal territory came to form parts of an extremely complex ethno-cultural mosaic stretching across the Prairie West.

HOMESTEADING AND THE BLOC SETTLEMENT PROCESS

Since the opening of Canadian prairie land to homesteading in 1872, much of the prairie (grassland and parkland) area of Saskatchewan has been settled by ethnic or, more specifically, ethno-religious groups who have formed their own bloc settlements.

Before considering how ethnic identity changes, we would do well to learn why these bloc settlements came into existence in the first place.[1] Description of the initial founding of the settlements should provide some explanation of the raison d'être of this form of social organization, thus a partial answer to its persistence. First, bloc settlements resulted from consolidation of a larger territory initially settled by a particular ethnic group that found itself in a minority position within the region. Such was the case of the Métis, who resisted by armed conflict (the North-West Resistance of 1884–85) anticipated incursions by later settlers. Second, bloc settlements resulted from importation of a similar form of social organization from Europe by immigrants who formerly occupied minority positions there as well. Associated with this importation might have been religious values advocating pacifism, as among Mennonites, Hutterites, and Doukhobors. Third, bloc settlements resulted from colonization schemes of the federal government and ethnic or religious agencies. Such schemes introduced to Saskatchewan German Catholics from the American Midwest; French from France, Quebec, and the United States; Ukrainians, Poles, and other ethnic groups from Eastern Europe; and Scandinavians from Scandinavia and the American Midwest. We can speculate that the decision to settle here rather than emigrate to, or stay in, the United States might have revealed a dislike for a proclaimed "melting-pot" attitude in that country and a preference for a Canadian "cultural mosaic," a belief that Canada would be more tolerant of ethnic minorities perhaps holding unique beliefs (e.g., an emphasis on pacifism), and especially an appreciation of less expensive and more readily available farmland in Canada.

The questions of why and how bloc settlements came into existence are basic to understanding the complexity of ethno-religious identity as well as the nature of identity change in those settlements.[2] Although, in a sense, group settlements also resulted from territorial consolidation, as among First Nations and Métis, and strictly speaking not all non-Aboriginal settlers were immigrants (many arrived from other Canadian provinces), the vast majority of settlers were in fact immigrants directly from Europe or via the United States. So let us now examine respectively the immigrants' motives for settling in Saskatchewan, then various schemes and organizations responsible for promoting or opposing the mass immigration of non-British settlers, before discussing the processes by which bloc settlements began to form. Subsequent chapters will describe the formation and expansion of the bloc settlements of each ethnic or ethno-religious group in the province.

To commence, then, with the reasons for migration, we can distinguish the factors pushing the migrant from a place of origin from those pulling the migrant to a new destination.[3] The principal "push" factors were overpopulation, impoverishment, political discontent, and persecution (perhaps leading to forced migration or mass expulsion) in the sending country. Among the most significant "pull" factors were the recruitment of immigrants by the government of the new country to offset low internal migration, the recruitment by agencies seeking cheap labour, the influence of settlers writing home, and the transportation of immigrants as a lucrative business; moreover, the establishment of planned utopian and religious settlements was particularly important. Admittedly, certain factors considered as "push" from one standpoint might be seen as "pull" from another standpoint. For example, Canada engaged in purposeful commercial colonization to exploit natural resources and to extend its political influence by importing continental European immigrants as pioneering grain farmers who would ensure stabilization of the restive Métis and First Nations out west. Doubtless virtually all of the "push" and "pull" factors affected migration into the bloc settlements of the Prairie Provinces.

Now let us turn from ultimate reasons for migration to specific schemes involving the actual process of migration. Immigration can be seen as primarily, though not entirely, an individual undertaking or a collective drift rather than an organized group movement. Yet whole villages have been known to migrate to another country, and governments regulate, direct, and encourage or discourage migration.[4]

What exactly were the Canadian government's policies on immigration during the decades when the vast majority of settlers arrived? Toward the end of the nineteenth century, in competition with the fairly open American immigration policy, the Canadian campaign for immigrants intensified. In 1891, census results indicated an unsatisfactory increase in population during the previous decade.[5] When Clifford Sifton became Minister of the Interior in 1896, he immediately began to encourage immigration.[6] Agents were appointed throughout Europe, even though most European countries had strict laws against emigration; the quest for migrants was publicized through circulars, exhibits, and advertisements; transportation companies were federally subsidized. Moreover, the flow of Central and Eastern European migrants to the Canadian prairies was soon enhanced, no doubt, by the imposition of American quota restrictions.

Settlement of the prairies by people of European origin (and to a considerable extent their descendants in Eastern Canada and the United States) assumed a utopian character with Christian religious references to the "Promised Land."[7] Every sort of device was employed to attract immigrants, including those who had first settled in the United States, to the Canadian prairies. One poster read "Good-bye South Dakota! Trainloads of settlers and their effects ... Bound for the Canadian North-West ... Free land ... plenty of timber ... pure water ... no more two bushels per acre ... no more five mile water haul ... no more grinding machine agents... Hurrah for Canada!"[8] Sifton was especially eager to encourage immigration from the United States.[9] American settlers arrived by every means, including covered wagons drawn by teams of horses, and those who had sold their farms before heading north could afford to pay the Canadian Pacific Railway (CPR) price of five dollars an acre for less remote railway land.[10]

Many of the 160,000 initial continental settlers in Saskatchewan by 1911 were secured through the efforts of the North Atlantic Trading Company, which had an agreement with the Canadian government since 1899. The company was obligated to spend a minimum of $15,000 annually to secure immigrants from various parts of continental Europe: the Low Countries (the Netherlands and Belgium), the predominantly German countries (Germany, Luxembourg, and Switzerland), Scandinavia (Denmark, Norway, Sweden, and Finland), and Eastern Europe (Austria-Hungary and Russia). The company was to be paid one pound sterling for every farmer who settled. The contract was renewed in 1904 for ten years but cancelled only two years later because of the hostility of European governments toward clandestine immigration propaganda and manipulation of finances. With regard to the latter, apparently payments had been made for immigrants who had actually come to Canada under other auspices. But by 1906 the company had already received immense sums of money from the Laurier government.[11]

The Sifton policy of fairly open immigration from continental Europe was not without its critics. In the first place, the attitude of the provincial government toward immigration differed markedly from that of the federal government. Provincial financial difficulties were only exacerbated by the influx of immigrants resulting from the immigration policies of the federal government; continuing and even accelerating immigration created demands for heavy expenditures on educational facilities, public works, and other provincial government services.[12] Moreover, Sifton's policy conflicted sharply with the desire of the province's population of British origin to preserve Saskatchewan "for English-speaking peoples." In fact, it was clear from the beginning that Englishmen would be preferred immigrants. As J.A. Smart, Deputy Minister of the Interior, pleaded in 1903,

> Send us good emigrants and we will make them prosperous and contented men; we will relieve your [over]population and your ever-congested labour market; we will keep these new settlers loyal to the Imperial flag in a land which is progressing faster than any other colony in the world. ... You will see

what this means for the home country. It solves the much-disputed problem of your food supply in time of war. That is the bargain the colony offers.[13]

The Commissioner of Immigration in Winnipeg simply explained in 1909 that "the men who are directing the Canadian immigration propaganda on both sides of the Atlantic are of British blood and several of them are British-born. ... Naturally they prefer British stock." Resentment against uncontrolled immigration, especially from Eastern Europe, grew steadily through the post–First World War years. The Empire Settlement Act in 1922 emphasized imperial cooperation. British authorities viewed direct emigration to the Dominion of Canada as a way of strengthening the British Empire. Canadian authorities continued to express concern over the effect that the massive "foreign" immigration initiated by Sifton might have on Canadian social cohesion. In fact, the Deputy Minister of the Department of Immigration and Colonization was reportedly "intensely interested in stemming the flow of undesirables from Central Europe." Attempting to pursue "a vigourous [sic] settlement policy to combat ... the large infusion of alien blood in the West," the Canadian government brought thousands of British settlers to the Prairie West.[14]

At the hearings conducted by the Saskatchewan Royal Commission on Immigration and Settlement in 1930, numerous briefs opposing open immigration were submitted.[15] The Saskatchewan section of the United Farmers of Canada suggested that the immigration of farmers be stopped until the native born were better provided for, that there be no solicited or assisted immigration, and that there be a quota system controlled to some extent by the provincial government. The Saskatchewan Command of the Canadian Legion believed that immigration from continental European countries should not exceed immigration from within the Empire. The Saskatoon Labour Trades Council advocated selective immigration "where assimilation is a certainty." The Regina Assembly of the Native Sons of Canada opposed assisted immigration, whether sponsored by Canada, the immigrant's country of origin, or group interests; special homesteading concessions to immigrants; as well as granting Canadian citizenship before five years of residence in Canada had elapsed. The Ku Klux Klan in Saskatchewan desired that immigration from "non-preferred" countries in Central, Eastern, and Southern Europe be stopped entirely for at least five years, after which a rigid quota of 2% of the 1901 census should be imposed, except for British, French, and Scandinavian immigrants; that "trained" British and Scandinavian families be allowed to settle on the land; that all handling of immigration be removed from religious organizations; and that any ethnic group settlement be prevented. And the Provincial Grand Lodge of the Orange Order in Saskatchewan advocated Anglo-Saxon predominance. It spoke out against the "unwise" policy of bringing in more immigrants than could easily be assimilated "to those British ideals which are fundamental to our national existence." It desired a quota system. It sought to confine immigration to "preferred" (Anglo-Saxon and Nordic) countries. It opposed group settlement of immigrants because "it is not conducive to the best interests of our province, or to the best ultimate interests of the immigrants themselves. ... It retards the problem of assimilation, and retains distinctions which are detrimental to national unity. ... We already have evidence of this throughout our province." It denounced assisted passages for immigrants. It sought a halt to immigrants entering without guaranteed employment. And, finally, it sought provincial government control of immigration and abolition of all colonization organizations.

Although the Saskatchewan Royal Commission on Immigration and Settlement did not appraise the situation in 1930 as negatively as did many of the organizations that submitted briefs, it did recognize that the development of such isolated bloc settlements was not readily conducive to an integrated Canadian society:

> Throughout the province will be found many group settlements, representative of diverse racial stocks. While group settlement has many good features, nevertheless there are grave objections to its further development. ... Doubtless these groups do add diversity and elements of richness to the cultural life of the community; and also doubtless by this very diversity there is greater opportunity to adapt newcomers to the new environment. This, in turn, may result in their more rapid economic progress. The warm welcome that may be expected from a racial brother, the overcoming of the nostalgia resulting from separation from the homeland, as well as other aids, are factors that appear to support group settlement. On the other hand, it is the rooted conviction of many of our people that group settlement tends to create blocks, thus preventing those intimate contacts without which it is impossible to create a sound citizenship.[16]

The commission thus concluded that "homesteading should be discontinued and remaining Crown lands should be sold, preferably to residents of this province; as a second choice to other Canadians; thirdly to British settlers; and lastly to other immigrants."[17] Therefore, the period of establishing primarily immigrant-origin bloc settlements in Saskatchewan extended mainly from the advent of Sifton's policy in 1896 to the commission's report in 1930, though certain areas were settled prior to that period, and some of the original bloc settlements have expanded considerably since 1930, and though the majority of settlements were formed during a more restricted period, the first decade of the twentieth century. Homestead entries increased rapidly, from 1,861 in 1896 to 32,682 in 1904; during the eight years when Sifton was in command, 115,479 entries were made.[18]

The process of settlement on the land and into blocs was rather complicated.[19] The homesteading system was first established in the Prairie West in 1872, in accordance with the Land Act, Section 33:

> Every person who is the sole head of a family and every male who has attained the age of 18 years and is a British subject or declares his intention of becoming a British subject, is entitled to apply for entry to a homestead. A quarter-section may be obtained as a homestead on payment of an entry fee of $10 and fulfillment of certain conditions of residence and cultivation. To qualify for the issuing of the patent, the settler must have resided upon his homestead for at least six months of each of three years, must have erected a habitable house thereon, and must have at least 30 acres of his holding broken, of which

20 acres must be cropped. A reduction may be made in the area of breaking where the land is difficult to cultivate on account of scrub or stone.[20]

The land survey system used in Western Canada originated in the United States. Each square mile constituted a "section"; thus, typically, each original homestead allotment was a quarter-section or simply a "quarter" (160 acres). Ideally, every section would systematically be bounded to the east and west by grid roads, which would then be a mile apart, whereas to the north and south the road allowances would be two miles apart.

Initial settlement tended to be primitive: "On the bald-headed prairie the settlers were restricted to sod houses or wooden shacks, dried cow dung for their cook-stoves, and winter fuel that had to be hauled from the faraway bush or from coal sheds in the nearest town."[21] The establishment of ethnic/religious bloc settlements would have a profound effect on the prairie landscape in both a physical and a cultural sense.[22] Women played a key role in settling on the land and establishing homesteads, yet they were rarely signatories in filing for ownership of homesteads.[23]

The federal government's settlement schemes were closely integrated with the railways' schemes and the latter in turn with those of ethnic and religious organizations; land grants to railway companies were an important adjunct to the Dominion Lands policy of the federal government.[24] The federal government subsidized settlement through the Colonization Department of the CPR (which had offices in Britain and France). The CPR settlement policy was already in full swing by 1894 along the Soo Line (a CPR subsidiary) linking Chicago with Moose Jaw; settlement along this line in Saskatchewan expanded in 1902 with the sale of more land by the CPR and Canadian North-West Land Company to the North-West Colonization Company. A similar Canadian Northern Railway promotional department would become a model for the Canadian National Railway Industrial and Resources Department in 1919, when the Canadian Northern Railway merged with the Grand Trunk Pacific and other lines between 1919 and 1923 to form the Canadian National Railway (CNR). The CNR Department of Colonization and Development was established in 1923, soon to be renamed the Department of Colonization, Agriculture and Natural Resources (DCANR) the following year, later reorganized as the Department of Colonization and Agriculture in 1930. In turn, the Canadian National Land Settlement Association (CNLSA) was closely affiliated with the DCANR as an ancillary organization to settle immigrants on vacant lands adjacent to CNR lines, with offices in Britain, the Netherlands, and the Scandinavian countries. The Canada Colonization Association (CCA), a CPR affiliate, chiefly placed continental immigrants with insufficient capital and was backed by loan and banking companies as well as wealthy individuals and landowners, suggesting some sympathy for continental immigration. Canadian Pacific had the advantage of a direct railway link with a shipping company, Canadian Pacific Steamships. The Railways Agreement of 1925 among the CPR, CNR, and federal government reinforced the railways' role in the settlement process until 1961.[25]

The railways operated through ethnic and religious organizations interested in establishing bloc settlements. For example, the DCANR and CNLSA collaborated closely with the British Immigration and Colonial Society, British Dominions Emigration

Society, Deutsche Verein, Kanadischen Katholiken, German Lutheran Immigration Board, Canadian Lutheran Immigration Aid Society, German Catholic Immigrant Aid Society, German Baptist Society, Mennonite Board, Norwegian Lutheran Church, Polish Catholic Immigration Society, as well as several Ukrainian organizations. These organizations were financed by the railways to some extent (five dollars per each adult in a family settled or one dollar per single agricultural worker).[26]

The development of ethnic enclaves is not unusual. Competition for space often results in the formation of segregated ethnic islands, each of which develops a distinctive culture. Members of each minority group tend to congregate in areas where they can speak their own language, practise their own religion, and follow their own customs. Immigrants were sometimes made to feel the hostility of the larger society and were segregated into well-defined areas. Many immigrants wanted to be among their co-ethnics, with whom they could identify and sympathize. Once such colonies have come into existence, moreover, other people of a given ethnic group tended to gravitate toward them.[27]

Four principal types of bloc settlement can be noted. First, planned bloc settlements were organized and settled by specific ethnic or ethno-religious groups through the work of group agents and associations. Second, the Canadian government and transportation and settlement companies were responsible for recruiting settlers of particular ethnic and religious groups. Third, bloc settlements came into existence gradually as the result of chain migration, a process by which people from a certain place of origin settled in a new locality in Saskatchewan, then established links with their relatives, friends, or other contacts back home, thereby inducing further emigration from the place of origin. Fourth, bloc settlements formed through a process of gravitation in which migrants were drawn together by forces of mutual attraction such as common origin, language, religion, and culture.[28]

The original character of the settlement could change over time, and some settlements could be offshoots of earlier ones. The bloc settlements of Saskatchewan conformed to all of these types. The Jewish, Mennonite, Hutterite, and Doukhobor settlements—as well as some German Catholic, German Protestant (mostly Lutheran), British, French, and Hungarian settlements—can be described as primarily of the organized type, whereas the Scandinavian, Ukrainian, Polish, and Black settlements tended to be more representative of the chain or gravitation types. The establishment of ethnic/ethno-religious bloc settlements in Saskatchewan was, in sum, partly due to organized colonization schemes and partly due to rather coincidental gravitation of co-ethnics.[29]

The effect of these settlement processes on the population of the Prairie West was profound. Since the opening of Canadian prairie land to homesteading in 1872, much of the prairie grassland and parkland areas of Saskatchewan had been settled, within little more than half a century (however, mostly within a far shorter period of only a couple of decades), by incredibly diverse ethno-religious groups who had formed their own settlements.

Despite an immigration policy favouring immigrants from "desirable" countries, by the 1920s Saskatchewan had twice as many immigrants of non-British as of British origin.[30] Vast areas of the prairie regions of the province had been incorporated into bloc settlements; some of the larger settlements each included over thirty towns and villages. Moreover, the Canadian prairies had received the diversion of unskilled Eastern European farm labour from the United States.[31] Ethnic enclaves had become a prominent feature of the prairies, helping to turn Canadian society into a cultural mosaic largely lacking the strong national identity and melting-pot consciousness emerging in the United States. These enclaves were characterized by isolation from other enclaves of different ethnic origins and religious affiliations and from the larger society. Social organization was extremely localized; most bloc settlements had decidedly local natures characterized by the dialects, customs, and traditions of particular areas in Europe.[32] As J.H. Gray has written, "Because nobody was under any compulsion to speak the language of the country," at least originally, "the foreign settlers tended to solidify in their individual ethnic blocs. ... [A]nd curiously enough, precisely the same things were happening with the English, Scots, Irish, and Welsh settlers and among the Roman Catholics and Protestants, the Greek Orthodox and Ukrainian Catholics, French Catholics and Irish Catholics."[33]

Some settlements were the products of incredible odysseys, such as Welsh who arrived from the Patagonia region of southern Argentina; Blacks who moved from Oklahoma; Acadians who had settled in Quebec for generations and Québécois who first settled in New England or Minnesota before coming to Saskatchewan; Mennonites whose predecessors had migrated from the Netherlands to Germany and then "South Russia" (Ukraine) and finally Saskatchewan; and Hutterites whose history had led them from the South Tyrol region of Austria (now in northern Italy) into Moravia (today in the Czech Republic), then Transylvania (now in Romania) and South Russia (Ukraine), before emigrating to the United States and finally moving into the Canadian prairies.

DEFINING ETHNIC BLOC SETTLEMENTS

How, exactly, are ethnic bloc settlements defined? What are their size and extent? And how does their extent relate to relative degrees of ethnic homogeneity/heterogeneity?

Ethnic bloc settlements are characteristic of the cultural mosaic in Western Canadian rural social organization. Social scientists and historians have sometimes referred to ethnic bloc settlements as ethnic colonies or enclaves. A *colony* can be "a group of people who leave their native country to form in a new land a settlement subject to or connected with the parent state"; or "the country or district settled, i.e. colonized"; or "any group of people having similar interests usually living in a particular locality." Although this term has obvious descriptive value for the form of social organization with which we are concerned, it lacks specificity. An *enclave* can be "a piece of territory entirely shut in by foreign dominions." Such a term can be applied to ethnic bloc settlements but tends to have political connotations, as evident in the more explicit definition of an enclave as "a country or outlying portion of a country entirely or mostly surrounded by the territory of another country."[34] And both of these definitions imply uniformity of the surrounding alien territory, whereas Saskatchewan is characterized less by such uniformity than by a plurality of contiguous group settlements and highly mixed areas.

Among the academic definitions of *settlement* are several that come close to describing the form of social organization characterized by ethnic bloc settlements: "the state of settling or of being settled"; "the settling of immigrants in a new country or place"; "a colony, especially in the earlier stages"; "a small community, village, or group of houses in a thinly populated area"; "a community formed or populated by members of a particular religious or ideological group." Moreover, sociologists have defined a settlement form, pattern, or type as "denoting the manner in which agricultural population is arranged on the land."[35]

Yet we are concerned with group settlements in particular. *Group settlement* has been defined by sociologists as a process "whereby the settlement or colonization of new lands results in the establishment of a new colony or community as an offshoot from an older one."[36] Thus, a group settlement can be defined as a result of this process. Implicit in these sociological definitions of settlements in general and group settlements in particular is the suggestion that such an area is entirely or largely rural. Before 1951, the Census of Canada defined rural areas simply as those outside an incorporated city, town, or village; that year, however, saw rural areas redefined more precisely as those outside any agglomeration of 1,000 persons or more: in other words, beyond a city or town within whose boundaries live at least 1,000 residents. Yet ethnic bloc settlements often include towns having a population of 1,000 or more, so they cannot always be viewed as completely rural, strictly speaking. Thus, we can assume that an ethnic bloc settlement is primarily though not necessarily exclusively rural and was originally developed and is still largely populated by a particular ethnic or ethno-religious group. But, as previously noted, Aboriginal reserves and settlements can also constitute virtual ethnic bloc settlements formed through a process not of colonization and settlement but of territorial consolidation.

As early as 1936–40, C.A. Dawson, a McGill University sociologist, described the development of ethnic group settlements in Western Canada. Two decades later C.A. Price, in a paper on immigration and group settlement (1959), attempted to clarify just how one goes about defining this unique form of social organization. He observed that members of a particular minority group tend to concentrate or settle in one geographical area and that their proximity makes for informal relationships within the group and few contacts with the host society. This situation can be defined as a group settlement. However, in his view, this concentration is not meant to imply that a group settlement must be homogeneous in ethnic terms, occupying a given geographical area to the exclusion of other ethnic groups. Group settlement, in the case of pioneering settlements, tends to coincide with the whole community settlement, colony, or bloc. Yet the monopoly of a given area is not essential for group settlement, according to Price: "in the sense we have defined the term *group settlement*—something which covers the greater part of members' lives, encourages within itself numerous social, cultural, and primary group relationships and which frequently acts as members' agent for contact with outside persons and organizations—it is quite possible for several group settlements to inhabit the same locality."[37] This seems to suggest, then, that bloc settlements can overlap, especially at their margins.

The population and extent of each bloc settlement can vary from the immediate land around a single small community to a vast area inclusive of many towns and villages. Yet it is important to emphasize that most rural communities in Saskatchewan are located within such settlements. In the *Atlas of Saskatchewan* (1999), the section on ethnic bloc settlements arbitrarily defines the extent of a bloc settlement as the area

INTRODUCTION

in which a particular ethnic or ethno-religious group constitutes at least a quarter or more of the general population.[38] Defined this way, though, there are many instances in Saskatchewan in which ethnic bloc settlements overlap. For example, around Esterhazy, Hungarian, Czech and Slovak, and Swedish settlements overlap; Ukrainian, Hungarian, German, and French settlements meet around Wakaw; in the Assiniboia area, German, Romanian, and French settlements converge; and, around Hanley, Norwegian, Mennonite, Scottish, and Croatian settlements meet.

Moreover, the areal extent of bloc settlements can change over time. For example, large Ukrainian settlements have expanded into historic Métis riverlots along the South Saskatchewan River south of Batoche as well as into areas originally settled by Icelanders around Wynyard, by French around Vonda and Prud'homme as well as Montmartre, by Germans north of Yorkton, and by Norwegians around Rose Valley, Norquay, and Preeceville.

Thus, the relative homogeneity of ethnic bloc settlements tends to be highly variable, especially in cases in which two or several settlements overlap, at the margins of settlements (it can become difficult in certain cases to define the extent—and therefore the ethnic population—of a settlement with any precision), and perhaps for smaller settlements. Communities located within bloc settlements can range from being entirely homogeneous in ethnic and possibly religious terms (e.g., where all residents are German Catholics) to having surprisingly low proportions of relevant ethnicities. For example, French communities in Saskatchewan range from very high proportions of residents claiming French ethnic origin (almost all of the residents of the small community of Ferland are of French origin and French speaking) to very low proportions (already by 1971 residents of French origin constituted a majority in just fifteen of the thirty-nine incorporated towns and villages having at least 10% of residents of French origin). And none of the communities situated within the largely Norwegian rural area between Outlook, Elbow, and Hanley has a Scandinavian majority, though in some of these communities residents of Scandinavian origin do outnumber people of other ethnic origins (i.e., constituting a plurality but not statistical majority). Yet Saskatchewan does have settlements where all of the residents are of a particular ethnicity, most obviously First Nations reserves and Hutterite colonies.

The size/extent of a bloc settlement can vary from settlements of at most a few hundred people of a particular ethnicity focused on a single community (perhaps even an unincorporated village or hamlet) to vast settlements where an ethnic or ethno-religious population can number in the thousands; these larger settlements can include several towns and even a small city plus many (more than thirty) other communities. There are many examples of very small settlements, including the French settlements of Forget, Dollard, Butte-St-Pierre, Sedley, Bonne-Madone, St-Front, Périgord; Hungarian Bekevar, Otthon, St. Laszlo; Romanian Kayville, Dysart, Wood Mountain; German Yellow Grass, Billimun/Mankota, St. Elizabeth, Marienthal; Welsh Bangor; Irish Sinnett; Dutch Cramersburg. ... On the other hand, some of the largest bloc settlements include the vast areas of Ukrainian settlement occupying much of east-central Saskatchewan, around Yorkton, Canora, Ituna, and Wynyard; several German Catholic settlements: St. Joseph's Colony in the west-central region between Unity, Kerrobert, and Macklin, St. Peter's Colony centred on Humboldt, and the contiguous settlements between Leader and Maple Creek; the large areas of Mennonite concentration between Saskatoon and Rosthern and around Swift Current; the Barr Colony founded by English immigrants, centred on the city of Lloydminster; and the French settlements near each other in southwestern Saskatchewan around Gravelbourg, Ponteix, Willow Bunch, and Val Marie and in the north-central region around St-Louis, Domrémy, St-Isidore-de-Bellevue, and Duck Lake.

COMMUNITY CLASSIFICATIONS

Throughout this book, reference is made to local "communities" and rural "districts." In Saskatchewan, communities are officially or conventionally classified in various ways, ranging from very large to very small. A city is normally recognized as having a population of at least 5,000 within corporate limits, but great variation is found in city size. Larger cities can be defined as Census Metropolitan Areas (CMAs), which include the population within a designated metropolitan area that can typically extend beyond the city limits, so the CMA population is larger than the city population. A city has a mayor and city councillors. A town is typically a community—often a regional service centre—having between 500 and 5,000 residents, with a mayor and town council. A community officially designated as a village (or incorporated village) usually had between 100 and 500 residents, when originally defined, within corporate limits; however, many villages have now declined to fewer than 100 residents (and some a lot less) yet have not been redefined. Communities officially designated now as organized hamlets (generally equivalent to "unincorporated villages" in previous censuses) are highly variable in size—some are actually larger than communities still officially recognized as villages—but most have fewer than 100 residents. In fact, some organized hamlets might have been downgraded from official village status. Far more hamlets are unorganized, having no official recognition as organized communities (again, some might have been former villages or well-defined communities); typically, they are very small communities with little remaining community infrastructure.

A named rural locality or district could have been a former or one-time school district, rural post office, railway station or point, church or cemetery, or simply traditional or historic place. Besides communities—towns, villages, and hamlets—a profusion of named rural localities or districts abounds in Saskatchewan, though now—two or three generations since most were eradicated from the map of Saskatchewan—the present generation might be unfamiliar with these local designations. A great many were rural school districts (mostly until the late 1950s and early 1960s). Some were rural post offices (gradually dissolved through the 1960s). Many rural districts or localities were named after rural churches and/or cemeteries (relatively few remain known). Some were named railway points that never became communities; they were often grain-shipping points and sometimes railway stations but never more, and they have mostly vanished with the gradual closure of many railway branch lines. And occasional localities were named traditional or historic locales, some of which have been recognized by the province or municipalities as official historic sites.

Well-defined communities—towns, villages, and even hamlets—tended, during the early years of settlement, to have schools, post offices, churches, grain elevators, and railway stations, yet a small rural locality that never really developed into a defined community could have two or more of these institutions (and some none). So, in this context, specific rural localities or districts might be mentioned without always indicating whether they were school districts, post offices, and so on given this overlap. Moreover, even when a certain rural district contained a school, post office, church, and/or railway point/station, they were not necessarily all in one specific place but scattered throughout the district. For example, within the Redberry Ukrainian bloc settlement (see Chapter 5), the Alberton district to the north of the town of Hafford contained Alberton School, Sts. Peter and Paul Ukrainian Catholic Church, Alberton three miles to the east and Holy Ghost Roman Catholic Church a mile south of the Ukrainian Catholic Church (which were actually closer to Lancaster School two miles farther east), while the Roman Catholic Parish of St. John the Baptist was three miles north and a mile west of Alberton School and served by Albertown Post Office (note the spelling change) another mile north and a mile west and near Comerford School. The closest railway station was Alticane, four miles west and a mile and a half south of Albertown Post Office; however, the Ukrainian Catholic Parish of St. John the Baptist, Alticane, was actually two and a half miles north of Alticane Station and Post Office, in the Orel School District. Farther west within the settlement, Whitkow School was actually five miles south of the community of Whitkow (where the railway station, post office, and churches were located); both Zoria School and Proswita School were closer to the community (each three miles). So identifying rural communities and districts can be a challenge!

ETHNICITY AND DEMOGRAPHIC DATA

Although current populations of many towns, villages, and organized hamlets are indicated where relevant (i.e., when communities are located within historical ethnic bloc settlements), much use is made in this book of 1971 census data because the way in which Canadian census data were collected changed markedly after 1971 in two respects.

First, census data on ethnic origin used to refer solely to paternal ancestry. This has always been problematic insofar as immigrants often came from territories or places of origin that were controlled by other states—so what used to be commonly conceived of as "nationality" could have meant either citizenship or ethnicity. However, most ethnic German immigrants who arrived in Saskatchewan to establish bloc settlements came not from Germany but from Eastern European countries—especially Russia (now Ukraine, to add to the confusion). And Ukrainians arrived with more awareness of their regional identities as Galicians or Bukovinians or Podcarpathian Ruthenians—and often their political status, coming from territories that at the time were in Austria-Hungary, Russia, or Poland—rather than having a conception of being Ukrainian. Moreover, tracing ethnicity only through paternal lineage was becoming increasingly misleading, for steadily increasing intermarriage over several generations meant that individuals tended to be of mixed ethnic origins. Therefore, after 1971, the census data on ethnicity became a lot more complicated, though perhaps more accurate, when Statistics Canada decided to permit individual respondents to claim more than a single ethnic origin. The complication, of course, is that an individual can claim a variety of ethnic origins without indicating which proportion he or she is of each ethnicity. So Canadian data on ethnicity, specifically on estimated size of ethnic groups or populations, can be highly variable; a distinction must be drawn between people claiming to be of only a single ethnic origin and those claiming to be only partially of a particular ethnic origin. In other words, estimates of ethnic group size or ethnic population now overlap considerably.

Second, after 1971, the Canadian census data on ethnicity refer to a 20% sample rather than to all respondents. This means that counts of ethnic populations at the provincial level are at best estimations, while at the local level data are either not available (ethnic origin information in the census now tends to be generalized rather than localized) or quite inaccurate. So, for an accurate localized count of populations of particular ethnic origins, we must resort to the historical 1971 data, the last census providing detailed information on *all* residents (not just one in five). This book, therefore, provides estimates of ethnic populations in settlements based on 1971 data on towns and incorporated villages (as well as some organized hamlets that have recently lost their status as incorporated villages) and rural municipalities (the data on rural municipalities must be added to the data on incorporated communities, whereas small, unincorporated communities are included in rural municipalities). Although noting 1971 census data does provide a very interesting (and most importantly accurate) count of ethnic populations within ethnic bloc settlements at the time, demographic changes, especially omnipresent rural depopulation, are also discerned up to the present time. Of course, the most recent data are provided on total local community populations as well as estimates of ethnic origin populations for the province as a whole.

Finally, it is important to recognize that "ethnicity" refers to everyone insofar as any individual has at least one ethnic origin. There has been a propensity in popular usage of the term "ethnic"—not the least by Canadian media—to refer to people who are different from a perceived majority population. Apart from the fact that, at least since the 1940s, there has never been a majority ethnic population in Canada, much less in Saskatchewan, everybody can be defined in ethnic terms, no matter how mixed. In this book on ethnic settlements, a relatively high degree of ethnic homogeneity can still be assumed within these settlements (though exceptions are noted). But, most importantly, almost all of the ultimately immigrant-origin (i.e., non-Aboriginal) ethnic groups established their own primarily rural settlements in the early period of settling the prairies (including the various groups that had originated in the British Isles and perhaps had settled in Eastern Canada for generations before moving west). However, certain smaller ethnic groups, while long in Saskatchewan, never established rural settlements because they were widely scattered in towns and villages (e.g., Chinese and Syrian/Lebanese) or settled primarily in urban places (notably Greeks). Then, in later years, with agricultural land long since occupied, more recent immigrants concentrated almost exclusively in the larger cities.

Some ethnic groups established extensive settlements that almost covered entire regions, while others comprised only small and widely scattered settlements. It might be tempting to reach the facile conclusion that these smaller settlements likely did not endure for long, but their endurance might have depended on factors such as the relative distinctiveness of the group, the strength of their culture, their sheer resilience and determination, or their networking with other settlements of the group. A case in point are the Hutterites, relative latecomers to rural Saskatchewan who nonetheless established numerous small colonies where they still practise their unique lifestyle and retain their German dialect.

HISTORICAL PERIODS

In discussing in the concluding chapter the impact of social change on the strength of ethnic identification within bloc settlements, the book returns to an examination of socio-demographic factors. At this point in this introductory chapter, though, historical periods in the evolution of bloc settlements can be outlined.

Apart from First Nations reserves, ethnic bloc settlements in Saskatchewan have undergone several historical trends: first, a period of original settling, primarily from the 1880s through the First World War; second, the further development and expansion of settlements as well as the creation of "daughter colonies," especially during the 1920s; third, a struggle for survival and continuity during the drought and depression years of the 1930s; and fourth, delocalization and rural depopulation since the 1950s. These periods or trends will be elaborated later within the description of particular settlements; finally, in the concluding chapter, an overview of more recent social changes will be provided.

In a sense, the group settlement process in what would become Saskatchewan in 1905 actually began with the consolidation of First Nations territories into reserves through the treaties of the 1870s, together with the widespread establishment of Métis settlements since the 1840s. But it was during the 1880s that the bloc settlement process really commenced in earnest. During that decade, eight English (or generally British) settlements were founded, including both Cannington Manor and the Saskatoon Temperance Colony in 1882 as well as seven distinctly Scottish colonies. More Métis settlements appeared, while French began to settle in the large Métis area near Batoche as early as 1881, and the fascinating French immigrant aristocratic colony commenced at St-Hubert in 1884. At least five areas of German concentration came into existence, notably the large Neu Elsass colony centred on Strasbourg and a series of colonies southeast of Regina. Scandinavian settlers began to arrive, establishing two Swedish settlements, a couple of Icelandic settlements, and one Finnish settlement. Adding to this early diversity were two Hungarian and three Jewish settlements.

The pace of European ethnic settlement accelerated during the next decade, the 1890s. Seven French settlements were established, three German settlements, the large Saskatchewan Valley Mennonite settlement, another Icelandic settlement, and a Norwegian settlement. But the greatest impact would come from the arrival of thousands of Ukrainians, who developed four settlements in quick succession after 1896. Other arrivals from Eastern Europe included Poles, who not only settled amid the Ukrainians but also developed at least two distinct settlements of their own, and Czechs and Slovaks, who concentrated in three areas, while a third Hungarian settlement and a fourth Jewish settlement developed. All five Russian Doukhobor colonies in Saskatchewan were established during the 1890s.

The first decade of the twentieth century, 1900-09, represented the peak of immigration and settlement in Saskatchewan. English immigrants founded the Barr Colony around Lloydminster, more Scottish settlements developed, and now distinctly Welsh and Irish settlements were added to the ethnic diversity of the new province. Aside from the role that French settlers played in the expansion of some Métis settlements into extensive francophone settlements, such as at Willow Bunch, a network of eleven completely new French settlements was added, including the almost contiguous large settlements around Gravelbourg and Ponteix. At least thirteen more areas of German concentration developed, including the vast St. Peter's Colony and St. Joseph's Colony founded by German Catholics respectively in the north-central and west-central regions. And Mennonites began to settle in large numbers in the Swift Current area and established another four smaller settlements. Most of the Scandinavian settlements developed during this decade: at least twelve more Norwegian settlements, three more Swedish, and two more Finnish. Eastern Europeans continued to arrive, developing three more Ukrainian settlements, five Polish, three Romanian, two Czech and Slovak, five Hungarian, four Jewish, and a single Croatian. To this remarkable diversity was added a settlement of Oklahoma Blacks.

During the next decade, 1910–19, the settling process slowed, not least because of the First World War. Yet still more settlements developed: seven French, three German, another Mennonite, two Dutch, a Norwegian, a Danish, a Finnish, and two more Romanian. With space for new settlement becoming very limited, after 1920 few new settlements were established—however, they did include two more French and two more German, while the latest influx of Mennonites from South Russia (Ukraine) not only settled in existing Mennonite settlements but also concentrated in at least seven new areas. Finally, more than sixty Hutterite colonies (each averaging only about 100 residents) have been established in Saskatchewan since the 1950s.

Although precise dates can often be determined for the original foundation of settlements, especially for the more systematically organized types of bloc settlements, this was not always the case for gravitation-type settlements, which tended to develop more gradually. Dates can differ for the arrival of the first settlers, the establishment of parishes, and the initial development of communities or their official incorporation. The ability of a bloc settlement to expand depended on a number of factors, such as continuing immigration, competition for space, and the strength of neighbouring ethnic settlements. Typically, for most settlements, the 1920s were characterized by population increase, the establishment and growth of new communities, the development of socio-economic infrastructure, and geographical expansion. But all this was soon to change.

In Saskatchewan, fairly intensive rural settlement, with each family farm often occupying a single quarter-section, became replaced by fairly scattered settlement, with one farm consisting of several sections (square miles) of land; increasing rural population by marked rural depopulation; and physical and social isolation and lack of mobility by increased physical and social mobility. Rural focal points such as country schoolhouses, churches, community halls, post offices, general stores, and grain elevators progressively began to disappear. During the early years of settlement, immigrants and other settlers often revealed a preference for rural as opposed to urban living, laying much stress on neighbourliness.[39] Farm size was generally small, just one or two quarters. Resistance to assimilatory tendencies was doubtless enhanced by spatial and social isolation, which corresponded with more intensive settlement patterns, small farm sizes, and close-knit ethnic community life.[40]

However, a long period of difficult, even prohibitive, economic conditions ensued. The international financial depression hit hard in 1929, drastically lowering prices for crops suffering from severe drought that would last through 1937, in turn resulting in depopulation. Then, though an economic recovery commenced around 1939, the Second World War years saw young men sent off to a distant war, many never to return. Not long before, rural ethnic bloc settlements were very localized, but a process of delocalization that began in the 1930s carried on into the 1950s and to a considerable extent even into the present day in the form of rural depopulation.

STRUCTURE OF THE BOOK

This book includes a thematic introduction (Chapter 1) and conclusion (Chapter 10), while the focus of intervening chapters, comprising the bulk of the book, is a successive description of rural ethnic settlements, commencing with a description of Aboriginal reserves and settlements. Each succeeding chapter then covers generalized ethnic categories in the order of overall size of each collectivity within the present provincial population: respectively, British (at least 606,000 Saskatchewan residents claiming a British ethnic origin, in whole or in part, according to the 2006 census), Germanic (at least 338,000), Slavic/Eastern European (together totalling some 273,000), francophone and Métis (together totalling at least 174,000 with related origins), Nordic (together totalling some 125,000), and finally other ethnic groups (primarily non-European), which have tended to concentrate in cities. This ordering of chapters is preferable to arranging them by historical sequence of settlement, starting with earliest settlement, for following the treaty establishment of Indian reserves almost all ethnic bloc settlements tended to be initially established within much the same time period, from the 1880s to the 1920s, with few exceptions. This ordering is also preferable to simply arranging chapters in alphabetical order by ethnic group (which would effectively turn the book into a less readable reference work). Rather, each particular ethnic group that established its own settlements is combined with other closely related groups in generalized categories representing each chapter. Yet subsections within each chapter focus on specific ethnic groups (again in order of size except for francophone Métis, who preceded and opened the way for French settlement). For example, the British settlements chapter (Chapter 3) includes subsections respectively on English, Scottish, Irish, and Welsh settlements.

It seems obvious that chapter length would be quite variable, with the chapter on non-European settlements (Chapter 9) being considerably shorter. Yet, given the complexity of the vast Slavic/Eastern European category, these groups are covered in two chapters: Chapter 5 on Ukrainians and Poles and Chapter 6 on other Eastern European groups (Russian Doukhobors, Hungarians, Romanians, Czechs and Slovaks, Croatians, and Jews).

Obviously, in organizing particular ethnic groups into these generalized categories, care must be taken to include qualifying explanations, such as the qualifier that "British" ultimately means origins in Great Britain and Ireland, considering that not all Irish prefer to be called British. Large numbers of ethnic Germans (*Volksdeutsche*) and Mennonites came to Saskatchewan, directly or indirectly, from their colonies in Eastern Europe but merit a chapter separate from Ukrainians, Poles, and other

Eastern Europeans. The chapter on "Germanic" settlements (Chapter 4) is subdivided by ethno-religious categories: German Catholic, Protestant (i.e., mainly Lutheran, Baptist, Adventist), Mennonite (strictly classified by religion today yet historically German speaking), Hutterite, and Dutch (who should absolutely be distinguished from Germans, though some Mennonites in the past claimed Dutch origin to emphasize their distinction from Germans and to indicate that their particular religious affiliation originated in the Netherlands). Again a qualifier is needed that certain Eastern European groups—notably Hungarians, Romanians, and Jews—are not Slavic. The chapter on Nordic settlements (Chapter 8) covers not only Scandinavian groups (Norwegian, Swedish, Icelandic, and Danish) but also Finns (who strictly, by linguistic categorization, are not actually Scandinavian); thus, the term "Nordic" might be more inclusive than the term "Scandinavian."

Although Métis settlement patterns are initially mentioned in Chapter 2, on Aboriginal reserves and settlements, since many or most historical Métis were francophone (though many also spoke Michif, considered an Aboriginal language yet infused with French) their contribution to opening the way to more general francophone settlement is considered in Chapter 7, on francophone settlements. The remainder of that chapter contrasts francophone immigrants from Europe with Canadian francophone migrants, including Québécois and Acadians, and francophone migrants from the United States.

The book focuses on primarily rural ethnic bloc settlements rather than urban minorities, though the urbanization of Aboriginal peoples is covered concisely in Chapter 2; moreover, Chapter 9, on other ethnic groups, describes not only a rural settlement of Blacks but also how "visible minorities" (at best an awkward and misleading yet common term in Canada) have concentrated in cities. Apart from most non-European ethnic groups who have concentrated in cities, certain European groups, notably Greeks, have done likewise, whereas among non-Europeans only Blacks formed a distinct rural settlement, yet Chinese and to a far lesser extent Syrians-Lebanese were widely scattered in rural communities but did not form their own settlements.

The concluding chapter essentially provides an overview of how social change, particularly rural depopulation, urbanization, and migration, as well as intermarriage and population mixing across ethnic and religious lines and other socio-demographic factors, might have affected the strength of ethnic identification, thereby the viability and character of ethnic settlements.

SOURCES

Saskatchewan Ethnic, Immigration, and Settlement History
Sections of this chapter and book are based on A.B. Anderson, "Assimilation in the Bloc Settlements of North-Central Saskatchewan: A Comparative Study of Identity Change among Seven Ethno-Religious Groups in a Canadian Prairie Region" (PhD diss., University of Saskatchewan, 1972). A concise summary of the principal findings of this study is found in A.B. Anderson, "Ethnic Identity in Saskatchewan Bloc Settlements: A Sociological Appraisal," in *The Settlement of the West*, ed. H. Palmer (Calgary: University of Calgary Press, 1977), 187–225. Other thematic sources based

on that study include A.B. Anderson, "Intermarriage in Ethnic Bloc Settlements in Saskatchewan," paper presented at the Annual Meeting of the Western Association of Sociology and Anthropology, Banff, December 1974; A.B. Anderson, "Ethnicity and Language in Saskatchewan Schools," paper presented at the Symposium on Ethnicity on the Great Plains, Center for Great Plains Studies, University of Nebraska, Lincoln, April 1978; A.B. Anderson, "Linguistic Trends among Saskatchewan Ethnic Groups," in *Ethnic Canadians: Culture and Education*, ed. M.L. Kovacs (Regina: Canadian Plains Research Center, 1978), 63–86; A.B. Anderson, "Generation Differences in Ethnic Identity Retention in Rural Saskatchewan," *Prairie Forum* 7, 2 (1982): 171–95. Parts of this chapter and book are also revised from A.B. Anderson, "Ethnic Bloc Settlements," in *Encyclopedia of Saskatchewan* (Regina: Canadian Plains Research Center, 2005), 305–09. Also see A.B. Anderson, "Ethnic Bloc Settlements, 1850s–1990s," in *Atlas of Saskatchewan* (Saskatoon: University of Saskatchewan, 1999), 56–58.

Early sources specifically on Saskatchewan immigration and settlement history, as well as more general sources that have contained information on Saskatchewan, include J.S. Woodsworth, *Strangers within Our Gates*, originally published by the Young People's Forward Movement Department of the Methodist Church in 1909 and reprinted by the University of Toronto Press in 1972; N.F. Black, *History of Saskatchewan and the North-West Territories* (Regina: Saskatchewan Historical, 1913); H.J. Boam, *The Prairie Provinces of Canada* (London: Sells, 1914); J.T.M. Anderson, *The Education of the New Canadian* (Toronto: J.M. Dent, 1918); J. Hawkes, *The Story of Saskatchewan and Its People* (Regina: S.T. Clarke, 1924); R. England, *The Central European Immigrant in Canada* (Toronto: Macmillan, 1929); *Report of the Saskatchewan Royal Commission on Immigration and Settlement* (Regina: King's Publisher, 1930); J.W. Dafoe, *Clifford Sifton in Relation to His Times* (Toronto: Macmillan, 1931); C.A. Dawson, *Group Settlement: Ethnic Communities in Western Canada* (Toronto: Macmillan, 1936); G.E. Britnell, *The Wheat Economy* (Toronto: University of Toronto Press, 1939); C.A. Dawson and E.R. Younge, *Pioneering in the Prairie Provinces: The Social Side of the Settlement Process* (Toronto: Macmillan, 1940).

Later sources include E. Rowles-Simpson, "Bannock, Beans, and Bacon: An Investigation of Pioneer Diet," *Saskatchewan History* (winter 1952), reprinted in *Pages from the Past: Essays on Saskatchewan History*, ed. D.H. Bocking (Saskatoon: Western Producer Prairie Books, 1979), 102–19; J.F.C. Wright, *Saskatchewan: The History of a Province* (Toronto: McClelland and Stewart, 1955); C. MacDonald, "Pioneer Church Life in Saskatchewan," *Saskatchewan History* (winter 1960), reprinted in *Pages from the Past: Essays on Saskatchewan History*, ed. D.H. Bocking (Saskatoon: Western Producer Prairie Books, 1979), 120–38; J.H. Archer, *Footprints in Time* (Toronto: House of Grant, 1965); N. Ward and D. Spafford, eds., *Politics in Saskatchewan* (Lindsay, ON: Longmans of Canada and John Dyell, 1968); C. Martin, *"Dominion Lands" Policy* (Toronto: McClelland and Stewart, 1973); M.R. Lupul, *The Roman Catholic Church and the North-West School Question: A Study in Church-State Relations in Western Canada, 1875–1905* (Toronto: University of Toronto Press, 1974); H. Robertson, *Salt of the Earth: The Story of the Homesteaders in Western Canada* (Toronto: James Lorimer, 1974); J. Bruce, *Last*

Best West (Toronto: Fitzhenry and Whiteside, 1976); J. DeVisser and H. Kalman, *Pioneer Churches* (Toronto: McClelland and Stewart, 1976); J.H. Thompson, *The Harvests of War: The Prairie West, 1914–1918* (Toronto: McClelland and Stewart, 1978); D.H. Bocking, ed., *Pages from the Past: Essays on Saskatchewan History* (Saskatoon: Western Producer Prairie Books, 1979); J.H. Gray, *Boom Time: Peopling the Canadian Prairies* (Saskatoon: Western Producer Prairie Books, 1979); H. Palmer and D. Smith, eds., *The New Provinces: Alberta and Saskatchewan, 1905–1980* (Vancouver: Tantalus Research, 1980); D. Smith, "Instilling British Values in the Prairie Provinces," *Prairie Forum* 6, 2 (1981): 129–41; K. Ondaatje, *Small Churches of Canada* (Toronto: Lester and Orpen Dennys, 1982); B.G. Smillie, "Religious Settlement on the Prairies," in *Visions of the New Jerusalem: Religious Settlement on the Prairies*, ed. B.G. Smillie (Edmonton: NeWest Press, 1983); J.N. McCrorie, "Historical Background to Prairie Settlement," in *Visions of the New Jerusalem: Religious Settlement on the Prairies*, ed. B.G. Smillie (Edmonton: NeWest Press, 1983); P. Berton, *The Promised Land: Settling the West, 1896–1914* (Toronto: McClelland and Stewart, 1984); A.W. Rasporich, ed., *The Making of the Modern West: Western Canada since 1945* (Calgary: University of Calgary Press, 1984); G. Friesen, *The Canadian Prairies: A History* (Toronto: University of Toronto Press, 1984); D.C. Jones and I. MacPherson, eds., *Building beyond the Homestead: Rural History on the Prairies* (Calgary: University of Calgary Press, 1985); M. Fieguth and D. Christensen, *Historic Saskatchewan* (Toronto: Oxford University Press, 1986); and Saskatchewan Association of Architects, *Historic Architecture of Saskatchewan* (Regina: Focus Publishing, 1987).

Recent sources include M. Lalonde and E. LaClare, *Discover Saskatchewan: A Guide to Historic Sites* (Regina: Canadian Plains Research Center, 1998); R.W. Widdis, *With Scarcely a Ripple: Anglo-Canadian Migration into the United States and Western Canada, 1880–1920* (Montreal: McGill-Queen's University Press, 1998); P.R. Magocsi, ed., *Encyclopedia of Canada's Peoples* (Toronto: University of Toronto Press, 1999), as well as its earlier American counterpart, S. Thernstrom, ed., *Harvard Encyclopedia of American Ethnic Groups* (Cambridge, MA: Harvard University Press, 1980); W.A. Waiser, *Saskatchewan: A New History* (Calgary: Fifth House Books, 2005); R.D. Francis and C. Kitzan, eds., *The Prairie West as Promised Land* (Calgary: University of Calgary Press, 2007); H. Schlichtmann, "Rural Settlements," in *Saskatchewan: Geographic Perspectives*, ed. B.D. Thraves, M.L. Lewry, J.E. Dale, and H. Schlichtmann (Regina: University of Regina and Canadian Plains Research Center, 2007), 288–92; H. Schlichtmann and M.L. Lewry, "Settlement Evolution since the Late Nineteenth Century," in *Saskatchewan: Geographic Perspectives*, ed. B.D. Thraves, M.L. Lewry, J.E. Dale, and H. Schlichtmann (Regina: University of Regina and Canadian Plains Research Center, 2007), 129–45; J.C. Lehr, J. Everitt, and S. Evans, "The Making of the Prairie Landscape," *Prairie Forum* 33, 1 (2008); and G.P. Marchildon, ed., *Immigration and Settlement, 1870–1939*, History of the Prairie West Series (Regina: Canadian Plains Research Center and University of Regina, 2009).

Local Community Histories
A vast amount of detail on the precise origins of settlers is found in innumerable local community and settlement histories, available in the University of Saskatchewan

Special Collections in Saskatoon and Saskatchewan Provincial Library in Regina. The most comprehensive and informative sources in a single volume for all of Saskatchewan are B. Barry, *People Places: Saskatchewan and Its Names* (Regina: Canadian Plains Research Center, 1997); B. Barry, *Geographic Names of Saskatchewan* (Regina: People Places Publishing, 2005); and D. McLennan, *Our Towns: Saskatchewan Communities from Abbey to Zenon Park* (Regina: Canadian Plains Research Center, 2008). Information can also be found in E.T. Russell, *What's in a Name? The Story behind Saskatchewan Place Names* (Saskatoon: Western Producer Prairie Books, 1973, 1997; F. Moore, *Saskatchewan Ghost Towns* (Regina: First Impressions, 1982); and, selectively, M. Hryniuk and F. Korvemaker, *Legacy of Stone: Saskatchewan's Stone Buildings* (Regina: Coteau Books, 2008).

Bibliographies and Directories

The Provincial Library in Regina is a repository for local histories, as is the Archives of Saskatchewan at the University of Saskatchewan. Through the mid-1980s, a comprehensive bibliography of sources on Saskatchewan ethnic groups is A.B. Anderson, *Ethnic Communities in Saskatchewan: Bibliographic Sources* (Saskatoon: Saskatoon Multicultural Council, 1986). Bibliographies on specific ethnic groups in Saskatchewan include A.B. Anderson, *Guide des sources bibliographiques des communautés francophones de la Saskatchewan/Guide to Bibliographic Sources on Francophone Communities in Saskatchewan*, Research Unit for French Canadian Studies, University of Saskatchewan, Report 13, 1987; and A.B. Anderson, *German, Mennonite, and Hutterite Communities in Saskatchewan: An Inventory of Sources* (Saskatoon: Saskatchewan German Council, 1989). An overview of earlier research on ethnic groups on the prairies is provided in A.B. Anderson, ed., *Ethnic Studies and Research in the Prairies*, special issue of *Prairie Forum* 7, 2 (1982).

Internet Sources

Statistics Canada (for demographic information); the Saskatchewan Genealogical Society (for detailed genealogical information); HOME: Historical Ownership Mapping Endeavour and the Saskatchewan Homestead Index (for details on original homesteads); rootsweb/Saskatchewan and Saskatchewan GenWeb (for histories of particular ethnic groups in Saskatchewan). Both the *Atlas of Saskatchewan* and the *Encyclopedia of Saskatchewan* are also available online, as are many sources located through the Saskatchewan Archives and Special Collections in the University of Saskatchewan Library.

Chapter 2
ABORIGINAL RESERVES AND SETTLEMENTS

This chapter describes the development and perpetuation of Aboriginal reserves and settlements within the territories incorporated into the newly formed Province of Saskatchewan in 1905. The word *Saskatchewan* came from *kisiskaciwan-sipiy*, meaning "swift-flowing river" in Cree. First, different types of Aboriginal peoples in Saskatchewan will be discerned and how they changed over time prior to the settlement of non-Aboriginal people. Then the consolidation of Aboriginal territoriality will be described, both through the treaty process with First Nations during the 1870s, which established a network of reserves, and through the attempted encroachment of the Canadian government on traditional Métis settlement patterns into the next decade. The locations of the reserve communities representing each of the five principal First Nations as ethno-linguistic groups will then be discussed in some detail, followed by a similar description of both former and extant Métis settlements. The chapter concludes with a contemporary analysis of the effects of urbanization on the Aboriginal population of Saskatchewan.

TYPES OF ABORIGINAL PEOPLES
It is conventional to divide the Aboriginal population of Canada into four broad categories. First, First Nations, or Registered Indians, originally settled on reserves primarily during the 1870s in the regions that would later comprise the Province of Saskatchewan, in accordance with various treaties. However, not all Registered Indians are Treaty Indians since certain bands were not involved, at least originally, in the treaty process. Moreover, today a majority of First Nations people (53.2% in 2006), thus equated with Registered Indians, no longer live on these reserves. Yet the term "First Nation" is commonly used in very different senses—not only as the equivalent of all Registered

Indians but also more generally as all North American Indians (thus including Non-Status Indians), more narrowly as a particular people or tribe (e.g., Dakota/Sioux First Nation), or even more specifically as a band or reserve community (e.g., Whitecap Dakota/Sioux First Nation).

Second, Non-Status Indians, who never did settle on reserves or sign treaties, today constitute only part of the "off-reserve" population (a large part of which consists of First Nations/Registered Indian people living in urban areas). Although not officially registered with a particular reserve or band, they are numerous, have often settled adjacent to reserves and intermarried extensively with Registered Indians, and generally can be considered part of the First Nations population.

Third, Métis generally are people partly of Aboriginal origin, though a distinction is often drawn between people who happen to claim some (perhaps remote) Aboriginal ancestry and *historical* Métis, who are far more narrowly defined—at least in the Prairie West—as the descendants of the original Red River (Manitoba) Métis, who were mixtures of Cree or Ojibwa and French (primarily) or Scots (to some extent). Despite being only partly Aboriginal, by definition at least historical Métis are considered to be an Aboriginal group in their own right. Beyond the Prairie West, a claim to being a historically identifiable Métis group can be made, apart from the more general claim to some Aboriginal ancestry, however remote. In this book, the designation Métis will normally refer to the narrower historical definition, though data on Métis population can include people who claim some Aboriginal ethnic origin.

Fourth, Inuit are not regarded as traditionally indigenous to Saskatchewan, though now several hundred do live in the province.

THE CONSOLIDATION OF ABORIGINAL TERRITORIALITY

Aboriginal people roamed the Saskatchewan plains and woodlands for thousands of years before contact with Europeans, as evidenced in provincial historic sites such as Wanuskewin near Saskatoon, where Aboriginal settlement dates back thousands of years; the St-Victor petroglyphs, rock carvings representing turtles, bison hooves, human heads, feet, and hands, and bear tracks, probably dating before 1750 (predating the introduction of horses to the prairie region); and numerous pictographs, rock paintings along northern waterways. The Northern Cree, Assiniboine (*Nakota*), and Chipewyan (*Dene*) have long occupied the territories that would eventually become Saskatchewan. Other early Aboriginal peoples who roamed these plains included the Snake/Shoshone (known to the Cree as *Kinepiko-wiyiniwak*) at least through the mid-eighteenth century, Hidatsa through the late eighteenth century, Gros Ventre (*Atsina*, or *Aaninin*—White Clay People—to the Blackfoot, *Pawisti-kowiyiniwak* in Cree) from the seventeenth century through the early nineteenth century (early Métis traders referred to the South Saskatchewan River as *la Fourche des Gros-Ventres*), Blackfoot peoples—Blackfoot, Blood, and Piegan (who called themselves respectively *Siksika*, *Kainai* or *Aapa-inni*, and *Apatohsi-Pikani* and *Amsskaapi-Pikani* or known to the Cree respectively as *Kaskite-wiyasitak*, *Mihko-wiyiniwak*, and *Pikano-wiyiniwak*) during the seventeenth and eighteenth centuries through the mid-nineteenth century, as well as occasional Crow (*Kahkakiwaitcanak*), Sarcee (*Tsuu T'ina, Tsotli'na*, or *Sasiwak*), Flathead (*Napakstok-wewak*), and Nez Perce (*Paipe-komak*). The Plains Cree and their allies the Ojibwa/Saulteaux soon came to dominate the Saskatchewan prairie yet did not actually begin to enter the region in significant numbers until the late eighteenth century through the early nineteenth century. Finally, the Sioux (*Dakota—Pwatak* to the Cree—and *Lakota*, related to the earlier Assiniboine/*Nakota*), were relative latecomers, not arriving in large numbers until the late nineteenth century, though they had certainly made earlier incursions into Saskatchewan. Collectively, hostiles or strangers were called *ayahtci-yiniwak* by the Cree; for their part, the Blackfoot referred to "our own way of life" (*nitsitapiisinni*), "people who speak the real language" (*nitsi-poi-yiksi*), "real people" (*nitsitapii*), and "our relations" (*niksakowe*), and more generally "plains people" (*sao-kitapiiksi*), to be distinguished from "other beings" (*matapi*), and especially White men (*napikowan*), some of whom were the "redcoats" (Royal North-West Mounted Police, *li-moh-ksi-so-ka-sii-ksi*). The Blackfoot also distinguished "earth beings" (*ksahkomi-tapiksi*) from "above beings" (*spomi-tapi-ksi*), "spirit beings" (*naa-to-yi-ta*), and "dream beings" (*papai-tapiksi*). The easternmost portion of their territory, which they viewed as "our land" (*nitawahsi*), extended from the North Saskatchewan River (*Ponoko-si-sahta*) south toward the Yellowstone River (*Otahkoi-tah-tayi*) in Montana and included the Great Sand Hills (*Omahksi-spatsi-koyii*) in Saskatchewan.

However, over time, there was considerable movement in the ranges and territories occupied by these various First Nations. During the seventeenth and eighteenth centuries, the Gros Ventre predominated in the south-central and southwestern regions and the Blackfoot in the west-central region, while much of the remainder of the prairie was occupied by the Assiniboine and Cree, and most of the north was dominated by the Cree, except for the farthest north, which was Chipewyan territory. Smallpox epidemics between 1781 and 1837 caused the depletion of some First Nations and much rearrangement of tribal territoriality: the Gros Ventre became restricted primarily to the southwest, Blackfoot territory became similarly constricted, the Assiniboine concentrated in the rest of southern and west-central Saskatchewan, most of the remainder of Saskatchewan became Cree, with the first movement of Saulteaux into several central areas, and the Chipewyan began to move south of Lake Athabasca. However, with increasing European infiltration, by the late nineteenth century the contemporary distributions had become evident, the Cree occupying much of Saskatchewan, overlapping with the Saulteaux in a broad band running from the southeast to the west-central region, with small pockets of Assiniboine and Sioux interspersed; in the north, the Churchill River had become the approximate division between Cree and Chipewyan.

Despite continuous competition for territoriality among all these migratory First Nations, over the course of centuries, but especially during the eighteenth century and early to mid-nineteenth century, when Aboriginal peoples encountered increasing numbers of White settlers, their broad sense of territoriality became severely circumscribed. Beginning in the 1870s and extending to 1906, a series of treaties effectively reduced First Nations territories to a network of fairly small reserves. This process commenced with Treaty 2 in 1871, which dealt mainly with Manitoba but extended into the Moose Mountain area in (what would become) southeastern Saskatchewan. Treaty 4 in 1874 (with later "adhesions" added in 1875–77) established numerous Plains Cree and Saulteaux reserves in southern and east-central Saskatchewan. Treaty 5 in 1875 (with adhesions in 1876) focused on the settlement of some Swampy and Woods Cree in the area west of The Pas. Treaty 6 in 1876 first settled many Plains Cree and some Saulteaux in the parkland belt of the north-central and west-central regions (later adhesions in 1878–79, 1882, and particularly 1889 focused on the Woods Cree of the northern boreal forest; still other adhesions followed in 1913, 1950, 1954, and 1956). Treaty 7 in 1877 dealt with a very small area where the South Saskatchewan River crosses the present Saskatchewan-Alberta border. Treaty 8 in 1899 and Treaty 10 in 1906 (with an adhesion the next year) dealt with the northernmost Chipewyan people and their Northern Cree neighbours. The Sioux were inserted into the existing Treaty 4 and Treaty 6 areas in their own reserves between 1878 and 1894.

It should be understood that, when referring to Saskatchewan regions prior to the official birth of the province in 1905, we are actually referring to territory that would be included in the new province. Before 1882, all such territory was undifferentiated land within the North-West Territories. Then in 1882 the District of Assiniboia encompassed all of the territory that now comprises southern Saskatchewan as well as the adjacent land west of the 110° west longitude, the present boundary with Alberta; the District of Saskatchewan comprised what is today central Saskatchewan as well as neighbouring portions of Alberta and Manitoba; while northern Saskatchewan still remained undifferentiated territory within the North-West Territories until 1895, when this northern territory was added to the District of Athabasca. Thus, the Province of Saskatchewan was formed in 1905 by combining most (but not all) of the former Districts of Assiniboia and Saskatchewan and the eastern half of the District of Athabasca (the western half became northern Alberta).

Today, within the Province of Saskatchewan, there are six principal Aboriginal languages. Cree (*Ininimowin/Ininokisowewin*) and Ojibwa/Saulteaux (*Nahkawewin*) are closely related languages of the Algonquian family. In turn, the Cree spoken in Saskatchewan is subdivided into three historically distinct dialects: Plains Cree, Woods Cree, and Swampy Cree. Over time, there has been considerable mixing of Cree and Ojibwa where these two First Nations settled together, resulting in a fused "Oji-Cree" dialect. Assiniboine (*Nakota*) and Sioux (subdivided into *Dakota* and *Lakota*) are historically related Siouan family languages. Chipewyan (*Dene*), an Athapaskan family language, prevails in northern Saskatchewan. These First Nations (broadly defined in a tribal sense) are divided into seventy-five First Nations (more narrowly defined in a band sense) on at least 158 rural reserves (not all of which are occupied and not including urban reserves). In addition, several traditional Métis dialects, collectively called Michif, have been spoken; they have been called French-Michif, Cree-Michif, and Chippewa-Michif, depending on the degree of influence respectively of French, Cree, and Ojibwa. Given this historical and to a considerable extent contemporary ethnic and linguistic complexity, Aboriginal peoples of Saskatchewan constitute by far the largest number of ethno-cultural settlements and communities in the province.

CREE/NEHIYAWEWIN

The Cree constitute the most numerous First Nation both in Canada and in Saskatchewan, the most widespread with the most reserves (forty-four main reserves in Saskatchewan alone). The term "Cree" originated in the French Jesuit missionaries' designation of *Kristinon* or *Kristineaux*, eventually shortened to *les Cris* in French and

Cree in English. The Cree nation as a whole (*Nehiyawewin*) is divided in Saskatchewan into two basic types with different cultural traditions and unique dialects: the Plains Cree (*Nehiyawak* or *Iyinow*, meaning real people), and Woods, Western Woodland, or Northern Cree (*Nihithawak* or *Sakaw-Iyiniwak*), though the actual division between these two distinct types might have become somewhat imprecise over time.

The Eastern Cree (*Omaskekowak*) migrated long ago from northern Quebec across northwestern Ontario into the boreal forest regions of northern Manitoba, Saskatchewan (by the early eighteenth century), and Alberta, becoming the Western Woodland/Woods/Northern Cree. Distinct subgroups formed: the Swampy Cree (*Maskekowak* or *Nehinawak*) were spreading from northern Manitoba into the adjacent area in Saskatchewan by around 1800, and the Rocky Cree (*Missinippi*) settled along the Churchill River.

The largest and geographically most widespread First Nations bands in Saskatchewan are the Lac La Ronge and Peter Ballantyne Cree First Nations. The Lac La Ronge First Nation (*Mistahi-sakahikanihk*) now contains 8,666 band members, of whom about 5,400 live on reserves (according to the most recent data), including part of the town of Lac La Ronge, Morin and Sanderson Lakes, Bittern Lake, Sikachu Lake, Egg Lake, Nemeiben River, Kitsakie, Grandmother's Bay, Stanley (*Amuchewaspimewin*), Keg Lake (*Mahkako-sakahikan*), Little Red River, Potato River, Sucker River, Old Fort, Four Portages, Fox Point, and Little Hills.[1] The Peter Ballantyne First Nation currently numbers 8,344 band members, of whom 5,511 remain on reserves. Their territories include the widely scattered reserve communities of Sturgeon Landing, Sturgeon Weir River (*Namiwi-sipihk*), Pelican Narrows (*Wapawikoscikan*), Southend Reindeer Lake (*Wapatihkwaciwanohk*), Deschambault Lake (*Kimosom-pwatinak*), Amisk Lake (*Amiskosakahikan*), Birch Portage, *Keewatinok Soniaw Aski*, *Kimosom Pwatinak*, *Mistik*, Sandy Narrows (*Wapaskokimow*), Woody Lake, Mirond Lake, and *Opawakoscikan*.

The beautiful Holy Trinity Anglican Church at Stanley Mission (*Amachewespimawin*) is the oldest continuously standing building in Saskatchewan and a designated provincial historical site. In 1850, the Church Missionary Society (CMS) established Stanley Mission. By 1854, the mission included a parsonage and Indian school, and construction of the church began. It was completed in 1860 and featured a seventy-five-foot steeple (later shortened) and thirty-seven gothic arched stained-glass windows. CMS missionaries in northern Saskatchewan used Cree and Chipewyan languages, and in the 1870s a printing press was operated by Reverend John Mackay, a Métis clergyman based at Stanley Mission.

Farther west along the Churchill River watershed, where historically the Northern Cree met the Dene, were the communities of Ile-à-la-Crosse, Beauval, and Pinehouse. Of the 1,903 band members of the Canoe Lake First Nation, 875 continue to live on the three reserves on the shores of Canoe Lake and Jans Bay. Almost all of these reserves were established by Treaty 10 in 1906, with the exception of Sturgeon Weir, which had been included in the area of Treaty 5 in 1876, and Montreal Lake, which had been included in the Treaty 6 adhesion in 1889. Of the 3,343 band members of the Montreal Lake First Nation, 2,121 still live on the reserve.

The Plains Cree had moved onto the prairie by the early nineteenth century and, like their similarly Algonquian-speaking Ojibwa neighbours migrating westward to the south, soon became acculturated to the plains peoples whom they encountered. They, too, became divided into distinct subgroups. To the southeast, the traditional land of the Moose Mountain people lay within the territory of Treaty 2 in 1871 (however, White Bear's band did not sign their treaty until 1874). Cree mixed with Saulteaux (Ojibwa) and Assiniboine here and on the re-created Ocean Man (*Osiya-mani*, or *Kihcikamiwiyin*, or *Kitchi-Kah-me-win*) Reserve. Of 2,118 band members of White Bear, only 785 still live on the reserve, and of 454 members of the Ocean Man First Nation 170 remain on the reserve. The "downstream people" (*Mamihki-yiniwak*)—consisting of the Qu'Appelle (Calling River) people (*Katepwewcipi-wiyiniwak*), the Rabbitskins of the File Hills (*Wapucwayanak*), and the Touchwood Hills people (*Pusakawatci-wiyiniwak*)—were all settled on reserves in their traditional territories in accordance with Treaty 4 in 1874. In the Qu'Appelle Valley were Ochapowace, with 571 of 1,436 band members now on reserve; Kahkewistahaw, with 605 of 1,742; Cowessess, with just 712 of 3,526; Sakimay, Shesheep, Little Bone or Leech Lake, and Minoahchak, together with only 250 of 1,412. Kahkewistahaw and Cowessess First Nations also included Saulteaux and Sakimay both Saulteaux and Assiniboine. Farther upstream were Pasqua, with 551 of 1,751 band members on reserve; Muscowpetung and Hay Lands, with 328 of 1,169; and Piapot, with 580 of 2,020. Cree mixed with Saulteaux on Pasqua and Muscowpetung and with Assiniboine on Piapot. In the File Hills (*Kiskimanaciy*) were situated Peepeekisis (including the former File Hills farm colony[2]), with 758 of 2,466 on reserve; Okanese, where almost half (257) of the 584 band members continue to reside on reserve; Star Blanket (*Wa-pii Moos-toosis*), 261 of 562; and Little Black Bear, 209 of 459. Cree were mixed with Assiniboine on Peepeekisis and with Saulteaux on Okanese. In the Touchwood Hills (*Posacanaciy*) were Muskowekwan, where 448 of the 1,503 band members reside on reserve; George Gordon (*Ka-newonaskasew*), with a present population of 3,177, but just 1,100 living on reserve; Day Star, with 142 of 447 band members on reserve; and Poor Man (*Kawacatoose*), where now only 731 of the 2,746 band members continue to live on reserve. Saulteaux were settled with Cree on Muskowekwan, George Gordon, and Kawacatoose. Far to the southwest, the Cypress Hills-Wood Mountain Cree were settled on a single reserve, Nekaneet, also in 1874; this is a small reserve, where only 197 of the 417 band members live.

The Willow Cree (*Nipisihkopa-wiyiniwak*) consisted, first, of the "parklands people" (*Paskukupa-wiyiniwak*) who were settled on the Beardy's, Okemasis, and recently added Willow Cree Reserves immediately west of Duck Lake, where today 1,085 of the 2,895 band members live; One Arrow (*Kapeyakwaskonam*), east of Duck Lake, where 568 of 1,465 band members live; Muskoday, southeast of Prince Albert, with 572 of 1,552 band members on reserve; and James Smith (*Notawkeecheekanis*) and Cumberland (*Chacastapasin*), where together 1,856 of the 2,908 band members continue to live. A reserve school (1905) at Muskoday and St. Stephen's Anglican Church (1930) at James Smith have been recognized as historic sites. Second, the "house people" (*Waskahikan-wiyiniwak*) were found at Muskeg Lake (the *Peteynakey* band, or Muskeg Lake Cree First Nation), where only 311 residents remain on the Muskeg Lake Reserve out of a band membership numbering 1,877 (most of the members live in Saskatoon, where the urban reserve *Asimakaniseekan Askiy* is used for institutional and commercial purposes, and many are widely scattered across Canada); and Snake Plain (*Mistawasis*), where 1,130 of the 2,350 band members live on reserve. The Muskeg Lake School is called *Kihiw-waciston*—Eagle's

Nest. Third, the "river people" (*Cipi-wiyiniwak*) lived on several reserves in the Battlefords area, in accordance with Treaty 6 in 1876: Red Pheasant (*Pihew-ka-mihkosit* or *Mikisiwacihk*), where about a third, 742 of the 2,042 band members, still live on reserve; Sweetgrass (*Nakiwaciy, Nakiwacihk*, and earlier *Weekaskookeeseyyin*—Old Man Sweetgrass—and *Nahweekahnickkahohtah-mahhote*—Strike Him on the Back), also little more than a third, 631 of 1,652 band members living on reserve; Poundmaker (*Pihtokahanapiwiyin*), with 774 of 1,412 band members on reserve; Little Pine (*Wasktowiyininahk*), with 793 of 1,687; and Moosomin, with a fairly high proportion—1,038 of the 1,475 band members—on reserve. The Lucky Man First Nation has been in a rather unique position: the band was rendered virtually landless during the 1880s, and the few remaining members—down to only nine persons by 1919—settled on the Little Pine Reserve; although new land was finally acquired in 1989 in the Thickwood Hills some sixty kilometres east of North Battleford, currently as few as two of the thirty-one band members living on reserves (out of a total of 106 band members) have actually moved there. Beyond Fort Pitt were the "upstream people" (*Natimi-wiyiniwak*).

Several bands were transitional between Plains and Woods Cree. In certain respects—such as their particular dialects—they could be considered Plains Cree yet lived along the southern fringe of the northern woodlands rather than the parklands or plains. For example, the Ahtahkakoop band (previously variously called *Assissippi*, Sandy Lake, or Shell River) migrated regularly between woodland and prairie. Other southern woodland bands were settled to the east by Treaty 5 in 1876: at Shoal Lake (*Pahkwaw-sakahikanikh*), where a significant proportion, 705 of the 812 band members, remain on reserve; Red Earth (*Ka-mihkwaskiwakahk*) and Carrot River, with 1,176 of 1,350 members on reserve; and Cumberland House, Pine Bluff, Budd's Point, and Muskeg River (and, as noted, Sturgeon Weir) Reserves of the Cumberland House First Nation, with 712 of the 1,094 members still living on these reserves. The unique Swampy Cree dialect was spoken around Cumberland House. Treaty 6 in 1876 created several Cree reserves north and northwest of Prince Albert: Sturgeon Lake (*Namiwi-sakahikan* or *Pakitahwakan-sakahikan*), where 1,677 of the 2,405 band members remain on reserve; Big River, where 2,185 of the 2,865 band members live on reserve; Ahtahkakoop (*Yekawiskawikamahk*), with 1,589 of the 2,905 band members on reserve, and where St. Mark's Anglican Church, built in 1916, is an official historic site; Witchekan Lake, with 455 of the 624 band members living on reserve; and Chitek Lake, with 1,012 of the 1,306 members of the Pelican Lake First Nation living on reserve. And in the Meadow Lake area, 473 of the 1,081 Flying Dust (*Ka-ohpawakastahk*) band members live on the Meadow Lake and Gladue Lake Reserves; Waterhen Lake (*Sihkihp-sakahikan*), where 895 of the 1,753 band members live; Joseph Bighead/Big Island Lake, with 559 of 851 band members living on reserve; Makwa Lake (*Makwa-sahgaiehcan/sakahikan*), with 926 of the 1,286 band members living on reserve; and the Ministikwan Reserve, where 978 of the 1,183 members of the Island Lake First Nation live. And farther west, at Thunderchild (*Ka-pitihkow*) and New Thunderchild, 1,122 of the 2,433 band members live on reserve; at Onion Lake (*Seekaskootch*, or *Seekaskoots-Makayo* or *Oskaskosiwi-sakahikan*), together with *Makaoo* and Frog Portage (*Athiki-sipihcikan*), 2,862 of the 4,517 band members live. Historic St. Barnabas Anglican Church at Onion Lake, a simple wooden church with a cemetery, was first constructed in 1883 and then rebuilt in 1905.

SAULTEAUX/NAHKAWINIWAK

The Woodland Ojibwa began to enter Saskatchewan after 1780 from the east. The westward migration of these *Anishinabeg* (simply, human beings) paralleled the movement of the Cree, and like the Plains Cree—who spoke a related Algonquian language—they soon became acculturated to plains peoples. The Plains Ojibwa became known by Métis traders as *Saulteaux* but referred to themselves as *Nahkawiniwak*. As noted above, they mixed freely with Plains Cree at Cowessess, Sakimay, Kahkewistahaw, Muscowpetung, and Pasqua in the Qu'Appelle Valley; Okanese in the File Hills; George Gordon, Muskowekwan, and Kawacatoose in the Touchwood Hills; and White Bear and Ocean Man in the Moose Mountain area. In fact, the term "Oji-Cree" is often used now (especially in Manitoba) to refer to Ojibwa-Cree mixing. However, specifically Saulteaux communities came into existence primarily through Treaty 4 in 1874: Cote, Keeseekoose, and Key (*Pakwank*) around Kamsack; Fishing Lake (*Nocikinonsewanink* in Saulteaux or *Pakitahwawin* in Cree) and Nut Lake/Yellow Quill (*Pakani-sakahikanink*) and Kinistin farther west. The Saulteaux Reserve in the Battlefords area was established by Treaty 6 in 1876. Today only about a quarter, 785 of the 3,041 members of Cote First Nation, live on reserve; about a third, 704 of the 2,107 members of Keeseekoose; 482 of the 1,526 members of Fishing Lake; 367 of the 887 members of Kinistin; over a third, 888 of the 2,528 members, of Yellow Quill; and just over half, 619 of the 1,138 members, of Saulteaux. The Key Reserve is the location of historic St. Andrew's Anglican Church and cemetery dating from 1883.

ASSINIBOINE/NAKOTA

The Assiniboine (*Nakota*) are a Siouan-speaking people who diverged from other Sioux in the United States more than two centuries ago. As was later the case for the western Cree and Ojibwa, the Assiniboine became divided into woodland and plains cultures; this was observed as early as 1737 by the explorer La Verendrye. The designation *Assiniboine* was a Frenchified version of an Ojibwa expression for "one who cooks with heated stones." By the seventeenth century, they had spread from southern Manitoba into central and southern Saskatchewan, and during the eighteenth century they had expanded farther west into Alberta, where they were identified as Stoneys (*Ahsinipwan* in Nakota or *Asiniwipwat* in Cree) and concentrated in the Rocky Mountain foothills west of Calgary. The Nakota became Cree allies and ranged far and wide into the plains and even as far north as the Swampy Cree territory. Under Cree influence, they adapted to plains culture, becoming one of the largest First Nations on the prairies during the early nineteenth century. Despite their American origins, by the early nineteenth century only one of eight bands remained in the United States, in the Souris Valley of North Dakota not far from the Canadian border. However, Assiniboine began to move southward into the Missouri Valley in North Dakota and Montana, where the Upper Assiniboine eventually were settled with Gros Ventre (*Atsina*) at Fort Belknap and Lower Assiniboine with Yanktonai (*Ihanktonwanna*) and Sisseton (*Wahpeton*) Dakota Sioux and Teton (*Hunkpapa*) Sioux at Fort Peck.

In Saskatchewan, Carry-the-Kettle (*Ciga-kina* or *Wichawostaka*), Long Lodge, and Pheasant Rump (*Sio-nide*, *Le-coup-du-pheasant*) were distinctly Assiniboine reserves located between the Qu'Appelle Valley and Moose Mountain, specified through Treaty

4 in 1874. However, in the case of the Pheasant Rump First Nation, a reserve was granted in 1881, only to be surrendered in 1898; band members were subsequently amalgamated into the predominantly Cree White Bear Reserve; in 1990, however, Pheasant Rump was recognized as a separate band, and a couple of years later it received a grant of land on the west side of Moose Mountain (White Bear is on the east side), where 152 of the 360 band members reside. The Ocean Man First Nation, consisting of mixed Assiniboine, Cree, and Saulteaux, had a similar history: a reserve was originally created in 1882 and then surrendered, and the band was amalgamated with White Bear in 1901; then, in 1988, the band was re-established, and a reserve was granted in 1992. This new reserve consists of various scattered pieces of land in the Moose Mountain Creek and Moose Mountain Lake area west of Pheasant Rump. This First Nation had the distinction of being the sole one in all of Canada having not only a female chief but also an all-female council. Approximately a third, 850 of the 2,387 members of Carry-the-Kettle Assiniboine First Nation, live on the reserve just south of Sintaluta.

The "Battleford Stoneys" consist of the Grizzly Bear's Head (*Waguksica-pa*), Mosquito (*Capaka*), and Lean Man (*Wicasa-hustaga*) bands. The Grizzly Bear's Head band was originally a signatory to Treaty 4 in 1877 in the Cypress Hills but five years later migrated north to join the Mosquito and Lean Man bands, signatories to Treaty 6 in 1878, in the Battlefords area. The Lean Man band had settled south of Battleford in 1882, but only a single band member remained by 1931. All three bands finally merged officially in 1951 into a single First Nation; now 674 members of the combined membership of 1,200 reside on these adjoining reserves.

The Saskatchewan Assiniboine became closely allied and mixed with Plains Cree and Saulteaux. In fact, all three First Nations were represented at White Bear and Ocean Man in the Moose Mountain area. At Peepeekisis in the File Hills, Piapot in the Qu'Appelle Valley, and the Cypress Hills (*Nehiopwat*), people descended from Assiniboine mixed with the Cree and became Cree speaking.

SIOUX / DAKOTA AND LAKOTA

Two other American-origin Siouan-speaking peoples, the Dakota and Lakota, commonly identified together as Sioux, eventually settled in Saskatchewan. The designation *Sioux* was first used by French-speaking traders as a shortened version of *Nadouessioux* (from Ojibwa *nadowessi*, meaning snake or enemy). The Dakota historically had subdivided into the Santee, consisting of the Mdewakanton, Wahpeton, Sisseton, and Wapakute. They first came to Canada as refugees in Manitoba in 1862 following the abortive Minnesota uprising. In 1862–78, Mdewakanton and Wapakute settled the Oak Lake Reserve; in 1865–75, Wahpeton and Sisseton settled the Birdtail Creek Reserve; in 1877, Sisseton settled the Turtle Mountain Reserve; and, during the 1870s, they settled south of Portage la Prairie on the Dakota Tipi and Dakota Plains Reserves. Sioux movement into Saskatchewan commenced in 1877 following the defeat of Custer's Seventh Cavalry at Little Big Horn in Montana the previous year. Between 1878 and 1910, the Wood Mountain Reserve was settled by Oglala and Hunkpapa, who were Teton/Tintonwan Lakota (the western division of Sioux). In 1876–77, an estimated 5,000 Lakota were camped in the Wood Mountain area; however, by 1880 they were facing starvation—the North-West Mounted Police (NWMP) who confronted them were instructed not to provide rations to "American Indians." Both Canadian and American officials attempted to get them to return to "their own country"; gradually, most of them—including their chief, Sitting Bull (*Tatanka–iyotake*)—did return, surrendered, and were assigned to reservations in the United States. This policy did not sit well with the NWMP officer in charge, Major Walsh, who reported in April 1880 that "I was forced to make small issues of food to save their lives. ... The conduct of those starving and destitute people, their patient endurance, their sympathy, and the extent to which they assisted each other, their strict observance of law and order, would reflect credit upon the most civilized community."[3] A "temporary" reserve was not established at Wood Mountain until 1910, and it was not officially recognized as permanent until 1930. But meanwhile the Dakota had also been migrating westward into Saskatchewan. A mixture of Dakota (possibly together with some Lakota) were settled on the Standing Buffalo (*Tatanka-najin*) reserve in the Qu'Appelle Valley in 1878. Soon after, in 1881, the White Cap (*Wa-pa-has-ka*) band, mainly Sisseton Dakota, began to settle in Moose Woods, just south of Saskatoon. And in 1894 the Wahpeton (Round Plain or *Tintamibena*) Reserve north of Prince Albert was settled by Wahpeton and Mdewakanton. Actually, the Dakota never entered into the treaty process, though they did establish these recognized reserves. Some Dakota also settled along with Assiniboine, as well as Cree and Saulteaux, on White Bear Reserve on Moose Mountain.

Chief Whitecap's band of about fifty lodges—mostly Cakute Sisseton Sioux/Dakota—had first entered Canada from the United States in late 1862, just west of Turtle Mountain on the North Dakota-Manitoba border, and hunted buffalo in southern Saskatchewan with the Standing Buffalo band, who were also Sisseton. By the spring of 1875, the band had camped in Moose Woods (some thirty kilometres south of present-day Saskatoon). Chiefs Whitecap and Standing Buffalo approached the lieutenant governor later that year to seek lands to be reserved for their respective bands. While Standing Buffalo's people were settled in the Qu'Appelle Valley by 1878, Whitecap continued negotiations through 1880, by which time his band had been joined by other Dakota—some Yankton as well as Lakota—in Moose Woods. The reserve arranged by Chief Whitecap (Wapahaska) by 1881 (subsequently expanded by adding contiguous lands in 1893, 1898, 1921, 1926, 1928, 1933, and 1941) was within the traditional territory of the Plains Cree; the Dakota were relative latecomers to this region. In fact, apart from earlier hunting forays, the first Dakota did not begin to settle in Canada until the 1860s and a decade later in areas where they finally settled on their reserves. Chief Whitecap was reputed to have assisted the Temperance Colonists to settle on the east side of the South Saskatchewan River (across from what would later become the townsite of Saskatoon) in 1882; in return, some band members reportedly found work in the new colony. However, the Whitecap Dakota became allied with their Métis neighbours during the North-West Resistance in 1884–85—a substantial Métis settlement existed at La Prairie Ronde just south of Moose Woods—and were likely perceived at the time as a threat to the Temperance Colony. Nevertheless, Chief Whitecap was known as an astute leader of his people and a friend of the colonists.

The more populous of these Dakota reserves is Standing Buffalo, where 433 of the 1,113 band members reside. Whitecap and Wahpeton are comparable in population: half (252) of the 512 members of Whitecap live on reserve, compared with two-thirds

(308) of the 464 members of Wahpeton. Whitecap has been developing rapidly, with a new championship-quality golf course, the Dakota Dunes Casino, an upscale housing complex, and a broader highway linking the reserve to Saskatoon. At Wood Mountain, only ten of the 219 band members still live on this small reserve.

CHIPEWYAN/DENE

The Chipewyan people of far northwestern Saskatchewan, now commonly called Dene (or *na-Dene* or *Denesuline*, which simply means people; *Chipewyan* was actually a Cree term), are an Athapaskan-speaking people who, unlike the First Nations to the south, have lived in Saskatchewan since time immemorial (they are not to be confused with the Chippewa in the United States, who are Ojibwa). They were settled in reserve communities in accordance with Treaty 8 in 1899: Fond-du-Lac, where 938 of the 1,673 band members remain on six reserves; Black Lake First Nation, with 1,439 of the 1,817 band members living on the Chicken/Black Lake, Stony Lake, and Stony Rapids Reserves; the Clearwater River Dene around La Loche, with 676 of the 1,557 band members living on three reserves; and Lake Athabasca. And, in accordance with Treaty 10 in 1906, the English River First Nation, with a total contemporary band population of 1,349, of whom 738 still live on reserves, settled at Patuanak (*Wahpaciwanahk*), where Father Louis Moraud ministered to the English River Dene Nation from 1916 until his death in 1965, Lac La Plonge, Knee Lake, Elak Dase, Dipper Rapids, Wapachewunak, Porter Island, and Cree Lake; the Birch Narrows First Nation has 369 of its 628 members living on reserves at Churchill Lake and Turnor Lake; the Hatchet Lake First Nation settled at Lac la Hache, where 1,137 of the 1,462 band members live on reserve; and the Buffalo River Dene First Nation has 633 of its 1,170 members living at St. George's Hill and Dillon on Peter Pond Lake (where the Roman Catholic rectory, built in 1932, is a historic site). The Churchill River marks the approximate frontier between the Dene and northernmost Woods Cree; Pinehouse (*Minahik Waskahigan*) and Lac Ile-à-la-Crosse were formerly Dene, but now Woods Cree predominate. The Young Chippewayan First Nation in Saskatchewan does not possess a legally defined land base.

MÉTIS

The early development of distinct Métis settlements in Saskatchewan is described in detail in Chapter 7, "Francophone Settlements," since Métis settlement opened the way to—in fact can be regarded as the initial stage of—francophone settlement in Saskatchewan. Historical Saskatchewan Métis were the descendants of mostly francophone fur traders and Métis who originally moved west from their earlier settlements in Manitoba: Rivière Rouge, St-François-Xavier, Rivière-Seine, Rivière-Salle, St-Laurent, and St-Lazare (the Cree called French people *mistikosoouk*). Yet the ethnic identification of Saskatchewan Métis has been somewhat enigmatic insofar as they bridged Aboriginal and European cultures while forging their own unique culture, identity, and sense of peoplehood. They were blood relatives of First Nations; they resisted European settlement and interference yet opened the way at least for francophone settlement. They have traditionally been multilingual: in varying proportions, they speak French and/or English, yet they developed and often retained their own Michif language based on Cree or Ojibwa with ample French admixture, and they were often conversant in these

Native languages. They developed a unique culture that borrowed not only from their Aboriginal roots but also from their French Canadian connections (e.g., fiddle-playing while seated and foot-tapping out the rhythm, the riverlot system of settlement that had been transferred from the Rivière-Rouge and St-François-Xavier settlements in Manitoba to the Batoche and St-Laurent-Grandin settlement on the South Saskatchewan River, and the adoption of the *ceinture-fleché*—woven waist belt—as the pre-eminent Métis symbol) as well as, to a lesser extent, their Scottish predecessors (e.g., the strong tradition of dancing reels). Métis often chose to settle together with non-status Indians close to First Nations, especially up north, so that over time the distinctions among these separate peoples became blurred, yet Métis also developed a network of their own distinct settlements across the Saskatchewan prairie, particularly during the 1870s.

Given the fact that Métis by definition are of mixed ethnic origins (while developing their own unique identity as an Aboriginal people), estimating their numbers today in Saskatchewan with any accuracy is difficult. There are far fewer registered members of the Métis Nation of Saskatchewan than even conservative estimates of Métis population. Moreover, there are twice as many Saskatchewan residents claiming partial Métis ethnic origin as those claiming only Métis ethnicity. Relatively few Métis today are familiar with Michif dialects. Over 97% of Métis in Canada under the age of forty-five do not speak Michif today.[4] The large majority of Saskatchewan Métis are primarily English speaking, though those still living in francophone settlements are most likely to speak French, while Métis still living—or who have lived—in northern areas are likely to be familiar with Cree. Even where Métis live among or near francophones, they might or might not choose to identify with the French; for example, in the historic Batoche and St-Laurent-Grandin settlement, they still live on their riverlots, host the largest annual Métis gathering (Back to Batoche), and proudly fly the Métis flag (rather than the Fransaskois flag). A series of annual national Michif-language conferences has been organized, including in Saskatchewan by the Gabriel Dumont Institute with the Métis Nation of Saskatchewan.

CONTEMPORARY DEMOGRAPHICS

How many Aboriginal people live in Saskatchewan? This is a difficult question to answer with any accuracy, for there are several different ways of defining the Aboriginal population: by national census data, Aboriginal Affairs and Northern Development Canada (AANDC) data (the Indian Register), health data, band rolls, membership in the Métis Nation of Saskatchewan, and so on. Even census data count Aboriginal population at least three ways: self-identification (as Registered Indian, Non-Status Indian, Métis, Inuit, or Undifferentiated Aboriginal), claimed Aboriginal ancestry (single or multiple responses), and people who are officially counted as Registered Indians. In Saskatchewan, 141,890 residents self-identified as Aboriginal in the 2006 census (14.7% of the total population of the province). Of these, 91,400 (64.4%) claimed to be only "North American Indian" (First Nation), 48,120 (33.9%) to be only Métis, and 215 to be only Inuit, while another 625 claimed more than one type of Aboriginal identity (likely First Nation and Métis) and 1,530 some other sort of Aboriginal identification. Examining data for people claiming Aboriginal ethnic origin, one can note that a slightly larger number of Saskatchewan residents claimed to be wholly or partially of Aboriginal descent. Over two-thirds of those claiming North American Indian ethnic origin claimed only this single ethnicity, whereas the remainder considered themselves to be only partially Aboriginal (which could in fact range from a very small part to primarily). The reverse was true for residents claiming Métis origin, fewer than a third of whom claimed to be completely Métis, compared with well over two-thirds who claimed Métis ethnicity as only one of several ethnic origins. However, we need to bear in mind that an individual claiming more than one ethnicity can still be entirely Aboriginal, for example someone claiming both Métis and North American Indian ethnicity (which would be captured in the data on total Aboriginal population, including both single and multiple responses). The count of Registered Indians again provided different data: 90,720, divided almost equally between those living on reserve and off reserve. In fact, there has been progressive urbanization of the entire Aboriginal population in Saskatchewan, with close to half now living in urban areas—by 2006, a majority (53.2%) of all Canadians claiming Aboriginal identity were living in urban places.

The 2006 census revealed that over 1 million Canadians (1,172,790) identified themselves as Aboriginal (3.8% of the total Canadian population). This represented an enormous 45% increase in just ten years, compared with just 8% for the rest of the Canadian population, so Aboriginal people were increasing almost six times as fast as others. In the same ten years, there was a 29% increase specifically in the North American Indian population of Canada, which numbered 698,025 in 2006. Saskatchewan accounted for 13.3% of the total Aboriginal population of Canada, including about 15% of both the Registered Indian and Métis populations of Canada. In absolute numbers, Saskatchewan currently ranks fifth for a province having the largest number of Aboriginal residents, but proportionate to the total provincial population it is ranked second (comparable to Manitoba).

The Aboriginal and Registered Indian populations of Saskatchewan have grown rapidly. In 1971, there were 36,040 Registered Indians and 54,720 total Aboriginal population. The Registered Indian population changed from 51,140 in 1981 to 62,232 in 1986 with the addition of women and children under Bill C-31, and it reached 84,075 by 2001. The Aboriginal identity population grew to 111,245 in 1996—twice what it had been in 1971—and, as noted, 130,190 in 2001. The Métis population of Canada almost doubled in just ten years, reaching 389,785 in 2006. Yet a substantial part of this increase must have been people identifying themselves as Métis or partially Métis in the census, including not only historical Métis but also numerous people of mixed Aboriginal/non-Aboriginal origin. According to recent census data, 48,120 Métis were counted in Saskatchewan in 2006; however, the Métis Nation of Saskatchewan estimates the Métis population to be at least 80,000, and some surveys suggest a population of perhaps 90,000–120,000.

The rapid growth of the Aboriginal population in Saskatchewan—an increase of 28% between 1996 and 2006, compared with a decrease of the non-Aboriginal population of 6%—can largely be attributed to the fact that the estimated total fertility rate among Registered Indian women is higher in Saskatchewan (3.1 in 1996) than in any other province or territory, while the regional patterns for both Métis and Non-Status Indians are similar. This growth has been countered somewhat, however, by Aboriginal mortality rates, which, while declining, are still higher than those among the non-Aboriginal population. Life expectancy rates for Aboriginals continue to lag behind those for the non-Aboriginal population. Certain illnesses and causes of death are still many times higher among Aboriginals in Saskatchewan than non-Aboriginals. Pneumonia has long been a prominent factor in neonatal, infant, and child mortality among Aboriginal people in the province. Deaths by fire, suicide, drug and alcohol abuse, and accidental poisoning have been more prominent among Aboriginal youth. Diabetes, circulatory and respiratory system diseases, and motor vehicle accidents have been above the provincial norm, especially for Registered Indians on reserve.

On the whole, the Aboriginal population of Saskatchewan is much younger than the non-Aboriginal population. Almost half (47%) of the Aboriginal identity population is younger than twenty, compared with just over a quarter of the non-Aboriginal population. Half of the Aboriginal people in Canada are under the age of thirty—the median age of Aboriginals is twenty-seven, whereas that of the general population is forty. In Saskatchewan in 2006, the Aboriginal median age was even lower (twenty-two), but this was little more than half the median age of non-Aboriginal people (forty-one). Only about 5% of the Aboriginal identity population was over sixty-five years of age in 2006, compared with approximately 13% of the non-Aboriginal population.

While a large number of young Aboriginal people will soon be entering the labour force, their occupational diversity will depend on educational levels attained. On the one hand, the proportion of Aboriginal people aged fifteen and above who have less than a high school education (52.6% in 2001) is disproportionately large compared with the non-Aboriginal population (37.8%). On the other hand, the proportion of Aboriginal people with a university education or trades or other higher education (39.3%) has been rapidly increasing. Today close to 10% of the total student body at the University of Saskatchewan is Aboriginal, and opportunities for higher education have multiplied for Aboriginal students, as evidenced in increasing enrolments at First Nations University of Canada (Regina and Saskatoon) and Saskatchewan Indian Institute of Technologies (Saskatoon). Still, the 2006 census revealed that literacy rates for many Aboriginals continued to be problematic: according to Statistics Canada, 70% of First Nations people and 56% of Métis in Saskatchewan aged between sixteen and sixty-five remained below the minimum level of literacy considered adequate for an individual to cope in a complex knowledge-based society, compared with 37% of urban non-Aboriginal residents. Yet 77% of adult First Nations people above that minimum level were gainfully employed. Nearly half of urban Aboriginal residents in these age cohorts with the lowest levels of literacy did not participate in the provincial labour force at all, whereas a large majority of those who had reached or exceeded conventional standards of literacy were employed. Literacy levels on reserves have been considerably lower.

Although the occupational diversity of the Aboriginal population will eventually improve, it still lags behind that of the non-Aboriginal population in certain respects. Compared with the non-Aboriginal labour force, the Aboriginal labour force is proportionately overrepresented in construction (8.2% compared with 5.2%), sales and service (30.8% compared with 22.8%), and trades (19.0% compared with 14.4%). It is still somewhat underrepresented in finance and insurance (1.6% compared with 3.9%); real estate (1.1% compared with 1.3%), management (6.4% compared with 8.6%); business, finance, and administration (12.0% compared with 15.1%); and primary industry (8.1% compared with 16.5%). Moreover, it is seriously underrepresented in other occupational categories. The unemployment rate for the potential non-Aboriginal labour force in Saskatchewan was 4.8% in 2001, whereas among the potential Aboriginal labour force it was 23.0%, among First Nations 29.4%, and among Métis 15.5%. On-reserve average individual income has been increasing yet has consistently lagged behind off-reserve, particularly urban, income. While the gap between Aboriginal and non-Aboriginal incomes has gradually been closing, the former still remain well behind the latter.

URBANIZATION

Approximately a third of Saskatchewan residents self-identifying as Aboriginal in the census were First Nations people on reserve; another 17% were rural Aboriginal people off reserve, while almost half were Aboriginal people in urban areas, a majority of whom were living in the two Census Metropolitan Areas (CMAs) of Saskatoon and Regina. In 2006, 21,535 Aboriginal residents were counted in the Saskatoon CMA (9.3% of the total population), whereas within the city proper the number was 19,820 (9.8% of the total city population). The Regina CMA had an Aboriginal identity population of 17,105 (8.9% of the total population), whereas within the city proper Aboriginal residents numbered 16,535 (9.2% of the city population). In absolute numbers, Saskatoon had the largest number of Aboriginal residents (19,820), followed by Regina (16,535), Prince Albert (13,570), North Battleford (3,550), Yorkton (1,830), and Lloydminster (2,220, of which 1,190 were in the Saskatchewan portion of the city). But proportionate to the total city population, Aboriginal residents were most significant in Prince Albert, inclusive of the Opawakoscikan urban reserve (34.1%), followed by North Battleford (20.5%), Lloydminster (14.7%), Yorkton (10.7%), Saskatoon, including the Asimakaniseekan Askiy urban reserve (9.8%), and Regina (9.2%). First Nations residents outnumbered Métis by a substantial margin in Saskatoon, Regina, and North Battleford, yet these two populations were approximately even in Prince Albert, and Métis far outnumbered First Nations residents in Lloydminster.

In absolute numbers, Saskatoon and Regina rank respectively sixth and ninth among CMAs in Canada by size of Aboriginal identity population, yet they have among the highest proportion of Aboriginal residents; among smaller cities, Prince Albert stands out as having a relatively high Aboriginal population, now exceeding a third of the city's total population.

A rapid urbanization of the "Native Indian" population in Saskatchewan occurred during the 1960s. The urban proportion within this population increased from just 5.5% in 1961 to 21.7% in 1971. Much of this change occurred in the two largest cities. In Regina, the "Native Indian" population increased from 539 to 2,860, and in Saskatoon it increased from 207 to 1,070. Since 1971, the urban Aboriginal population has continued to increase, though at a slower rate each decade. By 1991, in both Regina and Saskatoon, 5.7% of the total city population identified as Aboriginal. Note, however, that a greater number of residents claimed some Aboriginal ancestry than identified as Aboriginal (entirely or partially). Using identity rather than ethnic origin data, one can note that the Aboriginal identity population has increased both in absolute numbers and proportionately during the past decade: in Saskatoon, for example, both the Aboriginal identity population and the proportion of total city population almost doubled in just a decade (1991–2001); today approximately one in every ten residents is Aboriginal. In just the five years preceding the 2006 census, the Aboriginal population of Saskatoon increased by 6.2%, but this rate has been far slower than the national rate (20.1%). Migration of Aboriginal people into cities will likely continue due to the lack of housing and educational and employment opportunities on reserves and in northern communities.

The Aboriginal populations of Saskatoon and Regina have gradually become more dispersed yet remain largely concentrated in poorer neighbourhoods. Today in Saskatoon, for example, out of sixty neighbourhoods, in two inner-city neighbourhoods, among the poorest in the city, over half of the population is now Aboriginal; in another two neighbourhoods (also relatively poor), over a third of the residents are Aboriginal; in another six, 20–29%; in eleven, 10–19%; thirty-six neighbourhoods contain less than 10% Aboriginal residents (many as few as 1–3%); only three neighbourhoods still lack any Aboriginal residents.

Examination of recent five-year gross migration rates of Aboriginal people in Saskatoon and Regina reveals that in-migration has usually been matched, more or less, by out-migration, yet this might now be changing in favour of in-migration. Recent research reveals that an increasing proportion of the urban Aboriginal population consists of long-term or "permanent" residents. In the Saskatoon CMA, the 2006 census revealed that, for the urban Aboriginal identity population that had lived in the city for at least one year (21,030), 63.8% had lived in the same residence the previous year, a quarter had lived in the same city but at a different address, 8.5% had lived in Saskatchewan but changed residence, and 2.7% had moved outside the province. For the Aboriginal identity population aged five years and older (19,150), 32.9% had lived at the same city address five years earlier, 43.5% had changed address within the city, 17.6% had moved outside the city but within the province, and 5.6% had moved outside the province. Thus, these findings seem to reveal a substantial pattern of mobility within the city every few years yet less movement between urban and rural (e.g., reserve) areas.

The urban Aboriginal population is young. In both Regina and Saskatoon CMAs, close to half of the Aboriginal population is under twenty years of age. In the cities having the largest numbers and highest proportions of Aboriginal residents—Saskatoon, Regina, and Prince Albert—an increasing number of young Aboriginal people are born and raised in the city, with little or no familiarity with reserve or rural life.

The cities provide more opportunities for education, and urban Aboriginal youth are becoming better educated. For example, in Saskatoon, of the total Aboriginal residents aged fifteen and older in 2006, 38.8% lacked a certificate, degree, or diploma, compared with 25.0% with a high school diploma (or equivalent), 9.8% with apprenticeship or trade certification, 12.6% with other non-university education, and 13.7% who were either currently in university or already had a university degree. Several thousand Aboriginal students are enrolled at the University of Saskatchewan, First Nations University of Canada, and Saskatchewan Indian Institute of Technologies in Saskatoon and at the University of Regina, First Nations University of Canada, and Gabriel Dumont Institute in Regina.

While the increasing urban Aboriginal presence is felt at virtually every level of education, it is especially dominant at the elementary level. In fact, several inner-city schools in Saskatoon and Regina now have a majority of pupils who are Aboriginal.

There are also high schools pursuing an Aboriginal curriculum, such as Oskayak High School in Saskatoon.

Clearly, with urbanization, Aboriginal people have been diversifying within the labour force and earning higher incomes. Now almost one-third of urban Aboriginals within the experienced labour force are in sales and service occupations; they are becoming relatively prominent in trades, business and finance, and education occupations; but fewer (though increasing numbers) are found in management, health, and science occupations. The unemployment rate (14.6%) as well as dependence on government transfer payments (19.6%) are still excessive, though steadily decreasing, compared with provincial rates for the non-Aboriginal population (respectively 3.7% and 9.8%) in Saskatoon. There is wide variation in average family income in neighbourhoods having the largest Aboriginal concentrations. In 1996 in Saskatoon, for example, average income for Aboriginal families was less than half that of Saskatoon families in general, though a marked difference could be noted among neighbourhoods. More recent data revealed that in 2005, of the total Aboriginal residents aged fifteen and older having gainful earnings that year, the median income was $16,480, compared with $26,112 for the total population in these age cohorts.

Saskatoon and Regina have the highest proportion of Aboriginal population living below the statistical poverty line (the Low Income Cut-Off or LICO) of any CMA in Canada. In 1996 in Saskatoon, 64% of the Aboriginal population was below the LICO, compared with only 18% of the non-Aboriginal population; in Regina, 63% of Aboriginals were below the LICO, compared with 14% of non-Aboriginals. In 2001, Aboriginal poverty had declined to 52% in Saskatoon and 53% in Regina, yet these rates still remained the highest for any CMA in Canada. Aboriginal unemployment rates and the LICO rate in all neighbourhoods having the highest Aboriginal concentrations far exceeded non-Aboriginal rates. With average income for Aboriginal residents lagging far behind that of non-Aboriginal residents in Saskatoon and Regina, on the whole, then, despite indications of increasing occupational diversity among the urban Aboriginal population in Saskatchewan, this population remains disproportionately poor.

Unfortunately, there is contemporary concern among urban Aboriginal residents over increasing crime rates in poorer inner-city neighbourhoods. These neighbourhoods, which have the highest Aboriginal concentrations, have the greatest prevalence of Aboriginal youth gangs and of violent sexual assault, armed robbery, both residential and business break and enter, vehicle theft, petty theft, and prostitution. In 2006, Aboriginals still constituted approximately one in every five prison inmates across Canada.

Housing conditions for the urban Aboriginal population are gradually improving. Much research and many policy recommendations have been reflected in increasing collaboration among Aboriginal organizations such as the Saskatoon Tribal Council and the Central Urban Métis Federation Incorporated and universities, civic government (particularly city planning), housing consortia, and community organizations, all recently linked in the comprehensive Bridges and Foundations Project on Urban Aboriginal Housing in Saskatoon. Among the urban Aboriginal population, home ownership is increasing (approximately one-third) and overcrowding lessening; however, many families are still struggling with relatively limited incomes and poor housing conditions: almost half of all Aboriginal homes in Saskatoon and Regina were reported to be in need of major or minor repairs. In Canada as a whole, the homes of Aboriginal residents are four times as often overcrowded as those of non-Aboriginal residents, and Aboriginal residents of Saskatoon are nine times more likely to live in overcrowded conditions than non-Aboriginal residents. Moreover, demand for affordable housing far exceeds availability; the current vacancy rate in Saskatoon is 0.6%, and newer housing costs have increased rapidly.

In Saskatoon, in all neighbourhoods where Aboriginal residents form significant proportions (over 10%), the proportion of Aboriginal families headed by lone parents (25.3%) exceeds that in non-Aboriginal families (17.8%), yet the proportion of Aboriginal lone-parent families in particular neighbourhoods ranged as high as 68.8%. Among Aboriginal residents of Saskatoon who were married or common law, the common law proportion was 40.1%, compared with just 12.8% for the general population.

Aboriginal businesses and institutions (e.g., Federation of Saskatchewan Indian Nations, Saskatoon Tribal Council, Saskatchewan Indian Gaming Authority, Métis Nation of Saskatchewan administrative offices, First Nations Bank, White Buffalo Youth Lodge, Career Village in Saskatoon, and institutions of higher education in Regina and Saskatoon) are becoming common parts of the urban scene in Saskatchewan, some located on urban reserves, notably Asimakaniseekan Askiy in Sutherland, organized by the Muskeg Lake First Nation. At the edge of the city limits of Saskatoon is the Wanuskewin Heritage Park, inclusive of the Tipperary Creek Provincial Archaeological Site, where remnants of tipi villages, hunting camps, bison kill sites, and sacred medicine wheels are testimony to thousands of years of Aboriginal settlement there; Wanuskewin serves as a lively centre for explaining historical as well as contemporary First Nations culture. These institutions not only serve the needs of the urban Aboriginal population but also reinforce First Nations and Métis identities within an urban context, a pressing need.

For example, attrition of Aboriginal language use has tended to be most pronounced in urban areas: of 20,275 Saskatoon CMA residents who identified themselves as Aboriginal in 2001, 11.8% recognized an Aboriginal language that they first learned and still understood, compared with only 4.4% of the 15,685 Aboriginal residents in the Regina CMA and 25.5% of the 130,190 Aboriginals in Saskatchewan. In Saskatoon, 8.2% still spoke that language at home, compared with only 2.0% in Regina and 22.4% in the province. Also in Saskatoon, 15.5% claimed at least some knowledge of an Aboriginal language, compared with 7.2% in Regina and 29.4% in Saskatchewan. Across Canada, some 29% of First Nations people can speak one of sixty recorded Aboriginal languages; Cree remains the most commonly spoken Aboriginal language in both Canada and Saskatchewan. In Canada, the number of Cree speakers has actually been increasing recently by 7% over five years, and an increasing proportion now recognize Cree as their second language. There has been widespread Aboriginal language revitalization across Canada. In 2006, there were 78,855 Cree speakers, 24,190 Ojibwa speakers, and another 11,690 "Oji-Cree" speakers.

While a synthesis of First Nations cultures, and the depletion of traditional languages, are more evident in urban areas, cities have also become focal points of changing and renewed Aboriginal identities, as evidenced in city and university pow-wows, employment fairs, business and financial meetings, cultural events, education meetings, housing conferences, storytellers' festivals, Indigenous food symposia, sporting events, music festivals, awards ceremonies, youth leadership retreats, and many more activities. And beyond the cities, the numerous First Nations and Métis gatherings held all over the province testify to a continuing interest in Aboriginal identification and traditions.

CONCLUDING THOUGHTS

This chapter has emphasized that for centuries—in fact for millennia—First Nations have occupied territories within what would finally become the Province of Saskatchewan in 1905. After contact with the vast numbers of settlers who were almost entirely of European ethnic origins, the First Nations remaining in Saskatchewan became regrouped into Indian reserves in accordance with treaties. These reserves, then, established largely during the initial period of contact, essentially constituted early ethnic group bloc settlements in their own right, yet they were unique in that they were legally defined with demarcated boundaries. Aboriginal peoples continue to add immeasurably to the great ethno-cultural diversity of the Saskatchewan population. Yet their cultures and identities have been changing—soon more Aboriginals will be living in cities than on reserves or in their own communities, fewer are speaking their traditional languages, and perhaps a synthesized urban Aboriginal identity transcending tribalism is emerging. While unfortunately too many Aboriginal residents continue to live in poverty, this situation, too, is changing—as evidenced in the already large and increasing numbers of Aboriginal university students and the increasing occupational diversity of Aboriginal people in the labour force. It seems vital not only to appreciate the long history and continuing traditions of the Aboriginal peoples of Saskatchewan but also to understand better the changing contemporary and future profiles of our Aboriginal residents.

SOURCES

Aboriginal People in Saskatchewan: History and Contemporary Issues
The most comprehensive and up-to-date concise source on all aspects of Aboriginal people in Saskatchewan is *Encyclopedia of Saskatchewan* (Regina: Canadian Plains Research Center, 2005).

Among the numerous more general sources on First Nations in Canada (including Saskatchewan) in historical perspective are the classic D. Jenness, *The Indians of Canada* (Ottawa: National Museum of Canada, 1960); and, more recently, J. Price, *Indians of Canada: Cultural Dynamics* (Scarborough: Prentice-Hall of Canada, 1979); H. Buckley, *From Wooden Plows to Welfare: Why Indian Policy Failed in the Prairie Provinces* (Montreal: McGill-Queen's University Press, 1992); O.P. Dickason, *Canada's First Nations: A History of Founding Peoples from Earliest Times* (Toronto: McClelland and Stewart, 1992); J.R. Miller, *Shingwauk's Vision: A History of Native Residential Schools* (Toronto: University of Toronto Press, 1996); P.R. Magocsi, ed., *Aboriginal Peoples of Canada* (Toronto: University of Toronto Press, 2002); S. Carter, "'We Must Farm to

Enable Us to Live': The Plains Cree and Agriculture to 1900," in *The Prairie West as Promised Land*, ed. R.D. Francis and C. Kitzan (Calgary: University of Calgary Press, 2007), 103–26; and S. Carter, "Demonstrated Success: The File Hills Farm Colony," in *Immigration and Settlement, 1870–1939*, ed. G.P. Marchildon (Regina: Canadian Plains Research Center, 2009), 235–63.

Among general sources on First Nations from a contemporary perspective that have included Saskatchewan content are R.H. Bartlett, *Indian Reserves and Aboriginal Lands in Canada: A Homeland* (Saskatoon: University of Saskatchewan Native Law Centre, 1990); P. Monture-Angus, *Journeying Forward: Dreaming First Nations' Independence* (Halifax: Fernwood Publishing, 1999); M. Battiste and J.Y. Henderson, *Protecting Indigenous Knowledge and Heritage* (Saskatoon: Purich Publishing, 2000); R.F. Laliberte et al., eds., *Expressions in Canadian Native Studies* (Saskatoon: University of Saskatchewan, 2000); J.S. Frideres and R. Gadacz, *Aboriginal Peoples in Canada: Contemporary Conflicts* (Toronto: Prentice-Hall, 2001); and J.R. Miller, *Lethal Legacy: Current Native Controversies in Canada* (Toronto: McClelland and Stewart, 2004).

History of Treaties and Legal Issues in Saskatchewan

Among the many sources that have dealt with the history of treaties and relations between governments and First Nations in Canada (including Saskatchewan) are a classic source, A. Morris, *The Treaties of Canada with the Indians of Manitoba and the North-West Territories, Including the Negotiations on Which They Were Based*, first printed in 1880; more recent sources are J.R. Miller, *Skyscrapers Hide the Heavens: A History of Indian-White Relations in Canada* (Toronto: University of Toronto Press, 1989); J.R. Miller, ed., *Sweet Promises: A Reader on Indian-White Relations in Canada* (Toronto: University of Toronto Press, 1991); B. Barry, *People Places: Saskatchewan and Its Names* (Regina: Canadian Plains Research Center, 1997), 6–36; J.R. Miller, *Bounty and Benevolence: A History of Saskatchewan Treaties* (Montreal: McGill-Queen's University Press, 2000); T. Flanagan, *First Nations? Second Thoughts* (Montreal: McGill-Queen's University Press, 2001); A.C. Cairns, *Citizens Plus: Aboriginal Peoples and the Canadian State* (Vancouver: UBC Press, 2001); J.R. Miller, *Reflections on Native-Newcomer Relations: Selected Essays* (Toronto: University of Toronto Press, 2004); D.J. Hall, "Clifford Sifton and Canadian Indian Administration, 1896–1905," in *Immigration and Settlement, 1870–1939*, ed. G.P. Marchildon (Regina: Canadian Plains Research Center, 2009), 183–211; and F.L. Barron, "The Indian Pass System in the Canadian West, 1882–1935," in *Immigration and Settlement, 1870–1939*, ed. G.P. Marchildon (Regina: Canadian Plains Research Center, 2009), 213–33.

Specific First Nations in Saskatchewan

See, under specific First Nations, *Encyclopedia of Saskatchewan* (Regina: Canadian Plains Research Center, 2005); and B. Barry, *People Places: Saskatchewan and Its Names* (Regina: Canadian Plains Research Center, 1997).

An informative source on the Plains Cree is D.G. Mandelbaum, *The Plains Cree: An Ethnographic, Historical, and Comparative Study* (Regina: Canadian Plains Research Center, 1979).

Sources on Dakota/Sioux in Canada include E. Nurge, ed., *The Modern Sioux* (Lincoln: University of Nebraska Press, 1970); J.H. Howard, *The Canadian Sioux* (Lincoln: University of Nebraska Press, 1984); and especially G. Laviolette, *The Dakota Sioux in Canada* (Winnipeg: DLM Publications, 1988). A couple of books specifically describing Sitting Bull and the Sioux at Wood Mountain are I. Allan, *White Sioux: The Story of Major Walsh of the Mounted Police* (Sidney, BC: Gray's Publishing, 1969); and C.F. Turner, *Across the Medicine Line: The Epic Confrontation between Sitting Bull and the North-West Mounted Police* (Toronto: McClelland and Stewart, 1973).

Demographic Data
Most demographic data on the Aboriginal population in Saskatchewan are drawn from Statistics Canada, the Census of Canada, 2001, 2006 (and earlier). For a concise summary, see A.B. Anderson, "Aboriginal Population Trends," in *Encyclopedia of Saskatchewan* (Regina: Canadian Plains Research Center, 2005), 10–11. An overview of Canadian trends is provided in J.P. White, P.S. Maxim, and D. Beavon, eds., *Aboriginal Conditions: Research as a Foundation for Public Policy* (Vancouver: UBC Press, 2003).

Urbanization
Sources on Aboriginal urbanization specifically in Saskatchewan include E.J. Dosman, *Indians: The Urban Dilemma* (Toronto: McClelland and Stewart, 1972); A.B. Anderson with Association of Métis and Non-Status Indians of Saskatchewan (AMNSIS), *A Preliminary Socio-Economic Survey of Métis and Non-Status Indian People in Saskatoon*, a report for AMNSIS with the Employment Development Branch, Canada Employment and Immigration Commission, 1979; F.L. Barron and J. Garcea, eds., *Urban Indian Reserves* (Saskatoon: Purich Publishing, 1999); A.B. Anderson, "Urban Aboriginal Population," in *Encyclopedia of Saskatchewan* (Regina: Canadian Plains Research Center, 2005), 975–76; E.J. Peters, "Are Aboriginal People in Regina and Saskatoon Forming Ghettos?," in *Saskatchewan: Geographic Perspectives*, ed. B.D. Thraves, M.L. Lewry, J.E. Dale, and H. Schlichtmann (Regina: University of Regina and Canadian Plains Research Center, 2007), 325–28; and A.B. Anderson, *Home in the City: Urban Aboriginal Housing and Living Conditions* (Toronto: University of Toronto Press, 2013).

More general sources on Aboriginal urbanization in Canada include *Aboriginal Peoples in Urban Centres* (Ottawa: Royal Commission on Aboriginal Peoples, 1993); C. Hanselmann, *Urban Aboriginal People in Western Canada: Realities and Policies* (Calgary: Canada West Foundation, 2001); and D. Newhouse and E. Peters, eds., *No Strangers in These Parts: Urban Aboriginal Peoples* (Ottawa: Policy Research Initiative, 2003).

Chapter 3
BRITISH SETTLEMENTS

This chapter describes the establishment of bloc settlements by people of British Isles ethnic origins, respectively English (as well as undifferentiated or mixed British), Scottish, Irish, and Welsh, representing the order in which these ethnic groups can be ranked today by population size and thus the proportion that they form within the Saskatchewan population. The 2006 census revealed that Saskatchewan residents claiming one or more of these British origins collectively numbered 606,875, well over half of the total provincial population. Clearly, these people constitute the largest generalized ethnic category in the Saskatchewan population, though not the largest single ethnic group (the largest of these British ethnic groups, the English, is outnumbered by people of German origin); in any case, no single ethnic group constitutes a majority of the Saskatchewan population. However, the vast majority (89.6%, or 543,565) of these people claiming British ethnic origin claimed more than a single ethnic origin: that is, one of these specific British ethnic origins and another ethnic origin; just 10.4% (63,310) claimed only a single type of British origin, either English, Scottish, Irish, or Welsh. Incidentally, a very small number of people claimed to be partially of Manx (175) or Cornish (35) origin; the Isle of Man is situated in the Irish Sea almost equidistant from Wales, England, Ireland, and Scotland, while Cornwall is the southwesternmost county in England; both were originally Celtic speaking, but Manx and Cornish have long been considered virtually extinct languages.

Yet several qualifications are necessary. First, "British" ethnic origin actually means penultimate British Isles origin: that is, Great Britain (England, Scotland, and Wales) as well as Ireland (both Northern Ireland, which remains nominally a part of the United Kingdom, and the Irish republic, which has been independent since 1916, so strictly speaking it has not been "British" since then, although it was considered part of Britain before then, when the predecessors of most Canadians of Irish origin arrived).

Second, British origin includes not only immigrants direct from Great Britain and Ireland but also descendants of original immigrants who might have immigrated several generations ago. Thus, the vast majority of these people in Saskatchewan would conform to the latter type; they might recognize that they are descended from predecessors who once came to Canada from Britain or Ireland, most likely two or more generations back.

Third, given that in most cases British origin would actually imply British Canadian ethnicity, many of these residents or their predecessors who settled in Saskatchewan moved to the province from other provinces to the east, especially Ontario and Manitoba. To call them "Anglo-Canadians" might be rather misleading, though quite conventional; "English Canadians" can be more misleading, for strictly speaking this term should refer just to Canadians whose predecessors once came from England, or who themselves are English immigrants, if the term is used in an ethnic sense rather than a more common linguistic sense (referring far more broadly to English-speaking Canadians regardless of ethnicity).

Fourth, in actuality many people in Saskatchewan claiming a British origin came not from other Canadian provinces but from the United States—which still does not alter the claim that their predecessors originated ultimately in the British Isles. But to add to the confusion of demographic data, in Saskatchewan in the 2006 census 12,845 residents were listed as American origin (solely plus partially) and a very large number (172,365) as undifferentiated Canadian. Many of these people likely did have at least some British ancestors but were not counted in the British ethnic origin data.

Fifth, not infrequently it is assumed that Saskatchewan people of British origins simply formed the general population, implying that they could not be considered "ethnic" (everybody has some sort of ethnic origin); that they set the standard to which everybody else was obliged to conform (true enough: "Anglo-conformity" was imposed not only on Aboriginal children through residential schools but also on other ethnic groups through the provincial educational system, yet it was often strongly resisted); and that they did not form bloc settlements (not true: a wide variety of specifically English, Scottish, Irish, and Welsh settlements developed, similar to the bloc settlements of other ethnic groups).

ENGLISH SETTLEMENTS

The "English" population in Saskatchewan included not only large numbers of Anglo-Canadians who moved there from Ontario and neighbouring Manitoba, as well as Anglo-Americans, but also many immigrants who came directly from England. The early English immigrants tended to be romantic idealists who mostly lacked any farming experience yet viewed the Canadian West as a wild colonial frontier of the British Empire. They came to escape industrial unemployment, poverty and class inequity, religious discontent, and agrarian depression in England. Yet many were from cities, so they were quick to become frustrated with the rigours of prairie rural life, and many soon gave up farming.[1] Clifford Sifton's first and foremost goal was to attract British farmers, yet they exhibited a reluctance to relocate to a forbidding land.[2] Except for several thousand experienced tenant farmers and crofters, British immigrants who were enticed tended largely to be "a motley crew of star-crossed store clerks, school teachers, students, and remittance men. Some migrated on their own initiative; others came in groups sponsored and subsidized by church organizations or by the colonization and charitable societies working to rid English cities of their unemployed poor. ... These British immigrants were encumbered by an all-pervading ignorance of agriculture. ..."[3]

Several early utopian settlements were established. In 1882, Cannington Manor, named after a village in Somerset, was founded by Captain Edward Mitchell Pierce (1832–88) with his four sons. The colony attracted English aristocrats, businessmen, and landowners. Mutual visits were exchanged between these English and French aristocrats at St-Hubert; together they went hunting with horses and hounds, and other typically Victorian British diversions included horse racing, cricket, croquet, and tennis. The cultural life of this small, isolated colony was extraordinarily lofty: no fewer than sixteen homes had pianos, and gala balls were staged. Dinner at home featured linen tablecloths, polished silver, and fine crystal, and families dressed for dinner; afternoon teas were also a regular tradition. The settlers were less interested in dirty farming, hauling firewood, building their own homes, cooking, and housework.[4] All Saints Anglican Church and Beckton Place manor house on the Didsbury Stock Farm were prominent features of the colony; the latter intended to train young men of British origin to become efficient prairie farmers. Cannington Manor thrived for two decades—it once had a trading company, flour mill, doctor, police detachment, land agency, school, hotel, general store, woodworking shop, blacksmith, shoemaker, post office, and town hall—but by 1905 had become all but deserted. Five years earlier the new railway line had missed the community by more than sixteen kilometres. One of the few remaining buildings now comprising a provincial historic site is All Saints Anglican Church (1884), combining Gothic and Tudor features to resemble an English country parish church; however, the other buildings are all replicas or partially restored, including the Maltby House (whose occupant had formed a partnership with Captain Pierce's Moose Mountain Trading Company). The now-ruined Beckton House (completed in 1889) had twenty rooms, lavishly furnished, with rich carpets, a writing room, a billiard room, and an adjoining bachelors' wing (now partially restored) for visitors. Nearby on the Turton farm is Rosemount, the well-preserved stone farmhouse; John Turton left England for Ontario in 1869, then settled in Saskatchewan in 1882, building Rosemount in 1890. Although Cannington Manor today is a historic site, the nearby village of Manor (pop. 312 in 2006) is a growing community.

As Cannington Manor was developing in the southeastern region, other utopian settlements came into existence elsewhere in what would become Saskatchewan. Methodists from Toronto formed the Temperance Colonization Society, which founded the Temperance Colony in 1882–83 on the east side of the river flowing through Saskatoon. Several historic sites are remnants of that original colony: Nutana cemetery (1884), the Marr residence (1884), said to be the oldest remaining home in Saskatoon, and Victoria School (1887) and Rugby Chapel (1911) on the university campus, while Temperance Street and Colony Street are reminders of the original Temperance Colony. The village of Saskatoon was established on the opposite (west) side of the river in 1901; it became a town just two years later; then it amalgamated with the villages of Riversdale (also on the west side) and Nutana—the former Temperance Colony—on the east side to form the city of Saskatoon in 1906, by which time the combined population had grown quickly to approximately 4,500. From these modest beginnings, Saskatoon would grow into a city of a quarter of a million people.

In 1882, two fundamentalist Methodist ministers brought settlers from Ontario and England to what became known as the Primitive Methodist Colony, originally centred on the one-time hamlets of Pheasant Forks, Finnie, and Lorlie in the Pheasant Hills and eventually extending throughout the area between the small village of Duff and the larger communities of Abernethy and Balcarres. Although today the historic markers describing the foundation of this colony and the role of colonization companies are located in a small picnic park three kilometres northeast of Duff, the actual centre of the colony, Pheasant Forks, is located eleven kilometres to the southwest. The Primitive Methodist Colonization Company managed to settle 107 settlers, most arriving via Brandon, Manitoba, by 1883 in and around Pheasant Forks.[5] Zion Methodist Church was soon constructed, and a second church was built in 1905 when the original church became too small to accommodate the growing congregation. The church remained active until 1963 and is still used occasionally. A succession of schools was also located at Pheasant Forks in 1885, 1894, and 1920 (finally a third and more substantial two-room brick schoolhouse). Many of the original members of the colony had been local preachers in England, and adopting the traditional Methodist preaching circuit they were able to provide services to the entire colony. Given what barely passed for roads in the early years of settlement, getting to and from church proved to be quite a challenge both for preacher and for congregation. One elderly lay preacher used to drive to his service at Lorlie School with an umbrella fastened to the front of his cutter as a protection from bitter winter winds. When itinerant Methodist or Congregationalist preachers were not available, it was common for a homesteader in such a new settlement to undertake services on his own initiative—here these Protestants had a definite advantage over denominations requiring formal clergy. During the summer, church services became vital social gatherings; although some Methodists did not approve of community picnics and outdoor socials, they soon began with settlement—at Pheasant Forks within the first or second year.[6] Little evidence remains today of this colony, just the Pheasant Forks cemetery hidden in a grove of trees out in the open country. The cemetery, with a historic marker, is well maintained, and burials there have been conducted right up to the present. The Stilborn family is particularly well represented—almost half of the graves in this fairly large rural cemetery. Sadly, the deaths of children were common. Today Duff has only thirty residents; in 1971, there were not more than 500 people of British origin in the rural municipalities of McLeod and Stanley.

The Hogg Colony began to develop north of Lipton in 1883 with the arrival of settlers sponsored by L. Hogg, a well-to-do Englishman. The East London Artisans settled in the Wapella-Moosomin area in 1884. Sponsored by Baroness Burdett-Coutts, they were also known as the "Coutts colonists," while the colony was called the East London Colony. The settlers were primarily tradesmen and townsmen and thus found adaptation to agricultural life challenging; many soon moved into larger centres to pursue the trades for which they had been trained.[7] The York Farmers Colonization Company brought settlers from York County, Ontario, to commence a prosperous farm settlement centred on Yorkton in 1882. The post office changed the community name from York City to Yorkton two years later. Both the post office and the rural municipality respectively north and east of town were named after N. Clark Wallace, then the president of the York Farmers Colonization Company. The church hewn out of poplar logs in 1893 was used until about 1911. Yorkton was designated a village in 1894, a town in 1900, and a city in 1928. The old Anglican church at Katepwa Beach in the Qu'Appelle Valley was built in 1886 and is now a designated heritage site. The Church Colonization Land Company attempted—with limited success—to settle urban immigrants on preplanned homesteads in the Christ Church Settlement east of Qu'Appelle in 1887. Selection of English immigrants, land purchases, and construction of a cottage on each homestead were directed by a professor who was a British government examiner in agriculture. The scheme was short lived, however, because of the ready availability of free homesteads in the region.[8]

Utopian idealism was certainly not lacking as a force in the founding of certain colonies. In 1895, the Harmony Industrial Association founded the Harmonia (also called Hamona) colony in the Qu'Appelle Valley near the Manitoba border just east of Tantallon. As colony founders Edward and William Paynter explained, "Feeling that the present competitive social system is one of injustice and fraud ... we do write under the name of the Harmony Industrial Association for the purpose of acquiring land to build homes for its members, to produce from nature sufficient to insure its members against want or fear of want."[9] Although the cooperative colony did not represent any particular religious sect, one of the founders, Samuel Hearne, was a Quaker. This highly structured association intended to become as completely self-sustaining as possible while pursuing the ideal of absolute equality and cooperation among the colonists. It advocated a carefully planned scheme for the division of labour, issued its own currency, and became the first to harvest grain by combining. Yet only five years later, despite the high expectations of the association, its members (just ten families and several single men) voted to dissolve the community and to divide its assets.[10]

By 1905, the Swarthmore settlement of Quakers, known as the Friends Colony, up in the Coteau northeast of Unity, had its post office. The hamlet of Swarthmore was named after the home in England of George Fox, the original meeting place of the Society of Friends, more commonly called the Quakers. This small settlement was founded by William Ira Moore and other Quakers from Heathcote, Ontario. The Quaker meeting house in Swarthmore was transformed into a United church in 1930.[11] Amos Kinsey, raised in a Quaker family that had moved from the United States to Ontario, moved out west to Cannington Manor, then became a colourful leading resident of Moosomin, where his large stone home was built.[12]

The Barr Colony, an extensive settlement centred on Lloydminster, on the Saskatchewan-Alberta border, was established in 1903 by Reverend Isaac Montgomery Barr, from Halton County, Ontario, who initially had anticipated recruiting about 500 settlers in London in 1902; much to his surprise, some 2,000 had responded.[13] They set sail from England aboard a Canadian ship, the SS *Lake Manitoba*, built to accommodate 550 passengers, whereas 1,962 colonists, replete with their personal and household effects, were crowded into its hold.[14] Reverend Barr was assisted—and soon replaced as leader—by Reverend George Exton Lloyd, a Canadian who had gone to England in

1901 in the service of the Anglican Church; Reverend Barr appointed him chaplain of the new colony. Employed by the Colonial and Continental Church Missionary Society, Reverend Lloyd accompanied the colonists from England; later he became principal of the Anglican theological college in Saskatoon and bishop of Saskatchewan (1922–31). Reverend Barr, for all his visionary zeal, often revealed his duplicity. On the one hand, he challenged would-be settlers to overcome the rigours of Western settlement:

> If you are afraid, stay at home ... don't come to Canada. It is a land of brave and conquering men. But if you are honest and brave, and intend to work hard, if you propose to lead the temperate and strenuous life, then come and cast in your lot with us, and we will stand together and win.[15]

On the other, he seemed remarkably naive: he was familiar neither with prairie farming nor with the rigours of the Western climate.[16] Yet he did recognize the need for experienced Canadian and (even American) farmers.[17]

En route, the immigrants, dressed in their finery (the men wearing bowler hats, ties, starched shirts and suits, the women flowery hats and floor-length dresses), camped in dozens of tents (exaggerated as "tent hotels") on the plains of Saskatoon.[18] According to one Canadian newspaper account, the colonists "were no common emigrants. ... All of them were of a fairly well-to-do appearance, as if they had not found it impossible to exist in England, but had decided that they might do even better in the fertile land out west."[19] *The Herald* was of the opinion that "they may be good businessmen in England, but unless they have had colonial experience it is safe to count on their mission being a failure."[20] One of Barr's associates suggested that "these young men had been hardened by cricket and football in the public schools for a life of outdoor labour" but unfortunately not for the type of outdoor labour that they were to encounter in Saskatchewan.[21] The settlers were "the victims of a complete ignorance of the necessities of Canadian life." Disillusioned by the rigours of living in a rudimentary tent village that the Canadian Department of Immigration had been obliged to set up, the incomplete rail line northwest from Saskatoon, and the delay in supplies and services, some of the colonists refused to proceed any farther and opted to stay in the new community of Saskatoon. The Canadian Immigration Branch soon found that the colony buildings were "so primitive as to be practically useless beyond the immediate present."[22] Moreover, the committee whose responsibility it was to run the colony was "one of the most incapable bodies of men to ever get together. ... [I]t is helpless beyond hope to provide work for [the colonists]."[23] Evidently, many Canadians had favourable impressions of the Barr colonists: the *Saskatoon Phenix* went so far as to call them "first-rate material, just the kind we need in this great West to develop its abundant resources. ... Two years will make excellent Canadians of them"; *The Herald* called them "all a splendid class of people ... the material of which good settlers are made."[24] Others were of very different opinions. In 1903, Senator Lougheed of Alberta commented that

> there are few immigrants so helpless as the English landing on our shores. He is not familiar with the conditions which obtain in this country. He has been living under fairly comfortable conditions and expects to have all the comforts

of civilization, and we very well know that if these are not accorded to him he is the very prince of grumblers.[25]

To which Professor James Mavor, a pre-eminent political economist at the University of Toronto, added, perhaps more tactfully yet still pointedly, in the *Manchester Guardian* the following year, that the new settlers were "unfamiliar with Canada and its ways; even experienced English farmers were obliged to relearn farming in Western Canada; most of the colonists were from cities and did not possess even a rudimentary knowledge of farming; moreover, the colony was initially a consuming rather than producing community."[26] Even Clifford Sifton himself bluntly admitted that he could not be interested in efforts to transfer people from the cities of Great Britain to the Western Canadian prairies: "Let it not be imagined that you can gather up tens of thousands of people who have neither any desire for, nor adaptability to, the life which is ahead of them, and turn them into farmers. It takes two generations to convert a town-bred population into an agricultural one. Canada has no time for that operation."[27]

The colony was variously called the Barr Colony after its founder until Reverend Lloyd took control, the British Colony, Brittania Colony, or simply Brittania, NWT, with the new town of Lloydminster named after its leader, while the surrounding rural municipality (RM) retained the name Brittania. Britishness was strongly emphasized. Reverend Barr foresaw an all-British colony that would be neither denominational (although the Anglican Church had clear priority) nor "communistic." He proclaimed his clarion call: "Let us take possession of Canada. Let our cry be CANADA FOR THE BRITISH!" He sought to counterbalance the steady influx of Americans into Saskatchewan. Even Canadian and American farmers who could assist the colonists, he strongly suggested, "shall be of British descent."[28] And clearly Reverend Lloyd concurred: for more than four decades, he "engaged in a personal, unwavering struggle to realize a British prairie Promised Land populated by loyal citizens 'possessing the same language, the same ideals, the same character, the same king, the same flag, and the same old Mother Church of England.'"[29] Even the lieutenant governor at the time, A.E. Forget, a francophone, was of the opinion that, despite the "discomforts" and "difficulties" of settlement, "British pluck, British energy and British cheeriness will make light of them."[30]

Reverend Barr clearly thought more highly of his English immigrants than he did of communistic Doukhobors—a sentiment popular among the British population of Saskatchewan at the time. An editorial in the *Saskatchewan Herald* referred approvingly to the Barr Colony as "a big undertaking," while an editorial in the adjacent column was titled "The Crazy Doukhobors." Reverend Barr later acknowledged in 1904 that "After my experience I am convinced that the English do not make the best immigrants for a new country. ... [E]ven the despised Doukhobors look down with contempt upon the average English settler."[31] Moreover, his paternalistic attitude toward Indians could be viewed as representative of Anglo-Canadian ethnocentric views of the day: "All Indians in North-West Canada are now practically civilized. ... I met many of the people and conversed with them. They are now quiet and law-abiding citizens. ... There is nothing to fear from our Indian friends, any more than from the Gypsies of England."[32]

St. Peter's Anglican Church at Stoney Creek in Brittania RM northeast of Lloydminster, dating from 1912, is a designated historic site. The colony soon extended southeast to Marshall, in the original Stringer district named after an early colonist who was the first postmaster in the colony and where the first Anglican church, St. George's on the Trail, was established; to Lashburn, preceded by Wirral (named after the original home of the postmaster in Merseyside) and Sisley (named after postmistress Laura Sisley, who had brought orphaned boys from England); and westward to Kitscoty in Alberta (named after a place in Kent). Other districts in the settlement included Albion (the original Latin name for England), Furness, and Trafalgar. The religious focal point of the colony was St. John's Minster, a simple wooden Anglican church in Lloydminster (a historic site now moved to a park). Although there are many historic sites throughout the colony, colony history and social life are perhaps best viewed today at the Barr Colony Heritage Cultural Centre in Lloydminster, the Centennial Museum in Lashburn, and the Maidstone Museum.

Lloydminster, Saskatchewan, became a town in 1907; it was amalgamated with Lloydminster, Alberta, in 1930, and together they became a single city in 1958. The Barr Colony expanded into an extensive area of British settlement; just the Saskatchewan portion was approximately sixty kilometres across from east to west and from north to south; the colony extended from Brittania RM into the rural municipalities of Wilton, Eldon, and Paynton. Back in 1971 (the last census taking detailed ethnic origin data for local communities and rural municipalities before a less accurate 20% sample was instituted), people of British origin constituted almost two-thirds (65.4%) of the population of Brittania RM at the heart of the Barr Colony and 57.3% of the residents of the city of Lloydminster (on both sides of the border), 63.7% of Maidstone, 63.6% of Lashburn, 58.1% of Paynton, 53.7% of Marshall, and 40.0% of Waseca. These rural municipalities and communities contained a British-origin population numbering approximately 6,100. Today the city of Lloydminster has a combined population of 24,028 (8,118 in Saskatchewan and 15,910 in Alberta in 2006) and continues to grow, with some 4,000 residents employed in the oil and gas industry; the towns of Maidstone (pop. 1,037) and Lashburn (pop. 914) are increasing in population, whereas the town of Marshall (pop. 608) and the villages of Paynton (pop. 151) and Waseca (pop. 144) are currently decreasing in population.

Yet some caution over such a large English bloc settlement (or reservation) was expressed by Canadian authorities. Even Clifford Sifton seemed rather reticent: in refusing Reverend Barr's request for forty additional townships for his colony, Sifton noted that "With the present movement of population it is absolutely impossible to make reservation. ... Government has no way of keeping squatters off this land. ... There is no need of reservation. ... Plenty of land for all Barr's settlers. ..." *The Herald* was similarly opposed to reserving so much land for a colony, arguing that "millions of acres [would be] tied up so that the free settler cannot get in. ... Big reservations have been the curse of this country." For his part, Professor Mavor thought it a mistake to distinguish between "British" and "Canadian," so he was opposed to setting up a British colony.[33]

The Barr colonists had high expectations: as one colonist explained, "We still visualized the land we could get as picturesque parkland, with grassy, gently rolling slopes interspersed with clumps of trees, a sparkling stream and possibly a silvery lake thrown in, and the whole estate alive with game of all kinds." Well, some of this dream might have been realized, but England this was not. Still, as one historian later concluded, "In spite of ... hardships, ... the colonists survived and prospered. They came, they saw, they conquered. The very hardships, indeed, steeled them to greater effort."[34]

Apart from these settlements, innumerable communities and localities in Saskatchewan were named after places in England: Banbury, Bickleigh, Birmingham, Bognor, Canterbury, and so forth. ... And one district, Helland (near Coronach), was given a Cornish name. Asquith once prided itself as "the centre of the British Empire"[35] A railway siding near Weyburn was called Union Jack. Some communities and localities were named by settlers after their places of origin in Ontario, such as Uxbridge and Unionville. And many other communities and localities were named after figureheads, such as Gainsborough. Often, however, railway builders—financiers, administrators, even foremen—were responsible for naming communities, so that many were given English names yet settled by other ethnic groups or perhaps originally settled by English immigrants and Anglo-Canadian migrants from Ontario who were soon outnumbered by settlers of other ethnic origins. This was the case, for example, at Speers, originally named after C. Wesley Speers, a Canadian immigration officer and local landowner; the area was initially settled in 1904 as the New Ottawa settlement by parishioners of Reverend John Grenfell of Ottawa, but increasing numbers of Ukrainians homesteaded in the area (coincidentally, Wesley Speers had been instrumental in settling large numbers of Ukrainians around Yorkton in 1897 and later the Doukhobors and Barr colonists).[36] Nonetheless, from the foregoing it should be clear that a number of distinctly English or Anglo-Canadian settlements (with specific names) were organized beginning in the 1880s in what would become the province of Saskatchewan, while English and Anglo-Canadian settlers rapidly spread throughout Saskatchewan in many other areas and communities. Many very small communities have long retained a typical English or Anglo-Ontarian character. At Edgeley (pop. 41), between Balgonie and Fort Qu'Appelle, English settlers from Edgeley, near Manchester, England, were joined by Scottish settlers from Guelph, Ontario, in 1882 and founded the Methodist church the next year and the Anglican church in 1899. Ellisboro, in the Qu'Appelle Valley north of Wolseley, was named by an early settler who had headed west in 1882 from Guelph, Ontario. Gestingthorpe, a unique fieldstone farmhouse with a three-storey square tower, was built in the Summerberry area east of Wolseley in 1890 for Bernard Serjeant, an English immigrant who was the son of the vicar of Acton, Suffolk; he was trained as a farmer at Winmarleigh Grange, a farm in the Grenfell area with a grand home established in 1883 by Richard Lake, who became lieutenant governor of Saskatchewan. Another fine stone building is the former public schoolhouse in Summerberry.[37] Bridgeford, southeast of Elbow, was named by the first postmaster after his original community in England in 1903; it once flourished with over 300 residents (reportedly over 1 million bushels of grain were loaded from the Bridgeford siding in 1911), but the community began to decline as early as the 1920s when it was bypassed by a competitive rail line, and by 1970 only two families remained. Burnham, northeast of Swift Current, was similarly named by English settlers after a village in England; with a peak population of only fifty-six in 1907, by 1916 the post office had already closed, and there were just seven residents left by 1972. Leney, just south of Perdue, once boasted "a hundred plus children"—and a hotel, two general stores, hardware store, lumberyard, restaurant, flour mill, livery stable, meat market, barber shop, pool room, bakery, car and insurance business, and Anglican and Presbyterian church services—but proximity to the larger Perdue on the railway and a devastating fire started a decline already by the 1920s; today only two homes remain.

Among the finest examples of English stone churches in rural Saskatchewan are St. John the Evangelist in Fort Qu'Appelle (1885), Christ Church Anglican in Wapella (1899), St. Mary the Virgin Anglican in Whitewood (1902), Fairview Methodist in Davin (1903), and St. Lucy's Anglican in Dilke (1914), while at Heward (pop. 20) early settlers of the New Hope Colony near Stoughton built the lovely stone church (originally Anglican in 1921, United in 1961, closed in 1968, and declared a heritage property in 1983).[38] In 1907, James Addison, a skilled carpenter, and his family immigrated from England and settled in Saskatchewan. The "soddie" home that he built in Kindersley is the only such structure in Canada still being used as a home; it was designated a National Historic Site in 2004 (originally, the exterior sod walls were covered by vines, replaced by wooden siding during the 1940s, then asphalt, and finally in 1996 vinyl siding).

It is interesting to note that English immigrants to Western Canada were advised to "unlearn" their skills, thereby their former status, in accommodating to the existing Canadian settlers—"the Eastern Canadian and the American"—with whom they would initially have to compete: according to one government document issued in 1912, it is

> usually the old countryman who will be considered last. ... Unless he arrives at a fortunate time, the Englishman and Scotchman seldom gets a good position till he becomes known personally in the town he chooses to settle in. ... The lawyer, architect, engineer, surveyor, accountant and journalist all have a great deal to learn, or unlearn. The doctor is handicapped in that it takes him a little time to become "unprofessional" and advertise himself against the competition of the Canadian-born. ... Clerks and shop assistants, and they are not encouraged to emigrate, cannot, in large numbers, hope for much in Western Canada as such. ... The mechanic, carpenter, bricklayer, smith, or painter has much to unlearn. He has probably had a more thorough training than the man he competes with, and he may be chosen for the finer work, but that won't help him to steady work in winter. ... Most of the work is outdoors. ... Stonecutters [and other tradesmen] are sometimes wanted badly during the summer months, and earn big money ... [but] there is always a slack time in winter.[39]

Such sage advice has more recently become all too familiar to immigrants of non-White racial origins who similarly must compete with existing Canadians and more than likely have their professional accreditation earned prior to coming to this country questioned or scrutinized with scepticism.

As the English—and more generally the British—population of Saskatchewan grew, it long exercised control over political, economic, and social interests. Anglo-conformity was emphasized in urban and rural schools and ensured the dominance of Anglo-Canadian culture, in keeping with strong resistance to "foreign immigrants." British and especially English settlers have often been seen by historians and social scientists as reinforcements for the dominant Anglo-Saxon culture; this was certainly the view held by imperialists prior to the First World War who desired "to keep Canada British" and later by xenophobic Canadians of British descent who predicted "race ruin" if "foreign" immigrants were let into Canada insufficiently checked.[40] The Anglican Church long played a significant role in the preservation of a British identity in Canada. At the Lambeth Conference of Anglican archbishops in London in 1910, no less than the archbishop of Canterbury (the titular head of the worldwide Anglican Communion) invoked the church's "special responsibilities in regard to the British Empire" and appealed for "money and men" as well as "interest and prayer" for the church in Western Canada "linked with England by the bonds of history and institutions, of language and affections." The church saw an opportunity to become involved with the work of Canadian immigration officers at every level, beginning with the quest for new immigrants from Britain; after all, the Anglican Church was a state institution in Britain and was presumed thus in Canada, a former British colony.[41] Despite its historic missionary work, the rapid and steady influx of what seemed a "foreign" population soon brought about a lessening of the church's influence. Protestant missionary societies—such as the Church Missionary Society of the Anglicans and the Home Mission Boards of the Methodists and Presbyterians—attempted to ensure financial solvency not only through grants from church headquarters but also from collections and fundraising in the local community.[42] By 1911, though, Presbyterians, who were largely of Scottish origin, had become by far the largest denomination in the Prairie Provinces; the Anglican Church also had fewer members in this region than the Roman Catholics and Methodists.[43]

Religious and philanthropic organizations collaborated with the British Child Migration Scheme, which shipped over 150,000 impoverished children aged nine to fourteen out from Britain to Commonwealth countries from 1869 through the 1940s—approximately 100,000 to Canada to work mainly as domestics. About 82,000 were settled in Ontario and Quebec, some of whom eventually were sent out to "industrial farms" and family farms in Manitoba and Saskatchewan to work as farm labourers.

The total British proportion of the Saskatchewan population (i.e., the areas that would be included within the province of Saskatchewan in 1905) has been estimated at just 10.7% of the 19,114 residents back in 1881; at the time, people of British origin were approximately equal to the number of people of French origin (10.9%), but both were far outnumbered by Indians (78.0%). However, by 1885 half (50.5%) of the 32,097 residents were British. But this majority was short lived: British-origin residents again became a minority in 1901, when they comprised 43.9% of the total population of 91,279. Then, for the next two decades, they again found themselves in a slight majority position (51.0% in 1911, 54.5% in 1916, 52.9% in 1921, and 50.8% in 1926). But since then British-origin residents have collectively been a minority. By 1931, the British-origin population had peaked at 437,836—slightly less than half (47.5%) of the total population. Then, during the "dirty thirties," massive depopulation caused both the total population and the numbers of British residents to decline substantially, followed by several decades when the population stayed fairly static, while the British proportion remained quite constant (fluctuating between 40% and 45%).[44] In fact, by the 1930s Saskatchewan had become the only province in Canada besides Quebec lacking a British-origin majority. Yet English and British-origin residents have been pervasive throughout much of the province, outnumbering other ethnic groups in numerous communities. Today, out of a total Saskatchewan population of 968,157 (2006), 253,110 residents (26.1%) claim to be of English ethnic origin, of whom 37,335 (14.8%) claim only English origin and 215,775 (85.2%) partially English origin. As already noted, 606,875 residents claim various British origins (almost 90% of them only partially), but there is considerable overlap between these categories (e.g., English and Scottish, Irish, or Welsh). People claiming to be specifically of English origin (in whole or part) are now outnumbered only by people claiming German origin. At the present time, the Anglican Church of Canada is losing members at a rate of about 20% every ten years.[45]

SCOTTISH SETTLEMENTS

The settlement of people of Scottish origin in Saskatchewan dates back more than two centuries to the fur trade. Scots headed not only the North West Company but also the rival McLeod and Company and played a prominent role in the Hudson's Bay Company, which recruited personnel from the Orkney Islands and Lewis in the Outer Hebrides. Last Mountain House, a trading post established in 1869 by the Hudson's Bay Company (HBC) on Last Mountain Lake as an outpost of Fort Qu'Appelle, was placed under the charge of Isaac Cowie, who had arrived from the Orkney Islands as a twenty-one-year old apprentice clerk; his second in command was Joseph McKay, a halfbreed officer who became well known to Métis and Indians. With many Scots involved in the fur trade as managers, factors, traders, explorers, buffalo hunters, and trappers, they commonly took Native wives, with the eventual result that many Métis were partly of Scottish origin, and Scottish surnames became frequent among Indians and Métis. Indeed, the intermixing among Scots, French, and Indians soon became complex. Some Scottish-origin settlers in Saskatchewan (then the North-West Territories) had immigrated directly from Scotland, especially from the Orkney Islands; some were second-generation sons and daughters of immigrants. In the region around the Métis settlement of Batoche and what would become Prince Albert, one of the earliest settlers was James Isbister, whose parents were John Isbister, an Orkneyman employed by the HBC, and Frances Sinclair, a Scots Métis; his wife was Margaret Bear. He was reportedly conversant in English, Gaelic, French-Michif, Cree, and Chipewyan. Thomas Scott, also an Orkneyman who had immigrated to work for the HBC, married a Métis woman and became an active advocate of the Métis cause. Eleanor (or Helen) Thomas, a Gaelic- and Cree-speaking Métis (who was born at Swampy River in the Red River settlement in Manitoba and died at St-Paul-des-Métis, Alberta), was married to Laurent Gareau, arrested as a Métis sympathizer. Christine Johnson married Philippe-Charles Chamberland, who immigrated from France. Allan Morrison, born in Scotland, moved to the West from heavily Scottish County Glengarry in eastern Ontario, and Pierre and Léontine McLeod moved from Quebec. Marguerite Sutherland (called/*dite* Kapetakus) was the daughter of Napotchiyis and Ke-Pukokatik and the wife of Edouard Kapupikanew (*dit* Dumont), the son of an Assiniboine Métis raised by Gabriel Dumont's uncle Jean-Baptiste Trottier. Many Scottish and Scots Métis families in this area (including Adams, Bruce, Halcrow, Harrison, Monkman, Morwick, and Spence) originated in the Selkirk Colony in Manitoba, a large settlement of Highland Scots north of Winnipeg established by Thomas Douglas, Earl of Selkirk, in 1811; these settlers were soon confronted by Métis led by Cuthbert Grant, partly of Scottish origin himself, and several decades later it was William MacTavish who advised the Métis to form their own "provisional government" in Manitoba in 1869. Many other Scots Métis families who resettled in the Batoche area in Saskatchewan originated in the St-François-Xavier settlement (west of present-day Winnipeg) and tended to be intermarried with French Métis (e.g., Burston, Fidler, McGillis, McKay, McLeod, McMillan, Ross, Sayer, Short, Smith, Wells, Whitford). The pervasive Scottish influence on hybrid Métis culture was apparent in music (fiddling, reels, and dancing) and food (bannock).

An extensive area of Scottish and Scots Métis settlement developed in the region between the North and South Saskatchewan Rivers, west and south of present-day Prince Albert. What was originally called the Isbister settlement first began to develop with James Isbister's homestead in 1862. It was renamed the Prince Albert settlement by James Nisbet, a Presbyterian minister. Later the Prince Albert Colonization Company was justifiably viewed by Métis as a threat to their landholdings—it took over the property of at least thirty-five Métis. This settlement along the south shore of the North Saskatchewan River just west of present-day Prince Albert is still characterized by the traditional Métis riverlot system. Many Scottish surnames are still found today (e.g., MacGregor, McKeown, McDougall, Scott, McCallum, McIntyre, McDonald, Sinclair, Dunbar, Bruce, McCormick, Stewart, McLaughlin, Bannerman). And just to the south the Halcro settlement, also characterized by riverlots, extended along the north/west shore of the South Saskatchewan River downriver from St-Louis. It was settled during the 1870s mainly by interrelated Scots and Scots Métis (then usually referred to as English Métis) families (notably Halcrow, Cook, Spence, Swain, Cromarty, Tate, Adams). This settlement—also known as the St. Andrew's settlement—was centred on St. Andrew's Anglican Church and Halcro (post office [PO] 1887–1926) and eventually extended westward through Aaskana (PO 1888–96), later called Red Deer Hill (PO 1897–1969), and Gerrond (school 1912–59) toward MacDowall (PO 1903–), and eastward toward the Fenton ferry. Halcrow is an Orkney surname, and Clouston was named for brothers who immigrated from the Orkneys. Downriver from St-Louis, where the South Saskatchewan runs through the Halcro settlement, Scottish place names are preserved: McKay Creek, McKenzie's Crossing (where Captain Norman McKenzie, who immigrated from Scotland in 1886, ran the first ferry in 1887), Galloway Crossing, Galloway Creek, and the Sinclair winter crossing. Present-day farms include the extensive Charles MacDonald Galloway farm (which once contained more than 5,000 sheep) and the Duncan, Geddes, Tweedie, McDougall, Isbister, Tait, Adams, and McNabb farms.

Métis partly of Scottish origin, closely allied and intermarried with francophone Métis, played an important role in the North-West Resistance in Saskatchewan in 1885. Most Scots Métis actively supported the resistance, and some assumed leading roles: Charles Adams, William Cromarty, and Joseph Halcrow had been members of the joint English-French Métis committee in Manitoba that met with Louis Riel to express their support but their reluctance to resort to armed conflict. Later, in Saskatchewan, Andrew Spence of Red Deer Hill served as the president of a joint French-English Métis council yet again did not favour armed resistance. Louis Riel held resistance meetings in the Halcro settlement in 1884, and following the battle of Batoche, after initially escaping capture, he hid in the Halcrow family's root cellar. A number of Scots Métis were incarcerated at Prince Albert for their suspected sympathy for the "rebel cause," including Thomas Scott, Henry Monkman, Charles Bird, Fred Fidler, Elzéar Swain, Caleb Anderson, and James Isbister. Caleb Anderson, born in Manitoba, married a Swain-Laviolette daughter at St. Peter's mission in Montana, where Riel hid following his deportation from Manitoba. James Isbister, regarded as a leader of the "English Halfbreeds," went in the small party with Gabriel Dumont to St. Peter's mission to persuade Riel to lead the second Métis resistance at Batoche. Thomas Scott, an influential leader of the "English and Scottish Halfbreeds of the area," was charged with treason, though he never actually took up arms. Jean-Baptiste Wilkie, who had led the Métis of St-Joseph, Dakota Territory, and was intermarried with a Pembina Chippewa, moved to St-Laurent and later joined the Montana Métis; his daughter Madeleine married Gabriel Dumont. William Jackson was a graduate of the University of Toronto; strongly anti-Conservative, he moved west to join his brother in Prince Albert and became known in Michif as Honoré Jaxon. Robert Jackson's parents were André Jackson and Emilie Munroe, a Scots Cree.

Some Scots Métis, intermarried with French Métis, took an active part in the actual fighting. Alexandre McDougall, the son of Duncan McDougall, fought in the resistance; his wife was Virginie Lepine, daughter of influential Métis leader Maxime Lepine, and his brother Sam McDougall's wife was Virginie Morin. The extended Ross family from the St-François-Xavier settlement in Manitoba was intermarried with French Métis (especially the Sansregret family) and took an active part in the resistance; Donald (Daniel) Ross was on the council of the provisional government formed by Louis Riel and was killed on the final day of fighting. The Fergusons (originally Farquarson or Farquharson) too were involved: intermarried with French Métis, Elise Farquarson's husband Daniel Dumas fought alongside his brothers, while her brother Antoine was married to Elise Jerome (*dite* St-Matte). One Ferguson had even fought on the Sioux side in the battle of the Little Big Horn. James "Timous" (Little Dog) Short (married to Mathilde McGillis of St-François-Xavier) led Métis fighters. Andrew Tate, of the Halcro settlement, fought with Gabriel Dumont in the Duck Lake skirmish (his father was intermarried with Cree, while his wife was French Métis).

However, not all of the Scots Métis were supporters of the resistance. For example, Richard Hardisty (whose mother and grandmother bore the Scottish surnames Allen and Sutherland), a Métis who was a career British soldier, ended up being killed at Batoche on the final day of fighting. "Jackfish Johnnie" Daniels was a scout for the North-West Mounted Police, married to Mary McIver from the Moosomin Reserve near Cochin. And the Cunninghams, despite being intermarried with French Métis, were active on the "Canadian" side. In fact, it was the prime minister, Sir John A. Macdonald (himself a Scottish Canadian) who sent Canadian troops westward to quell this perceived Métis rebellion.

Gaelic-speaking crofters who had been considered "surplus population" in the Highlands and Outer Hebrides (Western Isles) during the Highland Clearances were sent to the Saskatchewan prairies during the 1880s. They had been driven from their homeland by a rising population in a fragile land, increased cultivation reaching capacity, high prices for livestock, a shift to the fishing industry, and precarious kelp manufacture.[46]

They lived in abject poverty in modest homes; a typical *shieling* was small and dark, with a dirt floor covered with heather or bracken, often lacking a chimney, and separated from the livestock that shared the quarters during the winter only by a low partition.[47] In 1883–84, inspired by the philanthropic efforts of Lady Gordon Cathcart of Aberdeenshire, initially "a total of forty-seven souls" that soon grew to nearly 300 crofters from Benbecula and South Uist islands in the Outer Hebrides settled the St. Andrew's and Benbecula Colonies near Moosomin and Wapella.[48] They included McDonalds, McKays, MacDiarmids. ... A large dockside banner read "We're sailing west ... we're sailing west ... to prairie lands sunkissed and blest ... the crofter's trail to happiness."[49] Lady Cathcart paid each family $500 for passage and supplies, at 5% interest; some have suggested that her intentions were not completely benevolent but in keeping with the objective of the Clearances of ridding the Highlands and outer islands of excess population. The settlers were predominantly Roman Catholic, initially served by French-speaking Oblates; soon St. Andrew's (Sancte Andrea) Parish was established in 1888, through the initiative of Father David Gillies, a young Gaelic-speaking priest from Nova Scotia. According to *A Short History of the Pioneer Scotch Settlers of Saint Andrew's, Saskatchewan*, this beautiful church in the countryside was expertly built by Donald McDougall, a stonemason, and Alex McPherson, a carpenter, in a style reminiscent of the Catholic churches in County Glengarry, Ontario.[50] A series of separate schools was established the preceding year: St. Andrew, St. Mary, St. Margaret, and St. Peter; later a convent school was operated by the Sisters of Our Lady of the Missions in 1942–48. Presbyterians concentrated in the northern portion of the colony. Near Langbank St. Paul's Anglican Church was built in 1938 completely in boulders, in a combined Norman and Hebridean style, by stonemason Charles Parker, described on his gravestone as "a man of faith who laboured with stone"—he had learned his trade in Ontario from his mother's brothers, who in turn had learned the stonemason craft in Scotland.[51] Presbyterians and Anglicans supported each other's efforts at Perth School near Rocanville in 1909.[52] The St. Andrew's and Benbecula Colonies expanded to include several Scottish-named communities in the general area around Moosomin (pop. 2,257) and Wapella (pop. 311)—Kennedy (pop. 187), Langbank (pop. 30), Kelso, Doonside, and Dunleath, as well as many rural districts—Ardine, Bavelaw, Carnoustie, Hopehill, Inchkeith, Iona, McKay, MacLeod, Maryfield, St. Andrew, and Cairnbank Farms near Langbank. The area of Scottish settlement covered portions of five rural municipalities: Moosomin, Martin, Silverwood, Walpole, and Wawken; together with the towns of Wapella and Moosomin, they contained a total British (including Scottish)-origin population numbering close to 5,000. Farmers in the settlement have typical Scottish names: McDonald, MacDougall, Cameron, Morrow, McLeod. ... Apart from the churches mentioned, other fine examples of traditional Scottish stonemasonry can still be found in the region, such as the lovely little Carpenter Cottage in Wapella, possibly built by Scottish-born Alex Sutherland of Tantallon around 1904; the Smithers home in Moosomin, built for a migrant from Ontario possibly by stonemason George Dagleish; and Granite Lodge, the large fieldstone home of Alex and Margarite Webster near Welwyn, north of Moosomin (Alex's grandparents had immigrated to Ontario from Inverary, Scotland).[53]

In April 1889, another forty-nine crofter families (282 persons) set sail from Scotland under the auspices of the newly founded Imperial Colonization Board. They came

CHAPTER 3

from the districts of Stornoway (Steornabhagh) and Barvas (Barabhas) on the Isle of Lewis (Eilean Leodhais), Harris (Eilean na Hearadh), North Uist (Uibhist a Tuath) and Benbecula (Beinn na Faodhla), and Loch—likely South Uist (Uibhist a Deas). Each district had a representative elected by the emigrants.[54] The immigrants settled fifty-six homesteads in the Lothian Colony north of Saltcoats and sixteen homesteads in the King Colony west of Saltcoats.[55] Saltcoats (pop. 467) was first named Stirling, after the birthplace in Scotland of a major railway shareholder, then with the establishment of a post office was renamed in 1888 after a town in Ayrshire, Scotland; it was situated on Anderson Lake, named after William Anderson, a Scottish immigrant who had settled there in 1882. Saltcoats became a village in 1894 and a town in 1910. The land originally designated for the Lothian Colony consisted of a township and a half relinquished by the York Colonization Company approximately twenty kilometres (twelve miles) north of town. Initially, it was thought that these settlers would be sent to the Wolseley area and Qu'Appelle Valley; however, the ready availability of land near Saltcoats close to a railhead proved an inducement to relocate there.[56]

The average cost of travel all the way from Glasgow, where they boarded a trans-Atlantic ship, to Saltcoats was only $163 per family. Each homesteader received an advance of $600; after travel, the balance was available for settlement in the colony. The actual balance varied between $358 and $521. The advance grant bore no interest for the first four years, then was 8% per annum. When all the required payments were met, the 160-acre homestead became the absolute property of the homesteader. However, each homesteader was obligated to sign a lien to safeguard the investment of the Imperial Colonization Board, which could exercise foreclosure if the settler failed to fulfill his obligations in sufficient time.[57] The settlers were obliged to purchase their supplies from Buchanan and Company, which generously allowed them a month of provisions at a time but at relatively higher cost. As their missionary, Reverend I.J. Macdonald explained,

> [these crofters] were born free and slavery is done away with, [yet] nearly three hundred poor innocent crofters [are] used, abused and treated according to the impure motives and selfish desires of disinterested individuals, [which should] in the latter end of the nineteenth century [be] absolutely out of the question. ... [I]n the contract with ... Buchanan and Co ... the poor crofter has to pay [excessive prices].[58]

Yet the Scottish settlers became noted not only for their resilience but also for their stubbornness. Only eleven families accepted the homestead locations originally assigned to them; twenty-five families selected different locations in the area, while eleven families took locations rejected by these families, and a couple of families left the colony entirely. Despite a pre-emption right that was part of the settlement agreement, just twenty-four families initially availed themselves of this right, though another twenty-four older sons later selected homesteads. Reportedly, men did not stay long on temporary railway jobs, soon choosing to return home; the majority of settlers took what was viewed by officials as an inordinate length of time to make up their minds in selecting homesteads; some of the lands that they rejected became prime farmland owned by the railway; much of the seed given to the new farmers was not planted (disappointed with cultivation in a dry year, some focused instead on livestock); some of the settlers who had been fishermen were not acquainted with farming; and the crofters clearly were thought not prepared to settle down at once.[59] According to the railway land commissioner, "The crofters are responsible for their fate," and other officials were of the opinion that

> the crofters and the Highland people generally are excellent settlers when they emigrate of their own accord, and are placed alongside people of other nationalities, but when settled in compact body they are like the Indians in that they spend a great deal of time in talking over their grievances, real or fancied. ... [T]hey are content to make very little progress when left to themselves.[60]

During the winter of 1889-90, the Imperial Colonization Board expended $400 a month for provisions and clothing for the crofter families.[61] The settlers' homes were perhaps an improvement over what they were used to in the Hebrides but nonetheless rudimentary: two basic types were made available, called the "new shanty" and the "McKay house"; the exterior walls were covered with sod for insulation, the roofs were covered with tarpaper, while the stables were built of wooden frames with sod walls and roofed with hay.[62]

These Highland crofter settlements in Saskatchewan were part of a series of such settlements. While these settlements were developing in Saskatchewan, not far away in Manitoba in June 1888 seventy-nine crofter families (183 settlers) from Lewis in the Outer Hebrides settled forty-two homesteads around Dunrea, north of Killarney and west of Pelican Lake, in the District of Turtle Mountain, and from Harris twenty-seven homesteads around Hilton, north of Pelican Lake, in the District of Argyle.[63] While the Pelican Lake settlements succeeded, the Saltcoats colonies had essentially failed by 1900 due to adverse climatic conditions—a dry year in 1892, followed by a tough winter in 1892–93, which resulted in the loss of livestock. By 1891, eighteen homesteads had already been abandoned; by 1894, forty-eight; by the next year, only twenty-two of the original settlers remained on the land; by 1899, only one of the original homesteaders remained on his land. In 1895, just 162 acres were under cultivation in the colony, and most of the settlers were anxious to give up their farms.[64] The years 1896 to 1900 saw the final dissolution of the colony. The settlers who had stayed this long were not in a position of debt to the board, but many who had left thought that they might never be in a position to pay off their obligations, so they sought their own homesteads independently, often close to those of other Scots.[65]

Thus, the Scottish settlement originally centred on the King and Lothian Colonies expanded to include many Scottish-named communities around Saltcoats (pop. 467 today) and throughout the east-central region—Dunleath, Stornoway, Kessock, Clonmel, Barvas, Rokeby, Calder (pop. 80), MacNutt (pop. 80), Tummel, McKim, Cana/MacDougall, as well as the rural districts of Alva, Anderson Bay, Anderson Lake, Barra, Campbelltown, Glasgow, Kinbrae, Loyal, and Zorra. Stornoway declined rapidly from about a hundred residents in the mid-1960s to just thirty-seven in 1971, and at last count only ten were left; the community's status as a village was cancelled in 2006 with so few residents left. In the Stornoway district, until 1906 religious services were held at first in homes and schools, then a simple log church was built out in the country, eventually replaced by a more substantial wood frame church, where services were held until 1966, when the Presbyterian church in Stornoway was relocated to Dunleath. The Scottish colonies had expanded to include, in whole or in part, six rural municipalities: Saltcoats in the centre, Cana to the west, Orkney to the northwest, Wallace and Calder to the north, and Churchbridge to the east, with a combined total of about 2,500 people of British (mostly Scottish) ethnic origin. In 1971, 70.6% of the residents of Saltcoats were of British ethnic origin.

Since the colonies around Saltcoats as such were abandoned, in this sense they failed, yet they succeeded in their original intention of alleviating population pressures and poverty back in the Hebrides and in introducing Gaelic-speaking Highlanders to the prairies.

During the 1880s, Scottish settlers were also attracted to the Qu'Appelle Valley, settling around Abernethy in the Qu'Appelle Farming Colony and Indian Head, where the extensive Bell Farm of the Qu'Appelle Valley Farming Company (featuring a unique stone round stable and farmhouse by 1883) was located.[66] But even before the establishment of the Indian Head Experimental Farm, a local farmer, Angus MacKay, had been experimenting with innovative prairie farming techniques, including fall plowing, early seeding, and packing (dragging heavy rollers across seeded land to improve moisture retention).[67] Many communities in this general area bear evidence of Scottish settlers—Abernethy (pop. 197), Cupar (pop. 566), Balcarres (pop. 598), Dysart (pop. 198), and the smaller communities of Markinch (pop. 59) and Kenlis—as do many rural districts—Balrobie, Blackwood, Braemar, McDonald Hills, Glen Murray, Invercauld, Motherwell, Saltoun, Tullymet, and Westlea. Abernethy Post Office dated from 1884, and the community was designated a village in 1904. Christ Anglican Church was built two kilometres south of the community in 1886, and the Little Stone Presbyterian Church west of Abernethy was built of fieldstone in 1892 by local stonemasons; Scottish surnames in the cemetery include Ferguson, Mackay, Mackenzie, Strath, Gillespie, McKee, Morrison, Lauder, Penny, Ballach—but several people of German descent are also found there. This church as well as Foster School (1896) to the northeast and Kenlis Methodist Church (1896) to the southwest are all heritage sites. The fieldstone Knox Presbyterian (now United) Church at Fort Qu'Appelle (pop. 1,919) was designed and built in 1884 by the minister, Alexander Robson, originally a stonemason. The centre of Abernethy is dominated by the Knox Presbyterian (now United) Church, built in 1905. Similarly, the elegant Motherwell Homestead, now a National Historic Site, just south of Abernethy was constructed of masterly fitted fieldstone in a style typical of County Lanark, Ontario. William Richard Motherwell (who co-founded the Grain Growers' Association in 1901, became Saskatchewan's first minister of agriculture from 1905 to 1918, then served as federal minister of agriculture from 1922 to 1930) came to Saskatchewan from Perth, Ontario, to homestead in 1882 at the young age of twenty-two and named his homestead Lanark Place (in turn, both Perth and County Lanark were named after Perth and Lanark in Scotland). Adam Cantelon, one of the most reputable Scottish stonemasons in Saskatchewan, was born in Ontario in 1857, moved west in 1883, and settled in the Duff-Lorlie area to the northeast; after building the

Little Stone Church in 1892, he built a fieldstone stable on the Motherwell farm in 1896 (enlarged in 1907) and the house in 1898.[68] Near Balcarres, the Anderson stone farmhouse exhibited typical symmetry, a centre gable, and a large porch; the Wright stone farmhouse in the Tipperary district was built in 1902 by Scottish stonemason John Barnes from Indian Head.[69] In 1971, 72.8% of the residents of Abernethy were of British (predominantly Scottish) origin; the total British-origin population of Abernethy RM (including Abernethy and Balcarres) can be estimated to be 1,100.

By 1890, Scottish Canadians from Ontario, encouraged by Colonel Andrew Duncan Davidson, who formed the Saskatchewan Valley Land Company to bring in settlers, homesteaded north of Regina and soon farther northward, following the Arm River Valley. Several communities and a rural municipality along the Qu'Appelle, Long Lake, and Saskatchewan Railway between Regina and Saskatoon were named after Scottish Canadian politicians, railway financiers, executives, civil engineers, and settlement promoters: Lumsden (pop. 1,523 in 2006), Bethune (pop. 369), Craik (pop. 408), Davidson (pop. 958), and McCraney RM. Or they were named after places in Scotland: the communities of Girvin (pop. 25 in 2001), Dundurn (pop. 647), Colonsay (pop. 425), and Findlater (pop. 49), Montrose RM, and the districts of Blair Athol, Brora, Dundee, Invernairn, Inverness, Kincardine, Kintyre, Lothian, and Seaforth. Or they were descriptive place names: the community of Glenside (pop. 86) and the districts of Glenbrea, Glen Valley near Disley, Bonnie Brae, and Burnside. Or they were named after first settlers: the districts of Blakely, Campbell, McCargar, and Melness. In the hills south of Last Mountain Lake, the Lauder residence, built of fieldstone in 1903 by a couple of immigrants from Berwickshire on their Eildon Vale farm (named after the Eildon Hills in the Southern Uplands of Scotland), became the Fieldstone Inn, a bed-and-breakfast and heritage property. Similarly, just west of Lumsden, the restored Miller farmhouse was constructed in 1902 of fieldstone typical of Scottish-settled areas of Ontario. The idyllic St. Nicholas Kennell Anglican Church was built near Lumsden in 1900. In Bethune, the Gillis Blakely Heritage Museum Site is inclusive of the former Huron Presbyterian Church (1892) and Blakely Homestead House (1905). A local resident at Carlea reported in 1911 that an annual haggis supper was served every Robbie Burns Day (January 25).[70] The Anglican church at Marquis (pop. 71), named St. Columba's, is a heritage property. In and around Glenside, streets and roads bear Scottish names: Arran, Islay, Kintyre, Inverness; the old Glenside School (1910) and Presbyterian church (1915) are heritage sites. After 1902, Scottish-origin migrants from Ontario and Nova Scotia, as well as from Scotland itself, settled neighbouring districts to the east of this railway line (e.g., Lothian, Allan Hills, and Burnmore). For example, families settling in the Hanley area, particularly east of town, were immigrants from Scotland (Smith, Bruce, Clark, Gillam, Patterson, Renny); migrants from strongly Scottish Cape Breton Island, Nova Scotia (Cameron, McRae, McKenzie, Coles); migrants from Scottish-settled areas of Ontario (Anderson from County Perth, McKee and Kilpatrick from Teeswater and neighbouring Lucknow, McPhee from West Lorne, Abernethy from Breadalbane, Archibald from Elora, Wood from McLean, as well as Rankin, McCann, McDaniel, Ross, Campbell); Scottish families from the United States (Andrews, Macdonald, McCallum, McGregor, Macbeth, Malcolm); and many others (Brodie, McClenaghan, McCormick, McLennan, MacFarlane,

CHAPTER 3

Armstrong, Duncan, Ferguson, etc.). The first town doctor was J.W. MacNeill from Prince Edward Island.

Meanwhile, during the 1880s, Scottish settlement spread from Wolseley southeast into the Moffat district, where a steady influx of Lowland Scottish immigrants from Ayrshire, Perthshire, Aberdeenshire, and the Lothians concentrated in four townships centred on the Presbyterian kirk in Moffat; forty families spread over 92,000 acres. Moffat was reportedly named in 1886 to honour a friend of the first postmaster (Alex Kindred); Dr. Moffat came from Motherwell, Scotland, to visit the new colony in 1889 and purchased land for the kirk, but he died back in Scotland two years later. In 1891, St. Andrew's Presbyterian Church, built by Adam Cantelon, replaced the original Moffatville Presbyterian Church, constructed in 1884; today it stands as a recognized historic site. In 1965, author Kay Parley, born in Moffat in 1923, wrote that "Moffat kirk is only seventy-six years old, but to the descendants of the Scottish pioneers, the stones of Moffat are much older than that. They are, in a sense, the stones of Scotland, part of a tradition that goes back to antiquity."[71] Moffat was known for its stonemasons—three Scottish stonemasons settled there in 1883–85—who built many fine stone homes: Loganston of the Gibsons, the McCall and Hutson homes (now gone), Craigfarg of the Fergusons (now abandoned), Berryhill (the "fairy house") of the Fergusons, the Scott home on Kenny's Lake (dismantled in 2007), Hayfield of the Parleys, Ladybank on Kindred's Lake. ... The kirk and just five of the original stone homes remain, when once in Moffat and neighbouring Greenville at least twelve homes, two churches, and a school were constructed of stone. With centralization and children leaving the family farms, few traditional stone buildings are left and few Scottish residents—today this district is more ethnically mixed. In this general area, Scottish settlers also concentrated around Glenavon (pop. 183) and Peebles (pop. now 20) and in the districts of Adair, Ferguslea, and Kegworth. Other examples of Scottish stonemasonry in the region include the McLean farmhouse on Paisley Farm (homesteader Robert McLean was born in Paisley, Scotland), built near Ellisboro in 1902 by John Jamieson, a Scottish immigrant, and Rossdhu in Broadview, dating from about 1890, named after the castle on Loch Lomond that was the seat of Clan Colquhoun (*rossdhu* is Gaelic for dark headland)—the Colquhoun family had left their home near Dumbarton, Scotland, in 1893, and Adam Colquhoun became the first mayor of Broadview in 1907 but died back in Scotland only a couple of years later.[72] And farther west, closer to Regina, the total British-origin population in the surrounding rural municipalities of Elcapo, Wolseley, Kingsley, and Chester can be estimated at about 1,600 in 1971 (excluding Wolseley and Grenfell).

Scottish settlers also concentrated in the southeastern region around Carlyle (pop. 1,257) and Carnduff (pop. 1,012), in the communities of Glen Ewen (pop. 120) and Douglaston, in the rural municipality of Argyle, and in numerous rural districts, including Annandale, Braeside, Calvin, Clarilaw, Fife, Glencoe, Glen Adelaide, Glen Morris, Hutton, Lomond, McAuley, McGregor, McNaught, Melrose, Minard, Munro. ... In the Clare district near Arcola (pop. 504), the first Presbyterian services were held in a log hut holding at best fifteen people; if more attended, they had to stand outside. Student ministers had to walk as far as twenty or thirty miles on Sundays to cover three or four services. Eventually, two log churches were constructed in this district, the first in 1885 (but burned just the next year in a prairie fire), the second ten years later (used just five years until the railway came through).[73] The fine work of Scottish stonemasons abounds in this region. In Argyle RM, the Reynolds stone house (1903) and the old stone church at Carievale (pop. 241)—Holy Trinity Anglican (1905)—are now designated heritage sites. The fieldstone farmhouses of the Mann and Purvis families in nineteenth-century Ontario style are found near Carievale. The Dagleish residence at Manor, also a heritage property, dates from 1904. The Knox Presbyterian Church (1895) at Whitewood (pop. 869), built by an expert local stonemason and bricklayer, is a historical site. Around Carnduff are found barns combining fieldstone bases topped with wood shingles. Around Arcola, Smithfield is a stone farmhouse that was successively occupied by Scottish immigrants Alexander and Mary Ann McNabb and James Smith and his wife Betsy Anderson; this home was possibly built by Robert McIlvenna of Oxbow, like the neighbouring farmhouse Restalrig, in typical Scottish style (named after a village now incorporated into the city of Edinburgh, birthplace of the first settler, John Peter McLaren). Doune Lodge was built by stonemason William Anderson of Arcola for Scotty Bryce, an agriculture graduate from the University of Edinburgh who had emigrated from Doune, Scotland, in 1882. The Langrish farmhouse near Oxbow was built for English immigrants by Bill McIlvenna.[74]

Farther west, in the south-central region, apart from the aforementioned Moffat settlement, other Scottish-named or settled communities included Balgonie (pop. 1,384), McLean (pop. 275), McTaggart (pop. 114), Mossbank (pop. 330), Lang (pop. 172), Macoun (pop. 168), and Trossachs (pop. 33), plus the rural districts of Airlie, Alloa, Banff, Breadalbane, Bruceville, Burnsville, Caledonia, Camlachie, Dunkirk, Glasnevin, Lockerbie, Sinclair Hill, Strathallen, Strathlorne. ... The former St. Andrew's Presbyterian (now United) Church at Halbrite (1908) has been designated a heritage property, as has been the former Presbyterian church (1901), now a community hall, in Balgonie, where the former King's Hotel (now demolished) was yet another example of fine stonemasonry, as was St. Thomas Anglican Church (1898) at Edgely Farm near McLean, named after the hamlet near the home in Scotland of the farming brothers.[75] Notre Dame School in Wilcox (pop. 222) was led for many years (from his arrival as a parish priest in 1927 until his death in 1975) by "Père" James Athol Murray, a grandnephew of Sir John A. Macdonald. Mount Joy School near Glasnevin, close to Ogema, was constructed of fieldstone in 1912.

Several communities in the southwestern region received Scottish names: Mortlach, Chaplin, Glen Bain, Glen Kerr, Glen McPherson, Orkney, Scotsguard. So did numerous rural districts: Caithness, Duncairn, Duncan Coulee, Edinburgh, Glenarchy, Glenbryan, Glendyeth, Glengarry, Glenrosa, Kincorth, McEachern, McKnight, McPhail, Macworth, Reid Lake, Duncairn, Rereshill, Scotia. The small lake in the centre of the Cypress Hills resort was Loch Leven. Glen Kerr, with nearby Calderbank, between Central Butte and Herbert, was once a hamlet with a grain elevator, post office, co-op store, general store, bulk service, blacksmith, school, and church; by the 1980s, no business was left and just fifteen residents. The town of Assiniboia had its St. Andrew's Presbyterian Church, built of fieldstone in 1920, now a heritage site. Near Cardross, around Lake of the Rivers, a stone farmhouse was built by the Parker brothers, Scottish stonemasons trained in Aberdeen; farther south, near Viceroy and Willow Bunch Lake, Scottish immigrant John Stevenson, born in Edinburgh, homesteaded in 1908 and built a typical stone farmhouse in 1914.[76]

Similarly, the strong Scottish presence in west-central Saskatchewan was reflected in the widely scattered communities of Arelee, Dunfermline, Kyle, Macrorie, Matador, Netherhill, Stranraer, Struan, and Dunblane. Rural districts bearing Scottish names and/or settled by Scots included Aberfeldy, Ailsa Aird,[77] Ardkenneth, Balmoral, Bonnie Doon, Bonnie View, Braeburn, Buccleuch, Craig, Duwar Lake, Glamis, Glenalmond, Glenellen, Glengarry Plains, Glenhurst, Glenloney, Glen Payne, Glenside RM, Glenuig, Greenan, Inverallen, Kintail, Learig, Lochaber, Mackinnon, McKellar, McLaren, McLead, McMorran, McNaughton, McNeill Junction, McTavish, Oban, Penkill, South Dean, Sporran, Tweedyside. … Keppel, southeast of Biggar, was founded by Scots; it declined since the 1940s and by 1966 was a virtual ghost town—by the 1980s, just the old post office building remained.

To the northwest of the Saskatchewan prairies, the districts of Glenbogie, Clansman, Kilronan, Strathmore, and Strathrock testify to Scottish influence, as does the old McMurray's trading post.

In the north-central region, we find a Scottish presence in the naming of the communities of Alticane, Broderick, Denholm, Glenbush, Kilwinning, MacDowall, and Melfort; of the rural districts of Balmoral, Campbellville, Fanford, Glen Mary, Glen Kelly, Kirkpatrick, Loch Side, Longfield, McAllister, McMillan, Morven, Mount Teviot, and Springburn; and of Invergordon RM. The McDonald residence (1905) in Prince Albert and St. Andrew's Anglican Church site and cemetery at Halcro are both heritage sites. Church picnics and sporting days in the Brightholm district south of Shellbrook featured tossing the caber along with horse racing.[78]

To the south, in the central region (east of the broad band of Scottish settlement between Regina and Saskatoon and north of the Qu'Appelle settlements), the only community with a Scottish name (but not much of a Scottish population) is Jedburgh, settled during the early 1900s by Scots and named in 1909 by the postmaster from Jedburgh, Roxburghshire, in the Scottish Borders. These Scottish settlers were soon far outnumbered by Ukrainians. But many rural districts testify to a substantial Scottish presence throughout the region: Bannockburn, Benchonzie, Blythewood, Caledon, Dunkeld, Dunrobin, Edenkillie, Garnock, Glen Afton, Kilmory, Lawrie, McKillop, MacMahon, McLeod, McMichael, Macfarlane, McDonald Hills, Tiree, Wyber, Ythanbank. … And the former bank in Nokomis, a heritage property, is now the Highlander Guest House. South of Nokomis, Keystown was founded by "hardy Scots" whose predecessors had fled clearances and potato famines, including six Keyes brothers, who all homesteaded, and McGillivrays, who donated land for the Cottonwood Presbyterian Church (incidentally, the youngest son became mayor of Regina during the 1940s). Besides this church, the community once included Wayside School and at least ten businesses—all now abandoned.

Finally, to the northeast, some communities were originally given Scottish names, such as Arran, Buchanan, and Invermay; however, while first settlers might have been Scottish, succeeding settlers were largely Eastern European. The Govan family immigrated from Scotland in 1906 to settle in the Valley Plain district north of the Quill Lakes.[79]

Scottish place names often were indicative of the exact origins of the settlers in Scotland or Scottish settlements in Ontario. It is interesting to note that Orkney Islanders founded their own communities, such as Orcadia in Orkney RM, fifteen kilometres northwest of Yorkton, and the tiny communities of Orkney, just west of Val Marie (down to only five residents in 2001), Birsay (pop. 53 in 2001) near Outlook (named after a village in the Orkneys), and Maeshowe near Simmie (named after a prehistoric site near the original Birsay), as well as the Halcro settlement (named after the Halcrow family, of Orkney origin) north of St-Louis. In the Orkney settlement northwest of Yorkton, immigrants from the Orkney Islands in Scotland arrived during the 1880s. They included John Reid of Eday Island, whose extended family was accompanied by four other Scots. The old Presbyterian church and schoolhouse were actually built—respectively in 1893 and 1897—by a Norwegian, Nels Holer Neilson, who had emigrated from Norway in 1856 and settled in Orkney RM in 1883, where he met his future Scottish wife, who had emigrated from Westray Island in the Orkneys.[80] These buildings, constructed of cut fieldstone typical of Scottish stonemasonry, have been designated as heritage sites.

Although many communities and rural districts in Saskatchewan were given Scottish names, not all of them are contained within distinct Scottish bloc settlements. Such settlements or colonies can be identified, but other areas represent concentrations of people of Scottish origin together with people of other ethnic origins, small Scottish settlements of just a few families, or a settlement named by just one settler or family or often a school trustee or postmaster. Because many communities were named by enthusiastic railwaymen who happened largely to be of Scottish origin, not all community names were indicative of Scottish settlement. Moreover, while the first settlers of a community or district might have been Scottish, and contributed a Scottish place name, over time they might have become outnumbered by people of other ethnic origins. For example, McMahon, Glen Bain, McLeod, and Gilnockie were settled mainly by Germans, Glen Mary by Norwegians, Kylemore by Icelanders and Poles, Murraydale by Cree, Buchanan and Arran by Russian Doukhobors, Jedburgh by Ukrainians, Glen McPherson RM by French, Germans, and Norwegians. ... Nonetheless, the Scottish impact on the settlement process and especially the topology of Saskatchewan can hardly be exaggerated. In Saskatchewan, there are some 400 place names with the prefix Mac or Mc and at least forty Glens.

Indeed, the Scottish impact in Saskatchewan was pronounced and omnipresent. Patrick Gammie Laurie founded the *Saskatchewan Herald* at Battleford in 1878. Thomas MacNutt was the first speaker of the Saskatchewan legislature. Walter Scott became the first premier of Saskatchewan and editor of the *Regina Leader*. Archibald Peter McNab was the lieutenant governor from 1936 to 1944. Premier Tommy Douglas led the Cooperative Commonwealth Federation and its transformation into the New Democratic Party.

By 1911, there were over a million Canadians of Scottish origin, 282,000of them in Western Canada and 70,000 in Saskatchewan. By 1941, the population of Scottish origin in Saskatchewan was over 108,000; people of Scottish origin were estimated to comprise 35% of the population of Avonlea, 29% of Lashburn and Wapella, 28% of Lumsden, 23% of Saltcoats. By 2006, 182,790 Saskatchewan residents claimed to be of Scottish descent, 14,125 (7.7%) solely and 168,660 (92.3%) partially. They comprised the third largest ethnic group in the province's population.

Lasting Scottish influence in Saskatchewan is reflected in pipe bands, Highland games, Presbyterian and United churches, and some Anglican and Catholic parishes.

The United Church of Canada was formed in 1924 by a merger of Presbyterian, Methodist, and Congregational denominations; however, this remained a contentious issue, and many Presbyterian churches (originally established in Canada by the Church of Scotland) retained separate identities. When Knox Presbyterian Church, the largest Presbyterian church in Saskatoon (constructed by 1914), became Knox United Church in 1925, St. Andrew's Presbyterian Church just down the road was founded. St. Andrew's Church in the Moffat settlement long served a Presbyterian congregation; Methodists in the area had attended the Greenville Methodist Church five kilometres to the south but joined what had become Moffat United Church by the 1940s.[81] After policing in Winnipeg had become a virtual Scottish monopoly, Regina and Saskatoon followed suit.[82] Scottish immigrants together with Scottish settlers from Ontario were quick to establish Sons of Scotland lodges and Burns societies, and Robbie Burns evenings continue to be celebrated by "piping in the haggis" in January (the frigid Saskatchewan temperatures making it a challenge to wear the traditional kilt). Local newspaper archives mention a Burns night celebrated in Davidson "in the usual enthusiastic way" in 1925. Regular entertainers in the Scottish pavilion at Folkfest in Saskatoon include the North Saskatchewan Regiment Pipes and Drums, Saskatoon Police Pipes and Drums, 96th Highlanders Pipes and Drums (formed in 1985 when the Saskatoon Boys Pipe Band, founded in 1961, merged with the Bonnie Blue Bells, a girls' pipe band established in 1963), Saskatoon Scottish Country Dancers, Saskatoon Highland Dancers, Glen Lily Dancers, and Back of the Bus.

Distinct Scottish settlements became part of Saskatchewan's cultural mosaic, and people of Scottish origin became pervasive throughout the province. Writing in *Maclean's Magazine* in 1922, Sir Clifford Sifton expressed his view that Western Canada "got a fairly steady stream of settlers from the north of England and from Scotland; and they were the very best settlers in the world."[83]

IRISH SETTLEMENTS

Irish place names in Saskatchewan do not necessarily indicate Irish settlement: for example, Limerick has been settled by Romanians, Meath Park by Ukrainians, Shamrock School District No. 38 near Foam Lake and Wynyard by Icelanders. Other Irish place names include the Enniskillen district near Oxbow, Erinferry near Big River, and the Connaught district near Tisdale. Street names in North Portal are Northern Irish: Belfast, Ulster, Antrim, Clair—revealing the origin of the first station agent. Some communities have been named after Irish Canadian politicians of renown, such as D'Arcy and McGee (after Thomas D'Arcy McGee, a father of Confederation) and Davin (after Irish-born Nicholas Flood Davin, who founded the *Regina Leader* and later served as a member of Parliament).

People of Irish origin tended to scatter throughout Saskatchewan, yet Irish settlers did concentrate in a number of areas. The "Irish Colony" around Sinnett, twenty kilometres northeast of Lanigan, was reportedly named by German Benedictine monks to distinguish this Irish-settled district from the neighbouring large German Catholic colony. This Irish settlement was originally founded in 1905 by Father John Chester Sinnett. Born in Ridgetown, Ontario, in 1855, he had served with the Jesuits from 1884 to 1894, during which period he had been the priest in Sheenboro, in a strongly Irish area in Quebec across the Ottawa River from Pembroke, Ontario, in 1890. He later returned, in 1902–04, to recruit Irish Canadian settlers to form an Irish colony in Saskatchewan, together with Irish settlers from Prince Edward Island and immigrants direct from Ireland.[84] Among the latter was Tommy Coughlin, born in Tipperary in 1880. According to a settler in the McGuire district in 1906, Father Sinnett initially was obliged to live in a simple shack with rain leaking and snow blowing through cracks.[85] He was an influential and active priest, also serving in Regina before becoming rector and vicar general of the Prince Albert Diocese. He established St. Patrick Parish at the northern end of the colony in 1905; this parish, located within the bounds of St. Peter's German Catholic Colony, served primarily Irish parishioners but also some Germans, Ukrainians, and Poles. It closed in 1966, and the church building was moved to Lanigan, where it became the Fellowship Church. At the southern end of the colony, near the community of Sinnett, a second parish, St. Ignatius (named after the founder of the Jesuit order) was built in 1907—the altar was constructed by Father Sinnett, the pews by church members[86] (a new church was constructed in 1915, replaced by a larger church in 1928). Father Sinnett returned to Ontario in 1922 to rejoin the Jesuits, and he died in 1928 without seeing the new church. Among family names—many of them original homesteaders—found in the St. Ignatius and St. Patrick cemeteries are Laverty, McEachern, Devine, MacDonald, Hearn, Coughlin, Sullivan, Bevan, Maguire, McGrath, McMahon, Downy, Cunningham, Allen, Dodd, Fisher, Cole, Carroll, Tallon, McTighe, Sinnett, Mulvihill, Casey, Dunne, Hall, Hollins, Miller, Leslie, Allen, and Doyle (including "Scots Irish" originally from Northern Ireland). A railway line passed through Sinnett in 1921, and stores and grain elevators were established there and in nearby Leroy. The Irish settlement extended as far west as the Shady Grove/Mulvihill district south of Humboldt. The colony was served by several school districts: Loyola School was established in 1907; in 1940, the old schoolhouse became a "continuation school" with a chapel and convent for the teachers, the Sisters of Service; the former schoolhouse was moved into Sinnett in 1948 to be the new community school and teachers' residence. Besides Loyola School District, the colony encompassed the Manresa, Caseyville, and Brindle School Districts. In its heyday, Sinnett had several businesses, a blacksmith, the Tipperary rural telephone company, two elevators, two grocery stores, elementary and high schools, a garage, a post office, a skating rink, a bulk oil station, and a credit union, but the last surviving business (Charlie Dunne's) closed in 1969. Today the once busy community has all but disappeared. The closest communities are Leroy, which currently has a stable population of 412, but the railway has been closed, and the elevator is gone, and Lanigan, a regional service centre, which has 1,233 residents yet is declining. In 1971, the total British-origin (i.e., including Irish) population of Lanigan, Leroy, and the rural municipalities of Leroy, Wolverine, Prairie Rose, and Usborne (which contained the Irish Colony) could be estimated at 1,700 at the most.

Other areas where smaller numbers of Irish settled included, in the southeastern region, Carnduff and the Calvin district (from County Down and Antrim in Northern Ireland), Enniskillen RM around Oxbow (from Northern Ireland and Ontario), the Orangedale district northeast of Oxbow (Northern Irish Protestants), the Dungannon and Orangeville districts respectively west of Arcola and north of Moosomin (from Ontario), and Carlyle, Kisbey, and the Dennington district east of Stoughton (where the Donnellys were early homesteaders), while the Erin district east of Lampman also had an Irish name. Farther to the west, Irish settled the Derganagh district north of Kennedy (from Ontario) and the Kilshannig district south of Cupar (from Cork), while other Irish place names included the districts of Skibereen south of Piapot, Glasnevin near Ogema, and Tipperary south of Balcarres. To the southwest, St. Patrick's Roman Catholic Church in Herbert was built in 1912 to serve mostly Irish Catholic families. The Donnellyville rural district south of town was named after the Donnelly family from County Armagh in Ulster. The church closed in 1983 due to a declining number of parishioners in this predominantly Mennonite area; the last service, a funeral for a Donnelly, was held six years later, and the church was sold to yet another Donnelly descendant now living in Montreal in 1996 to be preserved as a historic site. Many Irish are buried in the cemetery north of town. Limerick (pop. 130 and declining), west of Assiniboia, was given Irish street names (Galway, Connaught, Shannon, Kerry, Killarney); homesteaders in the Netterville district north of Palmer included several Davies families from Ireland via Manitoba; the community and rural municipality of Shamrock north of Gravelbourg and the Erinvale and Maypole districts were settled by several Irish families; the Carnagh district north of Eastend and the Roscommon district southwest of Gull Lake also bore Irish names; and the St. Patrick Separate School in Swift Current was solidly Irish at one time. In the west-central region, Irish place names included the rural districts of Ballinora east of Neilburg, Dungloe south of Eatonia, Kincora at Glidden, Sparling's Coulee east of Luseland, and O'Malley near Ardath. To the northwest, Irish settled around Mullingar south of Spiritwood (from Kilkenny, Ireland, and Ontario), and the Kilronan district west of St. Walburg (from Cork), while other districts with Irish names included Erinferry and Clonfert respectively north and southeast of Debden and Glocca Morra south of Choiceland. In central Saskatchewan, Irish place names included the districts of Athlone south of Foam Lake and Boyne north of Colonsay and to the northeast the districts of Glengariff west of Lintlaw, Lurgan north of Tisdale and Connaught RM, Shannon southwest of White Fox, and Wexford south of Canora. Finally, in the east-central region, Ulster Irish joined Scots around Dunleath.

Irish settlers in Saskatchewan were sharply divided between Catholics and Protestants. The latter tended to be Ulstermen who were strong supporters of the Orange Order, as was J.T.M. Anderson, born in Ontario to an Irish immigrant family from Ulster. He arrived in Saskatchewan in 1908 and joined the Saskatoon Orange Lodge in 1920; he was destined to become the provincial Conservative Party leader in 1924–26 and 1928, then the premier of Saskatchewan in 1929–35. This was a period of widespread nativism directed against non-British immigrants, anti-Catholicism, and francophobia, represented in the close ties between the Orange Order and the provincial Ku Klux Klan.[87]

The Irish influence in Saskatchewan was further reflected in the strong Irish presence in city fire departments. The Loyal Orange Order was imported with Northern Irish immigrants and regularly celebrated the "Glorious Twelfth" of July, historically a Protestant victory over Catholic forces—although in Saskatchewan the most distinct Irish settlement was in fact Catholic. Today the Irish connection in Saskatchewan is still celebrated annually on St. Patrick's Day and at the Irish pavilion at Folkfest in

Saskatoon, and regularly in Irish pub evenings in Saskatoon, while the Blakey Saskatoon School of Irish Dance recently held a *Feis*, a festival of Irish music and dance. Irish, Scottish, and Welsh events are regularly advertised by Clans, Celts, and Clover, a shop in Saskatoon specializing in imported Celtic knitwear, jewellery, recordings, and foods.

In 1911 (the first year that Saskatchewan's population was counted as provincial), of 492,000 people in the new province, some 58,000 (12%) claimed Irish origin, at least 70% of them likely from Ontario.[88] Of 145,480 people in Saskatchewan claiming Irish origin (2006 census), 9,600 (6.6%) claimed only Irish origin and 135,875 (93.4%) partly Irish origin.

WELSH SETTLEMENTS

Although people of Welsh origin constitute one of the smallest segments of the diverse population of Saskatchewan, the early history of Welsh settlement in Saskatchewan is fascinating. The sole distinctive Welsh settlement was centred on the small village of Bangor, about thirty kilometres southeast of Melville. Yet these Welsh settlers did not arrive from Wales but from a unique Welsh colony in Patagonia, the southernmost region of Argentina, established in 1865, originally by only 153 settlers who set sail from Wales on a two-month voyage on board a ship proudly flying the Welsh dragon flag. They included coal miners and quarry workers in addition to farmers. The most prevalent reason why they would choose to leave their native homeland to resettle in such a remote locale in South America was a Welsh nationalistic movement led by the influential professor Michael Daniel Jones (1822–98) at a Congregationalist college; other motivations included a depressed economic situation in Wales, fear of the loss of Welsh language and culture, dislike of English domination, and advertisement by the Argentinian government for British and continental European settlers, combined with the recent creation in 1861 of a Welsh colonization society. Their utopian dream was to build a Welsh colony "where their language, cultural achievements, distinctive customs, and non-conformist religious traditions would be preserved free of the compulsions of the British political and religious establishment and the blandishments of the assimilative nationalism which had absorbed so many Welsh migrants to the United States earlier in the century."[89]

The colony established in Patagonia could not have been more isolated. It was situated far from Argentinian control, some 700 kilometres from the closest White settlement, and approximately 1,500 kilometers from Buenos Aires. As more Welsh settlers arrived from Wales as well as the United States—by 1875 the original population had more than doubled, by 1882 it numbered 1,286, and by 1896 it was 2,500[90]—the colony came to include the communities of Gaiman, Trelew, Rawson, and Puerto Madryn in what the settlers called the Vale of Camwy, the Chubut River Valley. Initially, the colonists sheltered in caves, then lived in sod homes, before building more substantial frame houses. The settlement flourished with the introduction of larger numbers of horses, the mechanization of grain production (primarily alfalfa and wheat), the establishment of a consumers' cooperative, and the building of a railway from the coast. In 1888, a second and far smaller colony was established more than 500 kilometres away, deep in the interior at the foot of the Andes, focused on sheep and cattle ranching, with an eventual population of about 200 settlers by 1902.[91]

For two or more generations, the colonists spoke only Welsh, the sole language in the schools, local government, and commerce. But the dream of an exclusively Welsh state deep in South America was unrealistic from the start. The task of preserving Welsh language and culture in the settlement was left to the schools, communal action, and family discipline. In the generations since colonization, today fewer than half of the estimated 20,000 people in the region who are wholly or partially of Welsh origin can still speak any Welsh; rather, those who still do tend to be trilingual in Welsh, English, and Spanish. There are still people speaking Welsh as their first language, but they tend to be the elderly grand- or great-grandchildren of the original settlers. Yet Welsh language courses are still offered by teachers from Wales, while other aspects of Welsh culture persist: a Welsh choir, *eisteddfod* (choral festival), museum, newspaper, farm stays, and tea houses such as Ty Cymmeg, serving traditional pastries such as *cacen ffrwythau*.[92]

When the Patagonian Welsh colony was first established, Argentinian control was far removed from the colonists (although there is evidence that the Argentinian government did help to save them from starvation). Argentina had no internationally recognized legal claim to Patagonia at the time; in fact, the territory was also claimed by Chile and Britain. The very remoteness of Patagonia placed it beyond the reach of Argentinian, Chilean, and especially British jurisdiction. However, this situation was soon to change. Argentina's claim was recognized by a treaty in 1881. Increasing Argentinian control led to a proposal delivered by two colonists to the British Foreign Office in 1899, emphasizing long-standing British interest in the territory; by then, however, the British government did not seem particularly interested in the plight of these displaced Welshmen.[93] Argentine repression and interference were increasing: military conscription was compulsory, and military training took place on Sundays (violating the Sabbath); the Spanish language was required in the schools (taken over by the government), and the central government decreed a policy of assimilation in the 1890s; Spanish-speaking Argentinians as well as Italians were settling surrounding areas, intermarriage between these Catholics and the Welsh Protestants was feared, and the Welsh were feeling increasing discomfort over being an isolated Protestant minority in a predominantly Catholic country; and land titles were challenged. To make matters worse, there was disastrous flooding along with a shortage of fertile farmland.[94]

With growing discontent in the Patagonia colony, by 1892 some settlers had started to think seriously about leaving the colony and resettling in Canada, where ample land was becoming available and there was an opportunity for bloc settlement; in fact, some had contemplated leaving as early as 1867, just two years after arrival. In 1892, the Canadian immigration agent in Liverpool arranged for a few Patagonian Welsh to emigrate to Winnipeg and settle along the line of the Manitoba and North Western Railway, which extended into Saskatchewan. Yet it was not until 1901 that a Canadian immigration agent in Wales, who had been appointed to this position in 1897, travelled to Patagonia to investigate conditions there and possibly to arrange for the removal of the settlers to Canada. In 1899, a delegation of three prominent Welshmen, David Lloyd George, a member of the British Parliament, W.J. Rees, a justice of the peace, and W. Llewellyn Williams, a distinguished barrister and writer, had visited

Saskatchewan and were favourably impressed. At the urging of David Lloyd George, who was to become the prime minister of Britain, sympathetic Welsh members of the Canadian Parliament, with the backing of the British secretary of the colonies, helped these immigrants to raise more than sufficient finances to charter a ship of the Pacific Steam Navigation Company to bring settlers from South America to England in May 1902 en route to Canada.[95]

One of the earlier former Patagonian settlers to arrive in Saskatchewan was Evan Jenkins, who had already established a homestead in the area southwest of Saltcoats in 1892. He was instrumental in guiding an advance party of about thirty Patagonian Welsh to this area in April 1902, with the assistance of the Canadian Commissioner of Immigration, who then arranged for the Department of the Interior to reserve a bloc settlement for the Welsh covering 100 square miles around what would become the communities of Bangor and Waldron along the Grand Trunk Pacific Railway about ten miles (sixteen kilometres) northwest of Stockholm. Led by Reverend David G.J. Davies, 234 settlers arrived in Saskatchewan in June 1902.[96] Together with the settlers who had already arrived earlier, they constituted about 10% of the population of the Welsh colony in Patagonia at the time. They included several Davies, Edwards, Evans, Hughes, Haines, Jenkins, Morris, Owen, Richards, Thomas, Williams, and Jones families and individuals. Initially, the new settlers stayed in tents on the Jenkins farm while they built their own homes, some of which were simple adobe or sod buildings, while others were more substantial. Three rural school districts were soon established in 1903–04—Llewelyn, Glyndwr, and St. David's—and a fourth, Wales, nearby northeast of Stockholm. Llewelyn, the original name for the settlement (about eight kilometres north of present-day Bangor), was named after Sir John T. Dillwyn-Llewelyn, chairman of the Welsh Patagonian Committee, which had been instrumental in bringing the Welsh settlers from Patagonia. Anglicans and Methodists concentrated in this district and Congregationalists in the Glyndwr district to the east (actually outside the original bounds of the Welsh reserve). Within the first decade of settlement, four mainly Welsh congregations were organized: St. Asaph's Anglican Parish in 1902 and St. David's Anglican Parish five years later, followed by two Methodist (later United Church) congregations—Llewelyn Bethel and Seion respectively in 1910–11.[97] St. David's district was centred on the village of Bangor, which soon became the hub of the settlement with construction of the Grand Trunk Pacific Railway in 1907. Bangor gained a post office in 1909 and was recognized officially as a village a couple of years later. The most residents that it has ever had was about 130 during the late 1940s; today fewer than half that number remain.

In the early years of settlement, the Welsh language was commonly spoken by the settlers; church services were all held in Welsh, and it was regarded as "an absolute necessity" for the schools to teach in Welsh at least for the first two or three years. Welsh church services and *eisteddfodau* were vital in the first generation of settlers to maintain Welsh identity, but their children soon became English speaking, and their grandchildren, now widely scattered, know little if any Welsh. Writing in the 1960s, Gilbert Johnson commented that "a few of the younger people understand the language, but its use in daily intercourse is fast disappearing—the process of assimilation is practically complete."[98] Be that as it may, the migration and settlement of

Welsh from Patagonia comprise one of the most interesting stories in the settlement of Saskatchewan.

Welsh settlers also concentrated in central Saskatchewan around the hamlet of Cymric, south of Govan, and the rural districts of Bryn Mawr, Dunkeld, Llanvair, Llanwenarth, Longnor, and Cardigan. Both Llanvair and Llanwenarth were named after communities in Monmouthshire. Elsewhere several Welsh-origin families settled in the district of Lloyd northwest of Webb, and Welsh names for rural districts were found at Llewellyn Road (a school during the 1890s) just east of Saskatoon, Brithdir northeast of Plunkett, Bryntirion southeast of Ebenezer (today largely settled by people of Ukrainian and Russian-German rather than Welsh origin), Cambria near Torquay, Cardiff southwest of Glenbain, Carnarvon (a misspelling of Caernarvon) northwest of Pangman, Colwyn (a CPR junction at Moose Jaw), Cymri at Midale, Glaslyn north of the Battlefords, Hawarden near Outlook, Pontrilas (named after a village actually in Herefordshire but near the Welsh border) south of Nipawin, Rhondda near Rosetown, Rhyl siding near Perdue, and Rhyl School near Handel. These communities and districts might have been given Welsh names by a particular early settler, or perhaps railway builder, but were generally not indicative of any substantial concentration of Welsh settlers. The Lloyd George district south of Alsask was named after the British prime minister who was instrumental in establishing the Welsh colony around Bangor; the Rhondda district southeast of Rosetown honoured a prominent British politician who visited Canada in 1915; and Lloydminster was named for Reverend George Exton Lloyd, originally from Ontario, then London, who led the Barr Colony. The mixed British-settled district of Ermine near Kerrobert was originally named Mackinnon, and the Anglican church was constructed in 1913 under the supervision of a Welsh clergyman to look like his church at home in Wales, with altar furnishings and communion service donated by his friends in Wales and England.[99] Near New Osgoode, northeast of Tisdale, Welsh immigrant Hugh E. Jones homesteaded in 1905; New Osgoode became a bustling community during the 1930s, but the last business closed in 1969, and few residents were left by the 1980s. Another Jones family of Welsh origin farmed along the north side of Manitou Lake near Watrous.

By 1921, only 1,587 people claiming Welsh ethnic origin were counted in Saskatchewan, yet many Welsh immigrants were simply designated by immigration officials and census takers more generally as British. Gradually, the Welsh-origin population in Saskatchewan continued to increase with the arrival of immigrants from Wales and likely more significantly of migrants from Ontario. By 2006, 16,640 people in Saskatchewan claimed Welsh ethnicity, of whom just 790 (4.7%) claimed to be only of Welsh ancestry, whereas 15,855 (95.3%) claimed to be partly of Welsh origin.

Clearly, people of Welsh origin became scattered widely throughout the province. By 1921, one in five was living in the three largest cities: Regina, Saskatoon, and Moose Jaw. By 1971, no more than twenty Welsh residents—about a third of the village population—remained in Bangor (pop. 50 now), whereas in the neighbouring village of Atwater British-origin residents comprised 72.7% (40 of the 55 residents). The Welsh settlement had retained a Welsh population of at most several hundred; in these communities and the surrounding rural municipalities of Fertile Belt and Grayson, people of British origin numbered between 600 and 700 in 1971. It is striking that in such a small community as Bangor a memorial cairn lists 63 veterans of the First World War and 116 of the Second World War. Over the course of a century, the descendants of these settlers have largely lost their Welsh language and culture. Surprisingly, the sole church in Bangor now is Catholic. Yet a pride in their Welsh heritage has survived, as evidenced in the homecoming centennial celebration in 2002 and a community history book detailing family histories of the many families with Welsh surnames. Bangor Heritage Day is still held every July. There is pride, too, in the fact that, despite their small numbers, Welsh have been well represented in the history of Saskatchewan and the West: they have included geographers—David Thompson, born to Welsh-speaking parents, responsible for much of the earliest mapping of Western Canada, Professors Howard Richards and Adrian Seabourne, both graduates of the University of Wales who respectively headed the Department of Geography at the University of Saskatchewan Saskatoon and Regina campuses; Premiers Woodrow Lloyd and Allen Blakeney; a pioneering archivist—Professor Lewis H. Thomas from Blackwood; and labour lawyer George Taylor and a union leader, Joe Thain, from Tredegar, Wales. Moreover, the Welsh heritage in Saskatchewan has been kept alive through Welsh societies in the major cities.[100]

CONCLUDING THOUGHTS

David Smith observes that,

> of the three great streams of immigration into the Canadian West—the American, the continental European, and the British—only the last has failed to attract significant academic attention [due to] the sheer size of the group, the mobility of its members, and the dispersed pattern of their settlement. Except in rare instances, land reserves were not set aside for the British, and Clifford Sifton's unhappy experience with the Barr Colonists ... confirmed his opposition to new reserves for any group.

So, he continues, studies of particular ethnic settlements, "often used with profit to examine the non-British in their isolated colonies, were less suitable for investigating the British who, except for exotic hybrids like the Patagonian Welsh, were widely scattered over the prairies."[101] In contrast, this chapter has emphasized that immigrants from Great Britain and Ireland and Canadians of British and Irish origins did in fact form bloc settlements; bloc settlements were not formed just by people of other European origins. Moreover, the various British nationalities—English, Scots, Irish, Welsh—tended to form their own settlements rather than always blend into a more generalized British identity. The *Atlas of Saskatchewan* identifies six distinctly English settlements, ten Scottish, two Irish, and two Welsh. Yet in this chapter many more rural communities and districts have been noted with smaller concentrations of settlers from these ethnic groups or named by early settlers and others who were of these particular ethnic origins.

Indeed, it would be hard to overstate the profound effect that British settlers collectively have had on the settlement of Saskatchewan. Today their descendants represent more than half of the total Saskatchewan population (if people who claim to be partially of British origin are counted). Fortunately, the more conservative people of British origin succeeded only to a limited extent in blocking or limiting the settlement of hundreds of thousands of people of other ethnic origins—this will be explored further in the concluding chapter. Nonetheless, all of these other settlers, along with Aboriginal people, were expected—not the least by the British-origin residents—to conform to British culture as represented in language, dress, politics, manners, education, and even vision of Canadian national identity. Yet again it has been fortunate that such conformity has had limitations and has been replaced in time by an appreciation of cultural diversity through multiculturalism.

In concluding this chapter, it should again be stressed that the British settlers of Saskatchewan did not constitute a single monolithic ethnic group but in themselves were evidence of remarkable diversity: aristocratic and working-class immigrants from English cities, farmers from the United States, Scots-Métis, Scottish Canadians from Ontario and Nova Scotia, Gaelic-speaking Highland Scottish crofters, Irish Catholics and Protestants, Welsh from South America ... .

SOURCES

English Settlements
English settlements in Saskatchewan are described by A.B. Anderson, "English Settlements," and H. Stoffel, "Barr Colony" and "Cannington Manor," in *Encyclopedia of Saskatchewan* (Regina: Canadian Plains Research Center, 2005), 298, 92, 155. Other sources have included G. Johnson, "The Harmony Industrial Association: A Pioneer Co-Operative," *Saskatchewan History* (winter 1951), reprinted in D.H. Bocking, *Pages from the Past: Essays on Saskatchewan History* (Saskatoon: Saskatchewan Archives Board and Western Producer Prairie Books, 1979), 79–89; D. Smith, "Instilling British Values in the Prairie Provinces," *Prairie Forum* 6, 2 (1981): 129–41; F. Peake, "Anglicanism on the Prairies: Continuity and Flexibility," and B.G. Smillie and N.J. Threinen, "Protestants—Prairie Visionaries of the New Jerusalem: The United and Lutheran Churches in Western Canada," in *Visions of the New Jerusalem: Religious Settlement on the Prairies*, ed. B.G. Smillie (Edmonton: NeWest Press, 1983), 55–90; R.W. Widdis, *With Scarcely a Ripple: Anglo-Canadian Migration into the United States and Western Canada, 1880–1920* (Montreal: McGill-Queen's University Press, 1998), reviewed by A.B. Anderson in *Saskatchewan History* (fall 2000): 54–55; S. Harris, *Forgotten Gardens, Abandoned Landscapes* (Regina: Your Nickel's Worth Publishing, 2007); L. Kitzan, "Adventurers in the Promised Land: British Writers in the Canadian North West, 1841–1913," and C. Kitzan, "Preaching Purity in the Promised Land: Bishop Lloyd and the Immigration Debate," in *The Prairie West as Promised Land*, ed. R.D. Francis and C. Kitzan (Calgary: University of Calgary Press, 2007), 29–52, 291–312; M. Hryniuk and F. Korvemaker, *Legacy of Stone: Saskatchewan's Stone Buildings* (Regina: Coteau Books, 2008); R. Loewen and G. Friesen, *Immigrants in Prairie Cities: Ethnic Diversity in Twentieth-Century Canada* (Toronto: University of Toronto Press, 2009); and D. Smith, "Instilling British Values in the Prairie Provinces," in *Immigration and*

Settlement, 1870–1939, ed. G.P. Marchildon (Regina: Canadian Plains Research Center, 2009), 441–56.

The broader context of English settlement in Canada has been described by B.S. Elliott, "English," and C.H. Williams, "Cornish," in *Encyclopedia of Canada's Peoples*, ed. P.R. Magocsi (Toronto: University of Toronto Press, 1999), 462–88, 378–81.

Scottish Settlements

For details on the genealogy of Scots-Métis in the Batoche, Halcro, and Prince Albert settlements, see L.J. Barkwell, *Veterans and Families of the 1885 Northwest Resistance* (Saskatoon: Gabriel Dumont Institute, 2011).

Sources specifically on Scottish settlements in Saskatchewan are A.R. Turner, "Scottish Settlement of the West," in *The Scottish Tradition in Canada*, ed. W.S. Reid (Toronto: McClelland and Stewart, 1976), 76–91; W. Norton, *Help Us to a Better Land: Crofter Colonies in the Prairie West* (Regina: Canadian Plains Research Center, 1994); and A.B. Anderson, "Scottish Settlements," in *Encyclopedia of Saskatchewan* (Regina: Canadian Plains Research Center, 2005), 844. The work of Scottish stonemasons in Saskatchewan is described in M. Hryniuk and F. Korvemaker, *Legacy of Stone: Saskatchewan's Stone Buildings* (Regina: Coteau Books, 2008).

More general sources on Scottish Canadians include J.M. Gray, *Lord Selkirk of Red River* (Toronto: Macmillan, 1963); W. Cavaick, *Uprooted Heather: A Story of the Selkirk Settlers* (Vancouver: Mitchell Press, 1967); D. Hill, *Great Emigrations: The Scots to Canada* (London: Gentry Books, 1972); A.B. Anderson, "The Scottish Tradition in Canada: Its Rise and Fall," in *Scottish Colloquium Proceedings*, vols. 6–7 (Guelph: University of Guelph, 1973), 35–47; G. MacEwen, *Cornerstone Colony: Selkirk's Contribution to the Canadian West* (Saskatoon: Western Producer Prairie Books, 1977); J.M. Bumsted, "Scots," in *Encyclopedia of Canada's Peoples*, ed. P.R. Magocsi (Toronto: University of Toronto Press, 1999), 1115–42; M. Shaw, *Great Scots: How the Scots Created Canada* (Winnipeg: Heartland Associates, 2003); and J. Calder, *Scots in Canada* (Edinburgh: Luath Press, 2003).

Informative sources on the historical background in the Scottish Highlands and Western Isles include I.F. Grant, *Highland Folk Ways* (Edinburgh: Routledge and Kegan Paul, 1961); J. Prebble, *The Highland Clearances* (Harmondsworth, UK, 1963); J.M. Bumsted, *The People's Clearance, 1770–1815* (Edinburgh: Edinburgh University Press, 1982); and D. Craig, *On the Crofters' Trail: In Search of the Clearance Highlanders* (London: Random House, 1990).

Irish Settlements

For details on Irish settlements in Saskatchewan, see J. Coughlin, *The Irish Colony of Saskatchewan* (Scarborough, ON: Lochleven Publishers, 1995); M. Cottrell, "The Irish in Saskatchewan, 1850–1930: A Study of Intergenerational Ethnicity," *Prairie Forum* 24, 2 (1999): 185–210, reprinted in *Immigration and Settlement, 1870–1939*, ed. G.P. Marchildon (Regina: Canadian Plains Research Center, 2009), 507–42; and A.B.

Anderson, "Irish Settlements," in *Encyclopedia of Saskatchewan* (Regina: Canadian Plains Research Center, 2005), 485.

More general sources on Irish Canadians include J.J. Mannion, *Irish Settlements in Eastern Canada: A Study of Cultural Transformation and Adaptation* (Toronto: University of Toronto Press, 1974); B.S. Elliott, *Irish Migrants in the Canadas: A New Approach* (Montreal: McGill-Queen's University Press, 1988); C.J. Houston and W.J. Smith, *Irish Emigration and Canadian Settlement* (Toronto: University of Toronto Press, 1990); and M.G. McGowan, "Irish Catholics," and B.S. Elliott, "Irish Protestants," in *Encyclopedia of Canada's Peoples*, ed. P.R. Magocsi (Toronto: University of Toronto Press, 1999), 734–83.

Welsh Settlements
A brief overview of Welsh settlement in Saskatchewan is W. Davies, "Welsh Settlement," in *Encyclopedia of Saskatchewan* (Regina: Canadian Plains Research Center, 2005), 1006. More detailed descriptions of the Patagonian Welsh settlement, both in Patagonia and in Saskatchewan, are G. Johnson, "The Patagonia Welsh," *Saskatchewan History*, 16, 3 (1963): 90–94; and L.H. Thomas, "From the Pampas to the Prairies: The Welsh Migration of 1902," *Saskatchewan History* 24, 1 (1971): 1–12, reprinted in *Pages from the Past: Essays on Saskatchewan History*, ed. D.H. Bocking (Saskatoon: Saskatchewan Archives Board and Western Producer Prairie Books, 1979), 90–101.

Other sources on Welsh settlement in Saskatchewan include "Patagonia Welsh—Welsh Colonists in Canada, 1902–1965," Saskatchewan Archives file S-A130; *History of Glyndwr District, Saltcoats, Sask., 1955*; L.H. Thomas, "Welsh Settlement in Saskatchewan, 1902–1914," *Western Historical Quarterly* 4, 4 (1973); W.I. Stevenson, "Welsh Settlement in Southwest Saskatchewan" (MA thesis, Simon Fraser University, 1974); and G. MacLennan, "A Contribution to the Ethnohistory of Saskatchewan's Patagonian Welsh Settlement," *Canadian Ethnic Studies* 7, 2 (1975).

An overview of Welsh settlement in Canada has been provided by C.H. Williams, "Welsh," in *Encyclopedia of Canada's Peoples*, ed. P.R. Magocsi (Toronto: University of Toronto Press, 1999), 1325–34; and W.K.D. Davies, "Welsh Americans in Rural Alberta: Origin and Development of the Wood River Welsh Settlement Area," *Prairie Forum* 24, 2 (1999).

Other sources briefly describe the contemporary Welsh settlement in Patagonia, such as R. Perry, *Patagonia: Windswept Land of the South* (New York: Dodd, Mead, and Company, ca. 1973); and B. Chatwin, *In Patagonia* (London: Pan Books, 1977).

The background on Welsh nationalism has been documented by Sir R. Coupland, *Welsh and Scottish Nationalism* (London: Collins, 1954).

Chapter 4
GERMANIC SETTLEMENTS

After the British-origin ethnic groups, Germanic ethnic and ethno-religious groups constitute the next largest generalized ethnic category in the Saskatchewan population, totalling at least 338,245 people wholly or partially of German and Dutch ethnic origins in 2006, together representing about a third of the total Saskatchewan population. Although some mixing was apparent in most settlements of German Catholics and Protestants, German Catholics usually tended to establish their own settlements distinct from German Lutherans, Baptists, and Adventists. So, too, did large numbers of Mennonites develop their own settlements, and much later—not until the 1950s—Hutterites began to move into Saskatchewan to establish a network of colonies. All of these ethno-religious groups—except Dutch—could claim German ethnicity, yet most immigrated to Canada either directly or indirectly from previous colonies in Eastern Europe—especially "South Russia" (Ukraine). The far fewer Dutch also established a couple of small settlements of their own.

Comprehension of the reasons behind the formation of German settlements in Saskatchewan involves some familiarity with Russian history, for a considerable proportion of these German immigrants came directly from German colonies in Russia or indirectly via Russian German settlements in the United States. Following her direction of the Russian conquest of Turkish-held territories north of the Black Sea from 1763 to 1774, Empress Catherine II wished to rapidly resettle Russia's new annexations with agricultural settlers loyal to her. As a result, an invitation was extended to farmers in Central Europe to establish ethnic colonies in Russia, on the condition that they would enjoy religious freedom, no taxation for ten years, freedom from serfdom, and permission to emigrate from Russia after paying all debts to the Crown. The first colonies in Russia were organized along the Volga River by Germans from the largely Protestant region of Hessia (Hessen) in 1764–78. These *Wolgadeutsche* (Volga Germans) were to be distinguished from the *Schwarzmeerdeutsche* (Black Sea Germans) who settled later north of the Black Sea. In this latter region—called South Russia (Sud-Russien) by the Germans, though actually in Ukraine—colonies were founded by German and Swedish Lutherans from the Baltic coast (1787–1804); German Catholics and Lutherans from predominantly Protestant Prussia and from mixed Catholic-Protestant Alsace-Lorraine, Rhineland, Baden-Wurttemberg, Switzerland, Silesia, Bohemia, Posen, and central Poland (1789–1855); Mennonites from East and West Prussia (1790–1854); Hutterites of Austrian and Moravian origin (1843); as well as Jews, Bulgarians, and other ethnic groups.

Among the specific factors causing Germans to emigrate from their colonies in Russia were the progressive deprivation of rights and privileges granted by Catherine II, particularly the *ukase* of June 4, 1871, which subjected Russian Germans to military service, removed their right to extensive political autonomy, and increased pressure toward Russification in community schools. Germans were forced to emigrate from their colonies in other regions in Eastern Europe—including Bessarabia (today in Moldova and Ukraine), Dobruja (now mostly in Romania, except the southernmost area, which is in Bulgaria), Bukovina (in Ukraine and Romania), Galicia (in Ukraine and Poland), Volhynia (in Ukraine), Transylvania (in Romania), and Banat (in Romania and Serbia)—for similar and other reasons. For example, in Dobruja, a severe drought in 1884 and the imposition of military service the previous year added to the existing problem of land shortage.

The German influx into the United States from Eastern Europe might have reached 200,000 annually during the early 1880s. Large areas of the Dakotas and Minnesota were converted into replicas of the Russian German colonies. Until the notion of German separatism became passé with the assimilated third and fourth generations and with the surge of anti-German feeling during the First World War, in these settlements the homes, schools, ethnic press, voluntary associations, and churches all collaborated in an attempt to preserve German identity, promote a segregated German lifestyle, and prevent intermarriage with non-Germans. Even political separatism was persistently encouraged, and as late as 1862 attempts were made to have German become an official language.[1]

As for the Germans who then migrated to Saskatchewan from the United States (many of whom had previously moved from Europe, particularly Eastern Europe, within the same generation), the increasing problem of finding large tracts of good agricultural land caused many to look northward at the rapidly developing Canadian West. Germans, from whatever specific origin, were lured to Saskatchewan because of the ready availability of inexpensive, good farmland; solicitation by Canadian immigration authorities and agencies; the promise of exemption from the military service feared in so many European regions; the encouragement of prominent Germans invited to tour the West and to organize large colonies (notably Count Hohenlohe-Langenburg, president of the German Colonial Association, and F.J. Lange, a founder of the Catholic Colonization Society); the successful precedent set by the earliest German settlers; and, not least, the influence of German newspapers and writers.

Shortly before the First World War, Gotthard L. Maron, writing for the leading German-language newspaper in Western Canada, *Der Nordwesten*, made some interesting observations about German settlers in Saskatchewan:

GERMANIC SETTLEMENTS

It is the Province of Saskatchewan that has the second largest German population of any of the provinces of the Dominion. You can find Germans scattered all over that province, ready to take their place in the ranks of all those who are desirous to further the interests of the country. The Germans—and I suppose this applies more or less to any other nationality—prefer, however, to settle in groups. Some of these German colonies have become very large in Saskatchewan and there are various districts where one can travel for miles and miles without hearing anything but German spoken. ... A considerable movement of Germans ... from ... various European countries has ... increased steadily from year to year, and the ranks of these German farmers have meanwhile been swelled considerably by thousands of German-Americans. ... It is estimated that one-fifth of the farmers in the Canadian west are German-speaking. And although only a small percentage of them hail from the German Empire, they nevertheless call themselves Germans ... because they belong to the German race. They all speak the German language. ... The ties which bind the Germans of the various countries ... become more and more pronounced on account of the aggressive policy which the Slavs are at present following up against anything that is German. This and their common language are the means of cementing the Germans of western Canada into one nationality irrespective of the land of their birth—they are Germans. ... There is no more law-abiding and peaceful citizen within the boundaries of the Dominion than the German. ... It has been said by some narrow-minded people that the "foreigners" in Canada must be taught to become Canadians, that is to say English-Canadians, that they must give up their own languages and become body and soul thorough Canadians. ... In the first place the Germans in Canada should not be classed with other nationalities as "foreigners." ... Everybody knows that the German is of good stock, of that stock from which the inhabitants of the British Isles themselves spring. On the other hand, nobody will deny the fact that we Germans would indeed be bad Canadians if we could strip off our nationality and our German sentiments like a man laying aside his coat.[2]

Most of the Germans who settled in Saskatchewan did not immigrate directly from Germany. In 1916, only 15,328 residents of the Prairie Provinces gave Germany as their country of birth, whereas 101,944 indicated that German was their mother tongue. According to one estimate, only 12% of the ethnic German immigrants who arrived in Western Canada before 1914 were *Reichsdeutsche* (homeland Germans) from Germany; the remainder were mostly *Volksdeutsche* (ethnic Germans) from Eastern Europe—44% from Russia, 18% from the Austrian Empire (Austria-Hungary), 6% from Romania— and another 18% came from the United States.[3] In 1911, 13.9% of the total population of Saskatchewan consisted of ethnic Germans, whereas only 1.1% were born in Germany; moreover, the ethnic German proportion in Saskatchewan was far higher than in the neighbouring provinces of Alberta (9.9%) and Manitoba (7.5%). Saskatchewan's ethnic German proportion peaked by 1931 at 15.0%.[4] Among the reasons why relatively few immigrants from Germany came to Saskatchewan were ignorance of Canada, fear of the northern climate, and German government discouragement of emigration.

CHAPTER 4

As Giesinger has written,

> The most striking fact about the numerous Germans who settled in western Canada in the pre-1914 era was the small proportion of them that came from Germany itself. The vast majority came from central Europe and from southern Russia; from the Austrian provinces of Bukovina and Galicia, from the Hungarian Banat, from the Romanian Dobruja, from central Poland, and in larger numbers, about one-half of the total, from the German colonies in Russia, from Volhynia, Bessarabia, the Odessa region, the Crimea, the shores of the Sea of Azov and the banks of the Volga. They settled on the prairies in groups, not so much on the basis of their country or province of origin, but on the basis of religious affiliation. German Catholic areas, for instance, often had people from various Black Sea colonies settling side by side with their co-religionists from the Banat. The diversity was even greater in most Protestant areas, where people from Volhynia, from Galicia, from central Poland, from the Bukovina, from Bessarabia, from the Crimea and elsewhere, were sometimes all represented.[5]

Some of the German settlements in Saskatchewan were homogeneous in both religious affiliation and precise regional origin (e.g., those founded by immigrants from a specific religious colony in South Russia). But other settlements revealed mixed origins yet common religion or, conversely, common origin yet mixed religious affiliations. On the whole, though, German Catholics, Lutherans, Baptists, Mennonites, and Hutterites tended to form their own settlements or colonies. Many of the German immigrants concentrated in their own bloc settlements; many others did not, electing to settle in ethnically heterogeneous areas. Some settlements were planned; other German concentrations came into existence gradually through chain migration.

The German-origin population of Saskatchewan grew extremely rapidly from only 299 (0.9% of the total provincial population) in 1885 to 11,743 (12.9%) in 1901 and 68,628 (13.9%) in 1911. It continued to grow, to 77,109 during the next five years, but the proportion had started to decline (to 11.9% in 1916). Both German and German Canadian organizations played a significant role in promoting and facilitating German immigration and settlement in Saskatchewan. These organizations included the interdenominational Verein für das Deutschtum im Ausland (Society for Germans Abroad), Deutsche Ausland Institut (German Foreign Institute), and Deutsch Kanadischer Verband von Saskatchewan (German Canadian Association of Saskatchewan); the German Catholic Verein Deutsch Canadier Katholiken (Society of German Canadian Catholics), Sankt Raphaels Verein (St. Raphael Society, Hamburg), and Deutsch Katholischen Volksverein (German Catholic People's Society); and the Lutheran Hamburg Auswanderermission (Hamburg Emigration Mission) and Canadian Lutheran Immigration Board.

However, with German immigrants designated as "enemy aliens" during the First World War, all German immigration to Canada was prohibited completely until 1923, when an exemption for agriculturalists and their families was made, followed by a lifting of restrictions four years later. In any case, during the period between the First and Second World Wars, the German government actively discouraged emigration from Germany. Initially, at least, if German citizens were permitted to leave, settling in South America was preferred, where well-defined, closed German settlements offered the best opportunity for them to retain their German identity and culture.[6] This would soon change, however; by 1920, German authorities recognized that Saskatchewan in particular had developed similarly cohesive German settlements, though public animosity toward Germans continued following the war. A total of 3,233 German nationals had immigrated to Saskatchewan by 1920, while another 2,791 arrived between 1921 and 1930, but after 1931 this influx greatly diminished (to only 273 between 1931 and 1939), then virtually ceased during the Second World War. Yet it is interesting to note that 1,021 of the 5,391 German nationals living in Saskatchewan in 1931 and still possessing German citizenship had actually been born outside Germany in other Eastern European countries.[7]

Both the German population and proportion counted in Saskatchewan declined, to 68,202 (9.0%) in 1921 (perhaps partly due to the reluctance of existing ethnic Germans and Mennonites who had not immigrated from Germany to acknowledge their German identity during and after the war). But then the population and proportion began to increase steadily until the Second World War: to 96,498 (11.8%) in 1926, 129,232 (14.0%) in 1931, and 165,549 (17.8%) in 1936. However, during the next three decades, the number and proportion of German-origin residents of Saskatchewan fluctuated somewhat: from 130,258 (14.5%) in 1941 to 135,584 (16.3%) in 1951, 158,209 (17.1%) in 1961, and 180,095 (19.4%) in 1971. In 1981, the 161,705 Saskatchewan residents claiming German origin comprised 16.7% of the total population; however, if ethnic Germans claiming Austrian, Swiss, Russian, and other origins were added, the German proportion would likely have been closer to one in every five residents.[8] Most of the Germans who immigrated to Saskatchewan since the Second World War have tended to come from Germany rather than ethnic German colonies in Eastern Europe, though shifting international boundaries during the immediate postwar years continued to bring ethnic Germans to Western Canada as refugees.

Since 1981, the Census of Canada has distinguished between residents claiming to be entirely of a particular (e.g., German) ethnic origin and those claiming this origin as well as other origins. According to 2006 census data, the German population of Saskatchewan numbered at least 286,040, about a quarter of whom (26.0%, or 74,425) claimed to be solely of German origin, whereas almost three-quarters (74.0%, or 211,615) claimed to be only partially of German origin. Another 16,115 people claimed Austrian origin, so they could be added to those claiming to be of German origin; moreover, 4,365 people claimed Swiss origin and 340 Luxemburger origin, but not all of these latter would have originally been German speaking. People of German origin (in whole or part) have become the largest single ethnic group in Saskatchewan, comprising 29.5% of the total provincial population (that is, if people of British origin are counted separately as English, Scottish, Irish, or Welsh). Yet in 2001, 32,515 people (which would represent only about 12% of the population claiming German origin or 39% of those claiming only German ethnicity at the time) reported German as their mother tongue, reflecting the fact that a large proportion of the descendants of earlier (prewar) ethnic German settlers no longer speak German.

CHAPTER 4

As with the settlements established by other ethnic groups, there are several ways to describe German settlements. First, they can be described chronologically. However, the earliest German settlements all began to develop within just four years, 1884–87, so almost at the same time, and other settlements and concentrations later but also within a few years, 1902–10. Moreover, these settlements and concentrations continued to develop and expand over a longer period of time, typically several decades, so in a sense they were all developing concurrently.

Second, German settlements can be described by religious affiliation. Many settlements and areas of concentration were almost exclusively Catholic, Lutheran, Mennonite, or occasionally Baptist or Adventist, and by definition all Hutterite colonies are exclusive. However, most Catholic and Mennonite settlements included Lutheran and other Protestant minorities; conversely, many predominantly Lutheran settlements included some Catholics; moreover, certain areas of German settlement were mixed Catholic, Lutheran, and/or Mennonite.

Third, German settlements can be described by size. Of course, there are two ways of considering "size": by areal extent and by ethnic population. German settlements range from very large, covering many rural municipalities and townships and including many communities, containing German populations numbering in the thousands, to very small, in both a geographic and a demographic sense. Not infrequently, smaller named German settlements coalesced into larger areas of settlement.

Again, as explained in the introductory chapter, exactly what should be considered a "settlement" is somewhat problematic; in many cases, (especially larger but also quite a few smaller) settlements and colonies were carefully planned and named. They tended to be very cohesive, where the German population predominated in many communities within an extensive area. Yet eventually German settlement extended beyond the original designated boundaries of such a settlement or colony (if in fact such boundaries were predetermined). But in many instances, specific named German settlements were not actually the case; rather, they were simply relative concentrations of German immigrants in various areas, which therefore tended to be less cohesive, with Germans not necessarily predominating in communities while still forming a considerable concentration within the particular area.

Taking all this into consideration, this chapter will describe first the original formation as well as the gradual development of the largest and earliest named German settlements and then the emergence and continued development of smaller and mostly later German concentrations throughout the regions comprising the prairie portion of Saskatchewan; in the process, religious affiliations will be described in detail. Clearly, German Catholics established the largest, most cohesive and planned, and among the earliest settlements, so first four of the largest German Catholic settlements will be described: St. Joseph's Colony, Katharinental Colony, and the Kronau-Rastadt and Odessa settlements (1886–), which soon fused together into a single extensive area of German Catholic settlement; St. Peter's Colony (1902–); a second, much larger St. Joseph's Colony in the west-central region (1905–); and the Prelate Colony (1907–), which expanded to include a series of German Catholic colonies and settlements between Leader, Maple Creek, and Medicine Hat, Alberta. Then several of the earliest and best-defined primarily German Protestant settlements will be described: Neu Elsass Colony

(1884–), centred on Strasbourg, which expanded into a large area of German settlement that, while primarily Lutheran, came to include Catholic, Baptist, and Adventist communities; Hohenlohe Colony (1884–), centred on Langenburg, predominantly Lutheran; the Edenwold settlement (1885–), where Baptists and Lutherans predominated; and the Volga German Colony (1887–), north of Yorkton, Baptist and Lutheran. Two of the larger mixed Catholic and Lutheran settlements will be described next: first, the Catholic Mariahilf Colony south of Melville and the Lutheran settlement around Neudorf and Lemberg (1890–), which eventually expanded into an extensive area of German settlement centred on Melville; second, the Catholic and Lutheran settlements around St. Walburg and Loon Lake (1901–, 1929, 1939). By 1910, German settlements and concentrations had proliferated and were found in virtually every region of the prairie portion of the province; this later stage of settlement will be described in some detail. The chapter then turns to the foundation and development specifically of Mennonite settlements, particularly the two largest: the Saskatchewan Valley settlement (1891–) and the expansive settlement originally centred on Swift Current (1903–); smaller Mennonite settlements (most of which came into existence during the 1920s, though some were earlier and others later) will also be noted. This discussion is followed by a description of the rapid and far more recent establishment of numerous Hutterite colonies throughout Saskatchewan (since 1949). Finally, two small Dutch settlements (around 1910) will be identified. Following these descriptions of settlements, a discussion of German resistance to change in Saskatchewan will lead to a historical review of the battle over education in the German language, and the chapter will conclude with some thoughts on the survival and resilience of German culture in Saskatchewan.

MAJOR GERMAN CATHOLIC SETTLEMENTS
St. Joseph's Colony, St. Peter's Colony, St. Paul's Colony, Katharinental Colony, and the Kronau-Rastadt and Odessa Settlements (1886–)

St. Joseph's Colony near Balgonie, in the south-central region just east of Regina, originated in 1886 with the arrival of families who had migrated from the Josephstal Colony near Odessa in South Russia or Ukraine, which had been founded in 1804 by Catholics primarily from Alsace and southwestern Germany (but also from Silesia, Bohemia, Switzerland, and German settlements in Hungary). The Russian czar had revoked their privileges as German colonists, reduced them from landowners to tenants, and took measures to assimilate them into Russian culture. Disillusioned by this arbitrary revocation of what they perceived to be their inherent rights, more than fifty families decided to emigrate.[9] Once they had arrived in Saskatchewan, they built a rudimentary mud and stone church within a year, then a more substantial St. Joseph's Church in 1897. In 1891, the settlers organized a *dorf* (communal village clustered around a church) in Russian German style, remnants of which still exist; this was recognized as having official village status in 1894 (which it lost in 1986, downgraded to an organized hamlet). St. Mary's Chapel, St. Joseph's Church, the rectory and Ursuline convent (1903), parish hall (1928), and Southgate School (1943)—originally located eight kilometres southwest of Wolseley, then moved to Kendal in 1952 and finally onto the colony site—all constitute the St. Joseph's Colony Heritage Site, established in 1984 (the original colony school, built in 1903, closed in 1967 and was moved to Balgonie the following year). The brick façade of the rectory was constructed by Dominic Deschner; born in 1881 in Neuhlin, Russia, he arrived in the colony from South Dakota in 1905, moved in 1929 to Macklin in St. Joseph's Colony in the west-central region (described below), and died in 1948.[10] The Ursuline sisters, based in Vibank, served the community through the mid-1930s.

Between 1890 and 1893, more families arrived from the communities of Rastadt and Munchen (founded in 1809 in the Beresaner colonies northwest of Nikolayev by immigrants originally from the Palatinate, Baden, and Alsace) as well as from Klosterdorf (founded in 1805 by Catholic settlers from Austria, Swabia, and southwestern Germany). These *Schwarzmeerdeutsche*—Black Sea Germans—settled south of St. Joseph's Colony, establishing St. Peter's Colony by 1894. Some of these Russian German immigrants decided to form *dorf* villages similar to St. Joseph's: Rastadt-Dorf, Katharinental (named after the original community of Katharinental in the Beresaner colonies, but later in Saskatchewan the rural post office serving the colony became Kathrinthal and the local school Cathrinthal), and Speier (named after another community in the same area in South Russia). The villages of Davin, Rastadt, and Kronau came into existence, the latter two named after communities in South Russia (the original Kronau colony in South Russia, west of Nikopol, had been founded in 1870 mostly by Baden-Württembergers); the Kronau area included the rural districts of Saar, St. Johannes, and St. Mary.

This Russian German Catholic settlement in Saskatchewan expanded rapidly, with the arrival of more immigrants from the Odessa region (in Ukraine) and German colonies in the Banat region (today in Romania and Serbia). By 1896, there were already more than 200 German families in this region, almost all of them Catholic immigrants from German colonies in South Russia.[11] The settlement expanded southeast into St. Paul's Colony, centred on St. Paul's Parish in Vibank. The church, together with Elsas School, were built just north of the community in 1904 (later they were both moved into the village). In 1919, Ursuline nuns arrived from Germany, and their Holy Family convent and boarding school were opened in 1923 (which became the village community centre, office, and post office after 1977 and were declared a heritage site in 1992 and now house the Vibank Heritage Centre). Vibank became an official village in 1911; by the 1920s, there were close to 400 residents, but the village population declined rapidly during the Depression years, then regained its former size. Russian German Catholics had settled around Odessa (named after the principal port city on the Black Sea) by 1901–04. They built their first church in 1908 and the large Holy Family Church in 1953. Originally called Magna Post Office in 1908, the community became Odessa Station a couple of years later, and the next year it was incorporated as a village. The German settlement soon expanded to include Kendal as well as south toward Sedley and Francis. Surrounding rural districts were heavily German: Andreasheim, Franzfeld, Josephstal, Mayerling, New Holstein, Seitz, Sibel Plains.

Substantial pockets of Lutheran settlement developed within the large Catholic settlement by 1898–99 with the arrival of Lutherans from the German Black Sea and Bukovina colonies. Lutheran congregations were organized at Kronau in 1909–12, Vibank in 1909, Davin (the Emmaus and Frieden districts), and Francis.

This extensive area of continuous German Catholic settlement covers (wholly or partially) six rural municipalities and extends approximately fifty kilometres east to west and seventy-five kilometres north to south. The communities within or near these settlements include the towns of Balgonie (2006 pop. 1,384), White City (pop. 1,113), Ogema (pop. 304), and Francis (pop. 148); the villages of Vibank (pop. 361), Sedley (pop. 319), Odessa (pop. 201), and Kendal (pop. 59); and the organized hamlets of Kronau (pop. 209) and Davin (pop. 49). Ogema and Kronau are currently increasing in population, Davin is holding firm, and Odessa, Francis, and Kendal are decreasing. From 1971 census data, we can estimate the total German-origin population in these settlements to have been approximately 3,400. In the towns, Germans constituted a majority of the residents of White City (60.0%), almost half of those of Francis (48.5%), and a quarter of those of Balgonie (25.2%) but relatively few in Ogema. In the villages, most of the residents of Kendal (82.4%), Vibank (75.0%), and Odessa (62.9%) were German, while Germans comprised a substantial minority of the residents of Sedley (37.7%).

St. Peter's Colony (1902–)

The settlers of a second, far larger St. Peter's Colony, centred on Humboldt in the north-central region, came largely from the American states. With the rapid opening of Saskatchewan to settlement during the 1890s, German settlers from the closest American states (most of them second generation) began to move north; in many instances, they sent petitions for further immigrants to found new colonies back to their former parishes. One such petition was received by a Benedictine priest in Minnesota; he then persuaded his superior, the abbot at St. John's Abbey in Collegeville, Minnesota, to establish a German Catholic colony in Saskatchewan. This abbey was in the heart of a large German Catholic colony covering much of Stearns County, centred on St. Cloud. An exploration party was sent to Saskatchewan, headed by Reverend Bruno Doerfler of the abbey and consisting of representatives from several parishes.[12] Upon their return to Minnesota, the decision to establish the colony was made, and the Volksverein German-American Land Company was founded. In 1902, this company, in conjunction with the priests of the Order of St. Benedict and the Catholic Settlement Society of St. Paul, Minnesota, obtained colonization rights to a vast area in north-central Saskatchewan—fifty townships covering 1,800 square miles. The German-American Land Company was responsible for buying 100,000 acres of railway lands in the district selected and for selling it to settlers desiring more than the usual quarter-section homestead. The Benedictine priests based at St. Peter's Abbey in Muenster were to develop parishes and be primarily responsible for expansion of the settlement; they actually led settlers into specific areas within the settlement. The Catholic Settlement Society extensively advertised the venture and assisted the settlers in filing for their homesteads and locating them thereon.[13]

With the arrival of the Benedictines from Cluny Priory, Wetaug, Illinois, in the new colony in 1902 and from Collegeville, Minnesota, the following year, settlement was under way. The Benedictine order, based at St. Meinrad Archabbey in Indiana, played a significant role in recruiting German American settlers for St. Peter's Colony. Settlers from Stearns County, Minnesota, had also been encouraged by the German Catholic Golden Valley Land Company to take up land and organize parishes served by German-speaking priests from Assumption Abbey, Richardton, North Dakota, in 1902.[14] By the end of 1903, over a thousand homesteads had been filed and eight parishes established. Besides Muenster, the other original parishes were St. Boniface (at Leofeld, southeast of Cudworth, today a heritage site), St. Benedict, Holy Guardian Angels at Englefeld (named after Abbot Peter Engel of St. John's Abbey, Collegeville—the Schmitz farm, formerly the Fritsch farm [1924], west of the village, is a heritage site), St. Ann at Annaheim (where the Dauk residence [1916] became the House of Treasures and Keepsakes), St. Bruno at Bruno (where the first mass was held in 1904), St. Joseph (Old Fulda), and Assumption of the Blessed Virgin Mary at Marysburg (the present grandiose church dates from 1921 and is now a historic site).

Within five years of the commencement of settlement, there were over 6,000 German Catholics in the colony.[15] Most were second- or third-generation German Americans whose forefathers had immigrated from the *Reich* who arrived from Minnesota, the Dakotas, Wisconsin, Iowa, Nebraska, and Kansas, but some were from Russian German colonies from the Banat region (today in Romania and Serbia). The Order of St. Benedict in the colony had been incorporated in 1904 as a complex organization governing schools, associations, and whole communities. A German-language newspaper, *Der Bote*, began publication at Muenster the same year. Humboldt was being converted from a "wilderness of sloughs and bluffs" into the largest town in the region (with a population of over 2,000 by 1914). Fast-growing Humboldt became an incorporated village in 1905 and a town just a couple of years later, Watson an incorporated village in 1906 and a town two years later.

St. Peter's cathedral at Muenster, built in 1908–10, today a designated provincial historic site, features lavish art by Count Berthold von Imhoff, who had been born in a castle in the Rhineland in 1868 and emigrated to Pennsylvania in 1892 and then to Saskatchewan in 1914. He became widely known for his *religiösen meisterwerke* (religious art) decorating the interior of St. Peter's in 1919, with the bold inscription on the arch over the sanctuary announcing *Du bist Petrus, und auf diesen felsen will ich meine kirche bauen* (You are Peter, and out of these rocks will I build my church). Imhoff also decorated churches in the colony at St. Benedict, St. Leo, Humboldt, and Bruno as well as in other German and French settlements; he eventually settled near St. Walburg. St. Peter's did not actually become a cathedral until 1921 when the abbot was given "ordinary" jurisdiction over the two dozen parishes of the colony, which by then constituted the *abbacy-nullius*, equivalent to an autonomous diocese. The pioneering monk Bruno Doerfler had become an abbot in 1911 and remained so until his death in 1919.

Many more parishes were added within the next several years until the advent of the First World War: St. Anthony at Lake Lenore (where the first mass had been said in 1904 in the tiny Gerwing home, a mud-caulked log home that housed thirteen people)—seven Gerwing brothers homesteaded there in 1903—and St. John the Baptist at Willmont (west of Fulda) in 1904; St. Augustine at Humboldt, Sacred Heart at Watson (originally Vossen, where mass was celebrated almost immediately upon arrival of the settlers[16]), St. Martin (east of Annaheim), St. Scholastica (south of Humboldt), and St. Patrick's (near Leroy) in 1905; St. Oswald at Romance, St. Maurus at Dana, and Immaculate Conception (south of Carmel) in 1906; St. Leo/St. Meinrad (near Cudworth), St. Gregor, St. Bernard (Old Pilger), St. Gertrude (south of Muenster), and St. Anselm at Spalding in 1907; Our Lady of Mount Carmel at Carmel in 1908; St. Agnes at Peterson in 1910; Beauchamp mission in 1911; and St. Michael at Cudworth in 1912. Muenster became an incorporated village in 1908, Bruno in 1909, and Cudworth in 1911.

As the colony continued to expand, its German identity was further ensured. The first *Katholikentag*, a conference of German Catholics, was held at Muenster in 1908, with delegates from various settlements in Saskatchewan as well as from Minnesota and Manitoba; other *Katholikentage* were held at Humboldt in 1910 and 1914. In 1909, the *Volksverein*, a German Catholic voluntary association, was formed in Winnipeg; it was to play an active role in St. Peter's Colony for many years. It was during this period that two women's religious orders were imported from Europe. In 1911, some Sisters of St. Elizabeth, from Klagenfurt, Austria, immigrated to Humboldt, where they founded the first of a series of hospitals. Because they did not speak English, they were sent back to Minnesota to learn sufficient English to practise nursing in Canada. Eventually, the work of the order expanded to four hospitals in Saskatchewan and 120 sisters, some of whom also worked as teachers and domestics in Catholic colleges and retreat houses.[17] A couple of years later Ursuline nuns left their convents at Cologne and Hasseluene, Germany, to organize a small convent at Dead Moose Lake (later known as Marysburg) in 1914 and serve St. Angela's Parish School, constructed in 1912.

In spite of the effect of the First World War on discouraging the preservation of German identity, the colony continued to maintain a distinctly Catholic, if not German, character and to expand. Two immigration delegates from Germany, Baron Eduard von Stackleberg and Dr. Pastor Friedrich Caspar Gleiss, visiting the colony in 1924, found an outstanding example of an extensive, successful German settlement, complete with churches, schools, a monastery and convent, and even a hospital.[18] In 1919, the Ursuline nuns established a larger convent and three years later St. Ursula Academy at Bruno. During the 1960s, there were over 100 sisters there. The school graduated its last class in 1982, by which time it had graduated over 2,000 students, then successively became a retirement home for nuns, a community cultural centre, a university conference centre, and recently again a Catholic education centre. In 1922, *Der Bote* became an English-language publication, the *Prairie Messenger*; *Der Bote* had been defunct since 1918 due to legislation against printing in German. The last important *Katholikentag* was held at Muenster in 1933. By 1951–52, the remnants of the *Volksverein* were merged with the Catholic Immigration Society for Western Canada. But progress as a colony was also evident. St. Peter's College was founded at Muenster in 1920 (though as early as 1903 the Benedictines had petitioned the government of the North-West Territories, of which Saskatchewan was part at the time, for a charter as St. Peter's University); construction of Michael Hall was completed the following year, Placid Hall soon after, and St. Scholastica by the mid-1950s (all three buildings now comprise a provincial historic site). And new parishes continued to be established: St. Hubert (later Canadian Martyrs) at Middle Lake by 1915; St. Bernard east of Pilger (today a historic site) in 1918; St. George at Naicam in 1925; St. James (east of Lake Lenore) in 1933; Holy Family mission (near Spalding) in 1945; and Holy Trinity at Pilger in 1948.

The colony, while strongly Catholic, was not exclusively Catholic; Lutheran congregations were established within the settlement—but many only temporarily: Zion at Bruno (1911–2002), St. John at St. Benedict (1911–48), a mission at St. Brieux (1913–34), Mt. Calvary at Verndale (1916–50s), a congregation (but no church) seven kilometres south of Muenster (1919–33), Grace at Middle Lake (1926–60), Good Hope at Daphne (1930s–51), St. John at Cudworth during the late 1930s, a mission at Carmel (1939–46), and St. Benedict mission (1939–41). Mt. Calvary Lutheran Church (1916) serving the Three Lakes district northeast of Middle Lake is a heritage site.

More villages became incorporated: Englefeld in 1916, St. Gregor in 1920, Lake Lenore in 1921. Cudworth and Bruno became towns respectively in 1961 and 1962, while Middle Lake became an incorporated village in 1963, St. Benedict the following year, and Pilger in 1969. Annaheim was designated as an organized hamlet in 1967, then an incorporated village in 1977. Humboldt was elevated to the status of a city in 2000.

The German-origin population of St. Peter's Colony, which has the largest German population of any of the German bloc settlements in Saskatchewan, could be estimated at approximately 10,400 in 1971 (the last year for which an accurate ethnic count at the community and rural municipality levels was possible).[19] The colony included forty-eight townships covering (in whole or part) eleven rural municipalities. This area of German Catholic settlement extends, at its maximum, approximately seventy kilometres north to south and ninety kilometres east to west. Included within and at the periphery of this vast bloc settlement are twelve rural municipalities; seven towns: Humboldt (pop. 4,998 in 2006), Wakaw (pop. 864), Cudworth (pop. 738), Bruno (pop. 495), Naicam (pop. 690), Watson (pop. 719), and Leroy (pop. 412); and nine incorporated villages: Muenster (pop. 342), Lake Lenore (pop. 306), Middle Lake (pop. 277), Spalding (pop. 237), Englefeld (pop. 227), Annaheim (pop. 218), St. Gregor (pop. 102), St. Benedict (pop. 78), and Pilger (pop. 74). In 1971, only a single town, Bruno, was predominantly German (62.9%); almost half (48.6%) of the residents of Humboldt, the largest town and centre of the colony (declared a city in 2000), claimed German origin, whereas residents of German origin comprised smaller minorities in Leroy (31.3%), Cudworth (30.5%), Watson (29.9%), Naicam (18.2%), and Wakaw (13.8%). However, with the exception of Humboldt and Bruno, most of these towns are situated in ethnically mixed areas at the fringe of the colony. Villages and smaller communities located within the colony all had substantial German majorities: Pilger (83.3%), Middle Lake (71.4%), St. Gregor (69.6%), Lake Lenore (64.8%), Muenster (64.6%), Englefeld (63.0%), St. Benedict (57.6%) (Annaheim was not an incorporated village at the time). Strikingly, all of these towns and villages experienced declines in population during the five years 2001–06. The colony has also included many smaller, unincorporated rural communities, including Carmel and Dixon (between Humboldt and Bruno), Peterson, Dana, Muskiki Springs, and Totzke (west of Bruno), Leofnard and Ens (near Wakaw), Fulda (between Humboldt and Middle Lake), Marysburg and Moseley (north of Humboldt), Verndale and Daylesford (north of Lake Lenore), and Daphne and Romance (respectively north and south of Watson). Besides its dominating church, Marysburg still had a school by the 1980s but no remaining businesses and few homes. Apart from the rural parishes mentioned above, other strongly German rural districts included Kloppenburg, Bay Trail, and Waldsee (around Humboldt); Banner (near Muenster); Sjollie and Pappenfus Lake (near St. Gregor); Wimmer—named for the Right Reverend Archabbot Wimmer, the first Benedictine abbot in North America, Korbel, Vossen Lake, Iron Spring, and Alton— originally Holfield (around Watson); Chelton, Bunker Hill, Hat Creek, Freyling Lake, and Schmidtz Lake (around Annaheim); Stuckel and Schuler (around Lake Lenore); St. Henry and Dead Moose Lake (near Marysburg); Willmont, Canvasback, and Langenhoff (around Fulda); Wilfred and Solmond (around Middle Lake); Rock Valley, Vier

Lake, Belmont, and Hoodoo (around St. Benedict); Crooked Lake (near Wakaw); Hull (near Cudworth); and Thiel-Krentz, Hoffman, and Sunlight (around Bruno). In addition to the German Catholics of St. Peter's Colony proper, there are several thousand people of German origin in the adjacent areas to the south and east.

However, rural depopulation has taken its toll on many parishes, especially out in the open countryside but even within communities: St. Leo near Cudworth, Immaculate Conception near Carmel, St. Oswald at Romance, and St. Patrick at Sinnett all closed in 1965 (though St. Ignatius north of Sinnett [1928] is preserved as a heritage site), followed by St. John the Baptist at Willmont in 1971, Holy Family near Spalding in 1973, St. Martin near Annaheim in 1985, St. Maurus at Dana in 1989, and St. James near Lake Lenore in 1995. An interesting case in point is provided by the Carmel area. The first substantial church in the village of Carmel was constructed in 1910, a second, larger church in 1926, and a third in 1947, indicative of steady growth, while at Immaculate Conception a few kilometres down the country road the first mass was celebrated in 1906 in a substantial church constructed in 1926. The district generated many vocations as priests and nuns over the years. In 1920, there were fifty-two confirmations at Carmel and twenty at Immaculate Conception; by 1965, there were only eight. The number of baptisms recorded in the two churches was rapidly decreasing: thirty-two in 1935, just a couple in 1975, an average of four a year during the 1980s through the early 1990s. At Immaculate Conception, thirty-six families decreased to twenty-two (representing 105 people) by 1965; there was only a single baptism and no funeral. The church was closed that year. Abandoned and stripped of furnishings (the 1,000 lb bell was moved to Mt. Carmel shrine, the hardwood floor donated to the Carmel parish hall), it was sold in 1972 for $500 to artist Mel Bolen, who turned it into North Star Pottery. The small churchyard cemetery is maintained in a clearing in the woods. Little remains up the road at Carmel: the church is unpainted and in disrepair, the school is derelict, only a few homes are occupied, and the last one in reasonable repair is currently up for sale.

St. Joseph's Colony (1905–)

Only a couple of years after the inception of St. Peter's Colony, plans were already being made for the establishment of an even larger German Catholic colony. F.J. Lange, a founder of the Catholic Colonization Society, conceived the idea of a vast German Catholic colony covering 200 townships—about four times as large as St. Peter's Colony. During the summer of 1904, Lange selected the Tramping Lake area in the west-central region as the focal point for a new colony. The resulting St. Joseph's Kolonie (the second German Catholic colony with this name) covered a larger land area than St. Peter's Colony, making it the largest German Catholic settlement in Saskatchewan in this sense, but it never attained the population of St. Peter's Colony. Lange's high expectations were not entirely fulfilled; government officials agreed to the bloc purchase by the Catholic Colonization Society of seventy-seven townships, of which fifty-five (equivalent to the extent of St. Peter's Colony) eventually had German majorities.[20] As in St. Peter's Colony, the Catholic Colonization Society collaborated with a religious order—in this case the Oblate Order from Hunfeld, Germany—in the planning, development, and settling of St. Joseph's Colony.

The first settlers arrived in the Tramping Lake area in early summer 1905. The colony did not develop quite as rapidly as St. Peter's Colony, but by 1911 it included over 5,000 people of German origin and an estimated 7,000–8,000 by 1914; by the mid-1950s, the colony included seventeen parishes and seven missions.[21] Most of these settlers were *Schwartzmeerdeutsche* (Black Sea Germans), many of the first arrivals in 1905–08 migrating after first settling in the Dakotas, whereas later arrivals in 1908–10 tended to come directly from South Russia. For example, the settlers who established St. Anthony's at Grosswerder in 1908 (the present church dates from 1912) originated in the villages of Grosswerder in South Russia and Schuck in the Saratov region of the Volga German settlement and in German communities in Crimea.

The parishes comprising St. Joseph's Colony included St. Paschal, together with Notre Dame Convent, Leipzig (1905); Our Lady of the Assumption, Handel (1905); St. Henry/Leibel, Salvador (1905); St. Charles/Selz, Revenue (1905); St. Michael, Tramping Lake (1906); St. Franziskus, Ulrich (1906); Our Blessed Lady of Mount Carmel, Karmelheim (1906); St. Anthony, Grosswerder (1908); St. Mary, Macklin (1910); St. Johannes (1910); Holy Rosary/Rosenkranz, Reward (1910); St. Joseph, Scott (1910); St. Francis Regis/The Assumption of Our Lady, Kerrobert (1910); St. Donatus, near Cactus Lake (1914); Sacred Heart, Denzil (1915); Holy Martyrs, Luseland (1915); St. Peterskirche, Cosine Lake (1916); St. Elizabeth, Primate (1916); St. Peter, Unity (1919); Broadacres (1928); St. James, Wilkie (1928), a later parish at Landis; and, eventually beyond the original boundaries of the colony, Our Lady of Lourdes, Coleville; Our Lady of Grace, Dodsland; Immaculate Conception, Major; and an early mission at Ermine. These dates refer to when the parish was first formed rather than to the date of original settlement in these communities and districts or to the exact date of a surviving parish church, which in many cases replaced the original church. For example, Leipzig was first settled in 1905; the first church of St. Paschal's Parish was built the following year, replaced by a second, larger church in 1913, then by the striking present edifice in 1932 after that second church burned down. Notre Dame Convent continued to operate as a boarding school under the direction of the Sisters of Notre Dame, a German religious order dedicated to education, from 1927 to 1968; in 1974, it was purchased by a local family but lay mostly unused until it was renovated in 1991 as a bakery and private residence. The parish of nearby Handel was organized in 1905, and the first church, a modest sod structure, was built within a year; in 1913, a more substantial wooden church was built, eventually replaced in 1956 by a large, modern church. Holy Rosary at Reward, with fifteen Imhoff paintings, now houses St. Joseph's Colony Museum. St. Anthony at Grosswerder held regular services until 1983 and has now been preserved as a heritage property together with the church hall and Palm School. Some of these former parishes seldom hold services, are closed, or have disappeared entirely—all that remains of St. Francis (St. Franziskus), for example, is the cemetery.

A number of German Lutheran congregations and missions (all Missouri Synod except where noted otherwise) were established within this strongly Catholic settlement; those in the major towns—Luseland, Kerrobert, and Wilkie—have survived the test of time, but most in smaller communities and out in the country have closed over time, and some were very short lived: St. John German Evangelical Lutheran Church (Manitoba Synod) at Heart's Hill near Luseland (founded by German immigrants from

Nebraska, 1910–53); the Wollerman congregation at Rose Valley near Denzil (Hauge Synod, 1911, then Missouri Synod, 1934–40); Emmanuel in the Eigenfeld district near Biggar (1912–) and later St. Paul's in Biggar (1925–), both merged with Redeemer in 1961; St. John at Leipzig (1917–67); Spyridge near Wilkie (1927–39); Thackery near Wilkie (1928–43); Phippen near Leipzig (1928–29); Holy Trinity at Ear Hill near Luseland (1934–46); Fusilier mission (1934); Thorndale near Luseland (1934); Immanuel at Elk, near Cactus Lake (1939–45); and Rockhaven near Wilkie (1944).

The dates when communities within the colony officially became incorporated villages or towns varied considerably and tended to follow the organization of the parishes, in some cases by many years. Scott and Wilkie became incorporated villages in 1908, then towns just a couple of years later; Macklin a village in 1909 and town in 1912; Kerrobert a village in 1910 and town the next year; whereas Luseland was a village in 1910 but did not gain town status until 1954. Smaller communities that became incorporated as villages were Denzil in 1911, Handel in 1913 (though it was downgraded to an organized hamlet in 2007), and Primate in 1922. Reward was a designated hamlet, and Leipzig, Revenue, Salvador, Broadacres, Grosswerder, and other very small communities were never incorporated as villages.

During the 1930s, Deutscher Bund chapters (*stützpunkte*) were organized at Wilkie, Macklin, and Biggar. However, St. Joseph's colonists showed little interest in this nationalistic organization, despite their strong retention of German identity and language. In 1930, 89% of the 1,326 families resident within the colony were German speaking.[22]

St. Joseph's Colony is vast; clearly, it is the most extensive German settlement in all of Western Canada. The area of German Catholic settlement now extends approximately 120 kilometres from east to west and seventy kilometres from north to south. Together the towns, villages, and rural municipalities within the settlement had an estimated total German-origin population of approximately 8,800 in 1971. Within or at the periphery of St. Joseph's Colony today are at least seventeen rural municipalities; six towns: Unity (pop. 2,147 in 2006), Macklin (pop. 1,290), Wilkie (pop. 1,222), Kerrobert (pop. 1,001), Luseland (pop. 571), and Scott (pop. down to just 91); five incorporated villages: Denzil (pop. 142), Landis (pop. 116), Major (pop. 81 in 2001), Tramping Lake (pop. 60), and Primate (pop. 50); and the "official" hamlets of Reward, Handel, Springwater, and Cactus Lake. Other communities within or at the periphery of the settlement included Broadacres, Leipzig, Revenue, Salvador, Dodsland, Evesham, Heart's Hill, Superb, and Kelfield. In the towns, villages, and hamlets, in 1971 Leipzig was totally German, followed by Primate (82.4%), Tramping Lake (79.6%), Macklin (69.6%), Denzil (66.6%), Handel (56.3%), Evesham and Kelfield (half German), Luseland (48.7%), Wilkie (45.1%), Major (44.1%), Scott (41.9%), Salvador (40.0%), Unity (34.5%), Kerrobert (32.9%), Landis (32.1%), Dodsland (20.5%), Springwater (18.2%), and Coleville (15.9%). Moreover, the area of German settlement extended westward into Alberta, Catholics settling around Hayter, Provost, Bodo, Altario, and Compeer, and Lutherans near Monitor.

Rural depopulation has taken a severe toll on many of these communities, especially the smallest ones; virtually all of these communities have been declining or static in number of residents in recent years—Handel is now down to twenty-five, Springwater just fifteen. Cactus Lake, despite being bypassed by a railway by more than twenty kilometres, had in its heyday more than sixty residents, three general stores, grain elevators, a blacksmith, pool hall, dance hall, rural municipality office, post office, and school; it survived the dirty thirties and Depression, only to begin to decline during the 1950s—by the 1980s, it had only fifteen residents and at last count only two. Only Primate has grown—but only by five residents in the past five years. Reward had about a hundred residents in the mid-1960s, but the last remaining store had closed by 1969 and the school in 1982, by which time fewer than a couple of dozen residents were left; then, by the mid-1990s, the rail line was abandoned and all four grain elevators torn down; the community lost its status as an organized hamlet in 1997. Leipzig was incorporated as a village in 1913; through the 1940s, it was an active business centre with a peak population of about 150; now very few residents remain. The surrounding rural schools—Pascal, Krist, Coblenz/Cavell, Aroma Lake, Medina (all established in 1908–10)—had all closed by 1958–60; the community school in Leipzig (1913) then became the central school in 1959, when students from these surrounding rural districts were bussed into the community, but it too was finally closed in 1981. Revenue and district began with thirty-nine families in 1906; the next year the community had two rural post offices (Memo and Pascal), by the 1920s two general stores, a hardware, pool hall, machine shop, and five grain elevators, but by the 1980s only the elevators remained (and these are fast disappearing all over Saskatchewan).

Apart from the many rural communities and parishes, numerous strongly German rural districts developed within and near the colony, including Allenbach, Gramlich, Park, Kokesch, and Walz (around Cactus Lake) and Palm/Schachtel at Grosswerder; Coblenz and Zimmer (near Landis); Donegal/Asor (near Salvador); Heiland and Warington (near Luseland); Kersor, St. Lucia, Gutenberg, and Uzelman (around Tramping Lake); Koemstedt, Leibel, Ollenburger, and Wollerman (around Denzil); Krist, Pascal, and Aroma Lake (near Leipzig); Medina (near Handel); Rhyl (to the southwest of Asquith); Seifert and Zoller Lake (near Macklin); Selz (at Revenue); Verulam (near Kerrobert); and St. Alphege (near Wilkie). The Meier farm near Salvador (1918) is a designated heritage site.

The Prelate Colony and Settlement in the Leader–Maple Creek–Medicine Hat Region (1907–)

As settlement in St. Joseph's Colony was nearing completion, a fourth major German Catholic colony—or rather a series of colonies—developed in southwestern Saskatchewan between the Alberta border to the west and the Great Sand Hills to the east and the South Saskatchewan River to the north and Cypress Hills to the south. As early as 1889, a large Russian German settlement of migrants from Volhynia and Galicia began to develop just across the border in Alberta; eventually, an extensive expanse of territory on both sides of the border (between Leader, Maple Creek, and Medicine Hat) would be settled primarily by Russian Germans, many arriving from earlier settlements that they had established in the United States. Beginning in 1908, Russian German Catholics established a series of colonies and parishes on the Saskatchewan side, which included the original parishes of Sts. Peter and Paul at Blumenfeld (the "mother church" of the colony, established in 1908–09, with construction completed in 1915, now a historic site and museum), St. Francis Xavier at Prelate (1910), Immaculate Conception at Krassna (1911), St. Mary at Richmound (1912), St. Mary at Rosenthal

(1913), St. Lawrence at Maple Creek (1913), St. Anthony serving Mendham and the Speyer district (1914), Sacred Heart at Liebenthal (1914), St. Joseph at Josephstal (1915), St. Joseph at Shackleton (1916), Sacred Heart at Lancer (1918), Prussia Colony, centred on Leader (1919), and Holy Trinity at Rastadt (1922). Later parishes included St. Mary at Fox Valley (1929), St. John at Johnsborough (1943—however, St. John's Parochial School, now a historic site, dates from 1925), St. Mary at Lemsford (1948), Golden Prairie (1949), and St. Michael at Burstall (1969). Down the highway southeast of Leader and Prelate, priests from Blumenfeld also served a series of Catholic parishes in the mixed communities of Sceptre, Lemsford, Portreeve, Lancer, Abbey, Shackleton, and Cabri, beyond the German Catholic settlement.

Leader became the de facto centre of the Saskatchewan side of the settlement. In 1913, it was incorporated as the village of Prussia. It had more than 500 residents by 1917, when it became the town of Leader, and over 1,200 in 1966. However, the village of Prelate, just ten kilometres down the road, became an important German Catholic centre with the establishment of St. Angela's Convent in 1919 and later Academy by the Ursulines. Prelate had over 500 residents by the 1920s, but it was hit hard by the Depression, then grew fast during the postwar years, reaching over 600 by the 1950s, only to begin a steady decline again—it now has little more than a hundred residents.

Liebenthal (south of Leader) was named after Liebenthal, Kansas, from which some of its settlers had migrated; this Russian German colony in the United States in turn had been established by migrants from the Liebenthal group of Catholic colonies immediately west of Odessa, founded in 1804–06 largely by migrants from Alsace and southwestern German regions. Germans from a variety of regions had settled in central Poland in 1795–1806, then moved to establish colonies in the southern Bessarabian region southwest of the Liebenthal colonies after 1814. In particular, these Bessarabian colonists were the forefathers of the settlers of the Krassna, Rastadt, and Rosenthal districts in Saskatchewan (to the south of Liebenthal); the original Krassna Colony had been founded near Akkerman (Belgorod Dnestrovskiy) in Bessarabia in 1815.

Although these adjoining colonies around Prelate were predominantly Catholic, they included several pockets of strongly Protestant settlement, such as Mendham, Burstall, and Kronsfeld. Within the region, German Lutheran congregations and missions once included St. John near Mendham (1910–59); Christ, originally located northwest of Mendham (Ohio Synod, 1911–70); Neu Kronsfeld near Golden Prairie (1911–70, linked with New Hope on the Alberta border); Schmidt Lake at Deer Forks near Burstall (1911–44); Good Hope, serving Hatton and Schuler across the border in Alberta (1912–55); Grace at Krimmerfeld near Forres/Hatton (1912–53, established by Crimean immigrants who purchased the Schmidt Lake church near Burstall for $1,000); Zion at Arbana or Downey Lake west of Maple Creek (1912–47); Peace at Prussia/Leader (1913–77); Sagathun (1914–35); Christ at Estuary (established by Volga Germans, 1916–58); Christ at Ingebright near Prussia/Leader (1916–54); Zion at Shackleton (1917–40); Zion at Buffalo Head near Horsham (1919–50); Martin Luther at Fox Valley (1919, congregation split in 1931, merged in 1952); St. Paul at Burstall (1921–); Neuheim (American Lutheran Church) near Fox Valley (served from Irvine, Alberta, during the 1930s and 1940s); Peace at Fox Valley (formed in 1931 from a split in the Martin Luther congregation, merged in 1952); Sceptre mission (1933–46); Westerham mission near Leader (1936–39); a mission at Kuest near Horsham (served from Schuler, Alberta); and Golden Prairie mission. Leader had Lutheran, Apostolic, and United Brethren churches in addition to its strong Catholic parish.

All of these Lutheran congregations and missions were strongly German: Neu Kronsfeld was a base for the Kanader Krina Sociashen (later called the Kanader Saut-Russien Sociashen), formed in 1922 to assist the "Kriner" (Crimean) immigrants; membership cost fifty cents. And, among the Crimean immigrants around Krimmerfeld, English hymnals were not used for the first time until 1954; however, a motion to have services in English only was defeated four years later. Similarly, services at St. John, Mendham, were held completely in German until 1945, then alternated between German and English. By 1925, this congregation had 178 baptized members.[23] In 1924, the congregation built a school, the sole Lutheran Missouri Synod parochial school in the province; it became a Catholic separate school in 1942 and closed in 1965. Sagathun held monthly services in German. The Buffalo Head congregation was the base for the Kongregeser or Bruder sect.[24] A large Deutscher Bund chapter (*ortsgruppe*) was operational at Leader, and there were smaller chapters (*stützpunkte*) at Burstall and Prelate during the 1930s.

In 1971, the total number of people of German origin in the settlement (just within Saskatchewan, excluding the portion in Alberta) could be estimated at 4,000. In Saskatchewan, the settlement extends approximately 125 kilometres north to south (from the South Saskatchewan valley down to the Cypress Hills) and fifty kilometres east to west (from the Great Sand Hills to the Alberta border), covering (in whole or part) eight rural municipalities. In 1971, people of German origin comprised a majority of the population at Leader; villages having the highest German proportions were Mendham (82.9%), Richmound (76.2%), Lancer (73.2%), Prelate (64.3%), Fox Valley (60.4%), and Golden Prairie (51.7%); residents of German origin comprised a substantial minority at Burstall (44.5%), Portreeve (41.7%), and Sceptre (26.1%). Other communities within the settlement with substantial German populations include Estuary (where the Smith barn site in the district, dating from 1914, is a heritage property), Westerham, Sceptre, Gascoigne (formerly Meusatz), Linacre, Horsham, Golden Prairie, Tunstall, and Hatton. Besides the rural parishes mentioned, there are many largely German districts in the region, including Happyland RM (around Leader); Hohelinden and Speyer (south of Leader); Herman, Schultz, and Selz (south of Prelate); Frohlich (near Mendham); Baden and Blumenfeld (near Liebenthal); Neigel Plains and Hoffnung (near Burstall); Krupp, Rosenthal, Krassna, Rastad, and Bern (around Fox Valley); Pontoville and Schmidt (near Richmound); Kuest (near Horsham); Kronsfeld, Neu Kronsfeld, Rosenfeld, Annenthal, Kassel, and Stahl (around Golden Prairie); Sagathun (east of Tunstall); and Neuheim and Schroeder (west of Maple Creek).

Moreover, the Russian German settlement extended across the provincial border well into Alberta, around the rural communities of Hilda, Schuler, Irvine, and Walsh, and as far as the city of Medicine Hat. This city is actually the largest urban centre at the periphery of the settlement. It contains the largest Catholic church of the entire settlement, with the Irish name of St. Patrick, built in Gothic Revival style, as well as five Lutheran churches, including St. Peter, which still has a German service. Hilda has Bethlehem Lutheran as well as Baptist churches, Schuler a Church of God congregation.

Rural depopulation has taken a severe toll on the rural parishes comprising the settlement. One by one, Catholic country churches have been closed and occasionally even removed or demolished, such as at Rosenthal in 1943, Krassna in 1944, Josephstal and Rastadt in 1962, Shackleton in 1963, Johnsborough in 1967, Lemsford in 1982, and Speyer in 2001.[25] And virtually all of the Lutheran congregations and missions eventually closed except for those in the larger towns. The largest communities within the region, after the town of Maple Creek (pop. 2,198 in 2006), were the towns of Leader (pop. 881) and Burstall (pop. 315) and the villages of Fox Valley (pop. 295), Richmound (pop. 159), and Prelate (pop. 126); Sceptre is now down to ninety-eight residents, Lancer sixty-five, Mendham and Golden Prairie just thirty-five; and all of these communities have been declining. Today the Fox Valley School (1928) is a museum. The other communities in the region are not even classified now as hamlets. The Estuary area was settled between 1885 and 1906; Estuary became a village in 1916, when it had forty businesses and over 800 residents. The population declined yet stabilized at about 100; the community retained a school, a general store, three elevators, and a bulk feed station. But serious decline has occurred since the 1950s—the last store closed in 1966, the post office in 1970; by the 1980s, just five families were left. Hatton (formerly Forres) was incorporated in 1912, when it contained forty-nine businesses and services and 275 residents; hit by drought and depression, it has witnessed a steady exodus of youth and men looking for work; one by one, businesses closed or moved to larger centres. Although Horsham had just twenty-five residents as early as 1938, a new four-room school was built here in 1959 but moved to nearby Richmound in 1970, by which time Horsham had become a virtual ghost town with few residents left.

MAJOR GERMAN PROTESTANT SETTLEMENTS

In his epic work *The German Canadians, 1750–1937: Immigration, Settlement, and Culture*, Heinz Lehmann suggested that German Protestants tended to be more scattered than Catholics, seemingly having less of an inclination to settle in colonies. Yet Lutherans, Baptists, and Adventists of German descent established four principal early settlements in Saskatchewan, almost simultaneously commencing in 1884–87, plus numerous later smaller concentrations, including within larger Catholic and Mennonite settlements and in German settlements where Protestants and Catholics settled together.

Most German Lutheran congregations in Saskatchewan were affiliated with the Missouri Synod, yet many belonged to the Ohio Synod, the Lutheran Church of America (LCA), the American Lutheran Church (ALC), or the Manitoba Synod (Evangelical Lutheran Synod of Manitoba and Other Provinces), while some belonged to the Unaltered Augsburg Confession or were independent. It was not unusual for several German Lutheran churches representing different affiliations to be found around one small community and in rural districts. In 1966, Canadian congregations of the ALC formed the Evangelical Lutheran Church of Canada (ELCC), which merged in 1986 with the Canadian section of the LCA to form the Evangelical Lutheran Church in Canada (ELCIC). In the meantime, numerous predominantly Scandinavian Lutheran churches (which originally had their own affiliations by specific nationality—Norwegian, Swedish, Finnish, et cetera—had merged into what would eventually become the ELCC (see Chapter 8). A vast number of distinctly

German Lutheran congregations (many out in the countryside), at least 139, have been closed over time due to mergers with larger congregations (mostly in towns and more sustainable villages), rural depopulation, and occasionally natural disasters such as lightning strikes and fires; an additional 104 "preaching points" have come and gone (many of very short duration).

Neu Elsass Colony (1884–)

The Neu Elsass (New Alsace) Colony could claim with some legitimacy to be the first German colony to develop in Saskatchewan. In 1884, twenty-two families took up homesteads around Strassburg, approximately eighty kilometres north of Regina.[26] They were led by D.W. Riedl, an enterprising German immigration agent from Winnipeg. Ultimately, this community might have been named after Strasbourg (Strassburg in German), the principal city of the German-speaking province of Alsace (Elsass in German) in France (but in Germany between the Franco-Prussian War, 1870–71, and the First World War, 1914–18, i.e. the period when Neu Elsass Colony was founded in Saskatchewan). However, it is more likely that both the community and the colony were named more immediately after the communities of Strassburg and Elsass within the Kutschurgan colonies northwest of Odessa, in South Russia (today Ukraine), which had in turn been established by Alsatian migrants back in 1808–09. Still another possibility is that, since some of the settlers in this colony in Saskatchewan came from Russian German colonies in the United States, the Alsatian nomenclature might have been imported into Saskatchewan from any of several American colonies founded by immigrants ultimately of Alsatian origin, for example in Kansas, South Dakota, and North Dakota. Strassburg was established as a post office in 1886; it officially became a village in 1906 and a town the following year. It is interesting to note that the community, post office, and railway station were all originally given the German spelling Strassburg; the town was not changed to the French spelling until 1919 (when the city in Europe was returned to France), and the railway station and post office were not changed until 1956.

The original bounds of Neu Elsass Colony (ca. 1885) included Strasbourg, Duval, Bulyea and the New Munster district, the Edelane district (south of Strasbourg), Earl Grey, Gibbs, Silton, Dilke, Holdfast, Penzance, and Liberty—in other words, the region around the central and southern portion of Last Mountain Lake. But the area of German settlement expanded into surrounding areas, in effect doubling the territory of the original settlement. The settlement remains predominantly Lutheran; soon an extensive network of German Lutheran congregations and missions had spread throughout the region, while German Baptists and Adventists settled a few areas, and certain districts in the general region—especially those located west of Last Mountain Lake—were strongly Catholic. Strasbourg itself eventually had not only Lutheran but also Catholic and Baptist churches.

To the south of Strasbourg, toward Regina, former German Lutheran congregations and missions were Bulyea (1939–46), Zion at Gibbs (mid-1930s–57), St. John at Silton (1914–68), and Immanuel in the Kennel district near Craven (1911–71, later restored after being sold to the Mormons, who donated it back decades later as a heritage site for one dollar).

GERMANIC SETTLEMENTS

To the southeast, north of the Qu'Appelle Valley, German Lutherans and Baptists settled around Earl Grey; the Baptist church there had originally been founded in 1906 not by Germans but by Swedes. The Southey area was settled by German Lutherans primarily between 1902 and 1905; they attended Bethlehem Lutheran from 1906 to 1935. Catholics mixed with Lutherans around Southey. St. Anne's Catholic Parish was established in the Arbury district near Southey in 1932, and it is now a heritage site. To the south and southeast, the Fairy Hill, Wheatwyn, Fransfeld, and Freudenthal districts were strongly German Lutheran. Fairy Hill was served by St. John from 1911 to 1957, when it was destroyed by lightning. The pioneer pastor Sigmund Manz, born in 1899 at Arbora, Bukovina, Romania, grew up on the homestead near Southey where his family had settled in 1904; ordained at Fairy Hill in 1925, he served Trinity Lutheran at Lemberg from 1952 to 1966 as well as in Melville, Hatton, and Alberta.[27] Farther east, in the nearby Wheatwyn district, Zion Lutheran, a little stone church out on the prairie, was built in 1906–07, and services were held in German until the 1950s. The German immigrants who settled there came from Bukovina and the Austro-Hungarian Empire. Among the earliest settlers were brothers Paul and Lorenz Blaser (they had left their homeland in 1893, when Paul was just fifteen, first arrived in Neudorf, then settled in Wheatwyn in 1899) and the Molder, Ulrich, Kaminski, Markwart, Orb, Appenheimer, and Lingner families (Johann Lingner died at the age of nineteen in 1902, his brother Georg at the same age two years later). The ruins of stone Bethlehem Lutheran Church, southwest of Markinch, reveal a different style of construction. At Zion, the highlight of the year was Christmas Eve, with lit candles on the Christmas tree. *Familien abend* (family evening) featured songs, a potluck supper, and skits. The church was closed in 1961, yet it continues to be well maintained as a historic site, in keeping with a German expression handed down: *Armut ist keine schandeaber deswegen brauch mann nicht schmutzig und zerrissen herum laufen* (There is an excuse for being poor but no excuse for being dirty and tattered). On the plain wall, a plaque in Old German reads *E R bann helfen* (God can help).[28] The Loon Creek district near Cupar was served by Trinity Lutheran since 1930. German Catholics settled the Kronsberg district south of Dysart, named after the Bukovinian village from which the pioneer Schuster family had emigrated. Kronsberg School was established in 1898, St. Henry's Catholic Parish in 1906; the church closed in 1960 and the school four years later. The Radant district south of Dysart was named after Radantz/Radauti, now in Romanian Bukovina. The Sambor district northeast of Dysart was named after the Ukrainian home community of Henry Sigmond Schneider, who settled there in 1905. Two Lutheran congregations served the Lipton area: Holy Trinity (Missouri Synod), from 1912 (it eventually merged in the 1980s), and the North Congregation (Ohio Synod), 1919 until the 1930s.

To the east of Strasbourg and north of Southey, Baptists settled around Serath and Gregherd (where the original school, dating to 1914, is now a historic site). Farther north, the Raymore area was settled by Danube Swabians. Raymore, Punnichy, and Quinton were predominantly Catholic areas. Around Raymore were the Charlottenhof Post Office and Charlottenburg School, and the Wallenstein district, while the Torondal district was settled by Catholics from the Banat region of present-day Serbia and Romania. A Lutheran mission served Lutherans in the Raymore area from the late 1930s through the 1940s. A Deutscher Bund *stützpunkt* was organized at Quinton during the 1930s.

Directly north of Strasbourg, Lutheran congregations were established at Duval (Zion, 1911–18), Govan (Zion, 1935–50s, and Christ, 1936–59), Nokomis (Good Hope, 1953–74), where Germans mixed with Scandinavians and Baptists also settled, and Lockwood (Peace, founded by Volga Germans in 1913, closed in 1964). At Lockwood in 1906, a single church building served the Lutherans in the late afternoon, preceded by the Methodists and followed by the Presbyterians.[29]

Catholics predominated in communities west of Last Mountain Lake—notably Holdfast, Chamberlain, Dilke, and Liberty (originally called Wolffton, with the Wolff Valley School District). The beautiful Assumption of the Blessed Virgin Mary Church at Holdfast was constructed in 1920–21. In the surrounding area, including the Schell, Frohlich, and Mannheim districts, the rural Frohlich Post Office and Mannheim School were named after early settler and first postmaster Gabriel Frolich, who had left the village of Mannheim in the Kutchurgan colonies in 1900 and settled there in 1905.[30] These German Catholic settlers were from very diverse origins—many arrived from American states such as Oklahoma, Missouri, Kansas, Michigan, North Dakota, and Illinois; others came from earlier German Catholic settlements in Saskatchewan, including Kronau; some were from Europe (German colonies in South Russia and Banat); and a few even came from South America. Former German Lutheran congregations and missions west of Last Mountain Lake included, from south to north, Pilgrim at Bethune (1943–93), Aylesbury (during the 1930s), St. John at Holdfast (1907–60), and Trinity at Renown (during the late 1930s).

The highest German-origin proportion is found at Markinch, where in 1971 three-quarters of the population claimed German descent, and Southey, where two-thirds claimed German descent; Chamberlain (59.4%), Earl Grey (58.5%), Holdfast (57.6%), and Lipton (57.3%) were predominantly German, while people of German origin comprised strong minorities at Duval (40.6%), Strasbourg (34.3%), Nokomis (34.7%), Aylesbury (35.7%), Quinton (34.4%), Liberty (30.3%), and Dysart (26.9%). Residents of German origin comprised lesser proportions (between 10% and 22%) in all other towns and villages in the region. In 1971, the total German-origin population of the settlement could be estimated at approximately 4,700.

This region of German settlement is vast—the area of contiguous German settlement covers (in whole or part) at least ten rural municipalities and extends some 125 kilometres east to west and seventy-five kilometres north to south. The largest community within the settlement and region is Strasbourg (732 residents in 2006), although Southey (pop. 711) comes a close second, followed by Raymore (pop. 581), Cupar (pop. 566), Nokomis (pop. 404), Imperial (pop. 321), Earl Grey (pop. 264), Govan (pop. 232), Semans (pop. 195), and Holdfast (pop. 173); fewer residents remain in Chamberlain (pop. 108), Quinton (pop. 108), Bulyea (pop. 104), Duval (pop. 94), Silton (pop. 91), Dilke (pop. 80), Markinch (pop. 59), Liberty (pop. 73), Aylesbury (pop. 45), Penzance (pop. 30), Lockwood (pop. 25), and Stalwart (pop. 20); while Serath, Gregherd, and Gibbs are mere hamlets. Strikingly, almost all of these communities of various sizes have recently been declining in population; only a couple—Southey and Chamberlain—increased during 2001–06, while two others—Quinton and Dilke—have been more or less stable.

Hohenlohe Colony (1884–)

The Hohenlohe Colony began to develop around Langenburg, close to the Manitoba border, at the same time that the Neu Elsass Colony was developing. It was named after *Fürst* (Count) Hermann Ernst von Hohenlohe-Langenburg, president of the German Colonial League, who had toured the West and encouraged German settlement. Under the guidance of D.W. Riedl (the immigration agent also instrumental in the founding of Neu Elsass Colony), German Lutherans began to settle around Langenburg in 1884–85; they came not only from Germany but also from "Russian" colonies (actually in Ukraine). The Russian German proportion was further augmented with the arrival of settlers from the Bessarabian colonies in 1888–91; by 1896, the colony included fifty to sixty Russian German families with approximately 300 members. St. Paul Lutheran Church in Langenburg, founded in 1889 as the *Evangelische Lutherische Kirke zu Sint Paulus Gemeinde*, is believed to be the oldest continuing Lutheran congregation in Saskatchewan. Former German Lutheran congregations and missions in the settlement and surrounding area included Zion, serving the Hoffenthal district—the congregation was organized in 1892, but the first church was not built until 1896 and was closed in 1968; Grace, serving the Beresina district from 1895 to 1962; Peace in Churchbridge, 1916–64; Peace in the Rothbury/Stryj district near Calder, 1916–62; Trinity in the Easter Lily district near Marchwell, 1917–46; St. Paul in Marchwell, 1918–69; Hope at Macnutt, 1927–41; and Immanuel, serving the Kinbrae district near Zeneta and Bredenbury (originally Scottish settled, but this congregation was predominantly German), from the 1930s to 1959. The Lutheran pastor across the Manitoba border in the Inglis area, Reverend Leonard Julius Frederick Koss, arrived from Glusha, Kowel, Volhynia, to join families from the same region in 1917.[31] Although the colony retained a Lutheran majority, in 1889 Catholics from Bavaria and the Black Sea colonies arrived to settle in the Landshut district. The Beresina district was named by four families who filed for their homesteads in 1888; they came from the village of Beresina, near Akkermann in southern Bessarabia (today in Ukraine, whereas most of the former Russian province of Bessarabia now constitutes Moldova). The Hoffman School was in Langenburg. A unique self-help organization that came into being in this colony in the early pioneering years was the Germania Mutual Fire Insurance Company of Langenburg, first advocated in 1909 by George Haas, a prominent farmer in the Hoffenthal district, who had migrated from Menno, South Dakota.[32] Langenburg was incorporated as a village in 1903 and a town in 1959.

Back in 1971, people of German origin comprised a little over half of the residents of Langenburg (52.5%) and MacNutt (57.1%). The total German population within the settlement could be estimated at about 2,000. The area of German settlement extends over four rural municipalities from Langenburg north into the Hohenlohe district, northeast into the Landestreu, Flower Valley, and German Hill districts and beyond to MacNutt and the Zorn district, east into the Landshut and Morning Glory districts, southwest into the Karlsruhe district, and northwest into the Beresina district and beyond into the Mostetz district north of Calder.

The Volga German Colony (1887–)

Only three years after the Hohenlohe and Neu Elsass Colonies first began to develop, primarily Baptist and Lutheran immigrants from the Volga colonies in Russia, Volga

Germans (*Wolgadeutsche*) settled around Ebenezer in 1887. The Russian colonies from which they had emigrated were founded in 1764–68 near Saratov, mostly by Protestant and Catholic migrants from Hessia. A strong Volga Baptist colony grew in the area around Ebenezer (e.g., the Langenau district to the northwest), Gorlitz, Hamton, Rhein (e.g., the Kitzman district to the northeast), and Springside (e.g., the Grunert district to the southeast and the Homestead district to the north, the original homestead of Reverend Ferdinand Blaedow of the Homestead Baptist Church). Ebenezer already had a Baptist congregation and school district by 1889 and a post office by 1891; by 1901, the community and district contained close to 400 Germans. Ebenezer was not incorporated as a village until 1948. A Lutheran congregation was also established at Springside, and to the east Volga Lutherans concentrated around Rhein (where Christ Lutheran Church was built in 1920), Stornoway (Lebricht School), Runnymede, and Togo, where they merged with the German Lutherans of the Hohenlohe Colony to the south. During the early 1950s, English services were started once a month on Sunday afternoons by the pastor of Christ Lutheran Church in Rhein, Reverend Edmind Johannes Krisch, while the main weekly service continued to be held in German; the English services represented an effort to accommodate the growing number of mixed German and Ukrainian marriages, resulting in English-speaking children, when the Lutheran churches were still using only German and the Ukrainian churches only Ukrainian.[33] A Lutheran congregation, Christ Lutheran, was first organized at Runnymede in 1917; this congregation joined with the Togo Lutherans in 1921, and both were served by an itinerant pastor based at Rhein; the church closed in 1969. The Brunendahl district west of Stornoway was named after Brunnental, a community in the Lutheran Samara colony along the Volga River. This district was served by Trinity Lutheran (Missouri Synod) from 1904 to 1987. Rhein was a rural post office in 1905 and a village in 1913; it had close to 500 residents by the early 1940s. Deutscher Bund *stützpunkte* were organized at Togo and Runnymede during the 1930s. In addition to these Volga Germans of Baptist or Lutheran religion, Volhynian Germans settled in Yorkton, and German Lutherans who settled in Canora were served by itinerant preachers during the late 1930s and early 1940s.

Expansion of the vast Ukrainian settlement around Yorkton has steadily diminished the German proportion in these communities, so that now none of them retains a German majority, though in 1971 almost half of the residents of Rhein (47.5%) and Ebenezer (45.8%) still claimed German origin, compared with little more than a quarter of those of Springside (26.9%) and Togo (26.2%) and even fewer at Stornoway (22.2%). Today the town of Springside (pop. 494 in 2006) is the largest community in the area, followed by the villages of Rhein (pop. 161), Ebenezer (pop. 139), and Togo (pop. 100); Stornoway is classified as a hamlet, while Gorlitz and Hamton are unclassified. Recent demographic data (2001–06) reveal that all of these communities have been losing population. The maximum extent of this German settlement, covering portions of five rural municipalities, would be almost sixty kilometres east to west and over thirty kilometres north to south.

Edenwold Colony (1885–)

In 1885, a group of Baptist immigrants from the region of Dobruja, Romania, founded the colony of New Tulcea (Neu Tulscha), northeast of Regina. Migrants from the German colonies near Odessa in Bessarabia had resettled in Dobruja during the 1840s–50s. During the 1860s, Baptist missionaries from the Danzig congregation in Russia were responsible for creating a Baptist majority in the Kataloi colony and a significant Baptist proportion in the other two Protestant colonies, Atmagea and Cincurova. Religious quarrels as well as difficult economic and political conditions (Dobruja became part of Romania in 1878, bringing about revocation of privileges, restriction on land holding, and state control of schools) resulted in the emigration of Germans from Dobruja to North Dakota in 1884 and Saskatchewan in 1885. Gradually, the Saskatchewan colony became more heterogeneous in terms of both the origins of its German population and their religious preferences. The colony's name was changed by German immigrants from Bukovina; other Germans arrived from German colonies in Poland, Galicia, and Russia and from Germany. During the early 1900s, more Germans arrived from Poland, Galicia, and South Russia, and some German Catholics settled later in the Edenwold area in 1907.

By 1889, when the first Lutheran service was held, the colony had a Lutheran majority; a strong Lutheran congregation had been formed by the following year, and Adventists concentrated around Edenwold village (originally Edenwald, then misspelled when a post office was established in 1890). About seven kilometres southwest of Edenwold, and two kilometres west of the original Baptist church and school established respectively in 1886 and 1887, the *Deutsche Evangelische Sankt Johannes Gemeinde* was founded in 1893 by Pastor H. Schmieder, who left just three years later for the United States. Later, in 1904, Pastor Sigmund Manz arrived; born in 1899 in Arbora, Bukovina, he was raised on a homestead in the nearby Fairy Hill district and eventually also served several congregations in the large German settlement straddling the Saskatchewan-Alberta border: Good Hope at Hatton and Neu Kronsfeld near Golden Prairie, on the Saskatchewan side, and Schuler, Alberta.[34] Today St. John's Lutheran Church (1919) is a historic site. The Lutheran pastor lived in an adobe house on his homestead built with the help of members of his congregation; similarly, the unusual original church was constructed with adobe walls and a wooden roof, and all of the furniture was handmade by a local carpenter.[35] In 1886, the Baptists at Edenwold held their first communal picnic following a church service, with the food spread out in one long column in the churchyard "to avoid any grouping into separate cliques," according to a congregation member.[36]

To the southwest, Emmanuel Lutheran Church (ca. 1900) at Frankslake recently became a heritage site. Peace Lutheran, an Ohio Synod congregation, served the Rosenberg district near McLean from the 1920s to 1983, while Zehner was served by a Missouri Synod congregation from 1920 to 1959. Near Zehner, Jacob Lolacher homesteaded in 1895 and three years later built his beautiful fieldstone farmhouse (among many stone farmhouses in the settlement) with the assistance of German stonemasons John Zinkhan and Ed Fuchs, who also built the nearby Arrat Roman Catholic Church (converted into a private home in 1980) and smaller Leibel home. The Lolacher farmhouse was the scene of German dances. In 1975, it passed out of the Lolacher family after three generations.[37]

Two-thirds of the population of Edenwold (pop. 242 in 2006) were still of German origin in 1971. The other communities in the settlement—Frankslake, Zehner, and Avonhurst—are unincorporated hamlets.

CHAPTER 4

MAJOR MIXED CATHOLIC AND PROTESTANT SETTLEMENTS

Two expansive areas of German settlement, where Catholics and Protestants mixed to the extent that neither predominated in the area of settlement as a whole, gradually emerged from localized smaller concentrations of Catholics or Protestants in particular districts. These settlements were the area around Melville, in the east-central region, and the St. Walburg–Loon River–Beaver River area, in the northwestern region. Other smaller settlements will be covered after this section.

German Catholic and Protestant Settlements around Melville (1890–)

An extensive area of German settlement had its beginnings in the predominantly Lutheran settlement around Neudorf and Lemberg, southwest of Melville, in 1890, and Catholic settlement south of Melville around Grayson in 1896 and in the Mariahilf Colony in 1900. Neudorf was first settled by Galician and Russian German Lutherans; both churches in the village, Trinity and Christ Lutheran, are German Lutheran. The first post office was established in 1895 when settler Ludwig Wendel, an immigrant from Neudorf, Galicia, donated the land for the community. Neighbouring Lemberg was settled by German Lutherans as well as Catholics from Galicia (Lemberg is the German name for L'viv, the principal city of Galicia in the western Ukraine) and eventually from Volhynia, Poland, Prussia, and the Volga. St. Michael's Roman Catholic Church at the edge of town dates from 1901, the present Trinity Lutheran Church in the centre of town from 1926. Near Lemberg, the fieldstone schoolhouse in the Weissenberg district, named after a German village in Galicia in 1900, is claimed to be the oldest known Roman Catholic separate school in Saskatchewan; although it was replaced by a larger wood frame building in 1922, it continued to serve as a teacherage for over four decades and was recently restored as a historic site.[38] The pioneering Pastor Senft, born in Winnipeg to Russian German immigrants, was raised on a farm near Lemberg and ordained by Pastor Pohlman; he later served German Lutheran congregations in Leader, Radisson, Meeting Lake, and Lanigan, Saskatchewan; Medicine Hat, Alberta; and a Swiss German congregation in Starbuck, Manitoba; he lived well into his nineties.[39] Pastor Kroeger, born in Hannover, Germany, also lived into his nineties (1889–1984); he served Trinity Lutheran Church in Lemberg from 1916 to 1929 and congregations at Yellow Grass and Lang, Saskatchewan, as well as Starbuck, Manitoba.[40] The Trinity Lutheran congregation at Lemberg had been organized in 1906 by missionary Pastor Gehrke, instrumental in organizing German Lutheran congregations throughout the province. Redeemer Lutheran Church in Lemberg was an independent congregation from 1901 to 1958. As in most Galician, Black Sea, and Bessarabian German colonies and their offshoots in Saskatchewan, in Lemberg the Germans spoke a Swabian dialect because their forefathers had migrated to the Russian colonies from Swabia and other southwest German regions. Surrounding Lemberg and Neudorf were the rural districts of Weissenburg, Hill Farm, Henry, Erlösser, Baber, Heil Lake, Peace, Piller, and Ulmer. The Gottinger rural phone company was based in Neudorf. In this area today, the Mariahilf pioneer farm, Pheasant Forks School (1920), Zion Methodist Church (1905), Weissenberg School (1900), and Zion Lutheran Church southwest of Neudorf (1896) all constitute historic sites. St. John congregation served the Rosewood district near Neudorf from 1911 to 1958.

Meanwhile, the area immediately south of Melville was settled largely by Catholic *Volksdeutsche* from Bukovina, Bessarabia, Galicia, and Poland. Grayson, first settled in 1896 by German immigrants from Galicia and Bukovina (which were then in the Austrian Empire), was first called Nieven but was renamed in 1903. The Mariahilf Catholic Colony south of Killaly was founded in 1900. Grayson and Killaly both had Catholic parishes; the Killaly parish came into being in 1910. German Lutheran congregations were established in the predominantly Catholic communities of Grayson, where Zion Lutheran congregation was formed in 1915 and lasted through the mid-1940s; Killaly, where St. John lasted from 1926 to 1968; and Waldron, where Redeemer was operational from the 1930s through the early 1960s (at Waldron, only German was used in services until the 1940s, when German and English services alternated). Ottenhouse Separate School was at Grayson, the Hauer and Gelowitz School Districts west of town. Ursuline nuns arrived in Grayson in 1915. A popular Polka Fest is held every July in Grayson.

West and northwest of Melville, both Lutherans and Mennonites settled around Duff and in the Reimer district; Lutheran congregations in the area were St. Peter (1921–67) and St. Paul (1941–59) in the Mona district. German Baptists and Lutherans settled at Fenwood, where Zion served the Lutherans from 1912 to 1969, and with German Catholics at Goodeve, where St. Petri Lutheran congregation was formed in 1905 and terminated in 1957; at Hubbard, Lutherans established Immanuel congregation by 1917 (until 1969). The Koenigsberg district was originally settled by German-speaking "Ruthenian Calvinists" whose evangelical church eventually was transformed into a Ukrainian Orthodox church. The Headlands or Beresford district near Kelliher was served by St. Paul Lutheran from 1922 through the late 1940s.

And in the small city of Melville itself, St. Paul Lutheran Church (originally Bethania Lutheran) was founded in 1907; the first members of this congregation included immigrants from the Baltic states. Both Luther Academy (now the Melville Heritage Museum) and St. Henry Separate School were established in 1913, the latter honouring Father Henry Kugener OMI, the first priest to celebrate mass in the area.

During the 1930s, Deutscher Bund *ortsgruppe* chapters operated in Melville and Grayson, while smaller *stützpunkte* meetings were organized in Lemberg and Goodeve. Interestingly, a Royal North-West Mounted Police detachment was stationed in Neudorf during the First World War to prevent any possibility of sabotage when Canada was at war with Germany and Austria-Hungary.

In 1971, almost a third (31.4%) of the population of Melville was of German origin. Neudorf contained 159 residents by 1906, more than 500 by 1921. The Depression, together with Neudorf's loss of status as a railway centre, resulted in continuous decline and loss of businesses for a while—the population was down to 420 in 1941, though the community rebounded somewhat to reach a population of over 500 in 1966. The railway line was finally abandoned completely in 1996. In 2001, the median age in Neudorf was fifty-five, compared with thirty-six for Saskatchewan. Lemberg had a population exceeding 300 in 1906; it became a village in 1904 and a town three years later; it had more than 500 residents by the 1950s. Lemberg (pop. 255) now has fewer residents than the village of Neudorf (pop. 281); back in 1971, they were considerably larger communities and comparable in population: 71.4% of the 455 residents of Neudorf and 58.4% of the 445 residents of Lemberg were of German descent. In 1971, two-thirds of the residents of Grayson (pop. 179 today, down from about 400 during the 1950s), almost three-quarters of Killaly (pop. 77), and 35.7% of Waldron were of German extraction.[41] West of Melville, in 1971, people of German origin comprised 68.8% of the residents of Duff and 39.1% of the residents of Fenwood.

All told, this is a very extensive area of continuous German settlement: we can estimate that in 1971 there were at least 2,200 people of German origin in the principal communities of Lemberg, Neudorf, Grayson, and Killaly and the two encompassing rural municipalities (Grayson and McLeod); almost 1,700 more people of German descent were in Melville; and hundreds more were settled west and northwest of Melville. So the total German-origin population (primarily Lutherans and Catholics with some Baptists and Mennonites) would have exceeded 5,000. Moreover, the total extent of German settlement was at least 100 kilometres east to west and sixty kilometres north to south. Thus, though these areas could not really be considered a single German settlement, they did collectively amount to one of the largest concentrations of German population in the province.

The St. Walburg, Loon River, and Beaver River Settlements (1901–, 1929, 1939)
German settlement in the northwestern region developed gradually in several stages. The St. Walburg area was settled first primarily by Catholics from the *Reich*, Bavaria, Austria, and Luxemburg, in 1901–12. St. Walburg (pop. 672 today) was named after Walburga Musch, who had immigrated from Minnesota in 1908 and ran a store with her husband, Rudolph. The Assumption of the Blessed Virgin Mary Church in St. Walburg (1925) became the District Historical Museum in 1984. A strongly German Lutheran church was established at St. Walburg in 1937. Other former Lutheran congregations and missions (all Missouri Synod) around St. Walburg include Grace in the White Eagle district (organized in 1927, church built in 1935, closed in 1952, but restored in 1988), Brightsand (1933–46), Hillside (1930s), Mervin (1934–39), and Paradise Hill (1934).

German Catholics settled north of the Beaver River, about 100 kilometres north of St. Walburg, around Goodsoil (pop. 253), during the 1920s and later around the neighbouring small community of Peerless as well as farther west with Mennonites around Pierceland (pop. 498) near the Alberta border. They were soon joined by German Lutherans, who established congregations and missions during the 1930s in the Flat Valley, Beacon Hill, and Northern Beauty districts near Goodsoil and Peerless.

In 1929, twenty families arrived directly from Germany (mostly from Thuringen, but others were from Holstein, Westfalen, Mecklenburg, and the Baltic coast) to establish the Loon River settlement between St. Walburg and the more northerly communities mentioned (today the principal community of Loon Lake has 306 residents). These immigrants, as well as the Germans who settled around Goodsoil during the 1920s, apparently were ardent nationalists. With the foundation of the Deutscher Bund (German Alliance) in Canada in 1934, Goodsoil boasted the strongest Deutscher Bund chapter in the province, and strong *ortsgruppen* (chapters having at least fifteen members) were organized at Loon River, St. Walburg, and Paradise Hill, as well as a *stutzpunkt* (chapter having from five to fifteen members) at Blue Bell near Pierceland. In view of their strong pro-National Socialist sentiments, eighteen families and individuals (all told numbering about fifty people) from the Loon River and Goodsoil areas departed in July 1939 to return *heim ins Reich*—home to the *Reich* (Germany). The pro-Nazi newspaper *Die Deutsche Zeitung für Kanada* congratulated them for serving as proof of the better opportunities of Nazi Germany compared with the assimilationist and discriminatory practices found in Saskatchewan. At least 650 Germans returned from Canada to Germany during 1938–39.[42]

However, a German presence in this region was maintained because the return migrants were replaced in 1938–39 by German refugees from the Sudetenland in Czechoslovakia, newly annexed to the *Reich*. About half of the 1,000 Sudetenland immigrants (totalling 352 families) who came to Canada settled in Saskatchewan; 150 families and twenty-nine single immigrants were sent to the St. Walburg area in Saskatchewan, while another 150 families were sent to the Tomslake settlement near Dawson, British Columbia.[43] Most of the Saskatchewan settlers were concentrated in the Klein (Little) Sudetenland settlement between St. Walburg and Brightsand Lake, including Sudeten beach and extending southward to the Beaverbrook (Carlsbad) district, with smaller numbers settling to the north around Loon River and Goodsoil. In 1939, their 156 children were in the Brightsand, Pine Ridge, Deer Valley, Loon River, and Flat Valley Schools.[44] At Goodsoil, the Teacherage (1932) and Central School (1945) now constitute heritage properties. A few kilometres southwest of St. Walburg, the Imhoff studio-museum, farmhouse, and barn (1914–22) were preserved as a historic site in 1993. In 1971, people of German origin constituted little more than a quarter of the population of St. Walburg but almost two-thirds of the population of Goodsoil and a majority of the population in the Barthel–Loon River district.

OTHER GERMAN CATHOLIC AND PROTESTANT SETTLEMENTS AND CONCENTRATIONS

Throughout the Saskatchewan prairie, smaller German Catholic and Protestant settlements and concentrations had developed by 1910. Let us now look at them by region.

The Southeastern Region
In the southeastern region, German Catholics concentrated around Lampman (pop. 634), where the Maryland Colony was established to the east in 1905 by Catholic *Banat-Deutscher*, and the Landau district to the south, Benson (pop. 95), with St. Francis de Sales Parish at Ossa and the Schell district, Arcola (pop. 504), and Steelman. But they had Lutheran neighbours: a concentration of German Lutherans and other German Protestants developed around Lampman and nearby communities, including the rural districts of Wabash and Woodley, where St. Luke Lutheran Church (1929) is a heritage site. Virtually all of the baptisms and confirmations at St. Luke (originally organized in 1911) recorded between 1913 and 1930 bore German surnames, as did all baptisms at St. Peter in Oxbow from 1915 to 1929.[45] Volga Germans settled in the Arcola area, which like Lampman became a mixed Lutheran and Catholic area. Former German Lutheran congregations were widely scattered throughout the southeastern region; they tended to be out in the country or in smaller villages, and many eventually merged with larger congregations in larger communities. Lutheran congregations in this area of settlement included Christ Lutheran at Arcola (1906–56), Trinity at Wordsworth (1920–), Grace at Willmar (1939–46), and St. James at Carlyle (1957–89). German Lutherans also settled around Stoughton (pop. 653). Deutscher Bund *ortsgruppen* were organized at

Stoughton and Oxbow during the 1930s. Germans constituted a third of the population of Lampman in 1971 and less than a quarter of that of Estevan.

German Catholic and Lutheran settlement also extended along the frontier above the Canada-US border. East of Estevan, there were settlers around Oxbow (pop. 1,139), Bienfait (pop. 748), Frobisher (pop. 145), and the Ernewein district. Peace Lutheran served the Alameda area from 1930 to 1993 (half the members of this ALC congregation split in 1956 to join the Missouri Synod congregation serving Frobisher, founded in 1929 and merged with a larger congregation in 1955). St. Paul Lutheran was established in the Forest Glen district near Roche Percee by 1920 (first served by pastors from across the border) and lasted until 1953, and a mission served the Hirsch area. West of Estevan, a small German Catholic colony, Marienthal, was established south of Torquay near the border. German and Scandinavian Lutherans established congregations and missions around Torquay (pop. 184), Bromhead, Oungre, Tribune (pop. 35), Lake Alma (pop. 30), Gladmar, Minton (pop. 60) and the Bergfield district, and Regway. St. John Lutheran was founded in 1921 and closed in 1966, while a mission served the Tribune area in 1915–18 and again during the 1930s–40s. In all of these mixed communities, the German population comprised only a small minority in 1971, the highest proportion being attained at Torquay, where a quarter of the residents were German.

German settlement also followed the Soo Line northwest from Estevan through Weyburn to Moose Jaw. Between Estevan and Weyburn, immediately west of the Lampman settlement, former German Lutheran congregations were established at Hitchcock (St. John, 1928–49), Macoun (Emmanuel German Evangelical Lutheran Church, founded in 1906, joined St. Luke's, Midale, in 1953, and St. John, 1906–36), and Midale (pop. 462). Near Weyburn, the Schneider district was settled by German Lutherans. And between Weyburn and Moose Jaw, into the south-central region, Volhynian Germans, mostly Lutherans but including some Catholics, settled around Yellow Grass as early as 1892; there their descendants made up a little more than a quarter of the village population in 1971. The Old Stone School (1903) became the town and RM office, then a regional library and Masonic Lodge, and it is now a heritage property. Beyond Yellow Grass, Catholics and Lutherans settled around Lang (pop. 172); Milestone (pop. 562), where St. Aloysius Catholic Church (1920) is now a heritage site; Corinne, where St. John Lutheran congregation existed from 1906 to the late 1940s; and Rouleau (pop. 400), where St. Paul Lutheran congregation lasted from 1924 to 1941.

Several concentrations of German population came into being farther north within the southeastern region, in communities along Highways 1 and 16. More than 2,000 people of German origin settled in three rural municipalities immediately south of the Qu'Appelle Valley, particularly in the Josephsburg district north of Grenfell, where Galician Germans from Josefsburg colony in Ukraine settled in 1888, and at Hoffman Coulee north of Sintaluta, where Prussian-born Reverend George Hoffman established one of several Lutheran Reformed congregations in the region. In Grenfell, St. Paul Lutheran congregation was founded during the 1930s and closed in 1959; Pastor Rudy Mensch came from Hoffenthal near Langenburg. Two former Lutheran congregations in the Josephsburg district were both founded in 1912: St. Paul (Missouri Synod) moved to Indian Head in 1953 (where the former St. Peter then became St. Paul), and Peace (United LCA) closed in 1959. The small village of Oakshela, immediately east of Grenfell, was settled by *Volksdeutsche* from Galicia and Volhynia. St. John Lutheran congregation was founded at Oakshela in 1907 and merged with the larger Broadview-Moosomin congregation in 1965. And west of Grenfell, Summerberry was served by Redeemer Lutheran during the 1930s. Windthorst (pop. 194) was named after Count Ludwig Windthorst, one of the organizers and leaders of the Centrist Party in Germany and an able opponent of Count Bismark. Windthorst was settled in 1907 by Lutheran Russian German immigrants from the Vladimir-Volynskiy area north of Lemberg (Lviv) and other Volhynian-Galician German communities. These particular German colonies in Russia had been established between 1783 and 1875; heavy German emigration from Volhynia and Galicia occurred between 1890 and 1914. Wilhelm Pusch (1878–1926) had emigrated from Vladimir-Volynskiy in Volhynia in 1909 to settle in Windthorst; he married Pauline Hirsekorn (1878–1952), born in Marindorf; and their children intermarried with other settlers in the colony— Dresslers, Zaisers, Schmieders. Near the neighbouring village of Peebles, once called Kaiser, the Schmidtz farm (1904) has been recognized as a heritage property. Other rural districts include Carlsberg and Edenland. Polish Germans, specifically from the Tomaszow-Mazowiecki and Wengrow areas in Poland, settled around Wapella (pop. 311) in 1928 and built their Lutheran church in 1936. Other German Lutherans settled around Kipling, Moosomin, Wawota (pop. 522), Fairlight (pop. 40), and the Maryfield district, establishing Lutheran congregations. The Whitewood area was settled by German Swiss as well as *Reichsdeutsche* from Hannover. The town of Whitewood had a declining population of 869 at last count in 2006.

The South-Central Region
Apart from the extensive, primarily Catholic settlement southeast of Regina, the primarily Protestant settlement around Edenwold northeast of Regina, settlement along the American frontier and along the Soo line southeast of Moose Jaw (all described above), and Mennonite settlement around Parry (to be discussed in the next section), several other German Catholic and Protestant concentrations within the south-central region merit mention. In the city of Regina itself, a German congregation, Trinity Lutheran, began to develop in 1906, while First English Lutheran existed from 1919 to 1943. In the city of Moose Jaw, a former German Lutheran congregation was Redeemer (1910–57), while just outside the city were Augustine Ecumenical at Davyroyd (1910–44) and Zion in the Grainland district (1930s–40s).

Among the diverse origins of people claiming German ethnicity in Saskatchewan have been the Danube Swabians (*Donauschwaben*), who established a number of settlements in Saskatchewan, beginning with the Zichydorf settlement just south of Regina. Following reincorporation of the Danube Basin into the Austro-Hungarian Empire and liberation from Ottoman Turkish control by the early eighteenth century, large numbers of ethnic German settlers were introduced into the newly acquired region. Farther east, Transylvanian Saxons (actually originally from the Rhineland and Mosel) had already established German colonies (the *Siebenburgen*) as early as the thirteenth century, setting the precedent for a greater, revitalized ethnic German influx into the Balkans. The new settlers became known as Danube Swabians, for they originated primarily in Swabia (*Schwaben* in German)—a broad region that historically had extended between Alsace and Bavaria and southward into what later became eastern Switzerland and the adjacent part of Austria. These ethnic German settlers concentrated particularly around Arad, Temeschburg/Timisoara, Reschitza/Resita, and Hatzfeld/Jimbolia in the eastern Banat region today in Romania; Werschetz/Vrsac, Gross-Kikinda/Kinkinda, Pantschowa/Pancevo, Weisskirchen/Bela Crkva, Gross-Betschkerek/Zrenjanin, and Zenta/Senta in the western Banat region in Serbia (east of the Tisza River); Neusatz/Novi Sad, Maria Theresiopel/Subotica, and Zombor/Sombor in the Batschka/Backa region in Serbia (between the Danube and the Tisza); Karlowitz/Sremska Karlovci in Syrmien/Srem formerly in Croatia, now in Serbia (between the Danube, Drava, and Sava); Esseg/Osijek in Slavonia in Croatia (across the Sava); and Funfkirchen/Pecs in the Baranya region straddling the Hungarian-Croatian border (west of the Danube and north of the Drava). The Germans of the Banat region (and their descendants in Saskatchewan) were known as *Banatdeutscher* (Banat Germans) or *Banatschwaben* (Banat Swabians).

Danube Swabians first began to emigrate to Saskatchewan during the 1890s. Beginning in 1897, the Zichydorf settlement was founded by eighteen families from the community of Zichydorf (or Zichyfalva/Mariolana) in the Banat region some seventy kilometres northeast of Belgrade. Although other emigrants from this one community eventually emigrated to St. Paul, Minnesota, other American destinations, and even South America, these early settlers in Saskatchewan settled immediately southeast of Regina. Other *Banatschwaben* arrived from the communities of Georghausen, Setschanfeld, Glogon, and Gross-Zsam. Due to its proximity to Regina, the Zichydorf Colony soon lost settlers to the city. By 1910, all of the original families were either living on individual homesteads or had already moved into the city.

With changing political conditions in the Balkans, especially the division of the former Austro-Hungarian territories among Hungary, Romania, and the newly created state of Yugoslavia following the First World War, and then the occupation of these territories by German and Axis troops during the Second World War, ethnic Germans were no longer a protected, much less favoured, minority, and increasingly they became placed at a disadvantage. So Danube Swabians continued to emigrate, including to Saskatchewan, where they had relatives and friends. Many joined the Zichydorfers in Regina's "Germantown"; in fact, one east Regina neighbourhood became known as "Klein Zichydorf." But most of the Danube Swabians in Saskatchewan are widely scattered throughout the southern regions of the province. The Sudom district northeast of Avonlea was named after Joseph Sudom, a Banat settler who immigrated with his extended family into this district in 1903. Other distinct Banat, Swabian, and Hungarian German colonies included Torondal near Raymore, Maryland near Lampman, St. Elizabeth Colony near Glenbain, and districts near Lemberg; Danube Swabians from Herzogendorf/Hercegfalva settled around Wakaw together with Hungarians. Over the course of several generations, the Danube Swabians in Saskatchewan have become progressively anglicized and less acquainted with their unique history.

Swabian settlers in Saskatchewan—part of *die wanderlustigen Schwaben*, the wandering Swabians, the Swabian diaspora—brought with them a rich folk legacy. They spoke their own melodic Schwabisch dialect, which had persisted for generations in their settlements in Bessarabia, Volhynia, and Volga; this dialect had incorporated some Slavic loan words, such as *holoptsi* (cabbage rolls) and *perahe* (perogies). Their traditional foods also included *aepfel kuchen* (apple cake), *kvach kuchen* (plum tart), *karpfen/kripfa* (doughnuts), *moen luchen* (poppyseed roll), soup with *knuckle/nookl* (dumplings), *noosz* (noodles), *nosz luchen* (light cake), and other traditional baking. Traditional weddings were an exhibition of unique Swabian folkways. They were always held on Tuesdays at 10 a.m. Invitations were delivered from home to home orally by two men in a decorated vehicle; these messengers were given a drink at each home; then coloured ribbons or handkerchiefs were tied to a cane or stick that they carried to indicate each home visited. The bride was led to the church by the best man, the groom by the bridesmaid. After a traditional dinner, the guests danced (usually Hungarian *czardas*) until noon the following day. The bride danced with each male guest, who was expected to place a sum of money on a plate held by the *brautmutter* (an older woman). An important event was the "selling" of the bride's shoe, "stolen" by the best man to be "auctioned" (*ein thaler, die bu'hon da shuk*—one dollar am I bid for the shoe). Mummers often performed at wedding celebrations. Unique practices were also evident around New Year's Eve and Day, *Fastnacht* (Shrove Tuesday night, when house parties were held), *Chitsunday* (Pentecost), and *Whitmonday*. However, some pietistic families disapproved of dancing and alcohol served at house parties. Swabian people were often named after saints, so relevant "name days"—saints' days—were as important as birthdays. Women were skilled at embroidery, but except for folk-dancing troupes there was no regularly worn uniquely Swabian dress in more recent times, though women tended to wear a *schupf* (scarf) tied behind the head.

To the southeast of Moose Jaw, German Catholics settled around Spring Valley, Bayard (including the Hapsburg district where Martin Beitel from Czernowitz—today Chernivtsi in Ukrainian Bukovina—settled in 1910), Claybank (pop. 20), Avonlea (pop. 381) and the Sudom district where the Swabians settled, and Truax and the Schutt/Rosebud district. Incidentally, the Claybank brick plant, founded in 1904, supplied firebricks for construction of the Chateau Frontenac in Quebec City, the Bessborough Hotel in Saskatoon, Hotel Saskatchewan in Regina, the Capital Theatre in Moose Jaw, and the Gravelbourg cathedral, among many other historic buildings. Former Lutheran congregations and missions around Spring Valley were Peace in the Blue Hills district (1913–91), Galilee (1941–46), and Cardross (1941–43). Farther south, Catholics settled around Pangman, Ogema and the Weicker Lake district, Horizon, Bengough, and Ceylon. Lutheran congregations and missions in this area included Christ at Ormiston (1916–), Hope at Kayville (1912–56), Trinity at Pangman (1924–96), Bures near Ogema (1930s–40s), St. John at Verwood (1913–90s), Hardy (1915–), St. Paul in the Oakville district near Ceylon (1916–56), Radville (1932–34), and Grace at Trossachs (late 1930s). Southwest of Moose Jaw, German Catholics settled around Mossbank, Congress and the Aldenburg district, Assiniboia, Pickthall, Scout Lake, Rockglen, and Coronach. German Lutheran congregations and missions were Trinity at Ardill (1932–40), St. Matthew at Mossbank (1910–59), St. John at Mazenod (1915–60), Assiniboia, St. John in the Luella district near Coronach (1912–80), and a mission in the Buffalo Gap district near Big Beaver (1930s–40s).

During the 1930s, a Deutscher Bund *ortsgruppe* was established at Claybank and *stützpunkte* at Mossbank, Avonlea, and Bayard. However, by 1971 only about half of the few remaining residents of Horizon were German, while in all of the other communities in the region people of German ethnic origin constituted less than half of the community population: Mankota (30.2%), Vanguard (25.8%), Rockglen (24.8%), Mossbank (21.6%), Khedive (21.4%), Spring Valley (21.4%), Mazenod (20.0%), Pangman (18.4%), Bengough (13.6%), Assiniboia (13.3%), Ceylon (12.7%), Avonlea (less than 10%). Yet community size should be taken into consideration since it pertains more to the distribution and concentration of German-origin population; some of these communities retain very few residents today. Horizon, established as a village by 1912, soon had over 200 residents and seventeen businesses, but it began to decline during the late 1940s, and by the 1980s only one operating grain elevator and three homes remained. At last count, Congress had only twenty-eight residents, Scout Lake twenty, Spring Valley thirteen. More viable communities in the region have been the towns of Assiniboia (pop. 2,305), Coronach (pop. 770), Bengough (pop. 337), Rockglen (pop. 336), Mossbank (pop. 330), and Ogema (pop. 304) and the villages of Avonlea (pop. 381) and Pangman (pop. 200).

The Southwestern Region
The southwestern region contained two extensive settlements: the predominantly German Catholic settlement between Leader and Maple Creek (described above) and the Mennonite settlement centred on Swift Current (described in the next section).

Along Highway 19, southeast of Swift Current, German Catholics, Lutherans, and Mennonites concentrated in the area around Flowing Well, Hodgeville, Kelstern, and Bateman. A predominantly Lutheran settlement of Volga Germans emerged around Hodgeville. Trinity Lutheran Church at St. Boswells (1916) and Zion Lutheran Church at Flowing Well (1919) are heritage sites. German Lutherans mixed with Catholics and Mennonites from German settlements in the United States, as well as immigrants direct from German settlements in Russia and Hungary, around Hodgeville in 1907–14; with Mennonites around Kelstern, St. Boswells, and Vogel; and with both Mennonites and Adventists at Flowing Well. German Catholics settled in this particular area in 1908–14; many came from the Midwestern United States, particularly from German American settlements, founded by immigrants from the original German colonies in Russia. The Rosenke farm is preserved as a heritage site near Flowing Well.

Hungarian German Catholics founded St. Elizabeth Colony during 1908–09 near Glenbain. In this colony, the first mission church was established around 1910 when Father Wilhelm homesteaded and built a small house and chapel, whereas the present church and cemetery date from 1927 and now comprise a historic site.

Farther south, Russian German Catholics from Crimea founded Billimun Colony in 1909–10, near Mankota (pop. 238), and settled the Rausch Creek district. Billimun was a mission in 1910, the first church was built in 1914, and a larger church was constructed in 1926 (destroyed by fire the following year, so the present church was then built). St. Martin's became a parish in 1925, Mankota not until 1946. St. Martin's Church and cemetery at Billimun today constitute a historic site.

Rural depopulation has taken a toll on some communities in the area: Bateman once had over 180 residents and during the 1920s at least eighteen businesses and services; however, most residents moved into nearby Hodgeville—only a few remained by the 1980s. St. Boswells once featured a wide variety of businesses and services, including both a Chinese restaurant and an Orange Hall, and more than 135 residents; however, decline escalated during the 1950s, and by the 1980s only a single family remained, living in the former schoolhouse. Hallonquist, west of Hodgeville, once had eleven businesses, but by the 1980s only a grain elevator marked the community. Hodgeville still survives as a regional centre, with 142 residents; when it was recognized as a village in 1921, it contained over 200 residents, and by the 1960s it had 400 residents. Glenbain had some sixty residents during the mid-1950s; they declined to approximately three dozen by the 1970s, and by 1988 only eleven were left.[46] In all of these communities, people of German origin now constitute only a minority, yet some rural districts retain stronger German concentrations, such as Ensz, Flowing Well, Grismerville, Henke, Marx, and Scottsburgh/Kramer around Hodgeville; and Arnold, Busch, Gooding, and St. Elizabeth Colony around Glenbain.

Southwest of Swift Current, Germans (primarily Lutherans) settled around Gull Lake (pop. 965), Simmie (pop. 15), Illerbrun (named after an early settler from North Dakota in 1907), and the Voll, Georgina, Grassy Creek, and Coal Valley districts around Instow. One-time congregations and missions in this area included Good Hope in the Aldag district south of Gull Lake (1912–67), Beaver Valley, Lac Pelletier and the Neu-Hoffnung district (1930s–40s), and Stone near Tompkins (1933–43). German Catholics began to settle near Shaunavon in 1907–08 and established a strongly German Catholic parish in 1914, assisted by German religious orders. In 1971, about one in five people in Shaunavon (pop. 1,691 in 2006) was of German origin.[47] And in the far southwest corner of Saskatchewan, German Catholics and Lutherans settled around Consul (e.g., the Zentner and Ziegler Coulee districts) and Vidora, where Lutheran missions existed during the 1930s. To the east, close to the American border, other German Lutheran missions served Orkney from 1932 to 1945 and Masefield during the 1930s.

The West-Central Region

The west-central region was dominated by the vast St. Joseph's Colony, founded by German Catholics (described above). Just across the South Saskatchewan River to the north from Leader, the Eatonia-Glidden area (including the districts of Dankin, Crimea, and Ebenau) was settled by German Lutherans as well as by Catholics, Mennonites, and most recently Hutterites. In 1971, a majority of the residents of Glidden (pop. 48 in 1996) were German and over a third of those of Eatonia (pop. 449 in 2006). Just to the northeast is the Rathmullen district. Other former Lutheran congregations and missions along Highway 44 included Alsask North and South (1934), Peace at Laporte (1912–74), Peace in the Cornfeld/Dungloe district near Eatonia (1912–27), Trinity at Eston (1946–50), Redeemer in the Tyner district near Eston (1946–50), the Saltburn district near Eston (1945), and Elrose (1933–43). Elsewhere in the west-central region, former primarily German Lutheran congregations and missions included communities and districts along Highway 7 between Rosetown and Saskatoon: Rosetown (1933–40), Marriott northwest of Zealandia (1911–43), Harris (1930s), Tessier (1933–34), Laura (1911–36), Delisle (1933–39), and the Donovan district near Delisle (1933); near Lake Diefenbaker: the Hill and Hollow district near Demaine (1916–42) and Macrorie (1930s); and in the far northwest corner of the region: the Artland district near Marsden (1930s), Lashburn (1930s–40s), Baldwinton (1930s–40s), and the Standard Hill district near Maidstone (1933). A Mennonite settlement around Fiske and Herschel will be described below.

The Central Region

Numerous communities in the central region were included within the extended area of German settlement that expanded from the Neu Elsass settlement (previously described). However, a couple of other smaller areas of German settlement merit mention.

Another small German Catholic colony, the Seltz or St. Aloysius Colony (named after a community in the Kutchurgan colony near Odessa in Ukraine), was centred on St. Aloysius Parish in the town of Allan in 1903–07. The original church, general store, and post office were actually situated southwest of the current community; the present large parish church in town was constructed in 1922. Allan became a village in 1910, the potash mine commenced operations in the mid-1960s, and with a growing population Allan became a town in 1965. Approximately half of the population of Allan (pop. 631 today) was of German descent in 1971. These German families tended to be large: in 1979, a reunion of the Moldenhauer family was celebrated by 260 members. The progenitor of this extended family was early settler Johannes Moldenhauer, whose predecessors had migrated from Bavaria to Bessarabia, where he was born; he and his wife, Lucia Breckner, produced five children in Russia, then another eight in Canada. After first looking for land in North Dakota, they came to the Allan settlement in 1904.[48] Fred Schumacher and Amelia Yetcha already had five sons and two daughters in Kronau, South Russia, when the mother died in childbirth; Fred soon married Rosa Stulberg, and together they had another nine sons, eight of them after they emigrated to Saskatchewan in 1912, where they farmed near Young, so altogether Fred raised sixteen children![49] The colony extended east along Breckner Road into the Zangwill district. The small neighbouring village of Zelma was named after Zelma Jacoby Thode from Dundurn, to suit the alphabetized naming of railway stations along the CNR main line; however, the first post office was Camholt, partially named after pioneer settler Frank Imholz. During the 1930s, a Deutscher Bund *stützpunkt* chapter was organized in the nearby community of Young.

German Lutherans also settled close to Mennonites in the Lanigan area, at Lanigan (pop. 1,233), Leroy (pop. 412), Watrous (pop. 1,743), Jansen (pop. 140), Esk, and Dafoe (pop. 10). In 1971, approximately two-thirds of the residents in the village of Jansen were German; their predecessors were Russian Germans, those in the nearby hamlet of Dafoe Volga Germans. Zion Lutheran Church was established in Jansen in 1907; many—but not all—of the pastors have been of German ethnicity.[50] Volga Germans who settled around Dafoe founded Emmanuel congregation in 1913; they originally called their church *Bethaus* (house of prayer) and the entranceway the *vorhaus*. A *frauenverein* (women's group) was active. Membership peaked in 1935, but eventually many joined the larger Zion congregation in Jansen, and the church finally closed in 1968. Nearby, the area around the hamlet of Kandahar had four Lutheran congregations—two German, a Norwegian, and an Icelandic. The German ones were St. John in the Product district (1911–56), an Ohio Synod congregation whose history was faithfully recorded in *Aus Frueneren Kirchenbuch*, and a United Lutheran Church of America congregation (1920s–40s), just a small mission meeting in private homes. Other primarily German Lutheran congregations and missions in the area included no fewer than three Trinity congregations: at Esk (1907–67), in the Attica district near Lanigan, and in the Eigenheim district, settled by Russian Germans, north of Little Manitou Lake (1920–56). A small mission at Guernsey met in private homes for many years. Closer to Saskatoon, former congregations were Zion at Viscount (1915–46) and Christ at Clavet (early 1930s–50), while south of Saskatoon, in the Haultain district, were yet another Trinity, a Missouri Synod congregation (1905–65) founded by Russian and Austro-Hungarian Germans from the United States, and St. Mark, a congregation of the Unaltered Augsburg Confession (1912–43). The Dundurn area was settled by German Lutherans (a couple of decades before Mennonites settled in this area) under the leadership of E.J. Meilicke, who brought German American homesteaders.

The East-Central Region

Three large areas of German settlement in this region have already been described: the Hohenlohe Colony around Langenburg, the Volga Colony north of Yorkton, and the extensive area of German settlement around Melville; some Mennonite settlement in this region will be mentioned in the succeeding section. Together these large settlements contained virtually all of the German concentrations in the region.

The Northeastern Region

Apart from the Carrot River Mennonite settlement (described later), most of the other smaller German concentrations within this region were in the Nipawin area, where former German Lutheran congregations and missions included Holy Cross in the Spooner district near Pontrilas (congregation organized in 1920, church not built until 1934, closed in 1947), a mission in the Crest/Blue Spruce district near Nipawin (1927–47), Torch River (early 1930s), St. John in the Connell Creek district near Arborfield (1931–mid-50s), St. Paul at Snowden (1931–64), Garrick (1931–52), and Love (1940s). Other scattered congregations and missions were Zion at Nut Mountain (1933–63), Carragana (1930s), Carrot River (1940s), Paswegin (1940s), and Concordia at Margo (1945–65).

The North-Central Region

The large St. Peter's German Catholic Colony has already been described, and several Mennonite settlements in this region will be discussed later, including German Lutheran congregations within these settlements, but several other German concentrations should be mentioned.

The Bergheim German Lutheran settlement near Saskatoon, and adjacent to the portion of the Saskatchewan Valley Mennonite settlement east of the South Saskatchewan River, began to develop in the early years of the twentieth century; by 1906, Pastor F. Pompeit of Rosthern was often travelling on foot to conduct services and religious instruction in the homes of the settlement across the river. St. Paul, a United Lutheran Church of America congregation, was organized by Pastor G. Juttner in 1912, and for the next seven years, until a church was constructed in 1919, services and Sunday School were conducted in Bergheim School. Religious instruction was provided in German on Saturdays and Sundays until 1945; then English was used. From the 1920s through the

1950s, a brass band played regularly at church services, picnics, and other community social events. In 1952, a Women's Auxiliary was formed, and since 1956 a Vacation Bible School has been held every July.[51] Bergheim was declared a municipal heritage site in 2002. Pastor Pompeit also conducted the first German Lutheran service in Saskatoon in 1909; two years later Trinity Lutheran Church was established, which for many decades conducted services in German. Another German Lutheran church in the Bergheim district, Trinity (an Ohio Synod congregation), came into being in 1909 but merged with nearby St. Paul (less than a kilometre away) in 1942. And a third congregation was the German Baptist *Gotteskinder*. The settlement, centred on Bergheim School (1912) and the churches, soon expanded into the Kilmenny and Blackley districts to the north, Strawberry Valley (school 1915) and Hesseldale (school 1917) districts to the east, and Patience Lake and Bainesville districts to the south. Many of the settlers were of Volhynian German origin, and their unique traditions included an elaborate wedding ritual: *schnappen mit wein* (rye and wine) were served for toasts, and a bidding game for the newlyweds was played as guests sang *schenk der braut ein thaler* ("give the bride a dollar").

German immigrants, including the pioneering Flaata, Meister, and Bronsch families from the Wilhelmswalde settlement near Lodz, Poland, arrived in 1902 to settle next to Mennonites near Radisson; they organized Zion Lutheran congregation in 1907 (church dedicated in 1912) in the Bronsch Road district (some sixteen kilometres northeast of Radisson) and today are widely scattered on farms throughout the neighbouring Grand Valley, Wheatheart, Turtle Lake, Twin Lakes, Waterbury, and Scottville districts.[52] At least thirty German family surnames are found in the area today (apart from many more Mennonite families in adjoining districts farther east). Zion Lutheran was closed in 1966 and moved into Radisson, where it is now the town museum, across the street from St. Paul Lutheran. Other former nearby missions were in the Lamoyle district to the southwest of Radisson (1925–27) and at Speers (until 1939).

A number of primarily German Lutheran congregations and missions were situated close to predominantly Scandinavian settlements in the region: St. Peter at Big River (late 1930s–late 40s), Amiens (1920s), and the Wood Hill district near Shell Lake (1930s); the Forester district near Melfort (early 1920s) and Fenton near Birch Hills (1930s); as well as St. Paul in the Silver Grove district near Leask (organized in 1917, made a heritage site in 1984, and still occasionally used). St. Paul's, a Russian German congregation, did not shift from German to English until 1957. St. John (Manitoba Synod), in the Brightholme district near Leask, was founded in 1919 but destroyed by lightning in 1966. A third church in the Leask area was St. John (LCA, 1956–2000). There was a German Lutheran congregation in the city of Prince Albert during the 1930s. And a number of German Lutheran congregations were situated within Mennonite settlements in the region; they will be covered later in the description of Mennonite settlements.

The Northwestern Region
Finally, in the northwestern region, all but a few of the German Lutheran churches and missions were located within or close to the areas of German settlement around St. Walburg, Loon River, and Beaver River (described above). The remaining few included St. John at Glaslyn (1934–40) and an ELCC congregation at Prince (1945).

MENNONITE SETTLEMENTS

The Mennonites date their origin back to the spread of Anabaptism from Switzerland during the sixteenth century. A then fairly radical group of Anabaptists appeared in the Netherlands under the leadership of Menno Simons (1492–1559), who had been a Catholic priest in a small community in Friesland. Faced with persecution not only by Catholics but also by less communal-minded Protestants there, these people, who became known as Mennonites, began to take refuge in northern Germany, initially in East Friesland (close to the Dutch border) and by the mid-sixteenth century in West and East Prussia, where they were invited to occupy undeveloped territories as part of a German eastern colonization scheme in which they were promised exemption from military service. But by the 1780s, facing numerous problems there from the Prussian government, the Mennonites began to leave Prussia to establish colonies in Poland and South Russia (present-day Ukraine). Invited by Catherine II and lured by military and taxation exemptions and permission to found their own schools and local governments, they first established the large Chortitza (1789) and Molotschna (1803) colonies, then numerous smaller colonies during the nineteenth century. Mennonites had become *das volk des eigentums* (a peculiar people), *das heilige volk* (a holy people), concentrated in *de gemeinde* (community), within *die Mennischde gesellschaft* (broader Mennonite community or society).

However, in 1874, Russian nationalism caught up with the German colonists of South Russia. Their military and taxation exemptions were revoked; their political autonomy was disrupted when their colonies were incorporated into larger Russian administrative units; records and schools had to use the Russian language; and "unqualified" Mennonite schoolteachers were replaced by Russian ones. That year Mennonites, Hutterites, and other Russian German Protestants emigrated to South Dakota. Other conservative Mennonites from the Chortitza colony moved to the East Reserve in the Steinbach area of Manitoba (southeast of Winnipeg). The following year the conservative Mennonites of the Furstenland and Bergthal colonies moved to the West Reserve in the Morden and Winkler area (southwest of Winnipeg). Already by the 1890s, the overpopulation of these Manitoba "reserves" led to the emigration of some of the Mennonites who had settled in Manitoba to new settlements in Saskatchewan.

Numerous small Mennonite villages and rural localities in Saskatchewan were given descriptive names; most of these Mennonite place names in Saskatchewan, though typical of Mennonite tradition, were named after earlier Mennonite communities in South Russia and then, in turn, Mennonite reserves established in Manitoba. Typical prefixes were Blumen- (flower), Rosen- (roses), Klee- (clover), Eigen- (own, particular), Ein- (one), Neu(an)- (new), Schoen- (beautiful), Halb- (half), Hoch- (high), Tiefen- (lower), Friedens- (freedom), Gruen- (green), Rein/Rine- (Rhein), Hoffnungs- (hope), Stein- (stone), Krons- (crown), Bruder- (brother), Wald- (forest, wood), Gnaden- (grace), Sommer- (summer), Oster- (eastern), Eben- (plain), Eben- (even, plain, level), Rudner- (round), Reichen- (plentiful), Schantzen- (shady), et cetera. And frequent suffixes were -ort (place), -feld(t) (field), -wiede (pasture), -wiese (meadow), -berg (hill), -stadt (town), -dorf (village), -lage (site, place), -thal (valley), -heim (home), -gart (garden), -bach (stream), -hof (farm), -land (land, soil, earth), -grund (ground), -wick (harvest), -werk (work), -ruh (peaceful), et cetera. Thus, for example, Blumenheim could be translated as flower home, Gruenthal as green valley, Neuanlage as new place, Hoffnungsfeld as field of grace, and so forth.

The Saskatchewan Valley Settlement (1891–)
The Saskatchewan Valley settlement developed rapidly into a major bloc settlement similar in many ways to its forerunners in South Russia. The settlement developed in several stages between 1891 and 1918. The initial nucleus of this settlement came into existence in 1891–94 with the settling of the immediate area around Rosthern by immigrants of the *Rosenort Gemeinde* (later General Conference Mennonites, who eventually became the Mennonite Church Canada [MCC]) from West Prussia, Russia, and Manitoba. For example, in the Tiefengrund district, Johann Fieguth homesteaded in 1896 after emigrating from West Prussia to Oregon in 1886. The first Mennonite homesteader in the Rosthern area was Gerhard Ens, who settled there in 1892, operated a store and post office out of a boxcar loaned by the railway, later became an influential immigration agent instrumental in recruiting Mennonite settlers to this area, and eventually was elected to serve in the first provincial legislature in 1905.[53] As this area developed, a network of local schools serving communities and rural districts came into being mostly between 1897 and 1910 (e.g., around the town of Rosthern and the smaller communities of Laird and Carlton were the rural districts of Rosenort, Tiefengrund/Diehl's Creek, Hamburg, Eigenheim, Friedensfeld, Johannesthal, Ebenfeld, Stony Hill, Riverlot, Snowbird, Elberfeld, Eigenfeld, Hoffningsort, Heidelberg, Silberfeld, Danzig, Blumenhof, Friesen Creek, Kohleschmidt Creek, Tadei Lake, and Rempel Lake). Rosthern was first established as a post office in 1893, then incorporated as a village in 1898 and a town in 1903; by 1911, it already had over 1,000 residents. The Rosthern German-English Academy (1910) became the Rosthern Junior College, then the Rosthern Mennonite Heritage Museum, while the Rosthern Experimental Farm became the Mennonite Youth Farm in 1944, then the Mennonite Nursing Home in 1964.

Furstenländer migrated from the West Reserve in Manitoba to settle around Hague in 1895. A compact reserve consisting of numerous small communities was then established by Old Colony (*Reinländer*) Mennonites from Manitoba in 1895–1905 around Hague, Osler, Warman, and Aberdeen. The *Reinländer* had been formed in 1875 by immigrants from the Chortitza and Furstenland colonies in the western portion of the West Reserve under the leadership of Bishop Johann Wiebe (who had been a bishop in the Furstenland colony) and their civic leader Isaac Mueller. Numbering over 3,400 at the time, they advocated a return to biblical principles that they thought had been abandoned in Russia. In his letter to church members in 1904, Bishop Wiebe prayed: "Oh God, grant us strength to withstand all evil, to walk in the truth, and to turn away from all unrighteousness."[54] In order to accomplish these aims, the church should have central authority in the schools and civic matters.

Most of the conservative Mennonites in the settlement arrived immediately from the West Reserve in Manitoba; they or their predecessors had formerly come to Manitoba largely from the Chortitza colony and some from the Bergthal colony in South Russia, but later arrivals from Russia as well as from Mennonite colonies in the United States included emigrants from the Molotschna colony. The *Kleine Gemeinde*, eventually closely related to the *Bergthaler*, originated in the Borozenko colony in 1812–14 as a renewal movement that reaffirmed a commitment to sixteenth-century Anabaptist principles. In 1874, the entire *Kleine Gemeinde* left Russia, more than two-thirds (just some 700) heading for the Manitoba East Reserve. There, under the leadership of Bishop Peter Toews, they sought to renew and unify the Mennonite church and to ensure its control of schools; moreover, the *Kleine Gemeinde* attempted successfully to elect village mayors. *Bergthaler* (*Chortitzer*) Mennonites numbered some 2,800 when they settled in the East Reserve. Led by Bishop Gerhard Wiebe, the cousin of the *Reinländer* bishop, their vision was also for the church to be central to the life of the community, particularly schools and civic affairs. Soon, during the mid-1880s, many (some 400 families) moved to the West Reserve, where Johann Funk became their bishop. The designation *Bergthaler* had become more or less limited to these West Reserve settlers by the 1890s, while those remaining in the East Reserve became known as *Chortitzer*. A further division of West Reserve *Bergthaler* over the issue of education formed the *Sommerfelder* Mennonite church. Out of some 450 *Bergthaler* families in the West Reserve, fewer than sixty (mostly original *Bergthaler* immigrants and former *Reinländer*) stayed under the authority of Bishop Funk; the remainder, numbering 1,500 members in the West Reserve by 1901, became the *Sommerfelder* under the leadership of Bishop Abraham Doerksen in 1893.[55]

Then, within a few years, all of these factions began moving into Saskatchewan. *Bergthaler* or *Sommerfelder* Mennonites concentrated after 1902 around Suedflus, Aberdeen, Krim, and Clarkboro in Aberdeen RM; Warman, Martensville, Osler, Blumenheim, Gruenthal, and Schoenwiese in Warman RM; Rheinfeld, Rosengart, Rosthern, Bergthal, Blumenhoff, and Heuboden in Rosthern RM; and Waldheim and Laird in Laird RM. Continuing *Bergthaler* congregations are found today in Suedflus, Gruenthal, Blumenheim, Martensville, Warman, and Reinfeld and likely number close to 1,000 congregants. Continuing Old Colony congregations are still found at Blumenheim, Hague, Neuanlage, and Neuhorst, but adherents were estimated to number fewer than 800 by 1990 and were declining. Smaller numbers of congregants belong to the Evangelical Mennonite Mission Conference (*Rudnerweider*), which has congregations at Hague, Hepburn, and Warman.[56] An offshoot of the *Kleine Gemeinde* was the Holdeman sect, officially the Church of God in Christ, founded by John Holdeman, a Swiss Mennonite from Ohio who had won over many Volhynian Mennonite settlers in Kansas. Holdeman was invited to Manitoba in 1881 to assist with the renewal of the *Kleine Gemeinde*. He advocated a return to traditional Mennonite values, including withdrawal from worldly matters; conservative dress, pacifism, refusal to hold public office or serve in such an office, together with fervent evangelism, conversion, and assurance of salvation, characterized this sect. Even the *Kleine Gemeinde* bishop, Peter Toews, joined, together with about half of the *Kleine Gemeinde* at the time; the remaining *Kleine Gemeinde* were reorganized by a bishop from Nebraska, Jacob Kroeker. A Holdeman (Church of God in Christ Mennonite) congregation is now found at Neuanlage, and conservative Mennonite congregations exist near Altona (west of Osler) and southeast of Rosthern.

The social organization in the conservative colonies in South Russia was systematically duplicated in Manitoba, then Saskatchewan. Old Colony villages were characterized by the *strassendorf* form of settlement—small villages with houses all lining a broad main street (a custom developed in Russia because of the possibility of thatched roofs catching fire). Each family held title to a house in the village as well as a homestead where the farming was done. A *herdschult* (herder) was responsible for tending the community cattle; there were no fences between farms (though communal pastures could be fenced to keep cattle in). Churches were in some but not all villages; in other villages, services were simply held in homes or a school. Each village had a *schultz* (overseer). The determination of conservative Mennonites to keep their German-language schools led inevitably to a clash with the provincial government and the departure of many of these traditionalistic Mennonites for Mexico and Paraguay during the 1920s (described in detail in a later section of this chapter).

Remaining examples of traditional Old Colony villages are Neuanlage (the first Old Colony village established, in 1895), Blumenthal, and Neuhorst in Warman RM and Edenburg in Aberdeen RM. Grace Mennonite Church at Neuanlage conducted services in German through the 1950s. Blumenheim and Osterwick in Warman RM as well as Friedland-Schonfeld-Steinreich in Aberdeen RM represent a dispersed *strassendorf* type. Most of these early conservative communities today have become communal hamlets, such as Halbstadt, Hochfeld, Chortitz, and Silberfeld in Rosthern RM; Hochstadt, Gruenthal, Rheinland, Gruenfeldt, Rosenfeld, Schoenwiese, Halbstadt, and Kronsthal in Warman RM; and Olgafeld–Suedflus–River Park and Halbstadt (North and South Lilly) in Aberdeen RM. With rural depopulation, many other communities are now simply dispersed rural localities: Rosengart, Reinfeld, Neuhoffnung, Halbstadt, and Blumenort in Rosthern RM; Rosenbach, Schlorrendorp (later called Freundrussendorp after the arrival of *Russländer* immigrants), Schlauberg, Rieferthal, and Schoenthal in Warman RM; and Schanzenfeld–New Steinbach and Krim in Aberdeen RM. Still others were country school districts, such as Steele and Altona in Warman RM.

These adjoining Mennonite settlements then expanded into a single vast settlement with the establishment of additional communities and congregations by Mennonite Brethren from the American Midwest (particularly Minnesota, Nebraska, Kansas, and Oklahoma), directly from Russia, or via Manitoba; Mennonite Brethren had immigrated to Kansas in 1874, then had sent missionaries to Manitoba in 1886. Mennonite Brethren drew converts from the *Reinländer*, from whom they differed in their emphasis on individual salvation through adult baptism and individual repentance rather than communal life; church services also differed, with Mennonite Brethren emphasizing "modern" sermons and hymns, evangelism, prayer, and Bible study. In Saskatchewan, Mennonite Brethren settled around Laird, Waldheim (and the Bruderfeld, Springfield, Salem, and Schmidtsburg districts), Hepburn (with the surrounding Hudson Bay, Carson, Richmond, New Home, and Lakeburg School Districts), Mennon, Dalmeny, Warman, Osler, and Aberdeen in 1898–1918. The Mennonite Brethren church at Hepburn had been established in 1910, but the community was not incorporated as a village until 1919; Bethany Bible College was founded there in 1927. One illustrious graduate of Bethany was Emma Lepp Baerg, born on a farm near Dalmeny in 1917; she served as a missionary in India from 1946 to 1978, then became with her husband co-pastor of Central Mennonite Brethren Church in Saskatoon. She passed away in 2010. Reverend Jacob Pauls, pastor of the Osler Mennonite Brethren Church for twenty-seven years, was born in Gregorievka/Naumenko, Ukraine, the fifth of six children; his parents died when he was only three, so he was raised by his grandparents, who took him to Canada at the age of ten; he became a pastor at twenty-two. He also helped to establish the Warman congregation, the Osler Mission Chapel, and German-language churches in Ontario and Mexico. When he died in 2010, he and his wife, Mary Schmidt, were the progenitors of eight children, twenty-six grandchildren, twenty-eight great-grandchildren, and two great-great-grandchildren. Aberdeen Mennonite Church has also just celebrated its centennial; it is widely known for its popular annual borscht supper, a fundraiser for Mennonite Central Committee projects. The Mennonite Brethren congregation at Bruderfeld (Brotherfield), northwest of Hepburn, formed in 1898; the first church was built in 1902 and replaced by a second church in 1911; in 1988, the congregation merged with the Waldheim Mennonite Brethren, and a lovely little memorial chapel was dedicated at the old cemetery in 2002, exactly a century after construction of the original church.

Krimmer Mennonite Brethren (KMB) from Kansas and Nebraska settled around Langham and Waldheim in 1899–1901. And *Bruderthaler* or Evangelical Mennonite Brethren (EMB) from Minnesota settled in the Langham-Dalmeny area in 1912 and in the Edenberg and Mierau districts, respectively to the north and southwest. The KMB congregation near Langham was founded in 1917 by *Prairieleut* (prairie people, former Hutterites who continued to maintain certain Hutterite social and theological traditions but lived non-communally). This congregation was established by several *Prairieleut* families who settled around Langham during the early 1900s, seeking improved economic opportunities. They settled together, but separately from other Mennonites, within a fifty-square-mile block. They long retained a unique identity well away from Hutterite colonies. Their unordained leader, Andreas Stahl, first conducted services in private homes; however, he encouraged the foundation of a church. Before his death in 1920, Stahl had a reputation for advising church members how they should act. Yet many of these *Prairieleut* in the Langham area never joined the Emmanuel congregation, preferring to continue to meet privately for Bible study and prayer, though it became expedient during the First World War for them to become more formally affiliated with a Mennonite church to re-enforce their claim to be conscientious objectors. Eventually, the then prevalent Hutterite practice of keeping children at home or at least separate from adults during church services caused young people to drift away from the KMB fold, yet the KMB did develop, with some success, "young people's meetings." Nonetheless, *Prairieleut* around Langham tended to maintain a strong Hutterite identity, with high moral standards emphasizing hard work, honesty, and piety. In the late 1990s, the Emmanuel Church continued to serve as a community centre, graveyard, and historic site for *Prairieleut*. Although Emmanuel had ceased to hold services on a regular basis, occasionally it was the scene of social/religious gatherings for a still active Ladies Aid group who made quilts to support missions, marriages, an annual Thanksgiving service, and communal barbecues.[57]

The EMB had originally formed in Nebraska and Minnesota, where they were first known as "Defenseless Mennonite Brethren" because of their strict pacifist stance. Their missionaries initially arrived in Manitoba in 1897, where they developed an unlikely combination of Russian pietism, American evangelism, traditional Mennonite theology, and acculturated business practices. Meanwhile, General Conference

Mennonites, largely from the Midwest (Kansas, Oklahoma, Minnesota) but also directly from Russia or via Manitoba, settled at Hague (and nearby Hochfeld and Neuanlage), the Hoffnungsfeld, Great Deer, and Concordia districts near Borden, Langham, Osler, Warman, and Aberdeen in 1910–12. General Conference Mennonites were similar to the Mennonite Brethren in many respects but had even freer sermons and did not practise immersion baptism; they emerged as the most liberal of Mennonite subdivisions. With the movement of the original *Rosenort Gemeinde* settlers around Rosthern into the General Conference, the latter became the most numerous Mennonites in Saskatchewan.

The exodus of several thousand conservative *Sommerfelder/Bergthaler* and Old Colony Mennonites from Saskatchewan and Manitoba to Mexico and Paraguay in 1922–28 was offset to some extent by a renewed mass influx of Mennonites, as well as German Lutherans, from Russia, though these latest immigrants usually did not choose to settle in communities evacuated by conservative Mennonites. The Canadian Mennonite Colonization Board was organized in 1922, and the Lutheran Immigration Board the following year, to assist the remaining Mennonites and Lutherans in Russia and postwar refugee camps to escape from famine and the new Communist regime, atheistic and unsympathetic to the German minorities. By the time the Soviet government forbade further emigration in 1930, 19,891 Mennonites and 12,310 Lutherans had come to Canada; 7,828 of the Mennonites, joined by small groups of Lutherans, settled in Saskatchewan (close to 3,000 in the Rosthern settlement in 1923 alone). The Canada Colonization Association, the boards, and the ministers cooperated in settling the immigrants on tracts of land recently placed on the market—often large farms were forced to divide and sell due to high overhead during deflation. Commissions of 1.25% were paid by the CCA to a board or vice versa for finding land and subsidizing settlement.[58]

The influx of *Russländer* (Russian Mennonites arriving in the 1920s distinguished from the *Kanadier*, who arrived earlier) was met with some opposition. In 1919, the Canadian government had passed orders-in-council prohibiting Mennonites as well as Hutterites and Doukhobors from entering Canada to settle. When the orders were repealed in 1922 by the new Liberal government, English Canadians continued their outcry against the Russian Mennonite "flood," which "flocked to church while our boys fight," "don't conform to Canadian school laws," and bring "unsanitary habits and Asiatic diseases."[59] Mennonite Brethren from Russia distinguished themselves from *Kirchliche*, non-Brethren or "church" Mennonites, though an intermediary group called the *Allianz* tried to mediate between these divergent viewpoints (and soon simply became general Mennonite Brethren).

Farther north, *Rosenorter* settled the more isolated Garthland-Wingard district in 1913; their schoolhouse operated from 1913 to 1965 and their church from 1934 to 1959. During the 1920s, Mennonites continued to extend the settlement farther north, beyond the French around Duck Lake, into the Stoney Lake, Horse Lake, and Wrench Lake districts. The Wingard ferry began operation in 1887, and a post office began the following year; Stoney Lake School District near Wingard Ferry dated from 1891 and the Anglican parish from 1892. With the later arrival of Mennonite settlers in the Stoney Lake and Wrench Lake districts, a community hall was built in 1923. The Garthland district, already settled by *Rosenorter*, became a strongly Mennonite area; a school was established in 1913, a Mennonite church was built there in 1934, and another was built at Horse Lake in 1941 (the former church at Tiefengrund was moved to replace the original church at Horse Lake in 1958). Despite rural depopulation of the area, this church still holds occasional services. However, the Garthland Church closed in 1960, Stoney Lake School in 1964, Garthland School the next year, and Wingard Post Office in 1982. The Mennonite-operated Shekinah Retreat Centre first began to develop in 1979; it now operates as an ecumenical spiritual and ecological centre.

Small numbers of German Lutherans also settled in this extensive Mennonite settlement, such as at Hague (where Volhynian migrants settled and founded the Zion Lutheran congregation), Laird, Langham, Rosthern, and Warman. The former Bethel Lutheran Church in Hague is now Bethel House, serving coffee and dessert. In Rosthern, the first Lutheran service was conducted by visiting Pastor Schmieder, and in 1899 Pastor Rucclus from Neudorf organized Christus-Gemeinde (Christ Lutheran Church), which merged in 1947 with Trinity Lutheran Church, organized by Pastor Gehrke of Lemberg in town in 1911. Another former German Lutheran congregation was St. Matthew at Waldheim (1937–43).

Today the Rosthern and Saskatchewan Valley settlement, originally covering at least forty-two townships in six rural municipalities, includes about 8,400 people of German origin. This largest Mennonite settlement in Saskatchewan—both in population and in area—extends about eighty kilometres north to south and sixty-six kilometres east to west. The settlement historically included the towns of Martensville (pop. 6,300 at last count), Warman (pop. 4,764 and rapidly growing), Dalmeny (pop. 1,560), Rosthern (pop. 1,382), Langham (pop. 1,120), Waldheim (pop. 868), Hague (pop. 707), and Aberdeen (pop. 527); the incorporated villages of Hepburn (pop. 530) and Laird (pop. 207); and at least seven remaining unincorporated villages or hamlets: Neuanlage (pop. 143), Neuhorst (pop. 126), Blumenheim, Blumenthal (pop. 74), Gruenfeld, Gruenthal, and Edenburg; and numerous other named localities. Back in 1971 the population claiming German origin in these towns and villages ranged from over 90% in Warman (92.4%), Osler (92.3%), and Hague (90.9%); to over 80% in Hepburn (88.7%), Waldheim (87.2%), and Martensville (83.8%); to over 70% in Dalmeny (77.6%) and Laird (77.1%); and to a majority or close to it in Langham (58.7%), Rosthern (47.0%), and Aberdeen (41.8%). However, with rampant suburban growth—especially in Warman, Martensville, and Dalmeny—the original Mennonite character of these communities close to Saskatoon will inevitably disappear. In fact, all three communities have surpassed Rosthern as the largest towns in the settlement. Martensville grew suddenly after Isaac Martens' land was subdivided for residential development during the 1960s: it had not become a named community until 1954, it became an incorporated village in 1966, it became a town just three years later, and it gained over 1,000 new residents in 1976–81, reaching over 3,000 by the end of the 1980s and over 6,000 today, qualifying for city status in November 2009. Warman, with more than 7,000 residents, became a city in October 2012. Martensville now has the greatest number of commuters into Saskatoon of any suburban community: 1,870 a weekday, followed by Warman with 1,400, Dalmeny with 470, Langham with 280, Osler with 235, and Aberdeen with 130.[60] Osler and Hepburn, also relatively close to the city, are growing, but all other communities within the settlement have recently been losing population, including Hague, which had been elevated to town status in 1991. The city of Saskatoon, just south of the Mennonite settlement, contained over 10,000 Mennonites by 1991, making it the third largest urban Mennonite population in Canada after Winnipeg and Vancouver.[61]

The Swift Current–Vermilion Hills Settlement (1903–)

A second and even more extensive Mennonite settlement developed around Swift Current and Herbert, then spread northeastward to include the Vermilion Hills region. This vast settlement had its origins in two rather different Mennonite colonies established immediately east and south of Swift Current. First to arrive were Sommerfelder Mennonites from Manitoba, who settled the Excelsior area—including Plumi Moos Hill or Rush Lake Butte—north of Herbert and Rush Lake by 1903. Mennonite Brethren were settling around Main Centre and Gouldtown by 1905; the Bethel Mennonite Brethren Church was established at Old Main Centre and Bethania School and Church between Main Centre and Gouldtown respectively in 1906 and 1912 (then finally closed in 1951 and 1969); and the Lobethal and Schonau School Districts north of Main Centre were established respectively in 1905 and 1913. Mennonite Brethren were joined by General Conference Mennonites at Herbert and Rush Lake by 1904–05; within a couple of years, at least a hundred Mennonite families had settled there, most from Russian German Mennonite colonies in the United States (the Wiens residence at Herbert [1912] is a heritage property). General Conference Mennonites also settled in the Capeland district northwest of Main Centre in 1913. Mennonites also settled in rural districts around Waldeck (between Swift Current and Rush Lake), including Moscow, Spenst, and Bode.

Meanwhile, a more conservative Mennonite colony was developing south of Swift Current. In 1904, Old Colony/*Reinländer* Mennonites from the Manitoba reserves petitioned the dominion government for a reserve of six townships. Within a year, twenty-two villages had been founded in this colony, many named after former Old Colony villages in South Russia and Manitoba and duplicating similar conservative communities in the Saskatchewan Valley settlement: Wymark, Blumenhof (which retains a *Rudnerweider* congregation), Blumenort, Chortitz, Rheinfeld, Rhineland, Schantzenfeld, Schoenfeld, and Springfeld continue to be well-defined villages, whereas Hamburg, Hochfeld, Hochstadt, Hoffnungsfeld/Hopefield, Neuendorf, Neuhoffnung, Nord-Gnadenthal, Sud-Gnadenthal, Rosenbach, Rosengart, Rosenhof, Rosenort, Schoenwiese, and Sommerfeld are remembered only as localities. Wymark, though depopulated by the large exodus of conservative Mennonites during the 1920s, became an incorporated village in 1928 — but not for long; it was downgraded to hamlet status, then designated as an organized hamlet in 1981. So, too, was Chortitz designated as an organized hamlet a couple of years earlier. Actually, the Wymark Evangelical Mennonite Conference Church is located there, six kilometres from Wymark. By 1911, there were already approximately 4,600 Mennonites in these settlements.[62]

From these two nuclei, Mennonite settlement expanded rapidly throughout the general region. General Conference Mennonites established Emmaus congregations within the Old Colony area at Wymark, Schoenfeld, Rheinland, Blumenhof, and McMahon and at Syke's Farm, Kidron–Gull Lake, and Pella-Neville, while Mennonite Brethren built a church at McMahon and the Evangelical Mennonite Mission Conference churches at Wymark and Blumenhof. Swift Current and Wymark have

Kleine Gemeinde Evangelical Mennonite Conference Fellowship congregations. To the southeast, Mennonite Brethren established churches in the Elim settlement around Kelstern (1907), Flowing Well (Gnadenau congregation, 1907), and Woodrow (1909); General Conference Mennonites established a church at Neville (1914). To the northeast, Mennonite Brethren congregations included Bruderfeld (1901), Main Centre, Herbert (1905), Lichtfeld (1908), Greenfarm/Grunfeld (1912), Turnhill (1913), Beechy (Friedensheim congregation, 1925), and Lucky Lake (1943); General Conference Mennonites were found around Morse (1920s), Gouldtown (1926), Eyebrow (1929), Tugaske, Central Butte, Lawson, Gilroy, and Elbow (all during 1920s). The Faresfield district north of Rush Lake was also settled by *Russländer* in 1923 and the neighbouring Friedensfeld district by Krimmer Mennonite Brethren during the late 1920s (today the former Friedensfeld KMB Church [1929] is Peace Lutheran Church, a heritage site). To the west, small Mennonite Brethren and General Conference Mennonite congregations were established in many communities.

Lutheran settlement extended north to the Chaplin-Ernfold-Uren area, and Lutheran minorities were found within extensive Mennonite settlement in the Swift Current and Vermilion Hills regions (e.g., at Swift Current, Waldeck, Herbert, and Rush Lake). Former Lutheran congregations and missions within this predominantly Mennonite settlement included St. Paul at Morse (1910–90), Christ at Rush Lake (1910–50), St. John at Rush Lake (1910–26), Trinity in the Green Prairie district near Central Butte (1917–90), Waldeck (1933), and McMahon (1940s).

Given the expansion and widespread distribution of Mennonite settlement in this region of Saskatchewan, it is difficult to estimate, with any real accuracy, the total Mennonite population, yet people claiming German origin numbered approximately 3,600 in 1971, excluding the city of Swift Current; if Swift Current is included, then another 4,000 should be added. But aside from the strongly Mennonite villages immediately south of Swift Current, only three towns or villages retained majority German proportions by 1971: Herbert (65.2%), Waldeck (54.2%), and Morse (50.5%). Swift Current now contains 14,946 residents and is growing. However, beyond this small city, virtually all of the original Mennonite communities are currently losing population, including Herbert (pop. 742), Waldeck (pop. 294), and Wymark (pop. 144); Rush Lake now has only about fifty residents and Chortitz only twenty-six; only five were left in Main Centre in 2001, and now none remains. The business district of Waldeck had all but disappeared already by the 1980s. Rush Lake, once a thriving community during the 1920s (some 700 farms were in the surrounding area), lost a third of its residents during the Depression years (only 100 remained by 1936); it rebounded, though, to over 200 by 1961, but by the 1970s fewer than half the number of farmers remained, and the community was characterized by vacant lots and abandoned businesses. Other communities, such as McMahon, are mere hamlets. Despite this decline, Herbert still tries to maintain something of a Mennonite tradition—*faspa* is served in the former railway station during summer months. Incidentally, Senator Jack Wiebe, a former lieutenant governor of Saskatchewan, hailed from this community. The extent of this settlement is virtually identical to that of the Saskatchewan Valley settlement: approximately eighty kilometres north to south and sixty-six kilometres east to west, covering all or part of six rural municipalities.

CHAPTER 4

Other Mennonite Settlements

Although the Rosthern–Saskatchewan Valley and Swift Current–Vermilion Hills settlements are really the only extensive Mennonite settlements in Saskatchewan, many smaller Mennonite concentrations are widely scattered throughout the prairie portion of the province, mostly dating from the *Russländer* migration—the last substantial emigration from the Mennonite colonies in Russia—during the 1920s. The migration of *Russländer* resulted not only in the expansion of existing Mennonite colonies in Saskatchewan but also in the foundation of new settlements as large farms were broken up in the Dundurn-Hanley area, Fiske-Herschel area, and other areas.

At an early date, a Mennonite concentration had developed close to the main Saskatchewan Valley settlement, in neighbouring rural districts northeast of the village of Borden (pop. 223). Mennonite Brethren had settled at Hoffnungsfeld as early as 1904; General Conference Mennonites had settled at Bethel/Great Deer by 1912 as well as in the Clear Spring and Concordia districts; and Mennonite settlement extended into the Walter Scott, Halcyonia, King George, and Thistledale districts.

Farther northwest, some ninety families settled marginal lands to form the Meeting Lake settlement, situated in the Thickwood Hills, in 1926–30.[63] By 1947, more Mennonites immigrated to the Meeting Lake settlement and other settlements from Eastern Europe in the wake of the Second World War. In 1971, the Meeting Lake and Thickwood Hills settlement included about 1,500 people of German origin in and near two incorporated villages (Medstead and Rabbit Lake), three unincorporated villages or hamlets (Fairholme, Mayfair, and Glenbush), and at least twenty named localities. The most recent census data counted 148 residents in Medstead and 113 in Rabbit Lake; Glenbush is an unlisted hamlet, and Mullingar is down to just five residents. Mennonites and other Germans formed about a third (34.3%) of the population of Medstead in 1971 and over a quarter (26.0%) of that of Rabbit Lake, but they probably predominated in the smaller communities. *Bruderthaler* established a congregation at Fairholme in 1927; the Mennonite Brethren church at Glenbush dates from 1928, the General Conference one from 1934; other General Conference congregations were established at Rabbit Lake in 1926 and Mayfair in 1928 and 1936. The Hoffnungsfeld congregation centred at Rabbit Lake served congregations at Bournemouth, Glenbush (including the Kunz district), Mayfair, and Mullingar (formerly Remnant). South of this settlement, some Mennonite families settled in the Lorenzo, Fielding, and Speers areas. Former German Lutheran congregations and missions in this small settlement included St. John at Meeting Lake (founded by German immigrants from Poland in 1928, closed in 1969), Peace at Belbutte (1928–67), Peace at Medstead (an Ohio Synod congregation, 1931–54), a Missouri Synod mission at Medstead (early 1930s), and Christ at Glenbush.

Other General Conference Mennonite congregations were established northwest of Meadow Lake: Daisy Meadow, Dorintosh, and Capasin (1931), Immanuel at Pierceland (1931), Compass (1933), serving also Barnes Crossing, and Meadow Lake (1935); Mennonite Brethren churches were also established at Meadow Lake (1935), Compass (1938), and Pierceland (1939). Pierceland is a fairly large community (498 residents and growing), Dorintosh smaller and less active (127 residents and static), Compass little more than an unlisted hamlet.

In the west-central region, an early Mennonite congregation was established by Mennonite Brethren in Christ at Alsask, on the Alberta border, in 1910 (Old Mennonites had settled around nearby Acadia Valley in Alberta); today Alsask has a declining population of 129. During the 1920s, *Russländer* Mennonites affiliated with the General Conference settled in the Herschel-Fiske area (the Ebenfeld congregation dates from 1925 and also serves Glidden, Kerrobert, Kindersley, and Superb) as well as around Springwater, Harris, Ardath, and Major. Fiske contained only eighty-one residents at last count, Herschel just thirty. During the 1920s and 1930s, Mennonite Brethren settled in the Lashburn-Waseca-Maidstone area.

Mennonites from a variety of different backgrounds settled in compact pockets in central Saskatchewan from an early date. Some Old Mennonite families from the Kitchener-Waterloo region in Ontario established the small Sharon congregation at Guernsey in 1905 and settled the Waterloo district. Nearby, General Conference Mennonites from Kansas and Oklahoma formed the Nordstern (North Star) congregation at Drake in 1906–13, served by homesteader-pastors. Among the early settlers were Jacob Schellenberg and his wife, Elisabeth Kroeker, who immigrated from Arkadok near Saratov. For the Christmas program held in one home in 1906, a small poplar tree was decorated with homemade candles; so many people arrived that they had to open a window to get fresh air despite the intense cold, as one settler reminisced.[64] Among the more interesting farm buildings with traditional architectural features in the Drake area are the Steiner home and barn (1915) and the round stone barn on the Bartel farm (1927).[65] Drake Meat Processors has been a family-run business for more than sixty years, long specializing in traditional farmer's sausage, summer sausage, and garlic coils. Today Drake has 232 residents, Guernsey eighty-eight. As Mennonite settlement spread, as far west as the Eigenheim district north of Little Manitou Lake, other General Conference churches were established in the general region: Bethany at Watrous (1930) and Lampard and the Philadelphia Mennonite Brethren congregation at Watrous. Mennonites also settled around Colonsay, Nokomis, and Lanigan. Wynyard has a *Rudnerweider* congregation. The village of Jansen was named after Peter Jansen, from Jansen, Nebraska, who envisaged a Mennonite colony of forty-four townships west of the Quill Lakes; this grand scheme was never brought to completion, but smaller numbers of Mennonites did settle in this general area centred on Prairie Rose RM.[66]

The *Nordheimer Mennoniten Gemeinde* (Nordheim Mennonite Congregation), affiliated with the General Conference, settled around Hanley and Dundurn in 1924–27. This settlement again was part of the immigration of *Russländer*. The Mennonite Settlement Board purchased twenty large farms. The Sheldon Farm Land Company was formed and controlled fifteen sections of farmland in a single bloc, which included ten individual and two communal farms, west of Hanley. Thirty-two families were settled there, another five on the smaller Rowse farm nearby. Four families were settled on the Peterson farm, in the Indi district at the edge of Blackstrap Valley between Hanley and Dundurn. Another large group of settlers, known as *der Dundurn Gruppe*, were settled between Dundurn and northeast around the Pleasant Point district: ten families on the Meilecke farm, fifteen on the two Schwager farms, eight on the Lietzaw farm, and six on the Strehlow farm. During the 1940s, the families around Pleasant Point were at last able to celebrate the final payment of the *reiseschuld* (transportation debt). And seven families settled on widely scattered farms well to the south near Elbow. The Hanley Mennonite Church had its humble beginning with the ordination of the first elder, Johann Klassen, by Reverend David Toews of the Rosenort Church in a machine shed on the Sheldon farm in June 1925. The church was dedicated in 1929, and a new church was built in 1956. Sheldon School operated from 1930 to 1957. The Mennonites around Pleasant Point were led by *vorsänger* (lead singer) Heinz Koop and reader Heinrich Klassen; the first minister was Reverend Isaac Epp, but he died in November 1925. The steepled church at Pleasant Point had originally been built by Moravians, who shared it with the rapidly increasing number of Mennonites in the district after 1928; in 1931, Reverend Gerhard Zacharius (ordained in his home community in Russia in 1921) arrived, but the Mennonites did not actually buy the church until 1950. The Dundurn Mennonite Church in Dundurn itself had originally been built by Methodists in 1906; later it became Adventist; then in 1929 it was sold to Mennonites, who had previously been led by a *vorsänger* on the Meilecke farm with congregants also from the first Schwager farm. A fourth church serving the few Mennonite families near Elbow was added in 1953, when a country school was purchased jointly by the Nordheim Congregation and Brethren and turned into a simple little church in 1956.

As a whole, the *Nordheimer* settlement was a cohesive and active Mennonite community that long made a consistent effort to maintain Mennonite traditions and the German language. During the early years of settlement, *Biblische Geschichten Deutsch* (Bible German) was used in the Hanley church, which held an annual *gemeinde feste* (community picnic) since 1933, with entertainment provided by *das Sheldon Blas Orchestra* (the Sheldon brass band), and *altenfeste* (honouring seniors) since 1961; a *Jugendverein* (Christian Youth Endeavour) was organized in 1937 and a *Kraenzchen* or *Schnettje verein* (Junior Aid); and German-language *Sonntagsschule* (Sunday School) and a German summer school "for religion and German instruction" were long active. At Pleasant Point, *Der Chor von Pleasant Point* sang German hymns; a German school taught during winter months until 1970, and language instruction was provided for two weeks during the summer in *die Deutsche sommerschule* (German summer school); religious instruction was given in German until 1969. Closer to Dundurn, *Hochdeutsch* (High German) was taught privately in a farmhouse on the first Schwager farm, then in town at a German school, since 1927. Over time, the original families who formed the *Nordheimer* settlement have expanded—adult members of the Nordheim Congregation in the half century from 1925 to 1975 included ninety Dycks, sixty-two Klassens, fifty-four Epps, fifty-one Friesens, forty-two Penners, forty-one Martens, thirty-six Thiessens, thirty-two Neufelds, thirty-two Froeses, thirty-two Hildebrands, thirty-one Peters, twenty-nine Koops, twenty-six Harders, twenty-six Zacharias, twenty-four Schellenbergs, twenty-four Patkaus, twenty-two Kroegers, twenty-two Loewens, twenty-two Wiens, twenty Remples, among many other family names.[67]

In the east-central region, a congregation at Wynyard was established by the Evangelical Mennonite Mission Conference. One was also established at Foam Lake by the Mennonite Brethren. Mennonites also settled around Parkview, Wishart, and Sheho, and General Conference Mennonites established Immanuel congregation at Beaver Dale.

To the northeast, a *Sommerfelder* Mennonite reserve was founded in the Carrot River area, including *Bergthaler* in the Blue Jay district, as early as 1908; later General

Conference congregations served Carrot River (1926), Bethany at Lost River (1916), Petaigan (1931), and Erwood, with a Mennonite Brethren one at Carrot River (1926) as well; *Prairieleut* moved from the Langham area to resettle around Nipawin and Kelvington during the 1930s but did not establish KMB congregations there. Similarly, an isolated Old Colony Mennonite settlement in the Swan Plain area, a marginal, heavily treed area near the Manitoba border, was later served by a General Conference mission. *Kleine Gemeinde* EMC Fellowship congregations are located at Endeavour, Creighton, Pelly, and Hudson Bay and a Holdeman (Church of God in Christ Mennonite) congregation at Hyas. The predominantly Ukrainian village of Dnieper, north of Yorkton, was originally called Menofield, then Mennofeldt. Newfield, west of Codette, was an anglicized version of Neufeld.

In south-central and southeastern Saskatchewan, Mennonites settled in the Truax-Dummer-Parry-Brooking area during the 1930s as well as around Carnduff and Fleming. Parry now has only eighteen inhabitants, while Truax, Brooking, and Dummer have never been more than hamlets or rural localities. Ukrainian Mennonites from Kansas and South Dakota settled the Reimche district near Woodrow by 1910; the school closed in 1951, and the North Country Mennonite Brethren congregation is now the Woodrow Gospel Mission. Woodrow has fewer than fifteen remaining residents.

Rural depopulation has taken an extensive toll on Mennonite settlements in Saskatchewan. Most of the more conservative Mennonite communities were already eradicated or depleted by the 1920s, though some have survived. Rural schoolhouses, post offices, and churches began to close as early as the 1930s; virtually all were gone by the 1950s, except for the occasional country congregation that likely had become part of an extensive network served by a centralized church. Nonetheless, Mennonites have clearly played a large role in the historical settlement of Saskatchewan.

The overall number of Mennonites in Saskatchewan has remained relatively stable since 1940 (11,518 then compared with 11,031 half a century later), as have the numbers of more "progressive" or "liberal" Mennonites (e.g., General Conference Mennonites/Mennonite Church Canada: 5,063 vs. 4,529; Mennonite Brethren—including Evangelical Mennonite Brethren and Krimmer Mennonite Brethren—3,604 vs. 3,215). Today the MCC has approximately 33,000 members and 224 churches in seven provinces, including the Mennonite Church Saskatchewan (established in 1959), which has 3,600 members in thirty-four congregations. The slightly larger Canadian Conference of Mennonite Brethren Churches claims 36,000 members in 248 churches in eight provinces, including 3,400 members in thirty congregations of the Saskatchewan Conference of Mennonite Brethren Churches (established in 1946). However, conservative Mennonites have declined or been minimal: back in 1917, Old Colony Mennonites totalled 2,015, but with many departures, combined with gradual movement toward less conservative branches, they declined to 1,200 by 1940 and just 750 in 1990. Today there are approximately 9,000 Old Colony or *Furstenländer* Mennonites in twenty-one congregations across Canada (mostly Ontario and Manitoba), including 264 members of a single congregation in Saskatchewan. The Chortitzer Mennonite Conference (*Sommerfelder/Bergthaler*), established back in 1874, now claims 1,700 members in thirteen congregations, ten of which are in Manitoba and only one in Saskatchewan. The East Reserve Bergthaler in Manitoba became the Chortitzer Mennonite

Conference, but the Bergthaler Mennonite Church of Manitoba joined the MCC in 1972. The Sommerfelder Mennonite Church of Manitoba counted 5,000 members in thirteen congregations, but just a single congregation, Swift Current, in Saskatchewan. This church has repeatedly been depleted by emigration to Mexico in 1922 (with some *Bergthaler* and Old Colony Mennonites from Saskatchewan), Paraguay in 1928, and both Mexico and Paraguay in 1948; Saskatchewan *Bergthaler* left for Paraguay in 1948, Honduras in 1951, and Bolivia in 1962. But most of the *Bergthaler* congregations in Saskatchewan were not connected to the Manitoba churches; their members numbered 958 in 1917, 900 in 1990, and currently over 800 in six congregations. However, as if this is not confusing enough, higher counts of *Bergthaler* (e.g., 1,537 in 1940) have included *Sommerfelder* (who numbered 556 just in the Swift Current region at the time). One independent *Bergthaler* congregation, called the Old Bergthaler Mennonite Church, located near Hague, is affiliated with the Reinland Mennonite Church in Manitoba. The Evangelical Mennonite Mission Conference (EMMC; the former *Rudnerweider*, which separated from the *Sommerfelder* in 1937) numbered over 4,000 nationally in twenty-nine congregations but in Saskatchewan numbered only 650 by 1990 and most recently 374 in six congregations. In 1958, half of the *Sommerfelder/Chortitzer* congregation in Swift Current split and joined the EMMC. The Evangelical Mennonite Conference (descended from the *Kleine Gemeinde*) had some 7,000 members nationally in fifty-nine congregations, including 517 members in Saskatchewan in 1990, down to 357 in six congregations according to the most recent data. The Holdeman Mennonites (Church of God in Christ Mennonite) now have over 4,000 members in fifty-two congregations across Canada and have grown in Saskatchewan from 350 members in 1990 to the present 541 in seven congregations. And the remaining descendants of the Old Mennonites of the Guernsey area are now affiliated with the MCC. The Brethren in Christ now have over 3,000 members nationally in forty-three congregations, all in Ontario except for four in Saskatchewan.[68]

HUTTERITE COLONIES

Both the Mennonites and the Hutterites trace their origins to the Swiss Anabaptist movements of the sixteenth century, and both groups immigrated, directly or indirectly, to the Canadian Prairies from German colonies in South Russia, as had most of the German Catholics. But in the intervening period of over two centuries, their histories were quite distinct. While the Mennonite group was forming in the Netherlands, another communal Anabaptist group was developing in the South Tyrol (then in Austria, now in Italy) as well as later in southern Germany and Moravia (now within the Czech Republic). In 1528, the first real *bruderhof* (communal village or colony) was established in Moravia. Five years later it was joined by a South Tyrolean preacher, Jacob Hutter, from whom the sect acquired its name. Despite repeated persecution (Hutter was burned at the stake in 1536), by the end of the century there were as many as 70,000 Hutterites and over ninety *bruderhofe*. Reduced in numbers by the Austro-Turkish and Thirty Years Wars, by 1622 they had all been driven from Moravia; some 20,000 had emigrated to Slovakia, Hungary, and Transylvania (now in Romania), where they had established over thirty new colonies. However, persecution continued, particularly by Jesuits seeking to convert them in Slovakia, and there was further attrition. A small number were briefly re-established at Kreutz, Transylvania, in 1763–70; caught in the midst of the Russo-Turkish Wars, 123 of them trekked to Russia (present-day Ukraine) to found the Vishenka and Radichev colonies (by 1802).[69]

Finally, their rather unsettled existence in Europe was terminated altogether in 1874 when all of them, numbering nearly 800 by then, moved to South Dakota, along with Mennonites and other Russian German Protestant groups escaping from the repeal of their military exemption by the Russian government. The *Schmiedeleut*, *Dariusleut*, and *Lehrerleut* sects separately founded three initial colonies from 1874 to 1877. But about half of the Hutterites decided to homestead individually rather than communally, thus becoming *Prairieleut*, merging eventually with the Mennonites who settled in the same areas (where some congregation names—Hutterthal, Neu Hutterthaler, and Hutterdorf—recalled their Hutterite origins). Six of these congregations in the Dakotas were Krimmer Mennonite Brethren; the rest were independent *Prairieleut*. Similarly, in Saskatchewan *Prairieleut* established the Emmanuel Krimmer Mennonite Brethren congregation in 1917 and settled in the Wurtzburg district near Langham; they also played a role in the Zoar congregations at Langham and Waldheim.[70] The First World War hastened the exodus of *Dariusleut* and *Lehrerleut* from the United States to Alberta and *Schmiedeleut* to Manitoba in 1918.

Each Hutterite colony averages approximately 100 men, women, and children. Hutterites have tended to have a high but recently declining birth rate and a large family size. So when a colony's population grows well beyond the average, a new "daughter" colony is founded, about every fifteen years. Thus, the Hutterite population as a whole and the number of colonies have grown rapidly. Prior to 1949, there were no Hutterite colonies in Saskatchewan; however, land restrictions in Alberta forced many colonies there to expand into neighbouring Saskatchewan (Manitoba Hutterites were less affected by such restrictions so did not move into Saskatchewan). Since then, at least sixty-two colonies have been established in Saskatchewan, equally divided between the *Dariusleut* and the *Lehrerleut*. The latest data reveal that there are approximately 30,000 Hutterites in Canada in 339 colonies.[71]

Hutterite colonies have tended to be concentrated in western regions of Saskatchewan, though they are becoming increasingly widespread. In the southwestern region, there are five colonies in the immediate vicinity of Maple Creek (in the following list, L = *Lehrerleut*, D = *Dariusleut*): Cypress L (1952), Spring Creek D (1956), New Wolf Creek or Downey Lake D (1958), Box Elder D (1960), and more recently Dinsmore L (1978).

Farther east, in the southwest region, another nineteen colonies are found in the Cypress Hills and around Swift Current. Bench L (1949–52) west of Shaunavon was the first colony in Saskatchewan and the initial *Lehrerleut* colony. During the 1950s and 1960s, it was soon followed by Tompkins L (1952), West Bench D (1960) near Ravenscrag, Simmie D (1961), Waldeck/Friesen L (1963), Main Centre L (1963), Sand Lake L (1964) near Masefield, and Hodgeville D (1971); during the 1970s by Ponteix D (1971), Swift Current/Ruskin D (1976), and Vanguard L (1980); during the 1980s by Carmichael L (1983), Spring Lake D (1988) near Neville, Bone Creek L (1988) south of Gull Lake, Webb D (1988), and Butte L (1989) near Bracken; and most recently by New Spring Creek D

(1993) northwest of Shaunavon, Earview D (1997) near Gull Lake, and Garden Plain L (2001) near Frontier.

Six colonies have been established in the Regina and Moose Jaw area: first Arm River D (1964) near Bethune, then Baildon L (1967), Huron L (1969) near Brownlee, Lajord D (1977), Belle Plaine D (1981), and Rose Valley L (1985) near Verwood.

In the Sand Hills area north of Maple Creek, five colonies have been founded: first Estuary D (1958), then Haven L (1967) near Fox Valley, Abbey L (1971), Wheatland L (1987) near Abbey, and Pennant L (2001).

Nineteen colonies are widely scattered through the west country farther north: during the 1960s Hillsvale D (1961) near Baldwinton, Glidden L (1963), Smiley L (1968), Fort Pitt D (1969), and Sanctuary L (1970) near Kyle; during the 1970s Lakeview D (1970) near Scott, Rosetown L (1970), Willow Park D (1977) near Tessier, Beechy L (1978), Golden View L (1978) west of Biggar, and Springwater D (1979); during the 1980s Big Rose D (1980) south of Biggar, Eagle Creek D (1981), Eatonia L (1985), Sunnydale D (1988) at Sonningdale, and Springfield L (1989) near Kindersley; and most recently Sovereign L (1995) east of Rosetown, Scott D (1997) near Scott, and Valley Centre L (2001) north of Rosetown. Several other colonies have been developed north and south of Saskatoon: Leask D (1953) and Riverview D (1956) near Saskatoon were the earliest *Dariusleut* colonies in the province, followed by Hillcrest D (1969) near Dundurn, Clear Springs L (1971) near Kenaston, and most recently Riverbend D (1996) west of Waldheim and Green Leaf D (2001) near Marcelin.

Finally, to the northeast, a couple of colonies have been established: Quill Lake D (1975) and Star City D (1978). By 2006, data sources indicate that there were already thirty-one *Lehrerleut* and thirty *Dariusleut* colonies in Saskatchewan (with more currently in the planning or construction phase).

All Hutterites continue to live in their own colonies, which are small in population yet often control extensive farmland. Although they sell their produce (grain, livestock, poultry, vegetable crops) on the public market, they live within sequestered colonies where strict conformity is ensured by unique dress, religious education (together with limited "public education" from an outside teacher at the colony school), language (they converse in an archaic German dialect), authority (each colony is ultimately headed by a male boss), occupational specificity (male and female jobs are assigned even before adulthood), property held in common, and orderly lifestyle (e.g., preparing meals and dining together, the daily routine, and even buildings arranged in rectangular order). Because Hutterites own their farmland and machinery in common, their farming is usually a profitable venture. However, the rapid expansion of Hutterites' territorial acquisitions has resulted in contested legislation restricting concentration and expansion of Hutterite colonies, initially in Alberta (as noted above) and then later, to a lesser extent, in Saskatchewan, where rather than comprehensive legislation occasional disputes have arisen over legislation enacted by particular rural municipalities. Moreover, Hutterites have traditionally tended to be non-political, to buy farm machinery on a wholesale rather than localized basis, and to claim tax exemptions as a religious organization, which have caused further problems in Hutterite relations with neighbouring local communities. Today, though, Hutterites are rightly respected as prosperous farmers and a most interesting part of the diverse Saskatchewan rural population.

DUTCH SETTLEMENTS

In 1981, 17,215 Saskatchewan residents claimed Dutch ethnic origin, whereas in 2006 the census revealed that 35,375 residents of Saskatchewan claimed to be of Dutch origin—5,895 (16.7%) completely and 29,480 (83.3%) partially. An additional 655 people claimed to be Flemish (hence originally Dutch speaking), and possibly some of the 9,125 people of Belgian origin were also Flemish; another sixty people claimed to be Frisian (though Frisian is a distinct Germanic language, it is spoken primarily in the Netherlands). Close to a million Canadians are entirely or partially of Dutch descent. However, in Saskatchewan far fewer people have ever claimed to be Dutch speaking than to be of Dutch origin, at least partly because some Mennonites—who traditionally have spoken a German dialect—have claimed Dutch origin (Menno Simons, the progenitor of the Mennonite faith, lived in Friesland in the Netherlands, and the common Mennonite surname Friesen is indicative of Frisian origin). In 2001, only 1,930 Saskatchewan residents recognized Dutch as their mother tongue.

The first Dutch settlers were lured to Western Canada by Canadian immigration advertising, which promised *200 millioen akkers voor kolonisatie ... eene vrije haardstede ... in het groote Noord Westen van* Amerika (200 million acres for colonization ... a free homestead ... in the great North West of America). In 1892–93, Frisian farmers from the northern Netherlands arrived in Winnipeg, the vanguard of a larger group of Dutch immigrants assisted by the Christian Emigration Society, to homestead around Yorkton, Saskatchewan, though only a small number actually made it to their destination—most remained in Manitoba. By 1904, Dutch immigrants, primarily from Iowa and Montana but including some directly from the Netherlands, settled in southern Alberta around Granum (originally Calvinists from Groningen), Nobleford, and Monarch (where their settlement was named Nieuw Nyverdal after their place of origin in Overyssel). Subsequently, a Dutch Catholic settlement developed around Strathmore, also in southern Alberta, in 1908 and a Dutch Calvinist settlement, Neerlandia, near Barrhead in northern Alberta, in 1912. These successful settlements would encourage further Dutch settlement in the Prairie Provinces.

In Saskatchewan, Dutch Americans settled near Moose Jaw in 1908, then in the Cramersburg rural district in the RM of Miry Creek near Abbey in 1910. The first settlers (named De Vries, Veltkamp, Vry, Van der Wall, Leep) were men who lived in tents while they built wood houses and barns, before being joined by their wives and children. The railway arrived in nearby Cabri in 1912, facilitating settlement. However, the settlement already started to break up in 1919–23 due to drought, influenza, hard winters, light crop yields, and low grain-buying prices; several families returned to the United States. After just twelve years of settlement, the church was sold to the Anglicans and moved to Cabri. The Cramersburg Post Office closed in 1964. Venlo School (named after the town of Venlo, Netherlands) operated from 1914 to 1948. The original Dutch Reformed Church (1913), now St. Andrew's Anglican Church, is a historic site.

Meanwhile, though, Edam (named after a place of origin of the settlers in the Netherlands), northwest of North Battleford, became a post office in 1908, continued to be settled in 1914–17, and became a bicultural Catholic community shared with French neighbours. By 1971, there could not have been more than seventy-five people claiming Dutch ethnic origin in Edam and area (fifty in the village plus another twenty-five in the encompassing rural municipality of Turtle River, comprising just 13.9% of the village residents and outnumbered almost two to one by French and more than three to one by residents of British ethnic origin). Nonetheless, today Edam tries to retain a unique Dutch character: lamp standards decorated with banners picturing windmills, the sign at the entry to the community announcing that this is a little bit of Holland in the prairies, the tidy garden of one family with a Dutch surname sporting a small model of a windmill, shop signs illustrating windmills. ...

Other rural Dutch concentrations emerged around Leoville and Morse, and the Dutch Hollow School District south of Willow Bunch (1913–55) was likely named by the Van den Heuvel brothers, Dutch-origin settlers who arrived in this district from Wisconsin and operated the Heuvel coal mine. The short-lived rural Slager Post Office near Tribune (1905–13) was named after its first postmaster, Mindert Slager, who first immigrated from Friesland to Illinois, then moved on to Saskatchewan. Dutch immigrants continued to arrive in urban Saskatoon, where they established a Dutch Reformed (later Christian Reformed) congregation that was long served by Dutch-origin pastors.

A small concentration of Flemish (Dutch dialect) –speaking immigrants from Belgium began to develop around Manor, in the southeastern region, after 1912. This settlement resulted from chain migration from the rural communities of Lommel and Kerkhoven in the Belgian province of Limburg (Lommel is just four kilometres from the Dutch border and within thirty kilometres from the Dutch city of Eindhoven, while Kerkhoven is about nine kilometres south of Lommel). Among the first settlers was Henri Clemens, who was instrumental in recruiting about thirty families from this district, with the assistance of the office of the Belgian vice-consul in Manor (the government of Belgium established a consulate in the predominantly francophone neighbouring community of Forget in 1911, then transferred it to Manor in 1915-21). The initial settlers were soon joined by a large contingent of First World War veterans from this same district in Belgium after 1919. At least fourteen Flemish family names were represented in the settlers; a smaller number, with some eight family names, were French-speaking Walloons who intermarried both with the Flemish and other francophone settlers. L'Abbé Hubert Heynen, from Limburg province in the Netherlands, based in Manitoba, reportedly served missions including Forget in both Dutch and French before 1897; however the Flemish-speaking Catholics of the Manor area were initially served respectively by Father Janssen from Forget, who said mass at the local hotel, or by the francophone priest at the nearby French community of Wauchope until 1925. Then in 1929 a vacant bank in Manor served as a church; an actual church, St. Joseph's, was not built until 1950 (it was downgraded as a mission in 1974 and finally closed in 2006). Crop failures due to drought during the 1930s caused the departure of many farmers and the dwindling of the Belgian settlement. However, meanwhile Flemish-origin farmers became widely scattered in the general region, such as at Antler, Fairlight, Moose Mountain, Radville, Weyburn, Gladmar, Ceylon, and Yellow Grass.

GERMAN RESISTANCE TO CHANGE

An extensive study conducted in 1969–72 among 190 families in St. Peter's German Catholic Colony, 244 in the Saskatchewan Valley and Meeting Lake Mennonite settlements, and six in the Riverview Hutterite Colony compared the capability of different generations in German bloc settlements in the north-central region to resist assimilation and to preserve their distinct ethno-religious identities.[72]

As a whole, virtually all of the Hutterites interviewed took for granted the preservation of their unique identity. Among the Mennonites, 21.3% strongly favoured ethnic identity preservation, 54.1% were generally in favour yet somewhat resigned to losing certain aspects of their identity, and the remaining 24.6% seemed indifferent. German Catholics were more mixed in their attitudes: just a single respondent was strongly in favour, almost a third (32.1%) generally in favour, just over a third (34.7%) indifferent, and almost a third (32.6%) actually opposed.[73]

Asked then whether they believed that there has been a loss of ethnic identification for youth, again none of the Hutterites found this to be true (though there have been occasional cases of young men leaving the colonies—but then they cease to be identified as Hutterites). A small proportion of Mennonites (6.6%) noted a major loss, a large majority (85.2%) a minor loss, and only a few (8.2%) little or no loss. German Catholics were of a completely different opinion: 41.1% noted a major loss, 58.9% a minor loss, and none little or no loss.[74] They attributed this to two world wars in which Canada fought Germany, and concomitant discrimination and suspicion of any German activities, together with the desire of younger German Canadians to be more accepted in Canada, to become "more Canadian." Since Mennonites traditionally were pacifists, they were not as affected by this wartime discrimination.

Generational differences were striking, especially for German Catholics, less so for Mennonites, and not at all for Hutterites: 73.0% of German Catholics in the first (immigrant) generation favoured German identity preservation, compared with 34.6% in the second and just 10.5% in the third; among Mennonites, change had come more slowly: 95.3% in the first generation favoured identity preservation, 81.7% in the second, and 64.2% in the third.[75]

The decrease in German-language use in Saskatchewan has been pronounced. Use of the German mother tongue declined among the German-origin population in Saskatchewan from 73% back in 1941 to 58% in 1951, to 40.6% in 1961, but then stabilized to 42.2% in 1971 (only about 10% were actually still speaking German at home). German-language use was more prevalent in the rural bloc settlements than in the urban communities but was declining rapidly: between 1951 and 1971, for example, German mother tongue use declined from 59% among the rural farm population of German origin to 44%, 50% among the rural non-farm population to 46%, and 44% among urban residents to just 16%.[76] As noted, recent census data (2001) reveal that, although the 275,060 people claiming at least some German ethnic origin now comprise over a quarter of the total population of Saskatchewan, just 32,515 (12%) of them were still speaking German as their mother tongue (but likely a much higher proportion—though still a minority—of those claiming to be exclusively of German descent).

In the study sample, all of the Hutterites were bilingual in German and English and were expected to speak their unique German dialect in the colony. Hardly any of the Mennonites (1.6%) and none of the German Catholics could speak only German; 52.5% of the Mennonites were bilingual but preferred to speak German both at home and in the community, compared with just 13.7% of the German Catholics; 14.8% of

Mennonites and 15.8% of German Catholics were bilingual, speaking German at home but English in the community; 28.3% of Mennonites and 64.2% of German Catholics could speak at least some German but used English both at home and in the community; and 2.9% of Mennonites and 6.8% of German Catholics were unfamiliar with German. In sum, all of the Hutterites, more than two-thirds (68.9%) of the Mennonites, and only 29% of the German Catholics were still using their German mother tongue at least fairly often. Yet at the time (ca. 1970), high proportions in the rural bloc settlements studied could still speak at least some German: all of the Hutterites, 97.2% of the Mennonites, and 93.2% of the German Catholics.[77] However, generational differences were particularly revealing for German Catholics: 45.9% in the first generation were speaking English primarily or exclusively, compared with 71.8% in the second and 82.7% in the third. This was less dramatic for the Mennonites: only 4.8% in the first generation, 31.7% in the second, and 40.0% in the third.[78] Among Mennonites in Saskatchewan, the highest use of the distinctive *Plautdietsche/Plattdeutsch* (Low German) dialect has clearly been *biem aunsiedle* (when the settlers came), among the first generation, especially Old Colony Mennonites who particularly appreciated the retelling of *jeschichte enn resse ut'e vegangenheit* (stories and humour from the past).

Perhaps, to some extent, the traditionally German-speaking groups in Saskatchewan generally failed to unite originally to preserve the German language partly because they spoke distinct dialects that were different enough to hinder easy communication. Hutterites still speak a unique dialect with roots in the Tyrol, little influenced by languages of the regions in Central and Eastern Europe where they settled—Bohemian German, Czech, Slovak, Hungarian, Romanian, Russian, and Ukrainian. The language of their own "German school" is *Hochdeutsch* (High German).[79] Mennonites have used a variety of dialects. The home languages spoken by the first Mennonites in the Netherlands were Dutch and Frisian. In fact, Dutch was retained for a long time by Mennonite refugees who resettled in the Vistula estuary, but by the mid-eighteenth century with their movement eastward their original languages were gradually transformed into the *Frankenische* (Frankish), *Niedersachsenische* (Lower Saxon), and *Ost-Friesische* (East Frisian) dialects of *Niederdeutsch* or *Plattdeutsch* (Low German). Later, in West Prussia, the dialect spoken by most Mennonites was *Westprussische Plattdeutsch* (West Prussian Low German). With migration to South Russia, a *Schwarzmeerdeutsch* (Black Sea German) dialect of Low German with some Russian and Ukrainian admixture developed. By the time they arrived in Saskatchewan, the Old Colony Mennonites used a *Plattdeutsch* (Plautdietsch) dialect as their daily speech; less conservative Mennonites tended to view this dialect as crude, boorish, corrupted German used only by the less educated—for their part, they initially used standard Low German (and increasingly English) in everyday speech and *Schriftsprache* (literary German), *Bibeldeutsch* (Bible German), or *Hochdeutsch* (High German) in their churches and schools.[80]

It is interesting to speculate why historically Mennonites quickly shifted from speaking Dutch and Frisian and adopted German as they moved eastward from the Netherlands, where Menno Simons had originated the unique Mennonite branch of Anabaptism; when Mennonites eventually moved on to their colonies in Ukraine, they retained German (or their unique dialect) with very little incorporation of Russian or Ukrainian; yet in North America they soon became divided over the adoption of

English. One explanation might be that German was regarded as a more important language than Dutch (and certainly Frisian); moreover, German language and culture were considered by Mennonites to be superior to Russian or Ukrainian, whereas the same could not be said for English.[81]

As already noted, a feeling of the superiority of German culture also initially affected the preservation of German identity and language among German Catholic settlers in Saskatchewan. Many of the older, first-generation, conservative Mennonites spoke very little (and poor) English. In fact, the German language was considered central to the avoidance of contact with the larger society; such avoidance was positively valued and perhaps backed by xenophobia (fear or mistrust of "strangers"). Moreover, German was considered the only "proper" language for church services. Although some younger conservative Mennonites were having trouble with sentence structure in English, using the German structure when talking or writing in English, linguistic assimilation seemed imminent and inevitable, especially among German Catholics, whose admiration for German cultural superiority—to a lesser extent shared by Mennonites—lessened markedly after two world wars in which Canada was at war with Germany. Soon younger Mennonites, especially in the more liberal churches, began to express disdain for what they considered an excessive use of the German language. The more liberal churches soon adopted English, and use of German in public schools was outlawed. The *Russländer* immigrants expressed their eagerness to learn English, in contrast to the Old Colony Mennonites who had emigrated from Russia several decades previously.[82] Even among Hutterites, it became possible that English would replace German due to schooling in the former language, though Hutterites effectively responded to this threat by obtaining permission to retain their own schools (partly using German in instruction) on colony premises. Linguistic assimilation, using English as a vehicle for assimilation, became an extremely important issue insofar as it tended to signal the end of what provincial authorities (who were mainly Anglo-Canadian) considered the introversion and seclusion of ethnic minorities reinforced by traditional language use within sequestered bloc settlements.

Regular church attendance was a different story—in the 1972 study, generational differences between German Catholics and Mennonites were relatively minor: among German Catholics, 94.6% in the first generation were attending regularly, 97.4% in the second, 89.3% in the third; among Mennonites, respectively 97.6%, 86.6%, and 81.7%; all Hutterites attended both the *lehr* and the *gebet* (respectively the morning and the evening services).[83] Old Colony and certain other conservative Mennonite groups held a long weekly morning *versammling* (service or meeting) characterized by the *prediger* (preacher) giving a lengthy sermon and the *vorsänger/forsinger* (lead singer) facing the congregation to conduct multi-stanza sombre hymns.

How have attitudes toward ethnic and religious intermarriage been changing with each generation? The study showed that a very high proportion (90%) of German Catholic respondents were endogamous (i.e., had German Catholic spouses), compared with almost all (97.6%) of Mennonites and all of Hutterites. What was more important, ethnicity or religion? Of German Catholics, 90% were indifferent toward marrying someone of a different ethnic background, yet they were far more mixed in their views on religious intermarriage (i.e., marrying a non-Catholic): 69.5% expressed their opposition. An identical proportion of Mennonites were opposed to religious intermarriage, while a far larger number (56.5%) were also opposed to ethnic intermarriage.[84] However, there has been an increasing tendency among Mennonites in general to consider themselves more a religious than an ethnic group, though in the bloc settlements they are almost completely of German ethnicity. In any case, opposition to both ethnic and religious intermarriage has been declining with each generation. Among Mennonites opposition to ethnic intermarriage declined from 76.2% in the first generation to 63.4% in the second and to 45.0% in the third; among German Catholics from 24.3% in the first to 12.8% in the second and to none in the third. Among Mennonites, opposition to religious intermarriage correspondingly declined from 92.9% in the first generation to 69.5% in the second and 60.9% in the third; among German Catholics respectively from 91.9% to 85.9% and to 41.4%.[85]

Of these German ethno-religious groups studied in 1969–72, Hutterites revealed a wide range of folk traditions, German Catholics very few, and Mennonites a changing situation. In the extensive German Catholic settlement studied, there was little use of traditional German foods, little practice of traditional German crafts, no German folk music except the recollection of a song or two "from the old country" by the older generation. However, since then there has been something of a revival of German culture, centred on Humboldt, the largest town in St. Peter's Colony. Fully half of the Mennonites interviewed regularly prepared and ate German or Mennonite foods. At the time of the survey, about every fifth respondent could practise a traditional Mennonite craft. Western Mennonites have not become as involved as their eastern counterparts in designing complex *gwilt muschder* (quilt patterns), much less now in the high degree of commercialization of traditional Mennonite crafts found in Ontario, Pennsylvania, Ohio, and Indiana. Yet most Mennonites in Saskatchewan are not conservative, being members of the General Conference and Mennonite Brethren churches. Gone are some of the traditional social gatherings, yet *freundschaft* (extended family gatherings) still occur, and *zodelteit* (spring seeding) and fall harvest have long been times of family and communal solidarity and pleasure despite the hard work involved . A *Friesenfest* brought together more than 500 Friesens at Tiefengrund in 1991, from as far away as Kansas and Germany. A recent reunion of the Giesbrecht family originally of Rhineland (but now spread far and wide) included all twelve siblings raised on the original farm, their forty-two children, and ninety-eight grandchildren. Among Hutterites, hog-slaughters are still practised, along with collecting goose feathers in a *federsöck* (feather bag) and then holding a *federscheissen* (feather-stripping gathering). Hutterite colonies might still have a *henna hüttel* (honey hut).

It is interesting to contrast *die Alt-Mennischde* (Old Colony/Old Order Mennonites) with Hutterites. Both Old Colony Mennonites and other conservative Mennonites and especially Hutterites have maintained separation from the outside world (which of course included less conservative Mennonites); they have adhered to a stricter interpretation of the biblical admonition *Gehet aus von ihnen und sondert euch ab, spricht der Herr* (Come out from among them, and be separate, says the Lord). Unique Old Colony *strassendorf* villages are still found in the Saskatchewan Valley and Swift Current settlements, as are occasional homes with the house and *scheier* (barn) connected by the *gank* (walkway), but few examples of this traditional style are left—a good example

(1908) is found at the Saskatchewan River Valley Museum in Hague, and house-barn combinations can still be seen in the Osler, Gruenfeldt, and other Old Colony areas. In the earliest Mennonite settlements on the prairies, barn roofs that reached almost to the ground were entirely thatched, reminiscent of the style still found in Friesland in the northern Netherlands, where the Mennonite faith originated. Each room in an Old Colony Mennonite home had a distinct name and purpose: the main entrance into the home led into the *vorderhause* (front of the house); the *grossestube/schtuub* (literally large room) was the living room; the *sommerstube* (summer room) was the boys' bedroom; the *hinterhause* (rear of the house) served as a large combined kitchen and dining room; the *kleinestube* (small room) was the girls' bedroom; and the *eckstube* (corner room) was the master bedroom.[86] Old Colony and other conservative Mennonite churches remain simple, unadorned white buildings, usually in the countryside or in hamlets. Hutterites live in small colonies centred on a single, exclusively Hutterite, community averaging 100 residents. Among Old Colony Mennonites, individual land ownership has generally replaced the former collective landholding with a common pasture supervised by a *herdschult*, though community pastures are still common. Another personage in some villages would have been the *schuster* (shoemaker). In a Hutterite colony, all land is held communally.

Among Mennonites in Saskatchewan, only female members of Old Colony, some *Bergthaler*, and conservative Mennonite churches continue to wear traditional clothing—a *frack* (knee-length simple print dress), perhaps with *bibschaetz/schaets* (apron) and *schnieawest* (laced undergarment intended to flatten breasts, thus ensuring modesty), and *weiwer summer/winder bannet* (women's summer/winter bonnet) or *weibsleit kapp* (simple prayer bonnet), and possibly a *kaep* (cape) or *schaal* (shawl). Men still tend to dress in dark suits for church—"modern" clothing is frowned upon—although in Saskatchewan the more traditional *tschaecket* (vest), *mutze* (coat), *latzhosse* (pants), *mannsleit Sundaags hut* (men's Sunday hat), and *winde kapp* (winter cap) have undergone modifications, if still worn at all. Hutterites are the only ethnic or ethnoreligious group in Saskatchewan who continue to dress completely in distinctive clothing on a daily basis—the women wear a *tiechel* (polka dot headscarf) or *mützen* (bonnet), *kittel* (floor-length plaid dress) with *fëttig* (apron), *pfaht* (shirt), *mieder* (vest), and *wannick* (jacket), the men black pants with suspenders, a dark shirt, and a straw hat or dark fedora. Moreover, Hutterite hairstyles are unique: women braid their hair and tuck it up under their headscarves, and adult men have beards.

Mennonites are familiar with traditional Mennonite, German, and Eastern European foods but might prepare and eat them only occasionally. For *friestik* (breakfast), they might eat *hovagret* (porridge), *pankucken* (pancakes), or *grevan* (pork cracklings). Then for *maddach* (mid-day lunch, *middag* or *mittag* in German) *summaborscht* (creamed potato borscht soup) or *kommstborscht* (cabbage borscht), and often *borscht-und-browt* (borscht with home-baked bread), *Mennoniten-wurst/waescht/wascht* or *riekya vorscht* (Mennonite smoked farmer's sausage) on a *schiev* (bun), *heina salot* (chicken salad), or other lighter meals such as *klupz* (burger) or *flinzen* (crepes). Once-common *faspa* (mid-afternoon lunch) usually consisted of *supsil* (bread with homemade jam *aun-da-zeid* [on the side]) and *toum drinken* (beverages), often *prips* (roasted wheat brew, an alternative to coffee). This practice was similar to the Hutterite *lunschen*, often brought by the women out to the fields at harvest time. *Ovenkost* (evening dinner) tended to be heavier, consisting typically of *riekya vorscht* served with *vereniki* (dumplings), or *noodlin-mett-schmaunfat* (noodles in cream gravy with fried onions and diced bacon), or *schinkefleisch* (ham steak), then *plume-mouss* (dried fruit and cinnamon) for dessert. The single restaurant in the settlement (in Osler) now offering a German/Mennonite menu is actually run by Swiss immigrants; there are a couple of more authentic Mennonite restaurants nearby in Saskatoon (Taunte Maria's and the Mennonite Kitchen). Mennonite sausage is still produced commercially in the settlement, such as at Neuhorst and by the Smokehaus in Martensville, but *schwein-schlachten* (hog-slaughters) and *schnitzen* (building-bees) have ceased to be the community social events they once were. Jams are now made commercially at Gruenfeldt.

Much Hutterite food is home grown, cooked in communal kitchens, and consumed in a communal dining room (*essenstuben*) with the sexes and children separated—children eat in their own area (the *essenschul*); all people in the colony are called to this communal dining by ringing the dinner bell (*glöckel der glucken*). Certain Hutterite recipes (e.g., *maultoschen, strankel-worsch*, and *tröplich suppen*) have long been handed down. Common foods are *specksaften* (bacon cuts) and *focken klops* (pork burgers), *milch gerstel* (milk soup), *schmond wacken* (breakfast dipping cream), homemade *schmuggi* (soft caraway cheese) and *schutten* (cottage cheese), *nukkela suppen* (dumplings), *krapflen* (poppyseed "pockets"), potatoes from the communal *kartoffel kammela* (potato bin), and *alla kartoffel* (egg potatoes). Hutterites bake their own *rescha zwiebach*, similar to Mennonite *zwiebach* (rolls made of two—*zwie*—pieces of dough). Apart from home-grown food (colonies have extensive vegetable gardens and sell potatoes, corn, ham, and chickens commercially), clothing also tends to be homemade, from fabrics stored in a large wooden cupboard (*schronk*), and even soap (*specksaften*).

Until at least the 1930s (and in some families a generation later), many Old Colony Mennonites were opposed to riding in cars unless necessary but did use mechanized farm machinery. Hutterites have long practised highly mechanized agriculture, yet vehicles are community owned—in striking contrast to Old Order Mennonites and Amish in eastern North America, who shun any mechanization, using horses and a *boggi, karitsch fer die familye*, or *dachweggli* (buggy, family carriage, or covered buggy) and plowing with horses. Old Colony Mennonites now have private telephones, whereas Hutterites have communal phones. Old Colony Mennonites avoid drinking alcoholic beverages; Hutterites make their own alcohol for home consumption, and men will drink alcohol at pubs outside the colony (though moderation is emphasized). As we will see in more detail below, Old Colony Mennonites, in contrast to more liberal Mennonites, have opted for limited education and fought many a battle not only with provincial school inspectors but also with their liberal co-religionists for the right to teach in German in their one-room schools through the 1950s. Hutterites later avoided this confrontation by winning the right to retain their own school on each colony, with an "English" teacher from outside and a "German" teacher (*die teacherin*, usually the *prediger*, the minister). Although both conservative Mennonites and Hutterites have discouraged any education beyond a rudimentary level, it is interesting to note the *Plautdietsch* term *schlope-metz* (slow thinker), similar to the Hutterite terms *longsäm* (slow) and *maulvoll* (mouth-lazy).

So, despite some interesting contrasts, there have been many similarities between conservative Mennonites and Hutterites. Both Old Colony Mennonites and Hutterites have a tendency to be apolitical; both stress simplicity in living exemplified in restriction of material possessions and absence of jewellery; both have long church services in German; both are pacifist; both avoid "worldly amusements" such as films, dances, partying, card games, smoking, and public displays of affection between the sexes. Old Colony Mennonites are parochial, while Hutterites limit contact with the outside world by intentionally restricting media. Conservative Mennonites and Amish aim at *gelassenheit* (humility) as a life model and frown on being *stolt* (overly proud or vain); Hutterites disapprove of *irdisch* (carnal) things and *reiche leut* (rich, materialistic people) and emphasize being *der gute* (a good one), *mochs gut* (making it good), and being *fein* (virtuous) in anticipation of *Jüngste Tog* (Judgment Day). Old Colony Mennonites were preoccupied with what is *im abschnitt steben* (forbidden by the church); they dealt with departures from such social norms, perhaps by a *bengel* (misbehaving rascal) or worse yet a *schlingel* (disreputable rogue), with an *undertalk* visit to a person or home by the *diener* (preacher or elder), which could lead to a *donnadach* (Dutch *donderdag*, Thursday) meeting to try a sect member who violated a norm. Punishment meted out was shunning or ostracism in mild cases, excommunication from kin and sect in severe ones. Today, however, the emphasis is more on impassioned pleas by conservative elders and preachers to better one's life. Similarly, Hutterites can be the recipients of a *vermohn* (warning), perhaps meted out at a *stübel* (men's conference). A *rechnung* (annual accounting) is expected of every home. Hutterite social control continues to operate in the traditional manner. For example, a young man who has consumed too much alcohol in public might be restricted to the colony and obliged to do arduous or less attractive jobs. Or, upon return to a colony after spending some time away in the outside world (*weglaufen*—running away—is discouraged, especially for females, yet seems to be fairly common among young men), he might simply be expected to submit fully to colony authority. But some colonies "bend with the wind" in accepting minor piecemeal changes as long as their Hutterite way of life and identity are not really threatened. As Hutterites explain, *gemeinschaft ist der einzege weg* (community is the only way). Conservative Mennonites might concur but traditionally have had a different interpretation of community.

Conservative Anabaptist communities are not completely no-nonsense strict. As they say, *lass die herzen immer fröhlich* (don't worry ... be happy). There are certainly occasions for levity, apart from the social gatherings already mentioned, reflected in family and communal life. *Hochzeit/hochzich* (marriage) is an important one among Hutterites, marking the transition from *diene* (young unmarried women) being *bubisch* (boy-crazy) to having *heiratsgedanken* (marriage thoughts) with *buben* (young unmarried men). This recalls the Amish tradition of adolescent *rumspringa* (running around), although Hutterite matchmaking is usually based on exchanges or visits between colonies. Similarly, conservative Mennonites pass from *die kinneryaahre* (childhood years) into adolescence—*beim uffwaxe* (growing up) when a young man is *uff sei eeyes* (on his own) but with *noch mehner pflichte auszurichde* (added responsibilities). Among Hutterites, weddings are communal affairs, and *hochzeit g'schirr* (special wedding table settings) might be used. A *weib* (wife, called *mumkje*, a married woman among Old

Colony Mennonites) might be assisted by a *luckela* (baby-holder), *abwärterin* (one who waits on you) or *magdelein* (maiden), perhaps somewhat similar to an Old Colony *kjäkshe* or *maad* (hired girl), though *oltvetter* and *ankelen* (grandfathers and grandmothers) can also play a significant role in early child care. Old Colony households also often included a live-in *gnecht* (hired man). At home, Hutterite children might play games such as *blinde-kuh* (blind-cow, sort of like blindman's bluff), and *feiertog* (religious celebrations) are joyfully participated in. At Christmas, children receive special *wiehnachtsgeschenken* (Christmas presents). In contrast to conservative Mennonites, much of Hutterite children's life is conducted communally: already noted was the separate children's dining area, and at nap time the youngest children in *kleineschul* (kindergarten) might have their *schlofbänk* (sleeping-bench).

The *Prairieleut* in the Langham area long retained some Hutterite cultural practices, phrases, and traditional foods, re-enforcing a distinct identity separate from Mennonites. Yet in due course they became more secularized than their counterparts remaining in the Dakotas and revealed aspects of societal assimilation despite cultural insularity.

Referring back to that detailed study of four decades ago, one might readily conclude that at the time Hutterites seemed to be virtually unaffected by change (and still are except in a technological sense and very minor ways); Mennonites in general as well as *Prairieleut* tended to be more conservative than German Catholics but were still quite affected by change between generations and were more diverse in their interpretations of religion; and German Catholics were drastically affected by external pressures causing them to devalue their German identity and culture. Nonetheless, through the work of the Saskatchewan German Council and not the least the arrival of more German immigrants during the past several decades, renewed awareness of and pride in German Canadian culture in Saskatchewan have become increasingly prevalent.

THE BATTLE OVER EDUCATION

It is instructive to revisit the controversies during the early years of settlement over the use of German in the schools of the German bloc settlements and colonies. As early as 1892, Mowat, a member of the Territorial Legislative Assembly, attempted in vain to introduce a bill that would have required that all schools in the territories be taught in the English language. Yet the Ordinance of 1892 reduced the Catholic vote in school matters from essentially joint control of the Board of Education, with non-Catholics sitting as non-voting advisory members of an Executive Council. German Catholics were assured in 1901 that a local school board could arrange to employ competent teachers to give instruction in their mother tongue; later it was further stipulated that such instruction should be restricted to the last hour of the school day and be in the form of reading, composition, and grammar.[87]

By 1907, Prior Bruno, founder and guiding light of St. Peter's Colony, had requested Premier Scott to allow German as a language of instruction at any time during the school day. Scott's government (1905–16) could not accept this proposal in view of the Ordinance of 1901 ensuring the further limitation of teaching in German, which the government reiterated and clarified in 1915.[88] The provincial government's lenient policy of "gradualism," whereby school inspectors would encourage the many country school districts to gradually adhere to regulations, was effective among German Catholics. At the same time, an authorized German text was being used: the *Eclectic Series for German*.

It is difficult to describe succinctly the actual situation in St. Peter's Colony at the time because of conflicting reports from various sources. The Saskatoon *Daily Phoenix* suggested that there were as many as forty-five private schools with 1,200 pupils using German rather than English as a language of instruction and established by the Catholic Church to be free from government control. But Prior Bruno countered with his own set of facts: there was a third of that number of private schools; they were all bilingual with ample teaching in English; and all students were expected to be proficient in English. According to government school inspectors' reports, there were at least fifteen major separate schools founded by the Benedictines in the colony, with about fifty to sixty students in each. Although it was the ideal of these schools to preserve the German language and Catholic religion through ethnic-oriented church control, they were bilingual and observed government expectations. As one report put it, "No case has arisen of neglect for the teaching of English." Apparently, both religious and secular teachers were employed. Although many of these schools were up to date, those in the western parts of the colony were reported as being overcrowded, ill equipped, unventilated, and staffed by unqualified teachers. One inspector complained that the public schools adhering to government regulations were "practically empty." Some of these public schools, however, were virtually indistinguishable from the separate schools insofar as they were definitely oriented toward German Catholic traditions and used the German language extensively, while other public schools probably used some German and still others possibly some German. It seems safe to conclude that during the Scott regime the vast majority of schools in the colony, separate as well as public, were strongly oriented toward ethno-religious group control.[89]

Yet this situation was to change rapidly during the following Martin administration (1917–22). Any tolerance by the provincial government of German-language instruction tended to disappear during the First World War when Canada was at war with Germany and Austria-Hungary. Revision of the School Act in 1919 meant not only the obliteration of German-language teaching during school hours but also the removal of Catholic religious symbolism from public schools. Only a couple of schools were now reported as still using German, and just one complaint was made to the provincial government over religious emblems.[90] However, schools with a German Catholic orientation continued to function despite all odds. By 1925, separate schools still operated in the colony; in fact, some had increased in size: two had between fifty and seventy-five students, three between seventy-five and 100, and a couple over 100. It was reported that virtually all of their teachers lacked Saskatchewan teaching certificates or had expired certificates. The instruction at one large school at Muenster, in fact, was reported as still being in German, given by Catholic nuns.[91] Apart from such an anomaly, though, in general during the 1920s a marked reorientation of schools in the colony occurred, with separate schools shifting from a strong ethnic and religious orientation to an almost exclusively religious one and with public schools moving away from a substantial ethnic link.

The first Old Colony Mennonites had arrived in Saskatchewan with attitudes inevitably destined to conflict with the public school system. They did not consider education per se as an ideal; education beyond the minimum level required by the provincial government was frowned upon and considered a waste of time and money. They had a traditional maxim: *yi yilchda, yi vekehda* (the more learned you are, the more abnormal you become). Moreover, any enthusiasm that they might have shown for education was related to a desire to completely control their own schools so that their language and religion could be taught and maintained. These Mennonites thought that preservation of their language and religion went hand in hand and that preservation was possible only in strict isolation from the general society and even from less conservative Mennonites.[92] Old Colony schools were originally entirely in the *Plattdeutsch* (Low German) dialect, while *Hochdeutsch* (High German) was taught (mainly to understand church services). Extremely few, if any, children spoke any English at home. Their German texts covered successively basic German, Old Colony catechism, and Old and New Testament. Their classes, given in very poor conditions, covered Bible history and interpretation (the *Bibel* was accompanied by *Die Febel*, a religious reading book) and, to a limited extent, arithmetic and *schoenschrieben* (good writing); no education in Canadian history, science, or the English language was offered.[93] Old Colony Mennonites tended to regard education as unnecessary after age twelve or thirteen (strikingly similar to later Hutterites); education ended by the eighth grade or sooner. Teachers were paid from twenty-five to forty dollars a month (plus amenities—room and board, hay to feed the teacher's horse, and fuel). Pupils sat on backless benches along crude long tables.

According to reports, in 1917 there were eleven private schools and no public schools in the four townships comprising the heart of the Old Colony within the Saskatchewan Valley Mennonite settlement. Each school had between thirty-five and sixty pupils. Few teachers were familiar with English or had any professional teaching qualifications; most had only five to six years of education; some were illiterate even in German. Several were community patriarchs with as many as eleven children. Any slight deviation from Old Colony conservatism meant immediate dismissal, as in one case at Rheinland. Old Colony religious leaders (ältester), notably Jacob Wiens of Neuanlage and Johann Klassen of Hochfeld, quoted scripture as evidence that it would be immoral to attend public schools that were inadequate in religious education while Old Colony private schools assured a better form of wisdom: "And that from a child thou hast known the holy scriptures which are able to make thee wise unto salvation through faith which is in Jesus Christ." Moreover, Old Colony children were expected to attend a private school even if they lived close to a public one. When more than twenty families were excommunicated in the Old Colony in 1908 alone for allowing their children to attend public schools, a Royal Commission on Mennonite Schools began a two-year investigation of the situation, hearing numerous complaints of coercion from excommunicated and progressive Mennonites, to which the religious leaders simply replied that their actions had been predetermined by scripture. Excommunicants were thoroughly ostracized from the Old Colony community as well as from their own relatives.[94]

The matter really came to a head in the Martin administration after 1916. The School Attendance Act in 1916 permitted private schools, provided that they conformed to provincial standards. If any school was found inadequate, it was condemned. The 1922 School Act required attending English-language schools. The provincial government built public schools near Old Colony villages between 1918 and 1928 and employed outside teachers. The Old Colony leaders were quick to point out that Mennonites had been assured of Canadian government non-interference in language or religion when they first immigrated and commented that "The Lord will surely bless the government if they are not hard on us. ... We want to be left alone." But the provincial government was no longer willing to make an exception for the Old Colonists. In 1918, there were still at least thirty-two Mennonite schools in the Saskatchewan Valley settlement instructing largely or entirely in German, including all of the Old Colony schools as well as many schools in other Mennonite settlements.[95] Premier Martin's School Ordinance of 1919 forbade any use of German during school hours. As a result, the Old Colony schools were replaced by public schools, and attendance at the latter was enforced by threatening fines of ten dollars a month per child not attending. However, little headway was made by the government. Within the Old Colony, despite fines amounting to more than $700 a family, not a single child attended; the threat of excommunication and ostracism was greater than the problem of being fined. In 1921 alone, sixty people were charged $1,000 each, some 1,500 together were fined $13,034, and one was sent to prison with a thirty-year sentence.[96]

By 1930, the fines had been lowered to just a token dollar a month, and Mennonites were permitted to teach for an hour and a half in German after 3:30 p.m. (the normal end of school hours). It was not, however, until the school consolidation process began in the late 1940s that teaching in German during the school day finally disappeared on a large scale—and with it the final dissolution of the Old Colony as a close-knit community.

Another group of conservative Mennonites was situated in the River Park–Friedland area near Aberdeen, across the South Saskatchewan River to the east. When Martin became premier, the three private Mennonite schools in this area bore a close resemblance to the Old Colony ones across the river. According to reports, instruction was given in German by unqualified teachers unable to speak English well; the schoolhouses were overcrowded, unventilated, and poorly equipped; few pupils were educated beyond the fourth grade. Although German instruction had been available at several public schools in the area, it declined with the replacement of German-speaking teachers by English-speaking ones and with an increasing insistence on qualified teachers, so Mennonites chose to send their children to private schools. The public schools were left practically empty: twenty-five enrolled at River Park, but only five actually attended out of a possible fifty; fifty-four enrolled at Friedland, but only five attended out of a possible sixty. As a result, at least one public school had to be closed. However, despite the intransigence of some tradition-bound families (one was reported to be skimping on clothing and food for the children in order to pay for fines for not attending the public school), within a few years some private schools were closed, and Mennonites in some areas of the settlement, such as Edenburg and Lilly, accepted the public school idea.[97]

Mennonite sects that were not overly conservative or markedly progressive tended to retain some German-language instruction but avoided conflicting with provincial school regulations. By 1917, all but a few schools in areas occupied by these middle-road Mennonites were public ones with qualified teachers proficient in English. Most schools were teaching in German for the final hour of the school day (e.g., Dalmeny,

Rosthern, Hepburn, New Home, Richmond, Hoffnungsfeld, Clear Spring, etc.). Some schools in the mixed Mennonite-Ukrainian area east of Rosthern were teaching Ukrainian rather than German in the specified hour, while as late as 1921 complaints were received that Bergthal School was still instructing in German (after the 1919 legislation had forbidden this). The Hague School District had used English only for the past six years, Waldheim for the past two years, though the school at nearby Bruderfeld taught German for an hour a day and was still poorly attended. Incidentally, in the Hague School District, established in 1902, William Diefenbaker was the teacher in 1905–06; his sons John (later to become prime minister of Canada) and Elmer were among the thirty-nine pupils. Some schools, such as the one at Schmidtzburg, taught in German only on occasion. It is interesting to note that many of these middle-road Mennonites opposed the *Russländer* immigration in 1922; they included the Mennonite Brethren of the Bruderfeld, Waldheim, Hepburn, Ebenezer, Neuhoffnung, and Aberdeen areas; the Bruderthaler of the Langham area; and the Krimmer Mennonite Brethren of the Langham, Immanuel, and Salem areas. The progressive General Conference Mennonites were the most willing to abandon the German language, as they tended to regard their Mennonite identity in religious rather than ethnic terms.[98]

Meanwhile, former conservative Mennonite communities bearing German names had been largely replaced by anglicized school districts with "neutral" names such as Renfrew, Steele, Embury, Pembroke, Lilly, River Park, Saskatchewan, Virtue, Malden, Venice, and Kenmare, but there were a few exceptions, such as Altona, Wurtzburg, Roseland, and Warman. Gruenthal School (originally West-Neuanlage) became a compulsory English-language school but was strongly resisted by the local farmers, while Pembroke replaced the original Old Colony school (Ost-Neuanlage).

During the First World War, Mennonites found themselves in a position in which they had to declare themselves conscientious objectors, more conservative Mennonites in particular being strict pacifists. Moreover, German language and culture were hardly popular at a time when Canada was at war with Germany and Austria-Hungary. Prior to the war, Germans in Saskatchewan were viewed as "well-behaved contributing members of Canadian society" but during the war they were branded as "enemy aliens," and their previous image of cultural superiority quickly became tarnished.[99] Increasingly concerned that the Canadian and Saskatchewan and Manitoba provincial governments were not likely to change their intolerant position, the *Altkolonier* and other conservative Mennonites soon began to look for alternatives to preserve their conservative religion, language, and culture. In 1919, conservative Mennonites in Saskatchewan and Manitoba decided that emigration was once again their only recourse, and they sent a delegation to explore land opportunities in several Latin American countries. So, beginning in 1921, land was purchased in Mexico to establish the Manitoba, Swift Current, Nord, Quellen, and Santa Clara Kolonien.[100] In June 1924, the first trainload of 140 emigrants left Hague, bound for Mexico. During the next couple of years, seven more trainloads would leave under the leadership of Johann P. Wall—amounting to about 1,000 emigrants in all. Soon other colonies were established, including one in Durango by *Altkolonier* from the Old Colony Reserve in the Hague-Osler area. All told, during the 1920s, an estimated 7,000 conservative Mennonites left Saskatchewan and Manitoba to resettle in four colonies in Mexico.

Since then, and particularly following the Second World War, when once again conscription became an issue, more colonies were founded, so that by the early 1980s fifteen colonies had a combined population estimated at over 50,000. Moreover, former Canadian Mennonites who settled in Mexico have also established at least nineteen colonies (with a combined population estimated at over 20,000) in Paraguay since 1926 as well as six colonies (with a population of over 5,000) in British Honduras (now Belize) and sixteen colonies (with a population in excess of 20,000) in Bolivia beginning in the 1950s. Numerous community names in the colonies duplicate what had become place names in Mennonite settlements in Saskatchewan and Manitoba; the Saskatchewan origins of these Mennonites are also reflected in colony names—there is a Swift Current Colony in both Mexico and Bolivia and a Hague Colony in Mexico; and numerous typical Mennonite community names were repeated in Mennonite colonies in Mexico, Belize, Paraguay, Brazil, and Bolivia. Yet at least 10,000 Mennonites had returned to Canada (especially to Manitoba, Saskatchewan, and Ontario) from Mexico by 1990, and thousands more from Paraguay, Bolivia, and other Latin American countries, driven by drought, indebtedness, lack of employment opportunities, shortage of land, and perhaps increasing resistance to conservatism, affecting especially the younger generation.[101]

During the 1950s and 1960s, virtually all of the one-room schools in the countryside within German and Mennonite settlements closed in favour of consolidation, with the exception of Hutterite colonies. So, among conservative Mennonites, *die Auswanderung* (scattering) continued well into the 1950s, when *Reinlander, Sommerfelder, Chortitzer,* and *Bergthaler* moved from Saskatchewan to resettle in remote bush areas up north: La Crete in northern Alberta and Prespatou-Altona in northern British Columbia. Intentionally seeking the availability of land and isolation, they sought to maintain a rural lifestyle and traditional culture. Church services were initially held completely in German, but since the mid-1970s they have been in a mixture of German and English. Meanwhile, back in Rheinland, Saskatchewan, fourteen *Bergthaler* and Old Colony families re-established a two-room private country school in 1979.

With the proliferation of Hutterite colonies in Saskatchewan since the late 1940s, one might expect a renewal of the German-language controversy with reversion to the conservative Mennonite style of education. But this has not exactly happened. Although closely resembling Old Colony Mennonites in many ways, Hutterites have long had a distinctive system of education that has attempted to conform both to their traditions and to provincial school regulations. Each Hutterite colony has two schools in the same building: a "German" school in which the teacher from the colony (usually the preacher) promulgates Hutterite beliefs, norms, lifestyle, and discipline and an "English" school taught by a teacher from outside the colony in accordance with provincial regulations. In order to check the possible erosion of Hutterite values by the English teacher (supplied by the public school board), the English school is preceded each day by its German counterpart; it might be visited by colony elders when in session, its décor must be kept simple, its teacher might be "advised" by the colony pastor, and its textbooks might be censored to conform to Hutterite expectations. Usually, though, its influence is sufficiently controlled through pupils' awareness that it describes worldly matters and cannot be considered to be completely moral (though Hutterites are very up to date in agricultural technology). Moreover, it is rare for Hutterites to have more than the minimum education required by provincial school regulations.

CONCLUDING THOUGHTS

We have seen that people of German, including Mennonite and Hutterite, and to a lesser extent Dutch origins have had—and continue to have—a profound impact on the cultural geography of Saskatchewan. Their settlements have not only contributed to the cultural diversity of the Saskatchewan population but also reflected their own diverse origins. They have been German-speaking colonists from South Russia (Ukraine) and many other Eastern European countries (today Russia, Romania, Bulgaria, Moldova, Hungary, Serbia, Austria, Slovakia, Czech Republic, Poland, and Lithuania); more recent immigrants from Germany and Austria; settlers from previous German settlements in the United States; Catholics and Protestants (particularly Lutherans, Baptists, and Adventists); Mennonites previously from colonies in South Russia and West Prussia (today in Poland) and from former settlements in Midwestern American states, Manitoba, and Ontario; Hutterites whose predecessors had followed an odyssey from Tyrol through Moravia, Transylvania, South Russia, and the United States; and Dutch-speaking immigrants from the Netherlands, Belgium, and the United States.

This chapter has provided and examined a lot of detailed data on linguistic and other changes affecting people of Germanic ethnic origins in the province. Yet it would be presumptuous to conclude that German, Mennonite, and Dutch identities and cultures in Saskatchewan have been steadily eroded over the past century. Rather, a significant revival of German culture and a continuing interest in its survival have been occurring in recent years. For example, Humboldt—named after the distinguished German scientist and geographer, Baron Friedrich Heinrich Alexander von Humboldt (1769–1859)—adopted a German theme on its main street in 1991. It also holds an annual *Oktoberfest* as well as other German festivals: a popular Polkafest in July, *Deutsche Kaffeestunde*, *Maifest* (with children in *tracht*—local costume—dancing the traditional *Maitanz* around the Maypole), *Sommerfest*, *Erntedankfest*, and *Sint-Nikolaustag*. The old courthouse and land titles office (1914), post office (1911, now a museum), and telegraph station (1874) are all preserved as heritage properties. Since 1991, Humboldt has advertised itself as *ein bitschen Deutschland*—a little bit of Germany in the heart of the prairies, and information on heritage events is available in the Willkomen Centre and the Humboldt and District Museum and Gallery. Shops offer *bauernmalerie* and other German crafts, while restaurants feature *schnitzel, bratwurst, sauerkraut, rotkraut,* and *spätzle*. A *volksmarsch*—German walking tour—is available. Nearby, in Bruno, the Pulvermacher family has been making sausages for more than a century since grandfather Alex arrived from Wisconsin in 1906 to establish his butcher shop. The Ursuline Sisters' convent and academy were closed in 1982 and became the Ursuline Centre, then leased in 1999 to the University of Saskatchewan as the Bruno Ursuline Campus; most recently, in 2003, the property reverted back into the Prairie Ursuline Centre, then the following year became St. Therese Catholic College of Faith and Mission, together with a Healing and Growth Centre. The grounds were developed as a cherry orchard, which has become the main contributor to the annual Bruno Cherry Festival since 2003. The large, beautiful Assumption Church in the countryside at Marysburg is used for a series of classical concerts during summer months.

The Saskatchewan German Council (SGC), founded in 1984, is a comprehensive "volunteer-based, non-profit organization dedicated to promoting the heritage, culture and interests of Saskatchewan people of German-speaking backgrounds."[102] It consists of a network of organizations concerned with historical/genealogical research, cultural/recreational activities, and education. Based in Regina are the German-Canadian Society Harmonie and Volksliederchor Harmonie (both founded in 1955); the Deutsche Sprachschule Regina, *wo das lernen spass macht*—where learning is fun (1955); the American Historical Society of Germans from Russia (1968); the Karnevalsgesellschaft Harmonie (1970); the Austrian-Canadian Edelwiess Club (1972); the Saskatchewan Association of German Language Schools (1990); the Zichydorf Village Association (1996); the German Harmonie Singers (1997); and at the University of Regina the Department of International Languages. In Saskatoon are the German-Canadian Club Concordia (1957), with its Volksliederchor Concordia and the Deutsche Sprachschule Concordia (1983); the Saskatchewan Association of Teachers of German (1968); the Skat Club Saskatoon (1969); the *Treffpunkt Deutschland* FM radio program (which started in 1977); the Saskatoon German Pre-Kindergarten (1985); and, at the University of Saskatchewan, a German Students Association (1995). Unfortunately, the original Concordia Club burned to the ground in 2009 but was soon reconstructed. Other SGC members now include the Melville and District German Heritage Club (1983); the Humboldt and District German Heritage Society (1985) and Folkart Co-op (1992); the Battlefords and District German Heritage Association (1985) and Battlefords and District German Heritage Language School (1988); the German Sudeten Association (1989) and Imhoff Heritage Society (2003) in the St. Walburg area; the Waldhorn German Club, Prince Albert German Language School, and German Junior Folk Dancers (1990) in Prince Albert; the Estevan and District German Freundschaft Society (1991); the Lloydminster German Heritage Society (1991); the Mennonite Heritage Village in Swift Current (1992); and the Village of Edenwold (2005).

For decades, continuous urbanization of Germans and Mennonites took a toll not only on the viability of communities and settlements but also on the preservation of their unique cultures. Within urban areas, it became a challenge for migrants from rural settlements to maintain their traditions, as they have said, *wege zur menschlichen stadt* (making cities livable). Many Mennonites in the Saskatchewan Valley settlement arrived at a compromise, moving to satellite communities between city and country; thus, Martensville grew rapidly during the 1960s and 1970s from a small Mennonite village into a large suburban community, and other once largely Mennonite communities—notably Warman, Dalmeny, and Langham—close to Saskatoon have advertised their new suburban-style housing and inexpensive lots. But with the arrival of new German immigrants primarily in the larger cities of Saskatchewan, these cities rather than rural bloc settlements have become the focal points of German cultural activities and in turn have encouraged a revitalization of German identity and culture in some towns. The German and Dutch pavilions in Folkfest, Saskatoon's multicultural festival, have been popular venues. Some Mennonite institutions have demonstrated remarkable durability and remain active, notably the Mennonite Central Committee, which carries out extensive international relief work and runs Ten Thousand Villages and the Village Green Thrift Shops locally, and Mennonite Trust (dating from 1917), which continues to be involved in will and estate planning, loans, investments, account and income tax management, notary/commissioner services, and "special ministries" and is situated next door to the Mennonite Historical Society of Saskatchewan.

SOURCES

German Settlements in Saskatchewan

Sources on German settlements in Saskatchewan have included A. Becker, "The Germans from Russia in Saskatchewan and Alberta," in *German-Canadian Yearbook*, vol. 3 (Toronto: Historical Society of Mecklenburg, 1976), 108–19; W.A. Holst, "Ethnic Identity and Mission in a Canadian Lutheran Context," in *German-Canadian Yearbook*, vol. 5 (1979), 20–24; H. Froeschle, "German Immigration into Canada," in *German-Canadian Yearbook*, vol. 6 (1981), 16–27; A.B. Anderson, "German Settlements in Saskatchewan," in *Roots and Realities among Central and Eastern Europeans*, ed. M.L. Kovacs (Edmonton: University of Alberta Press, 1983), 175–227; B.G. Smillie and N.J. Threinen, "Protestants—Prairie Visionaries of the New Jerusalem: The United and Lutheran Churches in Western Canada," in *Visions of the New Jerusalem: Religious Settlement on the Prairies*, ed. B.G. Smillie (Edmonton: NeWest Press, 1983); H. Lehmann, *The German Canadians, 1750–1937: Immigration, Settlement, and Culture*, trans. G.P. Bassler (St. John's: Jesperson Press, 1986); A.B. Anderson, *German, Mennonite, and Hutterite Communities in Saskatchewan: An Inventory of Sources* (Saskatoon: Saskatchewan German Council, 1989); G. Grams, *German Emigration to Canada and the Support of Its Deutschtum during the Weimar Republic* (Frankfurt: Peter Lang, 2001); A.B. Anderson, *German Settlements in Saskatchewan*, 2nd ed. (Saskatoon: Saskatchewan German Council, 2005); A.B. Anderson, "German Settlements," in *Encyclopedia of Saskatchewan* (Regina: Canadian Plains Research Center, 2005), 389–95; and G.W. Grams, "Immigration and Return Migration of German Nationals, Saskatchewan, 1919–1939," *Prairie Forum* 33, 1 (2008): 39–64, reprinted in *Immigration and Settlement, 1870–1939*, ed. G.P. Marchildon (Regina: Canadian Plains Research Center, 2009), 413–37.

The broader context of German settlement in Canada has been described by G. Bassler, "Germans," in *Encyclopedia of Canada's Peoples*, ed. P.R. Magocsi (Toronto: University of Toronto Press, 1999), 587–612.

Historical Background in Russia and Eastern Europe

German colonies in Eastern Europe have been described in Reverend P.C. Keller, *The German Colonies in South Russia*, trans. A. Becker (Odessa: n.p., 1905); Reverend P.C. Keller, *The German Colonies in South Russia, Vol. II*, trans. A. Becker (Odessa: Jakob Zentner, 1914); A. Giesinger, *From Catherine to Kruschev: The Story of Russia's Germans* (Winnipeg: Marian Press, 1974); A.B. Anderson, "Emigration from German Settlements in Eastern Europe: A Study in Historical Demography," in *Proceedings of the First Banff Conference on Central and East European Studies*, ed. T.M.S. Priestly

(Edmonton: University of Alberta, 1977), 184–223; A. Giesinger, "The Background of the People of German Origin in Saskatchewan," *Saskatchewan Genealogical Society Bulletin* 9, 2 (1978): 38–53; A.B. Anderson, "German Migration from Romania to the Prairies," paper presented at the Meeting of the Central and East European Studies Association of Canada, Université du Québec à Montréal, June 1980; and S.A. Welisch, *Bukovina Villages, Towns, Cities, and Their Germans* (Ellis, KS: Bukovina Society of the Americas, 1990).

Mennonite settlements in Russia have been described in W. Quiring and H. Bartel, *In the Fullness of Time: 150 Years of Mennonite Sojourn in Russia*, trans. K. Janzen (Waterloo: Reeve Bean, 1974); A. Reimer, *My Harp Is Turned to Mourning* (Winnipeg: Hyperion Press, 1985); J. Friesen, ed., *Mennonites in Russia: 1788–1988: Essays in Honour of Gerhard Lohrenz* (Winnipeg: CMBC Publications, 1989); J. Urry, *Mennonites, Politics, and Peoplehood* (Winnipeg: University of Manitoba Press, 2006); and R.P. Friesen, *Building on the Past: Mennonite Architecture, Landscape, and Settlements in Russia/Ukraine* (Moscow: Raduga Publications; Altona, MB: Friesens, 2004).

Specific German Settlements and Communities in Saskatchewan

Data and other details on St. Peter's Colony are drawn primarily from A.B. Anderson, "Assimilation in the Bloc Settlements of North-Central Saskatchewan" (Ph.D. diss., University of Saskatchewan, 1972). See also Reverend P. Windschiegl, OSB, *Fifty Golden Years, 1903–1953* (Muenster, SK: St. Peter's Abbey, 1953); "Father Bruno's Narrative, 'Across the Boundary,'" reprinted in *Saskatchewan History* 9, 9 (1956): 26–31, 70–74; B. Hubbard, "St. Peter's: A German-American Marriage of Monastery and Colony," in *Visions of the New Jerusalem: Religious Settlement on the Prairies*, ed. B.G. Smillie (Edmonton: NeWest Press, 1983), 153–64; A.B. Anderson, "Abbot Bruno (George) Doerfler," in *Dictionary of Canadian Biography*, vol. 14 (Toronto: University of Toronto Press, 1995), 1–4; *A Journey of Faith: St. Peter's Abbacy: 1921–1926* (Muenster, SK: Muenster Diocese, 1996); and C.O. White, "The German Catholic Parochial Schools of Saskatchewan's St. Peter's Colony, 1903–34: Their Teachers, Curriculum, and Quality of Instruction," *Prairie Forum* 24, 1 (1999).

An informative source is Archdiocese of Regina, *Golden Jubilee, 1911–1961*, for parishes in southern Saskatchewan. For parishes in St. Joseph's Colony, see Father W. Schulte, OMI (with Oblate priests of the colony), *St. Joseph's Colony: 1905–1930*, trans. L. Schneider and T. Schneider (Regina: Order of Mary Immaculate, 1930). A detailed description of the historical background, early development, and social life of St. Joseph's Colony, Balgonie, is provided in A. Becker, "St. Joseph's Colony, Balgonie," *Saskatchewan History* 20, 1 (1966): 1–18. A historical novel set in Neudorf and Lemberg is C. Jeffery, *Arriving 1909–1919* (Edmonton: Roadie Books, 2011).

Historical details on German Lutheran churches in Saskatchewan are found in L.K. Munholland, *Pulpits of the Past* and *Bread to Share* (Strasbourg, SK: Three West Two South Books, 2004, 2006).

National Socialism in Saskatchewan and more generally in Canada is described in J. Wagner, "*Heim ins Reich*: The Story of Loon River's Nazis," *Saskatchewan History* 29, 2 (1976): 41–50; J.F. Wagner, "The Deutscher Bund Canada in Saskatchewan," *Saskatchewan History* 31, 2 (1978): 41–50; J. Wagner, *Brothers beyond the Sea: National Socialism in Canada* (Waterloo: Wilfrid Laurier University Press, 1981); and L.R. Betcherman, *The Swastika and the Maple Leaf: Fascist Movements in Canada in the Thirties* (Toronto: Fitzhenry and Whiteside, 1975). The Sudeten settlements have been described in A. Amstatter, *Tomslake: History of the Sudeten Germans in Canada* (Saanichton, BC: Hancock House, 1978); and R. Schilling, *Sudeten in Saskatchewan: A Way to Be Free* (St. Walburg, SK: Sudeten German Club with the Saskatchewan German Council, 1989).

Danube Swabians
See B. Anwender, "Zichydorf Colony: A Brief History," *Saskatchewan Genealogical Society Bulletin* 27, 3 (1996): 103–05; and G. Schwartz, "Danube Swabians," in *Encyclopedia of Saskatchewan* (Regina: Canadian Plains Research Center, 2005), 238–39. Detailed descriptions of Swabian traditions in Saskatchewan have been provided by G. Johnson, "Swabian Folk Ways," *Saskatchewan History* 13, 2 (1960): 73–75; and M. Carlson, "The Swabian Germans at Wakaw: The Portable People Who Found a Permanent Home," 1988, author's archives.

General Mennonite History
Useful sources are C.H. Smith, *The Story of the Mennonites* (Newton, KS: Mennonite Publication Office, 1957); and C. Dyck, ed., *An Introduction to Mennonite History* (Scottdale, PA: Herald Press, 1967).

History of Mennonites in Western Canada
Sources on the general history of Mennonites in Western Canada include F.H. Epp, *Mennonite Exodus* (Altona, MB: D.W. Friesen and Sons, 1962); G. Lohrenz, *The Mennonites of Western Canada* (Winnipeg: privately published, 1974); F.H. Epp, *Mennonites in Canada, 1782-1920: The History of a Separate People* (Toronto: Macmillan of Canada, 1974); L. Klippenstein and J.G. Toews, *Mennonite Memories: Settling in Western Canada* (Winnipeg: Centennial Publications, 1977); F.H. Epp, *Mennonites in Canada, 1920-1940: A People's Struggle for Survival* (Toronto: Macmillan of Canada, 1982); T.D. Regehr, "Mennonites and the New Jerusalem in Western Canada," in *Visions of the New Jerusalem: Religious Settlement on the Prairies*, ed. B.G. Smillie (Edmonton: NeWest Press, 1983), 109–20; A. Schroeder, *The Mennonites: A Pictorial History of Their Lives in Canada* (Vancouver: Douglas and McIntyre, 1990); T.D. Regehr, *Mennonites in Canada, 1939-1970: A People Transformed* (Toronto: University of Toronto Press, 1996); and H. Loewen, "Mennonites," in *Encyclopedia of Canada's Peoples*, ed. P.R. Magocsi (Toronto: University of Toronto Press, 1999), 957–74.

Mennonite Settlements and Local History in Saskatchewan

A principal source is A.B. Anderson, "Mennonite Settlements," in *Encyclopedia of Saskatchewan* (Regina: Canadian Plains Research Center, 2005), 597–98; also see T. Regehr, "Mennonites," in ibid., 598–99.

Data and other details on the Saskatchewan Valley Mennonite settlement are drawn from A.B. Anderson, "Assimilation in the Bloc Settlements of North-Central Saskatchewan" (Ph.D. diss., University of Saskatchewan, 1972). A related source is A.B. Anderson and L. Driedger, "The Mennonite Family: Culture and Kin in Rural Saskatchewan," in *Canadian Families: Ethnic Variations*, ed. K. Ishwaran (Scarborough, ON: McGraw-Hill-Ryerson, 1980), 161–80.

Other sources include *A Historical Review of Rosthern Superintendency* (1967); *Nordheimer Mennonite Church of Saskatchewan, 1925–1975*; J.G. Guenther, *"Men of Steele": Lifestyle of a Unique Sect: Saskatchewan Valley Mennonite Settlers and Their Descendants* (1981); P.W. Riegert, *2005 Memories: A History of the Hamburg School District No. 2005, Laird, Saskatchewan* (1979); Aberdeen Historical Society, *Aberdeen* (Edmonton: Friesen Printers, 1982).

Historical Divisions within Mennonites

Apart from Epp, *Mennonites in Canada, 1782–1920* and *Mennonites in Canada, 1920–1940*, and Regehr, *Mennonites in Canada, 1939–1970*, all noted above, sources describing sectarian divisions among Mennonites, particularly conservative Mennonite groups, in Western Canada include Leo Driedger, "A Sect in Modern Society: A Case Study of the Old Colony Mennonites of Saskatchewan" (MA thesis, University of Chicago, 1955); H.J. Gerbrandt, *An Adventure in Faith: The Background in Europe and the Development in Canada of the Bergthaler Mennonite Church of Manitoba* (Altona, MB: D.W. Friesen and Sons, 1970); W. Schroeder, *The Bergthal Colony* (Winnipeg: CMBC Publications, 1974); J. Levy, "In Search of Isolation: The Holdeman Mennonites of Linden, Alberta, and Their School," *Canadian Ethnic Studies* 11, 1 (1979); J.W. Friesen, "Social Change as the Inevitable: A Case Study of the Holdeman Mennonites of Linden, Alberta, from the Perspectives of History, Sociology, and Education," paper presented at the Meeting of the Central and East European Studies Association of Canada, Montreal, June 4–5, 1980; L. Doell, *The Bergthaler Mennonite Church of Saskatchewan, 1892–1975* (Winnipeg: CMBC Publications, 1987); L. Driedger, *Mennonite Identity in Conflict* (Lewiston, NY: Edwin Mellen Press, 1988); and J.J. Friesen, *Building Communities: The Changing Face of Manitoba Mennonites* (Winnipeg: CMU Press, 2007).

Personalized accounts of life in conservative communities in Saskatchewan and Western Canada include K. Martens, *All in a Row: The Klassens of Homewood* (Winnipeg: Mennonite Literary Society, 1988); W. Driedger, *Jakob Out of the Village* (Regina: Your Nickel's Worth Publishing, 2007); and T. Friesen, *Pushing through Barriers: A Canadian Mennonite Story* (Dawson Creek, BC: Peace PhotoGraphics, 2011).

More general sources on conservative Mennonites include A.M. Buehler, *The Pennsylvania German Dialect and the Life of an Old Order Mennonite* (Cambridge, ON: privately published, 1977); J.W. Fretz, *The Waterloo Mennonites: A Community in Paradox* (Waterloo: Wilfrid Laurier University Press, 1989); C. Redekop, *Mennonite Society* (Baltimore: Johns Hopkins University Press, 1989); S. Nolt, *An Introduction to Old Order and Conservative Mennonite Groups* (Intercourse, PA: Good Books, 1996); I.R. Horst, *A Separate People: An Insider's View of Old Order Mennonite Customs and Traditions* (Waterloo: Herald Press, 2000); I.R. Horst, *Separate and Peculiar: Old Order Mennonite Life in Ontario*, 2nd ed. (Waterloo: Herald Press, 2001); and J.F. Peters, *The Plain People: A Glimpse of Life among the Old Order Mennonites of Ontario* (Kitchener: Pandora Press, 2003.

Data on types, locations, and populations of various Mennonite churches can be obtained from M.L. Reimer, *One Quilt, Many Pieces: A Guide to Mennonite Groups in Canada*, 4th ed. (Waterloo: Herald Press, 2008), as well as from sources such as the *Mennonite Yearbook*, the *Mennonite World Handbook*, and *Unity amidst Diversity: Canadian Conference of Mennonite Brethren Churches*.

Saskatchewan and Other Mennonite Settlements
Detailed maps and descriptions of Mennonite settlements in Saskatchewan, Canada, and other countries—including in Central and South America—are found in W. Schroeder and H.T. Huebert, *Mennonite Historical Atlas* (Winnipeg: Springfield Publishers, 1990). Mennonite settlements in Central and South America have been described respectively in C. Redekop, *The Old Colony Mennonites: Dilemmas of Ethnic Minority Life* (Baltimore: Johns Hopkins University Press, 1969); C. Redekop, *Strangers Become Neighbours* (Kitchener: Herald Press, 1980); and R. Loewen, *Diaspora in the Countryside: Two Mennonite Communities and Mid-Twentieth Century Rural Disjuncture* (Toronto: University of Toronto Press, 2006).

German/Mennonite Language, Culture, Change, and Modernization
On the Low German and *Plautdietsch* dialects, see R. Epp, *The Story of Low German and Plautdietsch* (Hillsboro, KS: Reader's Press, 1993); and A.M. Buehler, *The Pennsylvania German Dialect and the Life of an Old Order Mennonite* (Cambridge, ON: printed by the author, 1977).

The German-language and schools issue has been discussed by K. Tischler, "The German Canadians in Saskatchewan with Particular Reference to the Language Problem, 1900–1930" (MA thesis, University of Saskatchewan, 1978); and K. Tischler, "The Efforts of the Germans in Saskatchewan to Retain Their Language before 1914," in *German-Canadian Yearbook*, vol. 6 (Toronto: Historical Society of Mecklenburg, 1981), 42–61.

A detailed study of Mennonite house-barn combinations is E.M. Ledohowski and D.K. Butterfield, *Architectural Heritage: Traditional Mennonite Architecture in the Rural Municipality of Stanley* (Winnipeg: Manitoba Culture, Heritage and Recreation, 1990).

Aspects of traditionalism and modernization of Mennonites and Amish have been described by A.B. Anderson, "The Sociology of Mennonite Identity: A Critical Review," in *Mennonite Identity: Historical and Contemporary Perspectives*, ed. C.W. Redekop and S.J. Steiner (Waterloo: Institute for Anabaptist and Mennonite Studies; New York: University Press of America, 1988), 193–201; D.G. Kraybill, *The Riddle of Amish Culture* (Baltimore: Johns Hopkins University Press, 1989); J.H. Kauffman and L. Driedger, *The Mennonite Mosaic: Identity and Modernization* (Waterloo: Herald Press, 1991); C. Redekop, V.A. Krahn, and S.J. Steiner, eds., *Anabaptist/Mennonite Faith and Economics* (Waterloo: Institute of Anabaptist and Mennonite Studies, Conrad Grebel College, 1994); D.G. Kraybill and M.A. Olshan, eds., *The Amish Struggle with Modernity* (Hanover, NH: University Press of New England, 1994); and A.J. Shaw, *Crisis of Conscience: Conscientious Objection in Canada during the First World War* (Vancouver: UBC Press, 2009).

The urbanization of Mennonites in Western Canada has been described in L. Driedger, ed., *Mennonites in Urban Canada: Proceedings of the Conference on Urbanization of Mennonites in Canada* (Winnipeg: University of Manitoba, 1968); of Germans, Russian Germans, Lutherans, Mennonites, and Dutch in R. Loewen and G. Friesen, *Immigrants in Prairie Cities: Ethnic Diversity in Twentieth Century Canada* (Toronto: University of Toronto Press, 2009), and L. Driedger, *At the Forks: Mennonites in Winnipeg* (Kitchener: Pandora Press, 2010).

German church life in the early years of settlement has been described by C. MacDonald, "Pioneer Church Life in Saskatchewan," *Saskatchewan History* 13 (1960): 1–18. The changing roles played by Mennonite women have been documented by M. Epp, *Mennonite Women in Canada* (Winnipeg: University of Manitoba Press, 2008).

Hutterites

See A.B. Anderson, "Hutterite Colonies," and P. Laverdure, "Hutterites," in *Encyclopedia of Saskatchewan* (Regina: Canadian Plains Research Center, 2005). Among many other sources are J.A. Hostetler and G.E. Huntington, *The Hutterites in North America* (New York: Holt, Rinehart and Winston, 1967); J.W. Bennett, *Hutterian Brethren: The Agricultural Economy and Social Organization of a Communal People* (Stanford: Stanford University Press, 1967); J.A. Hostetler, *Hutterite Society* (Baltimore: Johns Hopkins University Press, 1974); W.M. Kephart, *Extraordinary Groups: The Sociology of Unconventional Life-Styles* (New York: St. Martin's Press, 1976); G. McConnell, "Hutterites: An Interview with Michael Entz," in *Visions of the New Jerusalem: Religious Settlement on the Prairies*, ed. B.G. Smillie (Edmonton: NeWest Press, 1983); K.A. Peter, *Dynamics of Hutterite Society* (Edmonton: University of Alberta Press, 1987); W. Janzen, *Limits on Liberty: The Experience of Mennonite, Hutterite, and Doukhobor Communities in Canada* (Toronto: University of Toronto Press, 1990); M. Holzach, *Das Vergessene Volk/ The Forgotten People* (Sioux Falls, SD: Ex Machina Publishing, 1993); R. Janzen, *The Prairie People: Forgotten Anabaptists* (Hanover, NH: University Press of New England, 1999); and L. Driedger, "Hutterites," in *Encyclopedia of Canada's Peoples*, ed. P.R. Magocsi (Toronto: University of Toronto Press, 1999), 672–81. Personalized accounts of life in Hutterite colonies are found in S. Hofer, *Born Hutterite* (Saskatoon: Hofer

Publishing, 1991); S. Hofer, *The Hutterites: Lives and Images of a Communal People* (Saskatoon: Hofer Publishers, 1998); M.A. Kirkby, *I Am Hutterite* (Prince Albert: Polka Dot Press, 2007).

German Organizations
A description of member organizations of the Saskatchewan German Council is found in B. McKinstry, *Bridges: A Book of Legacies for Saskatchewan People of German-Speaking Backgrounds* (Saskatoon: Saskatchewan German Council, 2005).

Dutch
See A.B. Anderson, "Dutch Settlements," in *Encyclopedia of Saskatchewan* (Regina: Canadian Plains Research Center, 2005), 264. A local history is *Memories of Yesteryear: History of the Rural Municipality of Miry Creek, 1913–1963* (Saskatoon: Modern Press, 1963). The broader context of Dutch settlement in Western Canada is described in H. Palmer and T. Palmer, "The Religious Ethic and the Spirit of Immigration: The Dutch in Alberta," in *Peoples of Alberta: Portraits of Cultural Diversity*, ed. H. Palmer and T. Palmer (Saskatoon: Western Producer Prairie Books, 1985), 143–73; G.P. Marchildon, ed., *Immigration and Settlement, 1870–1939* (Regina: Canadian Plains Research Center and University of Regina, 2009); H. Ganzevoort, *A Bittersweet Land: The Dutch in Canada, 1890–1980* (Toronto: McClelland and Stewart, 1988); and H. Ganzevoort, "Dutch," in *Encyclopedia of Canada's Peoples*, ed. P.R. Magocsi (Toronto: University of Toronto Press, 1999), 435–50. Flemish settlement in Saskatchewan has been described in detail by C.J. Jaenen, *Promoters, Planters, and Pioneers: The Course and Context of Belgian Settlement in Western Canada* (University of Calgary Press, 2011).

Chapter 5
UKRAINIAN AND POLISH SETTLEMENTS

People of Ukrainian and Polish origins have had a profound impact on the settlement of Saskatchewan. Examined first in this chapter will be the general historical background to Ukrainian settlement. Then major areas of Ukrainian settlement in Saskatchewan will be described in detail, taking into account the formation of ethnic bloc settlements, the precise origins of the settlers, and the establishment of Ukrainian Orthodox and Ukrainian Catholic parishes. Ukrainian ethnic identification and resistance to assimilation will be discussed, followed more specifically by Ukrainian language use, religious affiliation, and folk culture. The chapter will focus next on institutionalization of the Ukrainian community and finally on the effects that rural depopulation and urbanization have had (though this topic will be pursued further in the final chapter). After the discussion on Ukrainians, the chapter will turn to a briefer description of Polish settlements before providing some concluding thoughts.

THE BACKGROUND TO UKRAINIAN SETTLEMENT
Settlement of the Canadian prairies by people of Ukrainian ethnic origin dates back at least to 1891, when Wasyl Eleniak and Ivan Pillipiw arrived from the village of Nebiliw, in the Kalush district of Galicia, today situated in western Ukraine. After visiting Manitoba and Saskatchewan, they settled in Alberta. Their temporary return to Galicia, as well as a favourable report from Dr. Osyp Oleskiw, who had been sent to the prairies in 1895 by the Proswita Society of L'viv to explore the possibility of large-scale emigration from Galicia, initiated the first mass migration. The federal minister of immigration at the time, Clifford Sifton, noted that there had been considerable emigration of Galician peasants to the United States and even South America, so he was convinced that these people would make desirable settlers for Western Canada, and he sent his agents after them. As he so famously put it, "I think a stalwart peasant in a sheepskin coat, born on

the soil, whose forefathers have been farmers for ten generations, with a stout wife and a half-dozen children, is good quality." Not every Canadian politician agreed: these "peasants in sheepskin coats" became a battle cry for the opposition in the next election, who referred to them as "Sifton's pets" and more nastily as "the scum of Europe." But Sifton never seemed to waver in his strong conviction that the Ukrainian immigrants would make a valuable contribution to settlement of the West.[1] With inauguration of the Sifton policy by the new Liberal government in 1896, the migration of tens of thousands of Ukrainians began in earnest; during 1896–1900, an estimated average of 35,000 Ukrainians a year crossed the Atlantic to settle in Western Canada, whereas Canadian government records indicated 63,188 Slavs admitted between 1898 and 1904. By 1916, an estimated 170,000 had settled in the Prairie Provinces, by 1930 more than 200,000. Most were assisted by the Ukrainian Colonization Board, a subsidiary of the federal government-sponsored CPR Colonization Department.[2]

In addition to the "pull" factors encouraging immigration into the bloc settlements of the prairies, there were strong "push" factors encouraging emigration out of Eastern Europe. Although the *panschyna* servitude had finally been abolished in 1848 by the Austrian imperial government controlling the crown land regions from which the mass emigration of Ukrainians occurred, the deplorable living conditions of the peasants were hardly alleviated. The peasants had owned little land and had to devote much of their time to working the lands of the landlords; they had been subjected to corporal punishment; they had been required to seek permission to improve their lot, to increase their few worldly goods; they had been forbidden by Austrian or German and Polish landlords to speak their own traditional language; and they had been heavily taxed. Few peasant farms were more than thirteen acres in size. Moreover, after 1848, landlords claimed the communal lands of whole villages as an indemnity, and taxation increased.[3]

The vast majority of Ukrainian immigrants to Western Canada settled in well-defined bloc settlements, almost all of which were concentrated in a broad swath extending from southeastern Manitoba through the Interlake and Riding Mountain areas in Manitoba, across east-central and north-central Saskatchewan, into a large area east of Edmonton in Alberta, a total distance of almost 2,000 kilometres. By the end of the first decade of the twentieth century, vast areas of all three Prairie Provinces began to resemble the western Ukrainian countryside. Hundreds of Ukrainian onion-domed churches (the Museum of Civilization in Ottawa estimates 500) were constructed. The most extensive bloc settlements, inclusive of tens of thousands of Ukrainian immigrants, formed largely self-sustaining and autonomous units within the traditional Anglo-Canadian norm. According to one account, "Old World communities were taken up wholesale and set down on the soil of our prairie provinces: a little spot of Canada that is almost Ukraine!" Not only individuals but also entire extended families and villages emigrated. Thus, a couple of neighbours in a bloc settlement in Saskatchewan might well have been neighbours back in Ukraine. They shared a common background and cultural tradition, community gossip, relatives and friends, language, religion, and customs—in sum, an entire lifestyle.[4]

The immigrants formed compact bloc settlements for a number of possible reasons: the availability of lands only in certain designated areas, their alleged propensity for fairly hilly and unbroken country, immigration recruiting and routing procedures, and social factors.[5] Although it is debatable whether many of the immigrants were directed into poor farming areas or whether they deliberately sought areas that reminded them of their homelands, the bloc settlement process did serve to assist the settlement of marginal areas, facilitated psychologically by living en masse in a well-defined cultural area. Although some difficulty was encountered by immigrants who failed to become British subjects within five years (actual Canadian citizenship was not established until 1946), thereby endangering their legal possession of homesteads, the bloc settlements expanded rapidly due to the settlers' ability to survive in rough conditions, their tendency to remain in rural areas rather than move into cities, their ability to take over farms vacated by earlier settlers (who were often of other ethnicities), and their relative independence from heavily subsidized settlement schemes.[6]

The process of settling was hard for these Ukrainians:

> Many of the Ukrainians had arrived at their bush country homesteads with little more than the clothes on their backs. ... Once the women and children were established in a log shack (and sometimes even before they were), the men sought work for wages with the railways or on other construction jobs. That might entail trekking many miles across the country and an absence from home of several months. ... There was work aplenty for anybody with a strong back, and that was the work that fell almost exclusively to the men in sheepskin coats. They got along well enough within their own enclaves ... but the language barrier effectively barred the eastern Europeans from all but the most menial jobs. ... The Ukrainians also got all the worst of it in land selection. ... In the parkland, every acre of productive soil had to be wrestled from the bush that claimed it. ... The Ukrainian settlers could never make spectacular grabs for acreage so quickly. They were fortunate to get their quarter sections into full production in five years.[7]

An interesting personal reflection on the hardships of settling on the prairies was provided over three decades ago by an elderly woman who had immigrated in 1899:[8]

> It was toward the end of September 1899 when seven of our families, five from Bukovina and two from Halychyna, arrived [in Canada]. The Bukovinian families had friends here, and on our third day they found a driver with a wagon, paid him $15.00 per family, and left for [the area where they were to settle]. We could have gone with them too, but we had only $7.50, and we needed it for food. Even that might have gone to the driver, but he wanted $15.00 to take us, and we didn't have it. Our husbands then decided to look for homesteads close to [the city], and all week they walked, hungry, through the forests, sandy land, and sloughs but couldn't find good land. ... All the good land was long gone. To get good land, one had to travel 100 miles farther east or north. The other man who searched for a homestead with my husband—I forget his name—came across a friend who had homesteaded on some sandy land near [the city]. He left us with his family to settle near his friend. I was left alone with my small children in

the immigration station. ... As long as the other families from Halychyna were there, it wasn't so lonely. But when my friend left, and my husband was gone for days, ... sometimes he would go to town and see if he might meet someone who could take us to the settlement, ... we had Pasichney's address there. I was so alone then ... I would almost get sick. ... My heart ached from the emptiness, ached for companionship. I cried—the children cried. I thought I would lose my mind from grief. But no one wanted to take us [to the settlement]. They wanted $20.00, but we didn't have it. There was no reason to stay [in the city]. Winter was coming, and we had no money to live.

Finally, my husband decided to build a raft and to travel the 120 miles to Pasichney's on the bank of the North Saskatchewan River. ... My husband was strong and healthy but a useless Hutzul. We were called Hutzuls because we lived in Halychyna in the Carpathian Mountains. My husband was a logger. He cut trees that travelled as great log booms on the Cheremosh River to Moldavia. In Bukovina, he had heard that people were leaving for Canada, and on a whim he decided he wanted to go to Canada too. He didn't consider that, while it might be easy to get there, how would we live once there? Our Hutzuls used to say "If you don't know the depth, don't go in the water." My husband didn't understand this. He would listen to anybody. That's why we both had such a hard life. But I haven't finished how we went by raft to Pasichney's. ... As soon as my husband built the raft on the river, ... we took our belongings from the immigration shed where we stayed for two weeks. All went not badly. But when it came to our large trunk where we had all our belongings (it weighed about 400 pounds), people ran and gathered to watch us and to laugh at the fools. My husband couldn't speak English and didn't know how to ask for a wagon to take the trunk to the river. Finally, someone drove up and, seeing us struggling as we rolled our trunk down the street, offered to take it on his wagon. My husband walked in front of the horses to show the way. When we reached the river, the driver roared with laughter, and all the children around gathered to watch us float off. All laughed and kept saying "Galeeshens go homestead." The driver took nothing for his help, just waved and said "Bye-bye."

It was about noon when we pushed off the bank. Next evening we had drifted to the ferry about 25 miles [downriver]. The water was shallow, and the raft floated slowly. We saw some Germans there that could speak our way who told us it would take a week to get to [the settlement]. We only had food for two days. My husband had to go to the fort to buy potatoes, lard, and bread. On the raft, we had a sheet of tin where we made a fire, baked our potatoes, moistening them with lard. That is how we ate. My husband also built a little hut on the raft to shelter us from rain and storms and for a place for the children to sleep. We travelled through the night. One of us would sleep a little, the other would watch the raft so that it would keep us away from sand bars and from hitting the banks. We were afraid it would break apart. The raft travelled very slowly, and on the third night, when it began to snow very heavily, we wrapped ourselves in blankets, quietly sat in the hut, and paid no attention to our drifting. The raft drifted upon a sand bar. We had to go barefoot into the water to try to push it off. No matter how hard we tried and how we struggled, we couldn't push the raft off the sand bar. We stayed there until morning, quietly sitting before the opening to the hut. And it snowed, ... as though for a prank, trying to cover us completely. We couldn't build a fire ... it snowed so heavily. Overnight more than a foot of snow fell. The firewood was wet and wouldn't burn. We thought we wouldn't make it through the night. We were so cold, our teeth locked.

I cursed my fate then. ... I cursed my husband. ... I cursed his Canada. Just before noon some Indians who lived on the banks saw us and took us to their home. They made hot tea and gave us some dry biscuits. We finally warmed up. The children had not felt as cold as my husband and I. They had slept through the night covered with a feather quilt I had brought from the old country. But we had caught a bad chill because we had to go into the water to get the raft off the sand bar. I won't forget that time for the rest of my life. Imagine ... in the river, in the mud, water all around, snowing so hard you can't see, and here, neither of us know where we are, how far we have to go, ... and try looking for people to help us get off the sand bar. We were blessed by good fortune from the almighty God that he sent us to the inquisitive Indians who came to find out what was happening. If it weren't for them, we would have perished. The Indians rescued us. All went well, but we had trouble again with our trunk. When we had warmed up a bit, the Indians tried to speak to us. We simply couldn't understand. My husband had been taught ... that when we met someone during our travels he could say "Me go homestead ... Pasichney." He said this to the Indians. Perhaps they understood, for they asked "You Galician?" He didn't understand what that meant, but he nodded yes. We understood that there were ten miles to go, because the Indians showed all ten fingers on both hands. My husband understood them and went all the way [to the settlement], where the halfbreeds sent him to Ratsoy, who had lived there two years and already had his own horses. Meanwhile, the children and I stayed with the Indians. The Indian children wanted to talk with mine, but they couldn't understand each other. At dusk, Stefan Ratsoy came in his wagon. My husband loaded all our goods from the raft, and we went to Ratsoy's place. ... The raft with its hut was left behind. Next morning we were driven 25 miles to Pasichney, now the site of [a post office].

The misery I lived through in Canada couldn't be recorded on the skin of an ox. It wasn't enough that we cleared land by hand. ... For 22 years, we cleared stumps [on the prairie], but my husband got it into his head to clear stumps in BC for 15 years. He died there. There I lost my only son. He drowned in the river while moving logs to the sawmill. I came back [to the prairies]. Now I get an old-age pension and live with my daughter, who is married. ... But I remember my native land and my youth, ... and when I do my heart aches so ... that I feel it will break. It was such a happy life there ... and here to toil, to work so hard, and not to know good fortune. ... Canada may be a good country ... but not for me.

CHAPTER 5

Ukrainians who formed bloc settlements in Saskatchewan came primarily from Galicia (contemporary western Ukraine but at the time of emigration within the Austro-Hungarian Empire). In turn, by far the largest number of Galicians emigrated from the easternmost region of Galicia, Ternopil's'ka (particularly from the areas of Ternopil, Zbarazh, Lanivtsi, Krasne, Terebovlia, Zoloch, Kopychyntsi, Chortkiv, Husiatyn, Ozeriany, Buchach, Borshchiv, Podillia, Zalischyky ...), and they spoke various Dniester dialects. Most others originated in the Belz region northwest of L'viv (the historic capital city of Galicia) toward the present Polish border (especially the areas around Sokal, Uhriniw, Zhovka, Belz, Rewa Rus'ka ...), and they spoke their own unique dialect. Across the border in western Galicia (now in Poland), some emigrated from the Jaroslaw area near Przemysl, and they spoke the Sianian dialect. Others arrived from the L'vivs'ka region (around Janow/Yaniv, Horodok, Peremyshliany, Komarno, Sambir, Drohobych, Stryi ...) and from the Ivano-Frankivs'ka region (Halych, Stanyslavtsi ...), speaking Dniester dialects. A unique dialect was spoken by emigrants from the Pokuttia region (Horodenka, Sniatyn, Kolomyia, Yavoriv ...) adjacent to Bukovina and from Bukovina itself (Chernivtsi, Khotyn ...). A distinctive culture and dialects were represented by emigrants from the Carpathian mountain regions (Hutsul, Boyko, Lemko, Transcarpathia). Some came from the northern region of Volyns'ka/Volhynia (or close areas such as Radekhiv) and spoke a southern Volhynian dialect. Still other dialects were spoken by emigrants from central and eastern regions of Ukraine (including Kiev, Poltava and Zaporozhe, Dobrowody in Cherkas'ka, Liubashiv in Odes'ka ...). So Ukrainians who emigrated to Saskatchewan more than a century ago represented a remarkable regional and often localized cultural and linguistic diversity. In fact, at the time, they had little sense of common Ukrainian ethnicity, much less political affiliation—they spoke many distinct dialects, were divided between Ukrainian (Eastern Rite) Catholic and Orthodox religious affiliations, and were citizens of Austria-Hungary, Russia, and later Poland, Romania, Hungary, and Czechoslovakia.

The beginnings of Ukrainian bloc settlements occurred slightly earlier in the neighbouring provinces of Alberta and Manitoba. In Alberta, the area around Star/Edna, east of Edmonton, was first settled in 1891–94; this small beginning would eventually grow into one of the largest rural Ukrainian settlements in Canada. In Manitoba, the Stuartburn area in the far southeast began to be settled in 1896–98, the Dauphin area north of Riding Mountain by 1896, the Interlake region by 1897, and the Strathclair and Shoal Lake areas south of Riding Mountain by 1899. Similarly, the initial establishment of Ukrainian bloc settlements in Saskatchewan occurred within a very short period of time, so dating the first such settlement or the sequence of the settlement process can be problematic. One major source providing details on Ukrainian settlement and local parish history in Saskatchewan, *Ukrainian Catholic Churches of Saskatchewan* (1977),[9] suggests that Ukrainian settlers arrived in the Candiac area in southern Saskatchewan "prior to 1895," which would make this the start of the first Ukrainian settlement in Saskatchewan; however, within just a couple of years, much larger settlements in the Yorkton region and east of Rosthern had their beginnings.

UKRAINIAN SETTLEMENTS AROUND YORKTON AND CANORA

There were three major foci of original Ukrainian settlements around Yorkton in 1896–98: what was called the Saltcoats settlement to the east and northeast, the Crooked Lake–Sliding Hills settlement to the north, and the Beaver Hills settlement to the northwest. In little more than a decade and a half, these three original settlements would merge and form the nucleus of the largest Ukrainian bloc settlement in Saskatchewan, which would quickly expand to occupy much of the east-central region of the province.

The settlement centred on Wroxton, but known as the Saltcoats settlement, approximately thirty-five to forty kilometres east and northeast of Yorkton and thirty kilometres northeast of Saltcoats, began to develop in 1896–1904. Immigrants from Horodenka and Husiatyn settled in the Wroxton area (including the Babyna Dolyna, Jablonow, Zayacz/Liberal, and Probizhna/Geddes/Elite districts) in 1896, followed by immigrants from Kopychyntsi county around Calder in 1897 in the Golden Jubilee (originally named Verboska, after the village of Verbivka/Wierzbowka near Hermakivka in Borschiv), Jarema, Toporoutz/Toporivtsi/Chaucer, Torsk, and Mostetz districts. Immigrants from Horodenka, Borshchiv, and Husiatyn settled around Stornoway in 1904. By 1913, the settlement had expanded eastward with the settlement of Galicians and Bukovinians around Runnymede and the Czernawka and Verboska districts near MacNutt. Ukrainian Catholic parishes were established at Calder in 1904, Stornoway in 1906–10, St. Volodymyr and Olha north of Wroxton in 1909, Runnymede in 1928, and Holy Apostles Sts. Peter and Paul in Wroxton in 1949–52. Ukrainian Orthodox parishes were founded in the Toporiwtzi/St. Elia district south of Wroxton, the Kurchakiv district east of Calder, Stornoway in 1927 (where the Ukrainian Greek Orthodox Church of Sts. Peter and Paul is now a historic site), and Wroxton in 1953 (where the striking Ukrainian Greek Orthodox Church of St. Elia, with its large central dome and two frontal cupolas representative of traditional Byzantine architecture, was designated a heritage site in 1996). In 1971, Ukrainians constituted almost all (93%) of the residents of Wroxton; the Ukrainian proportion in both Stornoway and Calder was increasing (respectively from 55% in 1961 to 78% in 1971 in Stornoway and from 68% to 83% in Calder), while they constituted three-quarters of the population of the surrounding Calder RM and a quarter of Wallace RM. At the time, Ukrainians in these communities and rural municipalities totalled about 1,400, excluding the city of Yorkton (pop. 15,038 in 2006), where another 4,000 Ukrainians and 800 Poles lived, together comprising more than a third (35.6%) of the city residents in 1971. Wroxton, which became an incorporated village in 1912, officially lost its status as a village in 1997 when its population fell below fifty and the railway line was abandoned; Calder (pop. 80) is still a village though also declining; Stornoway had only ten remaining residents at last count.

The adjoining Crooked Lake, Sliding Hills, or New Yaroslav settlement immediately to the north first began to develop in 1897–1906 in the Dnieper area (approximately thirty kilometres northeast of Yorkton) and around Canora (forty-five kilometres north of Yorkton), where 180 families from western Ukraine settled in 1897. Immigrants from Borshchiv and Horodenka settled around Dnieper and in the Dnipro, Dniester, Scalat, Stawchan/Stavchany, Verenczanka, and Oleskow districts in 1897. They were followed by settlers from Volhynia, Bukovina, and Halychyna (Galicia), especially

Chortkiv, around Canora the following year, including the Dniester, Franko, Mazeppa, Wysla, and Brena districts. Then Whitesand (about equidistant, twenty-five kilometres southwest of Canora and northwest of Yorkton) and the Beblo district were settled by immigrants from the village of Lytsivka in Dolyna in 1903, Antoniwka (nine kilometres north of Canora) by settlers from the village of Antonivka in Chortkiv county the next year, and St. Philips and the Doroshenko/Bear Stream district north of Kamsack also in 1904 by immigrants from Terebovka. Others settled north of Veregin in 1906 and had expanded into the Kamsack area by 1928, while the Zhoda district southwest of Veregin was settled. South of Canora was the Fedoruk district, and the Bridok district was named after a village in Bukovina. At Dnieper, a church served the Seraphim sect from 1904 to 1918, when it became a Catholic parish. The Ruthenian Greek Catholic Church of the Assumption of the Blessed Virgin Mary, now a historic site, was established in 1906 at Antoniwka (Amsterdam); other Ukrainian Catholic parishes in the settlement were established at St. Philip's in 1907, Whitesand-Pakrov in 1911, Canora in 1917 and 1931, Dnieper (the Greek Catholic Church of the Transfiguration, 1931, now a historic site), St. Nicholas north of Veregin in 1932, and Kamsack in 1941. However, twice as many Orthodox churches were established: the earliest at Uspenska (immediately south of Canora) and Boychuk (fifteen kilometres southeast) in 1902, Donwell (eleven kilometres southeast) and Kaplychka (fourteen kilometres south of Veregin) in 1903. At Kaplychka, a rare abandoned log church hidden in the woods, a couple of the oldest burials are dated 1906, another couple 1912; most of the graves there indicate that these pioneer settlers had been born during the 1860s–70s and died during the 1920s–30s, though a few graves are more recent. At least two were infant deaths—the babies died the same year that they were born. The cemetery has twenty-two graves with markers (three with just plain wooden crosses). Other Orthodox churches in the settlement were Hampton (about twenty-five kilometres southeast of Canora) in 1908, St. Elias (nineteen kilometres south of Veregin) in 1909, Mohyla–Swiatoho Mychaila (just northeast of Canora) in 1912, St. Michael's (thirteen kilometres south of Veregin) in 1924 (today a heritage site, this tiny church has a unique traditional Eastern European roof line capped with three small cupolas), Mazeppa (about twenty kilometres southeast of Canora) in 1926, Canora in 1927 (Holy Trinity Ukrainian Greek Orthodox Church, a fine remaining example of traditional Kievan architecture, is a heritage site), Gorlitz and the Annak district in 1939 (midway between Yorkton and Canora, where Sts. Peter and Paul Church exemplifies classic Ukrainian Byzantine architecture with an exterior bell tower), Kamsack in 1945, as well as Burgis. Canora was a railway station, post office, and school district in 1904; it became an incorporated village in 1905 and a town five years later. By 1921, it had more than 1,200 residents and peaked at 2,700 in 1966. During the 1960s, the Ukrainian proportion in Canora was actually increasing (from 58% in 1961 to 63% in 1971). Ukrainians comprised almost two-thirds of the population of Sliding Hills RM and over a third (38.2%) of Cote RM. Although they were still a minority (only about 30%) in Kamsack, they now outnumbered the Russian Doukhobor population for whom this town was a centre. The town of Canora had 2,013 residents in 2006, Mikado had been designated an "organized hamlet" with just fifty-six residents, while Dnieper, now simply a rural locality, had seen better years. The Ukrainian population of the Crooked Lake/Sliding Hills settlement could be estimated at approximately 2,100 in 1971, adding Ukrainian-origin population in Kamsack and the rural municipalities of Sliding Hills and Cote but excluding Canora. Residents of Ukrainian and Polish origin constituted almost three-quarters of the population of Canora; so, with the inclusion of Canora, approximately 2,000 Ukrainians and Poles would be added. The strong Ukrainian presence in Canora is announced by "Lesia," a statue of a woman wearing traditional Ukrainian garb offering bread to visitors.

The Beaver Hills settlement initially began to develop during 1898–1905. The original nucleus of this settlement was around Theodore, Insinger, and Sheho, approximately forty to eighty kilometres northwest of Yorkton, along the Canadian Pacific Railway line between Yorkton and Saskatoon (today the Yellowhead Highway 16); the settlement soon expanded southward toward the Beaver Hills. Sheho already had a post office and school (Sheho Lake) as early as 1891–92 (three kilometres north of the present community). In 1898, immigrants from the village of Volkivtsi in Borshchiv county in Galicia and from Bukovina settled around Insinger, including in the Lysenko and Wasileff districts, and Sheho, including the Malyk Lake district to the north and the Wolkowetz district to the east, then were joined by others from Volkivtsi as well as from Zoloch and Terebovlia counties, settling to the south of Sheho in the Kolo Shevchuka/Kolo Kozakevychiv, Okno, Fosti, Pohorlowtz, and Krasny districts in 1903. The beginnings of the present community of Sheho were when a railway station was located there in 1904; the community became an incorporated village the next year. That year settlers from the village of Bartativ in Horodok county arrived in the Tuffnell area. Theodore already had a country post office in 1893; by 1904, a nucleus of the community had formed with a school, post office, and general store. The community became an incorporated village in 1907. North of Theodore were the Drobot and Kenaschuk districts, and the Czernowitz School District dated from 1909; it was named after Czernowitz, the German version of Chernivtsi, the capital of Bukovina. The Walawa and Horosziwci/War End districts were located west of Theodore, most likely named after the village of Horokhivtsi south of Przemysl, today in Polish Galicia. The typical Ukrainian pattern of establishing churches and cemeteries in the country soon became characteristic of this settlement. In or close to the community of Insinger, Ukrainian Catholic and Orthodox parishes were established as early as 1904, and a second Orthodox parish—Descent of the Holy Spirit— was established in 1942 (recognized as a municipal heritage property in 1988). Insinger was an incorporated village and had a school in 1921. In Sheho, Orthodox parishes came into being in 1905 and 1922, Catholic ones not until 1954. At Tuffnell, the Catholic parishes were founded in 1909 and 1924, and St. Mary's Orthodox cemetery dates from 1919 and church from 1927 before moving into the village in 1961. The Orthodox parish at Theodore was not established until 1948. Out in isolated rural localities, north of Theodore at Mamornitz an Orthodox parish was organized in 1905 and a Catholic parish in 1913, and an Orthodox cemetery was located at Riverside. Beyond Insinger, an Orthodox parish was established in Westbrook to the south in 1919, and an Orthodox cemetery was located at Lysenko to the northeast, where the Aysgarth district was settled. South of Sheho, Orthodox parishes were formed at Kuprowski in 1908, Melnychuk in 1909, and Stadnyk in 1924, and Orthodox cemeteries were located at Sochawski and Fedyak and a Catholic cemetery at St. Mary's. The Ukrainian Greek Orthodox Church of the Holy Ghost near Insinger (1942) became a heritage site in 1988. Ukrainians comprise almost three-quarters of the population of Insinger RM. The Ukrainian proportion in the village of Insinger seems to have fluctuated somewhat: in 1961, Ukrainians constituted 84%, ten years later just 60%; however, if residents claiming Polish ethnicity are added, the combined Ukrainian-Polish proportion came to 93%. Conversely, at Theodore the Ukrainian proportion increased from 53% to 71% in the same period. At Sheho, Ukrainians have made up approximately 80% of the population. In Sheho, Tuffnell, and Foam Lake, by 1907 Protestants were already far outnumbered, so that Presbyterians and Methodists shared churches.[10] In 1971, the Ukrainian populations of these communities and encompassing Insinger RM could be estimated at about 1,300. Foam Lake had 1,123 residents in 2006, Theodore 339 (but almost 400 residents already by 1931), and Sheho 121 (compared with over 400 in 1956). But Insinger, which once had over 100 residents from the 1930s through the 1960s, then declined to just seventy-two in 1971, fifty-six five years later, and thirty-nine in another five years, and now it is down to only twenty. The school was closed in 1967, the grain elevators were demolished in 1999, and the village was dissolved in 2003, becoming a hamlet. Tuffnell now has only ten remaining residents. Moreover, all of these communities have continued to decline.

These original three settlements rapidly expanded to the west, northwest, and north. Ukrainian settlers moved into the area immediately west of Yorkton as soon as 1897–1907. The Jaroslaw district was settled in 1897 by immigrants from the villages of Vitlyn, Makovys'ka, and Liashky in the Jaroslaw area of western Galicia; they also settled around Jaroslaw in 1897 and Jedburgh in 1905. The secluded church there is one of the earliest Ukrainian Catholic churches in Saskatchewan, dating back to 1902. It has long been derelict and has often been vandalized, but the cemetery is still well maintained by local farmers, and historic plaques tell the story of these earliest pioneers. The earliest gravestones date back to the 1850s–60s; most burials were carried out through the 1930s–40s, but a few more recent gravestones can be found, for example from the 1960s. Jaroslaw School used to be five kilometres to the south of the church, but the schoolhouse has been removed to a farm. Jedburgh and the Kvitka district to the south were similarly settled by people from the villages of Liashky and Makovys'ka; Beaver Dale was settled by people from Liashky in 1905. The settlers around Plain View came from Borshchiv in 1906, those around Parkerview and Beckenham the following year from Khotynets and other villages in Yavoriv. During the 1920s, Ukrainian settlers moved from Beaver Dale and Plain View into the Willowbrook and Radimno area. This general area became strongly Ukrainian Catholic, with parishes established at Jaroslaw in 1903 (one of the earliest Ukrainian Catholic parishes), Beaver Dale in 1907, Plain View and Beckenham in 1911, Willowbrook in 1941, Parkerview in 1943 with Sawiuk cemetery, and Jedburgh in 1948. Ukrainians and Poles comprised half of the residents of Willowbrook, 43.8% of those in Jedburgh, and 17.9% of those in Springside in 1971, yet in surrounding rural areas they had far higher proportions. In 2006, only twenty people still lived in Jedburgh, while Jaroslaw, Beaver Dale, Plain View, Beckenham, Willowbrook, and Parkerview had never become more than hamlets. Adding together the Ukrainian population in these communities and the rural municipalities of Orkney and Garry yields a total estimate of about 1,400 in 1971.

Farther southwest of Yorkton, Ukrainians settled heavily in 1901–10 within the corridor extending between Melville and Ituna, along the CNR main line from

UKRAINIAN AND POLISH SETTLEMENTS

Winnipeg to Saskatoon (and today Highway 15), skirting the File Hills, through the Beaver Hills, to the Touchwood Hills. The Melville area was settled by both Galicians and Bukovinians in 1907; the settlers around Fenwood arrived from Drobych county in 1901; Goodeve and the Halech and Stryj districts from Sokal, Husiatyn, and Drohobych in 1902 and from Yavoriv and Liubachiv in 1904; Hubbard from Stryi county, Dolyna city, and the village of Lublinets in 1903 and from Zbarazh in 1908; Bedfordville from the village of Yamnytsia in Stanyslavtsi county in 1906; Birmingham from Ulychno in Halychyna in 1904; Ituna from Stryi in 1905 (the old Ituna public school, dating from 1920, became a designated heritage property in 1983); the Jasmin area from the village of Kobylnytsia in Rava Rus'ka county in northwestern Galicia in 1904 and from Yavoriv the following year. Ukrainian settlement already extended as far west as Herzel by 1910, and Ukrainians had moved into the Kelliher area during 1928–34. Ukrainian Catholic parishes formed throughout the region: at Fenwood (1905), Goodeve (1906, 1909—Holy Trinity Ukrainian Catholic Church north of Goodeve is a heritage site), Hubbard (1909), Immaculate Conception in the Jasmin area (1909), St. Nicholas-Stanyslavtsi (1910) in the Bedfordville–Church Hill district (where the Michael Hrushewski Community Hall was located), Birmingham/St. Paraskevia (1912), Melville (1916), Ituna (1919), Plain View (twenty kilometres north of Melville, where St. John Ruthenian Greek Catholic Church, also known as St. John the Baptist and the Holy Ghost Greek Catholic Church, was built in 1934 and declared a heritage site in 1992), Herzel (1938), Moleski near Kelliher (1942), Jasmin (1948–49), and Kelliher (1950); missions were also established at Leross and Barvas. Orthodox parishes formed at Fenwood (where the original Keningsberg School, constructed in 1905, became Sts. Peter and Paul Ukrainian Greek Orthodox Church in 1914, when it was purchased by the former Ruthenian Presbyterian Church, and a designated historic site in 1986), Melville (1916, 1928—respectively St. George's and Intercession of St. Mary Churches were designated as heritage sites), Goodeve (1918), and Ituna (1923). In 1971, Ukrainians and Poles together comprised strong majorities of the residents of Goodeve (85.0%), Hubbard (73.9%), and Ituna (83.0%) and lower proportions of those of Jasmin (50.0%, down from 74.0% just ten years earlier), Fenwood (34.8%), Kelliher (30.0%), and Melville (22.7%). Among these communities, apart from the city of Melville, only the town of Ituna (pop. 622 in 2006) reached a substantial size; the villages of Goodeve (pop. 50), Hubbard (pop. 43), and Fenwood (pop. 35) have few residents; Jasmin has lost all of its final five residents counted in 2001. The Ukrainian populations of these communities, including Melville, and the surrounding rural municipalities of Stanley, Tullymet, and Ituna–Bon Accord was approximately 3,300, to which could be added another 1,000 people of Polish origin. Incidentally, at the time of writing, the oldest living Canadian, at age 112, is Pearl Lutzko of Ituna; born in 1899 in Chortikiw, Ukraine, she immigrated in 1907 and after marrying farmed near Goodeve until 1959.

Another corridor of Ukrainian settlement soon extended northwest from Canora toward Wadena, along another CNR line (today Highway 5) in 1903–12, and was further expanded during the late 1920s to early 1930s. Northwest of Canora, Tiny/Kovalivka was settled in 1906 by immigrants from Buchach, Borshchiv, and Ternopil; Buchanan in 1903, from various counties of Galicia, as well as Mitchellview Post Office to the north, serving the Chechow, Monastyr, Hryhoriw, Vasloutz/Vasyliv/Kolo-Vasyleva, and Olesha School Districts (north of Buchanan, a wooden cross erected to honour the early pioneers is a historic site); Kolo Vasyliev/Wasyliw (about eight to ten kilometres southwest of Buchanan) and the Dobronoutz or Dobranovetz district in 1905 from Borshchiv; Dobrowody (about ten kilometres northeast of Rama) and the Wolna district in 1904 and later Rama in 1912 from Dobrowody in Pihaitsi county; Kyziv-Tiaziv (about ten kilometres southeast of Rama) in 1904–07 from Oleksyatsi and Tiaziv in Borshchiv and Stanyslaviv counties; Kulykiv (eleven kilometres north of Invermay) in 1912 from the village of Kulykiv; and Kuroki and the Chorney Beach district on Fishing Lake by 1926. Early Ukrainian Catholic parishes were formed respectively at Wasyliw (1906), Kovalivka (1907), Kyziv-Tiaziv (1910), Dobrowody (where St. Mary's, built in 1911, is dominated by a magnificent central *bani*, covered in shiny textured tin), Rama (1928), Kulykiv southwest of Okla (1930–32—the Ukrainian Catholic Church of the Holy Eucharist, Kulikiw, is now a historic site), Kuroki (1934), Buchanan (1935), and Invermay (1953). Orthodox parishes were formed at Rama (where St. Michael's Church has been a heritage site since 1994) and Buchanan in 1936. The present head of the Ukrainian Orthodox Church of Canada (UOCC), His Eminence Metropolitan John, born in 1935 into the Stinka/Spizawka family with twelve children, received his earliest education in the Dobranovetz School near Buchanan; he became the Ukrainian Orthodox bishop of Saskatoon in 1983, the bishop of Edmonton in 1985, the archbishop of the Western Diocese in 1990, and finally the metropolitan of the UOCC in 2005. In Buchanan RM, Ukrainians comprised just over half (53%) of the population, but 78% combined with Poles and Russians, in 1971 and about one-third (67%) in Good Lake RM. Similarly, in the village of Buchanan, only half of the residents claimed Ukrainian ethnic origin, whereas the combined proportion of Ukrainians, Poles, and Russians was 83%. At Rama, Ukrainians made up just one-third of the residents yet 88.9% combined with Poles. It is interesting that in just one decade—the 1960s—at Invermay the combined Ukrainian-Polish proportion declined sharply from almost two-thirds of the residents to just one-third. The 2006 population of Invermay was 262, Margo ninety. Both of these communities, as well as Buchanan, Rama, and Kuroki, have all been declining, and suffice it to say that Tiny lives up to its name. Buchanan became an incorporated village in 1907; it had over 500 residents by 1951 but underwent a dramatic decline during the 1970s; it now has less than half that number. Rama became an incorporated village in 1919 and had almost 300 residents in 1961, but now only seventy-five remain. Kuroki was also incorporated as a village in 1919, but it lost its status as a village just seven years later and was downgraded to an organized hamlet; still, it had over 200 residents by the early 1970s; today it has just sixty-five. The total Ukrainian population of this settlement (in these communities and the rural municipalities of Good Lake, Buchanan, Invermay, and Sasman) was approximately 2,600 in 1971, to which could be added at least 900 Poles.

Ukrainians from Buchach and Horodenka settled in Wadena in 1909, while north of Wadena immigrants from the village of Bobulyntsi in Buchach had settled in 1907–09 in Fosston, the Bobulynci district (west of Fosston), the Zazula district near Hendon, and Rose Valley; the Ponass Lake district in 1907 from Horodenka, Buchach, and particularly the village of Lemkivshchyna; and Nora by 1933 from various earlier Ukrainian Canadian settlements. Ukrainian Catholic parishes were formed at Ponass Lake

UKRAINIAN AND POLISH SETTLEMENTS

(where the Ruthenian Greek Catholic Church of St. Michael the Archangel, constructed in 1910–11, became a heritage site in 1990), Bobulynci (1920), Fosston (1937), Nora (1938), Wadena (1950), and Rose Valley (1958–60). Ukrainian Orthodox churches came into existence at Fosston and Wadena (1951). In 1971, Ukrainians and Poles comprised 42.9% of the residents of Fosston, 23.8% of those of Rose Valley, and 22.1% of those of Wadena. At that time in these communities and the rural municipalities of Ponass Lake and Lakeview, the Ukrainian and Polish population numbered approximately 1,400. Rose Valley (pop. 338) is a substantial community, whereas Fosston (pop. fifty-five) and Nora are far smaller; all are losing population.

Ukrainian settlement also expanded rapidly north, northwest, and northeast of Canora, into the Porcupine Hills and Swan Plain, primarily in the 1902–14 period, then further during the late 1920s and early 1930s. North and northwest of Canora, immigrants from Buchach settled around Preeceville and Sturgis in 1902, in the rural districts of Halycry to the southwest and Buchach (twenty kilometres to the west) in 1904–06, Chekhiv (named after their village of origin) and Hryhoriv (to the southwest) in 1902, and Muchowsko to the northeast; Hazel Dell in 1904 and the districts of Stove Creek/St. Elias/Byrtnyky (about twenty kilometres north of Okla and Lintlaw) and Lodi in 1914 from Hryhoriv and Byrtnykiv in Buchach; Tadmore in 1904 from Borshchiv; and later Endeavour, the Cheremosz and Borszczow districts, and Usherville; Hudson Bay in 1925 from Borshchiv and Liubachiv counties; Porcupine Plain after 1920; and particularly the High Tor district in 1928–33 from Buchach. In these areas, early Ukrainian Catholic churches were established at Chekhiv (1906), Hryhoriv (1907), Buchach (1913), and later Stove Creek (1924), High Tor (1936), and Hudson Bay (1937), while the Porcupine Plain Parish (1941) served missions at Carrot River, Endeavour, Prairie River, Chelan, and finally Hazel Dell (1944–48). Tiny Holy Ascension Russian Greek Orthodox Church near Sturgis, now left abandoned in a field, was built by poor immigrants in 1905; it resembles a peasant cottage, with rough, saddle-notched log construction, a single window, a shingle roof in traditional hexaform style, and only a dirt floor.[11] Swiatoho Mychaila Ukrainian Greek Orthodox Church (1912), also known later as Mohyla or St. Michael's, northeast of Canora, a small clapboard church that was originally Ukrainian Catholic, was made a heritage site in 1985. Other Orthodox parishes were found at Sturgis (n.d.) and Endeavour (1942). Little more than a third of the residents of Preeceville, Sturgis, Rusally/Endeavour, and Porcupine Plain claimed Ukrainian origin in 1971 (respectively 37%, 34%, 41%, and 33%), yet in surrounding rural districts there was a far higher proportion (e.g., 71% in Clayton RM). After Canora, the largest of these communities is Preeceville (pop. 1,050), with neighbouring Sturgis (pop. 575), while Kelvington had 866 residents and Porcupine Plain 783 in 2006. But all four towns have been losing population, as have Lintlaw (pop. 145) and Endeavour (pop. 118). Other communities in the region are far smaller: Okla now has only twenty-five residents, Usherville and Hazel Dell twenty, Ketchen fifteen. Altogether we can estimate the Ukrainian population of this settlement area—including these communities and the rural municipalities of Preeceville, Hazel Dell, Kelvington, and Porcupine—to have been about 2,800 or a combined Ukrainian-Polish population of 3,500 in 1971.

Northeast of Canora, Ukrainians from Hryhoriv in Buchach county settled near Norquay in 1902–03 and from Borshchiv in 1904; from Zalishchyky and Borshchiv around Arran, in the Kobzar and Paseika districts to the south and Vesna to the southeast, and in the Whitebeech/Sopoff district (twenty-three kilometres north) in 1907 and the Osin and Podolia districts; from Chortkiv and Bukovina around Stenen in 1904 (there is a Halicz cemetery north of Stenen); from Borshchiv around Paniowci/ Swan Plain and Hyas in 1904; from Galicia and Volhynia in the Maybridge area near Pelly in 1908 as well as in the Poelcapelle (originally known by settlers' names—Baran, Kurytnik, Tataryn, Phylipowich) and Maloneck districts north and northeast of Pelly; and from Borshchiv in Glen Elder/Kolo Lazaruk in 1912. Later Ukrainians from Yavoriv settled in the Erwood district in 1927 (from Yavoriv), in Weekes in 1927–28, and in the village of Pelly in 1940. Ukrainian Catholic parishes were organized in rural districts outside Canora at Kovalivka/Kowalowka, at Norquay (1906–07, 1935), and at Vesna (southeast of Arran, 1910), Swan Plain (1912), Arran (1916), Maybridge (1918), Glen Elder (1935), Erwood (mission 1941, parish 1946), Weekes (Doncrest mission, 1946), Pelly (1948), Norquay (1951), and Hyas (1954). Orthodox parishes were organized at Sturgis (n.d.), Norquay (1921), Danbury/St. Volodymyr (thirty kilometres northwest of Norquay, 1925), Kobzar (southeast of Arran, 1929—the present Ukrainian Greek Orthodox Church of the Ascension dates from 1934–36), Swan Plain (1940), and Stenen (1955); cemeteries were also located at Podillia and Zalishchyky near Arran. A significant majority of residents in these communities have claimed Ukrainian origin: three-quarters at Arran in 1971, 81% at Stenen, 55% at Hyas (a decline from two-thirds in 1961). According to recent (2006) census data, Norquay (pop. 412) was the largest community in this region, followed by Pelly (pop. 287), Hyas (pop. 11), Stenen (pop. 91), Arran (pop. 40), and Swan Plain (pop. 15). All of these communities have been declining. Arran, which became an incorporated village in 1916, had more than 200 residents in 1951, and now fewer than a quarter of that number remain; the school was closed in 1994. All told, back in 1971, the Ukrainian populations of these communities and the surrounding rural municipalities (St. Philips, Keys, Livingston, and Clayton) totalled approximately 3,200; between half and over two-thirds of the populations in these rural municipalities was Ukrainian.

Meanwhile, Ukrainian settlers had started to move into the region to the west of the original Beaver Hills settlement, south of the Quill Lakes and north of the Touchwood Hills, initially in 1903–10 and continuing through the 1930s. South and west of Wadena, Ukrainians from earlier Ukrainian settlements around Arran and Swan Plain in Saskatchewan and Ethelbert in Manitoba had settled in the town of Watson by 1925 but the nearby district of Wimmer several years earlier. Immigrants from Borshchiv in southeastern Galicia and Peremyshl and Jaroslaw in western Galicia (today in Poland) first settled at the Model Farm in the West Bend area in 1903–05. Immigrants from Husiatyn and Rava Rus'ka joined them around Bankend in 1905, and settled around Wishart in 1907, including in the Halicz (named after Halychyna, or Galicia), Larisa, and Honey Bank districts. Wishart was a post office as early as 1884, but Ukrainians and Poles did not pour into the district in significant numbers until 1906–07. A Canadian Pacific branch line from Foam Lake reached Wishart in 1928. Wishart was incorporated as a village in 1937. The rural district of Holar (southeast of Wynyard) was settled in 1908 by immigrants from the villages of Uvysla, Zvyniach, and Khvorostkiv in Husiatyn and Chortkiv counties; the Krasne district (west of Wishart) was settled in 1910 by immigrants from Husiatyn and Stanyslaviv counties. The Michael Hrushewski

Community Hall was located in the Stanyslavtsi/Stanisloff district south of Foam Lake. Typically, the first Ukrainians settled in rural districts and did not move into towns in significant numbers until much later—for example into Wynyard, especially from the Krasne district, and into Foam Lake, from the Model Farm, Tuffnell, as well as Ukrainian settlements in Manitoba, during the 1930s. Ukrainian Catholic parishes were organized throughout the region: outside Wishart (1907), Patronage of the Blessed Virgin Mary in the Model Farm district near West Bend (1909), at Beckenham (twenty-five kilometres south of Foam Lake, 1911), Krasne/Kolo Pidkowich (1914, replaced by St. John Apostle the Theologian, a brick church constructed in 1940 in Byzantine cruciform style with a large central dome bracketed by two frontal cupolas, which together with the cemetery and community hall now constitute a historic site), St. Demetrius/Kolo Syrota (1919), St. Michael's north of Wishart (1924, now a historic site), Wynyard (1937), Foam Lake (1940), Bankend (1942), Watson (1952), and Wishart (in town, 1958). Orthodox parishes included Edmore (sixteen kilometres south of Foam Lake, 1905), near Foam Lake (where the Russian Greek Orthodox Church of St. Mary, now a historic site, was established in 1909), Wimmer (1919), Punnichy (1936), St. John Bohoslow at Krasne, Foam Lake (1943), Watson (1948), and Wynyard (1950). Apart from the nearby towns of Foam Lake, Wynyard, and Watson, the only real remaining small village (now reclassified, though, as an organized hamlet) is Wishart (pop. 95); Bankend at last count retained only ten residents, and West Bend was just a hamlet. To put this in perspective, Wishart had attained a population of almost 300 by 1966; the community lost its status as a village in 2002. In 1971, Ukrainians with some Poles comprised a high proportion of the residents of Wishart (72.4%) and West Bend (71.4%) and a substantial minority in Foam Lake (41.0%) and Wynyard (34.5%). In these communities and the encompassing rural municipalities (Foam Lake, Emerald, Elfros, and Big Quill), the Ukrainian population numbered about 3,200 and Polish another 1,000. Despite its declining population, Wishart still maintains a strong Ukrainian identity: *Malanka*, a Ukrainian folk holiday, is still celebrated every January 13; New Year's Eve is celebrated according to the Julian calendar; and the Hopak Dancers have been performing for more than three decades.

All together, by the 1920s, these neighbouring areas of Ukrainian settlement had merged to form a single vast Ukrainian settlement, arguably not only the largest Ukrainian bloc settlement in the Prairie Provinces (especially since this region in Saskatchewan is contiguous with the large Ukrainian settlements around Riding Mountain in Manitoba) but also the largest ethnic bloc settlement in this region of Canada. The total area of Ukrainian (and often Polish) settlement in Saskatchewan extends over at least twenty-eight rural municipalities, an area stretching over 180 kilometres from east to west and the same distance from north to south. Within this vast settlement, Ukrainian Canadians constitute a majority or plurality (i.e., they outnumber other ethnic groups) in most towns and incorporated villages and in numerous rural districts, smaller villages, and hamlets. These contiguous areas of Ukrainian and Polish settlement (including the cities of Yorkton and Melville) contained at least 27,700 people of Ukrainian origin and another 5,800 of Polish origin in 1971.

This is not meant to imply that all of this territory comprising the east-central region of Saskatchewan is solidly Ukrainian, for there are smaller ethnic settlements of

Germans, Scandinavians, French, Hungarians, Romanians, and Doukhobors in this region. Nonetheless, not only have Ukrainians completely surrounded these smaller settlements of other ethnic groups, but also in many cases they have progressively penetrated them. In recent decades, people of Ukrainian origin have been steadily moving into areas formerly settled largely by people of Scandinavian origin, both north of Wadena and south of Foam Lake and Wynyard. Comparing data from the 1960s for four mixed Ukrainian and Scandinavian communities, we can note a consistent increase in Ukrainian population and a consistent decrease in Scandinavian population: Ukrainians made up 25.6% of the residents of Foam Lake in 1961 and 34.7% in 1971, whereas Scandinavians were 19.2% in 1961 and 14.4% ten years later; in Wadena, Ukrainians increased from 17.6% to 18.9%, while Scandinavians decreased from 20.7% to 18.6%; in Wynyard, Ukrainians increased from 22.7% to 25.0%, whereas Scandinavians in this traditionally Icelandic town declined from 22.6%—virtually equal in number to their Ukrainian neighbours—to 18.3%, now outnumbered by Ukrainians; and in Rose Valley, Ukrainians were outnumbered by Norwegians more than two to one in 1961 but increased from 14.4% to 16.4%, while Scandinavians decreased from 30.1% to 28.7%.

THE FISH CREEK AND YELLOW CREEK SETTLEMENTS

Meanwhile, several other Ukrainian bloc settlements were developing in other regions of Saskatchewan. A large Ukrainian settlement formed in the north-central region from 1897 to 1912 and continued to expand well into the 1950s. Between Rosthern and the South Saskatchewan River, the Rosthern Farms district (inclusive of Kolo-Kaminskykh, Nichlava, Kolo-Blokhiv, Dobraniwka, Adamiwka, and Hnatiw Lake) was settled by immigrants from Borshchiv in 1897; thirty-two families had settled in this district by 1901 and another thirty-two across the river. However, according to accounts, initially these settlers "stubbornly resisted" being settled there. The *Toronto Globe and Mail* (May 21, 1898) reported a situation of "open revolt." The immigrants threatened to kill a government interpreter. Since they wanted to proceed to join relatives already settled in Alberta, they refused to even inspect the proposed area of settlement. At last, twelve families did agree to settle there, but forty-seven left (thirty for Alberta, seventeen for Manitoba). A heavy frost in June encouraged the remainder to leave, but French Catholic priests from Duck Lake persuaded them to stay. But by 1901 a government inspector was already able to report that "the Galician settlers are in a very prosperous condition." In his report to Frank Pedley, the superintendent of immigration at Ottawa, on August 28, 1901, C.W. Speers, the government inspector based at Brandon, commented that

> The settlers were busy cutting a very good crop and they have made ample provision for their stock for the winter. They have excellent gardens and ... I was very much impressed with the progress they are making. Their buildings are very much improved, their families much more comfortable. They are very industrious and I think all the early difficulties of settlement have been fully overcome. These people are good settlers and will do their share in developing the country.[12]

UKRAINIAN AND POLISH SETTLEMENTS

Ukrainian settlers rapidly moved eastward across the river to settle the Fish Creek settlement around Alvena (where a post office was established as early as 1899). North of Alvena (and west of Wakaw), the St. Julien and Sniatyn districts were settled in 1897 by immigrants from Horodenka, Sniatyn, and Sokal (St. Julien was served by a rural post office from 1904 to 1969 and a country general store from 1930 to 1962); the Sokal district was settled in 1901 by immigrants from Sokal and Radekhiv (the Sokal Post Office operated from 1912 to 1939 and the Farmers Trading Store from 1907 to 1911); while the Kolomyia and Kyjiw/Kiev districts were also developed by early settlers. West and southwest of Alvena, immigrants from Borshchiv, Sokal, and Ternopil settled in the Svoboda/Alvena Farms (where there was a country store between 1915 and 1930), Laniwci, and Vladimir districts in 1998–99. From Alvena northeast toward Wakaw, immigrants mainly from Borshchiv, Buchach, and Horodenka had settled around Carpenter/Hory by 1900 (where a post office operated from 1930 to 1969) and in the Zalischyky and Horodenka districts; from Alvena east toward Cudworth in the Kolo-Pidskal'noho/St. Demetrius, Kotzko, and Skala districts; and southeast of Alvena in the Ozeriany/Carpathian and Ruthenia districts. Southwest of Alvena, immigrants primarily from Borshchiv and Horodenka settled in 1900–04 around Smuts/Na-Prymovin, in the surrounding Borszczow, Poltava/Poltawa, Torhovytsia/Torhowycia, Pitt, Riel-Dana, Bodnari, Pretty Lake, Delena, and Rak districts. Farther south, immigrants from Borshchiv settled among French around Vonda in 1904 and Prud'homme in 1910 as well as in the Borshchiv, Ozeranko, Kolo-Havrylyukiv, and Trojan districts south of Prud'homme in 1905. The settlers in the Vonda area (185 Ukrainians and eleven Poles, divided almost equally by gender) complained about being sold poor, stony land by English Canadian "real estate sharks" at $700 a quarter.[13] The hamlet of Dana and surrounding districts (Kolo-Solomyanoho, Drahomanow) were settled in 1902 by immigrants from Horodenka and Borshchiv. Still farther south and southeast, immigrants from Horodenka and Husiatyn predominated around Meacham and the Siczynsky district in 1907, while immigrants from Borshchiv settled near Bruno in 1903 and around Peterson in 1909, and they were joined by people from Yavoriv in the Wolverine district toward Lanigan in 1905.

Northeast of Wakaw, the Yellow Creek settlement was also forming. Tway (and the Kaminka district) were settled as early as 1899 by immigrants from Radekhiv and Horodenka; Tarnopol (and the Madraga Farm district) the next year by immigrants from Borshchiv; and the village of Yellow Creek (and the Trepannia district to the north and Hazel Lake/Sheremata Farm to the south) by various Galicians in 1912. The Lepine and Bukowina area (ten kilometres southeast of Wakaw) had been settled by 1900 by immigrants from Borshchiv and Horodenka, though Ukrainians did not move into the main towns of Wakaw and Cudworth in significant numbers until the 1930s. Wakaw Lake has beaches named Schitka, Osze, and Siba. Despite its increasing Ukrainian and Polish population, the community and rural municipality of Yellow Creek long maintained Anglo dominance, evidenced in English speakers controlling the RM administration (the first Slavic reeve was in 1937) and punishing Ukrainian children caught speaking their mother tongue at school.

An extensive network of Ukrainian Catholic parishes was rapidly built throughout the settlement and beyond. The Descent of the Holy Spirit Parish at Rosthern Farms/

Kolo Kaminskykh, established in 1902, claimed to be the first Ukrainian Catholic parish in Saskatchewan (the present church dates from 1927 and became a heritage site in 1995); the neighbouring Nativity of the Blessed Virgin Mary Parish was formed soon after in 1904. A Basilian mission and monastery, St. Basil the Great, was established at Alvena Farms, several kilometres northwest of Alvena, in 1902 and served the district until 1925, when it was moved to Alberta—the monastery became a rectory and then a parish hall until it was destroyed by fire. The Assumption of the Blessed Virgin Mary congregation was organized in 1903, a first church built in 1905, and the present church built in 1925. The tiny Ascension of Our Lord Jesus Christ Church in the Hory (*v horakh*, meaning in the hills) district near Carpenter, constructed in 1904, is the second oldest extant church in the entire eparchy. Other early Ukrainian Catholic churches in the settlement were St. Paraskevia near Tway (1904, destroyed by fire in 1973), Holy Trinity at Sokal (1904), Smuts (the first St. John the Baptist Church dated from 1905 but was destroyed by fire in 1925; the present church was built the next year and was designated a heritage site in 1985), Ascension of Our Lord Jesus Christ at Laniwci (the first church was built in 1906 but the present church not until 1965), Sts. Peter and Paul at Bodnari/Kolo Bodnariv (the first church built in 1906, the present church in 1936), Sts. Peter and Paul at Borshchiv (first church 1907, present church 1947), Holy Trinity near Bruno (first church 1909, present church 1925), St. Demetrius/Kolo Pidskal'noho (the first church, built in 1911, originally eight kilometres east of Alvena, was reconstructed in 1948 and moved in 1964 to the Shrine of Our Lady of Sorrows close to Cudworth), Ascension of Our Lord Jesus Christ at Meacham (first church 1911, present church 1952), and Patronage of the Blessed Virgin Mary at Wolverine (first church 1913, present church 1953). Later parishes in the settlement were St. John the Baptist at Dana (first church 1915, present church 1945), Spasa Transfiguration of Our Lord/"Kolo Solomyanoho" near Cudworth (first church 1915, destroyed by fire in 1934, replaced by a second church, which also burned down in 1967), Patronage of the Blessed Virgin Mary at St. Julien (1926), Descent of the Holy Spirit at Peterson (1926), Sacred Heart at Vonda (original parish formed 1927, present church constructed 1942–43, now a heritage property), Sacred Heart/"Kolo Havryliukiv" east of Prud'homme (1928), a chapel at Gabriel's Crossing (fifteen kilometres east of Rosthern in 1931), Dormition of the Blessed Virgin Mary at Yellow Creek (1937), St. Michael at Alvena (1939), St. John the Evangelist at Prud'homme (1945, became a heritage site in 1998), Sacred Heart at Wakaw (1945–46), Sts. Peter and Paul at Tway (1947), Sts. Peter and Paul in the town of Rosthern (1952), and Assumption of the Blessed Virgin Mary in the town of Bruno (1970). Farther afield were Holy Eucharist at Guernsey (1925, closed 1974), All Saints at Humboldt (1950), Sacred Heart at Lanigan Farms (built in 1925 and moved from Wolverine in 1952), and Holy Mother of God at Manitou Lake (1974).

The original parish of St. Mary the Protectress at St. Julien (1903) could be recognized as one of the earliest Ukrainian Orthodox parishes in Western Canada (though St. Michael's Ukrainian Orthodox Church in Gardenton, Manitoba, dates from 1899). One of the local pioneers was ordained by a bishop of the Ukraine; however, in 1918 the congregation divided, and those sympathetic to Ukrainian Catholicism organized a separate parish. A similar split occurred at Meacham in 1912. The small Ukrainian Orthodox Church of the Assumption (1912) on a hill overlooking Meacham is noteworthy for its unique architecture: rather than a central dome, it has a hexagonal shingled roof, a decorated *ikonastas*, with a finely crafted *bani* over the centre.[14] Other Ukrainian Orthodox parishes included an Independent Greek Church of Canada congregation in the Sniatyn district for a few years (1907–15)—now only a small cemetery remains, St. Michael's at Bukowina/Lepine (1907), St. Mary's Ukrainian Orthodox Church and cemetery just east of Wakaw (1912)—now a historic site, Holy Trinity at Tarnopol (1920), Holy Trinity west of Smuts (1925), Holy Trinity at Cudworth (1928), Sts. Peter and Paul at Yellow Creek (1936), All Saints at Alvena (1940), and Dormition of the Blessed Virgin Mary at Wakaw (1946). The beautifully maintained St. Mary the Protectress Ukrainian Orthodox Church at St. Julien is one of the finest examples of traditional Ukrainian Byzantine architecture in rural Saskatchewan, rising majestically out of the fields and its silver domes seen from afar; the present church, constructed during the mid- to late 1940s, was preceded by a first church as early as 1903 and a second in 1912. Today services are held several times a year; however, special occasions, such as the annual blessing of the graves in April, draw relatives of local and former farm families back from the city and other communities. St. Michael's Orthodox Church in the Bukowina district, about ten kilometres east of Wakaw, is now a historic site; it features unique architecture: an attached bell tower looking more like a Buddhist pagoda or a Hindu temple, profuse domes despite the church's relatively small size, a fairly small central dome surrounded by six smaller cupolas topping octagonal towers with eight windows.[15] Unfortunately, today there are just forty remaining adult members of this congregation and very few young people; the church now holds services only four times a year. And Holy Trinity Ukrainian Greek Orthodox Church near Smuts, despite its relatively small size, remains a classic example of Ukrainian Byzantine architecture, with metal roofing and an embossed shingle pattern; it too became a designated heritage site in 1984—but again virtually all of its members now live in Saskatoon, and services are rarely held.

Scarcely a dozen years after the first immigrants arrived at Rosthern, the Fish Creek and Yellow Creek settlements had merged into a single large bloc settlement centred on Wakaw; this settlement almost reached its present limits, forming a rather non-compact circuitous shape between areas occupied earlier by settlers of other ethnic origins. The settlement continued to develop internally after its expansion slowed. Wakaw was a post office in 1905, an incorporated village in 1911, but did not become a town until 1953. By 1914, Rosthern had as many as 1,500 residents, Wakaw and Cudworth each 300, Prud'homme 185.[16] The progress of some Ukrainian settlers in the district closest to Rosthern was already evident by 1911, for they had immigrated with total assets averaging about $100 apiece and now had productive farms typically ranging in size from five to six quarters.[17]

In 1971, Ukrainians constituted a majority or plurality in just one town, Wakaw (42.4%), and two incorporated villages, Alvena (73.9%) and Yellow Creek (52.8%), within this settlement as a whole, yet many other communities contain substantial Ukrainian minorities, and surrounding rural districts and smaller villages and hamlets remain almost exclusively Ukrainian and Polish. In some areas, such as the districts around Wakaw between the Fish Creek and Yellow Creek settlements, Ukrainians competed with Hungarians, Germans, and French for farmland. Ukrainians and Poles shared Wakaw with Germans and Hungarians, Cudworth (44.8% Ukrainian) with Germans,

Vonda (39.6% Ukrainian) and Prud'homme (37.5%) with French (in fact, this village was equally divided between Ukrainians and Poles, on the one hand, and French, on the other). In Alvena, in the heart of the Fish Creek settlement, Ukrainians and Poles together make up virtually the entire village population. Ukrainians comprised a very high proportion (83% alone, 92% with Poles) of the population of the surrounding Fish Creek RM. From detailed data in the 1971 census, we could estimate that the total Ukrainian population of the settlement was approximately 4,300.

Today, however, virtually all of the communities, larger and smaller, within the settlement are losing population. The most recent data (2006) reveal that, of the towns, Wakaw now has 864 residents (yet there are more than 1,000 summer cottages on Wakaw Lake), Cudworth 738, and Vonda 322. Of the villages, Prud'homme has 167, Meacham seventy, Alvena fifty-five, and Yellow Creek forty-five. Tway now has only ten residents, while Tarnopol, Carpenter, and Dana are also very small communities with few remaining residents. Dana, incorporated in 1905, at its peak reportedly had some 300 residents and nine businesses, but ever since the closure of a salt mine it has undergone a decline, despite the establishment of a Royal Canadian Air Force (RCAF) radar base nearby during the 1960s. Alvena became an incorporated village in 1936 and had over 200 residents in 1961; now, with less than a quarter of that number, it is in an advanced state of decline, characterized by overgrown sidewalks, vacant lots, and abandoned businesses. Incidentally, Alvena was the birthplace of Ed Tchorzewski (1943–2008), one of nine children in a poor Polish family; he became one of the youngest ministers of the provincial New Democratic Party (NDP) at the age of twenty-eight soon after he was elected in 1971. He served the provincial government as minister of culture and youth, minister of consumer affairs, minister of finance in both the Blakeney and Romanow governments, and deputy premier. He then became president of the federal NDP and chief of staff and finally returned to Saskatchewan to serve as an executive officer and special adviser to the Calvert government. Yellow Creek began a marked decline during the 1970s; the rail line was abandoned in 1981, the school closed in 1990, and almost all businesses have shut down. Only twenty-five members remain in the Ukrainian Catholic church, sixteen in the Orthodox one. The median age in this community was fifty-eight in 2006, compared with thirty-eight in Saskatchewan. Smuts has been a virtual ghost town for decades; well-aged trees have grown up in the middle of what used to be stores along the main street.

Nonetheless, the vast extent of this settlement is impressive: it covers portions of eleven rural municipalities and extends about seventy-five kilometres east to west and over ninety kilometres north to south (but many more kilometres by road).

THE REDBERRY SETTLEMENT

Another extensive area of Ukrainian settlement developed around Redberry Lake, in the region east of the Battlefords, between 1904 and 1912 and continued to expand to about 1920. Immigrants came primarily from Sokal (in northwestern Galicia close to the present-day Polish border), settling in 1904–05 around the towns of Hafford (together with immigrants from Horodenka) and Blaine Lake (with settlers from Horodenka, and particularly the community of Lis'ko, as well as Kiev and even Siberia), in the village of Krydor, and in the surrounding rural districts of Zaporozhe, Oukrania,

Redberry Station, and Lost Lake between Hafford and Krydor and north of Redberry Lake as well as Fedeyko Bay, Zbaraz, Uhriniw/Kolo-Bilya Parchomy, and Orolow/Orliv (Teshliuk's) in the forested hills south of Krydor and east of the lake. Hafford became incorporated as a village in 1913, a year after the railway reached the community, and Krydor became a village in 1914. The settlement expanded rapidly to include the Nauka, Zypchen, Tomman Lake (named after homesteaders Dmytro and Katherine Romansky Tomman), Bereziw/Slawa, and Krasne/Roseberry districts south of Hafford and west of the lake. It also included Swystun Bay, Welechko/Bilya-Velechka, Rus, Pysklyvetz, Redberry Park/Grant, and Concordia southeast of Hafford and south of the lake with the arrival of immigrants from Stanyslaviv, Horodenka, and Borshchiv in 1906. Immigrants from Sokal settled the Nesdoly Lake district south of Blaine Lake (primarily Ukrainian Orthodox); the area inclusive of Oscar Lake, Krivoisheim, Kleczkowski, and Bohdan (a common Ukrainian name meaning God given) in the northernmost extent of the settlement; and the Albertown/Alberton, Alticane, Canada, Orel, Ravenhead, and Galician Lake districts north and northwest of Hafford in 1907–08. The outlying Pearl district much farther north near Spiritwood was also settled by several Ukrainian families. Farther to the northwest, Whitkow and the districts of Zoria and Proswita were settled in 1911 by immigrants from Radekhiv (Whitkow was named after Vytkiv in Radekhiv), Sokal, and Horodenka; also settled were Mayfair, Green Canyon, and Redfield east of Whitkow and the Wolia district near Glaslyn. The Wasyl Kurish (originally Kuryaz) homestead west of Whitkow is now preserved as the pioneer Ukrainian home in the Western Development Museum in North Battleford. Immigrants from Horodenka and Sokal had settled in the Radisson area farther south from Hafford by 1912. The Sich district (thirteen kilometres north of Krydor) was settled by immigrants from Horodenka, Sokal, and particularly Lis'ko in 1914. Richard and Speers had been settled by 1920 by immigrants from Ternopil, and earlier the Langley, Whiteberry, and Keatley districts west of Hafford were settled.

Ukrainian Catholic parishes were established successively at Uhriniw (1909), Krydor (1910), Orolow (1910), Hafford (1911), Welechko (1911), Albertown (1912), Alticane (1916), Whitkow (1917–21), Sich (1934–37; Virgin Mother Mary of Perpetual Help Church was built in 1947–48, now abandoned), Blaine Lake (1947), Speers (1948), and Radisson (1955–56), with missions at Richard, Marlin, and Junor. The Ivan Franko National Home and Cooperative Association (named for the Ukrainian nationalist and writer of the late nineteenth and early twentieth centuries) were established on the Belyk farm across from the Assumption of St. Mary Ukrainian Orthodox Parish in the Redberry Park (Rebryna) district south of Redberry Lake during the 1920s. Other Orthodox parishes were Hafford (1911), Glaslyn-Wolia (1912 and 1932), Whitkow (1917 and 1933–34), Krydor (1921; the present St. Peter and St. Paul Church was constructed in 1934–35), and Redfield (east of Whitkow, 1920s and 1933–34). As in other Ukrainian settlements, though, these dates are subject to some interpretation. For example, though a Ukrainian church was established just east of present-day Hafford by three priests from the Fish Creek settlement in 1911, the separate Ukrainian Catholic and Orthodox congregations in the town itself were not actually organized respectively until six and fourteen years later, and the present Orthodox church was not built until 1936. In 1985, both the Ruthenian Greek Catholic Church of the Presentation of the Blessed Virgin Mary (1911) and the Ukrainian Greek Orthodox Church of the Assumption of the Virgin Mary ("Belyk's church"), southeast of Hafford, were designated as heritage sites. There were also small Ukrainian evangelical congregations in the settlement, such as an early one established in Blaine Lake by "Russian" Baptists who immigrated from the village of Boridianko near Kiev. Dalmeny Bible Church, in a traditionally Mennonite community, is currently partnering with an Evangelical Baptist Church in Talnoe, midway between Kiev and Odessa, Ukraine.

Although the ultimate origins of the settlers were in Ukraine, many had moved on to the Redberry settlement after initially settling in the Fish Creek settlement, motivated by a desire to escape from what they considered to be a "miserable existence" there little alleviated by the government. These migrants from Fish Creek were soon joined by others from Dana as well as directly from Ukraine. At Hafford in 1917, there were 102 Ukrainians and four Poles originally from Galicia and four Ukrainians originally from Russia (likely central or eastern Ukraine today), divided equally by gender. Twenty-six men had immigrated directly to the settlement from Ukraine, six had spent one year already on farms in Canada, seventeen from two to five years, and the remainder from five to twelve years. Twenty-seven men had lived in Canada for at least ten years.[18]

By 1920, the Redberry bloc settlement had reached its full extent: approximately eighty kilometres from east to west and forty-five kilometres from north to south, covering portions of at least seven rural municipalities. Within this area, Ukrainian Canadians comprise a large majority of the population, especially in many rural districts, though they are mixed with people claiming Polish origin in some areas and merge with Russian Doukhobors around Blaine Lake, French Catholics north of Hafford, and German Protestants toward Radisson. In 1971, Ukrainians constituted a majority of the residents of Hafford (77.7%), Krydor (88.5%—and together with Polish residents virtually the entire population of the village), and Richard (54.5%), as well as a strong plurality in Blaine Lake (43.9%), where most of the rest of the population was Doukhobor. Street signs in Hafford are now bilingual, in English and Ukrainian, and various community events tend to have a Ukrainian flavour. In Blaine Lake, predominantly Ukrainian and Russian Doukhobor, a Ukrainian Dancing Club was founded in 1975, and a local branch of the Ukrainian-Canadian Committee existed from 1949 to 1970. In the centre of the settlement, the Ukrainian proportion in Redberry RM was already declining during the 1960s (from 70% in 1961 down to 58% in 1971, though combined with the Polish population the proportion would have been more than three-quarters of the total population in 1971); this trend has likely continued to the present day with the purchase of cottages around Redberry Lake and other lakes by non-Ukrainians. Nonetheless, it is important to recognize again that throughout this settlement area most of the rural districts originally settled by Ukrainians still remain strongly Ukrainian. Altogether about 2,500 Ukrainians and another 400 Poles were living in this settlement in 1971.

Hafford had over 600 residents by the late 1960s; it became a town in 1981. Today Hafford (with 360 residents in 2006) remains the most viable community in the settlement, though it—like all of the other communities—has been losing population. Speers still had 175 residents in 1961, despite the loss of its main business, a creamery; at last count, it was down to seventy-five, and today the community is characterized by vacant businesses and empty lots. Mayfair now has only thirty residents, Richard and Krydor no more than twenty-five, Whitkow even fewer. Incredibly, not that long ago, Krydor had almost 200 residents in 1961, but the age structure revealed that, with older people dying and an increasing number of younger people leaving, before long the community—like so many others—would become a virtual ghost town. Just a few homes are still occupied, the Orthodox church is occasionally used, but most homes, all businesses, and the former school have been abandoned.

THE WILLOW CREEK SETTLEMENT

While the Redberry settlement was developing, Ukrainians began to settle in the area northeast of Melfort in 1904; they came predominantly from Zalischyky and Zbarazh to the Brooksby district, and they were followed by more immigrants from Zbarazh who settled around Gronlid and the Taras district (named after Taras Shevchenko) in 1908. Later immigrants from Borshchiv and Stanyslaviv settled in Melfort in 1927, and settlers from diverse earlier Ukrainian settlements in Saskatchewan (notably Ituna, Yorkton, Cudworth, and Sheho) resettled around Nipawin during the 1930s drought in search of better land. Within and near this settlement, Ukrainian Orthodox congregations were established at Gronlid in 1918, Brooksby in 1925, Codette in 1934, Nipawin in 1952, and Melfort in 1954. Ukrainian Catholic congregations were established at St. Nicholas/Kolo Yurchyshyn at Old Maryville (eight kilometres southeast of Brooksby) in 1912, Gronlid in 1919, Nipawin Farms (sixteen kilometres east of Nipawin) in 1939–40, and Melfort and Nipawin in 1954. The Evan Franko Community Hall was located southeast of Nipawin. Gronlid has only sixty residents and continues to decline, while Brooksby had sixty-six back in 1966 but had already declined to thirty-six by 1972. In 1971, there were approximately 600 Ukrainians and Poles living in Willow Creek RM around these communities.

THE GARDEN RIVER SETTLEMENT

The Garden River settlement centred on Garden River RM (originally Russia RM to 1928) northeast of Prince Albert was settled within just a couple of years, 1906–07, though it continued to expand into the 1920s. During 1912–16, the settlers were joined by poor farmers from the Stuartburn ("Stombur") settlement in southeastern Manitoba who had become disillusioned with sandy, stony soil and frequent flooding. Within a few years, 139 families had left communities in that older settlement, vacating some 362 sections of land to resettle in the Garden River settlement in Saskatchewan and in the Peace River country of northern Alberta. Although the farmers seemed reasonably satisfied with their new lands in Saskatchewan, the older women expressed their nostalgia for the neighbourly and traditional lifestyle in the less spread-out settlement that they had left in Manitoba. In that settlement, the population had been divided equally between Ukrainians and some Poles from Galicia, on the one hand, and Bukovinians, on the other. Similarly, in the new Garden River settlement, thirty-six settlers were recorded as Galicians, sixty-seven as Bukovinians, four as Ukrainians from Russia, and one couple as Poles from Russia. Only one woman was Canadian born, and just five men had immigrated directly to the settlement from Europe.[19] The settlers came ultimately from Ternopil, Horodenka, and Sambir to the Samburg district (south of Meath Park) in 1906, and from Sokal, Borshchiv, Redekhiv, and Ternopil to Meath Park the following year, as well as to the neighbouring community of Weirdale and the rural districts of Janow Corners, Kalyna, Honeymoon (phonetically spelled Honejmun by the Poles in the local cemetery), Husiatyn/Claytonville, Podole (named after the Podolia region in Ukraine), Zamok, and Strong Pine. Moving eastward, they settled around Foxford, Shipman in 1925 from Horodenka, Sokal, and Ternopil, and Smeaton. To the south across the North Saskatchewan River, the Cecil area was settled in 1927 by Ukrainians from Sokal, Ternopil, and Borshchiv. The Macdowall area (isolated from the main settlement, approximately thirty kilometres southwest of Prince Albert) was not settled until 1928–30 by Ukrainian-origin people from both the Rosthern–Fish Creek settlement and the Redberry Lake settlement.

Most of the Ukrainians from Galicia were Eastern Rite (Ukrainian) Catholics, whereas the Bukovinians tended to be Orthodox, and the Poles were Western Rite Roman Catholics. Ukrainian Orthodox parishes were organized at Samburg in 1914, Honeymoon in 1926, Weirdale in 1959, and Shipman; Ukrainian Catholic ones were organized at Samburg and Janow Corners in 1917, Shipman in 1931, Cecil in 1945–46, and Macdowall in 1946–47; the Poles tended to concentrate around their church at Janow Corners. Meath Park was originally six kilometres south of its present location; when it relocated north to the railway in 1937, the original location was first known as Old Meath Park and then renamed Janow Corners to avoid confusion in the post office. But already by 1971 all that remained of Janow Corners was the seldom-used Roman Catholic church, the foundation of which had been the first general store, a boarded-up schoolhouse, and just a few occupied homes—the rest were deserted.

Ukrainians and Poles made up close to two-thirds of the residents of Weirdale and just over a third of the residents of Meath Park in 1971; however, they comprised far higher proportions in the rural districts immediately south of these communities where they originally settled—Ukrainians and Poles formed almost three-quarters of the population of Garden River RM. At the core of the settlement, Meath Park (pop. 179) and Weirdale (pop. 83) have been losing population. Weirdale, not incorporated as a village until quite late, in 1948, witnessed many of its residents leave during the 1970s and 1980s; its school closed in 1983, and the railway was abandoned in 1998. To the east, Smeaton (pop. 183) remains active, but Shipman now has just fifteen residents, Foxford even fewer. Macdowall has 123 residents. Counting Ukrainian and Polish populations in these communities and the surrounding rural municipalities (Garden River, Buckland, Paddockwood, Torch River, Prince Albert, and Duck Lake), there were about 2,100 people of Ukrainian origin and 800 of Polish origin in 1971, plus another 1,100 Ukrainians and 500 Poles in the nearby city of Prince Albert. All told, this settlement—including the Macdowall area to the southwest—extends over 100 kilometres from east to west and at least fifty kilometres from north to south at its maximum extent.

UKRAINIAN SETTLEMENTS IN SOUTHERN SASKATCHEWAN

Although not exactly constituting a bloc settlement, except perhaps in the immediate Montmartre-Candiac area, Ukrainians did concentrate in several areas of southeastern Saskatchewan between the Qu'Appelle Valley and the US border, initially in 1895–1905 and later from 1910 to 1951. In fact, the small settlement around Candiac could be viewed as the first rural Ukrainian settlement in Saskatchewan: immigrants from Yavoriv settled there by 1895, and the settlement expanded with further immigration from Yavoriv to the neighbouring Montmartre area in 1904. To the north, immigrants from Buchach settled around Grenfell in 1897 and from Yavoriv (particularly the villages of Tuchap and Muzhylovych) around Dysart in 1895–1900. Ukrainian immigrants from Ternopil settled to the south near Weyburn in 1905, though not in town significantly until around 1951, and from Synkiv in Zalishchyky around Tribune (over forty kilometres south of Weyburn) in 1905. Elsewhere in the southeastern region, immigrants from Rava Rus'ka settled around Bienfait in 1905, from the city of Lubach around Estevan in 1910, and from Yavoriv and Peremyshl around Broadview in 1913–16 and 1948–49. Still others settled at Balcarres and Kipling. Ukrainian Catholic parishes were organized at Candiac and Dysart in 1913, Kipling in 1916 (closed in 1972), Tribune in 1919, Grenfell in 1923, Montmartre in 1950–52, Weyburn in 1952, Balcarres and Bienfait in 1958 (however, a Ukrainian community centre that occasionally held religious services had been established as early as 1921), Estevan in 1960 (now also serving Bienfait, Weyburn, and Tribune), and Broadview in 1961. A single Ukrainian Orthodox parish was organized at Montmartre in 1931. In the rural municipality of Montmartre, shared with French, Ukrainians and Poles together made up over a third of the population and 22.4% in the village of Montmartre in 1971. Roughly 500 Ukrainians and 300 Poles were found in this one small settlement around Montmartre and Candiac and in the surrounding rural municipalities of Montmartre and Chester. There were 413 residents in Montmartre at last count (2006), while Candiac was now down to just twenty residents. In 1971, another 200 Ukrainians and 300 Poles were living in the Weyburn-Tribune-Cedoux area to the south (scattered through the rural municipalities of Souris Valley, Lomond, Weyburn, Fillmore, and Wellington), but in Tribune itself there were only five people claiming Ukrainian ethnicity and at most fifty in this immediate vicinity; Tribune had only thirty-five residents in 2006.

Similarly, small concentrations of Ukrainians—but no real bloc settlements—are found throughout the western and southwestern regions. Some settled in the main towns: Swift Current, where immigrants from Husiatyn arrived in 1907 and a Catholic parish was organized in 1955–68; Biggar, settled by Ukrainians since 1912, with a Catholic parish organized in 1952–71; and Meadow Lake, where immigrants arrived from L'viv and Sokal in 1918 and an Orthodox parish dates from 1935 and a Catholic parish from 1957–58. But Ukrainians also chose to settle in isolated rural locales such as St. John the Baptist (twenty kilometres southwest of Kindersley), where settlers came in 1912 from Husiatyn and Buchach, and organized an Orthodox parish during the late 1930s and a Catholic parish in 1944; Thunder Creek (sixteen kilometres northeast of Chaplin), settled in 1911, with a Catholic parish since 1943–44; Cactus Lake (near Major), where a former German Roman Catholic parish was converted into a Ukrainian Catholic one in 1958; Hodgeville, settled in 1909, with a Ukrainian Catholic parish since 1916; and Glentworth, settled by immigrants from Borshchiv in 1908, with a Ukrainian Catholic parish dating from 1926. Moreover, Ukrainian Catholic missions were established at Assiniboia, Findlater, and Maple Creek.

UKRAINIAN SETTLEMENT IN THE CITIES

Ukrainians gradually moved into the six largest cities of Saskatchewan. In fact, Bukovinians and Galicians were already in Regina as early as 1890. The Ukrainian

Orthodox parish Descent of Holy Spirit was founded in 1924; the present church was constructed in 1960 and declared a *sobor* (cathedral) in 1978. The Ukrainian Catholic parish St. Basil the Great dates from 1928, though the present church was constructed in 1960. A second Catholic parish, St. Athanasius Byzantine, was added in 1966 as well as a second Ukrainian Orthodox parish, St. Michael. In Saskatoon, Ukrainians were arriving by 1910; in 1911, it was estimated that there were just seventy-five Ukrainians in the city, 228 by 1913. St. George's Ukrainian Catholic Parish was established in 1912, a church was moved onto the present location in 1918, and it became the cathedral seat of the entire Saskatoon Eparchy, serving all parishes in Saskatchewan, in 1951. During the 1960s, the parish contained more than 2,000 parishioners, today little more than a tenth of that number; the choir once had sixty-two members, today only eight. Across the street from the cathedral is the Venerable Nun Martyrs Shrine (*Khram*) erected by the Ukrainian Sisters of St. Joseph in memory of Sisters Olympia and Laurentia, martyred in 1952 during the postwar liquidation of the Ukrainian Catholic Church in Ukraine. Today there are just ten sisters of this order resident in Saskatoon (worldwide the order has 100 members working in orphanages, schools, and health care in Ukraine, Canada, Poland, Russia, Italy, and Brazil). The shrine was officially blessed in 2012 by the present patriarch of the international Ukrainian Catholic Church, His Beatitude Sviatoslav Shevchuk. Two other Catholic parishes were organized to serve the city's large Ukrainian population—Holy Apostles Peter and Paul in 1954 and Dormition of the Blessed Mother of God in Sutherland three years later—while St. Volodymyr was constructed in 1959 in Ukrainian Park (a youth camp) in classic Carpathian architectural style. Holy Trinity Orthodox Cathedral was established in 1922 as the seat of Ukrainian Orthodox parishes in Saskatchewan, and All Saints Church was built in traditional Carpathian style in 1969. The Ukrainian Museum of Canada is affiliated with the Ukrainian Orthodox Church, while the Ukrainian Catholic Cathedral also has a smaller museum in Saskatoon. The Orthodox Church in America, tracing its origins back to the Russo-Greek Catholic Orthodox Church, also has parishes in both Saskatoon and Regina. In Yorkton, the focal point of the most extensive Ukrainian bloc settlements, Ukrainian Catholics (the first of whom arrived in 1902 from Uhryn, Hryhoriw, and Chekhiv villages in Buchach county) have been served by the parishes of St. Mary's since 1911 and Our Lady of Perpetual Help since 1914, Ukrainian Orthodox by Holy Transfiguration since 1920. The area around Prince Albert, situated close to the Garden River settlement, was settled by immigrants from Husiatyn, Zhovka, and Sokal in 1903–04, and within four years the first Ukrainian immigrants had started to live in the city. Both Holy Trinity Ukrainian Orthodox Church and St. George's Ukrainian Catholic Church date from the 1920s. North Battleford is relatively close to the Redberry settlement. There Ukrainians were living in substantial numbers at least since about 1924, served by St. John the Baptist Ukrainian Orthodox Church since 1935 and All Saints Ukrainian Catholic Church since 1949–53. Moose Jaw has had Ukrainian residents at least since the arrival of immigrants from Rava Rus'ka in 1910; they have been served by Dormition of the Blessed Virgin Mary Ukrainian Catholic Church since 1948 and St. Volodymyr Ukrainian Orthodox Church since 1953.

UKRAINIAN ETHNIC IDENTIFICATION AND RESISTANCE TO ASSIMILATION

Certain writers have argued that the resistance of Ukrainians in Canada to assimilation has not been due as much to nativism as to other factors, such as having a distinctive culture, the relative recency of settlement, and segregation necessitated by limited availability of good agricultural land. Yet in the Ukrainian Canadian case, it could be argued, nativism in the form of ethnic nationalism played an important role that was reflected in the comparatively high proportion of people in this ethnic group, compared with those in other ethnic groups, exhibiting a conservative attitude.[20]

A strong sense of Ukrainian identity was not necessarily imported into Canada with the arrival of the first Ukrainian immigrants. The development of national consciousness—be it Ukrainian or Canadian—can often be a long and difficult process dependent on the strength and uniqueness of cultural traditions and the stage of social development, education, and politicization of a people. In a sociological sense, in its incipient stage, nationalism is an effort to develop pride in an ethnic group identity; ultimately, nationalistic movements aim at acquiring the status of a nation-state. However, at the time when Ukrainians were immigrating in large numbers to the Canadian prairies, the regions from which most of them came—primarily Galicia and Bukovina and to a lesser extent Podcarpathian Ruthenia (constituting the western regions of contemporary Ukraine)—were parts of the Austro-Hungarian Empire, and what was then called the Ukraine (today central and eastern Ukraine) was part of the Russian Empire. Thus, all Ukrainians in Europe living in their homeland territories were by definition in a minority position within these empires—there was no such thing as Ukrainian citizenship or nationality (in the strict political sense). Despite their geographical contiguity, Ukrainian areas in Europe have been under Russian, Austrian, Polish, Lithuanian, Hungarian, Turkish, Romanian, and Czechoslovakian rule. It is small wonder, then, that Ukrainian Canadians first considered themselves primarily as Galicians, Bukovinians, Ruthenians, and so on and secondarily possibly as Austro-Hungarians, Poles, Russians, Czechoslovaks, or Romanians. Only gradually did a common identity as Ukrainians emerge. In fact, certain aspects of Ukrainian Canadian culture—such as particular Ukrainian words, a unique Ukrainian alphabet (to emphasize the distinctiveness of the Ukrainian language, Ukrainian nationalists in Canada replaced letters of the Russian Cyrillic alphabet with new "Ukrainian" ones), and unique Ukrainian churches—emerged in Canada.[21]

Beliefs about alleged national roles or missions are closely related to national self-characterizations; moreover, ethnic self-awareness can increase among immigrants because of differences from the majority. This is a crucial point in understanding the development of ethno-nationalism among minorities in Europe as well as in Canada. The quest of Ukrainian nationalists in Europe for cultural and political autonomy, official recognition of the Ukrainian language, and permission to have their own schools, which culminated only in recent years with the independence of Ukraine from the Soviet Union, was gradually introduced by Ukrainian immigrants into Canada, where an awareness of being a single people was intensified by a deep consciousness of nationality among British Canadians, not unlike that found in many British colonies.[22]

If the various religious subdivisions of the collective Ukrainian-Polish group—Ukrainian Orthodox, Ukrainian (Eastern Rite) Catholics, and Polish (Roman Western

Rite) Catholics—today form a single fairly unified ethnic collectivity, or at least separate Ukrainian and Polish Canadian ethnic groups, was any conflict among them as distinct groups imported into Canada from Europe? The Ukrainian Orthodox had the strongest representation in what was then the Ukraine proper and in Bukovina; the Ukrainian Catholics in Galicia and Podcarpathia; the Polish Catholics in Galicia (especially western Galicia, which today is in Poland). Orthodox metropolitan (archbishop) seats were located at Chernivtsi in Bukovina and Kiev and eparch (bishop) seats at Radauti in Bukovina, Kamenets-Podol'sk in Podolia, and Zhitomir, Ostrih, and Volodymyr in Volhynia. There was a Ukrainian Catholic metropolitan seat at L'viv, and there were bishops at Stanyslaviv in eastern Galicia, Przemysl in western Galicia, and Mukachevo, Uzhorod, and Presov in Podcarpathia. A Roman Catholic archbishop was located at L'viv, and there were bishops at Volodymyr, Luts'k, Zhytomir, and Kamenets-Podol'sk. All three groups shared resistance to Austrian rule in Galicia, Podcarpathia, and Bukovina, but Polish Ukrainian antagonism had been enhanced by centuries of Polish domination over Ukrainians. On the Canadian prairies, the long-standing animosity between Poles and Ukrainians periodically gave rise to troublesome incidents in the bloc settlements, such as Ukrainians occasionally cutting down a wayside crucifix erected by Poles. But by the end of the 1920s, such incidents were lessening. As one writer commented, "It is an interesting fact ... that the Ukrainians and Poles who have lived and fought together in the Old World and who continue to hate each other, are invariably to be found in the same settlements out here—usually a small minority of Poles in a large settlement of Ukrainians." In Europe, Poles and Ukrainians fought each other as well as coercive assimilation by Austrians and Russians; in North America, they united to a considerable extent and were less successful in resisting coincidental assimilation. Not that all Ukrainians were opposed to Russians; on the contrary, especially in the period before the Russian Revolution of 1917, "Russophiles" (i.e., pro-Russian Ukrainians) existed in small numbers in the Canadian bloc settlements (e.g., among Bukovinians who settled near Vegreville, Alberta), and many of the earlier Ukrainian Orthodox worshipped in Russian Orthodox churches.[23]

A strong pro-Ukrainian feeling was easily aroused by nationalists, including intellectuals who had been forced to emigrate, among Ukrainian immigrants in Canada. In virtually any large group of Ukrainians in Canada, definite factions emerged, based on similar factions in Europe. In addition to splits among Ukrainian Orthodox, Ukrainian Catholics, and Polish Catholics, there were differences of opinion between assimilationists and traditionalists, republicans and monarchists, Canadian pluralists advocating multiculturalism and ardent advocates of Ukrainian independence, people who insisted on Canadian non-interference in foreign (e.g., Ukrainian or Soviet) affairs and "old guard" reactionaries, secular nationalists and religious ones.[24] The League for the Liberation of Ukraine was active in Saskatchewan.

An acute awareness of Ukrainian politics did not necessarily imply disinterest in—or opposition to—Canadian issues, though some non-Ukrainian Canadians certainly believed that it did. In general, Ukrainian Canadians were concerned with the condition of friends and relatives still in the Ukraine, the denial of status by other Canadians, and the recollection of centuries of subjugation by foreign powers in Europe.[25] Noted American sociologist Robert Ezra Park once wrote that "The rise of nationalist ...

movements within the limits of a state ... strikes me as a natural and wholesome disturbance of the social routine, the effect of which is to arouse in those involved a lively sense of common purpose and to give those who feel themselves oppressed the inspiration of a common cause."[26] However, Saskatchewan newspapers editorialized against Ukrainians as well as Mennonites, Hutterites, and Doukhobors, who purportedly resisted Canadian influences, suggesting that ethnic nationalist leaders who were using their power to prevent Canadianization should be deported.[27]

According to numerous accounts, Ukrainian immigrants were slow to be assimilated in any way, which was hardly surprising. When first settling, they were reportedly driven along like cattle and abused by government agents, treatment that could only have inspired resentment.[28] One newspaper report referred to the anger of the "stubborn" Bukovinians arriving in the Yorkton region:

> The stubborn Bukovinian immigrants ... had to be turned out of the immigration hall yesterday by main force. Some of them threw themselves on the floor and had to be carried out. An old woman who had been very outspoken in her foreign way, finally pulled off her long boot and threw it at the commissioner's ... head, fortunately missing her aim. The men also became so excited that four policemen had to be called in clearing the place. The immigrants had been in the hall over a fortnight and longer than the time allowed and it was necessary to get rid of them to make room for the new arrivals. Many of their number refused work.[29]

Clifford Sifton's exuberant remark that Canada needs "the man with the sheepskin coat and the big, broad wife" was sharply contrasted with the difficult-to-remedy reality of Ukrainian separatism, nationalism, illiteracy, and low intermarriage and general Canadians' alienation from the peculiar language, church service, customs, and folk dances of the Ukrainian immigrants.[30] Moreover, the support of some Ukrainians in Saskatchewan, such as in the Vonda area, for the Austro-Hungarian war effort allied to the German campaign and opposed to the British and Canadian efforts, during the First World War, added to the separation between the Ukrainian minority and the general Canadian society.[31]

But according to N.F. Black, a Saskatchewan historian writing in 1913, the Ruthenians were "especially marked by their desire to become real Canadian citizens." Even those living in remote rural areas exhibited an early sympathy for "things Canadian."[32] By 1926, out of about a quarter of Saskatchewan's people who were foreign born, 29% of the immigrants claiming to be from Galicia, 46% of those from Poland, 26% of those from Romania, 50% of those from Hungary, 38% of those from Russia, and 33% of those from the Ukraine had not yet taken out Canadian citizenship.[33] Elderly immigrants tended to be more reluctant than younger ones to adopt a new citizenship. A sociologist, Stanley Lieberson, once appropriately observed that naturalization is not a perfect indicator of assimilation.[34] This seemed especially to be the case for rural Saskatchewan, where naturalization tended to be more indicative of the relative amount of homesteading, evidence of the Ukrainian peasant's desire for his own *faruma* (homestead), than of assimilation.[35] In fact, the Orange Order complained that tens of thousands of

Central Europeans were dumped in settlements remote from Canadian influences, yet those immigrants had become enfranchised, in accordance with homesteading regulations, before they had learned their duties as citizens or the English language.[36] For their part, Ukrainian Canadians responded with the suggestions that it was regarded as their foremost duty to learn "the Canadian language," that they had adapted themselves to Canadian traditions in a "short space of time," and that their children mingled with those of other groups and all spoke "one tongue." But they also suggested that Ukrainian cultural learning and especially traditional language were essential to Canadian life, that "the learnings of various groups" be moulded to make a strong and united Canada, and that what was best should be picked out to work for a greater Canadian nation embodying various cultures.[37]

How strong has Ukrainian culture remained from generation to generation within these bloc settlements? In an extensive study of intergenerational cultural change conducted in 1969–72 among 237 households (154 Ukrainian Catholic and eighty-three Orthodox) in the Fish Creek–Yellow Creek, Redberry, and Garden River settlements, it was learned that almost half (48.5%) were of the opinion that ethnic identity must be preserved under any circumstances, almost a third (32.5%) were in favour of preservation but seemed resigned to some loss, and all but one of the remainder (18.6%) were indifferent, while only a single respondent was actually opposed to preservation. 14.3% foresaw a major loss for youth, 55.7% a minor loss, and 30.0% little or no loss. A large difference in opinions favouring ethnic identity preservation was noted between relatively younger and older respondents: among teenagers interviewed, 40.7% favoured identity preservation, among respondents in their twenties 44.4%, whereas 85.5% of those aged thirty–forty-nine 90.6% of those aged fifty–sixty-nine, and all of those aged seventy and older favoured the preservation of Ukrainian identity. More specifically, comparing the Ukrainian Catholic with the Orthodox respondents, a significantly higher proportion (45.0%) of Catholic teenagers were in favour, compared with just 28.6% of Orthodox teenagers. Otherwise the data were similar: 44.4% for both Catholics and Orthodox in the twenty–twenty-nine cohort, 83.1% and 94.2% in the thirty–forty-nine group, 95.4% and 85.7% in the fifty–sixty-nine cohort, and all of the group seventy and older. Again, by generation, it was clear that with each new generation emphasis on ethnic identification was declining: all of the first generation (immigrants) favoured identity preservation, compared with 82.1% of the Catholics and 73.9% of the Orthodox in the second generation (i.e., the first generation to be born in Canada) and respectively 55.5% and 68.4% of the third or later generation.[38]

Yet the cities have become repositories and popularizers of Ukrainian Canadian culture in a major way. For example, in Saskatoon the Vesna Festival in the spring has long been a popular showcase of Ukrainian food and entertainment and a significant gathering of the Ukrainian community. The Karpaty Ukrainian Pavilion, organized by the Tryzub Society of All Saints Orthodox Church, in Saskatoon's annual Folkfest in August, is likely the busiest, most active, most entertaining of all the pavilions, with three days of non-stop entertainment featuring excellent dance troupes such as the Yevshan Ukrainian Folk Ballet Ensemble (founded in 1960), Pavlychenko Folklorique Ensemble (established in 1967), and more recently the Vesnianka Academy of Ukrainian Dance and Boyan; the exuberant contemporary band Tyt I Tam; and the outstanding Lastiwka Ukrainian Orthodox Youth Choir and Orchestra (organized in 1983). The kitchen dishes out thousands of helpings of *borscht, varenycky, perohi, kowbassa* (Ukrainian sausage), and *holubtsi* (cabbage rolls), followed by *makivnyki* (poppyseed cake), *deed moroz* (crepes), and *rishky* (cinnamon pastries), all washed down with *Slavutich pyvo* (Ukrainian beer). And, soon after this event, there is an annual Ukraine Day in the Park. An annual King of the Kovbasa Challenge to declare the best local sausage makers is hosted by the Ukrainian Canadian Professional and Business Association of Saskatoon.

UKRAINIAN LANGUAGE USE

In the early years of settlement, frequent use of the Ukrainian language—and a corresponding failure to prefer English—was enhanced by the illiteracy of Ukrainian immigrants, certainly in English and not infrequently in Ukrainian, by what other non-Ukrainian settlers considered to be the backwardness of Ukrainian settlers, by a lack of familiarity with English, reinforcing seclusion from the outside world, by a deep-rooted nationalistic pride in an emerging Ukrainian identity and a love for the mother tongue, and by traditional institutions resisting all attempts to tamper with that language.[39]

For example, in the Vonda area in 1917, two decades after the establishment of the Fish Creek settlement, out of ninety-eight male settlers of Ukrainian and Polish origin, only sixteen could speak any English, and only eight could also read English; yet forty-five of them were literate in Ukrainian or Polish. Of an equal number of women, only eight could speak English, and just one could read English; thirty-one were literate in Ukrainian or Polish. They had 395 children; of the 175 who were between six and fourteen years of age, ninety-eight could read English and ninety-nine their mother tongue; of the eighty-six who were more than fourteen years of age, fifty-two were able to read English and sixty-nine their mother tongue. Forty-one families had home libraries in their traditional language; all told they held 659 books (an average of about sixteen books per home), chiefly fiction and Ukrainian history. Of course, books would have been heavy to carry all the way from the Ukraine, and Canadian publications in Ukrainian or Polish were still a rarity. One family who had lived an isolated existence in a forest in the Ukraine was illiterate yet expressed their regret over this situation. Another illiterate family, however, reportedly was backward in many other respects, farming with oxen, caring little for their children.

A similar situation prevailed in the Hafford area. Out of fifty-six male Ukrainian and Polish immigrants, only eighteen spoke some English, and nine were literate in English, whereas thirty-six were literate in their mother tongue. Of an equal number of women, three could speak English, two of whom were also literate in English, compared with twenty-nine who were literate in Ukrainian or Polish. Of their 197 children, ninety-four were from six to fourteen years old, and of them fifty were literate in English and fifty-seven in their respective languages; of the thirty who were over fourteen, thirteen could read English and sixteen their mother tongue. Thirty-two homes lacked libraries of any sort, while the other homes had books in Ukrainian (including prayer books).

In the Garden River settlement, there were fifty-eight male immigrants, of whom seventeen could speak a little English, eleven could read a little English, and thirty-two could read and write Ukrainian, Polish, or Russian. As for the fifty-two women, only three could speak any English, one could read a little English, and thirty-two were literate in their mother tongue. There were 157 children, forty-nine of them from six to fourteen, of whom ten could read and write English and fourteen their traditional language; another twenty-one were over fourteen, of whom only three were literate in English, compared with eleven in their traditional language. Only one family had some literature in English, thirty-seven no literature at all, the remainder Ukrainian literature (generally fiction and religious material).[40]

It seems small wonder, then, that such a high proportion of the Ukrainian people interviewed in the 1969-72 study could still speak Ukrainian. But some changes in language use merit mention. Evidently, considerable anglicization of the Ukrainian dialects began to occur at a fairly early date in the bloc settlements. Numerous Ukrainian Canadian words were derived from English, though others actually from the Ukraine were already similar to English. English combined with Ukrainian was increasingly used, though English verbs were conjugated by the settlers as if they were speaking Ukrainian, and Ukrainian sentence structure was imposed when speaking English. This practice became typical of the second generation, whereas the third generation often tended to reverse the process, imposing English structure on Ukrainian.[41]

When the first Ukrainians immigrated en masse to the Canadian prairies, an estimated half of them were still illiterate; by 1921, 40% of the immigrants were still illiterate; by 1931, almost a third of them in Saskatchewan were probably still not able to speak English, much less read and write it.[42] When interviews for the study were completed in 1969-72, almost all of the Ukrainian respondents could still speak Ukrainian, to variable extents of fluency, while about two-thirds were using their mother tongue fairly often, albeit in different circumstances at home or in the local community.

Ukrainian language use has steadily declined in Saskatchewan. Back in 1941, 94% of people claiming Ukrainian ethnic origin recognized Ukrainian as their mother tongue, but this proportion had declined to 87% by 1951, 72.3% by 1961, and 62.1% by 1971. In 1971, Ukrainians in rural areas of Saskatchewan retained their traditional language better than those in urban areas: 70.0% compared with 55.2%. By then, a high proportion (87.1%) of Ukrainians in Saskatchewan had been born in Canada, compared with 12.9% who were immigrants (most of whom had immigrated decades before). As one might expect, these immigrants had far higher Ukrainian language capability (90.3%) than the Canadian born (52.4%); moreover, they tended to speak Ukrainian at home (73.7%) far more than the Canadian born (19.5%). Since the 1981 census, ethnic origin was measured by a 20% sample; moreover, a distinction was made between people claiming just Ukrainian origin and people claiming Ukrainian and at least another ethnicity or even multiple ethnic origins. That year 76,810 people in Saskatchewan claimed only Ukrainian origin, compared with 23,280 claiming two or more (multiple) origins; thus, the total population in the province claiming to be wholly or partially Ukrainian had now passed the 100,000 mark (specifically 100,090). The number speaking Ukrainian was 44,175—therefore the equivalent of 57.5% of the Ukrainian-only population. By 1991, approximately 110,000 people were claiming to be partially Ukrainian; not more than approximately 50,000 could have been just Ukrainian. In a single decade, the number speaking Ukrainian had fallen drastically to 27,610—little more than half of the Ukrainian single-origin population. By 2001, there were 40,710 people claiming to be solely of Ukrainian ethnicity, compared with double this number, 81,025, claiming more than this one ethnicity: that is, a total of 121,735 people who were entirely or partly of Ukrainian descent. The number who still spoke Ukrainian was 19,650, slightly less than half (48.3%) of the single-origin Ukrainian population. It is noteworthy that in 1981 approximately three-quarters of the people claiming at least some Ukrainian predecessors specified that they were completely Ukrainian, compared with a quarter who specified Ukrainian plus other ethnic origins; twenty years later twice as many people were claiming Ukrainian plus other ethnic origins as just Ukrainian origin; this seems to indicate increasing intermarriage.

Within bloc settlements, considerably higher proportions of Ukrainians speaking their mother tongue tend to be found than for the Ukrainian population of the province as a whole. In fact, the 1941 and 1951 censuses actually counted more people speaking Ukrainian than people claiming Ukrainian ethnicity in the census divisions within which the Fish Creek–Yellow Creek, Redberry, and Garden River settlements were located: the correlation was 107.6% in 1941, 103.6% in 1951, and still a high 95.3% in 1961. Perhaps this can be explained by the fact that many people claiming Polish rather than Ukrainian ethnicity actually immigrated from Ukraine and spoke Ukrainian or dialects closer to Ukrainian than Polish, and "Russian" Stundists (Baptists) actually immigrated from Ukraine. Just 4.2% of the total respondents in the 1969–72 survey in these particular settlements could not speak English at all or hardly at all. The largest number (40.5%) were bilingual, preferring to speak Ukrainian both at home and in the community; another 21.9% spoke both languages, preferring Ukrainian at home but mostly English in the community; and 32.5% could speak Ukrainian yet spoke mostly English both at home and in the community. Only two people were found to be familiar only with English, with little or no acquaintance with Ukrainian. Yet age differences were most revealing. Most of the younger Catholic and Orthodox respondents were speaking English primarily or exclusively: respectively 50.0% and 57.1% of the thirteen to nineteen cohort and 55.6% and 66.7% of the twenty to twenty-nine cohort, compared with 42.4% and 47.1% of those from thirty to forty-nine, 18.6% and 31.0% of those from fifty to sixty-nine, and none of the older group. Again, for each generation, clearly Ukrainian-language use was declining though still quite high: for Catholics and Orthodox respectively 10.5% and 13.6% speaking English primarily or exclusively in the first generation, 35.9% and 38.1% in the second generation, and 44.4% and 63.2% in the third or later generation.[43]

Personal name change can be closely related to language change as part of ethnic identity change. As linguistic shift occurs, names undergo change and therefore become progressively less reliable indicators of ethnic identity. Name changing is not necessarily a deliberate attempt to obscure one's ethnic origin; rather, it can be a practical attempt to alleviate the embarrassment over people of other ethnic origins not being able to pronounce a name typical of a particular ethnic group. Given names tend to change before inherited and legal family surnames. Yet either type of name can be altered without being converted entirely into—or exchanged for—an English-sounding name; the name can be shortened for convenience, or the spelling can be changed for easy phonetic pronunciation by English speakers. For example, relatively few of the

Ukrainian farmers in the bloc settlements retained traditional names, though back in the early 1970s many varieties could still be detected (e.g., Wasyl, Dmytro, Orest, Jaroslaw, Bohdan, Slawko, Taras, Metro, etc.). But English translations of popular saints' names were increasingly encountered (e.g., Steve, Peter, John, Mike, Paul, Nick, etc.). Often individuals went by two first names, one Ukrainian (Olenka) and the other an English version (Elaine), depending on whether that individual was interacting with the older generation (especially within the family) or the younger generation and outsiders.[44]

Even in Yorkton, Ukrainian-language use has been slowly declining. This small city still has the highest proportion of allophones (people whose mother tongue is neither of Canada's official languages). In 2006, Ukrainian was still the language claimed by the most residents after English; 1,425 residents recognized Ukrainian as their spoken mother tongue, compared with 1,545 five years earlier, but German speakers have been declining faster, and there are far more residents who consider Ukrainian as their mother tongue than German.

UKRAINIAN RELIGIOUS AFFILIATIONS

Ukrainian and Polish immigrants brought with them a centuries-old rivalry between Western Rite Roman Catholicism and Eastern Rite (Byzantine) Russian Orthodoxy. Ukrainian Catholicism had become a third force since it was sanctioned by the Union of Brest in 1595, recognizing the papacy while retaining the Eastern Rite.[45] As early as 1896, separate parishes were being organized by Orthodox Ukrainian immigrants from Bukovina, backed by Russian Orthodox priests, and by Ukrainian Catholics from Galicia, backed by Belgian and francophone Redemptorist priests (notably Père Delaere).[46] In 1912, the Most Reverend Nykyta Budka was installed as the first Ukrainian Catholic bishop of Canada to serve some 135,000 Ukrainian Catholics. Ukrainian immigrants arriving in Saskatchewan tended to concentrate in particular areas, depending on whether they regarded themselves as Catholic or Orthodox, reportedly because of religious differences between them which appeared to cause friction. Even though most Ukrainian immigrants had come from Galicia, where the Ukrainian Catholic Church was strongest, in the bloc settlements this church found itself challenged by the Russian Orthodox Church, especially from 1905 to 1911, by the All-Russian Patriarchal Orthodox Church created by Metropolitan Seraphim in 1903–08, and by a Presbyterian-financed Independent Greek Church or Ruthenian Independent Church in 1903–12.[47] Encouraged by the Ukrainian newspapers the *Ukrainian Voice* and the *Canadian Farmer*, as well as by friction between the Ukrainian Catholic hierarchy and the Mohyla Institute, a *bursa* or Ukrainian student hostel in Saskatoon, the independent Ukrainian Orthodox Church of Canada was founded in 1918, with priests ordained by Russian Orthodox and Polish National Catholics (the latter had parted company with Roman Catholicism in Pennsylvania in 1897). Within a single year, this new church already had 107 parishes (only twenty of them urban) served by forty to fifty priests. Although almost two-thirds of the parishioners were Bukovinians, compared with 20% Galicians and the remainder Ukrainians and Russians from Russia (likely the regions of eastern Ukraine and Volhynia then in Russia), only a couple of the priests were Bukovinians—the rest were all Galicians.[48] In Saskatchewan, St. Julien in the Fish Creek settlement became the first independent parish, yet many other Orthodox parishes in this settlement (including Lepine and Meacham) and in the Crooked Lake–Sliding Hills, Beaver Hills, Melville-Ituna, Quill Lakes, Redberry, and Garden River settlements actually predated the official foundation of the Ukrainian Orthodox Church of Canada. In fact, some country churches seem to have either been independent or wavered between identifying as Ukrainian Orthodox or Catholic before becoming officially Ukrainian Catholic; such was the case, apparently, at Laniwci and Alvena Farms, according to local farmers. In Meacham, in 1910–11, a common church building served Orthodox, Catholics, and even Protestants; a priest supplied by the Russian Orthodox Mission ministered to both Eastern Rite Catholics and Orthodox.[49] Then, in 1911–12, a Roman Catholic congregation was formed; in 1913, Orthodox and Roman Catholics shared a church, but in 1917 the Orthodox separated because they outnumbered the Catholics, though a resident Orthodox priest was not installed until 1928. In Wakaw, separate Ukrainian Catholic and Orthodox parishes were first organized during the First World War years. Within a decade of the foundation of the official Ukrainian Orthodox Church of Canada, there were 26,500 members, some 38,000 under pastoral care, and at least 152 parishes with twenty-one priests.[50]

Rivalry with Ukrainian Catholics had become intense. In Hafford, for example, it was carried into social relations, marriage, control of businesses in the community, control of community centres such as the Ukrainian National Home, voting behaviour, the building of separate parish churches, relations with neighbouring Polish and French Catholics, the election of school trustees and boards, the granting of scholarships to teachers, and so on.[51] One is reminded of early German sociologist Georg Simmel's observation that conflict sets boundaries between groups within a social system by strengthening group consciousness and awareness of separateness, thus establishing the identity of the groups within the system. The Ukrainian Orthodox movement was perhaps not as religious in origin and impetus as nationalistic. It surged ahead in 1917 when feelings among Ukrainian Canadians for an independent Ukraine were running high. Thus, the Ukrainian Orthodox regarded the Ukrainian Catholics as "mothered by Rome, fathered by the Polish state." For their part, Ukrainian Catholics exhibited their ethnic nationalism by placing the flag of independent Ukraine in their churches and by vehemently decrying both czarist and communist despotism of the Russians. They prayed to God "for all Orthodox Christians ... that He may unite them to His holy, catholic, and apostolic church." Yet both Orthodox and Catholic Ukrainians revealed a paranoia about Western Rite Catholicism. Ukrainians' dislike of "latinization," a different rite, liturgical language, music, vestments, customs, non-marriage of priests, centralized hierarchy, canon laws, and so on drove many of them into the Orthodox Church. But in spite of their official link with Roman Catholicism, Ukrainian Catholics rigorously defended their Eastern Rite, calling it "a sacred symbol of one's own people and a banner of faith and love for one's nation" and cautioning children: "Remember always that God made you a Ukrainian Catholic and that He wants you to serve Him and to save your soul in the Byzantine rite church."[52]

In Saskatchewan, Ukrainian Catholics have continued to outnumber Ukrainian Orthodox. Ukrainian Catholic churches are found in almost every Ukrainian community, though within the bloc settlements Ukrainian Orthodox outnumber Ukrainian

Catholics in some communities and in certain rural areas, especially where Bukovinian immigrants concentrated. With increasing intermarriage, there has been a steady decline in the proportion of Ukrainians in Saskatchewan who are members of the Ukrainian Orthodox and Ukrainian Catholic Churches. In 1941, 36.6% were Orthodox and 55.7% Catholic (including some attending Western Rite Roman Catholic parishes), so at most 92.3% together; by 1951, 34.9% were Orthodox and 43.4% Catholic, together 78.3%; by 1961, 30.0% Orthodox and 38.0% Catholic, together 68.0%; and in 1971, 31.0% Orthodox and 39.8% Catholic, totalling 70.8% (actually a slight increase). Since the 1981 census, the data have been less accurate, for only a 20% sample of population has been gathered, and people can now claim to be wholly or partially of Ukrainian origin; nevertheless, we can note that population claiming to be Orthodox declined sharply from 26,670 in 1971 to 15,095 twenty years later (a decrease of about 1,000 every couple of years), then to 5,050 in 2001. Similarly, people claiming to be Ukrainian Catholic decreased markedly from 34,175 in 1971 to 18,700 in 1991 (an even greater loss of almost 16,000 in just two decades), and the decrease has continued, to 17,615 in 2001. The combined Orthodox and Catholic total came to 33,795 in 1991 (fewer than the number of Ukrainian Catholics alone in 1971). Currently, the international Ukrainian Catholic Church claims more than 4 million members (served by 4,500 priests), approximately 110,000 in Canada and 7,500 in Saskatchewan. After Ukraine itself and Russia, Canada reportedly has the third largest Ukrainian population in the world.

However, both Catholic and Orthodox parishes have been facing dwindling and aging congregations, a pressing need for renewal and retention of youth, difficulty in recruiting priests, and declining attendance, contributing to many local church closures when small and elderly congregations can no longer afford to maintain church upkeep. Within the next couple of decades, as older members pass away, hundreds of Ukrainian churches dotted across the prairies will be endangered. The most visible aspect of Ukrainian culture in Canada, these rural churches represent outstanding and diverse examples of traditional Ukrainian Byzantine architecture, both externally and internally (typically every church contains a *kyvot* tabernacle for the blessed sacrament that is a scale model of the church's architecture).

The 1969–72 survey provided some interesting information on differences between Ukrainian Catholics and Orthodox in frequency of religious attendance and on changing trends in this regard. In general, a higher proportion of Catholics (81.8%) attended church "as regularly as possible," compared with 69.9% of Orthodox; respectively, 13.0% of Catholics and 18.1% of Orthodox attended "usually" or "sometimes," 4.5% and 10.8% "rarely," and only a few—0.6% and 1.2% "never." For Ukrainian Catholics, there was a slight decline in regular attendance from first generation (94.7%) to second generation (84.3%) but then a marked decline to third generation (55.5%); this pattern seemed less consistent among Ukrainian Orthodox, among whom the greatest decline was between first and second generations (96.4% down to 57.1%) but then an increase in third generation (back up to 78.9%). A later study of Sts. Peter and Paul Ukrainian Catholic Parish in Rosthern in 1990 revealed that, of nominal members of the congregation interviewed, almost one-third (32.9%) were attending regularly (especially those speaking only Ukrainian), slightly over a quarter (27.1%) sometimes, and some (15.3%) not at all; regularity of attendance seemed clearly to increase with age.[53] However, the same year another study, of the Ukrainian Catholic parish in Foam Lake, found a fairly even distribution in participation in communion among various age groups.[54]

Back at the time of the survey in 1969–72, very few people of Ukrainian origin were intermarried across ethnic or religious lines—hardly surprising given the ethnic solidarity of the bloc settlements. Respectively, among the Catholic and Orthodox respondents, respectively 22.1% and 13.3% were not married, 68.2% and 77.1% were married to other Ukrainian Catholics or Orthodox, and 9.7% and 9.6% were married to spouses of other ethnic origins and/or religious affiliations. But the study probed further into just how similar or different intermarried spouses were. Most of the Ukrainian Orthodox who intermarried had married Ukrainian Catholics and Polish Catholics, though a few cases of marriages to spouses from completely different ethnic groups or religious affiliations were found. Half of the intermarried Ukrainian Catholics were married to spouses of completely different ethnic groups and religious affiliations, the remainder to people of Ukrainian origin but completely different religious affiliations, to Russian Doukhobors, to Ukrainian Orthodox, and to Polish Catholics. Conversely, virtually all of the intermarried Polish Catholics had Ukrainian Catholic or Orthodox spouses. Despite a relative lack of intermarriage, were Ukrainians becoming more open minded about intermarriage? The study clearly revealed that opposition to ethnic intermarriage increased with the age of the respondent: respectively, among Catholics and Orthodox, 20.0% and 28.6% of teenagers, 44.4% and 33.3% of the twenty to twenty-nine cohort, 57.6% and 29.4% of the thirty to forty-nine group, 72.1% and 40.4% of the fifty to sixty-nine cohort, and 95.7% and 87.5% of the elderly. Moreover, we can note that the Ukrainian Catholics seemed generally to be more opposed than the Orthodox, both to ethnic and to religious intermarriage. Ukrainian Catholics and Orthodox respectively expressed their opposition to religious intermarriage quite differently among age categories: 45.0% and 42.9% of teenagers, 44.4% and 33.3% of those from twenty to twenty-nine, 61.0% and 35.3% of those from thirty to forty-nine, 81.4% and 40.4% of those from fifty to sixty-nine, and 95.7% and 87.5% of the elderly. It is particularly striking that opposition to religious intermarriage increases most substantially for the elderly among the Orthodox but more steadily among age categories among the Catholics. This finding was also reflected in the data on generational differences. Among both Ukrainian Catholics and Orthodox, there was a marked decline in opposition to ethnic intermarriage, respectively 89.4% and 68.2% in the first generation, through 58.5% and 33.4% in the second generation, to 33.3% and 26.3% in the third or later generation. Similar results were found for concern over religious intermarriage expressed by Ukrainian Catholic respondents: 89.4% in the first generation, 66.3% in the second generation, and 48.1% in the third or later generation. However, the data were less consistent for the Ukrainian Orthodox: 68.2% in the first generation, 33.4% in the second generation, and 36.8% in the third or later generation. The Foam Lake study mentioned above learned that the church took a pragmatic view of intermarriage—the couple would have to work out any problems themselves.

UKRAINIAN FOLK CULTURE

Traditional Ukrainian folk culture has remained popular in Saskatchewan, though certain art forms might be dying with the passing of the older generation. In the 1969–72 study, 86.5% of the Ukrainian Orthodox and 92.2% of the Ukrainian Catholic respondents acknowledged that they ate traditional Ukrainian foods such as *borscht* (beet or cabbage soup), *perohi/perogy* and *varenyky* (dumplings), *blintzi* (pancakes), *kapusniak* (buckwheat and sauerkraut), poppyseed bread, *holubtzi* (cabbage rolls), *kasha* (grain pudding), *kulesha* and *mamalyga* (cornflower bread), *studenetz* (headcheese), *dushenya* (cooked meat with gravy), *stynanka* (potato dough soup), *paska* (Easter bread), *kutia* (hulled wheat grains and honey at Christmastime), *medivnyk* (honey torte), *uzvar* (cooked dry fruit). ... Some of these foods can be regarded as daily fare, others as dedicated only to special occasions, especially Christmas and Easter dinner, or an extended family affair. At Christmas, twelve traditional meatless dishes are served to symbolize the twelve apostles.

Relatively few examples remain in rural Saskatchewan of the traditional Ukrainian thatched roof homes that were once so common in the bloc settlements through the 1930s. Around Hafford in 1917, out of a sample of fifty-eight Ukrainian homes, twenty-five were small log and clay huts with thatched roofs, twenty-one log with shingle roofs, and twelve frame houses. They were generally crowded: four homes were single room (including one with twelve inhabitants!), thirty-eight were double room (including seven with nine people each, one with ten, and a couple with eleven), and eleven were three room. This is explained by the practice of having extended family members, including married sons, share a single extended family dwelling and of having hired hands living in the house.[55] Now relatively rare examples of traditional Ukrainian pioneer homes can still be found near Smuts, where the Slywka homestead (1902) is built of reinforced log and sod, with external boards and plaster now exposed to reveal this original construction; remnants of classic thatched roof homes are still found in the Smuts, Alvena, and St. Julien areas; near Glaslyn, homes were constructed of logs with cross-hatched sapling strapping covered with mud plaster; near Tway, one home had an expertly woven thatched roof, with handwoven straw ropes holding thatched bundles onto a sapling roof frame; at Theodore, one could find an example of later construction, a two-storey log house with mud plaster held in place by vertical strapping, framed glass windows, and shingled roof.[56] Traditionally, each room had a distinct name and purpose: *siny* (entrance hall), *velykakhata* (larger room, which doubled as living and sleeping quarters in smaller, simpler homes), *malakhata* (smaller room, doubling as a living area and kitchen containing a *peech*—clay oven that provided warmth).[57] Up to the present day, Ukrainian homes are commonly decorated with traditional Ukrainian pottery, wall hangings and table runners, religious icons, and *pysanka* (decorated Easter eggs). Respectively, of the Orthodox and Catholic respondents in the 1969–72 study, 86.7% and 92.2% still utilized certain traditional crafts, including *kylymy* (handwoven tapestries and rugs), *pysanka* (Easter egg painting), inlaid woodcarving, and icon painting, but such arts were being practised less and less.

While older women can still be seen wearing *babushka* headscarves, the men's sheepskin coats have long ago been relegated to museums. In the early years of settlement, for example around Sheho, Ukrainian women typically wore wrap-around headscarves, loose-fitting embroidered blouses, piles of beaded necklaces, floor-length skirts covered in front with colourful aprons, and *obhortkas* (thick wool petticoats); poorer peasant women usually wore simple bandanas, layers of vests and heavy decorated jackets, and shin-length simple skirts, and they were often seen barefoot or wearing boots. Men wore less distinctive clothing—often dark pants and a vest over a loose-fitting shirt (sometimes embroidered) and broad straw hats, fedoras, or tweed caps. Weddings were occasions to dress up: in the Samburg district, for example, women dressed in their finest traditional Ukrainian clothing: finely embroidered blouses, richly decorated vests, skirts, and aprons, while the bride wore a floral headdress; men as usual were less colourful, dressed simply in dark suits and ties.[58] However, Ukrainian choirs and dance troupes still abound (there are at least forty-four Ukrainian dance groups plus many choral groups in Saskatchewan). And, typically, their members wear traditional clothing (embroidered shirts and blouses, *obhortkas* (petticoats and smocks), ribbon headdresses, billowing Cossack pants, leather boots).

Ukrainian immigrants brought with them a culture rich in folk and traditional music. In the early years, it was not unusual to hear women and children singing as they toiled in the fields. At St. Julien, there was the annual folk dancing of *Haiwka* (Easter Monday). Ukrainian musicals, usually depicting Cossack days, were once common (e.g., those held at the Siczynski School at Meacham) and remain popular. So, too, are Ukrainian weddings in a traditional manner; in the Tarnopol area, weddings were elaborate affairs, lasting days still in the 1950s.[59] Ukrainian churches typically reflect traditional architectural styles and are lavishly decorated with hand-painted *ikonastas*; the liturgy is still sung by innumerable fine choirs. One of North America's foremost iconographers is Vera Lazarowich Senchuk, originally from Hafford. Saskatchewan has several fine Ukrainian museums, research centres, and libraries. Hafford holds a popular annual polka fest. So, despite indications of a decreasing ability to practise certain folk arts, many aspects of Ukrainian culture are well maintained today in the bloc settlements and their urban legacy.

In Alvena, for example, Ukrainian traditions are still observed on Christmas Eve, not only in homes of generations of Ukrainian settlers but also in the home of new immigrants from Ukraine, the Maruschak family. The dinner table is elaborately set in a festive manner reflecting the religious and cultural significance of the occasion. Decorative braided bread (also used at Easter) is set on the embroidered tablecloth. Hay is placed upon and under the table to recall the stable where Jesus was born. Garlic, said to ward off evil, is placed at the four corners of the table. An extra table setting is in memory of those who have died and are with them now in spirit. Twelve meatless dishes are served to symbolize the twelve apostles, together with platters of *kutia, borscht, varenyky,* prune *perohi,* poppyseed bread, *holubtsi, uzvar, pampushkiy, makivnyk,* pickled herring, and other traditional Ukrainian dishes. But the *sviata vechera* (holy feast) cannot commence until the grandchildren sight the first evening star in the east, indicating the birth of Christ.[60] Ukrainian culture, engrained in generations of descendants of the original settlers, continues to prove important to younger generation Ukrainian Canadians even after they have left the bloc settlements to live in the city. One recent example was provided by Stacia Vesalia Horbay, from an Alvena family, recently the recipient of an award by the Ukrainian Canadian Congress for cultural contributions to the Ukrainian community; she perhaps typifies younger generation Ukrainian Canadians who retain a strong interest in maintaining Ukrainian traditions—she sings in a Ukrainian choir, has danced Ukrainian dances, teaches Ukrainian language at a summer camp, serves on the board of a Ukrainian museum in Saskatoon, hosts a Ukrainian program on FM radio, and has visited Ukraine as a young teenager.[61]

INSTITUTIONALIZATION OF THE UKRAINIAN COMMUNITY

An important consideration in the preservation of Ukrainian identity in Saskatchewan has been the institutional completeness of the community, represented in the availability of educational institutions, associations, and media. Although Orthodox Church Brotherhoods had established schools oriented toward the Ukrainian ethnic group in Galicia for several centuries prior to that region's reunification with the Ukraine proper, few of the peasants who were to become Canadian immigrants had received even three or four years of elementary education in the local *narodna shkola*. In the early years of settlement, there were few schools, though the first were organized by the immigrants themselves in conjunction with the Department of Education. The Ordinance of 1892 had not outlawed foreign-language teaching, though it had made clear that English was to be stressed, and the Ordinance of 1901 had actually permitted teaching in Ukrainian during the final school hour.[62] The local one-room schools established during the government of Premier Scott in the Ukrainian bloc settlements had a decided ethnic orientation that was to continue, albeit in modified form, through the Premier Martin government into the 1920s. Schools became the focal points of rural districts named after Ukraine and Ukrainian regions (e.g., Ukraina, Rus, Carpathia, Ruthenia, Galicia, Bukovina, etc.) or after provinces and communities in those regions (e.g., Borshchiv, Jaroslaw, Kiev, Kolomia, Krasne, Skala, Sniatyn, Sokol, Tarnopol, Zaporozhe, etc.). Still others were named after descriptions of local settings (e.g., Kolo-Pidskalnoho, Kolo-Blokhiv, Kolo-Solomyanoho, Kolo-Havrylyukiv, etc.). Many more were named after Ukrainian institutions or personages (e.g., Proswita, Slava, Svoboda, Zamok, Zoria, etc.). By 1917, there were at least twenty-seven largely Ukrainian schools in the Fish Creek settlement, ten in the Redberry settlement, and several in the Yellow Creek and Garden River settlements.[63]

It is difficult to ascertain the extent to which the Ukrainian language might have been used in these schools. According to one source, as early as 1915 only one-fifth to one-quarter of predominantly Ukrainian schools were still using the Ukrainian language in the primary grades and during the final school hour. One inspector reported in 1917 that, out of twenty Ukrainian schools that he visited, only two or three still used any Ukrainian. However, at least since 1913 government-approved Ukrainian-language texts were in use, and some schoolteachers might have been intentionally deceiving school inspectors regarding the amount of foreign-language instruction in their schools. Moreover, after foreign-language instruction during school hours was abolished in 1919, Ukrainian was still taught after school hours. In the Fish Creek settlement, by 1917, much Ukrainian was actually being used in perhaps three-quarters of the schools. The situation seemed less clear in the Redberry settlement, though. Apparently, most of the schools taught Ukrainian during the final school hour. At least one school was reported as illegally using more Ukrainian. At Proswita, most students spoke "broken English," and the teacher used Ukrainian words "only once in a while to render the meaning of an English word clear to a pupil who had heard only Ukrainian at home." It was reported that a few schools (including Dominion, Rus, and

Krasne) did not teach any Ukrainian (possibly due to a shortage of qualified Ukrainian teachers). It is most important, whatever one makes of these conflicting reports on language use in the schools, to recognize that virtually all of these schools served as vital rural community centres. They were perhaps not as much assimilatory agents of Anglo-Canadian society as they were focal points of rural life oriented to Ukrainian Canadian culture. Most schools had exclusively Ukrainian pupils, many had Ukrainian trustees, and quite a few had Ukrainian teachers.[64] At celebrations in Wroxton in 1914, Toporoutz and Chernowka schoolchildren gathered for a photograph under the Union Jack flag (doubtless representing Anglo dominance), but otherwise they could not have looked more like a scene from Ukraine: the girls were miniatures of their mothers, in wrap-around headscarves, embroidered blouses, and floor-length skirts cinched by broad woven belts, the boys in less distinctive overalls and broad-brimmed straw hats (some, though, in homemade suits with neckties).[65]

According to a harsh report by H.W. Foght on conditions in rural schools in 1918, schools in Ukrainian settlements had numerous deficiencies: unsanitary conditions, aging buildings, unkempt interiors and pupils, illiterate parents opposing the government and school system, no classes on Canadian history, unqualified teachers speaking limited English and teaching grammatical errors, poor discipline, the illegal closure of schools in winter due to a lack of adequate heating, and so on. Although all of these problems undoubtedly applied to some schools in the Ukrainian settlements, probably most teachers were qualified by that time, many schools did not correspond to such a negative portrayal, and parents in general were anxious to have their children learn English (in fact, some parents in the Hafford area set an example by organizing and attending night schools in 1920). In at least this area, no instance of Ukrainian people being fined for failure to comply with public school attendance regulations was noted.[66]

The ethnic-oriented schools had to face not only the opposition of the provincial government to foreign-language teaching after 1919 and to degrading conditions but also the opposition of other minorities in areas settled by more than one ethnic group. The Ukrainians in the Fish Creek area asked in 1908 for their own schools because they feared Roman Catholic control even though Roman Catholics (mostly Poles) were relatively few in number. Nine years later Polish Catholic priests complained that Ukrainian priests and teachers were using the schools for their own nationalistic purposes. Similarly, when a teacher began giving Ukrainian-language classes on Saturday mornings at Redberry Lake in 1921, the Polish ratepayers protested and declared their desire to have an English rather than Ukrainian teacher. In 1920 in the Wakaw area, Hungarians, Germans, and English Canadians expressed their opposition to Ukrainian schools, whereas the next year Ukrainians nearby at Kaminka were opposed to what they perceived to be French control. In 1916, the secretary-treasurer of Invergordon RM (the Yellow Creek area), an English Canadian, suggested that, "where the language of their native land has been used to any extent in the education of their children, they are consequently hindered in the learning of the English language." In 1920, ratepayers of the mixed English and Ukrainian Grant School District at the southern edge of the Redberry settlement expressed their desire to have an English rather than Ukrainian teacher.[67]

CHAPTER 5

Ukrainians continued to emphasize a multicultural outlook. This gave rise to the establishment of "Ukrainian schools," part-time schools of Ukrainian language and culture organized by the churches. Ukrainian Orthodox ones first met around 1927 in church halls; during the 1930s and 1940s, they were supported by the Ukrainian Women's Association of Canada and the Ukrainian Self-Reliance League. In 1916, the Mohyla Institute in Saskatoon developed its Ukrainian schools office, which became the Ukrainian Education Council of Canada, centred in Winnipeg, five years later. Through this council, the Ukrainian Orthodox Church of Canada has proclaimed its intention to make "better Canadians of its young members by helping them to become better Ukrainians." Although public schoolteachers had encouraged Ukrainian children to call themselves Canadians, they had to face considerable opposition from the parents (e.g., at Zalischyky in the Fish Creek settlement in 1922), with the result that such a dual Ukrainian-but-Canadian identity emerged.[68] Landmark Ukrainian educational developments in Saskatchewan have included the authorization in 1909 of the School for Foreigners in Regina and the Ruthenian Training School (based in Manitoba). The Ruthenian Training School in Regina, training teachers to serve Ukrainian school districts in Saskatchewan, occupied the former Territorial Administration Building (which operated from 1891 to 1905, served the new provincial government until 1910, then became the school, and after changing hands several more times was designated a provincial heritage site in 1982). The Mohyla Institute at the University of Saskatchewan was established in 1916 and was to play a significant role in the founding of the Ukrainian Orthodox Church of Canada two years later. The university offered the first course in Ukrainian in 1943, and the Department of Slavic Studies was established in 1945. Ukrainian as a high school subject was officially recognized in 1952. The Sheptytsky Institute was founded in 1953 at the University of Saskatchewan to serve Ukrainian Catholic students. The Ukrainian language was offered as a high school correspondence course in 1963. The Saskatchewan Teachers of Ukrainian chapter of the Saskatchewan Teachers Federation formed in 1966. An exchange between the University of Saskatchewan and Chernivtsi State University developed after 1976. A bilingual Ukrainian-English program began at a high school in Saskatoon in 1979 (by which time over fifty centres were offering Ukrainian-language courses to over 2,600 students). In 1990, an educational cooperation agreement with Ukraine was signed; the Prairie Centre for the Study of Ukrainian Heritage at the University of Saskatchewan formed in 1998; and another exchange between this university and the Ukrainian Catholic University of L'viv occurred in 2003.[69]

Lysenko pointed out that Ukrainian Canadians are highly organized and gregarious, functioning most effectively in organized groups, and that their organizations permeate every Ukrainian community, large or small.[70] Various types of *narodni domi* (community halls) were long-standing centres for localized cultural activities; participation in them was taken for granted. The Ukrainian Catholic and Orthodox *chulanyi proswitas* and *tovaristvos*, serving as cultural halls, social centres, libraries, and folk music, dance, and drama theatres, were once common in the bloc settlements. Some voluntary associations were specifically nationalistic, such as the Ukrainian National Federation, the Ukrainian Hetmans Association, and the pro-monarchist, ardently anti-communist Sich organization of the Ukrainian Catholic Church. However, with each new generation, participation in such reactionary "old guard" organizations was dying, and if they were to retain the sympathies of the younger generations they were faced with reinterpretation of their raison d'être. On the other hand, an increasing variety of associations with combined benevolent, cultural, social, and religious ends was found in Ukrainian bloc settlements and nearby cities, including the Saskatchewan Provincial Council of the Ukrainian-Canadian Congress (which now represents 209 Ukrainian organizations), the Workers' Benevolent Association, Ukrainian-organized cooperatives, the Ukrainian Benefit Society, the New Community Credit Union (1939), the St. Nicholas Mutual Benefit Association, and the Ukrainian Self-Reliance League (*Soyuz Ukrayintsiv Samostiynikiv*). The last organization was in turn linked to other Orthodox associations, such as the Ukrainian Self-Reliance League for Men (*Tovaristva Ukrayintsiv Samostynikiv*), the Ukrainian Women's Association of Canada (*Soyuz Ukrayinok Kanadi*), the Canadian Ukrainian Youth Association (*Soyuz Ukrayinskoyi Molodyi Kanadi*), and the Union of Ukrainian Community Centres (*Soyuz Ukrayinskih Domiv*). The Mohyla Ukrainian Institute (*Mohyla Bursa*) was a students' residence with a cultural centre originally supported by youth to "save the Ukrainian heritage," having its Ukrainian Catholic counterpart just down the road in the Sheptytsky Institute, inclusive of the Obnova Club.

Among the original officially declared objectives of the Ukrainian Orthodox organizations were to organize and financially support centres of Ukrainian activity in the community and Ukrainian Orthodox schools, churches, associations, camps, newspapers, and so on; to cultivate love and respect among Ukrainian people for their traditional language, faith, and customs and to develop brotherly love among all Ukrainians; to ensure the religious, moral, and national training of Ukrainian youth; to promote the recruitment of candidates for the Orthodox priesthood; to provide responsible leadership for the Ukrainian people in Canada; to fight communism and other anti-democratic activities harmful to community and political life in Canada; and to fight for the independence and freedom of Ukrainians in Europe.[71] With reference to the last point, reports of the Royal Commission on Bilingualism and Biculturalism suggested that voluntary associations can reflect sectarian divisions, political divisions in Europe, and narrow nationalistic fervour, which can limit immigrants' sphere of interest to events back in the homeland. But this last type of voluntary association, it was reported, tended to have difficulty recruiting members.[72] This was apparently increasingly the case for such Ukrainian organizations in Canada, with each new generation, as travel to Ukraine became easier with gradual liberalization during the final years of the Ukrainian Soviet Socialist Republic, then declaration of the independence of Ukraine with the dissolution of the Soviet Union during the early 1990s. Yet National Holodomor Awareness Week continues to commemorate the Ukrainian famine (regarded as virtual Stalinist genocide) of 1932–33 every November in Saskatchewan. The Saskatchewan-Ukraine Relations Advisory Committee, created in 1993, provides advice to the provincial government and businesses.

Even Ukrainian museums in Saskatchewan have tended to be divided between Orthodox and Catholic. For example, in Saskatoon, the Ukrainian Museum of Canada has had an Orthodox affiliation. Linked originally with the Ukrainian Women's Association of Canada, it was first formed in 1936, thus claims to be the first Ukrainian museum in Canada. It was not opened to the public until five years later, in the Mohyla

Ukrainian Institute (linked to the University of Saskatchewan). A new museum was constructed in 1979 and opened the following year. It is "dedicated to the advancement of the knowledge of Ukrainian-Canadian history. ... It collects, documents and preserves those items which reflect the life of Canadians of Ukrainian heritage ... and also acts as a resource centre for information. Research and study in all fields relating to the traditional and contemporary lifestyles of Ukrainians [are] promoted and supported by the museum." Similarly, the Museum of Ukrainian Culture was originally located in 1953 within the Sheptytsky Institute (now the Ukrainian Catholic Religious Education Centre, linked to the University of Saskatchewan); in 1966, it was relocated next to the Ukrainian Catholic Cathedral of St. George as the Museé Ukraina Museum. It has focused on collections of *rizba*, weaving, pottery, musical instruments, folk dress, embroidery, and *pysanky*. The Catholic college on the university campus now houses the new Prairie Centre for the Study of Ukrainian Heritage.

Ukrainian-language periodicals reinforced contacts between Ukrainian settlements and specific causes. The *Ukrainian Voice* began publication in Winnipeg in 1910, followed by *New Country* in Rosthern from 1912 to 1930 and the *Canadian Ruthenian* in Winnipeg by 1917. The *Winnipeg Herald* in 1924 and *Veestnik* were Orthodox oriented; the *Voice of the Saviour, Ukrainian Life*, and the *Edmonton Ukrainian News* in 1929 were Catholic oriented; while *Ukrainian Life* and *Robitnik-Toilu* were conservative and monarchist. Later other periodicals were circulated from Toronto, but after 1930 no widely circulated periodical in the Ukrainian language was published anymore in Saskatchewan.

The distance that Ukrainian Canadians in Saskatchewan have travelled in over a century has been reflected in recent years in this ethnic community having contributed a governor general of Canada, a provincial premier, as well as lieutenant governors, mayors, and civic councillors.

RURAL DEPOPULATION AND URBANIZATION

Rural depopulation has taken its toll on Ukrainian local rural life within the bloc settlements. The prolonged drought of the dirty thirties, combined with the Depression years and followed by country school closures during the 1950s, served to accelerate an exodus from the settlements. The Ukrainian settlers who arrived a generation earlier had revealed a marked preference for rural as opposed to urban life, laying much stress on neighbourliness. Farm size generally was small; concomitantly, rural settlement was fairly intensive. For example, in 1917, out of 106 farms in the Vonda area, forty-five were one quarter (160 acres) and thirty-eight two quarters (a half section); out of fifty-eight in the Hafford area, twenty-five were one quarter (or less) and twenty two quarters; and out of sixty in the Garden River settlement, fifty-six were one quarter and a couple two quarters. It is interesting to note, however, that in the Garden River settlement settlers complained that the farms seemed too spread out; in the Ukraine, their farms had been only a dozen acres or so in size, so that "you could hear the sound of bells from the village," which brought "a great pleasure in your heart." Resistance to assimilation doubtless was enhanced by spatial as well as social isolation or segregation that corresponded to fairly intensive settlement and close-knit community life.[73] However, this relative proximity of neighbouring farms would soon change. The smaller Ukrainian villages, such as Smuts and Whitkow, would become virtual ghost towns, their once busy main streets and shops now overgrown, and only a few homes remain occupied. One-time rural families eventually became extensive kin networks. For example, one elderly woman born near Alvena in the Fish Creek settlement in 1917 was one of ten children in this farm family; her immediate descendants include ten living children and twenty-five grandchildren. Yet few descendants of such extended families remain in the settlement; they are now found in the cities and widespread across the province and beyond.

The Ukrainian population of Saskatchewan remained almost exclusively rural for decades. In 1911, only 1,291 people of Ukrainian origin resided in urban areas; although there were twice as many (2,807) in 1921, Ukrainians still comprised just 1.3% of the total urban population of Saskatchewan. The Ukrainian population grew rapidly from 28,907 in 1921 to 50,700 in just ten years. However, with out-migration because of depressed economic conditions, Ukrainians still numbered 50,030 by 1941. By this time, they had started to move into the cities. In Regina, there were only 179 Ukrainian residents in 1921, compared with 1,619 in 1941; in Saskatoon, 352 compared with 2,499. By 1941, more than a quarter (28.2%) of the gainfully employed Ukrainian population in the province were engaged in non-agricultural occupations. By 1941, Ukrainians had become 8.9% of the total provincial population, and over a quarter (26.1%) of the total Ukrainian population of Canada lived in Saskatchewan. With a renewed influx of Ukrainians into Canada after the Second World War, almost all of the new immigrants settled in Toronto and other eastern cities; during 1947–54, only 6.2% of these immigrants selected Saskatchewan as their destination. In 2001, Saskatoon, Regina, Yorkton, Prince Albert, Canora, and North Battleford respectively contained the largest numbers of Ukrainian residents, though the bloc settlements still retain the heaviest concentrations of Ukrainians.

POLISH SETTLEMENTS

Most of the early Polish settlers in Saskatchewan arrived from Galicia, at the time also known as "Austrian Poland," then part of the Austro-Hungarian Empire. Following the First World War, Galicia again became part of Poland, and after the Second World War western Galicia remained in Poland. Early Ukrainian settlers in Saskatchewan often identified themselves as Polish or Austrian when asked for their nationality by Canadian immigration officials; conversely, Polish settlers spoke localized dialects that they shared with Ukrainians and that differed from standardized Polish or Ukrainian. One respondent in the 1969–72 study in the Garden River settlement commented that she used to be Ukrainian but now had become Polish. She went on to explain that she had been raised in a Ukrainian Catholic family but had married a Polish Catholic and was now attending the Polish church. Any sociologist would point out that ethnicity is inherited, so cannot be changed, whereas religious affiliation is subjective, so can be changed. This conventional academic wisdom was lost on this respondent.

Polish settlers and their descendants in Saskatchewan tended to remain loyal to their Roman Catholic faith; moreover, the Ukrainian Catholic Church frowned on intermarriage between Eastern Rite Ukrainian Catholics and Western Rite Polish Catholics. Polish settlers organized or contributed to the development of more than fifty parishes in Saskatchewan, and they served as beacons to identify the locations of Polish concentration.[74]

As early as 1894, Polish immigrants first arrived in the Otthon Hungarian settlement, where St. Cunegunda Parish was soon founded. However, almost all of the early Polish immigrants settled amid the far larger Ukrainian population, forming small concentrations within Ukrainian settlements. Perhaps an exception was the Polish settlement around Cedoux, north of Weyburn, but even this settlement was close to the earlier mixed Ukrainian-Polish settlement around Candiac, just to the northeast. Thirty Polish families followed the Soo railway line from Chicago to Weyburn to settle Cedoux and neighbouring communities in 1902–03. They founded Krakow and Polish Draw School Districts in 1906 and Holy Trinity Parish in 1907. Father Francis Pander served the Candiac congregation since 1908; he was appointed pastor of St. Joseph's in 1931. The following year he created the extensive Calvary Shrine—landscaped gardens with stations of the cross carved out of the land by local artisans, a pool traversed by a bridge, a small summer home, an artificial valley and hill dominated by a high cross, and a square tower (topped by a statue of the Virgin Mary), in which was kept a portrait of the Virgin Mary carried during processions. During the mid-1930s, thousands of pilgrims—many of them Polish—would gather there every Dominion Day, but with the increasing cost of gasoline during wartime these pilgrimages ended by the Second World War years. In 1981, the shrine became a heritage site. In 1961, the Polish population of Weyburn and contiguous Wellington, Fillmore, Griffin, and Montmartre rural municipalities numbered 847. Griffin was formerly called English-sounding Roxboro and then Hastings before receiving its present name in 1910. Situated at the intersection of two active rail lines, the community once had twenty businesses and services and some 200 residents; only one general store remained by the 1980s. Poles, together with Germans from Galicia, established the community of Lemberg (the German name for Lwow/L'viv) during the mid-1890s, and they were instrumental in the establishment of St. Michael Parish in 1901. They also contributed to the founding of St. Mary at Grayson (1907) and St. Elizabeth at Killaly (1911).

Significant numbers of Poles from the Borszczow (Ukrainian Borshchiv) district of Galicia began to arrive in the Fish Creek settlement by 1898. They shared the old Immaculate Conception Parish at Fish Creek with francophone Métis from 1901 to 1957 and established a number of predominantly Polish parishes, including St. Stanislaw in Cudworth (1903–20, 1933–60), Our Lady Queen of Peace near Prud'homme (the congregation formed by Polish immigrants from Galicia in 1904, the present church constructed in 1918), Holy Trinity at Alvena (first organized in 1905), St. Mary's "Pidsudski" (1916), about fifteen kilometres south of Prud'homme (now only Esperance cemetery remains, the original church used as a granary on a nearby farm), and Sacred Heart at Tarnopol (1920).

A study of Queen of Peace Church in 1988[75] found that the membership had declined from eighty-nine adults and 148 children in 1953 to just fifteen adults and seven children in 1988, even though the ethnic composition of the area had not changed. Services had been conducted exclusively in Polish but now were mainly in English unless some older people were present. Finances used to be adequate to run the parish but had become insufficient to pay the priest. Intermarriage, especially with the surrounding much larger Ukrainian population, had been increasing. Church attendance had been regular but now could best be described as variable, depending on the family interviewed, though substantial decline was noted in some families. In general, certain families were becoming more open to intermarriage outside Catholicism, though some were more accepting than others, and none of the families interviewed seemed concerned about marrying non-Poles. The language spoken at home had changed from exclusively Polish in the first generation, to a mixture in the second, and completely to English in the third.

Northwest of Canora, Poles from the Buczacz (Ukrainian Buchach) district of Galicia had settled at Tiny, Buchanan, the Oleksince/Oleksyntsi district to the southwest, and Rama by 1901, establishing St. Mary Parish at Tiny/Kowalowka (1905), Sts. Peter and Paul at Dobrowody north of Buchanan (1907), St. Anthony at Rama (1922), St. Anne at Buchanan (1929), and St. Andrew Babola near Invermay.

Polish settlers had entered the Redberry settlement by 1904 and established a number of parishes: Holy Trinity at Orolow (1909), Holy Ghost at Albertown (1912), St. Michael the Archangel near Krydor (1913), St. Joseph at Alticane (1918), and St. Anthony at Redfield (1918); Poles also settled in the Kleczkowski district. St. Michael became the principal Polish church for the whole settlement, and the Sobieski hall was a focal point for the Polish community. Many of these Polish immigrants came from the Sokal area near the present Polish border with Ukraine, as did their Ukrainian neighbours. St. Michael's (1913) as well as St. Joseph's east of Mayfair (1932–35) became designated heritage sites respectively in 1992 and 1988. In Hafford, Poles have comprised a large part of the congregation together with French.

Polish immigrants from Wielkie Oczy began arriving in the Ituna, Goodeve, and Hubbard area northwest of Melville in 1904, where they founded St. Stanislaus Parish (1906), originally located between Ituna and Hubbard, Our Lady of Perpetual Help at Goodeve (1907), "Little Church in the Bush" near Jedburgh (1909), and Sacred Heart at Beckenham (1915).

Polish immigrants began arriving in the early 1900s in the area north and east of Canora. They established a "Country Catholic Church" at Stornoway (1908), St. Thomas Parish at Mikado (1912), Borszczow cemetery (1913), Holy Cross and Ruda cemetery near Sturgis, Corpus Christi at Ormside, St. Elizabeth at Stenen, St. Joseph at Moss Lake (1923), and St. Thomas at Norquay. The Tarnoville School District (1918) southeast of Hubbard (west of Yorkton) was also settled by Poles. Silesian Poles settled around Brewer in Cana RM just northeast of Melville; they founded a small Lutheran congregation with a long name—Evangelical Lutheran Christ's Ascension Congregational Church—where services were conducted in Polish until 1938; the congregation disbanded in 1964, and the church building was torn down in 1980.

In the Quill Lakes area, Poles founded Our Lady of Perpetual Help Parish (1908), originally in the countryside north of Wishart and later relocated in Wishart, followed by smaller parishes: Sacred Heart at Model Farm (1915) and Our Lady of Visitation at Krasne (1928). North of Wadena, Poles first came to the Fosston area in 1914 and were followed by a much larger influx in the 1920s. St. Mary Queen of Poland at Fosston was soon established, followed by the missions of St. Rose of Lima at Rose Valley and St. Felix at Archerwill, while a Polish presence increased in several parishes that had already been established in the general region: St. Mary at Wadena, St. Joseph at Kelvington, St. Theresa at Lintlaw, St. Helen at Kuroki, and in the High Tor district near Porcupine Plain.

Polish immigrants arrived in the Melfort area in 1904. In 1912, they were joined by twenty-five families from Manitoba and soon established St. Helen Parish at Brooksby (1914). Within the Garden River settlement east of Prince Albert, Polish settlers arrived in 1906 and formed several parishes: Sts. Peter and Paul at Claytonville (1910), Sacred Heart of Jesus at Janow Corners (1922), St. Mary of Perpetual Help at Honeymoon (1924), and St. Thaddeus at Henribourg (1928).

Of course, many Poles also settled in urban areas. Our Lady of Czestochowa Parish (Parafia Matki Boskiej Czestochowaskiej) was established in Saskatoon as an explicitly Polish congregation in 1965. Services continue to be at least partially in Polish (a Polish mass is the main service), and many of the parishioners are first-generation immigrants. Between eighty and 100 families are currently registered with the parish. The church has a Polish-language school, attended in 1991 by fifty children.[76] Saskatoon has been a base from which Polish priests have gone out to serve various Polish parishes far afield in Saskatchewan, such as Kuroki and Fosston. An early and still functioning Polish parish in Regina is St. Anthony (Sw. Antoniego). The influential superior of St. Charles Scholasticate in Battleford during the 1950s was Father Leo Engel, who despite his German ethnicity had been impressed by a Polish priest who was a family friend in Regina, so he trained as an Oblate priest in Poland in 1936–38 and founded the Oblate House of Studies, a residence for Polish immigrants studying at St. Michael's College, University of Toronto, before returning to Saskatchewan in 1953.

The total number of people in Saskatchewan claiming Polish descent (through the male line) was 28,951 back in 1961 and 26,910 ten years later; then, in 1981, 18,335 people claimed to be exclusively of Polish origin; moreover, those claiming only Polish origin declined substantially during the two decades before 2001. The Polish population of Saskatchewan, once almost all of whom were living in rural areas, has become progressively urban: by 1981, a majority (59.0%) of the people claiming only Polish origin were living in urban areas.

Polish-language use has declined in Saskatchewan. Back in 1961, less than half (42.7%) of the Polish population preferred English as their primary language, a third (33.4%) considered Polish to be their mother tongue, while almost another quarter (23.6%) considered other languages (likely Ukrainian) to be their mother tongues. Of the people speaking Polish or Ukrainian (together totalling 57% of people claiming Polish ethnicity), 66.4% were rural residents. Ten years later, in 1971, the proportion speaking Polish as their mother tongue had declined to 28.5%, almost equally divided between rural and urban residents. Of the 22,035 people claiming Polish ethnicity, 81.9% had been born in Canada, of whom 67.5% were English speaking, 17.0% Polish speaking, and 15.4% Ukrainian speaking (and other languages other than French), whereas of the remaining 4,875 people not born in Canada 13.6% were English speaking, 64.2% Polish speaking, and another 21.6% speaking other languages. The number of people speaking Polish at home was declining: from just 2,190 in 1971 to 1,670 ten years later. The number of people in Saskatchewan considering Polish to be their primary mother tongue declined steadily from 9,684 in 1961, to 7,675 in 1971, to 5,080 in 1981, and to 3,015 in 2001.

A high proportion of Poles in Saskatchewan remained Roman Catholics: 65.2% in 1961 (18,873, while 1,931 were Ukrainian Catholics and 1,089 Ukrainian Orthodox) and

66.1% in 1971 (17,800 Roman Catholics, 1,325 Ukrainian Catholics, and 580 Ukrainian Orthodox).

People of Polish origin have tended not to predominate in any Saskatchewan community. For example, in Ituna in 1961, just 16.1% of the residents were Polish, compared with 66.3% Ukrainian; in Buchanan, 18.2% were Polish, 45.0% Ukrainian; in Rama, 54.2% Polish and 32.3% Ukrainian; in Emerald RM (centred on Wishart), Poles constituted 20.1%, Ukrainians 45.3%; and in Ponass Lake RM (the Fosston area), Poles were 12.3% and Ukrainians 28.1%. Nonetheless, specific rural districts have remained strongly Polish to the present day, and Poles remain the second most numerous ethnic group after Ukrainians in many areas and small communities.

CONCLUDING THOUGHTS

During the early years of settlement, Ukrainian schoolchildren literally had "the Ukrainian beaten out of them." Then, during the First World War, Galicians and others were declared "enemy aliens" because Austria-Hungary, which ruled Galicia, was an ally of Germany, thus officially at war with Canada; under provisions of the War Measures Act (1914), more than 8,000 Ukrainians and other nationals (present or former) of countries at war with Canada were interned as prisoners of war. It is testimony to the strength of Ukrainian Canadian culture and character that this ethnic group concentrated primarily in Western Canada survived intact if wounded.

These western settlers were the "first wave" of Ukrainian as well as Polish immigration to Canada; as their children became adults during the interwar years, a far smaller second wave arrived to settle primarily in Eastern Canadian cities, followed by immigrants and refugees displaced by the Second World War, then immigrants in the greatest wave of immigration since western settlement—again staying mostly in eastern cities. Now a "fifth wave" is bringing some Ukrainian and Polish immigrants to Saskatchewan, most recently at a rate of about 500 a year, of whom 300 have arrived in Saskatoon. Many are skilled labourers—welders, mechanics, drivers—drawn by urban job opportunities, liberalization of independent Ukraine and post-communist Poland allowing easier emigration for the first time in a century, and not least the existence of a large Ukrainian-speaking and substantial Polish population in Saskatchewan. The Ukrainian Canadian Congress currently assists 350 workers from Ukraine and their families to immigrate to Saskatchewan each year, arranges partnerships with some sixteen sponsoring employers, and introduces immigrants to English-language classes.[77] Doubtless these new immigrants could help to revitalize aging Ukrainian and Polish communities, yet they are primarily settling in urban areas rather than rural Ukrainian and Polish bloc settlements. Again, new immigrants help to increase Ukrainian and Polish language use, yet they tend to stay in the larger cities.

According to the 2006 census, people of Ukrainian descent now number 129,265 in Saskatchewan, of whom just 27.7% (35,850) claim to be only Ukrainian, whereas 72.3% (93,415) claim Ukrainian along with other ethnic identities. The proportion of Polish population that is ethnically mixed is even higher: out of 56,855 people claiming Polish ethnicity, 11.4% (6,465) claim to be only Polish, while 88.6% (50,390) are mixed. Therefore, intermarriage has clearly made significant inroads into both Ukrainian and Polish ethnic homogeneity (though perhaps a significant amount of this intermarriage has been between Ukrainians and Poles). Yet people of Ukrainian ethnicity (wholly or partially) now constitute the fifth largest ethnic group in Saskatchewan, those of Polish ethnicity ninth.

SOURCES

Ukrainians in Canada
Apart from more general sources on immigration and provincial history, among the great variety of sources on Ukrainians in Canada, the following (listed in chronological order) are particularly informative.

Among the earliest writings are M.A. Sherbinin, *The Galicians Dwelling in Canada and Their Origin*, Historical and Scientific Society of Manitoba, Transaction No. 71 (Winnipeg: Manitoba Free Press, 1906); R. England, *The Central European Immigrant in Canada* (Toronto: Macmillan, 1929); C.H. Young, *The Ukrainian Canadians: A Study in Assimilation* (Toronto: Thomas Nelson and Sons, 1931); and V. Lysenko, *Men in Sheepskin Coats: A Study in Assimilation* (Toronto: Ryerson, 1947).

During the 1950s and 1960s were J. Skwarok, OSBM, *The Ukrainian Settlers in Canada and Their Schools, 1891–1921* (Edmonton: Basilian Press, 1959); C.C. Englert, CSsR, *Catholics and Orthodox: Can They Unite?* (New York: Paulist Press, 1959); M. Schudlo, CSsR, *Ukrainian Catholics* (Yorkton: Redeemer's Voice, 1962); V.J. Kaye, *Early Ukrainian Settlements in Canada, 1895–1900* (Toronto: University of Toronto Press, 1964); W. Darcovich, *Ukrainians in Canada: The Struggle to Retain Their Identity* (Ottawa: Ukrainian Self-Reliance Association, 1967); P. Yuzyk, *Ukrainian Canadians: Their Place and Role in Canadian Life* (Toronto: Ukrainian Business and Professional Federation, 1967); *Ukrainian Greek Orthodox Church of Canada Golden Jubilee, 1918–1968* (Winnipeg: n.p., 1968); *Ukrainian Greek Orthodox Church of Canada, 1918–1968* (Winnipeg: n.p., 1968); O. Woycenko, *The Ukrainians in Canada* (Winnipeg: Trident Press, 1968); A. Royick, "Ukrainian Settlements in Alberta," *Canadian Slavonic Papers* 10, 3 (1968); and O.S. Trosky, *The Ukrainian Greek Orthodox Church in Canada* (Winnipeg: Bulman Brothers, 1968).

During the 1970s were O. Semchishen, *Byzantine Churches of Alberta* (Edmonton: Edmonton Art Gallery, 1976); M. Kostash, *All of Baba's Children* (Edmonton: Hurtig, 1977); Z. Keywan and M. Coles, *Greater than Kings: Ukrainian Pioneer Settlement in Canada* (Montreal: Harvest House, 1977); H. Potrebenko, *No Streets of Gold: A Social History of Ukrainians in Alberta* (Vancouver: New Star Books, 1977); M.R. Lupul, ed., *Ukrainian Canadians, Multiculturalism, and Separatism: An Assessment* (Edmonton: Canadian Institute of Ukrainian Studies, 1978); H. Piniuta, trans., *Land of Pain, Land of Promise: First Person Accounts by Ukrainian Pioneers, 1891–1914* (Saskatoon: Western Producer Prairie Books, 1978); A.B. Anderson, "East European Ethnicity in Canadian Society: Recent Trends and Future Implications," in *Proceedings of the Second Banff Conference on Central and East European Studies*, vol. 3, ed. M. Gulutsan (Edmonton: University of Alberta, 1977), 1–26; and J. Kolasky, *The Shattered Illusion: The History of*

Ukrainian Post-Communist Organizations in Canada (Toronto: Peter Martin Associates, 1979).

During the 1980s were W.R. Petryshyn, ed., *Changing Realities: Social Trends among Ukrainian Canadians* (Edmonton: Canadian Institute of Ukrainian Studies, 1980); W.A. Czumer, *Recollections about the Life of the First Ukrainian Settlers in Canada* (Edmonton: Canadian Institute of Ukrainian Studies, 1981); P. Yuzyk, *The Ukrainian Greek Orthodox Church of Canada, 1918–1951* (Ottawa: University of Ottawa Press, 1981); M.R. Lupul, ed., *A Heritage in Transition: Essays in the History of Ukrainians in Canada* (Toronto: McClelland and Stewart, 1982); S. Hryniuk and R. Yereniuk, "Building the New Jerusalem on the Prairies: The Ukrainian Experience," in *Visions of the New Jerusalem: Religious Settlement on the Prairies*, ed. B.G. Smillie (Edmonton: NeWest Press, 1983); M.R. Lupul, ed., *Visible Symbols: Cultural Expression among Canada's Ukrainians* (Edmonton: Canadian Institute of Ukrainian Studies, 1984); J. Balan, *Salt and Braided Bread: Ukrainian Life in Canada* (Don Mills, ON: Oxford University Press, 1984); J. Petryshyn, *Peasants in the Promised Land: Canada and the Ukrainians, 1891–1914* (Toronto: Lorimer, 1985); O.T. Martynowych, *The Ukrainian Bloc Settlement in East-Central Alberta, 1890–1930: A History*, Occasional Paper No. 10, Alberta Culture and Multiculturalism, 1990; L.Y. Luciuk and B.S. Kordan, *Creating a Landscape: A Geography of Ukrainians in Canada* (Toronto: University of Toronto Press, 1989); and O.J. Goa, ed., *The Ukrainian Religious Experience: Tradition and the Canadian Cultural Context* (Edmonton: Canadian Institute of Ukrainian Studies, 1989).

And most recently have been J. Kolasky, *Prophets and Proletarians: Documents on the History of the Rise and Decline of Ukrainian Communism in Canada* (Edmonton: Canadian Institute of Ukrainian Studies, 1990); B. Rotoff, R. Yereniuk, and S. Hryniuk, *Monuments to Faith: Ukrainian Churches in Manitoba* (Winnipeg: University of Manitoba Press, 1990); B. Kordan and P. Melnycky, eds., *In the Shadow of the Rockies: Diary of the Castle Mountain Internment Camp, 1915–1917* (Edmonton: Canadian Institute of Ukrainian Studies, 1991); O. Subtelny, *Ukrainians in North America: An Illustrated History* (Toronto: University of Toronto Press, 1991); B. Waiser, *Park Prisoners: The Untold Story of Western Canada's National Park, 1915–1946* (Saskatoon: Fifth House, 1995); F. Swyripa, "Ukrainians," in *Encyclopedia of Canada's Peoples*, ed. P.R. Magocsi (Toronto: University of Toronto Press, 1999), 1281–1311; B. Kordan, *Enemy Aliens, Prisoners of War: Internment in Canada during the Great War* (Montreal: McGill-Queen's University Press, 2002); J.C. Lehr, "'Shattered Fragments': Community Formation on the Ukrainian Frontier of Settlement, Stuartburn, Manitoba, 1896–1921," *Prairie Forum* 28, 2 (2003): 219–34; and F. Stambrook and S. Hryniuk, "Who Were They Really? Reflections on East European Immigrants to Manitoba before 1914," in *Immigration and Settlement, 1870–1939*, ed. G.P. Marchildon (Regina: Canadian Plains Research Center, 2009), 457–82.

Ukrainians in Saskatchewan
Sources specifically on Ukrainians in Saskatchewan include E. Tremblay, CSsR, *Le Père Delaere et l'Eglise Ukrainienne du Canada* (Berthierville, QC: l'Imprimerie Bernard, 1960); Ukrainian Catholic Directory for Saskatchewan, 1961; M. Stefanow, "A Study of

Intermarriage of Ukrainians in Saskatchewan" (MA thesis, University of Saskatchewan, 1962); Ukrainian Orthodox Directory for Saskatchewan, 1965; A.B. Anderson, "Ukrainian Identity Change in Rural Saskatchewan," in *Ukrainians in American and Canadian Society: Contributions to the Sociology of Ethnic Groups*, ed. W.W. Isajiw (Cambridge, MA: Harvard Ukrainian Research Institute, Harvard University; New York: Ukrainian Centre for Social Research, 1976), 93–121; A.M. Baran, *Ukrainian Catholic Churches of Saskatchewan* (Saskatoon: Modern Press, 1977); M. Harbuz, *Ukrainian Pioneer Days in Early Years, 1898–1916 in Alvena and District, Saskatchewan* (North Battleford: Appel Printing, ca. 1978); A.B. Anderson, "Ukrainian Ethnicity: Generations and Change in Rural Saskatchewan," in *Two Nations, Many Cultures: Ethnic Groups in Canada*, ed. J.L. Elliott (Scarborough: Prentice-Hall of Canada, 1979), 250–69; J. McCracken, "Yorkton during the Territorial Period," in *Pages from the Past: Essays on Saskatchewan History*, ed. D.H. Bocking (Saskatoon: Western Producer Prairie Books, 1979), 64–78; A.B. Anderson, "It Started with a Plow: Ukrainian Settlements in Saskatchewan," invited talk presented to the Saskatchewan Ukrainian Historical Society and Ukrainian Canadian Congress, In Baba's Trunk Conference, Saskatoon, May 2004, and Regina, November 2004; B. Kordan, "Ukrainian Settlements," in *Encyclopedia of Saskatchewan* (Regina: Canadian Plains Research Center, 2005), 694–95; and J.C. Lehr, "Governmental Coercion in the Settlement of Ukrainian Immigrants in Western Canada," in *Immigration and Settlement, 1870–1939*, ed. G.P. Marchildon (Regina: Canadian Plains Research Center, 2009), 267–84.

Details of local Ukrainian communities are found in numerous local community histories as well as B. Barry, *Ukrainian People Places* (Regina: People Places Publishing, 2001); B. Barry, *Geographic Names of Saskatchewan* (Regina: People Places Publishing, 2005); and K. Pidskalny, *Saskatchewan's Ukrainian Legacy* (Saskatoon: Saskatchewan Ukrainian Historical Society, 2006).

Polish Canadians and Polish Settlements in Saskatchewan
General sources on Polish Canadians and Poles in North America include W.I. Thomas and F. Znaniecki, *The Polish Peasant in Europe and America*, 2 vols. (New York: Dover Publications, 1958); H. Radecki and B. Heydenkorn, *A Member of a Distinguished Family: The Polish Group in Canada* (Toronto: McClelland and Stewart, 1976); H. Radecki, *Ethnic Organizational Dynamics: The Polish Group in Canada* (Waterloo: Wilfrid Laurier University Press, 1979); W. Kurelek, *The Polish Canadians* (Montreal: Tundra Books, 1981); F. Renkiewicz, ed., *The Polish Presence in Canada and America* (Toronto: Multicultural History Society of Ontario, 1982); D.H. Avery and J.K. Fedorowicz, *The Poles in Canada*, (Ottawa: Canadian Historical Association, 1982); A.M. Kojder and B. Glogowska, *Marynia, Don't Cry: Memoirs of Two Polish-Canadian Families* (Toronto: Multicultural History Society of Ontario, 1995); and H. Radecki, "Poles," in *Encyclopedia of Canada's Peoples*, ed. P.R. Magocsi (Toronto: University of Toronto Press, 1999), 1281–1311.

Specifically on Saskatchewan, see L. Kasperski, "Polish Settlements," in *Encyclopedia of Saskatchewan* (Regina: Canadian Plains Research Center, 2005), 696–97.

Chapter 6

THE SETTLEMENTS OF OTHER EASTERN EUROPEAN GROUPS

Apart from Ukrainians and Poles, as well as most Germans, several other ethnic groups of Eastern European origin developed their own settlements in Saskatchewan. This chapter successively describes the bloc settlements of these groups, in order of group population size today: Russian Doukhobors, Hungarians, Romanians, Czechs and Slovaks, Croatians and Yugoslavs, and Jews.

RUSSIAN DOUKHOBOR SETTLEMENTS

During the seventeenth century, a number of dissident sects in Russia broke away from the Russian Orthodox Church. One of these sects gradually emerged as the Doukhobors (originally derisively named *dukhoborets*, or spirit-wrestlers, by a Russian Orthodox bishop). They first congregated in South Russia (today Ukraine), where the similarly communal and pacifist Mennonites and Hutterites had already settled, then were banished into the Caucasus Mountains. In 1898, they started to leave their many secluded villages, dissatisfied with continuing persecution by both the Russian czarist government and the Russian Orthodox Church due to their refusal of military service and their rejection of the established church and with overcrowded agricultural lands.[1] As many as 1,200 settled temporarily in Cyprus that summer, but 5,882 from the Elizavetpol, Kars, and Tiflis districts in the Caucasus emigrated to Saskatchewan during the winter. Early in 1899, they began to settle in two almost contiguous colonies and an annexed area near Kamsack and later that year in a third colony near Blaine Lake, which included 1,472 Doukhobors who had taken refuge in Cyprus and much of the fourth and final shipload of 2,318 from the Caucasus.[2]

CHAPTER 6

Assisted by Russian and English philanthropists, notably Leo Tolstoy and Quaker Aylmer Maude, they had been promised good, cheap land, religious freedom, and exemption from military service in Canada. As the federal minister responsible for immigration, Clifford Sifton was quick to respond to the solicitation that Canada should find a home for some 7,500 refugees expelled from Russia in 1898. Tolstoy wrote that they were the best farmers in Russia; the British consul at Batumi (then in the Russian Empire, now in Georgia) testified to their "diligence and sobriety by which they had brought prosperity to the barren localities in which they were originally settled"; Lord Strathcona thought them likely to be an asset to Canada.[3] The immigrants paid the required ten dollar homestead fee per quarter of land (160 acres) and acquired some 750,000 acres of land specifically reserved for their use. They seemed impressed with financial aspects of the settlement agreements, remarking that "In Canada things are, one may say, based on God's law; for instance, the freehold of land is sold for about seven cents an acre." Moreover, they believed that they were receiving good pay as manual labourers: $1.50–$2.00 for ten hours of work. But they were reluctant to take the oath of allegiance required of homesteaders by the Canadian government.[4]

The North (Thunder Hill) Colony, centred in the Swan River Valley immediately east of Arran (about 110 kilometres northeast of Yorkton), contained six townships with twenty-four villages (though four were short lived). A typical village contained about forty families. The villages of Kaminka, Techomeernoe, and Simeonovo were situated on Bearhead Creek east of Arran; the villages of Bogdanovka, Techomeerovka, First and Second Osvoborsdennie, Stradaevka, Libedevo, and Lubomeernoe around the upper reaches of the Swan River north of Pelly; Hlebedardoe, Pocrovskoe (where the ruins of a meeting house can still be seen), Vera, First and Second Voznisennie, Michaelovo, and McVey Camp farther down the Swan River north of Arran; Boghumdanoe and Gromovoe farther north in the Thunder Hill district; Oospennie and Troitzkoe lower down Whitebeech Creek, near Whitebeech; and Pavlovo, Perehodnoe, and Archangelskoe between Whitebeech Creek and Maloneck Creek northeast of Norquay. All of these villages were originally communal, but Michaelovo and Troitzkoe later became mixed. The Peaceful Cove (Spokoene Zaleev) cemetery was located east of Pelly, and the rural Sopoff Post Office north of Arran operated from 1913 to 1939. Independent Doukhobors settled Vozvyshenie near Hyas in 1903–07.

The main part of the South Colony, south and west of Kamsack and around Veregin (approximately fifty kilometres northeast of Yorkton), was larger, containing fifteen townships and originally twenty-four villages, later increased to thirty-five (of which six were soon abandoned). The villages of Terpennie, First and Second Petrovka/Orlovsky and Cyprus, Kaminka, and Nickoliaevka were situated in the vicinity of Stony Creek, west of Togo. Along the Assiniboine River south of Kamsack and west of Cote were the villages of Voszennie, Radionovka/Old Riduonovo, Tomboscoe, and Troodeloobevoe. Along Kamsack Creek west of Kamsack and around Veregin were Old and New Voskrisennie, Trusdennie/Tooshdennie/Stradenofka, Old and New Effromovo, Slavenska, Lubovnoe, Verovka/Vernoe, Blagodarovka/Blagodarnoe, Terpennie/Kars, and Riduonovo. The Luzan School District, created in 1911, was just south of Veregin; the Terpenia School District, formed in 1924, was just west; Tolstoi Road was north.

Beyond the colony, Community Doukhobors ran the Vurtsovo communal stock farm northeast of Yorkton. Peter Veregin once occupied the upper storey of the impressive and ornate wooden Doukhobor prayer home in the village of Veregin, constructed in 1917–18. This large prayer home or *dom* was built with a double-storey wrap-around verandah topped with decorative metalwork. A smaller prayer home is also exhibited at Veregin, and the ruins of a similar one are found in the countryside south of Veregin.[5] The community of Veregin was not typical of Doukhobor villages, insofar as it did not consist of a single broad street bracketed by homes. Named after Peter Vasilevich Verigin (1859–1924), despite the different spelling, it had its beginning in 1906 as a post office (though it had already assumed some importance as a Doukhobor economic centre—the previous year the local brick factory had produced an astonishing 1.5 million bricks); Verigin relocated his headquarters there from the village of Otradnoe. Veregin became an incorporated village in 1912.

The remaining villages were spread around the Whitesand River between Kamsack and Canora and included Oobezhdennie, Spaskoe, Pokrovka, Najersda (Nadezhda), Smyrennie, Otradnoe, Kapustina, Slavnoe, Blagovishennie, Novoe Golubovo, and Bisednoe. All were communal villages except for Trusdennie, Oobezhdennie, Pokrovka, Slavnoe, and Novoe Golubovo, which were mixed or other types of villages. An elaborate prayer home was constructed at Otradnoe (Russian for joy) in 1908, but it burned down during a protest of radical communal Doukhobors just eight years later, as did the prayer home at Veregin (the second prayer home at Veregin was modelled after the original one at Otradnoe). Outside the colony, Doukhobors operated a sawmill at Chernoff Lake in Duck Mountain east of Kamsack, and the Verdant Valley School District and Post Office were created to serve the Swan River Valley respectively in 1911 and 1913.

The small separate territory between Good Spirit Lake and Buchanan (southwest of Canora) known as the Good Spirit Lake Annex was considered part of the South Colony. It contained eleven villages: Blagosklonoe, Ootishennie, Old Moisayovo, and Kyrilovo were communal villages, Old Gorilloe/Gorelovka a mixed type, and Kalmakovo, Novo Troitzkoe, New Moisayovo, New Gorilloe, Nova Slavenska, and Troitska/Razbegallovo other types.

The Saskatchewan (or Prince Albert) Colony along the North Saskatchewan River was similarly subdivided into two actual settlements: the Blaine Lake area (about eighty kilometres northwest of Saskatoon) and the Great Bend–Eagle Creek district west of Langham (thirty kilometres west of Saskatoon). Initially, six villages were established in the northern (Blaine Lake) portion and three in the southern (Langham) portion; soon they would respectively increase to nine and four. In the Blaine Lake area were First Spasofka (about twenty-three kilometres by road northeast of town, originally beyond the colony boundaries), Pasariofka/Pazeraevka (originally called Second Spasofka, almost seven kilometres east of town), Slavyanka (another eight kilometres farther east), Oospennie/Oospenia (eighteen kilometres by road southeast), Terpennie/Terpanie (also eighteen kilometres from town but farther south), Petrofka (twenty kilometres directly south), Troitzkaja/Troitzka (originally Third Spasofka, about ten kilometres by road southwest), and Small and Large Horelofka/Chorolofka (respectively about nine and thirteen kilometres by road northwest of town). By 1905, only Large and Small Horelofka and Pasariofka were still communal villages; all of the other villages were mixed. At Petrofka and other villages along the river during the first year of settlement (1899), homes were dug out of the hillside of the river valley; within a year or so, the settlers had moved to a better location up on the plateau. Other Doukhobor-settled districts within the settlement were the Postnikoff Creek district (around the former Petrofka), the Radouga Creek district (where a Doukhobor flour mill was situated in 1904–05), Tallman (a railway grain elevator on the shore of Blaine Lake), Nesdoly Lake, Harmonia, and Makaroff Lake (between the town and Petrofka). Blaine Lake became an incorporated village in 1912 and a town in 1954.

In the southern (Langham) portion of the colony were Karilowa (First Kirilofka) and Bodanofka (originally Second Kirilofka, and later Ceepee, respectively about six and ten kilometres west of Langham), Tambofka/Tambovka (later Henty, across the river, about three kilometres east of Borden), Pakrofka/Pakrowka (originally Third Kirilofka, and later Henrietta, about twenty-one kilometres west of Langham by road on the south side of the river). Bodanofka and Tambofka were communal, whereas Karilowa and Pakrofka were mixed. Today Doukhobors and other Russians (many of them former Doukhobors) are scattered throughout this area, around Arelee and Environ; the Petroffsk School District (1913) near Arelee was settled by Russian Baptists.

By 1905–10, the population of the North Colony exceeded 3,000; the South Colony (excluding the Annex) 3,700; the Annex close to 1,000; and the Saskatchewan Colony (both parts together) 3,800.[6]

The communal villages that the Doukhobors established in the Saskatchewan colonies were similar to those that they had left in the Caucasus. Even the village names were reproductions. A typical Doukhobor village consisted of an average of twenty houses lined up along either side of a broad main street, with the ends of the houses facing the street. The houses in the North Colony were usually log plastered with clay, whereas they were more commonly sod and clay in the other colonies, though the more individualistic settlers in the Saskatchewan Colony favoured house-barn combinations. Each house, unpainted and with a thatched roof, was set off from the street by a vegetable garden and split-rail fence. The upper storey of each house jutted out over the lower. It was usually the older men and women and children who constructed the villages, for the able-bodied younger men were away working on railway construction or on neighbouring farms. No more than fifty families were found in each village. The layout of the village reflected the Doukhobors' beliefs in egalitarianism and common ownership. Many villages featured a separate *dom* (prayer home or meeting house), and in central larger and more diverse communities such as Veregin there were grain elevators, flour mills, and even brick factories.[7]

However, Doukhobor communities were short lived in Saskatchewan. The Canadian government initially agreed to the establishment of reserves containing communal villages in 1899 because this did not set a precedent; Mennonites had already established similar villages within reserves in Manitoba in 1874. In fact, the Hamlet Clause in the Dominion Lands Act specifically permitted the establishment of communal villages, provided that they would be located within three miles (five kilometres) of the homesteaded quarters, as an alternative to the prerequisite of living on the homestead. Moreover, in February 1903, Clifford Sifton, the Minister of the Interior, reaffirmed this settlement arrangement by allowing a three-person committee to make common entry on behalf of all the Doukhobor settlers. Sifton seemed defensive, to say the least, about his decision to bring these strange Russians to Canada. In 1901, he wrote that

> The cry against the Doukhobors and Galicians is the most absolutely ignorant and absurd thing that I have ever known in my life. There is simply no question in regard to the advantage of these people. The policy of exciting racial prejudice is the most contemptible possible policy, because it is one that does not depend upon reason. You can excite the prejudice of one nationality against another by simply keeping up an agitation. ... All you have to do is to keep hammering away and appealing to their prejudices, and in the course of time you will work up an excitement; but a more ignorant and unpatriotic policy could not be imagined.[8]

By November 1904, 422,800 acres representing 2,640 homesteads had been entered.[9] But this agreement was soon countered by Frank Oliver, the new minister, in 1906 when he accepted the advice of Reverend John McDougal, Land Commissioner, to cancel the reserves. In 1907, the refusal of Doukhobors to accept individual homesteads and to take oaths of citizenship led to the dissolution of the colonies as special reserves. Although naturalization toward obtaining citizenship was a prerequisite of the Homestead Act, the Doukhobors had a history back in Russia of refusing to take state-enforced oaths since they feared that doing so would negate their exemption from military service.[10] As early as 1900, a Doukhobor petition had stated that

> The laws of your country require that every male immigrant, 18 years of age, who wants to settle on vacant government land, has to record it in his name, and after a certain term, such land becomes his property. But we cannot accept such a law, cannot record homesteads in our own individual names, cannot make them our private property, for we believe that in so doing we would break directly God's truth. Who knows this truth knows also that it opposes the acquisition of property.[11]

Protests proved to be in vain. In 1907, some 1,618 Doukhobor quarters were opened to non-Doukhobor homesteaders, and three years later Doukhobor lands were restricted to fifteen acres per man, woman, and child, while all other acreage was opened to homesteaders. Soon 2,500 homesteads were cancelled, representing 400,000 acres of land, at an estimated loss of some $11 million to the Doukhobors.[12] Professor James Mavor of the University of Toronto, who had assisted Doukhobors in their negotiations with the government, referred to a "breach of faith" by the government. As Doukhobor historian Koozma Tarasoff has commented, "To this day forty thousand Canadian Doukhobors remember this as a deliberate betrayal of government to break up their cooperative structure, their non-traditional way of looking at morality, and their anti-military social movement."[13]

In October 1902, an estimated 1,700–1,900 Doukhobors set off on a march eastward to protest the dominion land policy; when they were confronted by authorities, they stripped—this was the first incidence of what would become a common form of protest for radical communal Doukhobors. With the cancellation of the Doukhobor reserves in Saskatchewan, by 1908–09 most of the conservative Community Doukhobors (variously estimated at from 2,000 to 5,000), including the radical Sons of Freedom, who strongly believed that land is God given, were led by Peter ("the Lordly") Veregin to new secluded mountain colonies in the Kootenays near Grand Forks and Brilliant, British Columbia.[14] Although the reserves in Saskatchewan were cancelled, the government did temporarily specify much smaller reserves around communal villages for the Community Doukhobors, based on fifteen acres per village resident. These reduced reserves dwindled, and by 1918 the remaining land had been sold. However, the village of Veregin survived despite the departure of most Doukhobors in this region for British Columbia; the community's residents were soon supplemented by an influx of Ukrainians, Poles, and others. By the mid-1950s, close to 300 residents lived there, but only half that number twenty years later, and the community's status as an incorporated village was finally cancelled in 2006.

With the mass exodus of Community Doukhobors to British Columbia, by 1917 only a few communal villages remained in Saskatchewan (not necessarily populated entirely by Doukhobors). Russian place names that had marked some of these villages were converted into anglophone names for school districts: in the Saskatchewan Colony, for example, Spasofka became Ottawa and Riverhill School Districts, Pazeroika/Balmoral, Troitzka/Trinity, and Terpannia/Brook Hill, while other country schools with Doukhobor pupils would have included Gillies and Shield between Blaine Lake and Spasofka and Sand Lake and Merry Home just west of Petrofka. Country schools serving largely Doukhobor districts within the settlement were gradually established mostly between 1901 and 1917; they all closed between 1954 and 1962 (except for Shield, which started later in 1930 and closed earlier in 1943).

In 1905, Petrofka had eighty-five residents, who kept 172 head of livestock (cattle, horses, and sheep). At that time, though, it was just an average-sized village; the villages of the Saskatchewan Colony ranged in population from as few as sixty (Oospennie) to as many as 217 (Spasofka)—four villages were smaller than Petrofka, eight larger.[15] In the spring of 1913, sixty-seven people (almost all of them Independent Doukhobors) lived in Petrofka, by fall seventy-three residents (now fifty-one were Independent Doukhobors, and twenty-two were non-Doukhobors). Four years later there were still eighty residents (including twelve "Germans"). Petrofka had become the ferry crossing in 1901 and had its own post office in 1907 (not closed until 1940), so it was surviving better than other villages; in fact, now it had become the largest remaining communal village in the settlement. Of thirteen original communal villages, besides Petrofka, only one had a population of about fifty, two had just over twenty residents, three had just one or two families left, and the rest were now vacant. Tambofka, the smallest (and perhaps most solitary) communal village, lasted only eight years before it was abandoned; at its height, it had only sixty-six residents, who farmed 800 acres and tended sixteen oxen, twenty-three horses, fifty-four cattle, and twenty-four sheep. By 1917, the total number of Doukhobors still living in communal villages in Saskatchewan numbered little more than about 500. Most villages had been entirely vacated; some had part-time or a few non-Russian residents; many contained just a few remaining families and were no longer functional socio-economic communities.[16] Sadly, today, hardly a trace can be found of all the once numerous little villages that had from 100 to 200 residents and typically more than twenty fenced homes built of stone, wood siding, or mud-plastered logs with shingled or thatched roofs lining a broad (100-foot-wide) street—perhaps now just grass-covered foundations along an obscured road (this would describe all that remains of Petrofka), piles of rubble, perhaps a few long-abandoned farmhouses, rarely the ruins of what was once an active meeting house, and occasionally a well-maintained cemetery with a historic commemorative marker.

The controversy over communal or individual ownership of land had heightened the sectarian divisions among Doukhobors. Not all Doukhobors agreed with Verigin, or resisted the government's homesteading policies, or participated in or sympathized with the nude demonstrations of the eastern reserves. Yet a demonstration almost did occur in the Saskatchewan Colony during the First World War when an RCMP officer, backed by a local magistrate, refused to recognize the Doukhobor military exemption; as a result, the Doukhobors threatened to burn their crops, destroy their farm machinery, and march on the town (Blaine Lake). The trouble was averted by a telegraphed order from Ottawa.[17] Settlers who in good conscience could opt to affirm rather than take the oath and settle on individual homesteads were allowed to remain. Over 1,000 Doukhobors had legally taken out homesteads and been sworn in as Canadians by 1912. Some of these people had settled in the Good Spirit Lake Colony. Originally from the Kars and Elisavetpol districts in the Caucasus, they included many fairly well-to-do individuals who had held individual property in Russia. Others were *yakutsi farmali* who arrived from Russia in 1905; they sympathized with the Independents over the land ownership question and regarded Verigin as a supervisor but not as divine.[18]

Strangely, Verigin returned to Saskatchewan in 1918 to purchase another 10,000 acres of land that had been part of the Fishing Lake Indian Reserve. This land, comprising the Kylemore Colony, was settled by some 250 Doukhobors of the Christian Community of Universal Brotherhood who moved back from British Columbia. Evidently, Verigin's intention had been to provide flour to the main settlement back at Grand Forks, but this small colony had continuous financial problems, and creditors foreclosed on it in 1928. With Verigin assassinated four years earlier at Grand Forks, the settlers soon scattered, most returning to British Columbia, others joining fellow Doukhobors still in Saskatchewan, though the Gooliaff family remained to give their name to the district.[19] Today Kylemore has been reduced to a hamlet with just thirty-seven residents.

The Doukhobors in the Saskatchewan Colony were generally more individualistic than those in the eastern reserves. From the start of the settlement, a few families had owned their own quarters; soon many did not hold land in common and cooperated with their brethren of the other colonies only to a limited extent. In 1916, the Society of Independent Doukhobors was founded by Peter Makaroff, a lawyer, at Blaine Lake. Peter the Lordly's successor, Peter II Chistiakoff, attempted in 1937 to reunite the destitute conservative Community Doukhobors of the Kootenays with Independents who had settled around Grand Forks, and the following year he carried his campaign to the Saskatchewan Colony. A few potential or actual sympathizers with the Sons of Freedom still remained in the latter colony, but the Doukhobor leader met with little success there. After a prolonged illness, he died in Saskatoon in 1939, having been rejected by Doukhobor spokesmen from the Saskatchewan Colony and having excommunicated all of the Doukhobors in this colony who had refused to join his organization. When Stefan Sorokin, a Russian displaced person posing as a Doukhobor leader, arrived in the colony ten years later from Europe, he was advised by these Independents—who by now tended to be suspicious of hereditary leadership (and many of whom were relatively affluent, well educated, and sophisticated)—that his leadership was not needed. He was more successful, though, in being accepted in the Kootenays as the replacement for Peter II's successor, Michael "the Archangel" Verigin.[20]

Although at the time the Independent Doukhobors were found largely in the Saskatchewan Colony, today they constitute most of the Doukhobors as a whole. The most radical, conservative, and communal of the Doukhobors, the Sons of Freedom (also known as *Svobodniki* or Zealots) still numbered from 2,000 to 3,000 in their Krestova and Gilpin communes in the Kootenays by the 1960s. The less radical yet still conservative Orthodox Doukhobors (the Union of Spiritual Communities of Christ) numbered about 5,000 and were concentrated in British Columbia. The largest and growing sectarian division, the Independents (the Society of Independent Doukhobors) numbered close to 13,000, mostly (some 8,000) in Saskatchewan, close to 4,000 in British Columbia, and another 1,000 in Alberta. They retain an emphasis on traditional pacifism and the Russian language but remain non-communal.[21] So at the time the total Doukhobor population in British Columbia was estimated at more than 10,000, divided between Vancouver and the Kootenays around Brilliant, Krestova, and Grand Forks.

Perhaps some 4,000 remained in the Saskatchewan colonies: about 900 in the North Colony, 700 in the South Colony around Kamsack and Veregin, 400 in the Good Spirit Lake Colony, and 2,000 in the Saskatchewan Colony, approximately equally divided between the settlement around Blaine Lake and the settlement west of Langham.[22] However, a closer inspection of the distribution of Russian population in 1971 reveals more modest figures. By far the largest remaining Doukhobor settlement in Saskatchewan was the South Colony—including Veregin, Kamsack, and portions of four rural municipalities: Cote, Sliding Hills, Keys, and St. Philips—which had a Russian population totalling 1,280; Russians comprised almost a quarter (24.2%) of the residents of Kamsack and more than two-thirds (68.6%) of those of Veregin (today Kamsack has 1,713 residents, Veregin just sixty-five, and both are losing population). Not far to the west, another 170 people of Russian origin were living in the town of Canora (pop. 2,013 in 2006); an almost equal number, at least 190 Russians, were living in the area of the former Good Spirit Lake Colony, in the rural municipalities of Good Lake and Buchanan, and in the village of Buchanan (225 residents in 2006; in 1971, only forty were Russian). And, just to the north of the South Colony, the area that had been within or near the North Colony—that is, Arran, Pelly, and Livingston RM—contained only 240 people of Russian origin. Farther west, few have remained around the former Kylemore settlement: not more than 100 people of Russian origin—seventy in Kylemore, Sasman RM, and Lakeview RM, plus thirty in the nearby town of Wadena. As noted, the large settlement straddling the North Saskatchewan River, formerly known simply as the Saskatchewan or Prince Albert Colony (rather a misnomer), has always consisted of two separate settlements separated by at least twenty-five kilometres of land where Doukhobors did not settle: these two settlements were Blaine Lake to the north and Langham/Eagle Creek to the south. By 1971, people of Russian origin comprised only

29.3% of the residents of the town of Blaine Lake (which had 472 residents at last count and has been declining), outnumbered by people claiming Ukrainian origin (41.5% of residents). There were 180 residents of the town of Russian origin and another 165 in the surrounding Blaine Lake RM, thus a total of 345 in the northern portion of the colony. Slightly more people of Russian origin were living in the southern portion: eighty-five in the town of Langham (where they constituted 16.3%—a relatively small proportion of the 1,120 residents today are of Russian origin), ten (18%) in the hamlet of Arelee, and another 305 widely scattered through the rural municipalities of Corman Park (in the districts around the former villages of Karilowa, Bodanofka, and Pakrofka/Henrietta west of Langham), Eagle Creek (west of Pakrowka Creek and around Eagle Creek, Environ, Arelee, and Struan), and Great Bend (very few in the Henty district around the former village of Tambofka, between Borden and the river). So a total of 400 people claiming Russian origin were found in this southern portion of the colony (including adjacent areas where they had eventually settled).

The Russian-origin population of Saskatchewan, totalling 35,050 in 2006, of whom 13.7% (4,785) claimed only Russian ethnicity while the other 86.3% (30,265) claimed multiple ethnic origins, is quite diverse today, including not only people who are religious Doukhobors but also people who are of Doukhobor descent yet are now members of other religious affiliations, people of Russian but not Doukhobor origin (such as Russian Baptists or Stundists who settled south of Blaine Lake in 1907), Doukhobors who have intermarried especially with Ukrainians, and more recent immigrants who might be Russian. However, we can surmise that the largest number of people claiming Russian ethnicity in Saskatchewan are still descendants of the original Doukhobors. Today the total number of Doukhobors in Saskatchewan (including many who are intermarried with other ethnic groups and who live in cities, particularly Saskatoon) has grown to over 15,000, almost all of whom would identify themselves as Independents.[23]

In a study conducted in ethnic bloc settlements in the north-central region of Saskatchewan in 1969–72, some interesting opinions were provided by twenty Doukhobor informants representing different ages and generations in the Blaine Lake settlement.[24] Seven thought that Doukhobor identity absolutely should be preserved, ten thought that it should be but were resigned to change, and the remaining three seemed indifferent. Five respondents predicted a major loss of identity in the near future, thirteen a minor loss of some aspects of Doukhobor culture, and two little or no loss. Strikingly, all of the respondents in the first (immigrant) generation, and 90% of those in the second generation, strongly favoured the preservation of Doukhobor identity, compared with 60% of those in the third generation. It seemed that these families were not as conservative anymore as one might have imagined, though it must be remembered that they were all Independents. Concerning their use of the Russian language, just one could speak virtually only Russian, hardly any English; five were bilingual in Russian and English yet still preferred to speak mainly Russian both at home and in the community; eight Russian at home but English in the community; five English both at home and in the community yet were familiar with Russian; and the remaining one just English. Put more simply, one could speak only Russian, fourteen used Russian fairly often, and all but one could still speak Russian. None of the respondents in the first generation was speaking English primarily or exclusively, compared with half of those in the second and—surprisingly—just 20% of those in the third. Another surprise was that only 60% of first-generation respondents attended Doukhobor religious services regularly, compared with 80% of the second generation but none of the third generation. Expression of opinions opposing intermarriage to non-Russians declined from 60% in the first generation to 50% in the second and to 20% in the third.

Prayer meetings and services were first held in homes of villagers or in open air during summer and later in schools. The earliest prayer home in this settlement was likely "Up the Hill" in Haralowka; it was eventually moved into the town of Blaine Lake and used as a doctor's office and residence during the 1950s and 1960s. In 1930, Trinity School was purchased and moved into town to be used as a prayer home. It was replaced the following year by the present larger brick building on Main Street. Doukhobors around Blaine Lake have long chosen to live independently rather than communally but still maintain close ties with the Orthodox Doukhobors of British Columbia. Thus, the contractor for the new prayer home came from Brilliant, British Columbia; the prayer home was constructed under the leadership of Peter Chistiakov Verigin with the cooperation of the Central Executive Committee of the "Named Doukhobors of Canada" and with contributions from Doukhobors in British Columbia. The prayer home motto is "Toil and Peaceful Life. ... The welfare of all the world is not worth the life of one child." Today the prayer home is designated as a heritage property.[25]

The Blaine Lake Gospel Chapel, attended by some Doukhobors, has long been linked with Mennonites. Herman Fast, a Mennonite, once taught the Russian language in Petrofka School, built by Quakers, after 1906 and held gospel services in the school and private homes. A church was constructed in the Harmonia district in 1912–13 with financial assistance from Mennonite Brethren, on land adjoining Ukrainian and Doukhobor farms; these farmers respectively became the first minister and deacon. After 1924, Mennonites joined Baptists for rural services there and in private homes. During the 1940s, this church (then identified as Mennonite) moved from Harmonia into Blaine Lake. Between 1944 and 1956, the minister was a Ukrainian storekeeper; most services were held in Russian. In 1954, Mennonite Brethren supplied another pastor, who conducted services in English, though some Russian was retained until 1959, when a succession of Mennonite pastors followed, by which time a Russian-speaking congregation was meeting separately. Although Mennonite Brethren dominated, the church also became known as the Baptist-Mennonite Union Church until the Russian-speaking Baptists moved away. Eventually, in 1967, the more inclusive (and less Mennonite) Blaine Lake Gospel Chapel came into existence.

Meanwhile, specifically Russian Baptists (including Ukrainians) settled in 1907 in the Doukhobor village of Troitzkaja/Trinity while developing their homesteads. Initially, they walked about twelve kilometres to the Mennonite-led services held in Petrofka School as well as worshipped in private homes. They constructed their own church in 1917, with Pastor Nestor Nesdoly of the Nesdoly Lake district. In 1924, they temporarily joined with Mennonite Brethren into a single congregation, then affiliated with the English Western Baptist Union until 1932, when their church became the Russian-Ukrainian Evangelical Baptist Union with Pastor Nesdoly as president (in 1948, he became pastor of a Baptist church in Saskatoon). Since the 1950s, this congregation has been led by a succession of Ukrainian pastors. A Russian Ladies Circle was organized in 1965 (actually led by Ukrainians), following the earlier formation of the Blaine Lake Doukhobor Ladies Club in 1947.

Doukhobor families shared many aspects of Russian customs with the larger Ukrainian population, whose members were their close neighbours; only minor differences distinguished Doukhobor customs from Ukrainian ones. The once typical Doukhobor dress for men was soon largely abandoned, whereas women continued to wear headscarves (and still commonly do, if not in the community certainly in the meeting house and choirs). Lace making, weaving, and furniture making were long-lasting traditions that now have unfortunately been dying out. Weddings have continued to be focal points of social gatherings, but with increasing intermarriage (especially to non-Slavic spouses) this tradition will inevitably change. Country dances replaced folk dancing, plays were seldom given in the Russian language, and "Russian baseball" and *kitchka* were games no longer played after the 1920s. However, an annual Doukhobor gathering long continued to be celebrated on St. Peter's Day (June 29).[26] As late as 1921, Premier Martin received requests from Russian Baptists and Doukhobors at Blaine Lake as well as Eagle Creek for permission to establish "Russian-Canadian Christian Schools," which would teach the Russian language and "Russian Christianity" while flying a Russian flag.[27]

Perhaps we can conclude that the Doukhobors of Saskatchewan, while far less numerous than their Ukrainian neighbours, and perhaps now more urbanized (a Doukhobor residence existed in Yorkton as early as 1932; sixty years later it was designated a heritage property), have succeeded in maintaining distinct rural settlements where they have concentrated and a unique identity, though these settlements have far fewer members than they originally did, and some aspects of Doukhobor culture will continue to undergo change with each new generation, while other aspects (not the least familiarity with their traditional mother tongue) have proven remarkably resilient. The Doukhobor prayer home in Veregin contains an extensive library with hundreds of Russian-language publications, manuscripts, and documents; declared a provincial heritage building in 1982, it is part of the National Doukhobor Heritage Village, which opened in 1980. The recent re-creation of a Doukhobor village (Oospenia in the Blaine Lake settlement) with the earliest homes literally dug out of a hillside (now an active archeological site, declared a provincial heritage property in 2005 and a National Historical Site in 2009, now called the Doukhobor Dugout House) helps to maintain consciousness of early Doukhobor settlement and holds annual events that have included re-enactments of a traditional Doukhobor wedding, the historic "burning of the arms" in the Caucasus, a treaty of friendship with the First Nations, the assassination of Peter Vasilevich Verigin in 1924, and Dedushka Day for grandfathers. Doukhobor artifacts are also housed in the Blaine Lake Historic Museum located in the one-time railway station. The Blaine Lake settlement has become an active artistic centre; local artists include artist, poet, and writer Edith Vereshagin, stone sculptor Cecil Burima, painter and decorative furniture maker Doreen Kalmakoff, fabric artists Florence Cheveldayoff and Pat Wasylkowski, spinner Wendy Stupnikoff, gallery owner Nadia Pobran, and the late painter Hazel Stupnikoff. Painter William Perehudoff (1918–2013), raised at Bogdanovka, received many honours, including the Order of Canada, membership in the Royal

Canadian Academy of Art, the Saskatchewan Order of Merit, the Queen's Diamond Jubilee Medal, the Saskatchewan Centennial Medal, and an honorary doctorate from the University of Regina. Occasional Doukhobor gatherings are also organized by the Saskatoon Doukhobor Society, such as observance of an annual Peace Day with Quakers and Mennonites; the Saskatoon Doukhobor community has had a booth at the annual Saskatoon Exhibition for more than four decades, where sixty volunteers produce and sell over 5,000 loaves of traditional Doukhobor bread.[28]

HUNGARIAN SETTLEMENTS

Over a quarter century, beginning in 1885, Hungarian immigrants developed at least ten named settlements in three regions of Saskatchewan. In the eastern region, Esterhaz Colony (*Esterhaz Magyar Kolonia*) was planned by the illustrious Count Paul Oscar Esterhazy. Born Johann Baptist Packh in 1831, he adopted his aristocratic name from a wealthy land-owning family in Hungary, of whom he claimed to have been an illegitimate son; his mother was rumoured to have been impregnated by Nicholas Esterhazy (eight years later she was suspected of murdering Johann's father, who was an architect).[29] Johann was quickly promoted in the Hungarian army (perhaps because of his illicit birth?), only to become exiled as a revolutionary and granted refuge in Britain. "John" now joined the British army and served in the British West Indies, but he eloped with the daughter of a British officer. He returned to Hungary and assumed a new identity as Paul Oscar Esterhazy. He emigrated to the United States in 1868, at the age of thirty-seven. Finally, after various enterprises, he obtained a contract, together with a Hungarian agricultural expert, with the Canadian Pacific Railway to settle Hungarian settlers in Western Canada. Although he was accused of being an imposter, he played a significant role in bringing to Western Canada numerous Hungarians (Magyars as well as other citizens of greater Hungary within the expansive Austro-Hungarian Empire, which included at the time territories that today are in Austria, Slovakia, Ukraine, Romania, Serbia, Bosnia, and Croatia). Acting as a CPR immigration agent, he obtained 125,000 acres in Saskatchewan in 1885. He succeeded in persuading Hungarian and Czech and Slovak coal miners and steel industry workers from Pennsylvania to move to the Canadian prairies, where abundant farmland was available at minimal cost. After some were settled in Huns' Valley (originally called Hungarian Valley and later called Polonia) near Minnedosa, Manitoba, in 1885, thirty-five families moved on to his larger Esterhaz Colony in Saskatchewan the following year. A CPR benefactor provided a $25,000 advance for houses and supplies.

This colony was focused on the new town of Esterhazy, served by the Esterhaz Post Office, Roman Catholic school district (1888), and public school district (1889), the latter located seven kilometres southwest, where the Czechs and Slovaks (including more Protestants) had concentrated. Despite the departure of two-thirds of the original settlers, with the arrival of larger numbers of immigrants in 1888, encouraged by Esterhazy's ambitious propagation (Esterhazy anticipated several more large colonies), Hungarian settlement quickly spread southward to the Qu'Appelle River, and by 1888 the extended colony became known as Kaposvar (the Esterhazy family estates in Hungary were centred on Esterhaza castle near the city of Kaposvar). Meanwhile, though, Count d'Esterhazy (as he now styled himself) had left for New York, where he died in 1912. By 1902, the Esterhaz and Kaposvar Colonies had a population of over 900 settled on 200 homesteads, and 14,000 acres were under cultivation. Esterhazy was incorporated as a village in 1903 after the arrival of the railway. The Esterhazy flour mill, originally built in 1907, was designated a historic site in 1996. Esterhaz Colony had the main town, while Kaposvar Colony had a large church that replaced a small log church that had been built on the same site in 1892 and was served by French and Belgian priests, Père Decorby and Père Pirot. The latter priest employed his two brothers and a brother-in-law, who were Belgian stonemasons, to construct the impressive Our Lady of Assumption Roman Catholic Church in 1907–08; incredulously, they hauled 1,600 loads of fieldstone by sleigh to the church site. The stone rectory predated the church, having been built in 1901–03.[30] By 1890, Kaposvar had its own separate post office and two rural school districts, including St. Istvan Roman Catholic School (honouring St. Istvan or St. Stephen, first king and patron saint of Hungary). Today the present church (1906–07) and rectory (1903) comprise a historical museum.

Count Esterhazy was concerned over the settlement of Swedes in 1886 west of Esterhazy, so Hungarian settlement was further extended, westward to Stockholm, when the priest at Esterhazy promoted the settlement of some fifty Hungarian families in the Cana Colony, which they called Sokhalom (many hills), an obvious play on words.[31] Hungarian settlement was also expanding northward to Yarbo and Zeneta and eastward to Gerald. St. Elizabeth School, established at Yarbo in 1905, was named by Louis Nagy, an early Hungarian member of the school board, after St. Elizabeth of Hungary. In 1971, the total Hungarian population of the Esterhaz-Kaposvar-Sokhalom settlement could be estimated at about 900, including Esterhazy (where the 255 residents of Hungarian origin had declined to just 8.8% of the population), Stockholm (where 175 Hungarian residents now outnumbered Swedes, forming 42.7% of the population), very few in Yarbo and Gerald, and over 400 in Fertile Belt RM and a few in the neighbouring rural municipalities. Before the first potash mine in Saskatchewan began production near Esterhazy in 1962 and Gerald in 1967, Esterhazy contained little more than 500 residents; it gained town status in 1957 and rapidly grew to more than 3,000 residents by the 1970s. Today the town contains 2,336 residents, Stockholm 323, Gerald 124, and Yarbo seventy-two; all except Stockholm have recently been losing population. Of more than 800 people employed at the potash mines (reputedly the largest potash mines in the world), almost half live in Esterhazy.[32]

In 1894, the Hungarian settlement of Otthon (meaning home in Hungarian, named by early settler Stephen Balint Sr.), or Cana Colony, located between Melville and Yorkton, was founded by Reverend Janos (John) Kovacs, a minister of the Hungarian Reformed Church in Pennsylvania. Later, in 1910, Reverend Kalman Kovasci became the pastor there; he would become an influential pioneer missionary of the Hungarian Reformed Church and co-editor of *Kanadai Magyar Farmer*, published in Winnipeg, and a driving force behind Reformed Hungarian settlement in several colonies. The Otthon Post Office opened in 1896, and the Debrecan Post Office to the west operated from 1912 to 1916. Two school districts were created in 1898: East and West Otthon. This small colony attracted immigrants both direct from Hungary and via the United States. Today the organized hamlet of Otthon contains just fifty-six residents. However, there are a considerable number of people of Hungarian origin in the general area: in 1971 almost 900, including 280 in Melville, 205 in Yorkton, and more than 400 in the rural municipalities of Cana and neighbouring Orkney and Garry. A plaque honouring the centennial of this settlement was erected in 1993 by the Saskatchewan History and Folklore Society.

The Bekevar Colony (originally called the Hazelwood Colony) around Kipling began to develop in 1902 after Janos Szabo, having read about the success of Reverend Kovacs at Otthon, decided to establish another Reformed colony. Kipling was incorporated as a village in 1909. The focal point of the Bekevar Colony was the large double-steepled Reformed (later Presbyterian) church, completed in 1911, though soon a smaller rival Hungarian Baptist congregation was very active, conducting baptisms in a slough dubbed *Jordan to*. The Reformed church had its *Bekevari dalarda* (choir), a Christmas concert called *viragfakardas* (blossoming time), and an annual picnic.[33] A sign over the entry gate still proclaims *isten hozott* (welcome). The initial settlers came from Botragy, northeast Hungary, which had a strong Reformed congregation. Bekevar Colony grew rapidly to include the Bekevar Post Office and School District in 1904, renamed Kossuth in 1906 (after Lajos Kossuth, who led Hungary's nationalist movement for independence from Austria during the mid-nineteenth century), and three other school districts: Magyar in 1905, Rakoczi in 1910, and Little Mountain. The Budapest Rural Telephone Company operated from 1916 to 1977. In 1982, the Kipling and District Historical Museum was established. With the closure of Magyar School in 1952 and the cessation of services in Bekevar Presbyterian Church in 1968, the settlement lost an important focus (though the church was designated a municipal heritage property in 1996, facilitating its preservation and restoration). The Bekevar Colony contained virtually the same number of people of Hungarian origin as the Cana settlement, almost 900 in 1971, including the town of Kipling (39.6% of the residents) and the surrounding rural municipalities of Hazelwood, Kingsley, Silverwood, and Wawken. Kipling, which became a town in 1954 (three years before Esterhazy), had 973 residents in 2006 but was losing population.

Many Hungarian immigrants settled in the north-central region of Saskatchewan. The town of Wakaw (originally conceived by Hungarian settlers as Idavar) became virtually surrounded by Hungarian settlements around the turn of the century. To the north, the Buda School District was founded in 1907 by Hungarian settlers, but today they are outnumbered by Ukrainians; the former Buda School, today the Buda Cooperative Community Centre, was designated a heritage site in 1993. Hungarian settlers were also found in the Ens district to the west (together with Ukrainians, Germans, and French) and the Lone Pine district to the east (with Ukrainians). West of Wakaw, the Dunafoldvar School District (1907) was settled by immigrants from Dunafoldvar, Hungary (between Budapest and Kaposvar); Venne's general store served this district from 1898 to 1911. South of Wakaw Lake, the Matyasfold (land of Matthias) settlement developed under the original guidance of Zoltan Rajcs. The Crooked Lake and Bukowina districts (including the hamlet of Lepine) were mixed Hungarian and Ukrainian. Farther east Hungarians mixed with French in the Belmont and Bonne Madone districts (including Reynaud). Hungarian settlement eventually extended continuously far to the east and northeast, around Basin Lake, Little Moose Lake (where French priests from St-Brieux served a largely Hungarian congregation at St-Philippe Mission), and Meskanaw. To the southwest, between Wakaw and Prud'homme, St. Laszlo

THE SETTLEMENTS OF OTHER EASTERN EUROPEAN GROUPS

Colony developed in 1900–05, receiving overflow from Matyasfold and Dunafoldvar; in fact, many original settlers, such as the extended Miskolczi family, arrived from Dunafoldvar, Hungary. Eventually, this Hungarian settlement spread to the southeast around Muskiki Lake, where Hungarians mixed with Ukrainian and German neighbours, and southward to predominantly French Prud'homme. St. Laszlo (*Szent Laszlo*) Church (named after the virtuous king of Hungary in the early eleventh century), constructed in 1911, long remained a focal point of Hungarian communal activity, together with the school and community hall.[34] Father Oscar Solymus moved from Lestock to St. Laszlo in 1911 and served the parish until 1930. However, throughout the north-central region, the very dispersion of Hungarian settlement into districts also settled by Ukrainians, Germans, and French would inevitably hasten assimilation through intermarriage, especially since these Germans and French shared their Catholic religion with Hungarians. Altogether these settlements included approximately 800 people of Hungarian origin in 1971. Most lived on farms—they formed only small proportions of the residents of Wakaw (13.8%), St-Brieux (15.8%), St. Benedict (9.0%), and Yellow Creek (16.6%) and even smaller proportions of other communities. Yet they were concentrated in these particular districts widely scattered through six rural municipalities—especially Three Lakes and Hoodoo and to a lesser extent Bayne, Lake Lenore, Invergordon, and Flett's Springs.

Finally, two other Hungarian settlements developed in the south-central region. Szekelyfold (land of the Szekelys, Carpathian Magyars who mixed with ethnic Romanians both in Bukovina and in this area in Saskatchewan), or Mariavolgy Colony, extending from Raymore, Quinton, Punnichy, Lestock, and Leross southward across the Touchwood Hills toward Cupar and Dysart, commenced in 1906 and included the Arpad, Apponyi/Arbury, Mathyas, Granatier, St. Imre (*Szent Imre*), and Virag and Bimbo (respectively Hungarian words for flower and bud) School Districts and the Magyar, Zala, Balatone, and Benchonzie/Marianum Postal Districts. Magyar Post Office operated from 1910 to 1919, closed for twenty years, then was revived from 1939 to 1966. St. Joseph and St. Elizabeth Roman Catholic Missions served the colony; the priest at Raymore now serves St. Mary's Hungarian Parish. Homesteads were constructed in traditional Szekely style. Szekely immigrants from six villages in Bukovina were joined by ethnic Hungarians and Romanians from southern Bukovina. This Touchwood Hills settlement eventually contained the largest number of people of Hungarian origin in the province—almost 1,300 in 1971—in the communities of Quinton (31.3% of the residents), Lestock (25.6%), Cupar (22.3%), Punnichy (16.5%), and Dysart (7.7%) and smaller proportions in Raymore and Leross; there were also significant numbers in the rural municipalities of Touchwood, Kelross, and Cupar, also some in neighbouring rural municipalities farther north. The town of Cupar had 566 residents at last count in 2006, the town of Raymore 581, the villages of Punnichy 277, Dysart 198, Lestock 138, Quinton 108, and Leross 42; most were declining.

The Pinkefalva Colony near Plunkett was founded in 1905 by Imre Pinke, an immigrant from western Hungary via the United States. He attracted settlers by writing about homesteading in Hungarian American newspapers. He first founded St. Luke's Colony north of Whitewood in 1895, which had 200 settlers of mixed nationalities and religious affiliations, then the more homogeneous Hungarian colony of Pinkefalva

(Pinke's village). The colony was served by the Golden Hill School District after 1908. In 1971, there were perhaps 120 people of Hungarian origin left in this settlement, mostly on farms in the rural municipalities of Viscount and Wolverine and very few—just fifteen—in Plunkett (which had seventy-five residents in 2006).

Elsewhere the Fischman School District northwest of Gravelbourg, founded by Abraham Fischman in 1911, was settled by Hungarian homesteaders. The Roka district south of Kamsack was named after the Hungarian word for fox. In the Rothermere district southwest of Spiritwood, the small Temesvar Hungarian settlement was served by a United Church minister during the 1920s.

The Hungarian population in Saskatchewan grew to 8,946 in 1921 (when it constituted two-thirds of all Hungarian Canadians), 13,363 in 1931, and 14,576 in 1941, then declined to 12,470 in 1951. Recent census data (2006) have revealed a total of 27,390 people claiming Hungarian ethnic origin, of whom 20.3% (5,555) claimed only Hungarian origin, compared with 79.7% (21,835) who also claimed other ethnic origins. With Hungarian concentration in Toronto during the postwar years and after the Hungarian revolution in 1956 (when over 36,000 Hungarian refugees arrived in Canada but fewer than 1,000 settled in Saskatchewan), the older Hungarian population of Saskatchewan formed little more than 12% of the total Hungarian Canadian population. None of the communities with a substantial number or proportion of Hungarian residents has been gaining population.

Hungarian traditions have been maintained by the Hungarian Prairie West Club and Fonyo Dancers, who have long provided an *isten hozott* (welcome) to their pavilion in Folkfest in Saskatoon, where traditional dishes such as *gulyas* (goulash), *kolbasz* (pork sausage), *langos* (deep-fried bread sprinkled with icing sugar), and *makos* and *dios beigli* (poppyseed and walnut rolls) are served. There is also the annual Western Canadian Hungarian Folk Festival, now in its thirty-fifth year, recently hosted by the Tilinko Hungarian Folk Ensemble of Saskatoon, bringing together more than 300 Hungarian folk dancers and musicians.

ROMANIAN SETTLEMENTS

Not only did immigrants of Romanian ethnic origin settle in Saskatchewan but also people of other ethnic origins—Ukrainians, Germans, and Jews—who had emigrated from greater Romania, which historically had included Bukovina (today partially within Ukraine), eastern Moldavia (today Moldova), southern Bessarabia (now in Ukraine), southern Dobruja (now in Bulgaria), western Banat (now in Serbia and Hungary), and Transylvania (long claimed by Hungary but primarily in present-day Romania). The complex ethnic settlement patterns of greater Romania (i.e., historical Romania at its maximum extent) were duplicated on the Canadian prairies. After 1895, Transylvanian and Bukovinian Romanians and Hungarians settled near Dysart, while Bukovinian Romanians and Ukrainians settled around Yorkton and Canora during the early 1900s as well as in the Boian-Ispas area in Alberta. From 1901 to 1908, some 200 Jewish settlers from Bukovina established forty homesteads east of Dysart near Lipton, and Romanian Jews settled in the Hirsch and Hoffer Colonies.

St. Nicholas Church in Regina, founded in 1902, claims to be the first Romanian Orthodox parish in North America. St. Nicholas Parish preserves more of a Romanian identity, whereas all services in St. George Romanian Orthodox Cathedral, also in Regina, are now in English. Although Romanians were already in Regina by the turn of the century, they were largely a rural farm population. During the 1890s, a Romanian settlement began to develop around Dysart, where St. George Romanian Orthodox Church was constructed in 1906–07 by immigrants from Dobruja.[35] The Lupescu School District (named after Pincus Lupescu, an influential Romanian Jewish settler) was formed north of the village in 1913 (the school was renamed Princess Elizabeth in 1948 and closed ten years later) and the Radant School District (the German name for Radauti in Romanian Bukovina) south of the village in 1914 (closed in 1960). Dysart was only a post office in 1906 when St. George was founded; the community would not be recognized as an incorporated village for another three years. This church and Dysart School (1917) became designated heritage sites in 1986–87; the school houses the Dysart and District Museum. After a divisive argument during the 1950s, some members of St. George took the unusual step of joining the local Anglicans. The Bukovinian Szeklers/Szekelys who settled in the hills to the north were Western Rite Roman Catholics who mixed Hungarian with Romanian cultural features.[36] An Eastern Rite Catholic church, Holy Eucharist Parish, was established at Dysart in 1957 (and demolished in 2012). In 1971, a total of almost 100 residents of Dysart and Cupar, plus another 300 in the rural municipalities of Lipton, Cupar, Kelross, and Touchwood, identified themselves as "other" ethnicity, many of whom could have been Romanian. Dysart had 198 residents in 2006.

Elsewhere in the province, the Kayville-Dahinda area in the Dirt Hills in the south-central region was also settled after 1905 where first Sts. Peter and Paul Parish was founded in 1906, then St. Mary by a dissident group in 1915, and Holy Trinity Russian Orthodox Church in 1923. Kayville Post Office and School were established respectively in 1912 and 1913; the village site was laid out in 1924, and the community was designated an organized hamlet in 1951. But by 2006 Kayville reportedly had only five remaining residents (down from fifteen five years earlier). Today the community is characterized by abandoned homes and stores on the main street. Dahinda, too, was once an active community but had already declined to just twenty-five residents by 1968. Just to the west, the Wood Mountain, Lakenheath, Stonehenge, Flintoft, Elm Springs, and Stefan districts west of Assiniboia were first settled by Romanians (including several families of Gypsies, according to a former resident) in 1905. Sts. Peter and Paul Parish was established at Flintoft in 1911 and designated a historic site in 1991; its fine iconostasis (altar screen) was reputedly imported from a Romanian Orthodox monastery at Mount Athos in Greece. At Elm Springs, the Ascension of Our Lord Parish was founded in 1926. The community of Wood Mountain (currently down to just twenty residents), settled by Romanians by 1914, was served by Holy Transfiguration Parish from 1929 and today is a historic site. The Stefan School District (named after the patron saint of Romania) operated from 1919 to 1949. Romanians had moved into the nearby town of Assiniboia (pop. 2,305 in 2006) by the 1930s; today the parish priest there, in Descent of the Holy Ghost Parish, founded in 1958, serves several parishes in surrounding districts.

By 1906, a Romanian settlement straddling the Saskatchewan-Manitoba border had developed; this settlement included the parishes of St. John the Baptist at Shell Valley, St. Elias the Prophet at Lennard, and Holy Trinity, a striking church with its three steeples, founded in 1903 some ten kilometres west of MacNutt (pop. 80 in 2006), all served by a single priest based in Inglis, Manitoba, together with Sts. Peter and Paul Parish founded at Canora in 1920. The Dormition of the Theotokos Church also serves Romanian Orthodox around MacNutt.

Other small and isolated Romanian settlements have included one near Pierceland on the Beaver River west of Meadow Lake, where the Romanian Orthodox Church of the Holy Trinity, founded in 1934, was designated a heritage site in 1983; another at Cavell/Coblenz, in the west-central region between Wilkie and Landis; and in the Moon Hills north of Blaine Lake, where a tiny Romanian Orthodox church, St. John the Baptist, was built in 1941. The church cemetery reveals that the progenitors of this latter settlement were born in Romania from 1859 through the 1890s. Their stories of hardship and determination are captivating. Nicolaie Pampu arrived around 1905 from Romania to homestead with his wife Todora and five sons (later two more sons were born in Canada); their six daughters all died in infancy. After acquiring his homestead in 1911, Yoil Banda brought his wife Vista and two sons from Romania in 1913. The trip reportedly took thirty days at sea; they arrived at Pier 21 in Halifax, then began the long trek west by train. Fortunately, the trip took so long that they missed their passage, originally booked on the *Titanic*. Today the descendants of these original families farm throughout the area; they do not form a cohesive settlement but are scattered amid and intermarried with French, Ukrainians, and Doukhobors in neighbouring districts: Moon Hills and Banda Lake, Paddling Lake, Windsor Lake, Ash Lake, Martin's Lake, Damour, and Crown Hill.

During the early 1960s, the congregation of St. Nicholas, together with that of St. George, Dysart, changed their official allegiance from the Missionary Episcopate based in Detroit to an anti-communist Episcopate based in Grass Lake, Michigan. Then, after a contentious divided vote, the congregation of St. George, Regina, decided to accept the offer of these breakaway churches to join them.[37] The forerunners of this church were the Romanian Orthodox Church of the United States and Canada (1925), directly under the Patriarchate in Bucharest (which had separated from the Greek Orthodox Church in 1885); then a split occurred between the Romanian Orthodox Missionary Episcopate of America (1949), based in Detroit but closely tied to the Patriarchate in Romania, and the anti-communist Romanian Orthodox Episcopate of America (1952), which is more independent. This division among Romanian Orthodox Christians continues today despite political changes in Romania. During the early years of Romanian settlement in Saskatchewan, priests were sent from Romania, but in more recent times they have more likely been trained in seminaries in Winnipeg or Detroit.

Most Romanian Orthodox churches in Saskatchewan eventually became affiliated with, or more recently founded by, the Romanian Episcopate Deanery of Canada (also known as the Romanian Orthodox Episcopate or the Western Canada Deanery of the Romanian Orthodox Episcopate of America (*Episcopia Orthodoxa Romana din America*), whose presiding bishop is based near Detroit; in turn, this Episcopate forms an autonomous part of the Orthodox Church in America (OCA), based in New York City. St. George Cathedral in Regina is the seat of the Archimandrite of the Western Canada Deanery, while the Romanian Orthodox Deanery Centre of Canada is located at Fort Qu'Appelle; other parishes of the Romanian Orthodox Episcopate of the OCA are St. Nicholas in Regina, Descent of the Holy Spirit in Assiniboia, St. George in Dysart, Holy Trinity in MacNutt, Sts. Peter and Paul in Canora, Sts. Peter and Paul in Flintoft, and Protection of the Holy Mother of God Mission in Fort Qu'Appelle. Although the OCA contains this autonomous Romanian Episcopate, it increasingly defines itself as an Orthodox church transcending ethnicity: that is, an interethnic church. Some Romanians participate in OCA congregations not specifically designated as Romanian; these parishes are under the jurisdiction of the OCA Archdiocese of Canada and would include Holy Trinity in Kayville, Holy Trinity in Moose Jaw, Sts. Peter and Paul in St. Walburg, St. Mark the Evangelist in Yorkton, and Holy Resurrection in Saskatoon. A few churches still identify as Romanian Orthodox but are not affiliated with the OCA, rather with the Romanian Orthodox Archdiocese of America and Canada (also called the Romanian Orthodox Archdiocese in the Americas); formerly, the Romanian Orthodox Missionary Archdiocese in America and Canada, it gained autonomy from the Romanian Orthodox Church of Romania in 1974, based on a 1950 decision of the Holy Synod of the Romanian Orthodox Patriarchate. Parishes have included Holy Transfiguration in Wood Mountain, Ascension of Our Lord in Elm Springs, Sts. Peter and Paul and St. Mary in Kayville, Dormition of the Theotokos in MacNutt, Holy Trinity in Saskatoon, and St. John the Baptist near Marcelin. Some people of Romanian origin in Saskatchewan (especially from Bukovina, who were likely to speak both Romanian and Ukrainian) have attended Eastern Rite Ukrainian Catholic churches (e.g., Holy Eucharist in Dysart) and Ukrainian Orthodox churches, others Western Rite Roman Catholic churches within or near Romanian settlements (e.g., in Lebret and north of Dysart). Some Romanians might be members of the Eastern Rite Greek Catholic Church in Transylvania (dating from 1697); however, their descendants in Canada have tended to participate in Eastern Rite Ukrainian Catholic or Western Rite Roman Catholic parishes rather than form their own parishes. Intermarriage between Romanians and Ukrainians, particularly in mixed settlement areas and in cities, soon became common.

The early Romanian immigrants to Saskatchewan were mostly young men; by 1920, husbands and fathers had been joined by their families and supplemented by second-generation migration from the United States. Over 80% of the early settlers were homesteaders; an estimated 15% were manual labourers, who helped to build the streets and sewer system in Regina; and about 5% ran small businesses (including grocery stores, bars, insurance companies, confectionaries, coffee shops and restaurants, hairdressers, and shoeshine parlours) established between 1905 and 1920. Many urban women homemakers earned extra income in cottage industries such as dressmaking. Romanian women shifted gradually from being farmwives to undertaking diverse urban occupations. Today at least two-thirds of Romanian women in the Prairie Provinces work outside the home. Romanian voluntary associations in Saskatchewan have included a mutual aid society in Regina, linked to American counterparts based in Detroit, that served diverse functions as credit union, bank, insurance company, and even funeral parlour. In 1928, the Bok-O-Ria Romanian Restaurant and Social Club appeared in Regina (bok-o-ria is a phonetic spelling of *bucurie* or pleasure). Informal Romanian neighbourhood associations have also developed in Regina, particularly on the east side. Women's and youth organizations, such as the Romanian Orthodox

Women's Auxiliary (ARFORA), have been closely tied to the church. However, with a weakening of Romanian identity, younger women have become less active in such organizations.

Progressive, inevitable assimilation and acculturation of Romanians in Saskatchewan have been reflected in the loss of ability to speak Romanian (by the 1970s, only about 6% of people claiming Romanian origin in Saskatchewan were still speaking Romanian as the primary language at home—94% did not); intermarriage, especially with Ukrainians, and high and increasing rates of exogamy since the second generation; changing family values among youth; involvement of women in the wider community after the first generation; a shift to the nuclear family from the extended family; and a continuous movement away from the specific Romanian Orthodox Church. Yet there have been signs of continuing interest in Romanian culture as well. For example, in 1965, the second generation formed the Eminescu Romanian Dance Group, which has performed widely in North America. To an appreciable extent, Romanian culture has long been preserved in Saskatchewan in various respects: traditional religious rites, songs and dances, home cooking, unique wedding ceremonies, baptisms, and funeral and memorial feasts (one priest recently lamented that he now performs more funerals than baptisms).[38]

Back in 1914, most of the over 8,000 Romanians living in Canada had settled in the Prairie Provinces. By 1921, this population had increased to over 29,000. Of all Romanian-speaking immigrants, some 85% were from Transylvania, Bukovina, and Banat; another 10% included Vlachs (or Aroumanians, speaking a Romanian dialect) from throughout the Balkans—Thrace, Bulgaria, Greece, Macedonia, Serbia. So perhaps only 5% were actually from the "Old Kingdom" of Romania. But with the arrival of a "second wave" of Romanian immigrants in Central Canada after the Second World War, the proportionate distribution of Romanians in Canada would change. In 1991, 28,665 Canadians claimed only Romanian ethnicity, compared with 45,405 who claimed other ethnic identities as well. Of this total 74,060 Canadians claiming Romanian ethnicity in whole or in part, 8,474 were residents of Saskatchewan. Moreover, of 33,790 Canadian residents born in Romania, an estimated third claimed Hungarian, German, Ukrainian, Gypsy, or Jewish ethnic affiliation. In 2006, 11,615 Saskatchewan residents claimed Romanian ethnicity, 18.4% (2,140) solely and 81.6% (9,475) in combination with other ethnicities. There has been a recent influx of new immigrants from Romania into Saskatchewan; although they have settled in the cities, they do serve the purpose of revitalizing Romanian culture in Saskatchewan.

CZECH AND SLOVAK SETTLEMENTS

The beginning of Czech and Slovak settlement in Saskatchewan was in 1884, when four Czech families (the Pangracs, Juneks, Dolezals, and Skokans) from Bohemia settled in the Kolin district near Esterhazy. Count Paul Esterhazy brought Slovaks to his primarily Hungarian colony of Huns' Valley, near Minnedosa, Manitoba, in 1885, then to the new Esterhazy Colony in Saskatchewan the next year. In fact, the ten-acre site of the first Kaposvar church was donated by the Smerekovsky homestead, and many graves of Slovaks and Czechs are found in the cemetery. Kolin Post Office was created soon after postmaster Joseph Knourek was appointed postmaster of Esterhaz Post Office and relocated it to his farmhouse in the western part of the colony, where Czechs and Slovaks had concentrated; in 1902, this post office, together with the Protestant school district, was renamed Kolin after a Czech city. Some of these Bohemian Czechs had actually originated in Galicia, where they formed settlements around Volkov and Nova Silki north of L'viv. Bohemian Czechs from the Volhynia region in Ukraine settled around Gerald, just northeast of the town of Esterhazy, in 1898. Near Gerald, the St. Wenceslaus Roman Catholic cemetery dated from 1913 and the church from 1919. North of Yarbo, the Tabor cemetery dated from 1903; settlers in the Tabor/Dovedale district included families from the Tabor area in Bohemia. Today Gerald has 124 residents, Yarbo seventy-two; both have been losing population. So the entire region around Esterhazy had small concentrations of Czechs and Slovaks, outnumbered by Hungarians.

In 1901, George (Juraj) Zeman, an American Slovak, was appointed as a CPR colonization agent. Anxious to help get his people out of dangerous, unhealthy work in mines, mills, and refineries (especially in Pennsylvania) and back into farming, he introduced Czech and Slovak settlers to the central region in Saskatchewan around Davidson, Kenaston and the Zid district to the northeast (homesteaded by a single Bohemian immigrant), Hanley, Glenside, Broderick, Hawarden, Strongfield, and Milden. Other Czech families settled farther west around Marriott in 1902 (the Czechoslovakian Pioneers Memorial Hall, decorated with murals of Czechoslovakian scenes, still functions as a community centre). And in 1905 several Slovak families (Mlazgar, Tomecko, Beros, Mantyak, Pletz) moved from Minnesota to settle in the Lipton area. Much later, large numbers of ethnic Germans from Sudetenland would settle around St. Walburg, Brightsand Lake, and Loon Lake. Elsewhere in Saskatchewan, the Chechow School District west of Preeceville, established in 1908 and closed in 1961, was settled by immigrants from the village of Chekhiv (Czechow in Polish) in Ukraine, one of several Czech settlements in Ukraine (the village name meant "of Czech background"). A Czech family, the Nerada family, were early settlers of the Nerada Creek district north of Climax in southwestern Saskatchewan; they arrived in 1886 and filed homesteads in 1915. Nearby, Tabor School District was established by the Kluzak family in 1914 and named after their Czech community in Minnesota from which they had come to Saskatchewan (Climax was also named after a community in the same region in Minnesota).

Most of the early Czech and Slovak settlers were Roman Catholic, and some Slovaks were Eastern Rite Catholics. They tended not to form separate parishes in Saskatchewan but to join their Ukrainian, Hungarian, Polish, and Croatian neighbours. Doubtless this facilitated intermarriage. But some Czechs and Slovaks were Lutheran, Reformed, or other Protestant. The Hus Church several kilometres southwest of Glenside was named after the progenitor of the Hussite or Moravian Brethren movements. Czechs settled there in 1905; in 1913, they built the Bohemian Presbyterian Church, renamed the Jan Hus Presbyterian Church in 1929; it joined the United Church in 1934, and when it finally closed in 1975 the congregation joined the United Church in Glenside. The present United Church in Dundurn (designated a heritage site in 1990) was originally a Moravian Brethren church in 1910.

Despite their relative isolation, Czechs and Slovaks in rural Saskatchewan became integrated into ethnic networks uniting them with their co-ethnics across North

America. The earliest Czech organizations in Canada were local community associations at Kolin and Esterhazy in 1912. They were responsible for a Czech cultural revival in these enclaves during the 1930s. Kolin also had a service club called the Good Companions led by the Czech minister of the United Church in Esterhazy, with the aim of promoting Czech culture and language in the next generation. A national Czech Benevolent Association was founded in Winnipeg in 1913, connected with the Bohemian National Alliance in the United States. Similarly, Slovaks founded local benevolent associations that became federated with the Canadian Slovak Benevolent Society in 1946. Czechs and Slovaks were united in Sokal, a sports and recreational society with many local chapters in Canada and the United States; one early chapter was established at Goldburg, Saskatchewan. The Canadian Slovak League was formed in 1932. The National Alliance of Slovaks, Czechs, and Subcarpathian Ruthenians,[39] established in 1939, later became the Czechoslovak National Alliance of Canada, then in 1960 the Czechoslovak National Association of Canada.

There have been wide variations in counting Czechs and Slovaks in Canadian census data. Although the earliest concentrations were found in the Prairie Provinces and British Columbia, later they were far outnumbered by co-ethnics in Central Canada. The most recent census (2006) data counted 5,645 residents of Saskatchewan who claimed Czech ethnicity, of whom 14.4% (815) claimed to be only of Czech origin compared with 85.6% (4,830) who also claimed other ethnic origins. In 1991, only 615 people in Saskatchewan specifically claimed Slovak ethnicity, whereas in 2006 there were 1,180, perhaps because of the separation of Slovakia from the Czech Republic. Of these 1,180, 20.3% (240) claimed to be only Slovak, and 79.7% (940) also claimed other ethnic identities. In addition, there were 2,245 people in Saskatchewan who claimed Czechoslovakian identity.

CROATIAN AND YUGOSLAVIAN SETTLEMENTS

People of Croatian ethnic origin began to settle in the Kenaston area in 1904, concentrating in homesteads east of Hanley and Kenaston and in the Smales district between Kenaston and Bladworth. At the time, Kenaston was called Bonnington Springs Post Office; Kenaston Post Office and School District came into being two years later, and Kenaston became an incorporated village in 1910. These Croatian settlers had come from Lovinac and surrounding villages in a valley across the coastal mountain range east of the port city of Zadar, in Croatia (then in Austria-Hungary). The first to arrive were the Pavelic(h)(k), Prpic(k), Masic(h), and Tomljenovic/Tomlenovich/Thompson families. In the next ten years, they were joined by other families, including Sekulic(h), Brkic(h), Vrkljan, Matevic(h), P(e)rsic(h), Sarich, Zdunich, K(e)rpan/Krypan, Rupcich, Stromatich, Yelich, and Obrigavi(t)ch. Already by 1914 Croatians occupied forty-one homesteads in the settlement—not in a single compact bloc but scattered throughout the general area. By the late 1920s, Croatian farmers had accumulated some 50,000 acres of land—a remarkable contrast from their recent background in the mountains of Croatia, where family farms seldom exceeded forty acres (some were as small as only one or two acres). The migrants had been forced to sell their shares of family farms to pay for their passage to North America. The first to leave had been younger men escaping from overcrowding on these small farms. In the mountain villages, young

THE SETTLEMENTS OF OTHER EASTERN EUROPEAN GROUPS

men were accustomed to having to find physical work. In North America, they took whatever manual labour they could find—the first settlers around Kenaston had worked in railway section gangs in Oklahoma, Kansas, Arkansas, and other Midwestern states, and as coalminers in the Crowsnest Pass in Canada, before hearing of homesteads on the prairies. So they initially arrived in Saskatchewan as single young men before being joined by wives and other family members; some temporarily returned to Croatia to find wives.

Typically, men in the mountain villages of Croatia were limited to only four years of formal education, women more. But they were used to hard work and had come to Saskatchewan to develop farms that their predecessors back in Croatia could hardly imagine. When they first settled, they made their own hand-sewn clothing. Mixed subsistence farming soon became large-scale grain farming. Farm buildings were concentrated, in keeping with the *zadruga* communal tradition, at the centre of four converging blocs of land in order to enhance mutual cooperation. *Susjed*—helpful neighbours—were highly valued. The cooperative tradition was reflected in strong support for the United Grain Growers, Saskatchewan Wheat Pool, and Cooperative Association. Country schoolhouses quickly familiarized Croatian children with the English language; in turn, children assisted parents and even grandparents to learn some English.

Assimilation became apparent as within one generation English given names—and even an occasional surname—were adopted. Strong rural communal life was evident in the religious calendar (Kenaston had an active Roman Catholic parish that the Croatians shared with other Slavs), especially at Christmas and Easter, school concerts, threshing, sausage making, agricultural fairs, church bazaars and harvest suppers, homemakers meetings, sports events, and the weddings, baptisms, and funerals marking the passage of life. The Masich farm, midway between Kenaston and Bladworth, dates back to 1911 and became a heritage site in 1992, and Meuse School northeast of Kenaston dates back to 1917 and was designated a heritage site the previous year. Today Kenaston has a declining population of 259. In 1971, there could not have been more than about 300 people of Croatian descent in this small settlement—not more than 100 in Kenaston and another 200 in the surrounding rural municipalities of McCraney, Rudy, and Rosedale. All three remaining grain elevators are now privately owned; the Rupcich elevator boldly advertises Farmers for Justice.

Although the Kenaston area remained the best-defined Croatian settlement in Saskatchewan, smaller numbers of Croatians did settle in other areas, such as near Leask and together with their Serbian and Slovenian neighbours also from Yugoslavia in several locations. The Ortopan district, east of Hearne in south-central Saskatchewan, was named after homesteader Josef Ortopan from Slovenia in 1905 (but soon renamed Long View). Holy Trinity Serbian Orthodox Church, founded in Regina in 1916, was the first Serbian Orthodox parish in Canada. In 1975, a congregation of Croatians and Slovenians was established in Saskatoon, with a pontifical mass to celebrate the event by visiting Bishop Mijo Skvorc of Zagreb, assisted by Reverend Vladimir Stanicovic, National Director of Croatian Migration. The congregation would meet monthly at different churches, first including Our Lady of Czestochowa (a Polish Catholic parish). Reverend Stanicovic commented at the time:

In 1969 the Holy See published regulations prescribing government support of national priests in national rites of all emigrants. It is imperative for these newcomers to be able to experience the sacraments in their own language and customs if they are not to lose their faith. ... Greater stress has been put on maintaining religious practices of immigrants since the introduction of Canada's multiculturalism policy [in 1971]. ... In keeping their religious tradition the Croatians and Slovenians become part of the Canadian multicultural mosaic. ... Only in preserving them as good Christians can they become good Croatian-Canadians.[40]

In 2006, the Croatian population in Saskatchewan was estimated at 1,670, a quarter of whom (425) were solely of Croatian origin, while three-quarters (1,245) were of mixed origins. All together, Yugoslavian ethnic groups counted 5,105, including these 1,670 Croatians plus 1,290 people claiming general Yugoslavian identity, 1,080 Serbian, 480 Slovenian, 455 Bosnian, ninety Kosovar, twenty-five Macedonian, and fifteen Montenegrin.

JEWISH SETTLEMENTS

For centuries, Eastern European Jews had been forced into ghettos and had not been allowed the privilege of farming, yet they were among the first ethno-religious groups to establish agricultural settlements on the Canadian prairies. Jewish immigrants, like many other immigrants who, to some extent, might have lacked farming experience, were lured by Canadian propaganda that advertised ample and almost free land. The Canadian Department of the Interior was anxious at the time—the late nineteenth century—to populate the prairies as soon as possible, so it admitted large numbers of potential settlers, not only from the preferred countries but from Eastern Europe as well. Despite a history of considerable anti-Semitism in Canada, Jews were also welcomed, at least initially. However, unlike other ethnic or ethno-religious groups who were encouraged to develop bloc settlements, the government soon ruled that Jews could not do so. Preferably, they were to be dispersed among their Gentile neighbours. Nonetheless, well-defined Jewish agrarian settlements did develop primarily in Saskatchewan and to a lesser extent in Manitoba and Alberta.[41]

Following a public outcry against the 1881 pogroms in Russia, Sir Alexander T. Galt, Canadian High Commissioner in London, convinced Sir John A. Macdonald that assisting a relatively small number of poor Jews to emigrate from Russia to Canada would be advantageous to both the refugees and Canada. Sponsored by the Mansion House Committee (Mansion House was the seat of the Lord Mayor of London), and organized by Jewish societies in London with the aim of assisting Russian Jewish refugees to emigrate, the future settlers arrived in Montreal in May 1882; however, they were not allocated land until two years later, by which time fewer than half of the original 247 were still available for settlement. So just twenty-six families finally formed the Jew Colony near Moosomin in 1884, and after crop failures they established the settlement of New Jerusalem in 1887, only to be forced to abandon their lands after a disastrous field fire in 1889. The colony included the Jew Lake district.

THE SETTLEMENTS OF OTHER EASTERN EUROPEAN GROUPS

From 1886 to 1907, the Wapella settlement in the same region was established by John Heppner, from Russia, sponsored by Herman Landau, an Anglo-Jewish financier; settlers were led by Abraham Klenman and his son-in-law Solomon Barish, from Bessarabia (southern Moldavia), after whom the Barish Lake district was named. Some fifty Orthodox Russian Jewish families became the first settlers. By the mid-1970s, only a single family descended from these original settlers remained, yet among the illustrious descendants have been the Bronfmans, who eventually moved to Montreal to develop Seagram's Distillery (the Bronfman residence in Regina, previously the Kerr residence, dates back to 1911 and was declared a heritage property in 1990).

In 1892, the Hirsch Colony (about twenty-five kilometres east of Estevan), named after Baron de Hirsch (1831–96), a Bavarian philanthropist who was instrumental in founding the Jewish Colonization Association and bringing Jewish settlers to agricultural colonies on the prairies, was organized by the Young Men's Hebrew Benevolent Society of Montreal, which intended to rescue more Jewish refugees from the Russian pogroms. A $500 loan per family was to be available for up to sixty families; in the end, forty-seven families were selected and sent to the Hirsch Colony. The Jewish Colonization Association (JCA) assumed supervision of this settlement six years later. The colony extended eastward into the Deborah district. The earlier-established Jewish settlers such as the Waxmans assisted young men, even teenagers such as Mayer Hoffer, to file for homesteads and begin farming.[42] Today the deserted buildings are all boarded up in weed-infested vacant lots.

The Lipton Colony (north of the Qu'Appelle Valley, approximately twenty kilometres by road northeast of Lipton), which included the Tiferes Israel (1905–35), Herzel ("old" Herzel 1906–47 and "new" Herzel 1954–59), and Jeshurun (1907–52) School Districts, was initially settled by Romanian Jews in 1901 (one family, for example, bore the surname Lupescu) and later by Russian Jews. The men were dressed in round Russian wool hats and long jackets, the women in headscarves, jackets and blouses, and ankle-length heavy dark skirts. They lived in plastered log cabins with roofs of hay on top of cross-laid saplings.[43] This colony represented the only attempt to delegate to Canadian government officials the organization and administration of a Jewish agrarian settlement, though the JCA was to assist the government. By 1904, there were already close to 400 Jewish settlers in the colony. However, the last Jewish residents had left by 1935, many of them to become members of Beth Jacob Synagogue in Regina; all that remains is the Herzel Hebrew cemetery. Many buried there had been born during the 1840s–50s and had died during the 1920s–40s. Jews quickly became replaced by Ukrainians: the original twenty Ukrainian families who settled in the Herzel district in 1937 soon grew to fifty families. They established the Assumption of the Blessed Virgin Mary Ukrainian Catholic Parish, demolished in 1969.

In 1906, three young graduates of the Baron de Hirsch Agricultural College at Slobodka Lesna, Galicia (Philip Berger of Kolomiya, Israel Hoffer of Kossov, and Majer Feldman of Zaleszczyki), were instrumental in the organization of the Sonnenfeld Colony, originally New Herman (in the Oungre area, approximately eighty kilometres west of Estevan). Today Oungre has only fifteen residents. During the 1920s, the Farm Labourers hamlet was established by the JCA by subdividing a quarter-section of farmland into six agricultural training farms near Oungre. The colony was served by the

Hoffer Post Office, named after the Israel and Mayer Hoffer brothers, who became very successful farmers, farming some eighteen quarters by 1924 while serving as postmasters, justices of the peace, school trustees, and RM councillors. The colony also included the Schneller School District, founded in 1908 and closed in 1950.

All of these colonies were in southeastern Saskatchewan. The one exception was the Edenbridge Colony (near Gronlid, northeast of Melfort), which started to develop the same year (1906) with the arrival of twelve Lithuanian Jewish families from South Africa and later from London and New York. The original settlers averaged only $300 per family. Most lacked farming experience, with the notable exception of Hershela Wolfovitch (Wolfowitz), who had been sent to find a suitable settlement site. Although the nearest railway station was twenty kilometres distant, this site was well wooded and along the Carrot River. When the settlers first arrived, they were housed in a cabin later known as the Edenbridge Hotel, constructed of poplar logs covered with sod and clay, on the Wolfovitch homestead; a loft reached by ladder served as the men's sleeping quarters, with the women and children sleeping on the main floor. During the summer months, most of the men selected homesteads and began learning the necessary skills of prairie farming, while often finding temporary work on road gangs.[44] The settlement was quite spread out—three stores were located over thirteen kilometres. But the community nucleus was the small Beth Israel (House of Israel) synagogue and cemetery, dating from 1907–09, which remain well-preserved Jewish historic sites, though the synagogue stopped functioning as a place of worship and was turned into a museum in 1964. There was also a community hall and two schools (one teaching in Yiddish, the other in Hebrew). A postal district was created in 1908 and finally closed in 1945; originally conceived as Jew Town or Israel Villa, but rejected as "too ethnic," the name Edenbridge reportedly was an acceptable anglicized version of Yedn (Yidden)-bridge (Jews' bridge).[45] Latvian-born brothers Samuel and David Vickar were storekeepers in Gronlid, Ratner, and Brooksby; Samuel also served as a school trustee and an RM reeve. Norm Vickar became a provincial MLA as well as the mayor of Melfort. Doubtless the most famous descendant of the colony was Senator Sid Buckwold, the long-time mayor of Saskatoon, whose parents had settled there. Where the settlement once contained as many as 175 Jewish settlers, farming 12,000 acres, only a single Jewish farmer was left by the 1980s.

Apart from these settlements, Jews were also scattered on an individual or family basis or in small numbers both as farmers and as local businesspeople throughout rural Saskatchewan. Often they were fairly close to the settlements, though, such as at Melfort, Oxbow, and Alsask. By 1914, the Montefiore Jewish Colony extended from Sibbald, Alberta, the neighbouring community west of Alsask, across the provincial boundary into Saskatchewan, to the Eyre district to the southeast. Although the Zangwill district north of Young (southeast of Saskatoon) was named after Israel Zangwill (1864–1926), the prominent Jewish writer in England, the district did not represent a Jewish settlement.

The decline of the Jewish farm settlements—sometimes rapid (e.g., when a fire destroyed the crops in the New Jerusalem Colony after just five years of settlement), sometimes gradual—was caused by diverse circumstances: lack of previous farming experience, prolonged drought, economic depression, two world wars, the mechanization of farming equipment, the increasing size of farms, the expense of farming, the failure of children to take over family farms after receiving higher education, omnipresent rural depopulation, combined with a desire to live in larger centres with more business opportunities and where a Jewish lifestyle could better be maintained. However, some descendants of the original settlers either continue to farm or own original homesteads and rent the land to neighbouring farmers. But very few descendants of the original settlers remain in these historic Jewish settlements. Most have long ago moved into the cities, so some commentary on this urban legacy seems appropriate here.

The Jewish community of Saskatoon dates at least from 1907, when reportedly the first Jewish family, the Landas, moved into their modest dugout along the riverbank. When other Jewish people soon followed, Jewish religious services began, and in three years the growing community obtained a *shokhet* (religious slaughterer) and a Hebrew teacher. In 1911, the classes moved into a permanent Talmud Torah. Land was bought for a Jewish cemetery. A small synagogue was built in 1919.

Saskatoon's early Jewish residents were very diverse with respect both to financial means and to specific origins. They included former Saskatchewan homesteaders, the descendants of families who had emigrated from Europe to the United States, and immigrants from Eastern European countries direct to Saskatoon and Regina. Some spoke Yiddish and never learned to speak English fluently, while others spoke just English (back in 1931, nearly 150,000 Canadian Jews spoke Yiddish as their first language, compared with little more than 15,000—mostly Hasidic Jews in Montreal and older Orthodox Jews in Montreal, Toronto, and Winnipeg). Saskatoon Jews did not always think of themselves as religious Jews; they ranged from non-religious communists to the ultra-orthodox. The modern synagogue established in 1958, Congregation Agudas Israel, was Conservative, a compromise between Orthodox and Reform Judaism. Although members of the Jewish community integrated into the larger society in various ways, their diversity occasionally resulted in tensions within the Jewish community. A second Conservative congregation, Congregation Shir Chadash, was formed when a dissident rabbi, hired in 1998, was dismissed two years later on the ground that he lacked a proper ordination and on the charge of harassment. He and fifty dissident congregants organized this new congregation, which meets in a local community centre just down the street from the older synagogue.

Where Jewish life was once centred on the home and synagogue, it quickly became more outward looking, not the least because of the small size of the Jewish community, in spite of incidences of a restrictive and prejudicial attitude toward Jews in the general society. In 1915, the local B'nai B'rith was already producing musicals; Jewish hockey and softball teams came into being; the Talmud Torah's Ladies Aid held its first bazaar in 1922; the Saskatoon Section of the National Council of Jewish Women presented a play in 1956; the annual Silver Spoon Dinner honouring voluntary service is still sponsored by Saskatoon Hadassah-Wizo. ... Prominent members of the Jewish community in Saskatoon have included doctors, educators, and businesspeople, apart from a mayor and senator. Yet the synagogues remain the focus of most Jewish activities in the city: Congregation Agudas Israel is home to a Hebrew school, a library, adult education programs, the Sisterhood of the Women's League for Conservative Judaism, a B'nai

B'rith youth organization, and the Saskatchewan Jewish Foundation (financial assistance for education); Congregation Shir Chadash holds adult and children's Hebrew literacy classes; and there is a Jewish Students Association on the university campus nearby. Very recently, in 2011, a Lubavitch Hasidic couple, Rabbi Raphael and Sarah Kats, arrived from Brooklyn, New York, to open a *chabad*, a sort of Jewish community outreach centre, in their home, to be called the Saskatchewan Jewish Discovery Centre. A *chabad* is intended to combine Kabbalah spiritualism with the intellectual pursuit of Jewish faith. This particular centre will ambitiously offer education (on Kabbalah, Jewish history, Hebrew reading and writing) and social services (including marriage counselling, hospital and home care visits, kosher cooking, and even vacation travel) to Saskatoon's small Jewish community.

The religious Jewish community of Saskatoon has been estimated in recent years at only about 200, and 2006 census data revealed that 2,125 people in all of Saskatchewan counted themselves as Jewish in ethnic terms; 85.2% (1,810) of them also claimed other ethnic origins, while just 14.8% (315) did not. It seems likely, however, that a larger number of people might view themselves as being wholly or partially of Jewish descent, but today they would be almost completely in the cities (especially Saskatoon) rather than the original rural settlements. Back in 1971, though, people claiming Jewish ethnicity numbered 865 in Regina and 585 in Saskatoon. Other cities with smaller numbers of Jews (counted by ethnic origin, not religious affiliation) were Moose Jaw (95), Prince Albert (55), Yorkton (55), Weyburn (40), and Estevan (35), while a wide variety of communities had between ten and twenty-five: Tisdale, Melfort, Swift Current, Wynyard, Kinistino, Lumsden, Canora, Esterhazy. Virtually none are left in the original colonies.

CONCLUDING THOUGHTS

Clearly, ethnic groups of other Eastern European origins have added immensely to the ethnic diversity of Saskatchewan. Russian Doukhobors, Hungarians, Romanians, Czechs and Slovaks, Croatians and Yugoslavs, and Jews all established their own bloc settlements, thereby adding to the cultural mosaic that was fast becoming characteristic of the Western Canadian prairies. Yet over time these settlements have had varying degrees of longevity. Dozens of Doukhobor communal villages were soon obliterated by the harsh policies of the federal and provincial governments, though in most of the areas originally settled by Doukhobors enough have remained to retain these settlements, and some have maintained a strong Doukhobor identity. Although several Jewish colonies were established, they were small and suffered from continuous rural depopulation until few original settlers were left. However, their descendants have formed the basis of an active Jewish community in Saskatoon. Other groups—Hungarians, Romanians, Czechs and Slovaks, and Croatians and Yugoslavs—while scattered have maintained their original concentrations in various rural areas and their distinct identities within the Saskatchewan population, albeit not to the extent of larger Eastern European groups. In addition to these particular ethnic groups, other Eastern Europeans have come to Saskatchewan but have not been numerous enough to form their own settlements. They have included not only 3,435 other Yugoslavs (who have been mentioned) but also other Balkan groups totalling at least 440 people—Bulgarians

THE SETTLEMENTS OF OTHER EASTERN EUROPEAN GROUPS

(240), Gypsies (120), and Albanians (80)—as well as Baltic groups totalling 1,260 people—Lithuanians (740), Latvians (380), and Estonians (140). Greek settlement will be described in Chapter 9.

SOURCES

Russian Doukhobors
Selected general sources on Doukhobors in Canada (including in Saskatchewan) are A. Maude, *The Doukhobors: A Peculiar People* (New York: Funk and Wagnalls, 1904); S. Holt, *Terror in the Name of God* (Toronto: McClelland and Stewart, 1964); G. Woodcock and I. Avakumovic, *The Doukhobors* (Toronto: McClelland and Stewart, 1968); K.J. Tarasoff, *Pictorial History of the Doukhobors* (Saskatoon: Modern Press, 1969); F.M. Mealing, *Doukhobor Life: A Survey of Doukhobor Religion, History, and Folklife* (Castlegar, BC: Kootenay Doukhobor Historical Society/Cotinneh Books, 1975); M. Malloff and P. Ogloff, *Toil and Peaceful Life: Portraits of Doukhobors*, Sound Heritage 6, 4 (Victoria: Provincial Archives of British Columbia, 1977); K.J. Tarasoff, *Plakun Trava: The Doukhobors* (Grand Forks, BC: Mir Publishing Society, 1982); K.J. Tarasoff, "The Western Settlement of Canadian Doukhobors," in *Visions of the New Jerusalem: Religious Settlement on the Prairies*, ed. B.G. Smillie (Edmonton: NeWest Press, 1983), 121–36; K.J. Tarasoff, *Spells, Splits, and Survival in a Russian-Canadian Community* (New York: AMS Press, 1990); J.W. Friesen and M.M. Veregin, *The Community Doukhobors: A People in Transition* (Ottawa: Borealis Press, 1996); and K.J. Tarasoff, "Doukhobors," in *Encyclopedia of Canada's Peoples*, ed. P.R. Magocsi (Toronto: University of Toronto Press, 1999), 422–35.

Details on Doukhobor history, settlements, and life in Saskatchewan can be found in A.B. Anderson, "Ethnocultural Identity and Traditions in a Doukhobor Settlement in Saskatchewan," paper presented at the Meeting of the Central and East European Studies Association of Canada, University of British Columbia, June 1983; S.G. Stupnikoff, *Historical Saga of the Carlton Region, 1797–1920* (Saskatoon: Modern Press, 1985); C.J. Tracie, *"Toil and Peaceful Life": Doukhobor Village Settlement in Saskatchewan, 1899–1918* (Regina: Canadian Plains Research Center, 1996); K.J. Tarasoff, "Doukhobor Settlement," in *Encyclopedia of Saskatchewan* (Regina: Canadian Plains Research Center, 2005), 254–56; and C.J. Tracie, "Religion and Tradition in the Cultural Landscapes of the Doukhobors in Saskatchewan," in *Saskatchewan: Geographic Perspectives*, ed. B.D. Thraves, M.L. Lewry, J.E. Dale, and H. Schlichtmann (Regina: University of Regina and Canadian Plains Research Center, 2007), 288–92.

Hungarians
Selected general sources on Hungarians in Canada (including in Saskatchewan) are J. Kosa, *Land of Choice: The Hungarians in Canada* (Toronto: University of Toronto Press, 1957); N.F. Dreisziger et al., *Struggle and Hope: The Hungarian-Canadian Experience* (Toronto: McClelland and Stewart, 1982); J.P. Miska, ed., *Canadian Studies on*

Hungarians, 1886–1986 (Regina: Canadian Plains Research Center, 1987); G. Bisztray, *Hungarian-Canadian Literature* (Toronto: University of Toronto Press, 1987); and N.F. Dreisziger, "Hungarians," in *Encyclopedia of Canada's Peoples*, ed. P.R. Magocsi (Toronto: University of Toronto Press, 1999).

Sources specifically on Hungarians in Saskatchewan include G.V. Dojcsak, "The Mysterious Count Esterhazy," *Saskatchewan History* 26, 2 (1973): 63–72, and in *Kaposvar: A Count's Colony: 1886–1986*, ed. J. Pask (Yorkton: Dowie Quick Print, 1986), 30–35; M.L. Kovacs, *Esterhazy and Early Hungarian Immigration to Canada* (Regina: Canadian Plains Research Center, 1974); R. Blumstock, ed., *Bekevar: Working Papers on a Canadian Prairie Community* (Ottawa: National Museum, 1979); St. Laszlo Historical Committee, *With Faith and Hope: St. Laszlo—Our Heritage* (North Battleford: Turner-Warwick Printers, 1979); M.L. Kovacs, *Peace and Strife* (Kipling, SK: Kipling District Historical Society, 1980); A.B. Anderson, "Hungarian Settlements," and M. Vajcner, "Paul Esterhazy, 1831–1912," in *Encyclopedia of Saskatchewan* (Regina: Canadian Plains Research Center, 2005); and J.F. Kovacs, "Con Artist or Noble Immigration Agent? Count Esterhazy's Hungarian Colonization Effort, 1885–1902," *Prairie Forum* 31, 1 (2006), republished in *Immigration and Settlement, 1870–1939*, ed. G.P. Marchildon (Regina: Canadian Plains Research Center, 2009).

Romanians
Details on Romanian settlements in Saskatchewan are found in G. Johnson, "The Romanians in Western Canada," *Saskatchewan History* 14, 2 (1961): 64–70; *Calendrul Solia*, Romanian Orthodox Episcopate of America, 1971; G.J. Patterson, "Ethnicity and Religious Affiliation in Romanian Communities in Saskatchewan," Central and East European Studies Association of Canada, 1978, later included in *The Romanians of Saskatchewan: Four Generations of Adaptation* (Ottawa: National Museum of Man, 1977); A.B. Anderson, "German Migration from Romania to the Prairies," paper presented at the Meeting of the Central and East European Studies Association of Canada, Université du Québec à Montréal, June 1980; B. Sapergia, *Foreigners* (Moose Jaw: Thunder Creek Publishing Cooperative, 1984); G.J. Patterson, "Romanians," in *Encyclopedia of Canada's Peoples*, ed. P.R. Magocsi (Toronto: University of Toronto Press, 1999), 1092–1100; and A.B. Anderson, "Romanian Settlements," in *Encyclopedia of Saskatchewan* (Regina: Canadian Plains Research Center, 2005), 775–76.

Czechs and Slovaks
For information on Czechs and Slovaks in Canada in general and more specifically in Saskatchewan, see J. Gellner and J. Smerek, *The Czechs and Slovaks in Canada* (Toronto: University of Toronto Press, 1968); M.M. Stolarik, *Immigrants and Urbanization: The Slovak Experience, 1870–1918* (New York: AMS Press, 1989); M.J. Jovanovic, "Czechs," and E. Jakesova and M.M. Stolarik, "Slovaks," in *Encyclopedia of Canada's Peoples*, ed. P.R. Magocsi (Toronto: University of Toronto Press, 1999), 397–405, 1168–79; and A.B. Anderson, "Czech and Slovak Settlements," in *Encyclopedia of Saskatchewan* (Regina: Canadian Plains Research Center, 2005), 232.

THE SETTLEMENTS OF OTHER EASTERN EUROPEAN GROUPS

Croatians and Yugoslavs
Details on the Kenaston settlement have been drawn from A.W. Rasporich, *For a Better Life: A History of the Croatians in Canada* (Toronto: McClelland and Stewart, 1982).

Other sources include L.A. Kosinski, *Yugoslavs in Canada*, Occasional Paper No. 2, Division of East European Studies, University of Alberta, 1980; A.W. Rasporich, "Croats," in *Encyclopedia of Canada's Peoples*, ed. P.R. Magocsi (Toronto: University of Toronto Press, 1999), 382–89; and A.B. Anderson, "Croatian and Serbian Settlements," in *Encyclopedia of Saskatchewan* (Regina: Canadian Plains Research Center, 2005), 218.

Jews
Informative general sources on Jewish Canadians include W. Kurelek and A. Arnold, *Jewish Life in Canada* (Edmonton: Hurtig, 1976); M. Weinfeld, W. Shaffir, and I. Cotler, eds., *The Canadian Jewish Mosaic* (Rexdale, ON: John Wiley and Sons Canada, 1981); A. Davies, ed., *Antisemitism in Canada: History and Interpretation* (Waterloo: Wilfrid Laurier University Press, 1992); and M. Weinfeld, "Jews," in *Encyclopedia of Canada's Peoples*, ed. P.R. Magocsi (Toronto: University of Toronto Press, 1999), 860–81.

On Jews in Saskatchewan and Western Canada, see C.E. Leonoff, *Wapella Farm Settlement* (Winnipeg: Historical and Scientific Society of Manitoba and Jewish Historical Society of Western Canada, 1975); C.E. Leonoff, *The Architecture of Jewish Settlements in the Prairies* (Winnipeg: Jewish Historical Society of Western Canada, 1975); A. Horowitz, *Striking Roots: Reflections on Five Decades of Jewish Life* (Oakville, ON: Mosaic Press, 1979); H. Gutkin, *Journey into Our Heritage: The Story of the Jewish People in the Canadian West* (Toronto: Lester and Orpen Dennys, 1980); T.R. Neufeld, "Jewish Colonization in the Northwest Territories" (MA thesis, University of Saskatchewan, 1982); M. Usiskin, *Uncle Mike's Edenbridge: Memoirs of a Jewish Pioneer Family* (Winnipeg: Peguis, 1983); A. Arnold, "New Jerusalem on the Prairies: Welcoming the Jews," in *Visions of the New Jerusalem: Religious Settlement on the Prairies*, ed. B.G. Smillie (Edmonton: NeWest Press, 1983), 91–108; A. Feldman, "The Jewish Community in Saskatoon: A Short History, 1907–1998," *Saskatoon History Review* 15 (2001): 1–17; A. Feldman, "Were Jewish Farmers Failures? The Case of Township 2-15-W2nd," *Saskatchewan History* 55, 1 (2003): 21–30; and A. Feldman, "Jewish Rural Settlements" and "Jewish Community, Saskatoon," in *Encyclopedia of Saskatchewan* (Regina: Canadian Plains Research Center, 2005), 490–92.

Chapter 7
FRENCH SETTLEMENTS

The settlement of French-speaking people in the regions that today comprise the province of Saskatchewan occurred in three distinct stages. First, during the exploratory era of the fur trade, from the mid-eighteenth century through the mid-nineteenth century, numerous trading posts were established on the principal river systems by *voyageurs* of French or part-French extraction. Second, from the mid-nineteenth century until the North-West Resistance in 1885, many small Métis (mixed French-Indian) communities came into existence, some on the old river routes but most widely scattered across the southern prairies. Third, for half a century after the resistance, French-speaking immigrants from Quebec, Europe, and the United States arrived in large numbers to establish bloc settlements on the prairies. Yet the French were not alone in settling by this time. Various other ethnic groups were also establishing their own settlements and soon greatly outnumbered the French. No longer was French the most widely spoken common language in what was to become, after 1905, the province of Saskatchewan. French settlement in Saskatchewan, compared with settlement by most other ethnic groups, covered a relatively long period of time. Although the proportion of French speakers declined, their absolute number greatly increased. By the 1930s, numerous settlements, communities, and parishes had been founded in which French was spoken.

BACKGROUND TO FRANCOPHONE SETTLEMENT: THE EARLY FUR TRADE

Following exploration of the Saskatchewan River by Sieur de la Verendrye in 1737–41, Fort-à-la-Corne (originally called Fort-St-Louis-des-Prairies) was the first European agricultural settlement, in what would later become Saskatchewan, on that river from 1753 to 1757, while Fort-la-Jonquière had already been established downstream in 1751 as the first European post. Fort-des-Prairies or Fort-St-Louis operated intermittently between 1753 and 1773. However, the region had been claimed by England since 1670 as the hinterland to the Hudson's Bay Company's (HBC) territory of Rupert's Land—a claim supported by the explorations of Henry Kelsey in 1690–91.

With the collapse of the French colony of Nouvelle France, the predecessor of Quebec, in 1763, a monopoly of the HBC in the West might have seemed imminent. This was not yet to be the case. From 1763 to 1779, independent traders based in Quebec established two trading posts on Saskatchewan river systems for every one built by the HBC. Fur-trading posts established during the 1760s included Fort Rivière-à-la-Biche (on the Red Deer River, possibly dating back to 1767 as an independent post—by 1800, it had become a North West Company [NWC] post) and François-Finlay Post or Fort-Prairie on the Saskatchewan River (1768–73).

Then, during the 1770s, were added Maison Blondeau (established by Barthélemy Blondeau, an early trader on the Saskatchewan River), Fort-de-la-Traite (an independent trading post taken over by the NWC in 1772 on the Churchill River near Frog Portage), Isaac's House (established as an independent trading post in 1773), Fort-aux-Trembles and Place-Darreaux (built on the Saskatchewan River in 1773 by traders Bartolomé Blondeau and François Leblanc), Cumberland House (the first inland HBC post in 1774), Fort-Primeau (an NWC post established by Louis Primeau on Lac-Ile-à-la-Crosse on the Churchill River system in 1775), the Eturgeon (Sturgeon River) Forts of the NWC (1776–93), Peter Pond's Post (1776), Fort-du-Milieu on the North Saskatchewan (1778–79), Fort-Montagne-d'Aigle farther upstream (1778), and later Fort-Bataille (Battleford).

Between 1779 and 1787, with the gradual consolidation of independent interests into the North West Company, based in Montreal, the HBC posts remained outnumbered by rivals. During this period, thirteen principal NWC and independent posts were constructed as opposed to only three HBC posts. Posts established during the 1780s included Fort-Providence (constructed at Prince Albert in 1781), Lac-Vert/Green Lake (an NWC post in 1782, then an HBC post in 1799), Maison-Canadienne-Tute in 1782 (on the North Saskatchewan), while along the South Saskatchewan between present-day St-Louis and Batoche Fort-des-Iles (an independent post in 1785) and South Branch Post (an NWC post that year), rivalled by the HBC's South Branch House (1786–94), by which time Pichet Post was operating on the Saskatchewan, and Fort-Brulé (an HBC post on the North Saskatchewan in 1786–93). Fort-Espérance on the Qu'Appelle River just west of the later Manitoba border served as a major provisions post of the NWC, supplying pemmican and other staples, from 1787 to 1810; situated on the river flats down in the valley (Prairie-à-la-Paille), it was abandoned in 1810; a more substantial fort was rebuilt in 1816 on a small knoll overlooking the valley, but it lasted just three years.

Meanwhile, the HBC increased its efforts to counter the Quebec concerns, especially in the north and upper Assiniboine River area. In this period, half of the new posts established were HBC ones. During the 1790s, Fort-de-la-Rivière-Tremblante was established on the Assiniboine in 1791, while on the North Saskatchewan Fort-St-Louis and Fort-la-Montée were constructed in quick succession in 1794–97, Fort Alexandria first served the NWC in 1795–1821, while Peter Fidler, destined to become the chief surveyor for the Hudson's Bay Company, ran Bolsover House near Meadow Lake in 1799.

CHAPTER 7

Fort-Maringouin operated until 1821 at the junction of the North and South Saskatchewan branches, while Carlton House of the HBC, just below the junction, operated from 1795 to 1804. But during the next couple of decades, the Quebec-based traders built twice as many new posts as did the Bay traders. Fort-du-Milieu on the North Saskatchewan was an independent post in 1800. Maison-Balleau was an NWC post on the South Saskatchewan in 1801. Carlton House was now replaced by Fort Carlton, constructed in 1810 upstream near the Great Bend of the North Saskatchewan, adjacent to the NWC post La Montée (abandoned six years later). This fort became a key provisioning post of the HBC at the strategic intersection of the Carlton Trail and the North Saskatchewan River. But competition between the Hudson's Bay Company and the North West Company had become so acute that a merger was forced in 1821, giving the HBC its long-sought monopoly of the fur trade. In 1873, Fort Carlton became the headquarters of the fur trade in Saskatchewan. However, less than ten years later, in 1882, it was closed by the HBC, then a couple of years later was resurrected as a North-West Mounted Police (NWMP) post—it was from there that the police patrol ran into the opening conflict with the Métis just west of Duck Lake in 1885. Subsequently, it was evacuated and accidentally burned, then intentionally destroyed by the Métis militants. It has been partially reconstructed as a National Historic Site. Far upriver, Fort Pitt had commenced operations as an HBC post in 1829 and subsequently was an NWMP post attacked during the North-West Resistance in 1885. Fort Battleford was constructed in 1876 for the NWMP.

At least eighty-six main trading posts had been established in what would become Saskatchewan between 1763 and 1821, though only about a dozen of them—mostly in remote northern areas—were to remain as permanent settlements. The French-speaking traders based in Quebec had constructed the majority of these posts. Approximately one-third of these posts were on the Churchill and other northern rivers, while two-thirds were on the North and South and lower Saskatchewan Rivers, on the upper Assiniboine, and on the Qu'Appelle. In 1810, a Métis trader, Jean-Baptiste Letendre *dit* (called) Batoche, operated a trading post some five kilometres upstream from the Saskatchewan forks near Fort-à-la-Corne; he was the grandfather of François-Xavier Letendre *dit* Batoche, who later established the store at Batoche. Gabriel "Meemay" Côte was an influential Métis trader operating north of present-day Kamsack; he was instrumental in negotiating Treaty 4 with the Cree and Saulteaux in 1874.

Despite the impermanency of most of the posts, that the era of the *voyageur* should be considered a significant chapter in the history of French settlement in Saskatchewan can hardly be doubted. Almost all of the posts established by the Quebec-based traders were given French names. However, apparently French-speaking *voyageurs* also worked for—or traded with—the arch-rival Hudson's Bay Company; so some instances of HBC posts with French names could be noted prior to the merger of 1821. Métis communities grew around the northern posts after the merger as well as around new posts established by *voyageurs* on the prairies. At this point, though, the initial stage of French settlement in Saskatchewan was ending, and a second stage was beginning. The mostly impermanent posts established by the *voyageurs* had, after more than a century, contributed relatively little French population. It was more the development of fairly permanent Métis communities that would lay a firmer base for French settlement.

FRANCOPHONE MÉTIS SETTLEMENTS

The designation "Métis" was originally applied to "halfbreeds" of French and Indian descent. However, eventually the term came to be applied to persons of mixed descent who were not French-speaking Catholics but English-speaking Protestants, mostly of Scottish origin. Both types were found in adjacent settlements along the Red River in Manitoba after 1812, with the French speakers around St-Boniface and the English speakers around Selkirk. The descendants of both groups were to move westward into Saskatchewan to establish new settlements. By 1870, the census of the North-West Territories and Manitoba listed 5,770 French-speaking Métis, 4,080 English-speaking Métis, and only 1,600 "European" settlers. But considerable numbers of French-speaking Métis were at least partly of Scottish origin, as had been their *voyageur* predecessors. It was not uncommon for French-speaking Métis to have Scottish surnames; in fact, a Scottish Presbyterian mission served the Isbister settlement near present-day Prince Albert. Saskatchewan Métis distinguished themselves from their close relatives, both *nehiyawak*, *li sauvages*, and *li premières nassions* (First Nations) and *opitotowiw*, *moniyaw*, and *li blancs* (Europeans, White people). The Métis continue to call themselves *la noovel naasyoon* (the new nation); they were known as *aysinowak ka tipimisocik* in their Northern Cree-Michif dialect or *monde qui sounntaien leur propres chefs* in their French-Michif dialect (the people who owned themselves).

The first francophone Métis settlements in Saskatchewan grew around the more permanent trading posts in the north, notably Ile-à-la-Crosse (pop. 1,341 today), La Loche (pop. 2,348), Buffalo Narrows/Lac-de-Boeufs (pop. 1,081), Green Lake/Lac-Vert (pop. 361), Beauval (pop. 806), and Meadow Lake/Lac-des-Prairies (pop. 4,771). Soon numerous communities and physical features across the north country bore French names. After an exploratory visit by Brother Thibeault in 1844, the mission of Chateau-St-Jean was founded at Ile-à-la-Crosse in 1846 by two Oblate priests, Père Alexandre Taché and Brother Laflèche (renamed St-Jean-Baptiste by Père Rossignol in 1911). With the arrival in the community of the three Soeurs-de-la-Charité (the "Grey Nuns" based in Quebec), including Soeur Marguerite Marie (Louis Riel's sister), in 1860, after an arduous sixty-seven-day canoe trip from St-Boniface, a school, St-Bruno Convent, and a medical clinic (later renamed St-Jean-Baptiste) were established under the supervision of Bishop Grandin. The school was named for Père Marius Rossignol. Beauval was originally known as La Plonge because of its proximity to Lac-la-Plonge. The small settlement of Sakamayak was just southwest of Beauval. St-Louis Parish and School at Patuanak honour Père Louis Moraud, a pioneer priest serving the Churchill River communities from 1916. St-Leo the Great Roman Catholic Church (1944) at Buffalo Narrows housed the North-West Historical Museum (burned down in 1993). At Green Lake, the Métis Commemorative Hall museum, now a designated heritage site, was originally constructed during the early 1900s. Southeast of Green Lake/Lac-Vert were Lac-Voisin and Lac-Delaronde. Lac-Lavallée on the northern edge of Prince Albert National Park had been the trapping territory of a Métis from the Cypress Hills, Louis Lavallée, who had settled there in 1884. Another area named after a Métis trapper was Lac-Theriau, south of Stony Rapids in the far north. Lac-Breynat, farther north, was named later after Gabriel Joseph Elie Breynat, OMI, born in St-Vallier, France, who became the Roman Catholic vicar-apostolic of the District of Mackenzie in the

North-West Territories in 1901 (to 1943). Pemmican Portage was originally part of the Cumberland House Reserve but became a Métis settlement in 1930. Souchez was in the Porcupine Hills south of Hudson Bay. While French was frequently used during the earlier years of northern settlement, it gradually became replaced by English during the next century, though most northern Métis were long familiar with their own Northern Cree-Michif dialect.

From the 1850s through the 1880s, small bands of French-speaking Métis buffalo hunters followed a network of traditional wagon trails between trading posts and settled all across the southern prairies. Fort-Espérance, near the confluence of the Assiniboine and Qu'Appelle Rivers, served as a vital supply centre. Near Roche-Percée, the Long Creek or Wood End Post was later established, aimed at intercepting Métis and Aboriginals attempting to flee from prosecution for their involvement in the North-West Resistance until 1897. Farther west, Métis traders followed the Val-Souris (Souris River Valley). At Marieval in the lower Val-Qu'Appelle (Qu'Appelle Valley), Sacré-Coeur-de-Marie Parish (originally Notre-Dame-des-Missions, Our Lady of Missions, or Immaculate Heart of Mary) and a residential school were established in 1897 and at Peltier Crossing, farther upstream at the south end of Katepwa Lake, where Clement Peltier arrived from Minnesota in 1876 to operate a ferry and build a settlement. Fort-Qu'Appelle, established in 1864 by Pierre Hourie, a Métis from the Rivière Rouge settlement, became a focal point for distant outlying Métis settlements. The Touchwood Hills Post, north of the Qu'Appelle Valley, was an important trail junction dating from 1849 (it was abandoned in 1909 and is now a historic park).

The *hivernements* (winter sheltering camps) were important Métis gathering places. They included Talles-de-Saules (Willow Bunch, where the influential Québécois trader Jean-Louis Legare settled during the 1870s), la Coulée-Chapelle, and la Coulée-des-Rochers, respectively a few kilometres northwest and north of Willow Bunch, in the region of la Montagne-de-Bois (Wood Mountain); around Lac-Pelletier (originally called Lac-la-Plume by the Métis) at Vallée-Ste-Claire and Point-Lemire; in the Cypress Hills at Chimney Coulee (where an early HBC post and NWMP station were situated) and Wapashoe (where Charles Oulette had developed a horse ranch during the 1870s); and at Red Deer Forks from 1870 to 1884. In 1840, as many as 1,210 oxcarts, accompanied by 620 Métis hunters, 650 women, 360 children, 403 fast "buffalo runner" horses, 655 slower cart horses, and 586 oxen left Rivière Rouge and headed west to hunt.[1] The *hivernements* developed so that hunters travelling long distances would not have to return all the way back to Manitoba each year. Independent Métis hunters had camped at Chimney Coulee since the 1850s. In 1871, Isaac Cowie built an HBC post to trade with these Métis hunters; in one season alone, 750 grizzly bear skins and 1,500 elk hides were traded there. However, the post was short lived; it was burned by Blackfeet. Fort Walsh, farther west in the Cypress Hills, was constructed as an NWMP post in 1875.

Archbishop Taché of St-Boniface visited the Qu'Appelle Valley in August 1864 and later received in St-Boniface a delegation of three Métis men who requested a resident priest; as a result, in 1865 Père J.N. Ritchot was sent from St-Boniface to serve an Oblate mission near Fort-Qu'Appelle. Originally called Point-Denomie after an early settler, the mission was named St-Florent after Père Florent Vandenbergh, an Oblate priest at Ile-à-la-Crosse, by two Oblate priests, Pères de Corby and Lestanc, who served the mission in 1868; the mission was commonly originally known simply as La Mission Qu'Appelle. The rectory dates from 1866; one of the oldest surviving buildings in Saskatchewan, it once housed the post office. The original thatched roof log church built by Père Ritchot in 1866 with the assistance of local Métis was replaced two years later by a larger church and residence, built under the supervision of Père Jules de Corby, but this new church was destroyed by fire the following year and replaced by another church in 1870. Père Louis Lebret arrived in 1884 and named the *paroisse* Sacré Coeur-de-Jésus; the post office originally had the same name but was later changed by Senator Girard to Lebret. To accommodate a growing community—there were 171 families by 1920—a magnificent stone church was constructed in 1925 in classic French Canadian style, with a silver sheet-metal steeple and bell tower. This last church was designed by Frère Jean-Théodore de Byl, a brother in the Oblate Order and a reputed architect who had also designed the Indian Residential School at Marieval in 1897, the Church of the Assumption at Holdfast in 1922, and St. Joseph's Church at Marcelin in 1923, and later, in 1927, he designed Sacré Coeur Scholasticat in Lebret. The Lebret mission became an Oblate seminary that trained francophone as well as German- and English-speaking priests. This *scholasticat* finally closed during the 1960s and was destroyed by fire in 1982. It had been a massive building, topped with a silver cupola in typical French Canadian style. The *scholasticat* was closely linked to the Indian Residential School served by the priests. The influential Père Hugonard continued to serve the Métis and First Nations of Lebret and area from 1874 until his death in 1917. An open-air mass was held on a hilltop shrine overlooking the village in 1921, but the Ku Klux Klan was suspected of burning it in 1928, after which stations of the cross wound up the hill to a tiny chapel in 1929—all comprising a designated heritage site.[2]

A considerable influx of both French-speaking and English-speaking Métis from Manitoba resulted from the Red River Resistance of 1869–70. These Métis had been concerned about the survival of their unique culture and settlements. With the transfer of the Hudson's Bay Company's North-West Territories to Canada imminent in 1869, the Métis feared that their traditional landholding system of riverlots, in turn patterned after the *rangs* of the St. Lawrence and Richelieu River Valleys in Quebec, would be disrupted. The arrival of Canadian government land surveyors confirmed their suspicions, with the result that, under the leadership of Louis Riel, the Métis organized their own provisional government to protect their traditions and their title to the riverlots. Although open conflict was generally averted and the province of Manitoba was created in 1870 as a part of Canada, the restive Métis still did not feel secure given the banishment of Riel and the continuing deprivation of Métis landholdings.

The French-speaking Métis who left the Red River settlements in Manitoba trekked westward up the Assiniboine River Valley, then split up, some heading southwest to Wood Mountain, others following the Qu'Appelle River past St-Lazare, Manitoba, and Lebret, then heading over the Touchwood Hills to the South Saskatchewan River. Forty families, largely from St-François-Xavier and Pembina, settled in the Wood Mountain area. An equal number of families moved to the banks of the South Saskatchewan to found the short-lived community of La Petite Ville, situated several kilometres southeast of Duck Lake. At the time, scattered Métis were reportedly visited by Pères Moulin and Fourmond from the mission at Ile-à-la-Crosse during the winter on snowshoes (though the first Mass had been celebrated at Carlton House by Pères Norbert Blanchet and Modeste Demers as early as 1838). The settlement soon shifted east across the river and several kilometres north, with the foundations of the communities of Batoche and St-Laurent-Grandin by 1871 in a more favourable site, where Père Jean-Baptiste Thibault had celebrated mass decades earlier in 1842. As early as the 1850s, the Métis *hivernement* of La Prairie-Ronde, some fifty families, had developed in the Moose Woods district south of present-day Saskatoon; the mission of St-André-de-la-Prairie-Ronde was visited by Père Moulin (the priest at La Petite Ville) and Père Bourgine during the winter of 1870 and in 1873.

The St-Laurent settlement developed rapidly with the arrival of more families from the Red River settlements. They came from the St-François-Xavier, Rivière-Rouge, and Rivière-Seine settlements, respectively west, south, and southeast of St-Boniface. Clergy emigrated directly from France to assist in the process of converting hard-living Métis buffalo hunters into sedentary, docile agriculturalists. The initial mission at La Petite Ville was founded by Père Julien Moulin, born in Dinan, Brittany, in 1832; soon after arriving in St-Boniface in 1858, he was posted to Ile-à-la-Crosse. In 1874, Père Alexis André took charge of the Oblate mission at St-Laurent-Grandin; he, too, was a Breton, born in 1833 at Guipavas, just outside Brest. He was succeeded by Père Vital Fourmond the following year, and in 1879 Frère Piquet, OMI, arrived to assist Père Fourmond. Père Fourmond was born in 1828 at Arou in Bas-Maine; he left for Alberta in 1868, then was transferred to St-Laurent in 1875. When Père André was in charge, the St-Laurent-de-Grandin settlement contained 250 families; at the mission were forty-four men, fifty-eight women, and 198 children, plus 577 horses. The original log church was built in 1874, a dormitory and residential school the next year, a convent in 1883, and the rectory in 1890 (the log church burned down in 1990 and was painstakingly rebuilt as an exact replica). The shrine of Notre-Dame-de-Lourdes was conceived by Frère Piquet, a missionary brother from Arudy, France, near the famous healing shrine of Lourdes; the first *pèlerinage* (pilgrimage) was held in 1879, and by 1881 a grotto shrine with a statue of Notre Dame had been constructed. Frère Guillet, a lay brother from Reindeer Lake (and later a priest at Fish Creek in 1901), claimed to have been healed there in 1893 from a crippled leg. More miracles had been claimed by 1905, and the pilgrimages grew to as many as 3,000 pilgrims under Père Delmas in 1916, then had declined to half that number when the shrine was visited in 1922 by Bishop Prud'homme.[3] The shrine is the scene of summer pilgrimages to this day.

Other parishes and missions were soon founded in the settlement. Following the arrival of Oblate priests in 1868, a mission on Lac-aux-Canards (Duck Lake) was established by Père Alexis André (previously in charge of the Lac-Ste-Anne mission in Alberta) in 1876; a church in the community of Duck Lake, Sacré-Coeur-de-Jésus, was planned in 1875 and completed in 1879. In 1882, Père André moved to Prince Albert and was replaced by Père Zacharie Touze, who was then replaced by Père Victor Pineau in 1885. In quick succession, Ste-Eugène was established west of Duck Lake by Père Valentin Vegreville, OMI, in 1880, St-Antoine-de-Padoue at Batoche by les Oblats de Marie Immaculée in 1881, and St-Louis-de-Langevin by Père Fourmond in 1882. Père Moulin arrived in Batoche in 1882 and within a couple of years had established a *bureau de poste* (post office), *salle de classe* (classroom), and *presbytère* (parsonage) in buildings constructed in "*le style typique de la Rivière Rouge*" (traditional Red River style). Assisting in this effort were a couple of priests from the Maine region in western France, Pères Vegreville (of Chartres, Mayenne) and Fourmond (born at Aron, Sarthe), as well as Père Lecoq (also from Sarthe, who had already founded the parish of Ste-Rose-du-Lac in Manitoba). Another early mission was Mission de l'Immaculée-Conception, north of St-Laurent.

The Carlton Trail stretched approximately 1,500 kilometres from Fort Garry (present-day Winnipeg) to Fort Edmonton. The journey to Batoche took at least fifty days. Long caravans made the trip—in one year alone during the 1870s, 1,871 Red River carts, 227 wagons, and thirty-five buckboards were recorded. The main river ferry on the trail was operated at Batoche (*Traversier-Batoche*) in 1872 and at Gabriel's Crossing (la Traverse-à-Gabriel) five years later, respectively run by Xavier-François Letendre *dit* Batoche (1841–1901) and Gabriel Dumont (1837–1906), two of the most influential men in the settlement. Batoche started a general store, a blacksmith shop, and a warehouse for the fur trade and trading goods, and he operated a freighting business to Fort-à-la-Corne and Carrot River. He lived in a fine gabled house with a wrap-around porch and double doors, known as *la belle maison*. Other stores were soon established by Baptiste Boyer, George Fisher, and others in what would become a village. Gabriel Dumont had settled at his crossing in 1866, where he also ran a store. Vandale Post Office operated there from 1891 to 1898.

The St-Laurent ferry (*l'bato* or *le bec* in Michif), originally situated upstream from its present location, dates from 1873, while farther downstream Pierre Gariépy operated a ferry at what became known as Gardepuis Crossing (la Traverse-de-Gardepuis). Other crossings became available during the winter: the old Branger crossing at La-Roche-à-Bougon, and eventually the crossing of Maurice Holligier (1920s), linking the Métis settlers on the north shore, at the Boucher Colony, originally settled by Jean-Baptiste Boucher in 1882, Ruisseau-Seguin (Seguin Creek, where a sawmill operated during the 1930s), Aaskana/Red Deer Hill, and Gerrond with the main settlement. Between Batoche and St-Louis, river flats good for farming were named after early Métis settlers Fayant and Lepine, while Ruisseau-Parenteau in this district and Ile-Dubreuil and La-Roche-à-Bougon, closer to St-Louis, were other named physical features. The Boucher *bureau de poste* operated from 1888 to 1897; the first postmaster was Père Eugène Lecoq, followed by Jean-Baptiste Boucher in 1893. Later the Lecoq School District served the area from 1915 to 1958. By the 1880s, the St-Laurent settlement included four communities of forty to sixty families each (largely from St-Norbert in the Rivière-Rouge settlement), eight separate schools instructing in French, at least seven churches and missions, several post offices (the Batoche *bureau de poste* operated for a century, 1884–1983, St-Laurent-Grandin from 1913 to 1968) and stores, a fire brigade, a grist mill, and at least one saloon.[4] Onésime Dorval (1845–1932) became the first certified schoolteacher in Saskatchewan; born and raised in Quebec, she came west in 1877 and for the next forty years was a teacher of l'Ordre de St-François serving Oblate missions—first Baie-St-Paul in the Métis settlement of St-François-Xavier in Manitoba, then Lac-Ste-Anne in Alberta for a year, before arriving at St-Laurent-Grandin in 1881; after a couple of years, she went to St-Vital (Battleford), then returned to teach at Batoche from 1896 to 1914 and finally at Duck Lake from 1914 to 1921. St-François-de-Taché school served the Batoche area after 1887. The Minatinas School District later (in 1911) served what the Métis knew as the Minichinas Hills around Bellevue. Fourmond School between Batoche and St-Louis was named after Père Fourmond, the first postmaster at Grandin, in 1889, Moulin School at Batoche after Père Moulin in 1891. Immaculée-Conception Church at Fish Creek served Métis and Polish families from 1901 to 1957, when it was closed, and a general store continued to serve the Fish Creek district from 1900 to 1962, while St-Paul School was established in the area in 1888.

Although the Métis settlement was originally situated within the North-West Territories, it was the seat of a self-declared Métis provisional government patterned after its predecessor in the Red River settlements. Métis leaders, elders, and members of this government included Louis Riel, who had led the Red River resistance in Manitoba in 1869–70; Gabriel Dumont, the leader of La Petite Ville and later St-Laurent-Grandin; Maxime Lépine, a member of the original provisional government in Red River (his brother Didyme had been in charge of the Métis forces there during the resistance), then a member of the Manitoba Legislative Assembly, before moving to St-Louis in 1882, where he ran a ferry and farmed; Patrice Fleury, buffalo hunter, leader of Métis resistance fighters, and respected elder of the community; and Jean Caron, carpenter, tradesman, and farmer, and his wife, Marguerite Dumas Caron. Yet the stability of this settlement should not be overemphasized. The priests from France found it difficult to divert the Métis buffalo hunters from their nomadic ways, from using a Michif dialect infused with Indian words, and from a traditional mistrust of the clergy, education, alcoholic temperance, and European morality. The adaptation to farming went very slowly, in the opinion of the priests. Some Métis were becoming increasingly dissatisfied with the likelihood of a repeat struggle with the Canadian government over the question of land titles; the government had already announced its intention to resurvey the riverlots and impose a grid system of land ownership (riverlots extended along the South Saskatchewan River from St-Louis down through St-Laurent-Grandin and Batoche to Gabriel's Crossing and Fish Creek, and they were found in the Riverlot district near Fort Carlton). The Métis, assisted by the church hierarchy, demanded more representation in the administration of the North-West Territories and the courts. By 1883, some Métis were already selling their lands to non-Métis farmers; reluctant to lead a sedentary life as farmers, they exhibited little enthusiasm for developing their lots and sought the charity of the church as they became progressively impoverished.[5]

In 1884, Gabriel Dumont and a small Métis delegation brought Louis Riel back into Canada from exile in Montana, and during the spring of 1885 the frustrations of the Métis in the St-Laurent settlement erupted into armed conflict with Canadian troops, commencing three kilometres west of Duck Lake on March 26, 1885, and continued with the Métis ambush of invading government troops at Ruisseau-aux-Poissons or l'Anse-au-Poisson (Fish Creek) on April 24 about fifteen kilometres south of Batoche. Also known as la Coulée-des-Touronds, the Tourond family had homesteaded there in 1883; the present-day National Historic Site (with memorial plaques in English, French, French-Michif, and Cree-Michif) includes not only the *champs-de-bataille* (battlefield) but also the archeological remains of this homestead. The matriarch of the homestead, Josephte-Paul Tourond (born in 1828), eventually lived into her nineties; she survived her husband and two sons killed in the fighting, another who died of tuberculosis the same year, and three more before 1900. Their homestead was destroyed during the fighting, but she rebuilt it as well as another at Batoche after the resistance. The Métis Resistance culminated with their inevitable defeat at Batoche on May 9–12. An equal number, about twenty-five lives, were reportedly lost on each side of the conflict. The events of the resistance are explained well at the Batoche National Historic Site/Lieu historique national de Batoche as well as in the Regional Interpretive Centre/le Centre d'interprétation historique régionale de Duck Lake just north of Duck Lake. The entire town of Duck Lake is decorated with hand-painted murals depicting these events and the life of the Métis in the area—Duck Lake continues to advertise itself as a *village frontière des sociétés premières nations, métisse, et pionnière* (a frontier village of First Nations, Métis, and pioneer societies). Today the time-worn, wooden Fish Creek church that long served Métis and Polish families stands on private property several kilometres north of the creek, beyond the boundaries of the Fish Creek and Batoche historic sites.

Far to the west, close to where the North Saskatchewan River crosses the Alberta border, Frenchman's Butte (today a National Historic Site) became the scene of an indecisive fight between Plains and Woods Cree led by Wandering Spirit and Ayimisis (militants from Big Bear's otherwise relatively docile band numbering about 1,000, only a third of whom were men) and the Alberta Field Force in May 1885, after the Frog Lake "massacre" the previous month (actually only nine Whites and Métis were killed) and a brief attack on Fort Pitt.

However, the North-West Resistance only served to increase rather than alleviate the difficulties of the Métis. The resistance was not entirely supported by all Métis, or backed completely by the clergy, and it resulted in an increasing exodus from the settlement, in more destitution, and in an identity crisis. The defeat and humiliation of the Métis marked the end of a fairly short period of Métis settling and predominance on the prairies. Louis Riel was tried for treason and executed November 16, 1885, at the age of forty-one. Members of the Métis provisional government were imprisoned or fled into exile. Gabriel Dumont fled to the United States, where he was recruited by Bill Cody's Wild West Show and exhibited with Wild Bill Hickok and Sitting Bull; later he returned to Batoche, where he died and was buried in 1906. Maxime Lépine was imprisoned for a couple of years but returned to St-Louis. Patrice Fleury, born in 1840, lived until 1941. The home of Jean and Marguerite Dumas Caron was destroyed but rebuilt ten years later; Jean died in 1903, while Marguerite lived until 1937. The village of Batoche was burned down and left in ruins. *La belle maison* of the Batoche family was heavily damaged and all the fine furniture looted, but the house was subsequently restored with the store for a while until it was demolished in 1906, after serving as a police post. Monsieur Batoche moved south to the country between Alvena and Prud'homme, where he operated a large cattle ranch; he died at the age of sixty in 1901 (as did his older brother Louis in his eighties) and was buried at Batoche, but his wife, Marguerite Parenteau Letendre, lived until 1937, when she died at the age of ninety-four and was buried in St-Louis. Métis elders, women, and children sought temporary refuge in a camp north of the village. Métis farms received little or no compensation from the Rebellion Losses Claims Commission for the destruction of their property and confiscation of their possessions. They were unable to obtain recognition of legal ownership of their traditional lands and scrip grants (*les scrips*) paid in cash (if at all).

Already by the spring of 1886, the greatly decreased Métis community was impoverished, marginalized, and isolated; only a single store remained in the area, which was bypassed by the railways and treated as a backwater. In 1885, Père Leduc and the Faithful Companions sisters left the St-Laurent settlement for Alberta. Métis faced increasing prejudice against "the rebels." Reduced to abject poverty, discouraged, hard pressed by hunger and misery, many Métis left and were soon replaced by new farming immigrants from France and Quebec in neighbouring areas, while south of Batoche almost all of the former Métis strip lands were taken over by Ukrainian and Polish immigrants.[6] Combatant Joseph Ouellette, born in the Rivière Rouge settlement in Manitoba and the father of twelve children, escaped to resettle in the Métis settlement around St. John's, North Dakota; he was reportedly the last of the original fighters to die, at the age of ninety-three.

Many of the Métis of Batoche and St-Laurent-Grandin were scattered, some moving to more isolated communities up north (including Ile-à-la-Crosse, Lac-Vert/Green Lake, and Cumberland House). At Cumberland House, a Métis community adjacent to a reserve community developed around an early fur trade post. Manitoba Métis from the Rivière Rouge settlement had moved there during the 1870s, a tiny schoolhouse made of rough-cut log planks plastered over was built in 1890, and a Catholic mission led by Père Charlebois to rival the Anglican mission was established during the 1840s. Some of the Métis diaspora eventually merged into larger surrounding French settlements, and some eventually moved into cities. The leader of the Métis at La Prairie Ronde (Round Prairie), Charles Trottier (born ca. 1840), had joined the Métis resistance at Batoche with Dakota Chief Whitecap and served as a member of the Métis provisional government; consequently, the settlement of La Prairie Ronde was dissolved soon after the resistance, and Trottier fled with his followers to the United States. Yet La Prairie Ronde and nearby Frenchman's Flats were resettled in 1902–12 by some 150 "French" (actually Métis) families (Genereux, Caron, Demars, Fayant, Landrie, Larocque, Letendre, Ouellette, Sangret, and Trottier or Trotchie) who had scattered, many down to Montana; however, the last Métis families had all moved out again, mostly into Saskatoon, by 1939 because of hardships. The Round Prairie and Genereux School Districts operated in this settlement respectively from 1906 to 1937 and 1915 to 1958.

Other areas and communities where Métis settled in the northern prairie regions in Saskatchewan included Bresaylor, west of Delmas, where three Métis families from the Headingly-St-Charles community west of Winnipeg settled in 1882, and the Bonne Eau district about ten kilometres southwest of Crystal Springs, where a francophone mission to the Métis was located. Métis and francophones (e.g., Morrisette, Dubuque, Letendre, Lamontagne, Isbister, Thurier, Delaronde) also settled in the area around Mont Nebo, east of Shell Lake, between Ahtahkakoop First Nation to the north and Snake Plain/Mistawasis to the south, including around Isbister Lake and Jimmy Lake. At Saskatchewan Landing, where the trail from Swift Current to Battleford crossed the South Saskatchewan River, stands the magnificent stone Goodwin House, with wraparound verandas and gabled windows. It was built in 1898–99 by a North-West Mounted Police member who had been involved in the North-West Resistance; the foundation had been dug by Métis and Indians—the Métis workers had included leader Jean-Antoine LaRocque, who had built a kiln to make mortar, and strongman Joe Desjarlais, who had carried stones onto the site for stonemason Old Moses Delorme. Goodwin House has been fully restored as an interpretive centre for the provincial park.[7]

Louis Riel once commented that *"Nous devons chérir notre héritage. Nous devons préserver notre identité pour les jeunes de demain. L'histoire doit être écrite et transmise"* ("We [Métis] should cherish our heritage. We should preserve our identity for the youth of the future. Our history should be written and transmitted"). Today the Métis continue to say that *Nimamihtisin/nikisteyimon li Métis niya*, in Northern Cree-Michif, or *Ji t'in Michif fier*, in French-Michif (I am proud to be Metis). Respect is shown for *aniskac wahkomakanak/anskotapanak* or *li arrières-parents* (ancestors) and *kihtesiyiniwak*, *li vius* (*les vieux* in French, elders). Métis identity and culture, a Métis *pimachesowin* (way of life), have been preserved at Batoche, not only by the bilingual National Historic Site, where Les Amis de Batoche, a cooperative organization, operates the food concession and a gift shop selling books, maps, and artifacts pertinent to Métis history and culture, and organizes special events depicting historic and cultural resources, but also by the Métis Nation of Saskatchewan (La Nation Métisse de la Saskatchewan or *li nasyoon Michif de Saskadjiwan*), which holds its annual *Fête des Michifs* or Back to Batoche Days gathering on its own grounds nearby. The distinctive Métis flag proudly flies not only at the festival grounds but also alongside the Canadian and Saskatchewan flags at the National Historic Site. Upisasik Theatre produces *Batoche Musical*, a humorous play describing the anniversary of a Métis couple who wed soon after the battle of Batoche. And, near Saskatoon, every August the four-day John Arcand Fiddle Fest draws hundreds to partake in fiddling and jigging workshops, competitions, concerts, as well as old-time dances; it was first organized in 1998 by John Arcand, known as "the master of the Métis fiddle," an art that he learned from his father while growing up near Debden; in 2007, he was named to the Order of Canada. Prince Albert holds a Métis Gathering in June and a Métis Fall Festival in September. The Métis Nation of Saskatchewan (MNS), with branches throughout the province, is headquartered in Saskatoon. Other active Métis organizations and institutions in Saskatoon (some affiliated with the MNS) include the Central Urban Metis Federation Incorporated, the MNS Genealogical and Archival Research Centre, the Gabriel Dumont Institute (which publishes a quarterly magazine, *La noovel nasyoon*) and Dumont Technical Institute, Infinity House, La Petite Ville (a seniors' home), Métis Family Community Justice Services, Métis Addictions Council, the Clarence Campeau Development Fund, and SaskNative Rentals. The Métis Urban Housing Association of Saskatchewan is based in Regina.

Métis culture is still alive and well today in Saskatchewan. The woven broad Métis sash—*li Métis sancire* or *la ceintchure flèchie*—is proudly worn at Métis events, though *tressage* (weaving) is becoming a dying art, often together with *la shimeezh flalanet* (a loose-fitting flannel shirt); fiddle playing (*li vyayloon*) and jigging (*la jig neemiwuk*), if anything, are becoming more popular; and efforts are being made to maintain and teach the Michif dialects (which, however, are now spoken by very few young people). Traditional or common Métis foods include, for example, *pikwaci pisikiwak* or *la viande sauvage* (wild game) such as *aen shouvreu* (deer), *moswa* or *arignol* (moose), *waskisow* or *serf* (elk), *paskewaw* or *di buff'loo* (bison), *li boulet* or *boulettes* (meatballs), *niska* or *outarde* (goose), *li kanawr* (duck), *misipiyow* or *poule di prairie* (prairie chicken), *li pwesoon/pouaisson* (fish), *misakwatomina pouaires* (Saskatoon berries), and *la gallette* (bannock). There were few occasions in the Batoche settlement when music and dance were not involved, except Christmas, observed properly as a religious event, though a *réveillon* (late supper) was often served after midnight Mass; on New Year's Day, families went from house to house greeting each other and kissing, so this day was called *ochetookesskaw* (kissing day).[8]

THE ESTABLISHMENT OF FRENCH SETTLEMENTS

Three explanations for the establishment of French bloc settlements across the prairies after the North-West Resistance can be suggested. First, the immigration of large numbers of French-speaking farmers to the prairies could serve to stabilize the restive, semi-nomadic Métis. The Métis would be provided with the opportunities not only to improve their farming but also to intermarry with French speakers and incorporate their stigmatized "halfbreed" identity into a broader French Canadian identity. Many Métis, however, chose to retreat further into isolation rather than have their mixed identity viewed unfavourably.[9]

Second, the establishment of specifically French bloc settlements should be seen as only one element in the general context of prairie settlement. Many other ethnic groups rapidly developed their own bloc settlements throughout the prairies because of immigration schemes of the federal government and specialized agencies, often operating in close connection to the railways, which were anxious to settle profitable grain farmers along their rights of way. Moreover, with the emergence of the bloc settlement as the typical pattern of settlement in this region of Canada, the gravitation of co-ethnics to appropriate settlement areas was likely. In short, people of French origin would settle in one of the new French settlements rather than in an area that had been settled predominantly by people of other ethnic origins.

Third, most of the French settlements resulted from a planned attempt to maintain a significant proportion of French speakers in the West. French clergy played a vital role in such colonization schemes. Most of the French settlements that developed in southeastern Saskatchewan were founded by Jean Gaire during the 1890s, while most of those in the south-central and southwest regions were established by Pères Royer and Gravel in 1906–10. Many of the immigrants from France and Quebec who settled areas adjacent to the St-Laurent settlement after the resistance arrived under the auspices of la Société d'Immigration Française, based in Montreal and supervised by Secrétaire Général August Bodard, himself an immigrant from Bretagne. The society had been formed to encourage immigration from France, Belgium, and "la Suisse Romande" (French Switzerland) to French settlements throughout the West. Bodard believed that such an immigration would re-establish an equilibrium between French speakers and English speakers in the West, as least in the rural areas. Instead of the French minorities being swamped by an anglophone majority, Bodard saw the chances for survival in Saskatchewan and Manitoba as better than those in Ontario; he pointed out that already the Franco-Manitobans had priests, parishes, and schools everywhere.[10]

Many of the tens of thousands of *Fransaskois* (Saskatchewan French) live in numerous francophone communities and parishes located within thirty-two distinctly French rural settlements. Two series of French bloc settlements were organized in

Saskatchewan, one across the northern part of the prairies (note, however, that the prairies constitute only the southern half of the province as a whole) and the other across the southern part; these two series were separated by a central belt in which no French settlements were organized. Let us now examine each settlement in some detail, paying particular attention to the origins of the settlers.

THE NORTHERN SETTLEMENTS
Expansion of the Duck Lake–St-Louis Settlement
With the arrival of the French immigrants after the Métis resistance, the Métis settlement of St-Laurent became the nucleus of one of the largest French settlements on the prairies, despite the scattering of the Métis. St-Louis long retained its character as a historic Métis community—illustrious Métis residents of the community and area have included Charles Eugène Boucher (1864–1926), Hélène Letendre (1866–1951), and Joseph Octave Nolin (1868–1925), as well as Pierre Parenteau, Maxime Lepine and Josephte Lavallée, and later Howard Adams. While a few immigrants from France settled in the Batoche area as early as 1881 and 1884, the main influx commenced in 1886 when settlers arrived in the St-Louis area. They came from Poitou, Bretagne, Maine, Savoie (Savoy), and Picardie (Picardy). In Paroisse St-Louis-de-Langevin, a new church and rectory were built in 1887 and a larger church in 1906. The District Scolaire de St-Louis-de-Langevin was created in 1886. Père Lecoq served as the *curé* (parish priest) until 1897, when he was replaced by l'Abbé Barbier, born in Languedoc, who was to prove instrumental in establishing several other parishes. That year the teaching religious order, les Filles de la Providence, arrived from France and established Couvent St-Louis. Père Pineau served the parish from 1909 to 1912, then returned to his native France. His successor was l'Abbé Carpentier, born in Picardie, parish priest at St-Louis for over thirty years. L'Académie St-Joseph operated from 1919 to 1980; Collège Notre-Dame, founded in Prince Albert in 1953, relocated to St-Louis in 1967 but closed in 1974. Marie Thérèse LeClaire, born in 1916, the daughter of the owner of the local general store, first taught school in the Bellevue area and later at Ponteix. St-Louis has an Association culturelle Coeur-franc de St-Louis maintaining francophone interests in the area, not the least through a bilingual *Bulletin communautaire de St-Louis* (published monthly), and a Centre francophone BDS (standing for Bellevue, Domrémy, St-Louis), which circulates a community bulletin, *Les Echos*, as well as a St. Louis Historical Society, le Club St-Joseph for seniors (since 1970), the Regnier Care Home, and a bilingual *caisse populaire* (credit union). Today the francophone residents of St-Louis represent diverse origins: they include Métis (St-Louis has a Métis local branch), immigrants from France and one family from Switzerland, Québécois, and residents from francophone settlements and communities in Manitoba and Saskatchewan (e.g., Duck Lake, Titanic, Prud'homme, Vonda, St-Denis, Sedley, Marcelin, Ponteix, etc.). Although it is a historic community, St-Louis did not receive official recognition as an organized hamlet until 1956 and an incorporated village three years later.

The small community of Hoey (with the Argonne district) was first settled at about the same time by immigrants from Belgium, Paris, and the Saintonge region. Hoey was selected as the administrative centre of St-Louis RM in 1910. The village of Domrémy (with the surrounding Ste-Therèse, Rompré, Pea Vine, Lac-Dubois, St-Jude, St-Julien,

Ethier, Lac-de-Jonc, and Lac-Croch districts) was settled in 1892–94 by settlers from Ste-Anne-de-la-Pérade and Ste-Geneviève-de-Batiscan, Quebec. St-Julien School was established in 1888, possibly named after the parish priest at the time at Batoche, Père Julien Moulin. In 1894–95, they were joined by immigrants from France, chiefly from Bretagne but also from Poitou. In 1896, l'Abbé Barbier came from St-Louis to organize a new parish, Ste-Jeanne-d'Arc (Joan of Arc, born at Domrémy-la-Pucelle, France). Domrémy continues to have a Centre communautaire fransaskois, l'Association culturelle de Domrémy, a bilingual *caisse populaire*, and le Club d'âge d'or for seniors. Domrémy was given village status in 1921 but was downgraded to a hamlet in 2006; Hoey was recognized as an organized hamlet in 1952 (four years before the larger neighbouring community of St-Louis).

At St-Isidore-de-Bellevue (and the surrounding Manatinaw, Lac-Chitac, Lac-Chicot, Gaudet, Coteau-Martin, Lac-à-Procul, St-Gérard, Lac-Godette, and Garonne—also known as Gareau or Gartou—districts), the francophone population was remarkably diverse. Several Métis families had settled in the district by the early 1880s, when Philippe Chamberland, a French Canadian, had close contacts with the Métis at Batoche. The first Québécois settler, Azarie Gareau, arrived in 1882, soon followed by descendants of Acadian exiles who had resettled in Quebec before coming to Bellevue in 1883–94; about 1902 by Québécois families from communities in the Cantons de l'Est/Eastern Townships and other regions of Quebec as well as New England; several families from a French Canadian (originally Québécois) settlement in Minnesota; and a few families who came directly from France. The first priest, l'Abbé Myre, arrived from Quebec in 1902 and built a primitive log church, which doubled as a school on his homestead, and a *presbytère* the next year. In 1907–10, a new church and *presbytère* were built, then in 1925–27 a larger brick church, replaced by a simple "modern" church in 1960, renovated in 1987 with an accompanying convent and *presbytère*.

Early schools were St-Julien (1888), Gareau (1890), renamed Bellevue (in 1902, a new school constructed in 1906), Ethier (1907), Gaudet (1912), St-Isidore (1930), St-Gérard (1950), as well as Argonne (1909) near Hoey. Bellevue was selected as the locus for the regional Ecole Centrale in 1954, now the *bureau-régional* of the Division scolaire francophone. That year les Soeurs de la Présentation de Marie arrived; a teaching order, they were put in charge of l'Ecole St-Isidore. Soeur Maria Gareau, born in Bellevue in 1921, joined the Filles de la Providence in 1940; a teacher dedicated to the maintenance of French culture in Saskatchewan, she taught in St-Louis, St-Brieux, Prud'homme, Victoire, and Vonda. A *caisse populaire* was established in 1944. And, during the 1940s, a *troupe de théatre* was formed; by the 1980s, it had been replaced by another theatrical troupe who called themselves les Quats'coins. La Congrégation des Dames de Ste-Anne existed from 1940 to 1970, but a children's religious group called les Enfants de Marie et les croisés eventually ceased to exist.

Today Bellevue remains an active francophone community, with the parish church offering mass and various social services in French. Le Centre culturel le Rendez-vous came into being in 1985 through the efforts of l'Association culturelle de Bellevue; it houses a café offering *"cuisine canadienne-francaise,"* a boutique selling crafts as well as detailed local histories, the *archives historiques de Bellevue*, and a *gallérie d'art* featuring exceptional woodcarving (one extraordinary hand-carved tableau portrays all of the original *pionniers*, the founding families). Le Club d'âge d'or for seniors, founded in 1974, which meets at the cultural centre, has been affiliated with la Fédération des aînés fransaskoises (founded in Zenon Park) since 1983. Health services are provided in French at the Foyer Jésus-Marie. Together with neighbouring Domrémy, Bellevue constituted a *conseil-régional* of l'Association catholique franco-canadienne (ACFC) and continues to have a representative of the Conseil pastoral francophone interdiocésain de la Saskatchewan. Since 1985, Bellevue has been the *bureau-régional* of la Fédération des femmes canadiennes-francaises. It has a chapter of l'Association jeunesse fransaskoise. The community continues to have its own *école francophone* (Ecole St-Isidore, Division scolaire francophone 310) with grades from *prématernelle* (a kindergarten, called les Petits Amis de Passe-Partout) through grade twelve. This school is open to children with at least one parent with French mother tongue who still understands French, or with a parent who has received an elementary education in French, or a family in which at least one child has received or is receiving education in a francophone school at the elementary level. In keeping with its intention to serve francophones throughout the settlement, the school provides free bussing. Contact is maintained with families on a regular basis through a newsletter, *Messages aux parents*. Belle Pulses is a peas, fava beans, and lentils processing plant established in 1979; peas have been grown in the area since the 1930s.[11] Bellevue's French heritage is further preserved by a park that has become a veritable outdoor art gallery, along the trail called the Piste de la Légende Fransaskoise. An artisan from Ontario, a blacksmith and glassblower, moved to Bellevue in 2007, attracted by its rural artistic prowess.

While these communities immediately east of the St-Laurent settlement of the Métis were developing, the historic Métis village of Duck Lake (Lac-aux-Canards) was being reinforced as a French-speaking centre after 1890 by immigrants from Poitou, Bretagne, Paris, Normandie (Normandy), Savoie, and Franche-Comté. In the local history of Duck Lake and area, at least twenty-nine original settler families can be identified as Métis, fifty-nine were immigrants from France and another four from Belgium and three from Switzerland, twenty-one arrived from Quebec and two from francophone communities in Ontario, eleven were from French settlements in Manitoba, nine hailed from other French communities within this settlement (e.g., St-Louis, Hoey, Bellevue, Domrémy) and other French settlements in Saskatchewan (e.g., Marcelin and Damour, Spiritwood, and Debden), and a couple arrived from the United States.[12] One Belgian was Baron Huysmans de Deftal, an agent for crown lands who was described as helping settlers "of all races and beliefs"; he noted in 1901 the progress of the several Belgian farmers in the area. A new church was constructed in Duck Lake in 1895 to better serve the growing parish of Sacré-Coeur. French-speaking students in Duck Lake went to Stobart School (1885), whereas English-speaking students tended to go to Victoria Protestant Separate School (1890), which was not reunited with Stobart until 1960. Sisters who taught at Stobart since 1895 (as well as at St. Michael's Indian Residential School and at St-Laurent-Grandin) included les Soeurs des Fidèles Compagnes de Jésus (the Sisters of the Faithful Companions of Jesus)—notably Soeur Philomène Allard—and les Soeurs Grises (the Grey Nuns). The first sister to serve as school principal, from 1905 to 195, was Soeur Marie-de-la-Trinité. Incidentally, the school principal from 1945 to 1951 was Soeur Thérèse de Jésus, born Kathleen St-Laurent, the former prime minister's sister. All ten principals of the school through 1966 were francophone nuns. From 1966 to 1974, les Soeurs de la Charité de Notre Dame d'Evron, a religious order based in France, taught there. The Pelletier general store was established in 1948 by Guy Pelletier with the assistance of his wife, Yolande Emma Sirois (from the largely francophone community of Smooth Rock Falls in northern Ontario) until 1960.

West of Duck Lake, the parishes of Ste-Anne-de-Titanic (originally named Mourey after the first priest, Père Maurice Mourey, but changed to Titanic in 1912 to commemorate the tragic sinking of the *Titanic* that year) and St-François-de-Carlton were established in 1902 to serve the newly arrived immigrants from Bretagne, Poitou, and Belgium. In 1888, the Mazenod Catholic Public School District was formed, but soon the *district scolaire catholique* (Catholic school district) of St-Jean-Baptiste, named for school trustee Jean-Baptiste Arcand, was founded in 1890 (in 1931, it became simply St-Jean-Baptiste School District, known locally as l'Ecole St-Jean-Baptiste-de-Titanic). The Carlton School District, where French mixed with Mennonites, operated from 1888, the predominantly French Carlton Siding School from 1918, and Riverlot School west of Carlton from 1930. In 1903, the mission at the nearby small community of Carlton officially became Paroisse Ste-Anne-de-Carlton. The *bureau de poste* of Mourey was established in 1911. L'Abbé Jean-Pierre Le Sann served this parish actively from 1930 to 1944; he had formerly served Zenon Park, White Star, Big River, and Périgord. However, this period of several decades of growth and development began to falter during the Depression of the 1930s; St-Jean-Baptiste School finally closed in 1959, the church rectory was sold in 1961, and then the church closed permanently in 1964. The *bureau de poste*, relegated to a private home since 1950, closed in 1967. Now all that remains is a memorial to the once active parish and a cemetery hidden in a quiet grove. Both schools at Carlton and Carlton Siding closed in 1962, that at Riverlot four years earlier.

North of Duck Lake, country schoolhouses served the Lac-Cheval district (where Jamontville School was named after early settler Charles Jamont, who immigrated from Paris) from 1919 to 1965 and the Dorval district from 1947 to 1962; to the east, the Magnolia district from 1913 to 1963; and to the south, the La Plaine/Leckford district (settled by immigrants from France during the 1890s) from 1903 to 1959 (a *bureau de poste* operated there from 1937 to 1945). A local physical feature near Duck Lake had the colourful name of Butte-des-Bâtards.

Virtually all of the parish priests of Duck Lake have been francophone, including Père Tharcissius Schmid from 1909 to 1916, born in Switzerland and ordained in Cannes, France; he also served Carlton and Bonne-Madone. Several subsequent parish priests were Québécois. One local priest was Roland Gaudet, born in Bellevue in 1922; he studied at Gravelbourg, St-Norbert, Manitoba, and Université Laval in Quebec City before serving many francophone parishes in Saskatchewan: Marcelin, Prince Albert, Leoville, Zenon Park, Duck Lake, and Debden. Another local priest was Gilles Doucette, born in Duck Lake in 1935, where he was also ordained in 1962; after receiving his theological education at St-Boniface, Manitoba, he returned to Saskatchewan to serve Prince Albert, Spiritwood, Batoche, St-Laurent, as well as many Native parishes. Duck Lake had its own *bureau de poste* as early as 1879. The community was incorporated as a village in 1894 and a town in 1911. La Société St-Jean-Baptiste de la Saskatchewan was founded at Duck Lake in 1909; it was a precursor to l'Association catholique franco-canadienne de la Saskatchewan, organized at Duck Lake in 1912; and that year it was a provincial chapter of la Société du parler français. The French-language newspaper *Le Patriote* was also established there in 1910. A branch of the Bank of Montreal was established in Duck Lake in 1905; after seventy-seven years of service to the community, it closed in 1982 and was replaced by the Credit Union. L'Association culturelle de Duck Lake and l'Association francophone de Duck Lake have long served the francophone community. Les Dames de Ste-Anne were active since the early 1900s through the 1930s but were disbanded during the mid-1980s, by which time they had already been effectively displaced by the Catholic Women's League, active since 1971. The Allouette Club (formerly the francophone Cercle Jeanne d'Arc) came into existence in 1948.

All together, the French-origin population of the expanded settlement (inclusive of the small outlying settlements of Bonne-Madone and Titanic-Carlton) could be estimated to number approximately 2,600 in 1971 (exclusive of many Métis), including St-Louis, Domrémy, and Duck Lake and portions of the rural municipalities of St-Louis, Duck Lake, Prince Albert, and Rosthern. So this is the largest French settlement in Saskatchewan, both in population and in areal extent: the settlement proper extends at least seventy kilometres from east to west and more than thirty kilometres from north to south; however, a virtually continuous band of francophone settlement actually extends as far as 160 kilometres from St-Brieux westward all the way to the Coteau hills ("as the crow flies" and much farther by road). Almost three-quarters (72.1%) of the residents of Domrémy claimed French origin, though just over half (57.1%) were still French speaking. A little more than half of the residents of Duck Lake were French origin (57.9%) and French speaking (55.6%), though many more could have claimed just Métis origin, and many Métis were francophone. In fact, at St-Louis, people claiming French origin (53.3%) were actually outnumbered by those speaking French (61.0%), whereas Bellevue has always continued to have an almost exclusively francophone population. In recent years, the organized hamlet of Bellevue (pop. 110 in 2006) has been the only community within the settlement with an increasing number of residents; the town of Duck Lake (pop. 610), village of St-Louis (pop. 431), and organized hamlets of Domrémy (pop. 124) and Hoey (pop. 47) have all been losing population, while Carlton is a very small unincorporated community.

Other Settlements in the North-Central Region

A second French settlement to develop in the north-central region of the province was situated about forty kilometres east of Saskatoon. The settlement began to develop in 1897 with the first establishment of the community successively called Marcotte Ranch, Lally Siding (in 1904), Howell (in 1906—it became an incorporated village in 1908), and finally Prud'homme (after Joseph-Henri Prud'homme, 1882–1952, the bishop of the French-language diocese of Prince Albert in 1922). The initial settlers were from Nantes in Loire-Atlantique and Arras, in Artois, France; some arrived after first settling in Ste-Rose-du-Lac and Grande-Clairière, Manitoba. In 1910, they were joined by immigrants from the Belgian province of Hainaut. L'Abbé Bourdel, born in Bretagne, arrived in 1904 to establish the parish of Sts-Donatien-et-Rogatien in 1907 (with an impressive bell tower added in 1922, designated a heritage site in 1984); he was succeeded in 1931 by Maurice Baudoux, a son of one of the families from Belgium, destined to become the bishop of St-Paul, a French-language diocese in Alberta, then the archbishop of St-Boniface. Decades later Prud'homme was the home community of Jeanne Sauvé, the governor general of Canada during the early 1980s. Les Filles de la Providence religious order opened its convent there in 1905 and then l'Ecole Providence (today the Musée multiculturel describes the early history of settlement in the area). A bilingual *caisse populaire* is situated in Prud'homme.

A second parish in the settlement was St-Philippe-de-Néri, established at Vonda (originally Vaunder) in 1907. Vonda was incorporated as a village in 1905 and became a town just a couple of years later. François Rentier, a graduate in agricultural science, Université de Louvain, Belgium, arrived in the area in 1908. L'Ecole Providence, an *école fransaskoise* serving the settlement, is located in Vonda. Lalonde Insurance now occupies the one-time Bank of Commerce, dating from 1906 and now a heritage site. Among the early settlers was the Hamoline family from Belgium. Later the Hamoline farm was purchased by the Loiselle family. François Xavier Loiselle, whose predecessors originated in Normandy, had initially homesteaded with his brother and friends in Manitoba, arriving by oxen wagon, and was joined by his wife from Quebec in 1886; with their son Aimé, born in 1895, they moved in 1909 to the Vonda area. Forced to move away during the 1920s because of poor crops, they eventually resettled during the 1940s near Prud'homme to farm. Lionel Loiselle bought the Hamoline farm in 1963; his son Henri was destined to become an accomplished opera singer while continuing to farm (hence, he was known locally as "the singing farmer"). Another illustrious resident was the Honourable Allyre Louis Sirois. Born in Vonda in 1923, he had a particularly interesting life: during the Second World War, he parachuted into occupied France to join the French resistance, for which he was decorated with the prestigious Croix de Guerre avec Palme and became a Member of the British Empire. Returning to Saskatchewan after the war, he practised law in Gravelbourg, then was appointed to the Court of Queen's Bench; he was the first judge to preside over a trial in the French language in Saskatchewan, and he was recognized for his legal service to the francophone community by l'Association des juristes francophones. He also served as the president of the ACFC in 1963–64. In 1999, the annual provincial Fête fransaskoise was held in Vonda.

The parish of St-Denis (presumably named after the patron saint of the first postmaster, Léon Denis), due south of Vonda, came into existence in 1910 (the present church and rectory, Manoir Beauséjour, were completed in 1918 and declared a historic site in 1984). It had been settled first by immigrants from Saintonge and Poitou on the west coast of France, Bretagne, and Flandres (Flanders) and Hainaut on the French-Belgian frontier, then by families brought out from Quebec by l'Abbé Berubé. L'Abbé Mollier, the first resident parish priest, came from the Rhone Valley in Languedoc, southern France. St-Denis, Prud'homme, and Vonda together constitute la Trinité (represented by l'Association communautaire fransaskoise de la Trinité, a *conseil-régional* of the ACFC). St-Denis has a chapter of l'Association jeunesse fransaskoise and le Club culturel de St-Denis, and the Champêtre Country guest ranch operates in the district. Repeatedly, we are reminded of the interconnectedness between francophone settlements in Saskatchewan: more than forty quarters of farmland around St-Denis are now in the Denis family name, farmed by members of the extended Denis

FRENCH SETTLEMENTS

family. One of the original settlers was Clotaire Denis; his son Clodomir in turn had two sons—Wilfrid (a professor and former dean at the University of Saskatchewan) and Gédéon (a farmer at St-Denis)—who married two sisters, Jeannine and Madeleine Poulin of Zenon Park. The community centre is called le Centre communautaire de St-Denis. St-Denis paroisse et communauté celebrated its centennial in July 2010.

In 1971, there were approximately 900 people of French origin in this settlement, inclusive of the town of Vonda, the incorporated village of Prud'homme, the hamlet of St-Denis, and the surrounding districts of Casavant (school district, 1913–61), Dinelles (school district, 1912–43), Espérance (*bureau de poste*, 1912–26), La Martine (formerly Napoleon School District, 1917), and Grierson, Glenmour, Canoe Lake, Sleaford, Knapton, and Buffer Lake School Districts in the rural municipalities of Grant and Bayne. In 1971, there were the same number of French as Ukrainian residents of Prud'homme (ninety-five); residents claiming French origin (only through paternal lineage) constituted 39.6% of the population, compared with almost half (45.8%) at Vonda. However, fewer residents were francophone: respectively 30.8% at Prud'homme and 33.6% at Vonda. The hamlet of St-Denis has tried to remain staunchly French (though many Ukrainian farmers now occupy land adjacent to French farms); about half (48.4%) of the community residents were francophone. Vonda now has 322 residents (it had more than 400 by the 1930s but declined to half that number by the 1960s), Prud'homme has 167 (compared with 268 by 1926 and 321 in 1966), while St-Denis remains a hamlet.

Originally, eighteen French families settled around Peterson, some twenty-eight kilometres by road southeast of Prud'homme, where German priests have consistently served St. Agnes Parish since the first church was constructed in 1924 (replaced by a larger church in 1952). The first mass was held in the home of Ephrem and Adele Dauvin in 1909, the first wedding when Louis-Marie Jule married Julien Collin in 1913. Of approximately thirty families and individuals who founded this parish, half were French, the remainder German and Polish. The community once had three churches, but the Anglican church was last used in 1961, and the Ukrainian Catholic church has been inactive for at least fifteen years and was recently sold as a private residence. Only six occupied residences remained by the mid-1990s; all businesses, elevators, and the local school have long been closed and abandoned (the school became the community hall in 1984). But St. Agnes continues to draw on largely French rural families, though weddings and baptisms are now infrequent. At least forty-one French-origin family farms were in the area in 1970. The districts of Givenchy (school district, 1918) or St-Hilaire, St-Alphonse, and St-Quentin in this general area were also settled by francophones.

East of the Duck Lake–St-Louis settlement, immigrants from Haute-Loire, Franche-Comté, and Dauphiné in France had settled by 1899 around Bonne-Madone and Reynaud (named in 1929 after Jean-François Reynaud, a widower who had arrived with five children) and the surrounding districts: Belmont, Lac-Olivier, Lac-Bassin (Basin Lake), Lac-Dubois, Lepine, Lac-Louis, Lac-Lucien, Lac-Lezard, Marne, Lac-Venne, Berard Beach, and Tway (named after the first postmaster, Franck Touet, in 1913). They were served by Père Laurent Voisin, himself an immigrant from the Jura area on the Swiss frontier, as well as l'Abbé Barbier from St-Louis. The Bonne-Madone church and rectory, completed in 1919–20, were made a historic site in 1982. Father

Clifford Tremblay, born in Wakaw in 1929, was ordained at Bonne-Madone in 1956; based primarily in Prince Albert, he became the vicar general in 2007. As recently as 2005, the Bonne-Madone church was still holding Mass on Saturday evenings during the summer. Some francophone Métis and French families (Turgeon, Beauchamp, Laroche, Dumonceau) settled immediately west of Crystal Springs and in the St-André district around Northway, and others (Suignard, Poncelet, Lamont, Mansiere, Beaulieu, Deschambault, Roualt, Beaudet, Soulier, Boisson, Gudelot) settled in the Omand, Struthers Lake, and Waterhen Marsh districts between Crystal Springs and Meskanaw. Mission St-Augustin served the Flett's Springs district as early as 1899. However, the general region quickly became quite diverse, with Ukrainians, Hungarians, Germans, and Scandinavians settling near and among the French. The total French population in this region could not have exceeded 300 in 1971, scattered through the rural municipalities of Hoodoo, Three Lakes, and Invergordon. Meskanaw had only eighteen residents at last count (2006), while the former village of Crystal Springs declined rapidly from eighty-seven residents back in 1966 to sixty-five in 1972, only twenty-five by 2001, and twenty-three at last count. Reynaud reportedly once had fourteen businesses and services and 200 residents, but by the 1980s all businesses were gone, and only five residents remained. Reynaud Post Office, established in 1909, closed in 1982.

In 1904, a large Breton settlement began to develop at St-Brieux (originally Plaine), about thirty-five kilometres southwest of Melfort, with the arrival of some forty families from St-Brieuc, Brittany, led by Père LeFloc'h, who also served as the immigration agent and local postmaster. The priest's vestments reportedly came from France.[13] Bretons continued to arrive through 1909. L'Abbé Barbier—formerly the priest at St-Louis, Domrémy, and Bonne-Madone—became the *curé* of the parish of St-Brieux (founded in 1904—the rectory built in 1919 is a heritage site and museum). Eventually, an extensive French settlement extended eastward and southeastward to Sacristan, Kermaria (where a second church, Notre-Dame-de-la-Nativité, became a mission of St-Brieux under l'Abbé Barbier in 1915), Folgoët, Tilly (where the school served French and Breton families from 1923 to 1962), Champlain, Beauchamp, and Pilon (renamed Spalding); southward to Lacombe, Lac-Bergot, and Lac-Delaine; and westward to Lac-Dezou, Lac-Dormouse, Lac-Leroy, Lac-Ignace, and Little Moose Lake, where the mission of St-Philippe (1930, a heritage site since 1983) served a mixed French and Hungarian population.[14] The Kermaria, Kerguelen, and Folgoët districts were strongly Breton: the church at Kermaria was built on the homestead of Albert Roenspies; the first burial in the cemetery was Francoise L'Henaff LeBorgne in 1916, and Breton family names came to abound (e.g., Breton, Couzic, Guegnen, Guezille, Jezegau, Jezeguel, Kerneleguen, Kerleroux, Klemex, Migadel, Rohel …). In 1971, people of French origin totalled almost 700 in St-Brieux and the surrounding rural municipalities of Lake Lenore and Flett's Springs. The town of St-Brieux remains predominantly French (59.6% French origin and 50.7% French speaking in 1971), yet in recent decades the priests of the parish of St-Brieux, by their own admission, have tended to diminish the use of French in church services in recognition of the participation of Hungarian and other non-francophone Catholics. A French network television transmitting station was located in St-Brieux, also a bilingual *caisse populaire* and le Comité culturel de St-Brieux. Health services are provided in French at Château Providence. Local history is documented by le Musée de St-Brieux, housed in the rectory built in 1919 (now a heritage site). St-Brieux was incorporated as a village in 1913; it had a static to declining population for several decades, then grew rapidly from 177 residents in 1946 to 411 in ten years, only to begin to decrease again until a long-time resident established Bourgault Industries, manufacturing agricultural equipment; the population again grew steadily to over 400 by the 1980s, and now it is close to 500.

Northeast of Prince Albert, the White Star area began to be settled in 1904 also by Breton immigrants (who had immigrated the same year as the Bretons of St-Brieux). Originally, this locality was called Edouardville or Edwardfield (after Frère Edouard Courbis, the director of an orphanage in Prince Albert, originally from the Aveyronne region in south-central France). The *chapelle* was first served by l'Abbé Noël Perquis, from the francophone community of Fannystelle, Manitoba. Chemin Lempereur (Lempereur Road) running south toward Prince Albert was named after Georges Lempereur, who immigrated from Paris to homestead there in 1907. The Lac-de-Charles district to the immediate east was settled by French, beyond which they encountered the Poles and Ukrainians who soon predominated in the Honeymoon district. To the north, the Cloarec district was named after Gérome and Marie Cloarec, Bretons who settled there in 1912. Spruce Home was originally the Centreville School District in 1910, while the Ste-Lucie mission served the Sturgeon Lake Reserve to the immediate west. In 1910, settlers from Plessisville, Quebec, settled around Henribourg, which had a *bureau de poste* by the next year. Still more settlers arrived by 1912, many brought from Quebec by Henri-Albert Morin (after whom both Henribourg—originally Morinville—and Albertville were named). The francophone settlement soon expanded eastward around Albertville and northward along Chemin Gobeil into the Bégin district. Bégin School was named for Archeveque Louis Nazaire Bégin (1840–1925) in 1914 when he became the first Canadian cardinal. Nearby Ruisseau-Christopher (Christopher Creek) was named after Christopher Gravel, brother-in-law of the district surveyor at the time, J.E. Morrier, who later became a francophone school inspector and secrétaire-général de l'Association catholique franco-canadienne de la Saskatchewan. East of Albertville, Aurèle Morin had a small general store serving the Piché and Emilbourg districts. The settlement eventually coalesced into a very diverse francophone population consisting of immigrants from France, especially Brittany (including Donatien Frémont, historian of the French settlement of the West and first *chef du secretariat provincial* of the ACFC), some from Guyenne and Normandy, Belgium and Switzerland, as well as Québécois especially from Plessisville but also from Princeville, St-Côme-de-Beauce, St-Lambert, Batiscan, and Joliette and via the United States: Maine, North Dakota, Wisconsin, Montana, and Minnesota. The Albertville *bureau de poste* was established in 1914, that of White Star (Carlton Trail Siding) the same year. In 1916, l'Abbé Albert LeBel was instrumental in founding la Caisse populaire d'Albertville, the first credit union in Saskatchewan, preceding the adoption of the provincial Credit Union Act by twenty years. La Fromagerie d'Albertville (a cheese factory) began operation in 1918. La Paroisse St-Jacques d'Albertville became the focal point for the small settlement; the church was constructed in 1922–23, with an impressive forty-five-metre (150-foot) steeple seen for miles around; the church was designated a historic site in 1992. One Québécois parish priest, Père Gregoire Lachance, had been an assistant priest at Duck

Lake in 1958–63 and subsequently became a missionary in the Philippines from 1972 to 1980 before retiring back in Quebec. In 1926, farmers were using oxen to pull hand plows (*une charrue-à-mancherons*); in hard times, dairy farms' sole income was local sales. During the "dirty thirties," francophone farmers forced by drought to leave southern Saskatchewan arrived in the settlement. The original *caisse populaire* closed in 1936 but was re-established in 1950. The cheese factory ceased operation in 1943, White Star Post Office in 1964, Albertville Station in 1966, Henribourg Post Office in 1991 (little remains of the hamlet today, just several boarded-up one-time businesses), and Bégin School long ago—all that is left is a co-op community pasture. Albertville became incorporated as a village in 1986, strung out along two crossroads; it now contains 110 residents, having lost twenty-two residents in the past five years. In 1971, there were 540 French in Garden River RM and Buckland RM, but an additional 3,915 lived in the nearby city of Prince Albert.

Settlements in the Northeastern Region
French and Belgian colonists from Manitoba had settled in three areas in the northeastern region of the Saskatchewan prairies by 1910: St-Front (about fifty kilometres southeast of St-Brieux); Périgord (forty kilometres east of St-Front); and Veillardville (immediately west of the town of Hudson Bay). They were joined by immigrants from Haute-Loire, Savoie, Limousin, and Beauce at St-Front (including the St-Raymond, Vallée de la Barrière/Barrier Valley, Festubert, Cuvier, Lac-Charron, and Ponass Lake districts); by immigrants from Auvergne, Poitou, Savoie, and Picardie at Périgord (including the surrounding districts of LaBell's Hill/Bellshill, Lac-Lemaire, and Pré-Ste-Marie); and by Québécois in all three settlements. St-Front was first served from 1912 to 1919 once a month by a priest from the next closest Catholic church forty kilometres away. St-Front and Périgord were served by les Filles de la Providence. At the first community picnic in St-Front in 1922, the food served included rabbit, "prairie chicken," and wild duck.[15] The parish of St-Front (1926) was established by the omnipresent Abbé Barbier. St-Front has a *caisse populaire bilingue*. The *district scolaire* de St-Front was formed in 1918 and terminated in 1985. Other early French parishes were St-Athanase-de-Périgord and the mission of Pré-Ste-Marie (almost thirty kilometres north of Périgord). Périgord, originally settled by Métis families, was likely named after the region of Périgord, France, by an early parish priest; Pré-Ste-Marie was named by Père Emile Dubois, who combined the French term *pré* for little prairie with the first name of the first postmaster, Marie-Eugène Lafont, who immigrated to this rural district from Paris in 1912. Surrounding rural districts also included Nobleville, Merle (*bureau de poste*, 1932–66, named for the first postmaster, Merle Tremblay), Lac-Vert (Greenwater Lake), Lac-Marneau, Lac-des-Noisettes (Nut Lake), Petit-Lac-Noisette, and Prairie Butte. This small community maintains an interest in its history through the Société Historique de Périgord. West of Hudson Bay, Veillardville was settled in 1910 by Louis and Angèle Nicollet Veillard, immigrants from Chateauneuf, Savoie; Louis soon returned to France to serve during the First World War, and he received the prestigious Croix de Guerre at Verdun in 1916; Angèle became the sole postmaster of Veillardville Post Office (1928–64). Ruisseau-Loiselle (Loiselle Creek) south of Hudson Bay was settled by homesteader Henri Loiselle. St. Anthony's Church in Veillardville,

constructed in 1939, became a heritage site in 1987. In 1971, the French population around St-Front numbered more than 400, in the rural municipalities of Spalding, Ponass Lake, Barrier Valley, and Pleasantdale. Not more than 300 people of French origin were in the Périgord area, the nearby town of Kelvington, and Kelvington RM and Bjorkdale RM. Perhaps 300 people claimed French origin in and around Veillardville and the town of Hudson Bay.

Zénon-Parc (Zenon Park) was settled between 1910 and 1917 by some 500 settlers recruited by l'Abbé Berubé. The first parish priest, Père Dubois, had originally suggested Mariemont as the name for the community in 1913, but the community received its present name three years later, named after Zénon Chamberland, an early settler who had arrived from New Bedford, Massachusetts; however, the post office was called Chamberland. The first post office was located at the road junction then called Quatres-Coins (Four Corners) in 1913. Most families arrived from Quebec and from the textile mill towns in New England where many Québécois worked: Nashua and Manchester, New Hampshire; Fall River, New Bedford, and Worcester, Massachusetts; and Providence, Woonsocket, and Pawtucket, Rhode Island. Père Berubé and Romulus Laurier (a nephew of Prime Minister Wilfrid Laurier) had been sent to recruit millworkers; they gave a rousing speech to a packed hall in Pawtucket during the winter of 1909–10. Zénon Chamberland rose to declare that he was ready to lead the way ... who would follow? Raymond and Maurice Courteau, Mederic Foucher, Frank Soucy, Louis Favreau, Louis Gelinas, Joseph Delage, and others would follow. They left in April, leading the way for 317 adults and 101 children—this number increased to over 500 when Québécois were picked up along the way, and these initial settlers were supplemented by more migrants from Quebec in 1911–13 (especially from the Cantons de l'Est/Eastern Townships, Ile Verte, Trois Pistoles, and la Gaspésie), while other families eventually arrived or were intermarried with francophone people from a wide variety of other French communities in Saskatchewan (including St-Front, Bellevue, Duck Lake, Prud'homme, St-Denis, Vonda, Dollard, St-Brieux, Montmartre, Fir Mountain, Willow Bunch, Vawn, Marcelin, Domrémy), as well as from La Broquerie, Manitoba, Legal, Alberta, the Lafontaine settlement near Georgian Bay, Ontario, and North Dakota. Family surnames recorded in the Zenon Park history book include at least thirty-seven who came from New England, twenty-four from Quebec, sixteen from other francophone communities in Saskatchewan, nine Franco-Ontarian, six Franco-Manitoban, five direct from France, two Franco-Albertan, and one North Dakotan.[16] Yolande Emma Sirois Pelletier, born in Smooth Rock Falls, northern Ontario, in 1927, was raised in Zenon Park; after marrying Guy Pelletier, they moved to Duck Lake, where they ran the general store. In 1930, the neighbouring small parish of Ste-Lucie (St. Lucy) was formed in Arborfield. The strongly French settlement extended into the former rural school districts of Goyer (1914–59), la Marseillaise (1915–54), Ditton Park (1921–62), Verchères (1924–54), and Treasure/Arborfield (1930–59). Zenon Park School in the village dates from 1928. Both the church of Notre-Dame-de-la-Nativitée (the first church constructed in 1913, the present church in 1930) and a convent with a long name, Soeurs-du-Sacré-Coeur-de-la-Charité-de-Notre-Dame-d'Evron (1936), were designated historic sites in 1982–83. The first resident priest was Père Emile Dubois, who came from Rembouillet Seine, near Paris. He was succeeded by Père Pierre Nicolet, from Fribourg, Switzerland. The terms of the resident parish priests have varied from three years to thirty-two years (l'Abbé Armand Arès served from 1930 to 1962). Two Polish priests (Zelinsky and Ulinsky) were posted there in 1970. In 1932, les Soeurs de la Présentation teaching order arrived, followed by les Soeurs Notre Dame d'Evron three years later and les Frères du Sacré Coeur in 1954. The first local priest was ordained in 1946; by the 1980s, at least twenty-three sisters had been recruited locally, serving in eleven religious orders.

A continuing active interest in *la francophonie* has been assured not only through the churches and schools but also through l'Association fransaskoise de Zénon-Parc, l'Association coopérative de Zénon-Parc, and la Caisse populaire Notre Dame limitée (1942), which had assets of over $3 million by the 1980s; l'Hôpital Notre Dame de l'Assomption (1952), staffed by les Soeurs de Notre Dame de Chambriac until 1972 and les Soeurs Grises from 1972 to 1973; a *conseil-régional* of the ACFC; chapters of la Fédération des femmes canadiennes-françaises in 1972 and l'Association jeunesse fransaskoise; the Caisse populaire Notre-Dame de Zénon-Parc; and a French FM radio station. L'Ecole Notre-Dame-des-Vertus is a francophone school, while the bilingual Ecole Zenon Park School offers a French immersion program. In 1976, the National Film Board facilitated development of a series of twenty-five videotaped satellite exchange programs between Zenon Park and Baie-St-Paul, Quebec. Léon Marchildon is a local woodcarver. The local hotel with a restaurant is the Hôtel Rendez-vous. Over in Nipawin, a summer camp—Fête du soleil—is run by Canadian Parents for French, and the town offers French immersion programs at four schools. The settlement became a rich producer and processor of alfalfa during the 1960s with the creation of Zenon Park Co-op Dehydrators in 1961 and Parkland Alfalfa Products in 1968. Zenon Park remains solidly French—close to 90% of the residents claim French origin (87.8% were French origin and 72.5% French speaking in 1971). In 1971, approximately 800 people of French origin were living in Zenon Park and the surrounding rural municipalities of Arborfield and Connaught. Zenon Park townsite was laid out by 1929; the community was incorporated as a village in 1941, and during the 1950s and 1960s it had close to 400 residents, today fewer than half that number (pop. 192 in 2006).

Settlements in the Northwestern Region
While French settlements were developing in the northeastern region of the Saskatchewan prairies, others began to develop in the northwestern region. In 1877, Paroisse St-Vital in Battleford was founded by Père Alexis André and named in honour of Oblate missionary Bishop Vital-Justin Grandin. During the early 1880s, Père Louis Cochin (born in Nancy, Lorraine) established missions to serve Indians and Métis at Cut Knife, Delmas, Cochin (originally Delorme), and Meadow Lake. Onésime Dorval, to become the best known and most respected French-language teacher in the settlements on the northern plains, arrived in Battleford in 1880, having come to the Red River settlement in Manitoba from Quebec three years previously; in 1896, she moved to Batoche and in 1914 to Duck Lake. The Prince brothers, one of whom was to become a senator, began farming in the country immediately northwest of the Battlefords in 1888, having immigrated from St-Gregoire, Quebec. By 1907, immigrants from France had settled at Delmas and Jackfish Lake (where Père Cochin had resettled in 1900 and established

the parish of Ste-Rose-de-Lima) and joined Québécois at Vawn (named partly after two early settlers, Louis Vallière and Joseph Nadeau, who settled the St-Hippolyte district between Vawn and the North Saskatchewan River). St-Hippolyte Church, built in 1911 to replace the original log church of 1905, was moved into Vawn in the late 1950s. Among the priests who served this settlement was Father Theodore Jerome; born to Zenon Jerome and Yvonne Montreuil in the Rosetown area in 1928, he made his vows to the Oblate order in 1957 and served as a parish priest at Arborfield, then Duck Lake and Batoche, and finally at the various parishes of the settlement (including Cochin, Jackfish, Vawn, Edam, and Meota) from 1995 to 2004. People of French origin concentrated on the north side of the river valley around the communities of Vawn (pop. 61 in 2001), Edam (pop. 399 in 2006), Cochin, Jackfish Lake (parish of St-Léon), Cavalier, and Prince (pop. 45). They also concentrated in the districts of Lac-Lavigne (homesteaded in 1905 by Amédée Lavigne, from Quebec) and Lac-Levasseur north and east of Edam; Ruisseau-Charette (Charette Creek), Chemin l'Heureux (l'Heureux Road), and Chemin Blanchette between Vawn and Jackfish Lake; Ness and St. Michael (named after rancher Michel Coté in 1894) to the north; Jubenville at Meota; Nolin (named for Joseph-Octive Nolin, homesteader in 1890), Rosalie Hill (after Rosalie Desjarlais, married at Batoche in 1902), and Chemin Lessard near Prince; St-Hippolyte (parish and post office, 1907) and Nadon (homesteaded by Venance and Joseph Nadon from St-Pierre, Manitoba) west of Vawn (Nadon School District, 1906–28, was renamed St-Cyril); Delorme and Lac-Hélène near Cochin; and Rivière-de-Saules (Crystal Creek) and Pierard farther to the east. And on the opposite (south) side of the river, French Canadians settled around Delmas (pop. 116, parish of St-Jean-Baptiste-de-la-Salle, founded by Père Henri Delmas, who also founded St-Henri Indian Residential School nearby in 1901, served as the postmaster after 1906, and established St-Jean-Baptiste School in Delmas in 1910) and on Iles Caplette, Ile Blais, Iles Michaud (settled in 1918 by Joseph Omer Michaud from Quebec), and Ile Bernier (settled in 1915 by Joseph Bernier from Quebec). Delmas, together with North Battleford, constitutes an ACFC *conseil-régional*, while in 1969 Jackfish with North Battleford became a chapter of la Fédération des femmes canadiennes-françaises. Father Ted Jerome served Cochin, Jackfish, Vawn, Edam, and Meota from 1995 to 2004, after North Battleford, Saskatoon, Prince Albert, and Duck Lake. In 1971, French constituted a large majority at Delmas and Jackfish Lake, almost half of the population (43.5% French origin but a higher proportion—exactly half—French speaking) of Vawn, and over one-quarter (26.4% French origin and 20.9% French speaking) of Edam. This settlement straddling the North Saskatchewan Valley contained over 1,000 people of French origin in 1971 in the communities of Delmas, Vawn, Edam, and Meota and the surrounding rural municipalities of Meota, Turtle River, Battle River, and North Battleford. Another 1,450 lived in the Battlefords. All told, the area of French settlement extends almost forty kilometres from north to south and the same distance from east to west.

Another French settlement to develop in the northwestern region was centred on the village of Marcelin, about midway between North Battleford and Prince Albert. In 1889, Antoine Marcelin, originally from Pont-Chateau, Quebec, immigrated from North Dakota to settle in the Muskeg Lake district west of the present village of Marcelin; later, in 1902, he purchased land where the village now stands. He reportedly attempted to recruit settlers from both France and Quebec. Breton immigrants soon settled in the area, and a school was established in 1906 in the community (originally to be called St-Albert but changed to Marcelin in 1912), and a *paroisse* was organized by Père Lejeunesse. During the 1930s, families from French settlements in the southern regions of the province, driven north by drought and the search for pastures for their livestock, settled among immigrants from France, Quebec, and Michigan in the Moon Hills, part of the Coteau plateau west of Marcelin. Most of the postmasters in the rural district of Aldina, west of the village, were priests who also served the Notre-Dame-de-Pontmain mission on the Muskeg Lake Reserve; Aldina was named after Aldina Venne, the adopted daughter of Antoine Marcelin, the first teacher in the district. This expansive settlement extended westward into the districts of Lac-la-Pèche, Lac-Casavant (where Joseph, Pierre, and Felix Casavant had homesteaded and later the Lamontagne, Boisclair, Lavallee, and Mazon families), and the Alberton area some forty kilometres west of Marcelin. The Alberton district, possibly named after the first postmaster, Justin Albert Fendelet, was settled as early as 1887 by immigrants from France, soon joined by Polish settlers; together they shared the small Holy Ghost Church, dating from 1912. In Alberton School, built the same year, a dispute arose in 1915 over the French teacher using English only part time. A student was elected to clean the schoolhouse once a month, haul water, and fire up the woodstove, for which he was paid two dollars a month (dropped to $1.45 during the Depression). School enrolment was forty-one at the time but had declined to twenty-four by 1947; the school was finally closed in 1961.[17] Many farmers in the district are descendants of the early French settlers (including Fendelet, Desmarais, Similet, Vurcke, Jacques, Lafontaine, Falque, Attrux, Agarand, Janostin). The French-settled area extends southward from Alberton toward Hafford into the Luxemburg district (where a rural post office was named in 1906 by postmaster André Choque, who had immigrated from Luxemburg) and the Whiteberry district (where French-origin farmers included Choque, Limet, Bedier, Taillon). The French settlement also extends north toward Lac-Martin (Martin's Lake, named for François Martin, who had immigrated from Fougères, France, in 1893 and homesteaded there in 1905), Moulin (named after the self-same Père Julien Moulin, who had arrived from Bretagne in 1878 and went on to serve the Métis at Batoche), Damour (named after an early Québécois settler, Gustave-Philippe d'Amour), Beausite, Lac-Adelard, and Lac-Royal (named after homesteader Royal Choquette). West of Hafford, Richard was settled by Emile Richard, from Arthabaska, Quebec, a well-travelled Western Canadian trader who finally settled there in 1901. St-Joseph Church in Marcelin, constructed in 1922 in typical French Canadian style, became a heritage site in 1984. East of Marcelin, francophones settled the Lac-Natal district, and south in the town of Blaine Lake most of the priests of St. Andrew's Roman Catholic Church (1914, today a heritage site) have been French, while the Tallman district just west of town was homesteaded by Donat Parent, from Rimouski, Quebec, in 1907. In 1971, 42.4% of the residents of Marcelin claimed French origin, while 36.1% were francophone. The total number of people of French ethnicity in this extensive area in 1971 could be estimated at about 700, in the village of Marcelin, a few in the towns of Blaine Lake and Hafford, and the rest in the encompassing rural municipalities of Leask, Blaine Lake, Meeting Lake, and Redberry.

Marcelin became an incorporated village in 1911; during the 1920s and 1930s, it had close to 400 residents but declined during the 1970s and currently has 169 residents.

The most extensive French settlement in the northwestern region began to develop in 1909, when labourers and their families—approximately 400 settlers—immigrated from Quebec (mainly les Cantons de l'Est/Eastern Townships, especially Ham-Nord—the place of origin of seventeen families—and Gaspésie) and New England (particularly Maine) to work in the new pulp mills at Big River, where the first parish of Notre-Dame-de-Sacré-Coeur was established that year. By 1912, many French Canadian families were settling around Debden, led by l'Abbé Philippe Antoine Bérubé, who had been the *curé* at Vonda. The first resident priest of Paroisse St-Jean-Baptiste was l'Abbé Laurent Voisin (formerly of Bonne-Madone) in 1912. Construction of the church began in 1917, but the present large church was constructed in 1953. Paroisse Notre-Dame-des-Victoires was established by the omnipresent Abbé Berubé at Victoire, thirteen kilometres by road west of Debden, in 1914. The first nuns taught in *l'école paroissiale* in 1922, but les Soeurs de la Présentation de Marie arrived in Debden in 1942 to teach and do community service; their first convent was replaced by a more substantial edifice three years later. In due course, Debden and the settlement exported a number of Oblate priests as well as nuns in several religious orders. Early community efforts included *le défrichage du terrain* (clearing the land), *la chasse* (hunting) to secure *viande sauvage* (wild game meat), and *l'élevage des moutons* (sheep shearing). Despite the predominant French presence in the area, Debden Post Office and Station were named by railway officials after a community in England. The Debden School District came into being in 1914–15 (originally proposed as Joliette, Frontenac, Duval, or St-Cyr), followed by l'Ecole d'Eldred (1919), le District scolaire de Lac-Winslow, in the village of Mattes (1921–56), and l'Ecole de Wanakena (1922–63). Debden was incorporated as a village in 1922. Former businesses and institutions included *la fromagerie* (cheese factory) in 1924, *le dray livraison de la marchandise* (goods delivery by horse-pulled wagon), *la cour-à-bois* and *le moulin-à-scie* (lumber mills), *l'écurie-de-louage* (stable rental), and *les forgerons* (blacksmith). A branch of la Banque d'Hochelaga was organized in 1920 and the Caisse populaire de Debden in 1939. The French history and identity of the Debden settlement continue to be maintained by the Musée de Debden and Centre culturel fransaskois de Debden, established in 1986, as well as le Comité culturel fransaskois de Debden and Centre communautaire de Debden (which also contains a *clinique de santé* [health clinic]). The town also constitutes a *conseil-régional* of the ACFC/ACF as well as chapters of la Fédération des femmes canadiennes-françaises (since 1974), preceded by le Club des femmes de la communauté (1960), and l'Association jeunesse fransaskoise; le Club pour la conservation de la faune (a wildlife conservation club) was organized in 1977 and l'Age d'or seniors' club in 1972. Paroisse St-Jean-Baptiste is now bilingual. Debden has an *école-fransaskoise*, a French immersion program and preschool. Street signs are bilingual. A community newspaper, *La Voix de Debden*, is published. Both Debden and Leoville have a French network television relay station and a *caisse populaire bilingue*. Debden has a very extensive program of *l'art par les aîné(e)s* (arts for seniors) involving music, dance, *musique-à-bouche* (mouth music), *courtepointe, crochetage, tricotage, dentelle* (various kinds of weaving and needlework), theatrical acting, woodworking, *artisanat* (crafts), fine arts, and sculpture. Clogging and *danse-en-ligne* (line dancing) are taught in Victoire. The Debden library offers bilingual services.

Meanwhile, Spiritwood was initially settled in 1911–12 as a centre for ranching but really grew with the arrival of the railway in 1929. The parish of Sacré-Coeur was established in Spiritwood in 1912. The post office was named in 1923 by its first postmaster, Rupert Dumond, after his former hometown in North Dakota. Spiritwood became an incorporated village in 1935. Several families from the Prud'homme-St-Denis settlement near Saskatoon settled in the Laventure district north of Spiritwood in 1911, where they established St-Bonaventure Parish that year, as well as the Lac-Bérubé district southwest of Debden in 1914. Laventure was named after Octave and Aurèle Laventure, who had settled in the district along with seven sons and two sons-in-law from Wolfe County, Quebec. With the construction of a railway westward through Spiritwood, immigrants from Bapaume, France, settled in a district of the same name immediately west of town in 1929; another railway point farther west was Arleux. Spiritwood, which became a town in 1965, is primarily Anglophone—there is little evidence of a French presence in this mixed community (other than the former Sacré-Coeur Church, now identified as Sacred Heart, and Rivier Elementary School next door).

Leoville (thirty-three kilometres north of Spiritwood and fifty-five kilometres northwest of Debden by road) was named after Leo Carpenter (whose family name had been Charpentier) from Minnesota, who homesteaded there in 1927. A post office and Paroisse Ste-Thérèse-de-l'Enfant-Jésus were established at Leoville in 1930, and the rail line from Debden was completed the next year, bringing francophone settlers from Debden as well as migrants escaping from drought conditions in southern areas, notably the Willow Bunch area. Initially, they were engaged mainly in forestry, but over time agriculture assumed increasing importance as the bush was cleared off the land. Leoville became an incorporated village in 1944. In both Leoville and Spiritwood, the church sign and Mass are now in English only, and no French business is found on the main street.

In 1971, people of French origin comprised slightly over two-thirds (67.2%) of the population of Debden (according to the most recent data, francophones still comprise the same proportion) and almost two-thirds (61.0%) of the residents of Leoville but less than a quarter (23.8%) of the population of Spiritwood, where 18.8% were francophones. Around Debden, the nucleus of the French settlement extended north to Eldred and the districts of Boudreault, Delisle, Park Valley, Bodmin, Lac-Doucet, and Lac-Frenette; east to Lac-Filion, Millard Lake, Stump Lake, and Marchantgrove (named for general storekeeper Henri Marchant); southeast to Mattes and Rue Grimard; south to Lac-Bérubé and Lac-Perran; southwest to Boutin, Happy Valley, Jolie-Prairie, and Rivière-aux-Ecailles or Rivière Coquille (Shell River); west to Victoire and the districts of Ormeaux, Bernadette, Lac-Morin (Parc Régional du Lac-Morin), Lac-Savard, and Pascal. However, French settlement soon extended a lot farther to include areas around Leoville and Spiritwood: Morneau and Capasin between Debden and Leoville (beyond the Big River First Nation) have literally been hacked out of heavy bush in the Big River Valley; the parish church that long marked the location of the farming community of Laventure, together with the districts of Beauvallon, Witchekan, and Lac-Gagné, between Leoville and Spiritwood (formerly called Goupil by the francophones), has been removed to Spiritwood; Bazentin, Ranger, Lac-Eauclair, and Lac-Fafard (named for Père Félix-Adélard-Léon-Fafard, who founded the Frog Lake Mission in 1882 and lost his life during the Frog Lake "massacre") around Leoville; and Bapaume, Moline, Belbutte, and Rastel west of Spiritwood (today Bapaume is a sleepy, heavily wooded little locality revealing no apparent evidence of its French origins). All of these communities and rural districts together formed an extensive French settlement with a combined population of at least 1,100 people of French origin in 1971, in Debden, Leoville, and Spiritwood, and in the surrounding rural municipalities of Canwood and Spiritwood. Currently, Spiritwood has 911 residents, Debden 348, and Leoville 341.

Farther northwest, in 1971, there were about 1,000 people of French origin mixed with originally francophone Métis in the Meadow Lake (once called Lac-des-Prairies) area. Almost two-thirds of them were living in the town of Meadow Lake itself (pop. 4,771 today), where they are served by the parish of Notre-Dame-de-la-Paix (where Père Cochin had established a mission in 1908). Many of the rest were in the vicinity of Makwa (pop. 96), Ruisseau-Morin (Morin Creek), and Nolinville and Ruisseau-Nolin, immediately to the southwest, where they were served by the parish of St-Thomas-Apôtre (the former mission of St-Pierre-Apôtre also served francophones in the Meadow Lake area); 58.3% of the residents of Makwa were of French origin and 48.0% French speaking in 1971. Makwa was first settled prior to the First World War, but the main settlement occurred during the late 1920s through the early 1930s when many francophones migrated north to escape from drought conditions in the southern regions. Makwa-Nord/North Makwa Post Office was established in 1926, followed by Makwa-Sud/South Makwa Post Office in 1939; when the northern post office closed in 1957, the southern one became simply Makwa Post Office. Makwa was designated an incorporated village in 1965. The remainder of the francophones in the region were scattered around the bush districts east and southeast of Meadow Lake: Lac-des-Marais, Cabana (settled by francophones from southern Saskatchewan—Willow Bunch, St-Victor, Coderre, and Dollard—around the mission of St-Girard organized in 1935 by the Oblate missionary priest Père J.B. Cabana, today a heritage site), Lac-Huard, Lac-des-Joncs, Lac-Eauclaire, Chitek Lake, St-Léon at Sergent (named for Léon Victor Sergent, who had been born in Paris in 1884 and settled there in 1908), Lac-St-Cyr, Prendergast, Rivière-Lavigne, Lac-des-Iles; and farther north around Lac-l'Heureux and Nault or Lac-Mudie (named for the first postmaster, Aimé Nault, in 1911); Napoleon, St-Pascal, and Lac-Poisson-Blanc around Lac-Vert (Green Lake, where Père Julien Moulin established St-Julien Mission in 1890); and the mission of Ste-Marguerite-Marie at Canoe Lake.

In addition to the French and Métis of the Meadow Lake area, in 1971 there were some 365 people claiming French origin in the Paradise Hill (Butte-Paradis) area west of St. Walburg, in these two communities, and in the rural municipality of Frenchman Butte. Following early Métis presence on *la petite montagne de la piche*, on the Carlton Trail, this settlement developed primarily from 1910 to 1914 with the arrival of French-speaking settlers from southwestern France and Bretagne. Paradise Hill was named before 1900 for the high plateau on which the community sits by brothers Ernest and Alphonse Beliveau, recently returned from the Yukon goldfields. The French settlers concentrated to the southeast in the rural district of Butte-St-Pierre, where St-Pierre Church was originally located in 1924, yet it was eventually moved into the village of Paradise Hill in 1973; all that remains at Butte-St-Pierre is the cemetery. The interior of Notre-Dame-des-Douleurs (Our Lady of Sorrows) is lavishly decorated with paintings by Count Imhoff. This general area of French settlement includes the surrounding rural districts of Archie (Lac-LeClair), Lac-LeBosse, Lac-Belliveau, Frenchman Butte, Pyramid Hill, Ste-Marguerite (with Marguerite School District and Mariaville cemetery), Emmaville, Sandall (Butte-St-Pierre), Monnery, Charlotte, Butte-du-Cheval, Butte-des-Français, Tangleflags, and the missions of St-François-Régis near Frenchman Butte and Notre Dame-du-Rosaire at Onion Lake. However, in 1971, French residents of Paradise Hill had already declined to 15.4%, and just 11.6% were francophones. The present townsite of Paradise Hill was laid out in 1928; the community became an incorporated village in 1947. A prosperous and consistently growing community, Paradise Hill had 234 residents in 1957, 344 in 1971, 455 in 1991, and 483 in 2006. Little evidence remains, though, of the French presence in the area, other than the family names of many farmers particularly in the Butte-St-Pierre district (e.g., Laboucane, Larre, Labrecque, St-Amant, Desilets, Villeneuve, Marchadour, Gaboury, Bertrand, Beauvillier, Theberge, Bonnet, Duriez …). The now-deserted LeGrand stone farmhouse in the district was a fine example of the work of stonemason Karl Gortzyk, who immigrated from Germany in 1927, as were his construction of the neighbouring Roussel farmhouse and tiny Holy Trinity Anglican Church at Deer Creek in 1935 with the assistance of farmer Jean LeGrand, who had been a baker in Quimper, Brittany, before emigrating in 1910 with his wife, Marie, and their eight children—Marie had yearned for a stone farmhouse like the ones in their native Brittany. Their youngest daughter, Genevieve Etcheverry, reminisces that her parents were "proudly French but not French-Canadian."[18]

Finally, two other small localities where French settled in west-central Saskatchewan should be noted. The Cochery district near Duperow, immediately southwest of Biggar, was settled by Hilaire de Moissac, who first immigrated from Nantes, Lorraine, to St-Claude, Manitoba, in 1900, then to Saskatchewan in 1906. The St-Hilaire-de-Cochery cemetery dates from 1911, the church from 1916 to 1971. The short-lived Bouillon School District near Harris (1913) was settled by francophone farmers from Manitoba, and the Roman Catholic parish priest at Harris from 1907 to 1911 was Father Bouillon; however, almost all had left by the mid-1920s, and the school was closed in 1922. The mission of Ste-Anne-des-Prairies at Delisle was served by the parish of Notre-Dame-du-Bon-Conseil at Tessier. However, francophones were few in number in the region, despite the French names of these communities (Tessier was named for a local doctor) and parishes.

THE SOUTHERN SETTLEMENTS
Settlements in the Southeastern Region
The earliest French settlements in southern Saskatchewan developed in the southeastern region. Doubtless the first of these settlements was the most interesting. A French-speaking aristocrat from Alsace, Dr. Rudoph Armand Meyer, arrived in Whitewood (formerly known as Coquille-Pillé) in 1884 to establish a settlement of Swiss farmers in the area. In 1889, he sold fourteen sections of farmland in the Pipestone (Pierre-à-Pipe) Valley sixteen kilometres southwest of Whitewood to eleven French and Belgian aristocrats. Together they developed the St-Hubert or La Rolanderie settlement. The

parish of St-Hubert (1889) and the convent of Ste-Jeanne-d'Arc were organized, and the convent school that operated from 1920 to 1924 was soon replaced by a nursing home from 1924 to 1967; the present church of St-Hubert was dated to 1935 and, together with the cemetery, turned into a heritage site in 1990. Branch missions served from St-Hubert in 1909 were St-Luc at Whitewood, St-Nom-de-Marie at Broadview, and St-Bernard at Moosomin, while Beynes (named after a community west of Paris) comprised an early school district. The priest later serving the parish and missions belonged to la Communauté des Fils de Marie-Immaculée, while the nuns in charge of *l'école publique* and *l'hospice pour personnes âgées* belonged to les Soeurs de Notre-Dame-de-la-Croix. Imposing homes were constructed, including Ranche St-Hubert, Château Bellevue of Count de Jumilhac, and Château Richelieu of Count de Sauras; at Bird's Point on Round Lake in the Qu'Appelle Valley (about thirty-five kilometres to the north), a large stone home was built in 1892–93 for Viscount Charles de Cazes, who homesteaded there in 1883.[19] Whole families were imported from France and Belgium to work for the aristocrats; they included house domestics, gardeners, craftsmen, horse grooms, and tenant farmers. Horse-racing days, held in conjunction with nearby Cannington Manor, where English gentry had settled, were especially popular social events. When the French counts visited their English counterparts, they did so in fine style—in coaches accompanied by coachmen and footmen wearing top hats. In lieu of fox hunting, coyotes were hunted with imported purebred dogs and thoroughbred horses. Expensive wines and foodstuffs, plus many other luxuries, were also imported. Gala balls were held; a brass band was formed. At its apogee, the colony numbered some 150. However, the curious colony was not without its problems. Cattle, sheep, and horse ranching was largely unsuccessful, as were brush-making and cheese factories and chicory and sugar beet farming. Count de Saurras developed a sheep ranch with 2,000 imported sheep linked with cheese production; a cattle ranch also imported stock. The Bellevue French Coffee Company was established by Baron van Brabant and Count de Roffignac; chicory grown on the Bellevue farm was dried, mixed with imported coffee, and packaged in a plant that unfortunately burned down in 1891. Subsequently, Van Brabant used Château Richelieu to develop the Richelieu French Coffee brand, but it had limited success; soon the buildings and extensive landholdings lay idle as the enterprise ran into major financial difficulty. By 1905, Archbishop Langevin had personally intervened, selling the company to les Missionaires de Chavagnes in Brittany, who nonetheless never proceeded to revive the operation or to bring over more immigrants. Two graduates in agriculture from the Université de Louvain in Belgium did arrive respectively in 1908 and 1911. Meyer, disillusioned, returned to France within five years, followed by the other aristocrats, the last of whom left in 1913.[20] But their entourage did remain to be joined by settlers from many parts of France and Belgium as well as from the Fannystelle area in Manitoba; together they settled St-Hubert and the Beynes district. They are quite widely scattered, but farmers with French surnames (e.g., Boutin, Dumonceaux, Jeannot, Beaujot, Poncelet, Payot) are still found around St-Hubert.

Nearby, other small rural settlements of French immigrants came into existence. Immigrants from the Lyons region in France settled around Dumas (about thirty-five kilometres southeast of St-Hubert), with the arrival of the railway in 1906; this community was named after the prominent French writers Alexandre Dumas *père et fils*. French farmers (e.g., Bourgon, Beauchesne, Bourhis, Filteau, Baudu, Jacques, de Nevers, Brehart) are primarily concentrated in the countryside between Dumas and northeast to Vandura. Paroisse Notre-Dame-de-Pitié (originally the mission of Notre-Dame-de-l'Espérance) is in Dumas, while St-François-Xavier is in Wawota. West of Dumas, the Belleville district was named in 1920 by Emile LeDressay, an immigrant from Brittany. L'Orignal was another district. And, in the Moose Mountain area farther west, Edmonde Zenoide Beaudin, from Laprairie, Quebec, was a homesteader in 1894. Similar to La Rolanderie, French aristocrats Pierre and Charles-Henri Brenon settled just to the west and attempted unsuccessful ventures such as fur farming. Other French-settled districts in the Moose Mountain area were Couléeville and Neuve-Chapelle and Ste-Marie School District southwest of Moosomin (1887). In 1971, the total population of French origin in these small settlements was about 300 in the areas around St-Hubert and Dumas and scattered in nearby towns and villages (including Whitewood, Wawota, and Kennedy), where they comprised a small minority, and in the rural municipalities of Silverwood, Willowdale, Kingsley, and Wawken. Dumas once had eleven businesses and services, but the railway line was abandoned in 1961; by the 1980s, only the rural *bureau de poste* was left. Although a French school once served Dumas, it never had many students, and the school at Kennedy (where the parish of Ste-Anne was situated) taught only in English.

Where the Qu'Appelle River crosses into Manitoba and joins the Assiniboine River, French settlers followed in the footsteps of the francophone fur traders and Métis who had settled there a century earlier. The settlement around Ste-Marthe-Rocanville was actually an adjunct to the larger St-Lazare settlement across the border, which dated back to Métis settlement; the Métis were joined by French immigrants (served by a priest from Reims) in 1904. The first church of Ste-Marthe was built in 1908 and was designated a parish a couple of years later; it was destroyed by fire in 1925, so a new church was constructed in 1927. The pioneering parish priest was l'Abbé J.C. Passaplan, born in Hauteville, Switzerland; he died at la Vallée-St-Joseph in 1929 at seventy-two years of age. Other districts in the settlement included Ruisseau-Chasse and Martheton. With the closure of the community school (down to only twenty-three students by the early 1950s) and post office, the church was also closed in 1965, and the parishioners merged with those of St-Alphonse in the nearby town of Rocanville, named after August Honoré Rocan Bastien, an original settler in 1884 and the first postmaster, from St-Vincent-de-Paul, Quebec.[21] In 1971, the French population of the settlement on the Saskatchewan side of the provincial boundary might have numbered some 200 (however, another 750 were just across the border in Manitoba, so this francophone settlement as a whole had a population of almost 1,000). At the time, only fifty-five of the 955 residents of the town of Rocanville were French. Rocanville had become an incorporated village as early as 1904 but did not achieve town status until 1967; in 2006, it had a population of 869. The celebrated sculptor Joe Fafard hails from the extended Fafard family of this settlement (other early settlers were Gagnon, DeCorby, Blondeau, Fouillard, DeCelles, van der Bussche).

Many of the French bloc settlements in the southeastern region were formed because of the colonization schemes of Jean Gaire. Gaire immigrated from Alsace to St-Boniface in 1888. After visiting the Wolseley area in southern Saskatchewan that year, he returned to France the following year to recruit potential settlers (and another eight times between 1897 and 1906), envisioning a francophone settlement of over 1,000 settlers, with the approval of Archbishop Langevin. Gaire founded la Société générale de l'oeuvre de la colonization catholique française du Canada in 1904 (an investment company to purchase farmland for resale to approved French Catholic settlers) and la Société de la ferme du clergé français (for French-speaking clergy to invest in reserved farmland) in 1905; however, the following year these grand schemes were effectively curtailed by the Canadian government, and Gaire was warned by the Roman Catholic hierarchy, terminating recruitment in Europe; by 1911, funds were exhausted. Responding to advertisements in French journals, French and Belgian immigrants first established the small colony of Grande-Clairière in Manitoba in 1890, then the communities of Cantal (Paroisse St-Raphael, 1902; les Soeurs de Notre-Dame-de-la-Croix Convent, 1949) and Bellegarde (Paroisse St-Maurice, 1899) in Saskatchewan respectively in 1892 and 1893–94. Gaire persuaded more settlers to move to these new parishes from Grande-Clairière. The original twenty-two founding households of Cantal grew to almost 100 parishioners within a decade. A new stone church of St-Raphael was completed in Cantal in 1914, with stone buttresses and a unique shingled bell tower. Cantal was named after the Cantal area in Auvergne, southern France, and Bellegarde after a parish near the Haute-Savoie birthplace of an early settler, Cyrille Sylvestre. The settlement, situated in the southeastern corner of Saskatchewan, expanded to include Wauchope (Paroisse St-François-Régis, which became the home of Gaire until his death in 1928, and the convent and school of les Soeurs de Notre-Dame-de-la-Croix) from 1901 to 1913, Storthoaks (Paroisse St-Antoine-des-Prairies was organized in 1899, and rural districts included St-Edmond and St-Thomas), Alida by 1912–13, and finally Redvers (where Paroisse Notre-Dame-de-Fatima was not organized until 1950). The original settlers included a few Métis families, but most immigrated directly from Belgium (Luxembourg and Hainaut provinces) and France (Bretagne, Lorraine, Provence, Auvergne, and Bourgogne) in 1894–99; later settlers arrived from Quebec. Until 1900, a number of families moved back to Grande-Clairière each winter. By 1905, there were 175 farmers around Bellegarde, many of them Belgians. The community was bypassed by the railway line in 1901, and when the first church burned down in 1905 the priest suggested moving the community north on the railway line, but that district had already been settled by anglophone Protestants. Five homesteads had already been established around Wauchope before the arrival of the railway line in 1901. An influential early settler in Wauchope was Maurice Quennelle, who homesteaded in 1902 and became a general merchant and postmaster. An early Belgian settler was Alphonse Tinant, who settled there with his brother Auguste, while another brother, Gaston, settled farther west near Ponteix in 1912. By 1911, two-thirds of the residents of Wauchope were francophones. The Lebel School District west of Alida was named in 1907 after Ferdinand and Marianne Lebel from Victoriaville, Quebec, and the St-Thomas School District at Storthoaks was named in 1903 after trustee Thomas Boulet from St-Isidore, Dorchester, Quebec; the Quebec School District southwest of Wauchope was established in 1907; and the Middleburg School District south of Wauchope was named in 1916 by Francis Ed D'autremont after a school in Iowa where his father had taught—his brother George settled in the Lac-D'autremont (Dautremont Lake) district to the south. Another rural district within the settlement was Chapelle.

CHAPTER 7

In 1971, the settlement included more than 1,300 people of French origin, in the communities of Redvers, Storthoaks, Alida, and Antler and in the rural municipalities of Storthoaks, Reciprocity, and Antler. The hamlets of Bellegarde and Cantal remain strongly French (in fact, the former has been called *la capital du Pétit-Québec*), yet francophones actually comprised fewer than half (48.1%) of the residents of Bellegarde. Residents of French origin comprised about three-quarters of the population in Wauchope, half (52.9%) at Storthoaks (but surprisingly French speakers were 57.1%), fewer than a third (31.9%) at Alida (where francophones were only 19.6%), and about a quarter at Redvers (22.7%—and 21.3% francophone) and Antler (exactly 25.0% French origin but 26.1% francophone). Today the town of Redvers (an incorporated village in 1904 and a town in 1960) has 878 residents, the villages of Alida (incorporated in 1926) 106, Storthoaks (incorporated in 1910) eighty-two, and Antler (incorporated in 1905) only forty, and the organized hamlet of Bellegarde forty-five; Wauchope is a small hamlet. Fertile, just east of Storthoaks on the Manitoba border, was settled in 1905 and called Council Post Office in 1911 but renamed in 1915; it had a school in 1914, a grain elevator, and a general store, but the community is virtually gone now. L'Association communautaire francophone de Bellegarde has helped to maintain a French interest in the settlement, as have an FM radio station, a chapter of la Fédération des femmes canadienne-françaises in 1971, an *école francophone*, l'Ecole de Bellegarde, and la Maison culturelle de Bellegarde. There is a *caisse populaire bilingue* located in each of Bellegarde, Storthoaks, and Redvers.

In 1892, Gaire also founded the settlement of Forget (named after the first lieutenant governor of Saskatchewan, Amédée-Emmanuel Forget), situated just east of Stoughton. The first settlers arrived from many regions in France, particularly from Lorraine and Dauphiné, as well as from the province of Luxembourg in Belgium. More settlers of Belgian origin arrived from a Belgian settlement around Bathgate and Joliette in Pembina County, North Dakota, still others from a Belgian settlement in Manitoba as well as from Michigan. Forget became a waystation for Belgian settlement in Saskatchewan; in fact, the Belgian government established a consular office there by 1911 (later transferred to nearby Manor from 1915 to 1921). In 1913, the vice consul, Gaston de Jardin, established an insurance office and implement dealership and served as secretary-treasurer of the village. The first postmaster, who likely chose the name for the community in 1904 (previously it was called Alma), was Frank Zoel de Gagné. La Salette School District, recognizing les Missionaires de Notre-Dame de la Salette religious order (founded in France in 1852), which came to Forget in 1899, functioned from 1902 to 1958; the local parish was Notre-Dame-de-la-Salette. The school emphasized a classical humanities education. The community was also served by la Congrégation des Soeurs de Notre-Dame de la Croix (a religious order founded in France in 1832), whose convent was opened in 1905–06, along with l'Académie St-Joseph.[22] South of Forget, the Menard district was settled by and named after William Menard, from Michigan; he donated the site for St. Francis de Sales Church and cemetery and served as a trustee of Menard School (1915). To the northeast, the rural Alma Post Office functioned from 1897 to 1904. Forget became an incorporated village in 1904. It once had thriving businesses and more than 300 residents but underwent rapid decline after the Depression: l'Académie-St-Joseph finally closed in 1964; the number of residents was halved during the 1960s (from 221 in 1961 to 118 in 1971); in 1985, the last remaining grain elevator closed, and in 1990 the railway was abandoned and the tracks torn up. In 1971, there were 175 people of French origin in this small settlement, in Forget, the nearby town of Stoughton, the Quebec and Menard rural districts, and the rural municipalities of Tecumseh and Brock. Yet they comprised only a quarter of the population in the small village of Forget itself, and francophones comprised only one in five residents (20.8%). Today only forty residents are left in Forget. However, the lovely church of Notre-Dame-de-la-Salette remains; the former rectory (1904) has been renovated as a centre for the arts; and Forget has survived as a dynamic artistic community. An annual summer arts festival is held there in July. The present owners of the Happy Nun bookstore and café also run the Arthouse, Blue Nun, and Seven Sisters bed and breakfast.

The settlement of Montmartre (Paroisse Sacré-Coeur-de-Jésus) began to develop some twenty-five kilometres southwest of Wolseley in 1893. Jean Gaire founded the parish of Ste-Anne-du-Loup at Wolseley in 1888. The settlers came from Montmartre, today an integral part of Paris, as well as other regions in France and Quebec, under the auspices of la Société Foncière du Canada, which constructed a *grande maison* while providing settlers with little assistance; it was demolished in 1901. A butter and cheese enterprise founded by two Belgian entrepreneurs in 1894 survived, whereas another Belgian rancher found his land repossessed by the government in 1906, forcing him to return temporarily to Belgium. In 1971, the settlement included almost 600 French living in and around the village of Montmartre, which was little more than one-third (39.8%) French in 1971 and 35.3% francophone, the hamlet of Candiac (Paroisse St-Joseph), the nearby town of Wolseley, and the surrounding rural districts in Montmartre RM, including Lac-Marguerite (named after Marie-Marguerite, the daughter of early settler Octave Hennequin), Mutrie (named after the sister of Joseph Mutrie, the postmaster at Wolseley at the time), Lac-Chapleau (named after Sir Joseph-Adolphe Chapleau, a former premier and at the time the lieutenant governor of Quebec, who visited the settlement in 1894), Lac-Kleczkowski (named after the consul general for France, who visited with Chapleau), Butte-aux-Poules, Butte-de-Tête-d'Homme, Très-Ste-Trinité mission at Cedoux, Vallée-du-Renaud-Rouge at Sintaluta, and Joffre (named for Joseph-Jacques-Césaire Joffre, a commander of the French army during the First World War). The Mutrie district, some twenty kilometres by road southeast of Montmartre, was first settled by Cyril Caron in 1885. The first Mass was celebrated in 1904 by Père J-A. Theriault in the Caron home. The church, Notre Dame-de-Bonsecours (Our Lady of Good Help), was constructed in 1907 (replaced by a new church in 1943), the rectory in 1913, and the general store in 1921. Incidentally, the first teacher in Alpha School was Jim Gardiner, later the premier of Saskatchewan and the federal minister of agriculture. The small community of Mutrie had been virtually abandoned by the late 1960s; today the district is settled by scattered French and Polish farmers. Montmartre has a *caisse populaire bilingue*. Montmartre Post Office was established in 1894, and the community was incorporated as a village in 1908. In 1966, there were 566 residents; currently, there are 413, but Candiac has only twenty. During the early 1950s, more than 200 students were in the care of les Soeurs de Notre-Dame-de-la-Croix in the *couvent*, *école publique*, and *pensionnat*. Reinforcing its French identity, a miniature Eiffel Tower was constructed in this "Paris of the Prairies" in 2009.

Another small French settlement developed about fifty kilometres to the west, around the village of Sedley (Paroisse Notre-Dame-de-Grace), named after Winnipeg lawyer Sedley Blanchard, whose family owned the townsite, and the rural district of Béchard, named after settler Abraham Béchard, whose extended family immigrated from St-Jacques-le-Mineur, Quebec, and the milltown of Manchester, New Hampshire. More francophone farmers arrived in 1906, the year before Sedley was incorporated as a village. The Sisters of Loretto taught at the large brick girls' boarding school from the 1920s through the 1960s. Residents of French origin constituted a very small proportion (only 11.1%) of the residents of Sedley back in 1971—they claimed that they were *pas forts, mais pas morts* (not strong, but not yet dead). The total number of people of French origin at the time was only 160 in Sedley and the rural municipalities of Francis, Lajord, and South Qu'Appelle. The old Sedley School (1923) was made a heritage site in 1997. As of 2006, Sedley had 319 residents.

French Canadians continued to supplement the Métis in the Qu'Appelle Valley. As noted, the mission of St-Florent at Lebret was established in 1866. Soon an extensive network of missions developed, widely scattered throughout the general region, serving both francophones and the local Aboriginal population: Sacré-Coeur-de-Lac-Qu'Appelle, Notre-Dame-de-Bon-Conseil, St-Félix-de-Valois, Sacré-Coeur-de-Marie at Marieval (named by Père Perreault, the first postmaster in 1909, who was followed by seven more francophone priests), Notre-Dame-des-Anges. ... Francophones also named Point-Fayant at Lebret, the Violette district near Balcarres, Pechet near Lipton, Hugonard, Denomie Point.... The Jasmin area, some fifty-five kilometres directly north of Lebret, was settled by Métis and French during the 1880s. St-Joseph-de-Dauphinais School was established there in 1887, and the Jasmin School District operated from 1909 to 1965 (early settlers included Lusignan, Morin, Carrière, Boucher, Martineau, Bonin, Carion, Hamelin). The French proportion in Lebret (pop. 203 in 2006) has fallen to only a small fraction (17.2% French origin and 10.7% French speaking in 1971); in other towns and villages of the general area, French constitute a small minority. But all told, people of French origin in the immediate Lebret area could be estimated at not more than 245 in 1971, including the village of Lebret, the nearby town of Fort Qu'Appelle, and the rural municipalities of North Qu'Appelle and Abernethy.

In the Val-Souris (Souris River Valley) west of Estevan, Métis were joined by immigrants from Auvergne and Languedoc in France and some Belgians. The town of Radville (originally intended to be named Conradville after Conrad Paquin, an original homesteader) had its beginning in 1905. In 1971, there were almost 800 people of French origin in the Radville area, including the town of Radville and the rural municipalities of Laurier and the Gap, yet French constituted little more than a third of the total population of Radville (36.8% French origin and 21.3% francophone). Although the Radville area now has a mixed population, the French presence is still represented in the Catholic church (Paroisse Ste-Famille), street names (two main streets are Labbie and Laurier), and a school served by les Religieuses de St-Louis (a 1953 report on francophone schools noted that 208 of 260 students were French or Belgian, but just fifty-two were enrolled in the ACFC course). The surrounding rural municipality of Laurier and neighbouring RMs contained the districts of Dandonneau (settled by the family of Octave Dandonneau from St-Bartholémy, Quebec, in 1911), Bourassa (named by

Lindorph-Joseph Bourassa, from L'Acadie, Quebec, in 1907), Paroisse Ste-Colette (1934, today a heritage site occupied by the local Lacadia Club; Lacadia School District, which operated from 1911 to 1972, was named after l'Acadie, Quebec), the Oblate mission of Notre-Dame-de-Bonsecours (1909), Reims, St-Olivier, and Val-Souris (Souris Valley, served by Paroisse Ste-Germaine from 1907 to 1970, made a heritage site in 1984, and now housing the Souris Valley Cooperative Memorial Club), and farther to the south the village of Beaubier and the Lorraine district. Farther down the Souris Valley, immigrants from Belgium worked in a brickyard in Weyburn, where their neighbourhood became known as "Belgium town"; still farther, Belgians from North Dakota worked as coal miners and farmers around Roche Percée (Coalfields Post Office and School, 1896), Estevan (Oblate mission of St-Jean-Baptiste, 1909), and Nivelle (school district, 1917–48). Radville was incorporated as a village in 1911 and a town just a couple of years later; as of 2006, it had 755 residents, down from over 1,000 in 1981.

Settlements in the South-Central Region
After the foundation of French settlements throughout the southeastern region, similar settlements rapidly came into existence in the south-central and southwestern regions, so that by 1910 a continuous series of French settlements stretched across southern Saskatchewan. Again the clergy played a key role in this colonization process. L'Abbé Marie-Albert Royer, *curé* of the parish of Ponteix in Auvergne, emigrated to St-Boniface in 1906, then set out to serve a small French-speaking community in Saskatchewan, Gauthierville or Villeroy, on Rivière-la-Vieille (Wood River). He moved farther west that year because of the arrival of l'Abbé Louis-Pierre-Joseph Gravel (born in Princeville, Nicolet, Quebec, in 1868) with Québécois colonists from the Eastern Townships (Victoriaville etc.) at nearby Ste-Philomène (later Gravelbourg). L'Abbé Gravel had impressive credentials: he had been appointed "missionary-colonizer" of southern Saskatchewan by Archbishop Langevin of St-Boniface and was reportedly a personal friend of Prime Minister Laurier, who materially aided his colonization schemes, aimed at luring Québécois to the prairies as an alternative to the milltowns of New England; Laurier's minister, Clifford Sifton, advocated the "repatriation" of French who had been lured to the industrial centres of New England by the hope of employment and their resettlement in Western Canada.[23] He was further assisted by his brothers Emile and Henri, who led the colonists by wagon train from Moose Jaw (Louis-Pierre-Joseph had arrived with his five brothers and a sister). L'Abbé Gravel supervised expansion of the settlement to include the parishes of Ste-Radegonde at Lafleche (named after Louis-François Richer *dit* Laflèche (1818–98), a missionary to the Métis and later the bishop of Trois-Rivières in Quebec) in 1906–08 (the present church, noted for its cruciform rose-tinted windows illuminating the aisles, was completed in 1922 and designated a heritage site in 1993), Sts-Coeurs Jésus-et-Marie at Mazenod (named after Bishop Charles Eugene de Mazenod of Marseilles, France, founder of the Oblate Order, which served many of the French communities in Western Canada) in 1907–08, and Notre-Dame-de-Lourdes at Meyronne (named after Meyronne, France, formerly Le Pinto) in 1908 (where les Soeurs de Jésus-Marie taught school). The street names in Laflèche are French Canadian and Québécois (e.g., Montcalm, Cartier, Papineau, Bigot, Brunelle, Frontenac, Québec, Laurier, La Salle, Champlain). The teachers at Ecole Mathieu at

Laflèche belonged to les Soeurs de St-André-de-la-Puye (also known as les Filles de la Croix), who arrived in 1915. But by the 1950s, Abbé Ducharme reported that just eighty of 143 students at Laflèche were enrolled in the ACFC program.

The settlement expanded rapidly into a cohesive francophone bloc settlement, inclusive of many strongly French rural districts: Gauthier and Poulin north of Gravelbourg; Lefort (named after Adélard Lefort, from Notre-Dame-de-Stanbridge, Quebec, in 1905) between Gravelbourg and Mazenod; Gagnier and Marquette south of Mazenod; Valence, Ruisseau–La Berge, and Assomption-de-la-Vierge south and southeast of Laflèche; Baie-Gaumond, Bois-Lagassé, and Pelletier between Gravelbourg and Laflèche; Melaval and Gollier east and southeast of Laflèche; Bonvouloir and Wood River near Woodrow, between Laflèche and Meyronne; Ruisseau-Gavelin and Ruisseau-Laville (settled by homesteaders from Switzerland in 1910) south and southwest of Meyronne; Vindictive, northwest of Meyronne; Royer (named after colonizing priest Père Royer) and Arbuthnot (formerly called Vieux Bouvier), north of Meyronne; Armorin and Aussant west of Gravelbourg; Carrignan, Piché, and Petit-Nord (later Coppen) to the northwest and the Poulin cabin (ruins of a trapper's cabin dating from the early 1930s, now a historic site) to the northeast. Gravelbourg itself grew into a major French centre, gaining the Couvent de Jésus-et-Marie in 1917–18, a "collège-classique" (Collège Mathieu) in 1918, la Co-Cathédrale de Ste-Philomène, renamed Notre-Dame-de-l'Assomption in 1965 (with murals painted in 1921–31 by Père Charles Maillard, who had been born in France in 1873 and served as a parish priest from 1917 to 1929) and bishop's residence in 1918–19, a monastery in 1926 and seminary (Grand Séminaire Mazenod) in 1931, and a couple of French-language radio stations in 1952; Ecole Beau-Soleil is the centre for the Gravelbourg French-language le Conseil scolaire fransaskois de la vieille.[24]

French immersion programs are conducted at l'Ecole Elémentaire de Gravelbourg and l'Ecole Secondaire de Gravelbourg, while le Service fransaskois de formation aux adultes offers adult education in French. Today the cathedral, bishop's residence, college, and convent have all been designated as historic sites. The diocese has always maintained close links with French Canada; the first bishop, Bishop Villeneuve, became the archbishop of Quebec and a cardinal, and later bishops became the archbishops of Moncton, New Brunswick, and Ottawa. Le Conseil des francophones de Gravelbourg, le Centre culturel Maillard, le Conseil des arts Maillard, the *bureau-régional* of l'Assemblée communautaire fransaskoise, l'Association communautaire fransaskoise de Gravelbourg, Radio communautaire francophone de Gravelbourg (CFRG, the sole French-language FM radio station in Saskatchewan), chapters of la Fédération des femmes canadiennes-françaises (since 1968), l'Association jeunesse fransaskoise, and l'Assemblée communautaire fransaskois (formerly l'Association culturelle franco-canadienne de la Saskatchewan), as well as a *caisse populaire bilingue*, have all served the francophone community, while le Musée de Gravelbourg, le Lien–Centre fransaskois de ressources culturelles et pédagogiques at Collège Mathieu, le Centre communautaire des arts de Gravelbourg, les Danseurs de la Rivière-Vieille, les Cireux d'Semelles, Maison Soucy, and Café Paris ensure continuing interest in the French presence. Hôpital St-Joseph, Foyer d'Youville, and LaBerge Dental Clinic provide health services in French. Emphasizing its French character, Gravelbourg is now advertised as *un avant-goût de l'Europe dans les prairies* (a touch of Europe in the prairies).

In 1971, there were over 1,800 French Canadians in the Gravelbourg area, including the towns of Gravelbourg and Laflèche, several hamlets, and the rural municipalities of Gravelbourg, Sutton, Wood River, and Pinto Creek. In the town of Gravelbourg, they comprised about two-thirds of the total population (64.9% of the residents were of French descent, 57.7% francophones). At Laflèche, more than a third of the residents were French (37.8%, yet just 16.1% were francophones). The Laflèche and District Museum contains an impressive collection of historical artifacts. And in the village of Meyronne, just over a third of the residents were French (38.7% French origin but just 14.3% French speaking). A French-language school, Ecole Mathieu, was located there. Gravelbourg was incorporated as a village in 1912 and became a town four years later; it now has just over 1,000 residents (1,089 in 2006). Laflèche became an incorporated village in 1913 but not a town until 1953; it now has 370 residents and like Gravelbourg is losing population. Meyronne, incorporated in 1913, lost its village status in 2006, when it was down to just thirty-five residents (it had grown rapidly from 109 residents in 1916 to 357 just ten years later). Similarly, few residents remain in Mazenod (twenty-six in 2001) and Woodrow (just fifteen left); these communities were incorporated respectively in 1917 and 1913, but both lost their status as villages in 2002.

While Gravelbourg was first coming into existence in 1906–07, settlers from St-Gabriel-de-Brandon and l'Acadie, Quebec, were joining the Métis at Willow Bunch (Talle-de-Saules), about eighty kilometres to the southeast by 1902. Originally, the Métis preferred to settle on the hill slopes, whereas the French preferred the more fertile farmland below the hills; for many years, the two groups settled separately, for the most part, so that parallel patterns of settlement were evident, but eventually with increasing intermarriage between them the distinction between Métis and French became less obvious.[25] Within ten years, the settlement had expanded to include an extensive area. Yet the surrounding rural districts remain strongly French. Francophone parishes and missions in this settlement have included St-Ignace-des-Saules at Willow Bunch (1906), St-Victor (1906, named after the first parish priest, Père Victor Rahard), the mission of la Rivière-aux-Trembles at Little Woody (1907), Ste-Thérèse-de-l'Enfant-Jésus at Lisieux (1916, originally called St-Joseph-des-Poissons or simply Joeville after Joseph-Hermenegilde Préfontaine, whose family were early settlers in this area), Notre-Dame-de-Lourdes with Ecole Lourdes at Verwood (1919), the mission of Notre-Dame-du-Perpétuel-Secours at Coronach (1929), and l'Assomption-de-la-Sainte-Viérge at Maxstone. Les Soeurs de Jésus-Marie and les Soeurs Grises taught school at Lisieux. Abbé Roger Ducharme, inspector of francophone schools throughout southern Saskatchewan during the 1950s and 1960s, was born at St-Victor in 1919 to parents from St-Cléophas-de-Brandon and St-Gabriel-de-Brandon, Quebec. All of the priests serving St-Georges Parish at Assiniboia (1913), and most serving Our Lady of Perpetual Help mission at Coronach (ca. 1919), St-Jean/St. John's Parish at Rockglen (1917), and Christ-Roi/Christ the King Parish at Fife Lake (1908 mission, 1928 parish) have been French (this parish consisted primarily of francophones from France, Belgium, and Quebec, some Métis, as well as Germans, Irish, and Poles). The latter ended as a parish in 1965, and the church was finally closed in 1977. Other francophone districts within the settlement included Bonneauville and Lac-Bonneau (after early rancher Pascal Bonneau from St-Brigitte-d'Iberville, Quebec), Lautier (after Jules-Louis-Jean Lautier, who immigrated from Paris to homestead there in 1905), Ruisseau-Girard and Lac-Rivard (after homesteader Alexandre Rivard) to the southeast; Marie Hill at Coronach; Lacordaire south of Rockglen; Loraine and Lac-Labatte near Big Muddy; St-Alexis west of Willow Bunch; Little Woody and Twin Valley east of Lisieux; Bayard southwest of Lisieux; Maisonneuve, Villefranche, and Montcalm near St-Victor; and Butte-de-Cheval-Caille farther west. The Couvent des Filles-de-la-Croix (1914) in Willow Bunch is today the local museum; both it and the rectory (1927) were designated as heritage properties in 1986–88. The sisters left in 2001 after eighty-seven years of service. Le Musée Beau Village in St-Victor documents the area's early Métis history and the arrival of the French Canadian settlers in 1902. Le Centre communautaire de Talle-de-Saules and les Francophones de Talle-de-Saules in Willow Bunch remain foci of francophone community activities, as do an *école fransaskoise*, a French television relay station, executive members of l'Association jeunesse francophone there and in Lisieux, la Société historique de Willow Bunch, a *caisse populaire bilingue*, and a Chorale française de Willow Bunch, while le Musée de Willow Bunch (originally housed in the former hospital in 1972 and now in the convent school) documents the life of the most famous former resident, the giant Edouard Beaupré (born in 1881). In August 2012, Terre-ferme, an outdoor music festival, was held at the Champagne family farm near Willow Bunch.

In 1971, there were more than 1,600 people claiming French ethnicity (possibly not including francophone Métis) in this settlement, including the towns of Willow Bunch and Assiniboia, the smaller communities of Rockglen, Coronach, and St-Victor, and the rural municipalities of Willow Bunch, Excel, Lake of the Rivers, Stonehenge, Old Post, and Poplar Valley. French-origin residents constituted a strong majority (71.6%) in the town of Willow Bunch, and most (60.4%) were francophones. In the small village of St-Victor, francophones (58.8%) actually outnumbered people claiming French ethnicity (half the residents). Today francophones have proportionately declined to 35.0% in Willow Bunch (pop. 395) and 42.6% in St-Victor (pop. 49). Willow Bunch was incorporated as a village in 1929 and achieved town status in 1960; by the mid-1950s, it had 800 residents but since then has declined to half that number. Recently, three ideological entrepreneurs from British Columbia constituting the Pacific Way Foundation purchased the former local schoolhouse, a garage, and several residential properties with the intention of creating some sort of philosophical centre. When St-Victor was incorporated as a village in 1964, it had over 100 residents. In 1986, the parish church was closed, when only about sixty residents remained, and the village was dissolved in 2003. Lisieux, recognized as an organized hamlet in 1964, now has only fifteen remaining residents. A former resident of Lisieux and Rockglen, Marie Beaudin LeChasseur Delorme, passed away in October 2012 at the age of 103.

The Wood Mountain (*montagne-de-bois*) area, south of Gravelbourg and west of Willow Bunch, began to develop when Québécois from Ste-Clair in Dorchester County founded the community of Ferland (named after Jean-Baptiste-Antoine Ferland, Catholic historian, but originally known at Ste-Claire-des-Prairies, then St-Edmond). This settlement, centred on the parish of St-Jean-Baptiste at Ferland, founded in 1909, continued to expand eastward with the establishment of new parishes and missions at Ste-Thérèse (1914, moved to Wood Mountain in 1954, destroyed by fire in 1978) and St-Marcel (1917) near Glentworth (destroyed by lightning in 1954), St-Joseph (1929) in Glentworth, and Fir Mountain (1939). The Roman Catholic church at Wood Mountain used to share the same organist (an Anglican) with the neighbouring Romanian Orthodox and United churches. Finally, at Mankota west of Ferland, most of the priests of the parish of St-Albert (1954) have been French. The former Ferland or Reliance School (1914) is now a community centre and designated heritage site. Ferland and the rural district of Fournierville to the north remain virtually completely French; in fact, in 1971, Ferland had the highest proportion of French population for any incorporated community in the province at 94.1%, while 90.9% were still French speaking. A reunion of two intermarried founding families, the Chabots and the Fourniers, in July 1979 brought together over 200 family members.[26] Thérèse Couture Laberge, born there in 1924, began her teaching career in one-room country schools at Ferland and Fife Lake. The neighbouring villages of Glentworth and Wood Mountain to the east have only small French minorities, though the Theresa (Ste-Thérèse) district near Glentworth and the Plessis district near Wood Mountain (named in 1915 by l'Abbé Gravel for Joseph-Octave Plessis, the first archbishop of Quebec City) testified to the presence of French settlers, as did the Monvoisin and Survivance districts in the vicinity of Ferland and the Milly, Festubert, Ruisseau-Laberge (Laberge Creek), Ruisseau-Tetrault, and Lac-de-Maronds districts to the south. One school district near Ferland was originally named Survivance (survival). Ferland constitutes a *conseil-régional* of the ACFC, and it has a chapter of la Fédération des femmes canadiennes-françaises, a *caisse populaire bilingue*, an *école fransaskoise*, and l'Institut culturel de Ferland. Noella Lemire runs a *gite-touristique*, the Belle Rose bed and breakfast/tea room. The Glentworth Museum, located in the original two-room brick schoolhouse, describes the early history of education in the district. All told, almost 400 people of French origin were found in the general area in 1971, in Ferland and other nearby communities and Waverley RM and Mankota RM, yet these have always been very small communities: Ferland was never more than a hamlet, Glentworth had eighty-eight residents in 1996, McCord now has about forty, while Fir Mountain is a hamlet.

A small French settlement developed about forty kilometres northeast of Gravelbourg when the hamlets of Courval (Paroisse St-Joseph) and Coderre (Paroisse St-Charles) originated respectively in 1908 and 1910. Settlers from the Eastern Townships in Quebec followed the pioneer settler Luc-Louis-Philippe Poulin de Courval from Arthabasca, Quebec, while others came from North Dakota. Coderre was originally named after the first postmaster, Eudore Bernard Coderre; he and his family served as postmasters for many decades. Between these two communities was the St-Charles district, where the parish of St-Charles (now in Coderre) was originally located in 1912, and where a rural post office was established in 1914, operated by the parish priest, Père Charles Poirier. Les Soeurs-de-Jésus-Marie ran the local school since 1942. The descendants of these francophone settlers in this small settlement numbered about 300 in 1971; however, few reside in these communities now: perhaps forty in Coderre and reportedly only five in Courval.

CHAPTER 7

Settlements in the Southwestern Region

The town of Ponteix, about seventy kilometres west of Gravelbourg, had its origins in 1907 when l'Abbé Albert-Marie Royer arrived. He was born at Combronde, Puy-de-Dôme, in the Auvergne region of France, and his mother was so devoted to the Virgin Mary that she named all of her children—boys as well as girls—Marie. After his ordination, he became the *curé* of Ponteix, France. He emigrated in 1906 and was instrumental in the French settling of the Old Wives River area (the beginning of the Gravelbourg settlement); however, he became disappointed when the main parish was named by Père Gravel after Ste-Philomène rather than the Virgin Mary, so he requested another parish and settlement farther west. First called Notre-Dame-d'Auvergne, this new community was renamed Ponteix in 1914 after Père Royer's home parish near Clermont-Ferrand, France (though the parish and rural municipality still bear the old name). The first settlers came from Auvergne as well as from Belgium in 1907–08. Of the families listed in the community history in 1980, fifty-nine had originated in Quebec, eighteen in France, twelve in Belgium, ten in Ontario (mostly from francophone communities in eastern Ontario such as St-Isidore-de-Prescott and Casselman), nine in Manitoba, at least eight in other francophone communities in Saskatchewan (including Bellegarde, Storthoaks, Montmartre, Ferland, and Val-Marie), and ten from francophone communities in the United States (e.g., Crookston, Minnesota, the mill-towns of New England, and Michigan and North Dakota).[27] The first parish church was constructed in 1909–10 (the *pieta* had been brought from France by a settler), a second in 1916 with a large *salle paroissiale* (parish hall), rebuilt after it burned down as the present grand 900-seat edifice in 1929 with a bold inscription over the apse: *Mon ame glorifie le Seigneur* (My soul glorifies the Lord). Père Royer returned to France in 1912 and secured the assistance of the Congrégation de Notre-Dame-de-Chambriac as teachers and nurses for the settlement the following year. The nuns established the school in Ponteix as les Soeurs de Notre-Dame d'Auvergne. Construction of a new convent was finished in 1916. New recruits, *postulants*, were sent to France to start their novitiate through the 1930s. The village of Ponteix was laid out by 1914; in 1923, it became the administrative centre of the rural municipality of Auvergne, and it would eventually become a town in 1957. The parish was served by twenty-six francophone priests until 1967, when it had its first priest not of French origin (he was German); at least nine local parishioners had become priests by 1980 and thirty-two nuns by 1981.

L'Ecole Poirier in Ponteix (1924) was named after the successor to Père Royer, Père Napoléon Poirier. An extensive network of country school districts around Ponteix was created: Notre-Dame-Est (1911–51), McKnight (1912–50), Val Blair (1912–13), Notukeu (1913–53), Westerleigh (1914–59), McPhail (1914–46), Quimper (1915–58), Comfort (1915–55), Golden Valley/Halbert (1915–49), Courcelette (1917–54), Pinto Head (1918–59), Atoimah—Hamiota, Manitoba, spelled in reverse (1918–53), Royer (1921–53), and Stove Lake (1927–62). Eventually, with the closure of these country schools, students were bussed into l'Ecole Poirier, while the centralized Ecole Secondaire de Ponteix was replaced by a larger new Auvergne School in 1966. L'Ecole Boréale is part of the provincial network of *écoles fransaskoises*.

North of Ponteix, the rural district of Bourgogne (originally proposed by l'Abbé Gravel in 1911 to be called Sarthe) and the villages of Vanguard (where St-Joseph Parish was established in 1908 and Pontivy School District was named after a community in Bretagne) and Pambrun (named after Pierre Chrysologue Pambrun, from L'Islet, Quebec, a trader with the Hudson's Bay Company from 1815 to 1824), with the district of Courcellette, were settled partly by French-speaking farmers from the Eastern Townships in Quebec, from the United States, and from Belgium and France in 1908–09. West of Ponteix, the settlement expanded to include the Gouverneur district by 1912 and, across le Plateau de la Houssière (after a community in the Vosges department in France), the village of Cadillac (possibly named after Antoine de Lamothe Cadillac, the governor of Nouvelle France during the early eighteenth century, or perhaps more likely after the city in Michigan, from where some of the early settlers—including the first postmaster, Claude-Ives Bristol—had come in 1910), where the parish of Notre-Dame-de-la-Confiance was organized in 1914. East of Ponteix, the post office at Aneroid was originally called Val Blair in 1911–13. To the south, the settlement expanded into ranching grasslands around Quimper (named after another community in Bretagne) and Wallard up on Butte-de-Cheval-Caillé (Pinto Butte).

Ponteix became the cultural, institutional, and commercial centre of the settlement. The Notre-Dame *bureau de poste* was established in 1910, la Banque de Québec in 1914 (it soon merged with the Royal Bank of Canada three years later), la Banque d'Hochelaga in 1915 (which merged with la Banque Canadienne Nationale in 1924), *les écuries-de-louage* (horse stables) in 1917, les Chevaliers de Colomb (Knights of Columbus) in 1928, l'Hôpital St-Gabriel in 1918 (from 1929 to 1967, it was simply Gabriel Hospital), le Musée héritage de Notokeu in 1940, le Manoir in 1954, la Société d'aide aux hôpitaux in 1955, l'Hôpital union de Ponteix in 1961, la Fédération des femmes canadiennes-françaises in 1967, le Centre culturel Royer de Ponteix in 1969, le Centre éducatif les étoiles filantes, Foyer St-Joseph, la Société des Lions de Ponteix et district in 1974, as well as les Auvergnois de Ponteix and la Société historique de Ponteix. Some of these institutions and organizations, as well as a large statue of Notre-Dame-des-Champs (Our Lady of the Fields) in Ponteix, continue to maintain an interest in the history and francophone life of the settlement, while l'Ecole Boréale, a French television relay station and a *caisse populaire bilingue* continue to serve the francophone community. A theatrical troupe is La Troupe Notre-Dame de Ponteix.

In 1971, there were approximately 1,200 people of French origin in these areas, including Ponteix, Cadillac, and the rural municipalities of Auvergne, Wise Creek, and Whiska Creek. The town of Ponteix (pop. 531 in 2006, down from almost 900 in 1961) remained largely French; in 1971, three-quarters (74.8%) of the residents were French and two-thirds (67.7%) francophone, while today 55.0% are still francophone. In the small villages of Cadillac (pop. 80), Pambrun, and Vanguard, French comprise a minority; in 1971, they constituted a little more than a third (37.0%) of the residents of Cadillac, including 27.9% who were francophone. Gouverneur, between Ponteix and Cadillac, once had sixteen businesses and services, including a *bureau de poste*, livery, grocery store, clothing store, furniture repair shop, and hotel; however, during the Depression, the sixty remaining residents at the time started to leave, the highway bypassed the community, and by the 1970s only the cemetery and abandoned homes were left.

Meanwhile, other French settlements had developed in the southwest. Northwest of Ponteix, the Métis who had settled at Vallée-Ste-Claire, Lac-Pelletier (originally called Lac-la-Plume but later named after Norbert Pelletier, a Métis trader who had homesteaded there in 1886), Point-Lemire, and La Fourche were joined by Québécois in 1906–07, then by immigrants from France in 1910. The parish of Ste-Anne was founded in 1906. Later Lac-Pelletier was served by Père Eugène Cabanel, the parish priest in Swift Current, who had been born in France and had worked in Louisiana before coming to Saskatchewan. To the southwest, the Lévis School District was established in 1926 on the land of Donat Chenard, from Ste-Hélène, Quebec. In 1971, there were only seventy-five people of French origin remaining in the rural municipality of Lac-Pelletier.

Southwest of Cadillac, the small community of Frenchville (Ville-des-Français or La Petite France) and the Lac-Driscol (Lake Driscol), Epinard, and Beauchamp districts were settled in 1909–10 by diverse francophones from France, Belgium, Switzerland, Quebec, and Manitoba. The parish of St-Joseph was initially organized in 1909, moved into the upper floor of what had been a combined general store, post office, and hotel ten years later (the post office and rectory shared the lower floor), and finally became a proper church in 1940. Before becoming Frenchville, this rural post office was known as Filiatrault from 1912 to 1917.

Almost fifty kilometres south of Cadillac, Val-Marie, originally a Métis settlement, developed in 1910 when immigrants from France were brought in by Père Claude Passaplan, who also contributed to the settlement of Lac-Pelletier. Originally, l'Abbé Gravel used the traditional name of the Frenchman River Valley—Rivière-des-Français—for the settlement, then changed it to Libreval in 1911, before Père Passaplan's suggested name of Val-Marie was preferred by the settlers. The rural district with the rather curious Latin name of Gergovia, to the southeast, apparently was named by Père Royer of Ponteix after a historic site in his native Auvergne. Ruisseau-Denniel (Denniel Creek), which flows from Frenchville to Val-Marie, was named after homesteader Jean-Louis Denniel, who served as the postmaster from 1912 to 1959. The central parish in Val-Marie is la Nativité-de-Val-Marie (1910); later a second parish, Notre-Dame-de-la-Présentation (1938), was organized to serve the Masefield area (to the immediate southwest of Val-Marie, settled in 1926), the Roche Plain district (settled earlier by 1913), Monchy, and the Marne School District (1918–67). Val-Marie became an incorporated village in 1926. A *bureau de poste* operated in the community between 1912 and 1926. A rural school district existed from 1914 to 1951, while the old red brick school in the village (opened in 1927) is now a heritage site. When he died in 1939, Pat Trottier was reputedly the last surviving buffalo hunter in Canada; he was the great-grandfather of professional hockey star Brian Trottier. In 1971, the descendants of these French and Métis settlers numbered about 300 in the community and rural municipalities of Val-Marie and Glen McPherson. Approximately half of the residents of Val-Marie (pop. 137 in 2006, compared with over 400 during the early 1960s) are French and 31.8% francophone (in 1971, 46.7%, and 34.4% francophone, revealing little change). Le Musée Perrault explains the natural and human history of the region.

In 1908–10, the community of Valroy (later Dollard, named after Adam Dollard-des-Ormeaux, a Quebec hero in 1660), seventy kilometres west of Cadillac, was established by settlers primarily from Quebec yet also from various French settlements on the prairies as well as from France and Belgium. During the 1970s, their descendants numbered about 500 in the predominantly French community of Dollard, where

Paroisse Ste-Jeanne-d'Arc was founded in 1908 and served by Père Jérôme Boutin, in the nearby towns of Eastend and Shaunavon (most of the priests serving St-Patrice/St. Patrick's Parish in Eastend and many serving Christ-Roi/Christ the King Parish have been French), and in the surrounding rural districts: Jeanne d'Arc north of Dollard; Madelon near Shaunavon; and, at the eastern end of the Cypress Hills and down to and beyond the Frenchman River Valley (Rivière-des-Français or Rivière-de-la-Maison-de-Terre), Chambéry (rural post office in 1911), Valroy (school district named after J-Adélard Roy, from St-Isidore, Quebec, who homesteaded there in 1910), St-Hilaire (a country store at the original location of Dollard), la Maison-de-Terre, Plateau, Wyle, Uxbridge, Jumbo Butte, South Fork, les Cypres, Coulée-Gallienne, Lac-Léon, Coulée-Gregoire, and Madelon (a school district near Shaunavon that operated 1930–42 and 1957–58, named after the wife of settler Baptiste Vinette). The diversity of the originally francophone settlers could hardly be overstated. Just in the Frenchman River Valley and districts near Eastend, for example, today they are descendants of Québécois families (at least eleven families); immigrants direct from France (sixteen families), Belgium (ten families), Switzerland (two families), as well as North and South Dakota (a couple of families); migrants from francophone settlements in Manitoba (six families) and Saskatchewan (seven families); and Franco-Ontarians (at least one family).[28] Over the years, they have mixed with the descendants of settlers of Anglo-Canadian, Scandinavian, and many other origins, so that in these areas at the periphery of a French settlement centred on a village with a decreasing population they have tended to adopt English as a common language. In Dollard, in 1971, a slight majority (58.8%) of residents were French and almost half (47.7%) still French speaking. Dollard became incorporated as a village in 1914, when it contained 150 residents; by the mid-1950s, it had almost 200 residents; but only sixty-nine residents remained in 1976 and thirty-five by 2001—the community lost its status as a village in 2002. A general store, café, garage, bowling alley, school, blacksmith shop, bank, municipal office, barber shop, lumberyard, butcher shop, two elevators, two bulk agencies and a machine agency, and two pharmacies have all disappeared. Rural depopulation has continued to take a severe toll. The total population of this French settlement could be estimated at about 300 in 1971, in Dollard and the rural municipalities of Arlington and White Valley, to which another 200 could be added if people of French origin living in the nearby towns of Shaunavon and Eastend were included. But with the disappearance of Dollard as the francophone centre of this small settlement, little remains to support maintenance of French heritage in the area.

French individual homesteaders and families also settled in a number of other rural locales scattered in the southwestern region, such as Oxarat (where Michel Oxarat, a Basque immigrant, developed an extensive horse ranch after 1883), Lacs-Orléans and -Belanger (rural post office, 1907) south of the Cypress Hills, and Claustre (French immigrant Jean Claustre ran a store in Maple Creek and a ranch on Piapot Creek) north of the Cypress Hills. Many of the clergy serving St-Laurent/St. Lawrence Parish in Maple Creek have been French. In the isolated area east of the Sand Hills, Nadeauville was named for Jean Nadeau, from Montreal, who homesteaded there in 1910; he was preceded by ranchers Hormidas Brais and Auguste Chouinard in 1908. Nadeau's large home served as the *bureau de poste* and a chapel on Sunday. Disillusioned with recurrent drought, he sold out and retired back east in 1928, followed by Chouinard. However, he returned in 1933, and his home then became a general store (the post office closed in 1920, then reopened from 1929 to 1962). A few districts in the general area were also named by French settlers: Lac-Boyer, Petain, Petit-Nord (post office, 1911–21), and Rideauville. A small concentration of twenty French Canadian families (notably Lefort and Beaudrais) formed the Colonie des Laplantes fifty kilometres north of Swift Current in 1905.

DISTRIBUTION OF THE FRENCH POPULATION AND URBAN MINORITIES

Approximately one-third of all the French-origin people in Saskatchewan live in the northern tier of settlements, an almost equal number in the southern tier, and the remaining third in the major cities and ethnically mixed areas not included within settlements. By 1971, there were almost 20,000 people of French origin in the six largest urban centres. Yet these urban minorities were proportionately insignificant within the total urban population, and they tended to be quite anglicized, the majority speaking English as their mother tongue. They were served by only five French-language parishes. Since the 1970s, however, the French-speaking population in urban centres has grown considerably due not only to migration from rural communities but also especially to the arrival of French-speaking immigrants. Urban centres have continued to develop extensive infrastructures allowing francophone culture to prosper. Approximately one-third of the *écoles-designées* (designated francophone schools) have been located in cities, and both bilingual university programs were in the two larger urban centres. Saskatoon and Regina have the largest *number* of French people, whereas Prince Albert and North Battleford have the highest *proportion*.

Today Saskatoon has a francophone population estimated to exceed 5,000 (amid a far larger French-origin population). The parish of Sts-Martyrs-Canadiens serves francophone residents. In addition to l'Ecole canadienne-française de Saskatoon, there is a new high school, Pavillon Gustave-Dubois, plus seventeen French immersion schools, including l'Ecole française de Saskatoon. Numerous other francophone organizations are found in Saskatoon: la Communauté francophone de Saskatoon (la Fédération des francophones de Saskatoon), a *conseil-régional* of the ACFC (now l'Assemblée communautaire fransaskoise), a French television station and an AM radio station, la Caisse populaire fransaskoise de Saskatoon, a branch of l'Association jeunesse fransaskoise, Camp franco-jeunesse, Centre éducatif Félix le chat, l'Association des parents fransaskois, Fête du soleil catholique/Canadian Parents for French, le Coin français, Unithéatre—la Troupe théatrale française, la Troupe du jour, la Rimbambelle, le Choeur plaines, la Librairie coopérative, les Beaux jours, les Productions Belle Bouche, the Cinergie French film festival (a four-day annual event now in its eighth year), and Saskamis centre culturel français. A new francophone centre, called le Relais/Galérie d'art, will serve as a focal point for these diverse francophone activities. A network of health services provided in French is called Santé- réseau en français.

Regina now counts 2,758 francophones. A francophone parish, St-Jean-Baptiste, was established in 1954.[29] The Division scolaire francophone is based in Regina, and in addition to a francophone school, l'Ecole Monseigneur de Laval, there are fourteen French immersion schools. The many francophone community, cultural, and professional organizations of Regina include l'Assemblée communautaire fransaskoise and l'Association communautaire fransaskoise, l'Association canadienne-française de Regina, a *conseil-régional* of the ACFC/ACF, Coalition pour la promotion de la langue française et la culture francophone en Saskatchewan, l'Association des traducteurs et interprètes de la Saskatchewan, Conseil culturel fransaskois, Conseil de la coopération de la Saskatchewan, la Fédération provinciale des fransaskoises, la Société historique de la Saskatchewan, l'Alliance française de Regina, a francophone *caisse populaire*, a French television station and an FM radio station, a French film week, Théatre Oskana, and branches of la Fédération des femmes canadiennes-françaises (established in 1970), l'Association des juristes d'expression française de la Saskatchewan, l'Association jeunesse fransaskoise, Camp Troubadou, Camp Voyageur, Fête du soleil. Le Carrefour des plaines serves as a focal point for the francophone community.

Prince Albert francophones—numbering 1,770 today—have long attended la Cathédrale Sacré-Coeur/Sacred Heart Cathedral, founded in 1880. By 1980, only one of four Sunday Masses and one of the two weekday Masses were still offered in French. The cathedral and diocese have been served by an astonishing variety of francophone or bilingual religious orders: besides les Oblates Missionaires de Marie Immaculée, omnipresent throughout Western and Northern Canada in the early period of settlement, there were nuns imported from France (Filles/Soeurs de la Providence, Soeurs de Notre-Dame-de-Sion, Soeurs de l'Enfant-Jésus, Soeurs de la Présentation, Soeurs de Notre-Dame-de-la-Croix), Belgium (Soeurs de Marie-Reparatrix), Quebec (Soeurs du Sang Precieux, Soeurs Grises/Grey Nuns, Petites Soeurs de la Famille-Sainte, Institution de Notre-Dame), Manitoba (Petites Missionaires de St-Joseph), New Brunswick (Sisters of Charity of the Immaculate Conception), and Saskatchewan (Sisters of Mission Service). In Prince Albert, the former McDonald residence (1905), which later became the administrative offices of the Sisters of Presentation and the Vandale residence, today is a historic site. The centre for the francophone community in the city and region is le Carrefour fransaskois. Prince Albert has been a *conseil-régional* of the ACFC and is the *bureau-régional* of l'Assemblée communautaire fransaskoise and home to a wide variety of francophone organizations: le Comité paroissiale—liturgie français, le Club de l'amitié, la Société canadienne-française de Prince Albert, a French television station, l'Ecole Valois (as well as six French immersion schools), a francophone *caisse populaire*, l'Association des parents fransaskois, Camp Franco-fun, Entr'amis, and a chapter of l'Association jeunesse fransaskoise. Hôpital Victoria offers service in French, as does Mont St-Joseph Home. Moose Jaw now contains just 685 francophones, yet they are served by l'Association communautaire fransaskoise de Moose Jaw, Paroisse Notre-Dame-du-Perpétuel Secours, l'Ecole Ducharme, and a French television station, while French immersion programs are offered at les Petits Orignaux, Bonjour House, and four schools. The city contains l'Association communautaire fransaskoise de Moose Jaw, Fête du soleil, and the Chez Nous seniors' home. Chant'Ouest, celebrating western French music, was held in Moose Jaw in 2008. The Battlefords have only about 500 francophones but a significant francophone population in the region. Besides St-Vital Church (1882) and School (1911), designated as historic sites in 1982, there is the francophone Paroisse St-André. Today the city offers francophones l'Ecole Père Mercure, French immersion programs at Ecole Monseigneur Blaise Morand and Ecole John Paul

II Collegiate, Camp Chaleureux, an ACFC/ACF *conseil-régional*, an FM radio station broadcasting in French, l'Association des loisirs et centre culturel de North Battleford, a branch of la Fédération des femmes canadiennes-françaises, and health services in French at Manoir Marchildon and Villa Pascale. Lloydminster has two French immersion programs and a new francophone school, Ecoles sans frontières, in 2010. Yorkton has three immersion programs, Swift Current also three. So an urban francophone infrastructure exists in Saskatchewan; in fact, l'Assemblée communautaire fransaskoise provides an *annuaire Fransaskois*—an extensive directory of services available in French in these cities and throughout the province. Thus, the cities represent not only the greatest extent of loss of their traditional language for people of French origin but also opportunities for innumerable activities now available in French.

ETHNIC ORIGINS OF FRANCOPHONES

In the early 1880s, there were fewer than 3,000 people claiming French origin, scattered throughout the entire North-West Territories (which then comprised most of Western Canada and all of Northern Canada, excluding British Columbia and a small central portion of Manitoba).[30] Moreover, according to some estimates, as much as half of the total population of the North-West Territories might have been at least partially francophone, for French—or a mixture of French and various Native languages—was widely spoken by the omnipresent Métis.

In 1882, the Districts of Assiniboia, Saskatchewan, Athabasca, and Alberta were created out of the western portions of the North-West Territories. The southern or prairie portion of the present-day Province of Saskatchewan occupied most of the Districts of Saskatchewan and Assiniboia. By 1891, just over 900 residents counted in the Districts of Saskatchewan and Assiniboia had been born in Quebec, while almost 100 had immigrated directly from France.

During the next decade, immigration from Quebec continued, with the establishment of francophone settlements across the prairies. By 1901, the number of Québécois had tripled to almost 2,700. However, immigration from France was still only a trickle: 167 by the turn of the century. A more substantial flow from francophone Europe—France and Belgium and to a minor extent Luxemburg and Switzerland—during the next decade lessened this Québécois dominance. In fact, many of the thirty-two French settlements in the new province of Saskatchewan (founded in 1905) had been established primarily if not exclusively by French-speaking immigrants direct from Europe. By 1911, almost 3,000 (12.6%) of the more than 23,000 people reporting French origin had been born in France, while almost all (82.6%) of the over 1,500 people claiming Belgian origin were immigrants from Belgium.

Three decades later, in 1941, census data indicated that a high proportion (87%) of the 50,530 people in Saskatchewan claiming French ethnic origin (excluding the 4,250 claiming Belgian ethnic origin) were Canadian born. Migration into Saskatchewan from other Canadian provinces, the United States, and Europe had virtually ceased. Almost two-thirds (63%) of French Canadians in Saskatchewan had been born in the province, compared with about 14% who had migrated from Quebec, almost 6% from the other western provinces (particularly Manitoba), and just over 4% from Ontario and the other eastern provinces. But a substantial if lessening proportion were immigrants from Europe and the United States: approximately 13%.

Prior to the 1981 census, respondents to the question on ethnic origin could claim only a single ethnic origin through the male lineage. Thus, the French Canadian population of Saskatchewan, for example, was actually counted as people with a French father (and presumably a French surname), regardless of whether the mother, or any other female predecessor, was French or not. People with a French mother but not a French father could not claim French origin. So it is conceivable that, on the one hand, the actual French Canadian population of the province was undercounted in each census. On the other hand, possibly it was overcounted, because intermarriage was not taken into consideration. The 1981 census attempted to correct this situation by permitting respondents to claim multiple ethnic origins.

In 1981, almost 47,000 people claimed to be only of French descent, plus almost 3,000 of Belgian, over 1,000 of Swiss, and a small number of Luxemburg (note, however, that in these latter three countries French is not the mother tongue of the majority of people). Another 15,000 people claimed Métis origin, yet it is not clear how many of these people would be more specifically of Franco-Métis descent or speaking a Franco-Métis Michif dialect (though a majority of Métis in Saskatchewan are probably of part-French origin, a substantial proportion could be of other Euro-Canadian ethnicity—especially Scottish—mixed with Native origin). Of the more than 22,000 people estimated to be part-French origin (apart from those claiming only Métis origin), the largest number— more than 9,000—also claimed British origin; almost as many—over 8,000—claimed other non-Native origins; while another 4,000 combined French origin with British origin plus other non-Native origins. Relatively few—just over 1,000—people who did not identify themselves exclusively as Métis claimed to be of part-French and part-Native origin. Adding up all of these data, we arrive at an absolute maximum figure for possible French or part-French origin of almost 89,000 (i.e., including all people of Belgian, Swiss, Luxemburg, and Métis origins). Obviously, a far lower number would have been French speaking.

Recent census data (2006) estimated that 118,200 people in Saskatchewan (12.2% of the provincial population) were of French origin (wholly or partially), to which could be added another 270 claiming Acadian origin and 125 Québécois origin. However, though the predecessors of these people would have been francophones originally, they are not necessarily all French speaking in Saskatchewan today. Again, many—but not all—people claiming Belgian (9,125), Swiss (4,365), Luxemburger (340), or Basque (30) ethnic origin could have become part of the broader francophone population in Saskatchewan: almost half of the population of Belgium speaks Walloon, a French dialect, but the majority of Belgians speak Flemish, a Dutch dialect; French-speaking Swiss are far outnumbered by German-speaking Swiss in Switzerland; French might be an official language of Luxemburg, but native French speakers are a relatively small minority—Letzeburgisch, a German dialect, is more widely spoken; and only a minority of Basques are in France—most are in Spain—and their native language is Basque (Euzkadi). Moreover, while most of the predecessors of the 42,100 Métis counted in Saskatchewan spoke French, and thus could be counted within the francophone population, only a minority of Métis today are French speaking, and the vast majority (especially younger people) are not familiar with Michif dialects—most Métis now speak English.

Clearly, the French-speaking community of Saskatchewan is becoming increasingly diverse; in fact, diversity was the theme of the annual Rendez-vous de la francophonie in 2009. "Fransaskois" has become redefined as someone who identifies with the francophone community in Saskatchewan, whether through birth, marriage, adoption, or simple identification with the society. Choosing to live at least part of one's life in French is central to the definition of what it means to be Fransaskois. A Fransaskois contributes to the vitality of the French language as well as the growth and development of the French-speaking community in Saskatchewan, and there are unlimited ways in which to contribute to this development. So, while familiarity with the French language is considered essential, a general interest in and commitment to French heritage and culture are also emphasized. As one recent definition puts it, a Fransaskois is anyone who speaks French and lives in or comes from Saskatchewan; a Fransaskois is also someone who identifies, in one way or another, with the French language or culture with or without necessarily speaking the French language.

The more recent arrival of francophones from Africa (e.g., Congo, Rwanda, Burundi, etc.) and the Caribbean (e.g., Haiti, Martinique, etc.) has contributed substantially to the French-speaking population in Saskatchewan. In 2010, the Assemblée communautaire fransaskoise (ACF) embarked on a mission to facilitate the immigration of skilled workers from French-speaking countries. Recruiting missions were sent to Europe and Africa. The following year an official agreement was signed with the government of Mauritius, a crowded country in the Indian Ocean where English is the official language yet French and a local dialect are widely spoken; the government is eager to provide employment opportunities to young skilled workers. Facilitating the importation of skilled labour from Mauritius are the International Organization for Immigration, Prudhomme International (based in Regina), and the ACF. It is now estimated that globally 200 million people speak French; French is used in at least seventy countries representing a third of the member states of the United Nations. The impact of French-speaking immigrants from many countries beyond Europe has been dramatic, giving francophone schools, institutions, and services in the province a more cosmopolitan quality. A process to welcome and assist newcomers is being developed.

POPULATION TRENDS IN FRANCOPHONE COMMUNITIES

In 1901, there were very few people of French origin (2,634), and fewer still of Belgian origin, living in what would soon become the province of Saskatchewan. However, during the first decade of that century, the French population would increase tenfold (to 23,251 in 1911), then again double in the second decade (to 42,152 in 1921). Much of this rapid increase doubtless was due to large-scale migration of francophones from Quebec and other Canadian provinces, from French settlements already established in American states such as Minnesota, and particularly from many regions in France and to a lesser extent francophone regions in Belgium and Switzerland. During the 1920s, this influx slowed down, and—with the exodus from French settlements in Saskatchewan because of the Depression and repeated droughts—the French population of the province remained static after 1931 (50,700 in 1931, 50,530 in 1941, 51,930 in 1951), reaching a peak in 1961 (59,824), then slowly declining again (56,200 in 1971). With the change in census definitions in 1981, 46,915 people claimed to be solely of French origin, yet by then an increasing proportion of French were intermarried, so their children were claiming mixed ethnic origins. Recent census data (2006) reveal that Saskatchewan residents claiming French origin constitute the sixth largest ethnic group in the province. However, only 11.5% (13,580) of them claimed to be of only French origin, compared with 88.5% (105,010) who claimed to be of other ethnic origins besides French.[31]

During the past several decades, the urbanization of the French population of Saskatchewan has been dramatic. Back in 1941, 70% of that population was living in rural areas, whereas by 1981 this proportion had fallen to 45%. Moreover, most of the rural French population consisted of farming families through the 1960s, whereas today most are non-farming rural families. A central question must be whether French identity and language could be preserved most easily in an urban or a rural context.

In 1971 (the last census in which detailed and complete data on ethnicity in rural communities are available), there were thirty-nine incorporated communities in Saskatchewan in which francophones comprised at least 10% of the total community population. Yet only thirteen of these communities had a francophone majority. In another eight communities, francophones made up between one-third and one-half of the population, between 20% and 33% in seven communities, and between 10% and 19% in the remaining eleven communities. People claiming French ethnic origin made up a majority in fifteen of these communities, 33%–49% in eleven, 20%–32% in six, and 10%–19% in the remaining seven. Of course, the difference between those two sets of data is due to the fact that not everyone of French origin in these communities was still speaking French as his or her primary mother tongue. Yet there were some striking discrepancies: in five communities, francophones outnumbered people claiming French origin. In one rural community, residents claiming to be of French origin outnumbered those who recognized French as their mother tongue by 4:1. As noted, the small village of Ferland had both the highest proportion of French origin (94.1%) and French speakers (90.9%). The largest predominantly French community was Gravelbourg.

Examination of demographic data over several decades since 1971 in thirty francophone communities in Saskatchewan reveals that seventeen communities have been consistently declining, though the rate of decline has varied from slow to rapid. Most of the rapidly declining communities are located in the southwestern region, more prone to drought. But the other sixteen communities have been increasing; again considerable variation in rates can be noted. Given the variation, any generalization about overall population trends is difficult. It can be pointed out, though, that seven of the smallest communities are declining and seem destined to become ghost towns. Moreover, besides these incorporated communities, most of the many francophone communities that are unincorporated small villages and hamlets have experienced rural depopulation more severely. Looking at the most recent trends, over just a five-year period between 2001 and 2006, out of fifty-one communities (towns, incorporated villages, and organized hamlets) with substantial proportions or numbers of residents claiming French origin, thirty-six have been decreasing, five have been clearly increasing, while the remaining ten have been static, either showing no change or increasing just slightly (by fewer than ten residents). Thus, the inevitable implication is that, in many traditionally French communities in Saskatchewan, the capability of maintaining French language and identity unfortunately has been dramatically reduced.

PATTERNS OF LANGUAGE USE

The proportion of French-origin population in Saskatchewan speaking French as their primary mother tongue has declined markedly over the past several decades. Back in 1921, 91.7% of the French-origin population over ten years of age were French speaking. By 1941, three-quarters of the French-origin population were French speaking. Ten years later this proportion had declined to slightly less than two-thirds (65%); it was becoming evident that the greatest attrition in French-language use was in urban areas, where just 46% were French speaking, compared with 71% in the rural non-farm and 72% in the rural farm population. By 1961, 54.5% of the French population was still speaking French: down to 42% in urban areas, 58% in rural non-farm areas, and 66% in rural farm areas. By 1971, little more than half (51.7%) of the French-origin population were French speaking, yet both the urban (46%) and the rural non-farm (66%) proportions were actually increasing during the past decade, while two-thirds of the French rural farm proportion continued to speak French. Yet this proportion has remained more or less constant since then, so linguistic assimilation might have been more effectively slowed during the most recent decades, perhaps largely because of the increased availability of French-language media and education. Moreover, within the French bloc settlements, French language use was more prevalent; for example, within the settlements in the north-central region, 97.0% of the French were speaking French in 1941, 79.7% in 1951, 71.5% in 1961, and 66.9% in 1971.[32]

By 1981, within the population claiming only French origin, for every person speaking primarily French at home, four were speaking English. Approximately half of those claiming exclusively French origin were bilingual; the other half spoke only English. Moreover, almost two-thirds of the bilingual population of exclusively French origin preferred to speak English at home. Similarly, of the total francophone (French mother tongue) population in Saskatchewan, almost two-thirds preferred to speak English at home. One in ten of these people claiming French mother tongue reported that they spoke only English; the vast majority were bilingual; very few—only several hundred—could speak only French. On the other hand, there were almost 800 people in the province claiming English as their mother tongue yet speaking primarily French at home. Francophones in Saskatchewan declined from 36,815 in 1951 to 19,515 by 2001; however, the rate of decline has lessened since 1991. The population speaking French as their primary language at home declined by about two-thirds from 1971 to 2001. Yet, with the rapid rise in the number of French-language immersion programs throughout Saskatchewan since the 1980s, there were twice as many people who were bilingual in French and English as there were bilingual French Canadians; apparently, familiarity with the French language was increasing among people who were not French Canadian, though still only a small proportion of these non-French were bilingual in French and English. Approximately 10,000 more people claimed familiarity with French in just five years from 1996 to 2001. Now almost 50,000 people in Saskatchewan (5.1% of the total population) are conversant in French, compared with about 54,000 people who speak German. Although fewer than half (approximately 20,000) of the people claiming only French origin are francophone, to this French-speaking, French-origin population can be added people speaking French as their mother tongue who are either partly of French origin or claim other ethnic origins.[33]

Does French tend to be spoken by a higher proportion of the French-origin population in urban or in rural areas? French Canadians in rural Saskatchewan (especially the farming population) have consistently been more likely to retain French. Moreover, a far higher proportion of the rural francophone population have continued to speak French at home than the urban francophone population (42.5% compared with 29.9% in 1981). Yet, with the steady shift of French population from rural to urban areas, there are now more francophones of French origin in urban than rural areas, though there are more people speaking French at home in rural than urban areas, in absolute numbers. In 2001, just 17,775 residents of Saskatchewan considered French to be their mother tongue, another 1,375 both French and English, and 8,280 French plus another language other than English.

Differences in age and generation in ethnic language retention in Saskatchewan, including among the French-origin population, are noteworthy. Retention, particularly actual use of French mother tongue, declines markedly from first generation through third or fourth generation and from older age cohorts to younger ones. The age structure of French Canadians in Saskatchewan is distributed evenly, both in urban and in rural areas, but patterns of language use are not. Far higher proportions of French language use in the home, and exclusive use of French, are found in the youngest (preschool) and oldest (postretirement) age cohorts. According to Statistics Canada data, in 2001 the median age of francophones in Saskatchewan was fifty-two. People over the age of fifty represented almost 60% of francophones; nearly 30% are older than sixty-five. In fact, the median age of francophones in Saskatchewan is the highest of any province at 52.3%, far higher than the median age of 36.7 for the total provincial population. Research has indicated that overall for francophones in Saskatchewan every age cohort from oldest to youngest revealed a steady diminution in the numbers speaking French.

In an extensive survey of seven French settlements in the north-central and northwestern regions (Duck Lake–St-Louis, Prud'homme, Bonne-Madone, St-Brieux, Albertville, Marcelin and Coteau, and Debden–Leoville) in 1969–72, 202 respondents were interviewed for their perceptions of intergenerational assimilation. Of the respondents, 24.3% strongly favoured preservation of French identity, compared with 46.0% who were generally in favour yet resigned to some loss, 24.8% who were rather indifferent, and 5.0% who were opposed. Asked whether they thought that there would be a loss of French identification for youth, 52.5% thought that the loss would be relatively minor, 13.4% thought that it would be major, while 32.7% thought that there would be little or no loss (and three respondents had no opinion). There was little difference of opinion between the first generation (i.e., original settler in or migrant to Saskatchewan) and the second generation (i.e., first generation born in Saskatchewan), but there was a significant change in the third generation: 87.5% in the first and 80.4% in the second favoured French identity preservation, whereas just 47.2% in the third did. Among the people interviewed, almost one in ten (elderly) spoke only French,

78.2% used French fairly often, and almost all (99.0%) could still speak French. Yet a detailed analysis of actual language use by generation revealed that only 10.0% of the first generation were speaking primarily English, 16.3% of the second, and 35.7% of the third. Moreover, a very high proportion (91.1%) of respondents were attending a French Catholic church "as regularly as possible," though a slight decline in regular attendance was noted from the first generation (all) to the second (94.6%) and third (81.4%). The data gathered on attitudes toward ethnic and religious intermarriage were interesting: 91.1% of married respondents had French spouses; the few (thirteen) who had intermarried had all married spouses of other ethnic groups, but all were Roman Catholic. In fact, opposition to marrying a non-Catholic (81.2%) was far stronger than opposition to marrying a spouse of different ethnicity (45.6%). But this opposition was changing: opposition to ethnic intermarriage declined rapidly from 70.0% in the first generation to 48.9% in the second and 27.2% in the third; opposition to religious intermarriage declined more slowly from 95.0% in the first generation to 90.2% in the second and then 61.5% in the third.

Although most of the French settlements in Saskatchewan were founded several generations ago primarily by immigrants direct from Europe rather than by Québécois, now eight out of every ten francophones in the province are Saskatchewan born, 20% were born in other provinces, and fewer than 3% were born in other countries. However, as noted, with increasing francophone immigration, especially from non-European countries, to urban centres, this could be fast changing.

The latest census data (2011) reveal that the number of French speakers in Saskatchewan has increased for the first time in six decades. The number of francophones has grown 7.7% during the five years since the previous census, compared with growth of the total provincial population by 5.1%. Moreover, the number of people speaking French regularly at home increased by 2,187. Now 59% of Saskatchewan residents speaking French are found in the major urban centres of Saskatoon, Regina, and Prince Albert. In rural communities, as many as 78% of the residents of St-Isidore-de-Bellevue speak French, compared with only 41% now in Gravelbourg. These data are all the more striking considering that the total proportion across Canada of francophones has been steadily decreasing: from about a third (30.0%) of the Canadian population in earlier decades to less than a quarter (23.5%) in 1996 and 22.9% in 2001; the proportion of Canadians who actually used French as their primary language was even less. The largest decline among provinces was in Manitoba, where the proportion fell 6.5% compared with little change in Saskatchewan from 1996 to 2001. At the time, 43.4% of francophones across Canada reported that they were bilingual in French and English; this was four times the proportion among anglophones. It is likely that virtually all of the francophones in Saskatchewan are proficiently bilingual.

LA LUTTE POUR LA SURVIVANCE — THE STRUGGLE FOR SURVIVAL

Especially during the early years of settlement, francophones' struggle for survival as a minority group in Saskatchewan centred on the school-language issue. Prior to the North-West Resistance of 1884–85, use of the French language in the voluntary schools of what was then the District of Saskatchewan within the North-West Territories was common, as was the use of English and even Cree or a combination of these languages.[34] In 1867, Article 133 of the British North America Act had confirmed both English and French as official languages of Canada. With the extension of federal financing and centralized administration to these schools after 1881, the use of French remained unchallenged, and official government statements concerning the schools were in English and French. The first school ordinances of 1884–85 still did not specify any necessary language of instruction. But the resistance put the francophone minority in disfavour, and a long fight for ethnic control of the schools commenced, focusing on the language question.[35] By 1887, Père Lacombe, the well-known pioneer priest, was complaining to Archbishop Taché of St-Boniface about the threat of being forced to teach exclusively in English. Actually, the situation had not progressed to such a point yet; the following year an ordinance simply obligated school trustees to see that at least a primary course was taught in English. A spokesman for the Métis at Batoche deplored what he considered to be an "unjust and altogether unnecessary invasion of their right to speak their mother-tongue" and claimed that they had the right to use their own language because they had been in the North-West Territories first. By 1896, only about half of the instruction of French children in schools following regulations was in the French language. An ordinance of 1901 restricted instruction in French to a single hour, from 3 to 4 p.m., on school days recognized by the school board, with instruction confined to reading, composition, and grammar, using only texts authorized by the Department of Education, provided that the trustees of each school agreed to allow even this limited amount.[36] The great influx of non-French settlers at the time, moreover, reduced the French to an even smaller minority when Saskatchewan became a province in 1905.

Notwithstanding, the French minority was to keep the school and language question a lively political issue through the Liberal regime of Premier Scott, 1905–16. In 1907, the archbishop of St-Boniface expressed to the premier the willingness of French Catholics to have a bilingual education yet also their desire to have the freedom to be taught in French at any time during school hours. By the following year, however, the premier's office was already receiving complaints concerning French Catholic control of schools in areas such as Fish Creek and Bonne-Madone. In 1909, English was recognized as the sole language of school instruction in Saskatchewan. Then, in 1910, a dispute erupted at Vonda when, in a public speech in the town hall, a Presbyterian minister called Catholic separate schools a "national misfortune … perpetuating race and religious prejudice." A couple of years later the first conference of l'Association Catholique Franco-Canadienne de la Saskatchewan was held at Duck Lake, with participants pledging to fight for *la survivance* with renewed vigour and to dispense French-language education in the province's francophone communities.[37]

The opportunity to do so soon appeared. Premier Scott amended the School Act in 1912, making it mandatory for the ratepayers of a religious minority to support their separate school, and in 1915, allowing some foreign-language teaching even in public schools. Although Canada was officially a bilingual country and French should have been recognized as an official language, the anglophone majority in Saskatchewan (and most other provinces) tended to regard French as a "foreign" language. Premier Scott thereby aroused the vehement opposition of Reverend Murdock MacKinnon, a most influential Presbyterian minister in Regina, and by 1916 the Orange Order, the Saskatchewan Grain Growers, the Saskatchewan Association of Rural Municipalities (SARM), the *Regina Daily Post*, the *Regina Evening Province and Standard*, the Conservative Party, and, not the least, the Saskatchewan School Trustees Association (SSTA). The separate schools were accused of perpetrating "non-Anglo Saxon ideals and features," the ACFC of attacking the public school system and using the schools to foster its own sectarian ends, and the provincial government of discriminating against "that great unifying agency," the public school, when it should have been observing its duty to "foster assimilation by eliminating sectarian ideals and racial segregation."[38]

Nonetheless, the Liberals were returned to power in 1917, this time under Premier Martin. The new premier recognized that the French in Saskatchewan were in a rather unique position: given their status as "charter members" of Confederation, they could not simply be classed with other non-British minorities.[39] But he was instantly put under considerable pressure by organizations sharing the common view that it was their duty "to see that this province shall remain British, first, last, and all time."[40] Imbued with strong pro-British sentiments during the First World War and bitterness over the resistance to conscription in Quebec, the Orangemen, teachers, Grain Growers, Presbyterians, members of SARM, and the press who had opposed Premier Scott were now joined by the Sons of England as well as the Baptist Conference and Anglican Synod.

Another Grain Growers convention in Regina and a School Trustees one in Saskatoon in 1918 became opportunities to pressure the provincial government into a firmer stand on the school and language question. However, if the pro-British element was adamant, so was the pro-French one. In anticipation of the SSTA convention, the ACFC and its organ, *Le Patriote de l'Ouest*, encouraged strong opposition to such a great offensive against bilingualism in Canada. The conference was attended by many francophone delegates, including prominent French community leaders such as Emile Gravel of Gravelbourg. Nonetheless, the convention succeeded in passing resolutions stating that "nobody shall be a school trustee unless he is able to read and write the English language" (there was no comparable resolution for the French language) and banishing "any other language than English" from Saskatchewan schools. Francophones regarded these resolutions as "a direct violation of the rights of parents to have their own language taught to children in schools for which they pay." They observed that "as French-Canadians who are the first colonizers of this country and who have undisputed constitutional rights to the teaching of our language in our schools we have particularly resented the insult lavished upon us." The French press in Saskatchewan attacked what they considered to be "an association of fanatics" as well as the "unschooled Orangemen's Association" and "infuriated fools." A separate French school association, l'Association des commissaires d'école franco-canadiens de la Saskatchewan, was organized. The trustees of many if not all French schools promptly resigned from the SSTA, and the provincial government was ceaselessly reminded of French rights by Archbishop Mathieu, Père A.C. Auclair (director of *Le Patriote*), and Attorney General Turgeon.[41]

It is instructive to examine the exact situation during the Martin administration (1916–20) in the schools of the French settlements in, for example, the north-central region. Out of sixty largely French schools, little more than half (thirty-six) were reported to have French teachers, though there were actually fifty-three French teachers, of whom twenty-nine had been trained in Quebec and fourteen in other French areas outside Saskatchewan; reportedly, sixteen of these teachers spoke English very poorly.[42] From these data, it is evident that a fairly high proportion of the almost eighty Saskatchewan schools teaching in French in 1918 were in this region and that many schools must have been decidedly French in character and orientation.

It is probable that most of the largely French schools taught the first couple of grades completely in French but the upper grades in French for about an hour a day, in compliance with Section 177 of the School Act. However, this was not the case in certain areas. For example, several schools in the Prud'homme settlement instructed more in French than English and had teachers who were either incapable of teaching well in English or reluctant to do so. By 1918, the Vonda separate school had almost double the enrolment of the public school. The French Catholic clergy were blamed by the school inspector for encouraging separatism, and he considered the separate school to be fully four years behind the public one. At Prud'homme, Ukrainian opposition to French teaching resulted in English being taught to the Ukrainian pupils in the first couple of grades, while the French ones were taught in French. Again Ukrainians were annoyed that in the Kaminka School District near Bonne-Madone the teacher instructed in French and was unsympathetic to the Ukrainian pupils, who outnumbered the French pupils three to one in this district. The premier received a suggestion from the Shell River School District around Boutin in the Debden-Leoville settlement that the first five grades should be allowed to have instruction in French in French majority areas because French pupils did not sufficiently understand instruction in English. Ethier School between Bellevue and Domrémy was the subject of a three-year (1921–23) dispute over violation of the School Act through too much instruction in French; the defending lawyer in this case was John G. Diefenbaker.[43]

The Martin government further refined the legislation restricting teaching in languages other than English on May 1, 1919, when it forbade all instruction in languages other than English during school hours, except French, which could now be used as a language of instruction in the first grade and not for more than an hour a day in subsequent grades. Presumably, prior to that date, Regulation 3 of Section 177 of the School Act had been in effect (since 1915), stating that, "when the board of any district passes a resolution to that effect, the French language may be taught as a subject for a period not exceeding one hour in each day as a part of the school curriculum, and such teaching shall consist of a French reading, French grammar, and French composition." But teaching other subjects in French had been prohibited. In short, the new legislation essentially bypassed the francophone minority, to their leaders' partial satisfaction but to the province's non-French population's ire.[44]

Thus, the controversy continued into the Liberal Dunning regime, 1922–26. In 1925, the ACFC continued to offer French-language courses to francophone pupils. The French attempted to consolidate their position by requesting that the new government supply bilingual teachers, require French to be taught to all French children, unless their parents objected, appoint special teachers to look after the French primary and advanced courses, and allow regular conventions of a French school trustees' association. The government responded by requiring any teacher imported from Quebec to be proficient in English and by suggesting that a general teachers' convention seemed more desirable than a separate French one. For their part, the Orangemen continued their pressure, even though by 1926-27 only 1,360 French students were writing the ACFC course examinations each year; only 133 schools taught French language, grammar, and composition through the seventh grade and only 171 other schools in both grades seven and eight; and there were only twenty-three Catholic separate schools in Saskatchewan compared with 4,776 public schools.[45]

Dunning was succeeded by a fourth Liberal premier, Gardiner, in 1926 (as noted, Gardiner himself had been a schoolteacher in the largely French Mutrie district near Montmartre). Now the Ku Klux Klan emerged in Saskatchewan. The premier was inundated with letters in opposition to ACFC resolutions informing him that "the Orange Order stands for unity among British people and we do not want this part of the British Empire divided by language into warring elements"; that the "country and province should stay British and the British language should be taught"; that "surely this is a white man's country there for a white man's language"; and so on. The *Orange Sentinel* warned of a quarter of a million French Canadians coming to turn Saskatchewan into another Quebec.[46]

Liberal control of the province was finally terminated when J.T.M. Anderson, a Conservative, became premier in 1929. During the election, the Conservatives had accused the former Liberal government of following "an insidious program for French and Roman Catholic political control"; of allowing French to be "used as a language of instruction in all grades in spite of the protests of the English and other nationalities"; and of "fostering and encouraging bilingualism." By 1930, the Conservative government had altered the School Act so that no emblem or garb of a religious group could be displayed on public school premises during school hours. And, by the following year, on the pretext that "some common meeting ground was needed in order that the children of these various peoples be prepared, in a common way, on common grounds, for carrying out the duties of citizenship," Premier Anderson saw to the demise of first-grade teaching in French and required all school trustees to read, write, and conduct meetings in English. Although French had now been virtually obliterated as a language of instruction in the province, the issue did not end there. Anderson's frequent inspections of schools still did not entirely wrest control from all of the non-British ethnic groups; a country school could conform completely to the provincial school regulations when visited by an inspector, then continue its own practices more in keeping with ethnic group ideals, as evidenced by the large volume of complaints continuing to pour into the premier's office.[47]

Despite eventual concessions for the teaching of French and religion, at least in separate schools, a new School Act in 1944 introduced the process of rural school consolidation that was largely completed by the late 1950s. This process had a profound effect on ethnic minority group control of schools, for it meant that most of the larger schools had more heterogeneous enrolments than the small country schools. Yet, by the 1960s, a French boycott of Saskatoon public schools represented an attempt to draw attention to the demand among French for their own schools; statements were reportedly "belligerent and militant in tone, somewhat reminiscent of the statements emanating from Quebec separatists."[48] Finally, in 1967, the year of the Canadian centennial, a new law on education in Saskatchewan permitted teaching in French, and the following year the federal government re-emphasized the status of French as an official language throughout Canada.

Then in 1977 a Saskatchewan branch of Canadian Parents for French was established to promote the learning of French by non-francophone Canadians. Speaking at a national conference of French teachers held in Saskatoon, the president of the Ontario Teachers' Federation declared that

> we must bother with school programs to make French a second language because such programs are an investment in our children and in the future of our country and of the world. ... Canadians possess an innate and inane ability ... to confuse second-language education, bilingualism and politics. ... The English backlash to bilingualism ignores that for decades English was shoved down the throats of Quebecers. In a country built on immigration, the English-speaking majority has encouraged other ethnic groups to retain their native languages and cultures. ... However, when our largest linguistic and cultural minority—the French—wants the same rights as others, and wishes to ensure those constitutionally guaranteed rights, we feel threatened. ... As a Canadian, I believe in two languages, two cultures, but not two solitudes. ... Our children can only do a better job than we have done in providing the bridge of understanding of language and culture necessary to ensure the continuance of our nation as we know it.[49]

Thus inspired, within days the ACFC boldly commented that francophones in Saskatchewan had been "subjected to a state of alienation, calculated inferiority and systematic exhaustion by the English majority." The association called for French to be recognized as an official language of the province with the same status as English, the immediate expansion of French television to all French communities in the province, and the resumption of publication of a French newspaper. Regarding education, the association pressured the provincial government to recognize French-language instruction as a right, not a privilege, and called for the establishment of a special department within the provincial education ministry for the development of French education, a French preschool program, and resolution of any problems transporting students to designated schools.[50] In June 1977, francophone parents in the Prud'homme-Vonda-St-Denis settlement staged a protest against perceived inaction of the Saskatoon East School Board in providing sufficient French-language instruction in the schools of the area.[51]

The next year Section 180 of the Education Act guaranteed the right of access to a French designated program, the establishment of a network of *écoles designées* (schools designated to have a full curriculum in French) in Saskatchewan, and the initiation of programs with courses taught in French (other than just language and literature) at both universities; these initiatives have substantially changed the opportunities for young francophones to maintain their language and to be educated in it right through the highest levels (albeit still rather selectively) in Saskatchewan. In 1979, further regulations in the Education Act distinguished between two types of designated programs, depending on the proportion of time to be spent teaching in French. By now, however, quite a debate had emerged over issues such as the relevance of requiring the teaching of French in Saskatchewan schools in general, the sagacity and purpose of French immersion schools for non-francophones (though it is noteworthy that enrolment had already reached full capacity at the Saskatoon French School), whether students from francophone families should have their own Fransaskois schools, and whether "pure French schools" (advocated by the newly elected head of l'Association jeunesse fransaskoise from Ponteix) would be preferable to designated schools as a more effective bulwark against assimilation.[52]

With the creation of the federal official language minority office in 1980 and the Canadian Charter of Rights and Freedoms two years later, official language minority rights in Saskatchewan received further recognition; specifically, Section 23 of the charter guaranteed the right of official language minorities to instruction in their language. Then in 1988, by virtue of that section, the Court of Queen's Bench ruled that, where the number of eligible children is sufficient to warrant the provision of a school, the minority group has the right to manage and control this school (though access to such a school would be restricted to children of eligible parents). With the conversion of the former ACEFC into the Commission des écoles fransaskoises in 1983, schools attended by francophone students (contrasted with French immersion schools catering primarily to students from non-francophone families) now became known simply as *écoles fransaskoises*. Meanwhile, the Mercure case would provide a legal challenge to official language minority rights in Saskatchewan. In November 1980, Père André Mercure of Cochin was given a ticket for exceeding the legal speed limit on a provincial highway. He requested a trial in French; however, this meant that several relevant provincial statutes would have to be translated into French. This depended on whether Section 110 of the North-West Territories Act of 1891 (which stated clearly that French could be used before the courts) continued to apply after Saskatchewan became a province in 1905. The same year, in 1980, Manitoba became Canada's third officially bilingual province following the legal challenge of St-Boniface businessman Georges Forest, which went all the way to the Supreme Court. So did the *Mercure* case, but the majority decision to give full recognition to French-language minority rights in Saskatchewan was not reached until 1988, after Mercure's death from cancer in 1986. Moreover, the ruling stated that courts in Saskatchewan could use either official language, that a defendant does not necessarily have to be provided with a translator (unless it is clear that a fair trial cannot be conducted without one), and that not all provincial laws would have to be translated into French (which would be extremely expensive, though this had been implied in Manitoba).[53]

Plus ça change. ... In March 2006, Justin Bell, a francophone teacher from Gravelbourg, was stopped by police for speeding while driving to Bellegarde. When he asked the officer whether he could speak French, the policeman's response was perceived as both intimidating and rude. Subsequently, after he complained of this treatment, Bell was informed that this incident had occurred in an RCMP detachment area where a designated bilingual officer was not available (there are now sixteen bilingual detachments in the province). However, in keeping with Canada's Official Languages Act, in other detachments one should be directed to service in French. But researching this case and taking any legal action could be very expensive.[54]

In another judgment of the Supreme Court, in 1990, the right of francophones to determine the education of their children was recognized. Perhaps this was easier said than done. Francophone parents expecting to send their children to francophone schools were becoming frustrated over the failure to create French school boards (the prime minister at the time, Brian Mulroney, even wrote to Premier Grant Devine to express his "deep regret for the legislative delay and the image it presented to Canada"; moreover, there was substantial debate over the application of the "where numbers warrant" clause to local communities.[55] It was not until 1993 that Saskatchewan put into practice the francophone community management of *l'éducation fransaskoise*, and the following year le Conseil scolaire fransaskois de la vieille, Gravelbourg, became the first school unit to assume full self-management of a francophone school. During the next several years, more schools were added, and by January 1999 twelve *écoles fransaskoises* were transferred to a new Division scolaire francophone under the direction of le Conseil scolaire fransaskois (CSF); it was created in 1994 when francophone parents petitioned the provincial government under Article 23 of the Canadian Charter of Rights and Freedoms, which specified that francophone parents have the right to have their children taught in French. Relations between this French school board and the provincial government have been strained at times, such as in 2010, when the CSF was criticized in the provincial auditor's report for failing to provide relevant documentation to the auditors, and in 2012, when the CSF successfully took the government to court for a claimed $3.7 million shortfall in provincial funding of francophone schools for outdated repairs and expansion of facilities. Yet l'Ecole canadienne-français in Saskatoon recently added a high school, Pavillon Gustave-Dubois, in support of which the provincial government contributed $7.3 million and the federal government another $3 million for a new theatre and lecture hall. Currently, this school has 215 elementary students and seventy high school students, but that number is expected to double over the next five years with elementary students reaching high school age and with increasing immigration. In fact, growth in enrolment is becoming more dependent on immigration, as French Canadians no longer tend to have large families. With only eleven students graduating a year from the francophone school in Bellevue (one of the most francophone rural communities in the province), the school now relies on the latest technology, such as video conferences, to link it to other francophone schools. Currently, there are sixteen *écoles fransaskoises* in Saskatchewan with a total enrolment exceeding 1,200; in addition, there are over 1,200 students enrolled in the public school division's immersion programs and more than 2,000 in the Catholic division immersion programs (currently increasing by about 5% a year). In some urban schools, immersion programs are attracting increasing numbers of students: for example, in Saskatoon at College Park, immersion enrolment has increased from 189 to 273 during the past five years and at Lakeview from 156 to 351. In five years, immersion enrolment has increased 37% in Catholic schools and 22% in public schools in Saskatchewan. The Institut français at the University of Regina offers six degree and certificate programs yet most recently had not a single graduate in the francophone studies program. It also contains le Centre de recherché sur les francophones en milieu minoritaire and recently held a conference on the status of French in Western Canada.

CHAPTER 7

INSTITUTIONALIZATION OF THE FRANCOPHONE COMMUNITY

The survival of francophones in Saskatchewan has owed much to the remarkable institutionalization of the Fransaskois. Already noted, in describing the various francophone settlements, were many of the francophone organizations that function at the local community level; also noted were the many francophone organizations that function in an urban setting. In describing the development of specific French settlements and communities, numerous institutions and organizations serving francophones have been mentioned—indeed, this particular minority ethno-linguistic community must be the most highly institutionalized in Saskatchewan.

First, there have been general organizations serving the francophone community as a whole and assisting in the coordination of a multitude of other organizations. The most comprehensive has been l'Association catholique franco-canadienne de la Saskatchewan, formed in 1912; not meaning to imply that it was an organization of the Roman Catholic Church (though the historically common expression among French Canadians, *nôtre foi, nôtre langue*, did imply a close link between Catholic faith and French language and culture), the ACFC changed its name to l'Association culturelle franco-canadienne de la Saskatchewan in 1964, then to l'Assemblée communautaire fransaskoise (ACF) in 1999. Over time, the ACFC/ACF has given birth to several other organizations with more specific mandates. The ACF continues to be regarded as the main organization of the Fransaskois, and as such it is one of a network of francophone organizations in every province across Canada outside Quebec; this network was formally established in 1975 as la Fédération des francophones hors Québec. Several other general francophone organizations have operated in Saskatchewan, including le Bureau de la minorité de langue officielle (1979).

Religious organizations have included French Roman Catholic organizations for women in Saskatchewan, such as la Congrégation des Dames de Sainte-Anne, la Congrégation des Dames de l'Autel, le Groupe d'action catholique, la Croisade eucharistique (all of which, for example, operated in Duck Lake), and la Cadette des paroisses du diocese (in the Prince Albert Diocese). Each parish had its *cercle paroissiale*. Numerous community activities were conducted by francophone religious orders, which also played a significant role as teachers and nurses in many communities. Additionally, there were numerous secular, though church-supported, organizations.

Francophone women in Saskatchewan have participated in la Fédération des femmes canadiennes-françaises (1918), through local community branches extended particularly during the 1960s and 1970s, and la Fédération provinciale des fransaskoises.

A comprehensive business organization is le Conseil de la coopération de la Saskatchewan (1946), which promotes francophone cooperative business enterprises and holds a Francophone Entrepreneurship Month. Cooperatives are linked through l'Association coopérative d'établissement ltée (1960). A network of *caisses populaires* (credit unions) consists of *caisses populaires françaises* (services in French only) and *caisses populaires bilingues* (services in either French or English), with branches in several cities and many communities (the network had already grown to twenty-nine by 1964). Le Foncier franco-canadien is a national financial and insurance organization that has operated in Saskatchewan. A professional legal association serving francophones is l'Association des juristes d'expression française de la Saskatchewan.

Educational organizations have included l'Association des commissaires d'école franco-canadiens de la Saskatchewan (1918), which became la Commission des écoles fransaskoises and then le Conseil scolaire fransaskois, and la Fédération des enseignant(e)s de la Saskatchewan, l'Association des professeurs de français en Saskatchewan (1980), l'Association des parents fransaskois (representing parents whose children participate in francophone schools and childcare centres), Saskatchewan étudiante voyage international, les Jeunes voyageurs (an exchange between Quebec youth and *fransaskois* youth), l'Association du préscolaire fransaskois, le Centre de ressources éducatives à la petite enfance, and Service fransaskois d'éducation aux adultes.

Historical and cultural organizations have included la Société historique de la Saskatchewan (1978), le Conseil culturel fransaskois (founded in 1973 as la Commission culturelle fransaskoise, renamed the Conseil culturel fransaskois in 2000), l'Alliance franco-canadienne (a national French Canadian organization), Coalition pour la promotion de la langue francaise et de la culture francophone en Saskatchewan, l'Association France-Canada de la Saskatchewan (a cultural exchange program between France and Saskatchewan), le Club Richelieu international (founded in 1944, with chapters in Saskatoon and Regina founded respectively in 1972 and 1974), Journées du patrimoine, Gala fransaskois de la chanson, and les Rendez-vous de la francophonie (now in its fifteenth year). 2011 was officially declared by the provincial government *l'année des fransaskois*. One week in March is National Francophone Week. Given its increasing diversity, the francophone community of Saskatchewan is linked to l'Organization international de la francophonie (formerly l'Agence de cooperation culturelle et technique in 1970 and l'Agence intergouvernementale de la francophonie in 1998), which has celebrated International Francophone Day every March 20 for forty years.

The arts have been promoted by l'Association des artistes de la Saskatchewan, theatrical performances in French, and popular singing groups such as Folle Avoine (six sisters and one brother of the Campagne family during the 1980s) and more recently La Raquette à claquettes (led by Francis Marchildon originally of Zenon Park). A Fête fransaskoise showcasing French culture in Saskatchewan is held in a different community every year, and a francophone pavilion has become a regular feature of Folkfest in Saskatoon and Mosaic in Regina.

The comprehensive francophone youth organization is l'Association jeunesse fransaskoise (1977), with many local community and city branches. L'Association des scouts du Canada has been active in Saskatchewan. Other specialized francophone organizations have included l'Association des juristes d'expression française de la Saskatchewan (for the legal profession), and la Fédération des aînés fransaskois for seniors.

Controlling the influence of the media representing the general (English-speaking) society has been vital to francophone minorities in Saskatchewan and across Canada. As George Stanley once observed, a factor of importance in bolstering French survival in the West was the French press. Until French-language radio stations were established at Gravelbourg and Saskatoon in 1952, for decades the sole form of French media available to the French in Saskatchewan was their French-language press; the omnipresent English-language press was increasingly offset by a growing French-language press that circulated in francophone communities in Saskatchewan. Aside from occasional Métis papers, such as *Le Métis* of St-Boniface, one of the first French-language papers to be printed in the Prairie Provinces was *Les Cloches de St-Boniface*, a monthly founded in 1902. What soon became the most widely circulating French-language newspaper in the Prairie Provinces, *Le Patriote de l'Ouest*, was founded at Duck Lake in 1910, then moved to Prince Albert the same year, and finally merged with *La Liberté*, founded in St-Boniface in 1913, to become *La Liberté et le Patriote*, published in St-Boniface from 1942 to 1970. A second Saskatchewan weekly in French, *l'Etoile*, was established at Gravelbourg in 1921; in 1963, this paper organized a network of local weeklies in several small francophone communities (Willow Bunch, Debden, Domrémy, Marcelin, and Zenon Park). *Les Bulletins de l'ACFC* was based in Regina and St-Victor in 1970. *L'Eau Vive* soon became the most widely circulated francophone community newspaper in Saskatchewan from 1971 to 1976, then was turned into an independent *hebdo* when it resumed in 1978. French publishing in Saskatchewan is supported by les Publications fransaskoises ltée, la Coopérative des publications fransaskoises, les Editions Louis Riel, and les Editions de la nouvelle plume in Regina.[56]

As Stanley has explained,

> the development of (English-language radio broadcasting during the 1920s and 30s posed new problems from a cultural and religious point of view. Hitherto his home had been for the French Canadian the sanctuary of his language. But the radio was an insidious thing which penetrated both the walls and minds of the population, and its language was English and its culture neutralistic, materialist, sometimes immoral, pagan, or frankly anti-Catholic. It was a matter of deep concern both to the church and to the national associations how to counter the new threat to their culture.[57]

Writing about Quebec at the time, Scott and Oliver more generally pointed out that "the social revolution is, roughly, the sum of industrialization, urbanization, and the impact of mass communication, especially television."[58] The advent of the penetrating English-language radio during the 1920s and 1930s must have had a substantial effect on younger francophones in Saskatchewan, and television was added during the 1950s. This was countered somewhat, however, by the first French-language radio broadcasting in 1954 by CKCK-TV in Regina and CFQC-TV in Saskatoon, then by Sunday morning television in French in 1971 and later full-time French-language television; today full-time radio programs are available in both AM and FM frequencies and several television channels in French.[59] La Société Radio Canada en Saskatchewan (French-language CBC) was established in 1952–53 and la Fondation de la radio française en Saskatchewan in 1976. Francothon, a single-day telethon to raise money for the Fondation fransaskoise, is now in its seventeenth year.

CONCLUDING THOUGHTS

The demographic trends discerned have not been indicative of a strong survival of the French minority in Saskatchewan, at least not until recently perhaps. Ethnic origin will continue to become more complex with increasing intermarriage; concomitantly, the number of Saskatchewan people claiming only French origin continues to decline. The proportion of French-origin population resident in urban areas has steadily been increasing, at the expense of the rural proportion, and it is in the urban areas that the greatest decline in actual use of French among these people has long been occurring, though with the most recent francophone immigration, together with the concentration of francophone institutions in urban centres, this trend might be reversed or at least stabilized. There are numerous communities in Saskatchewan with substantial proportions of French residents, but most of them have been losing population; out of forty-four communities in which data were available in 2006, thirty-two were losing population during the previous five years, four were static, and eight were gaining population (but often only by several people). There has been a marked decline, over the past several decades, in the proportion of people of French origin still speaking French as their primary mother tongue (but most recently not necessarily in the numbers of Saskatchewan residents—including those not of French or Belgian ethnic origin—speaking French).

The steady drift into English-language use might have been slowed down in recent years because of the increased availability of French-language programs and immersion classes, French media, and organized activities conducted in French. But examination of age structure and language use seems to indicate that as a whole younger generation French Canadians in Saskatchewan are not significantly reversing the trend of linguistic assimilation. Even among young adults who claim to be francophone, only about one in five actually speaks French more than English at home. A core of committed French-speaking residents of Saskatchewan represents a relatively small and declining proportion of the total population in the province claiming, in whole or part, French origin. Although familiarity with the French language has increased somewhat among the non-French population, the vast majority of Saskatchewan people are not familiar with French; neither are more than half of the people who claim to be of French descent.

Yet the historical impact of French settlement in Saskatchewan has been profound, represented in the many French settlements and communities scattered across the province; indeed, Saskatchewan toponymy might include over 3,000 French place names. Since 1979, the *fransaskois drapeau* (flag) has flown proudly over the many francophone communities in Saskatchewan. Francophones continue to form relatively strong proportions of the population of certain rural regions of the province, where the French fact plays an important role in community life.

Indeed, it is hazardous to generalize about the current strength of *fransaskois* identity in the many rural communities in French bloc settlements across the province, for clearly there is a great deal of variety, or even to generalize about the toll taken by inexorable urbanization, when cities become the very bases for the plethora of francophone organizations in Saskatchewan. Every year the French fact in Saskatchewan is celebrated in special events that often encourage the participation of youth. It is anticipated that few francophones could be attracted from other provinces or more developed countries in Europe, with relatively high standards of living, whereas French-speaking immigrants could come from African and Caribbean countries, thus contributing to the French-speaking population but not to the French-origin population.[60]

CHAPTER 7

SOURCES

Saskatchewan Métis History

Classic sources on Métis history in Western Canada and Saskatchewan have been l'Abbé C. Rondeau, *La Montagne de Bois: Willow Bunch, Saskatchewan* (Québec: Imprimerie l'Action Sociale, 1923); Reverend J. LeChevallier, *St-Laurent-de-Grandin: A Mission and Shrine in the Northwest of America* (Vannes, France: Lafolye and J. de Lamarzelle, 1930); A-M. de Trémaudan, *Histoire de la Nation Métisse dans l'Ouest Canadien* (1936; reprinted, St-Boniface, MB: Editions des Plaines, 1984); M. Giraud, *Le Métis Canadien* (Paris: Institut d'Ethnologie, Université de Paris, 1945); and G. Charette, *Vanishing Spaces: Memoirs of Louis Goulet, a Prairie Métis* (Winnipeg: Editions Bois-Brûlés, 1980).

More recent sources include, for example, G.F.G. Stanley, *Louis Riel* (Toronto: Ryerson, 1963); J.K. Howard, *The Strange Empire of Louis Riel* (Toronto: Swan Publishing, 1965); D.B. Sealey and A.S. Lussier, *The Métis: Canada's Forgotten People* (Winnipeg: Manitoba Métis Federation Press, 1975); G. Woodcock, *Gabriel Dumont* (Edmonton: Hurtig, 1975); *A Pictorial History of the Métis and Non-Status Indian in Saskatchewan* (Regina: Saskatchewan Human Rights Commission and AMNSIS, 1976); A.S. Lussier, ed., *Louis Riel and the Métis* (Winnipeg: Pemmican, 1979); T. Flanagan, *Riel and the Rebellion of 1885 Reconsidered* (Saskatoon: Western Producer Prairie Books, 1983); M. Beaucage and E. LaRoque, "Two Faces of the New Jerusalem: Indian-Métis Reaction to the Missionary," in *Visions of the New Jerusalem: Religious Settlement on the Prairies*, ed. B.G. Smillie (Edmonton: NeWest Press, 1983), 27–38; M. Taft, "The St. Laurent Pilgrimage: A Religious Ritual of Faith and Healing," in *Discovering Saskatchewan Folklore* (Edmonton: NeWest Press, 1983), 83–111; B. Beal and R. MacLeod, *Prairie Fire: The 1885 North-West Rebellion* (Edmonton: Hurtig, 1984); J. Peterson and J.S.H. Brown, *The New Peoples: Being and Becoming Métis in North America* (Winnipeg: University of Manitoba Press, 1985); C.H. Shillington, *Historic Land Trails of Saskatchewan* (West Vancouver, BC: Evvard Publications, 1985); D. McLean, *Home from the Hill: A History of the Métis in Western Canada* (Regina: Gabriel Dumont Institute, 1987); D. Purich, *The Métis* (Toronto: Lorimer, 1988); D.P. Payment, *"Les gens libres—Otipemisiwak": Batoche, Saskatchewan, 1870–1930* (Ottawa: Environment Canada, 1990); F. Pannekoek, *A Snug Little Flock: The Social Origins of the Riel Resistance, 1869-70* (Winnipeg: Watson and Dwyer, 1991); D. Russell, "Fur Trade" and "Fur Trade Posts," D.R. Préfontaine, "Métis History," and A.B. Anderson, "French and Métis Settlements," in *Encyclopedia of Saskatchewan* (Regina: Canadian Plains Research Center, 2005), 605–06, 359–60; P. Douaud, ed., *The Western Métis: Profile of a People* (Regina: Canadian Plains Research Center, 2007); and L.J. Barkwell, *Veterans and Families of the 1885 Northwest Resistance* (Saskatoon: Gabriel Dumont Institute, 2011).

Detailed descriptions of specific Métis settlements in Saskatchewan include, for Batoche, D.P. Payment, *The Free People — Li gens libre* (Calgary: University of Calgary Press, 2009); for la Prairie Ronde, R. Schilling, *Gabriel's Children* (Saskatoon: Saskatoon Métis Society, 1983); and, for Willow Bunch, R. Rivard and C. Littlejohn, *The History of the Métis of Willow Bunch* (2003).

Contemporary Saskatchewan Métis Culture and Issues

Among the many sources that have described contemporary Métis culture and salient issues in general have been H. Adams, *Prison of Grass: Canada from a Native Point of View* (Saskatoon: Fifth House, 1975); H.W. Daniels, *The Forgotten People: Métis and Non-Status Indian Land Claims* (Ottawa: Native Council of Canada, 1979); J.D. Harrison, *Métis* (Calgary: Glenbow-Alberta Institute, 1985); P.C. Douaud, *Ethnolinguistic Profile of the Canadian Métis* (Ottawa: National Museum of Man, 1985); K. Zellig and V. Zellig, *Ste-Madeleine: Community without a Town: Métis Elders in Interview* (Winnipeg: Pemmican, 1987); S.W. Corrigan and L.J. Barkwell, eds., *The Struggle for Recognition: Canadian Justice and the Métis Nation* (Winnipeg: Pemmican, 1991); H. Adams, *Tortured People: The Politics of Colonization* (Penticton, BC: Theytus Books, 1999); O.P. Dickason, "Aboriginals: Métis," in *Encyclopedia of Canada's Peoples*, ed. P.R. Magocsi (Toronto: University of Toronto Press, 1999), 70–79; L.J. Barkwell, L. Dorion, and D.R. Préfontaine, eds., *Métis Legacy* (Winnipeg: Pemmican, 2003); N. St-Onge, *Saint-Laurent, Manitoba: Evolving Métis Identities, 1850–1914* (Regina: Canadian Plains Research Center, 2004); D.R. Préfontaine, "Métis Communities," "Métis Culture and Language," and "Métis Nation," in *Encyclopedia of Saskatchewan* (Regina: Canadian Plains Research Center, 2005), 603–07; and V. Ahenakew, *Nehiyawewin Masinahikan: Michif/Cree Dictionary* (Saskatoon: Gabriel Dumont Institute, 2009).

French Settlements in Saskatchewan and Western Canada

Early sources on French in Saskatchewan included G. Giscard, *Dans la Prairie Canadienne*, republished as Canadian Plains Studies No. 11 (Regina: Canadian Plains Research Center, 1982); L. Gilbert, *La Saskatchewan*, edité par *La Canadienne* (Paris: La Canadienne, 1914); and D. Frémont, *Les Français dans l'Ouest Canadien* (1959; reprinted, St-Boniface, MB: Les Editions du Blé, 1980).

Other publications and research included, during the 1960s and 1970s, G.F.G. Stanley, "French and English in Western Canada," in *Canadian Dualism/La dualité canadienne*, ed. M. Wade (Toronto: University of Toronto Press, 1960), 311–50; l'Association Catholique Franco-Canadienne de la Saskatchewan, *L'album-souvenir cinquantenaire de l'ACFC: 1912–1962* (Saskatoon: ACFC, 1962); M. Jackson, "Les Franco-Canadiens de la Saskatchewan," *Revue d'études canadiennes/Journal of Canadian Studies* 7, 3 (1972): 1–20; R.J. Joy, *Languages in Conflict* (Toronto: McClelland and Stewart, 1972); A.B. Anderson, "Ethnic Identity Retention in French-Canadian Communities in Saskatchewan," paper presented at the Annual Meeting of the Canadian Sociology and Anthropology Association, University of Toronto, August 1974; and A.B. Anderson, "French Ethnicity in North-Central Saskatchewan," in *Two Nations, Many Cultures: Ethnic Groups in Canada*, ed. J.L. Elliott (Scarborough: Prentice-Hall Canada, 1979), 262–69.

During the 1980s and 1990s were R. Breton and P. Savard, eds., *The Quebec and Acadian Diaspora in North America* (Toronto: Multicultural History Society of Ontario, 1982); R.J.A. Huel, "Gestae Dei Per Francos: The French Catholic Experience in Western Canada," in *Visions of the New Jerusalem: Religious Settlement on the Prairies*, ed. B.G. Smillie (Edmonton: NeWest Press, 1983), 39–54; *Perspectives sur la Saskatchewan française* (Regina: Société Historique de la Saskatchewan, 1983); A.B. Anderson, *French Settlements in Saskatchewan* and *Ethnic Identity Retention in Francophone Communities in Saskatchewan*, Research Unit for French-Canadian Studies, University of Saskatchewan, Report Nos. 5 and 6, 1985; A.B. Anderson, "L'avenir de la Société Fransaskoise," invited lecture, Club Richelieu, Saskatoon, March 1986; G. MacEwan, *Les Franco-Canadiens dans l'Ouest/French in the West* (St-Boniface, MB: Editions des Plaines, 1986); R. Lapointe and L. Tessier, *Histoire des Franco-Canadiens de la Saskatchewan* (Regina: La Société Historique de la Saskatchewan, 1986); G.J. Brault, *The French-Canadian Heritage in New England* (Montreal: McGill-Queen's University Press, 1986); Hanover, New Hampshire and London: University Press of New England, 1986); A.B. Anderson, *Guide des sources bibliographiques des communautés francophones de la Saskatchewan/Guide to Bibliographic Sources on Francophone Communities in Saskatchewan*, Research Unit for French-Canadian Studies, University of Saskatchewan, Report No. 13, 1987; R. Lapointe, *La Saskatchewan de A à Z* (Regina: La Société Historique de la Saskatchewan, 1987); R. Lapointe, *100 noms: Petit dictionnaire biographique des Franco-Canadiens de la Saskatchewan* (Regina: La Société Historique de la Saskatchewan, 1988); A.B. Anderson, "Les Fransaskois: Tendances demographiques," paper presented at Les Communautés Francophones hors Québec: Alienation ou Non?, University of Calgary, November 1989; and A.B. Anderson, "Francophones and Francophobes in the Prairies," paper presented at the Eleventh Biennial Conference of the Canadian Ethnic Studies Association, Winnipeg, October 1991.

Informative series are the Revue Historique of la Société Historique de la Saskatchewan and the proceedings of the colloquia of le Centre d'Etudes Franco-Canadiennes de l'Ouest, including *La langue, la culture, et la société des francophones de l'Ouest* (1983 and 1984), *Héritage et avenir des francophones de l'Ouest* (1986), *L'Ouest Canadien et l'Amérique Française* (1988), *Etudes Oblates de l'Ouest* (1989), *A la mesure du pays* (1990), and so on. See also A.B. Anderson, "Profil demographique des Canadiens-Français de la Saskatchewan: 1885–1985," in *Héritage et avenir des francophones de l'Ouest*, les Actes du Cinquième Colloque du Centre d'Etudes Franco-Canadiennes de l'Ouest Tenu au Collège St. Thomas More, Université de la Saskatchewan, octobre 1985, 175–95.

And most recently have been M.D. Behiels, *Canada's Francophone Minority Communities* (Montreal: McGill-Queen's University Press, 2004); A.B. Anderson, "Francophones" and "French Settlements," in *Encyclopedia of Saskatchewan* (Regina: Canadian Plains Research Center, 2005), 356–58, 362–66; and the reminiscences of Abbé Roger Ducharme, *Servir et non etre servi: Un Fransaskois se raconte* (Regina: Les Editions de la Nouvelle Plume, 2005).

Belgian settlement in Manitoba and Saskatchewan has been described in K. Wilson and J.B. Wyndels, *The Belgians in Manitoba* (Winnipeg: Peguis Publishers, 1976) and C.J. Jaenen, *Promoters, Planters, and Pioneers: The Course and Context of Belgian Settlement in Western Canada* (Calgary: University of Calgary Press, 2011).

The Controversy over Education

The struggle for francophone schools in Saskatchewan has been described in detail in K.A. McLeod, "Politics, Schools, and the French Language, 1881—1931," in *Politics in Saskatchewan*, ed. N. Ward and D. Spafford (Lindsay, ON: Longmans of Canada and John Dyell, 1968), 124–50; R. Huel, "The French Canadians and the Language Question, 1918," *Saskatchewan History* 23, 1 (1970): 1–15, reprinted in *Pages from the Past: Essays in Saskatchewan History*, ed. D.H. Bocking (Saskatoon: Western Producer Prairie Books, 1979), 181–96; M.R. Lupul, *The Roman Catholic Church and the North-West School Question: A Study in Church-State Relations in Western Canada, 1875-1905* (Toronto: University of Toronto Press, 1974); W. Denis and P. Li, "The Politics of Language Loss: A Francophone Case from Western Canada," *Journal of Education Policy* 3, 4 (1988): 351–70; W. Denis, "Politics of Language," in *Race and Ethnic Relations in Canada*, ed. P. Li (Toronto: Oxford University Press, 1990), 148–85; W. Denis, "La gestion scolaire fransaskoise," in *A la mesure du pays*, ed. J-G. Quenneville (Saskatoon: CEFCO, 1990), 11–30; and E. D'Almeida, "French Education in Saskatchewan," and M.E. Reeves, "French Immersion Education in Saskatchewan," in *Encyclopedia of Saskatchewan* (Regina: Canadian Plains Research Center, 2005). Details on enrolments in French schools during the 1950s and 1960s are provided in Ducharme, *Servir et non etre servi*, noted above.

Local Histories

Aside from several of the sources listed above, which provide ample detail on specific francophone communities, a vast amount of information is found in local histories, such as Paroisse de St-Brieux, *Reminiscenses d'un pionnier, St-Brieux jubilé d'argent, 1904-1929*; *Cinquantenaire de la Paroisse de St-Brieux, Saskatchewan, 1904–1954*; Diocèse de Gravelbourg, *Croquis historiques des paroisses du Diocèse de Gravelbourg, Saskatchewan* (Gravelbourg, SK: Diocèse de Gravelbourg, 1956); G. Hébert, *Les débuts de Gravelbourg, 1905–1965*; Père Denis Dubuc, *Généologie des familles de la Paroisse de St-Isidore-de-Bellevue, Saskatchewan, 1902–1970*; St. Louis Local History Committee,*"I Remember": A History of St. Louis and Surrounding Areas* (Altona, MB: Friesen Printers, 1980); R. Lacoursière-Stringer, *Histoire de/History of Ponteix* (Steinbach, MB: Derksen Printers, 1981); Reverend A. Chabot, *Histoire du Diocèse de Gravelbourg, 1930–1980* (Willow Bunch, SK: 1981); Comité du livre historique, *Echo des pionniers: Histoire de Debden et district, 1912–1985* (Altona, MB: Friesen Printers, 1985); Duck Lake History Committee, *"Their Dreams ... Our Memories": A History of Duck Lake and District* (Altona, MB: Friesen Printers, 1988); *Souvenirs, 1902–2002, St-Isidore-de-Bellevue* (2002); Sisters of the Faithful Companions of Jesus, *Journeying through a Century: Sister Pioneers, 1883–1983* (Edmonton: Technical Graphics, 1983).

The most comprehensive source on the origins of French place names in Saskatchewan is Carol Jean Léonard, *Mémoire des noms de lieux d'origine et d'influence françaises en Saskatchewan* (Québec: Les Editions GID, 2010).

Certain graduate theses have also provided much interesting information, including G.M. Marcotte, "Being French-Canadian in Zenon Park, St-Isidore-de-Bellevue, and

Marcelin, Saskatchewan (MA thesis, University of Saskatchewan, 1994), and B.R. Hamilton, "Francophone Settlement in the Gravelbourg Bloc Settlement and Francophone and Métis Settlement in the Willow Bunch Bloc Settlement in Southwestern Saskatchewan, 1870–1926 (MA thesis, University of Regina, 2007), partially published as B.R. Hamilton, "Francophone Settlement in the Gravelbourg Area," in *Saskatchewan: Geographic Perspectives*, ed. B.D. Thraves, M.L. Lewry, J.E. Dale, and H. Schlichtmann (Regina: University of Regina and Canadian Plains Research center, 2008), 146–52.

Chapter 8

NORDIC SETTLEMENTS

During the latter nineteenth century, large areas of Minnesota and the Dakotas became compact bloc settlements of Scandinavians, even more highly organized than their German counterparts in the preservation of ethnic identity; by 1890, close to 20,000 Norwegian immigrants had settled in South Dakota alone.[1] Relatively few Scandinavians had immigrated as yet to Saskatchewan, but this situation was soon expected to change markedly; already numerous Scandinavian settlers in the Midwestern states were contemplating resettlement in Canada. According to a Canadian government report in 1895,

> The falling-off of Scandinavian immigration during the past year is in a great measure due to the prevailing depression in the United States, news of the unfortunate condition of that country having reached Europe and deterred many would-be immigrants from leaving their homes. In previous years immigration has been, to some extent, a necessity, but the improved condition that has characterized European affairs during the past summer has placed it within the power of a good many to act independently. It may be assumed that this damming-back of the stream which has annually left the coasts of Scandinavia must be followed at no distant date by a correspondingly increased flow. When this takes place we may reasonably expect to benefit by the movement. … Our colonies are growing stronger, and better known every day, and the fact that so many of their countrymen are comfortably settled and doing well is a source of much confidence in the new arrivals. … It is satisfactory to note that a number of Norwegians from … Minnesota are turning their thoughts to our country; hardy and thrifty, accustomed to farming, they make the best of settlers, as the success that has attended their efforts in the past amply testifies. The increase in numbers, and the want of good land, is forcing them to seek

fresh fields of settlement, and we may look forward to a large immigration from this source next year. Already many have taken up lands with us, and their friends will unquestionably follow them as soon as the season sets in. ...[2]

So, despite relatively little active encouragement of emigration in Scandinavia itself by the Canadian government, the number of people of Scandinavian origin resident in Saskatchewan leapt from only 1,452 in 1901 to 33,991 in 1911.[3] During that decade, large areas of the province were settled by people of Scandinavian origin, thus adding to the compact bloc settlements that had already been established by Swedes in 1885 and 1889, Icelanders in 1886–93, and Finns in 1887.

Beginning in the mid-1880s, by 1911 Scandinavian and Finnish immigrants and Scandinavian Americans had founded a dozen primarily Norwegian settlements, half a dozen smaller Swedish settlements, three Icelandic, one Danish, and several Finnish settlements. By 1971, there were approximately 50,000 to 60,000 people in Saskatchewan who claimed Scandinavian or Finnish origin, including 22,000–36,000 of Norwegian origin, 10,000–15,000 Swedish, 3,000–6,000 Danish, 2,000–3,000 Icelandic, and almost 2,000 Finnish.[4] Recent census data (2006) estimated that a total of 125,700 Saskatchewan residents claimed Scandinavian (including Finnish) ethnic origin(s), the vast majority of whom claimed more than a single ethnic origin. More than half were of Norwegian origin, and over a quarter of Swedish origin, while smaller proportions were respectively of Danish, Icelandic, and Finnish ethnic origin. A relatively small number (3,065) simply claimed Scandinavian origin in general rather than a more specific Scandinavian origin.[5]

As we will see in the following description of the historical development and present extent of Scandinavian and Finnish settlements in Saskatchewan, almost two-thirds of the people of Norwegian origin in the province continue to live in settlement areas where they form a substantial proportion of the local population; the remaining third live in more mixed areas and in cities. On the other hand, only a very small proportion of people of Swedish origin now live in Swedish settlements, unless we consider communities and districts where Swedes have settled together with or adjacent to other Scandinavians and Finns. Hardly any people of Danish descent live in what could be called a Danish settlement. Yet, though they are less numerous, almost all people of Icelandic origin continue to reside within Icelandic settlements. And about half of the people of Finnish origin still live in well-defined Finnish settlements.

Divisions in the Lutheran Church tended to reinforce the separate ethnic identification of Nordic peoples for many decades in Saskatchewan, and traditional languages were initially used in church services but not as long in Scandinavian churches as in German churches. Not infrequently there were several Lutheran churches close together, each representing a different ethnic affiliation and an allegiance to a different synod. As we saw in Chapter 4, German Lutherans were divided into several rival affiliations that consisted entirely of Germans. Norwegian congregations belonged largely to the Norwegian Synod, the Norwegian Lutheran Church of America, the United Norwegian Lutheran Church, and occasionally the Lutheran Free Church and the Lutheran Brethren; Swedish congregations were affiliated with the Augustana Synod or the Augustana Evangelical Lutheran Church; Icelandic congregations adhered to the Icelandic Evangelical Lutheran Synod of North America or occasionally the United Lutheran Church in America or the State Church of Iceland; Finnish congregations were affiliated with either the Suomi Synod or the Laestadian movement; and Danish congregations had their own affiliation.

NORWEGIAN SETTLEMENTS

According to recent census data (2006), of 68,650 Saskatchewan residents claiming Norwegian ethnic origin, just 12.2% (8,410) claimed no other ethnic origin, whereas the vast majority, 87.8% (60,245) claimed other origins besides Norwegian, signifying extensive intermarriage. Almost all towns, villages, and hamlets with substantial Norwegian proportions have been declining, and the few exceptions have gained only a few residents. Norwegians, however, have tended overwhelmingly to concentrate less in communities than in open farmlands; there, too, rural depopulation has taken a heavy toll on the prospective cultural survival of this ethnic group, though quite a few Norwegian Lutheran country churches have survived to maintain at least some sense of historic continuity.

It seems rather arbitrary to attempt to determine the chronological sequence in which Norwegian settlements were founded in Saskatchewan. The Birch Hills settlement was probably the earliest, as it began to develop as early as 1894. The first Norwegian Lutheran congregation was Kopperud, near Northgate on the American border, in March 1903, but the oldest congregation still in existence is Hanley, founded soon after in September 1903, followed almost immediately by congregations near Langham and Birch Hills. In the meantime, other Norwegian settlements had started to develop; virtually all of the Norwegian settlements in the province had come into existence by 1910. It is therefore expedient to briefly describe their historical development and contemporary extent in geographical rather than strictly chronological sequence. In just a single decade, the number of Norwegians in Saskatchewan grew rapidly from 7,625 in 1911 to 31,438 in 1921. During the short period from 1903 to 1916, 224 Norwegian Lutheran congregations were established in the province.[6] But over time rural depopulation as well as church mergers and consolidation processes have taken a significant toll especially on smaller country churches: at least 137 Norwegian Lutheran congregations in Saskatchewan, as well as 159 preaching points (which usually met in private homes, community halls, or country schoolhouses), have closed (yet some have been preserved and renovated as heritage sites and might still be rarely used for special occasions).[7]

The Southeastern Frontier and Soo Line

Around the turn of the century, large numbers of Norwegians migrated northward across the international border from earlier settlements that they had established in Minnesota, North and South Dakota, and Montana. Many settled in areas just north of the border. Today Norwegian Canadians form a substantial proportion in most of the rural municipalities along the border as well as a corridor along the Soo Line extending northwest from Estevan through Weyburn, mixed with Germans. In 1971, they constituted between half and a quarter of the population of eight communities and a substantial proportion (but less than a quarter) in another eight communities.[8]

CHAPTER 8

But in certain rural districts and unincorporated hamlets, Norwegians predominated. Today there might be several thousand people of Scandinavian (mostly Norwegian) origin in these communities and rural municipalities.

Estevan has active ELCIC (Evangelical Lutheran Church in Canada) congregations; a former Norwegian congregation was Zoar or Trinity (1913–53). In the rural area around Estevan, Immanuel (founded in 1903) was fifteen kilometres to the south, toward the US border; the Rasmussen School District was formed in 1906; the Hildahl Rural Telephone Company was established in 1914 by the Hildahl families who arrived from Willmar, Minnesota, in 1902; and the Nygren School District was named in 1912 after school trustee Gustav Nygren. East of Estevan, Zion congregation served the Hirsch area from 1903 to 1910 and from 1916 to 1950. Kopperud Church near Northgate was actually the first Norwegian Lutheran church to be established in what is now Saskatchewan, in March 1903; all that remains is a historic plaque—the tiny frame church blew down in a strong wind in 1995.

Heading west from Estevan, Bethel congregation (1906–47) served the Outram area. Near Torquay (pop. 184), the Flaata district was settled by homesteaders Halvor Flaata with his six sons from Appleton, Minnesota, in 1905; the Solheim (Norwegian for sunny home) School District operated from 1913 to 1954; the Tenold School District was named in 1904 for Ole Tenold, born in Vik, Sogn, Norway, who came from Aberdeen, North Dakota, two years earlier; and the Hagen School District was named in 1906 for Ole Hagen, from Trondheim, who homesteaded there in 1902. The resilience of Norwegian Lutheran country churches can hardly be overstated: the Salem Lutheran congregation in the country near Torquay was first organized in 1906, and the church was built in 1911, destroyed by lightning in 1929, finally closed in 1963, then restored as a historic site in 1999. Torquay was a Norwegian Lutheran preaching point from the 1930s to 1945. The church at Bromhead was named after Hamar, Norway; a former congregation (1905–95) long served the Lac Qui Parle district. St. Olaf was formed in 1927 with the merging of two older congregations, Zion and Hauge; this church served the Oungre area for forty years, to 1967; originally, services were held in private homes, and Norwegian was the preferred language through the 1930s. The Bansgrund district outside Tribune was named in 1912 after the sole postmaster, Olaf Bansgrund, who immigrated from Norway with his father, Ludvig. The Hauge congregation was founded in 1907, the Immanuel congregation at Maxim in 1910 (closed in 1974). Near Beaubier, the Norge School District came into being in 1912. At Lake Alma, Skjerdal Park was named after the Skjerdal brothers (Torger, Haakon, and Louis), who homesteaded nearby, and around Lake Alma Nordalen Lutheran Church (1914–64) and its cemetery were named after the Nordalen region in Norway; Saron Church (1918) merged with Overland Church (1910) in 1957. The Overland School District was formed in 1910. On the Torkelson farm, the barn (1915), granary (1918), and windmill (1924) became designated heritage sites in 1989. And, to the north, near the Karl Lake–Olson Lake district, Ole K. Lein, who arrived from North Dakota in 1911, donated the site for Lein School the next year. Both Lake Alma and nearby Gladmar continue to have active ELCIC congregations. Half of the 170 residents of Lake Alma in 1971 were Scandinavian, but now only thirty residents remain; there are fifty-three at Gladmar. Lesja cemetery near Minton was named after Lesjaskog, Oppland, the Norwegian home of settler Ole C. Boe.

Between Estevan and Weyburn, near Hitchcock, Snaasen Church once served Norwegian Lutheran settlers; the congregation was organized in 1903, but the church was not actually built until 1919; it closed in 1956 but was temporarily revived again in 1974, 1984, and 1991. Hitchcock was a Norwegian Lutheran preaching point from 1908 to 1915. At Macoun, the Bethany congregation was organized in 1905; the church was built in 1919 and closed in 1976. Several Norwegian Lutheran preaching points served Macoun and area, including the Macoun community (1904-10) and the Long Creek and Paul Lies districts (1914-15). Midale (pop. 462) continues to have active ELCIC and LCC (Lutheran Church Canada) congregations. Near Midale, Bromsted School (misspelled) was named in 1911 for Peter Bromstad, who arrived from Trondheim in 1903; Herman Hoium, born in Fresvik, Sogn, Norway, arrived from White Rock, South Dakota, in 1902, and the local school was named after him three years later; the Olmstead School District was established in 1905; the Sorsdahl School District was named in 1911 after Andreas Sorsdahl, who arrived there in 1902 from De Smet, South Dakota; and Thorson School was named in 1904 after Norwegian homesteaders Anton and Olava Thorson, who arrived from Minnesota a couple of years earlier. West of Midale, Goodwater was a Norwegian Lutheran preaching point in 1914-15. The Thingvold mission served the Halbrite area from 1904 to 1908, while Ralph was a preaching point from 1904 to 1910.

Farther along the Soo Line, northwest of Weyburn, Ibsen was named in honour of the famed Norwegian playwright Henrik Ibsen. The Heiberg district near Lang (pop. 172) was settled by the Heibergs—a father with three brothers—from from Blair, Wisconsin; Lang was an early preaching point. Bethesda Lutheran Church (1912), now a heritage site, was located west of Milestone, a preaching point. Farther north, settler P.E. Thompson, from Barnsville, Minnesota, named Lajord (post office in 1905) after his home in Norway; there the Bethlehem Lutheran cemetery dates back to 1895 and became a heritage site ninety years later. About forty kilometres west of Weyburn, Forward, a railway terminus at the time, reportedly had as many as 1,200 residents from 1906 to 1911. The story is told of Ole Rude, a bachelor, who was so dismayed when his friend Whiskey Smith was locked up that he hitched up his horses and hauled the small jail out of town![9]

Finally, one more isolated small Norwegian Lutheran concentration in the southeastern region merits mention: Maryfield, near Moosomin, was established as a preaching point in 1915.

The South-Central Region
Farther west along the frontier, many Norwegian Americans from neighbouring Norwegian settlements in Montana spread northward across the border into the south-central frontier region, extending through the Big Muddy Badlands and Wood Mountain into the Cactus Hills to the cities of Regina and Moose Jaw and beyond. Today many people of Scandinavian origin (mostly Norwegians but also quite a few Swedes) are widely scattered throughout this region. However, in 1971, they formed a majority only in two of the smallest communities; in many other communities and in rural municipalities, they never formed more than from 15% to 20% of the population. Yet, again, specific rural districts were settled originally by Norwegians. In 1919, Nidaros Norwegian Lutheran cemetery near Big Beaver (pop. 15) was named after the

historic region around Trondheim, Norway. Norwegian settlers were widely scattered throughout the area to the west toward Wood Mountain. Former Norwegian Lutheran congregations were established in or near Willow Bunch, St. Victor, Hart (Bethlehem or Trinity, 1912–79), Scout Lake (Grand Valley district, 1911–93), Limerick, Verwood (Nidaros, Hart Butte–Beaver Creek districts, 1918–29, then intermittently until 1956), Viceroy (St. Olaf, 1910–, Nidaros, 1913–14, and Una, 1910–15). Southeast of Wood Mountain (pop. 20), Solvey and Reah Solverson arrived from Mound City, South Dakota, in 1908 to homestead along what became known as Solverson Creek. Gus Bolstad arrived from Minnesota in 1912 and homesteaded about sixteen kilometres south of Meyronne; his son Wes Bolstad was destined to become a long-serving senior administrator for four Cooperative Commonwealth Federation (CCF)/NDP provincial governments (under Premiers Douglas, Lloyd, Blakeney, and Romanow), a cabinet secretary and deputy premier in the provincial government, the founding director and dean of the School of Public Administration at what would become the University of Regina, and the first director of the Meewasin Valley Authority in Saskatoon. Norwegian families settled along Pinto Creek between Meyronne and the Pinto River School (1916) farther upstream (now a heritage site); still farther southwest, where the creek flows down from Pinto Butte, the rural Norge Post Office served this backcountry district from 1912. Norwegian settlement extended from Norge near Pinto Butte southward to Flaata Creek (today between two sections of Grasslands National Park), where homesteaders Guri, Sten, and Gunder Flaata settled. Norwegian congregations were established at Pinto Creek (1911–30s) and Norge (1915–69), while Meyronne was a preaching point. At last count, Meyronne contained only thirty-five residents.

West of Hodgeville, settler Benjamin Knut Nybo bestowed his name on Nybo School District in 1913 and Nybo Norwegian Lutheran congregation (1912–99). Bethany congregation served the Neidpath area from 1912 to 1949, another congregation the Blue Hill district from 1912 into the 1940s. Esther School District near Shamrock (pop. 20) originated in 1927 when it was named after the eldest daughter of settler Anton Venaas, an immigrant from Norway who owned the land. Norwegian settlers scattered through the districts around Assiniboia, Lake Johnston, and Old Wives Lake. One-time Norwegian Lutheran congregations included St. Lukas, Congress (1910–59), Ada and Gilbert Plains near Mossbank (Concordia, 1913–52), Dewdrop in the Westerheim district (1911–21), Lake Johnston (1913–52), Ettington (Grand Scandinavian Lutheran Church, 1912–48), and Emmanuel at Ardill (1915–37), while Expanse was a preaching point. Ole Hoffos, from North Dakota, settled near Congress (pop. 28) in 1907 and donated the site for a Lutheran cemetery three years later. The Lillestrom-Orland district north of Old Wives Lake was likely named after Lillestrom, Akershus, Norway; south of the lake at Mossbank (pop. 330), a large majority of burials in the Lutheran cemetery were Norwegian, though some were German.[10]

West and northwest of Moose Jaw, former Norwegian congregations were established near Mortlach (pop. 254) (Zoar, 1917–64), Herbert (Nidaros or Highland, 1911–63), the Antelope Creek district near Halvorgate (1942–60), the Horfield district near Central Butte (Rolling Prairie Scandinavian Lutheran, 1911–16), Lawson, the Lake Valley district near Brownlee, and the Beaver Flat district near Waldeck (Nordland, 1911–78). The long-time pastor of the Nordland congregation was Lars Olsen Tysseland, born in 1877 on a farm at Sand, Ryfylke, near Kristiansand; he immigrated to the United States in 1898 and to Saskatchewan in 1906. He homesteaded in the following year and taught at Bethania, Broderick, and Skudesnes in the Hanley-Outlook settlement in the central region. He later served as pastor of Nordland from 1911 to 1935 (also occasionally serving North Immanuel, Admiral, Simmie, and Lac Pelletier congregations), then from 1936 to 1939 Hagen, Tiger Hills, Mont Nebo, and other congregations in the north-central region.[11] Tobiason Coulee, named after homesteaders Wilhelm Andrew and Helmer Orlands Tobiason, ran from Keeler to the Qu'Appelle River.

Short-lived Scandinavian Lutheran congregations were found in the cities of Moose Jaw (1911–24) and the nearby Wolendale and Aldrich districts and Regina (1925–30). Finally, south of Moose Jaw and Regina, Norwegian congregations and missions were established at Briercrest and Drinkwater (Scandinavian Evangelical Lutheran Church, 1904–10), Readlyn (Scandinavian Lutheran, 1912–20s), Wilcox (Bethesda, 1904–60s), Ogema, Radville (Luther, 1916), Ceylon with the Big Four and Surprise Valley districts (Trail, 1915–56, settled by immigrants from North Dakota and Wisconsin, Lesja Scandinavian Lutheran Church, 1916–40s), the Darmody district north of Parkbeg (Zoar Free Lutheran, 1913–64), and the Beaver Creek district near Bengough (Zion, 1911–65).

The Southwest Region

There are fewer people of Norwegian origin in the southwestern region: in 1971, people of Norwegian descent did not form a majority in any incorporated community or rural municipality in the region, but in many smaller, unincorporated hamlets and rural districts they still predominate. Along the American frontier, they began to form a well-defined settlement in 1909–10. Moving north across the international boundary from Climax, North Dakota, they settled in and around Climax, Saskatchewan (pop. 182), where over a quarter of the residents were of Scandinavian ethnicity in 1971 and where a primarily Norwegian Lutheran church is still active, and Frontier (pop. 283), where Scandinavians comprised almost half of the residents and where Elim Lutheran Brethren congregation (1912–99) was located. White Valley Lutheran Church, southwest of Shaunavon, constructed in 1928, became a heritage site in 1983. A continuous area of Norwegian concentration extends south across the border into the adjacent Norheim and Hogeland districts in Montana.

South of the Cypress Hills, Robsart and Vidora were settled in 1909–10 by Norwegian immigrants from North Dakota and were incorporated as villages respectively in 1914 and 1917. In the Olga district near Robsart, the rural post office was named for the daughter of homesteader Ole Strand in 1915. Former Norwegian Lutheran congregations were found in the Cypress Lake district (1914–82) to the northwest and the Montrose district (by 1916) thirty kilometres to the south close to the border. Robsart once had thirty businesses; however, fires in 1929–30 destroyed businesses, homes, and grain elevators, which were never rebuilt. Years of drought and the Depression hit this dry region particularly hard. The last passenger train passed through in 1957. The community lost half of its 100 residents during the 1960s. Downgraded from village to hamlet in 2001, today Robsart is a virtual ghost town, with only fifteen remaining residents.[12] Nearby Vidora has not fared any better. It once had sixteen businesses and services serving over 100 residents. The last grain elevator closed in 1974, and only two homes were still occupied by the 1980s. Experiencing steady decline, the community was reduced to a hamlet, then simply a rural locality.

Many Norwegians settled around Shaunavon (pop. 1,691), which has an active Lutheran church, notably in the Stoneside district (where a congregation existed from 1913 to 1923), and northeast around Instow (Garden Valley congregation, 1910–64), Scotsguard (congregation, 1915–68), the Austenville and Thompson Valley districts, Admiral (which still had an active ELCIC church—former country congregations were North Immanuel congregation in the Wise Creek district, 1912–66, South Immanuel, 1913–66, and St. Olaf, 1913–14), Simmie (Bethesda, 1915–61, and Trinity, 1955–2001), Lac Pelletier, and Vanguard. A small concentration of Norwegians from North Dakota settled around Simmie in 1906; in the Sederstrom district near Simmie, John Sederstrom organized the school district in 1913, and farther south near Admiral the Dahlia district honoured pioneer settler Ragnvald Dahl in 1938. But today only thirty residents remain in Admiral, fifteen in Simmie, few in Scotsguard.

Today congregants of Norwegian origin are well represented at St. Olaf's in Swift Current. An extensive area of Norwegian settlement developed to the north and northwest of Swift Current, beginning in 1906. Leinan was named for Axel Ludwig Leinan, who served as postmaster from 1909 to 1915; former Norwegian congregations around Leinan were Bethel in the Atlas district (1910) and West Prairie (1915), which merged in 1959 to form Bethel Prairie (closed in 1984), and Grant (1911–13). Ole Jenson Marken, born in 1868 at Nordre Etnedal, Valdres, immigrated to the United States in 1902, where he served as a pastor in Minnesota in 1904; in 1919, he moved to Saskatchewan, homesteading in the Atlas district the following year, and he served as the pastor of the West Prairie congregation in Leinan and Bethel in Atlas between 1919 and 1936.[13] The Norwegian Free Lutheran Church was established in the Nordland district, east of Stewart Valley (pop. 100) in 1911. The Hovdestad district was named after homesteader Dedrik Hovdestad in 1908 and Jorgenson after settlers Sigvald and George Jorgenson in 1912. And, to the northwest, Battrum Post Office was named in 1912 after settler William Battrum, who donated the land; this community once contained some 200 residents and at least fifteen businesses and services, but by the late 1960s nearly all were gone—just two homes were left and one of four original grain elevators. Also located in this area were the Graydahl district (served by postmaster Ole Sannes from 1915 to 1927) and Vergland School District near Pennant (pop. 119) in 1913. Former Norwegian Lutheran congregations included St. John's Norwegian Lutheran Church north of Fosterton (congregation organized in 1912, church built in 1919, closed in 1979, but commemorated as a historic site), Zion (1910–) and Trinity (1912–53) serving the Pennant area, Bethania (1915–17) and Bethany (1917–93) in the Hazlet-Sanford area, and Three Butte mission near Battrum, while the Scandia Lutheran cemetery was at Cabri (pop. 439). Farther west, across the Great Sand Hills, Sagathun Post Office was named in 1917 after the family farm in Norway of settler Hjalmar C. Hjelmeland; Ingebrigt School District was named in 1913 after settler Ingebrigt (or Engebregt) Selseth; and Richmound was an early preaching point.

Finally, Norwegian settlers were scattered between Maple Creek and Swift Current: former specifically Norwegian Lutheran congregations and preaching points included Kincorth (1913) and Rolling Prairie (1917), Crane Lake Valley at Piapot (1914), Tompkins,

Gull Lake (1912) and Zion (1911) twenty-five kilometres north of town, and Bruflat at Webb (1912).

The West-Central Region

Norwegian settlers formed small concentrations in rural districts throughout the west-central region. The area of Norwegian settlement extended across the South Saskatchewan River from the settlement north of Swift Current to Kyle (pop. 423) and White Bear (pop. 15). A former Lutheran congregation (First Lutheran) in the Isham-Tyner area served both Scandinavian- and German-origin people during the 1930s and 1940s. Just north of Isham is Richlea (near Eston), where Sigurd Torleif Ostevik (1922–2010), who often visited Norway, grew up and farmed; his innovations in agricultural technology led to service in the Agricultural Engineering Department at the University of Saskatchewan. Another small concentration was in the area around Pinkham, Hoosier, and Ashford near Coleville—all Norwegian Lutheran preaching points. Fusilier was originally the rural Scandia Post Office in 1913, and the Dorcas congregation served Norwegians in the Court and Loverna areas from 1912 to 1936. Laporte was down to only five residents by 2006. In the Gorefield district south of Laporte, it was common in 1911 for a Norwegian Lutheran family to invite an entire congregation of twenty-five people to Sunday dinner after a morning service or supper after an evening service.[14]

Farther north, Norwegians settled between Marshall and Marsden: a Norwegian congregation served the Layco district near Marshall from 1906 to 1961; Oslo School District near Lone Rock, between Marshall and Marsden, was established in 1925; and in 1914, at Fram School near Marsden, all three of the founding trustees were Norwegian (one an immigrant direct from Norway, the other two from North Dakota).

South of Battleford, Bjelde Creek School District was named for early settler Ole Bjelde in 1913, and Urland Lutheran Church (1910–2001) was named after a church in Minnesota and ultimately Norway. Akerlund Lake near Unity was named after homesteaders Ole, Alfred, and Clarence Akerlund. Lars Orjasaeter homesteaded in the Winona district near Herschel in 1906. Asgard School District near Sonningdale was established in 1912. And Cando and Plenty were Norwegian Lutheran preaching points.

A very small concentration of Norwegians developed in the area between Langham, Asquith, Vanscoy, and Delisle, about thirty kilometres west of Saskatoon. The still-active Norwegian Lutheran congregation founded near Langham in 1903 is one of the oldest in the province. Nearby, another Norwegian Evangelical Lutheran congregation came into being in Dalmeny in 1908 but was closed in 1939. Four other but much shorter-lived Norwegian Lutheran congregations and preaching points were established in the Eagle Creek district near Asquith: East and West Eagle Creek (both 1905–09), Asquith–Eagle Creek Church (1910–26), and Eagle Bank–Dreyer (1911–13). Fronka School District north of Delisle was partially named in 1909 after a trustee named Kjelland; a Norwegian Lutheran congregation was formed there in 1907 and lasted until 1962, while preaching points once included Vanscoy and the Goose Lake district near Harris and Valley Park in the Pike Lake area close to Saskatoon (1925–61).

Norwegians also settled west of the great bend in the South Saskatchewan River Valley, establishing congregations at Demaine (Land Meninghet, 1911–30s) and Beechy (Ostervoll, 1913–29), while Forgan and Bernard (Urdahl) were preaching points.

Across the North Saskatchewan River to the north, some Norwegians formed congregations and preaching points at North Battleford (Bethlehem, 1911–50), Dulwich (1911–31), Radisson (1903–mid-20s), and Fielding.

The Outlook-Hanley Settlement

One of the largest primarily Norwegian settlements in Saskatchewan had begun to develop in the central region around Outlook and Hanley by 1903–06. Many of the original settlers came immediately from largely Norwegian communities in the United States, particularly the Cottonwood–Hanley Falls area in Minnesota, Langford and Veblen in South Dakota, and Grafton in North Dakota, as well as Wisconsin, Iowa, and Illinois. Yet most of these settlers had been born in Norway and were joined around Hanley by immigrants who arrived directly from Norway. They originated from diverse regions in Norway, including Vardal (Ole Nelson and the Frydenlunds), Vestre Toten (Johanna Hoiness), Valdres (Ragna Johnsrud Sira), and Gudbrandsdal (the Slettens) in Oppland; the Stavanger area (the Torgusons and Stanglands) and Haugesund (the Hamres) in Rogaland; Hallingdal in Buskerud (the Andersons); Drangedal in Telemark (the Wicks); Eikesdal (the Bohrsons) and Romsdalen (the Siras) in Möre og Romsdal; Trondheim (the Bertsons) and Overhalla in the Namsendal in Nord Tröndelag (the Opdahls); and the Lofoten Islands in Nordland (the Pedersons).

Norwegian family names tended to be changeable. For example, in the Hanley area, three full brothers all had different surnames: Thomas Bohrson, Anton Utigaard, and Magnus Opegaard; they were born the sons of Baard and Marit Opegaard and raised in Eikesdal; upon emigration, Thomas adopted the Bohrson surname used by his uncle, who had emigrated earlier; Anton returned to Norway and adopted the name of their farm, Utigaard; while Magnus initially changed his surname to Baardsen when he emigrated and finally to Bohrson when he settled in Hanley. Similarly, Ole Kristian Nelson was born Bratvold near Hov on the Randsfjord, went by the farm name Føllingstad where he was raised nearby in Vardal, near Gjovik, then changed his name again upon emigration to Canada to Nilson (which became anglicized to Nelson).

The earliest Norwegian Lutheran congregation in Saskatchewan that is still active was founded at Hanley in September 1903 by Reverend H.O. Holm, the home mission superintendent of the United Norwegian Lutheran Church of America; within a week, he was instrumental in establishing two other Norwegian Lutheran congregations near Langham and Birch Hills; all three congregations were originally called *Skandianviske Lutherske Kirke* (Scandinavian Lutheran Church); the Hanley congregation was soon redesignated as the Hanley Evangelical Lutheran Church in 1907. Pastor S.H. Njaa, based in Hanley Falls, Minnesota (the origin of some of the Norwegian families who settled there), conducted the first service at Hanley in October. Most Norwegian Lutheran churches tended to become focal points for compact, solidly Norwegian districts in the country. The Bethlehem Scandinavian Lutheran congregation, about twenty-two kilometres by road southwest of Hanley, was first organized in 1909 by Norwegian immigrants from Norway and Minnesota; construction of the church was completed by 1914. The former Zion congregation served the Sunny Valley district in the hills east of Hanley from 1926 to 1964, when its members joined the Hanley Lutheran congregation. The settlers who built the Saskatchewan River Church north of

Broderick (pop. 77) followed Hans Mollerud from Grafton, North Dakota, who came in 1903 to file homesteads by proxy for eighteen Norwegian families and himself in a single bloc around Nary School;[15] the church is still active today, even though it had to be completely reconstructed after being burned to the ground by a lightning strike in 1948. The Spring Creek congregation was organized in 1909; the church was built in 1917 and turned into a community arts centre in 1987. The Bethania congregation served the Eden Valley district near Broderick from 1905 to 1987. The Green Valley Church southwest of Glenside was constructed in 1917 and was recognized as a heritage site in 1988. Skudesnes, east of Loreburn, continues to be another active Norwegian church. Bethel Scandinavian Lutheran Church in Elbow was organized in 1909, built by 1918, but closed in 1971, and it has been a heritage site since 1998. Another former congregation was in the Sand Hills or Rensby district near Elbow from 1907 to 1918. Other former Norwegian congregations in the settlement included Bethania at Strongfield (1918–42) and Prairie College at Bladworth (1919–58). The settlement extended across the South Saskatchewan River from Outlook to include Our Saviour at Ardath, Bethania and West Point at Macrorie (1911–30s), and Zion at Anerley (1912–15). Swanson was originally founded by Abraham Swanson, who as postmaster hauled mail all the way from Hanley via the Rudy ferry; the community once contained eighteen businesses at its peak, but only four services and a few residents were left by 1973. Swanson and Conquest were early preaching points.

People of Scandinavian ethnic origin did not comprise a majority in any community in the general region in 1971: the highest proportion was in Hawarden (36.1%), followed by Elbow (30.6%), Outlook (26.3%), Loreburn (21.7%), Strongfield (11.1%), and Hanley (10.0%). Yet together more than 2,100 people of Scandinavian (almost all Norwegian) origin lived in this region in 1971, making it one of the largest concentrations of Norwegian people in Saskatchewan. These Norwegians settled a vast area covering parts of at least eight rural municipalities—Rudy, Rosedale, Loreburn, Fertile Valley, Montrose, Milden, McCraney, and Lost River—and live within and around at least twelve incorporated towns and villages. The town of Outlook (pop. 1,938 in 2006) has the largest number of people of Scandinavian descent for any essentially rural community in the province (with the possible exception of Melfort, almost triple the size of Outlook). Outlook is the home of a Lutheran college with a strong Norwegian tradition; the Saskatchewan Norwegian Lutheran College Association was organized in 1911 to build a college that was completed five years later (it closed during the Depression from 1936 to 1939 but reopened as the Saskatchewan Lutheran Bible Institute and became the Lutheran Collegiate Bible Institute in 1953). The college had been the inspiration of the Norse Society of Outlook. Among its aims were "to foster the noblest traditions of our race, and to this end we are keeping in contact with the cultural life of Norway and give assistance to immigration." What has been described by participants as "a great convention" was held at the college in 1925; eleven *bygdelags* (country districts) were formed representing some 2,000 Norwegian Canadians.[16] Hanley (pop. 464), the second largest community within the settlement, is only a quarter of the size of Outlook and now has a very diverse population of Norwegian, Mennonite, Scottish, Croatian, and other origins.

People of Norwegian origin predominate in many rural districts that together comprise the core of this extensive bloc settlement: the Saskatchewan River, Nary, Rudy

Ferry, Larsen, and Spring Creek districts of Rudy RM (centred on Outlook); Ardath and the Bethania and Sjovold Creek districts in Fertile Valley RM (west of Outlook); the Bethlehem, Cosmopolitan (1918), Hamre (1907), Sunrise (1911), and Bohrson (1907) districts in Rosedale RM (centred on Hanley); and the Skudesnes and Green Valley districts in Loreburn RM. Moreover, they were far more widely scattered throughout other districts with more mixed ethnic populations: in Rosedale RM, Norwegians shared the Box Elder (1905) and Farmington (1914) districts with Mennonites; Avonlea (1912) and Smilesville (1906) with Croatians; and Rainbow (1912), Strong, Crescent View (1914), and Bell Rock (1920) districts with Scots. Other districts farther afield settled by Norwegians included the Odel district in Dundurn RM (Odel School operated from 1907 to 1953) as well as around Hawarden (pop. 75), Strongfield (pop. 47), Loreburn (pop. 113), and Elbow (pop. 294) in Loreburn RM; and particularly in the Sunny Valley (1917) and Little Norway districts in the Allan Hills (school district, 1917) in Lost River and Morris RMs (east of Hanley and south of Allan and Young). In the Little Norway district, the pastor once noted that his congregation consisted of "thirty-seven souls and two Swedes."[17] Beyond the core area between Hanley, Outlook, and Elbow might not comprise a compact, well-defined, Norwegian bloc settlement, yet one could drive a circuitous route by back roads more than 200 kilometres all the way from the Allan Hills southwest to Macrorie, literally without ever being out of sight of a farm originally homesteaded by Norwegians that once would have been close to a Norwegian Lutheran church. These churches scattered over the countryside were important centres for localized Norwegian life: for example, the Saskatchewan River Church was the scene of song fests, a church orchestra, picnics, *lutefisk* suppers, Norwegian-language classes, and of course Lutheran Bible studies, with the Ladies Aid always playing an active role.

Other Norwegian Concentrations in Central and East-Central Saskatchewan

Norwegian settlers also concentrated in a couple of other areas in central Saskatchewan. Northeast of the large Norwegian settlement centred on Outlook and Hanley, Norwegians concentrated in certain rural districts around Viscount (pop. 251), Young (pop. 263), and Watrous (pop. 1,743). The Kolstad district and Austenson and Gjosund Road districts (where Severin Gjosund homesteaded) were near Viscount. St. John's Lutheran, originally Kolstad Scandinavian Lutheran congregation, was organized in 1911 by homesteaders Olaus and Andrew Kolstad; St. Peter congregation also served the area in 1908–11 and Vinje congregation in 1909. Watrous Post Office was originally briefly called Mandal in 1906–08, after the port in south Norway where postmaster Tom Bjorndahl and homesteader Boruf Haaland had lived; St. Olaf served the area from 1905 to 1958. A Norwegian congregation was organized at Young in 1909; the church was built in 1916 and closed in 1971. Not far away, near Saskatoon, a small Norwegian settlement called the Minnesota Settlement was a preaching point in 1904–06. And, farther east, former Norwegian congregations existed at Burr, near Humboldt (Hoiland, 1908–55), Kandahar (Aarnes Scandinavian Lutheran, 1909–98), and Jansen Lake, twenty kilometres north of Jansen (1914–).

North of Regina, in Southey (pop. 711), there were two LCC churches with both Scandinavian and German members; the surrounding districts of Lunner and Snarum were particularly Norwegian. A Norwegian Lutheran congregation existed at Lunner from 1909 to 1968; Lunner had been named after a small community in Oppland, Norway, where Hans Korsrud had lived before becoming a homesteader in Saskatchewan in 1903. His brother John Honerud built Snarum School in 1905 (named after Snarum, in Buskerud *fylke* near Oslo). Near Bulyea (pop. 104), the first Norwegian congregation was Our Saviour (1906–10); in 1921, most of the Norwegians in the Uneeda district split from the Norwegian Lutheran Church of America to join the Lutheran Free Church. Norrona Evangelical Lutheran Church was built in 1917 and became a heritage site in 1988. Elsewhere in this region, across Last Mountain Lake, Norwegians settled in the Iduna district near Liberty (pop. 73), where Iduna School was named in 1906 after a Norse goddess. In the Nordal district near Simpson (pop. 118), Nordal School was named in 1905 perhaps after Nordal in Vestfold (though this is descriptive nomenclature simply meaning north valley); the Nordal congregation served the district from 1908 through the 1930s). The Orvold School District near Renown was originally named in 1907 after settler Arne Orvold. Norwegian congregations around Renown were Our Saviour (1912) in the village, the Hawkshaw district (1909–54), and the Horseshoe Lake district twenty kilometres west of town (1913–14). Other former Norwegian congregations and preaching points in this general region were situated at Craik (Trondhjem, 1904–30s), Dilke (1919–24), Holdfast (Kindred, 1911–16), Penzance (Zion, 1911–40s), the Saline Creek district sixteen kilometres west of Nokomis (1910–14), and Punnichy (1913–14).

The Shellbrook Settlement
A large Scandinavian settlement around Shellbrook (pop. 1,215), west of Prince Albert, began to develop by 1904. Parkside (pop. 129), southwest of Shellbrook, was settled by people of both Swedish and Norwegian origin who had immigrated via the Midwestern states (e.g., into the Yankee Valley district) as well as immigrants directly from Sweden and Norway. Immanuel Lutheran Church at Parkside became a museum in 1998; in the Silver Grove district near Parkside was St. Paul's Lutheran Church (1917), now a heritage site. Stene was an early congregation in the countryside near Shellbrook from 1911 to 1914.

The Ordale area, due west of Shellbrook, was settled primarily by people of Norwegian origin related to those at Hagen in the Birch Hills settlement. In Norwegian, *ordal* would mean elder bush valley. Early congregations around Ordale were Southern Shell River (1903–07), Shell River (founded in 1904, became Concordia in 1919), and Aaseral (1912–). Both the Aaseral Lutheran cemetery in 1914 and Bygland School in 1915 near Ordale were named respectively after Åseral and Bygland, Vest Agder, at the southern end of Norway. Local crafts artists in the area include the Jensens, who operate Nisse Foundry at Ordale, a traditional log foundry creating bronze sculptures, and stone carver Lise Olson at the Honeywood Heritage Nursery near Parkside. South of Mont Nebo (a Norwegian Lutheran preaching point during the 1950s), Ole Tollefson built a ski jump on what henceforth became known as Tollefson's Hill. A Norwegian congregation served Norwegian settlers scattered around the Bapaume district during the 1930s and 1940s. The Scandia Lutheran cemetery was located south of Shell Lake. At Krivoisheim, Ignal, Paul, and Fedor homesteaded near the school that was to bear their family name in 1911.

Canwood (pop. 337), northwest of Shellbrook, became the focal point of a large area settled by people of diverse Scandinavian origins—chiefly Norwegian and Swedish but also some Danish. Early Norwegian congregations around Canwood were Northern Shell River (1905–07 and 1910–19) and Zion Scandinavian Evangelical Lutheran (formed when the former Dry Creek, Summit Prairie, and Merchant Grove congregations merged in 1915). The post office there was called Forgaard in 1912 (after pioneer settler Jens Forgaard, a Norwegian immigrant who arrived from Minnesota) but only for a year; it became Canwood the following year.

Scattered Norwegian settlement extended eastward into the districts of Deer Ridge (organized during the 1920s, church built in 1938, closed in 1958), Valbrand (where Minnesota-born postmaster Ted Odegaard had settled in 1910 and became postmaster in 1914, and later Agdar Johan Fjerwold, an immigrant from Fjaervoll in the Lofoten Islands, settled there in 1927—Zion congregation served this district from 1940 to 1951), Moose Valley (a preaching point), Cookson (where he operated a general store in 1934 and served as postmaster), Stump Lake (Zion, 1939–48), Nestledown, Blue Heron (Calvary congregation, 1943–51), Marchant Grove, Foxdale, Mayview, Sturgeon Valley, Silent Call, Park Valley, Brightholme, and so on and southeast as far as Spruce Home (where Hanna School was named in 1908 after Hanna Haugen, the daughter of homesteaders Andrew and Kari Haugen). The city of Prince Albert had a specifically Norwegian Lutheran congregation from 1904 to 1911, when it was redefined as more generically Scandinavian. And, to the north, a congregation served the few Norwegian settlers around Paddockwood from 1932 to 1952.

Early Norwegian Lutheran congregations were established at Parkside, Shell Lake, and Shellbrook; today all of them, together with Canwood, continue as ELCIC churches. In 1971, there were at least 1,300 people of Scandinavian origin within these areas, including Canwood (where they comprised 30.9% of the residents), Parkside (37.5%), Shellbrook (just 7.8%), and the surrounding rural municipalities of Canwood, Shellbrook, and Leask—this nucleus of Scandinavian settlement extends roughly seventy kilometres from north to south and over thirty kilometres from east to west.

The Birch Hills Settlement
Some thirty kilometres southeast of Prince Albert, the Birch Hills settlement was probably the earliest primarily Norwegian settlement, and remained one of the best defined, in Saskatchewan. The Glen Mary district near the town of Birch Hills was first settled by Norwegian immigrants from Solor, Hønefoss, Numedal, and Kongsberg as early as 1894.[18] In 1903, Reverend H.O. Holm travelled through parts of Saskatchewan to determine the need for home mission work among Norwegian settlers. Four days after he organized one of the earliest Norwegian congregations in the province at Hanley (in the Hanley-Outlook settlement south of Saskatoon), he founded the *Norden Skandianviske Lutherske Kirke* (Norden Scandinavian Lutheran Church) at Glen Mary, declared a heritage site in 1984. Later that year (1903), Pastor Sven H. Njaa was sent from Hanley Falls, Minnesota, to Hanley, Saskatchewan, by a church board that had met at Canton, South Dakota; then he was located in the Birch Hills settlement because it had been longer and more heavily settled by Scandinavians than Hanley. Bethania Norwegian Evangelical Lutheran Church in Hagen was established in 1913 and became a heritage

site in 1987. Today little evidence remains of the one-time small communities of Hagen and Fenton, west of Birch Hills. Fairly close contact seems to have been maintained among the various settlements within the province, between them and similar ones in the Midwestern states, and between them and certain areas in Scandinavia. It was largely through these contacts that the settlement around Birch Hills grew, as more and more people of Scandinavian origin migrated to this settlement from other Scandinavian areas in the province, from the American settlements, and from Scandinavia itself.

Scandinavian people do not predominate in any town or incorporated village within the settlement—in 1971 forming 40.4% of the population of Weldon (pop. 205 in 2006), 31.5% of Birch Hills (pop. 935), 19.2% of Kinistino (pop. 643), and 13.3% of Melfort (pop. 5,192)—yet they do form a very high proportion (over 90%) in many smaller communities and rural districts. In 1971, over 3,300 people of Scandinavian origin were living in these and many smaller communities within seven rural municipalities: Birch Hills, Kinistino, Willow Creek, Star City, Flett's Springs, Invergordon, and St. Louis. Thus, this is one of the largest Scandinavian settlements in population if not in areal extent, some eighty kilometres east-west and about forty kilometres north-south.

The Hagen area (named for Andreas Christianson Hagen, a Norwegian immigrant from Minnesota who homesteaded there in 1903), for example, is virtually completely Norwegian, as are other districts north of Weldon: Queen Maud (honouring the queen of Norway); Prestfoss (originally Norden in 1903, then renamed five years later for the home of postmaster Anders Reiersen Bergrud in Sigdal, Buskerud; a congregation was organized there in 1915); Viking; Northway; Lake Park (where the school was named in 1909 after a community in Minnesota at the suggestion of Ingebret Dragseth, and where Zion congregation functioned from 1903 to 1983, while the *bedehuset*—house of prayer— was constructed as a Baptist congregation in 1933); Neshem (named for postmaster Ivor Neshem in 1903; Scandia congregation dated from 1904, Roosevelt from 1911); South Valley; and Njaa's Hill (where Pastor Njaa had settled in 1903). Weldon was originally called Luther, after pioneer storekeeper and postmaster Luther Larson. A congregation serving the Rose Hill district was organized in 1912, the church was built in 1929 and closed in 1971, another one was built in the Windermere district in 1911, and a congregation served the nearby Chelan district from 1934 to 1993. St. Markus served Birch Hills from 1907 to 1920. South of these communities were other strongly Norwegian districts: Saron (where a *Norsk Evangelisk Luthersk Menighed*—Norwegian Evangelical Lutheran Congregation—was organized in 1904), Bastness, Tiger Hills, Waitville (a former preaching point, where the Ingvald Opseth Provincial Wildlife Refuge is located), Bonnie Hill, Braaten or Melfort Creek (a congregation served this district from 1904 to 1955), and Wolverine Lake. Hjalmar Gronlid settled in the community named after him in 1908; as a pastor, he initially assisted Pastor Njaa at Norden and Glen Mary, then eventually served Norwegian Lutherans in an extremely wide area, including South Star, Melfort Creek, the Carrot River Valley, Fairy Glen, Lost River, Mount Forest, and Beaver Creek–Ratner.[19] The Norwegian Lutheran churches in the Carrot River Valley near Fairy Glen (pop. 35) and Beaver Creek district near Ratner north of Melfort date respectively from 1909 and 1912. The latter was constructed by local men who hauled the logs, seats were homemade, and a local carpenter built the chancel furnishings. At their first communal picnic in 1911, moose meat sandwiches, home-grown vegetables, pies from freshly picked berries, and homemade ice cream were served.[20] Bagley, about twelve kilometres west of Gronlid (pop. 50), once had a general store and post office serving over 100 farm families in the district; by the 1980s, only the well-maintained Lutheran church (originally Bethel Norwegian Lutheran, 1903–23) was left. People of Norwegian origin still constitute a majority of members of the remaining ELCIC churches at Birch Hills, Weldon, and Kinistino and, together with people of Swedish origin, the LCC church at Melfort.

The Northeastern Settlements
It is often difficult to determine where one Norwegian settlement dwindles and the next begins. About fifty kilometres south of Melfort, another Norwegian settlement developed around Naicam (pop. 690). Immanuel Norwegian Lutheran congregation, founded at Naicam in 1910, held all of its services exclusively in Norwegian during the early years (as did most, if not all, Norwegian Lutheran congregations) and has long held a Norwegian Christmas service. Virtually all of the pastors who served this congregation, as well as the Dovre congregation, founded near Spalding in 1915 (the church was constructed in 1918 and moved into the village in the early 1950s), were Norwegian, as in many other Norwegian Lutheran congregations in rural districts in Saskatchewan. During the early years at Dovre, a morning service was held in English and an afternoon service in Norwegian; men sat on one side and women on the other. A bilingual sign in Norwegian and English welcomes visitors to Naicam. Naicam Pioneer School (1923) is now a heritage site. Former Norwegian congregations and missions were Our Saviour at Naicam (1921–45), Bigstone (1906–21) as well as Bethany and Our Saviour Free Lutheran near Spalding (1906–21), Iron Spring near Daphne (1905–mid-20s), and Clearview near Spalding (1913–14). Dovre was holding services once or twice a month by 2009 and closed in 2010. In 1971, the Scandinavian proportion was less than one-third (31.8%) in Naicam (current pop. 690) and a quarter in Spalding (pop. 237) and Pleasantdale, yet surrounding rural districts tend to be heavily Norwegian, as early place names suggest: Dovre, Norwegian Grove, Olson, and Ives School southwest of Norwegian Grove, named in 1904 after Olen and Harry Ives, homesteaders from Minnesota.

East of Naicam and Spalding, Scandinavian settlement continues fifty kilometres into the Rose Valley area. However, Ukrainians outnumber Scandinavians in the village of Rose Valley (pop. 338), where people of Scandinavian origin comprised slightly over a quarter (28.7%) of the population in 1971; they were a quarter of the residents of Archerwill but only 18.6% of those of Wadena. Sigstad School District was named in 1911 for Emil Sigstad (who had emigrated from the Ringsaker district north of Lake Mjösa in central Norway to South Dakota and then on to Saskatchewan in 1910; reportedly, eleven of the fourteen pupils in this school once bore the Sigstad surname). To the south, only one in five residents of Fosston (pop. 55) is Scandinavian—many Poles settled there; however, the community received its name from five Rustad brothers from Fosston, Minnesota, who settled there in 1908. But the next village, Hendon, was largely Swedish and Norwegian; outside the village is the Scandia cemetery. North of Rose Valley, Norwegians concentrated around Nora, Archerwill (pop. 185), and Dahlton. Like Hendon, which now has only ten residents, Nora was never more than a very small community; at its peak in 1925, it had six businesses and fifty residents, but by 1960 it had declined to a small hamlet. Southeast of Rose Valley, Bethel Norwegian Lutheran Church (1927) is now a heritage site. Some Norwegians also settled within the largely Icelandic settlement south of Wadena in the Quill Lakes area: Rotnum School near Wadena was named in 1920 for early homesteader Oscar Rotnum; Aarnes cemetery (1906) near Kandahar was named for the home in Norway of the Sather brothers Karl, Lars, and Gilbert; Marshall cemetery near Foam Lake was named in 1909 for Marshall, Minnesota, where the Norwegian settlers originated; and Nystrom Lake was near Wynyard. Early Norwegian Lutheran congregations were founded at Nora, Rose Valley, Hendon, and Wadena; today Dahlton-Archerwill, Wadena, and Rose Valley still have active ELCIC churches. Former congregations and preaching points include a Lutheran Free Church congregation at Algrove (1928–61), Bethany at Dahlton (1910–45), Bethel Norwegian at Fosston (organized in 1915, church built in 1927, turned into a heritage site in 1988), Scandia at Hendon (1911–2003), Ponass Lake (1911–46), Dovre Scandinavian Lutheran (1917–60s), Archerwill, the Cluffield district near Hendon, and the Scrip district near Fosston.

Norwegians were also widely scattered around Tisdale (pop. 2,981): former congregations and preaching points include Mount Olive at Eldersley (1935–41), Stene, Bethel at Star City (1904–68), and Lost River near Codette.

Norwegian settlement continued eastward past Kelvington (pop. 866) into the areas around Nut Mountain (pop. 15), Lintlaw (pop. 145), Margo (pop. 90), Okla (pop. 25), Hazel Dell (pop. 20), Invermay (pop. 262), Ketchen (pop. 15), Preeceville (pop. 1,050), Sturgis (pop. 575), Buchanan (pop. 225), Stenen (pop. 91), and Norquay (pop. 412). These tend to be mixed communities, with substantial Ukrainian proportions; in 1971, people of Scandinavian origin formed over a quarter of the residents of Margo (26.7%) but lower proportions of those of Norquay (21.0%), Sturgis (18.3%), Hyas (16.3%), Preeceville (14.4%), Kelvington (13.6%), Lintlaw (13.0%), and Invermay (5.9%).

The many early Norwegian Lutheran congregations and preaching points included Kelvington, High Hill Creek near Kelvington, Nut Mountain, the Bond district near Lintlaw, Hazel Dell, and Poplar Grove near Ketchen (1916–94). Around Preeceville, St. John Scandinavian Lutheran Church (1904) merged with North Prairie Church (1908) in 1988; other congregations in this area were in the Whitehawk district, Emmanuel Scandinavian Evangelical Lutheran at Stenen (1905–27), and at Fort Pelly and Endeavour. Around Buchanan and to the west were Zion (1910–58), Trinity in the Wergeland district (1906–27), North Prairie in the Hinchcliff district (1906, made a heritage site in 1988), Bethlehem at Invermay (1915–27), Whitesand southeast of Invermay (where a Norwegian Lutheran church was established in 1921 and made a heritage site in 1985), Moe United Norwegian Lutheran Church (later Moe-Concordia Evangelical Lutheran Church) near Margo (1904–65, made a heritage site in 1997), Margo, Good Hope at Kuroki (1908–68), Kylemore, the Whitesand district near Sheho (1910–55), Edfield, the Bromberg district near Foam Lake, Theodore. ... Again, virtually all of the pastors for decades have been Norwegian. Today Norwegians and other Scandinavians continue to predominate in ELCIC churches at Preeceville, Norquay, Margo, and Buchanan. The congregation in the Neewin district near Norquay was initially served by pastors who had come all the way from Winnipeg to Kamsack by train and then by horse to Norwegian homes in this district. North Prairie Scandinavian Lutheran Church, located northwest of Lady Lake in Preeceville RM, was constructed in 1918 and turned into a heritage site in 1990.

Although people of Scandinavian origin constitute relatively low proportions in the principal communities, far outnumbered by Ukrainians, they form higher proportions in certain surrounding rural areas, such as the Netherton district south of Invermay, where a large fieldstone farmhouse was built in 1897 by a reputed stonemason, Nels Holer Nielson. Born in Norway in 1856, he had immigrated in 1881. Near Buchanan, Norwegians settled in the districts of Christiana and Dydland (where the school was named in 1912 after Sivert Dydland, born in Norway in 1884); Scandinavian School District was established in 1910; Wergeland School was named after Henrik Wergeland in 1905. Among the early Norwegian settlers around Buchanan were Per and Evalina Carlson, who arrived from Minnesota; their four sons, John, Sten, Hjalmar, and Thorsten, continued to run the family farm. Near Stenen (named for settler Johannes Amundson Stenen, who came from the Dakotas in 1904) was the Goodhue district (post office, 1910, named after Goodhue county in Minnesota, where many of the Norwegian settlers originated). Around Preeceville and Sturgis, Strand (post office named in 1908 for early settlers Fred and Mathilda Strand, who had come from Minnesota in 1905), Lady Lake, Sunny Brae (where Norwegian immigrant Thomas Louvstad settled), and Waler (where the school was named in 1903 by Albert Hanson for his original home farm, Sjolli Kvern in Asnes-Valer, north of Oslo). And Norwegians settled the Bures district near Hazel Dell.

Within this total area of Norwegian settlement, covering portions of ten rural municipalities (Lakeview, Sasman, Hazel Dell, Invermay, Preeceville, Kelvington, Ponass Lake, Barrier Valley, Pleasantdale, and Spalding), and including at least nineteen communities, there were altogether more than 3,800 people of Scandinavian origin in 1971. Although these Norwegian-settled areas do not constitute a single well-defined bloc settlement, rather a series of rural districts where Norwegians concentrated, this pattern of contiguous settlement covers an enormous distance, from Norquay in the east to Naicam in the west, a distance of 228 kilometres by road.

The East-Central Region: Melville Area
A few scattered Norwegian-settled districts can be noted in the vicinity of Melville (pop. 4,139) in the east-central region. Northwest of Melville, in the Plain View district, Norwegians founded Zion congregation in 1904; in 1956, it elected to join Prince of Peace congregation in Melville until 1964. The Birmingham district was a preaching point. To the southeast, small Norwegian congregations were found at Atwater (Kristiana, 1906, now a heritage site) and Dubuc (Bethel, 1907–52), while Cana and Waldron were preaching points.

The Far North
Finally, Norwegians and other Scandinavians were omnipresent in the far north of Saskatchewan, and their legacy has been widespread in place names such as Ausland Lake, Einarson, Hanson Lake, Lofvendahl, Marken Lake, Sveinson Lake, Thoreson Lake. ...

SWEDISH SETTLEMENTS

Throughout Saskatchewan, Swedes often tended to mix with Norwegians and other Scandinavians; however, they also developed their own settlements. The first distinctly Swedish settlement in Saskatchewan was the New Stockholm Colony, developed between 1885 and 1887, immediately west of Esterhazy. The Swedish Lutheran congregation near Stockholm, founded in 1889, was the earliest Scandinavian Lutheran congregation in Saskatchewan and the first Swedish Lutheran congregation in Canada (today still a strongly Swedish ELCIC congregation). Itinerant American pastors served the New Stockholm Church until a resident pastor arrived in 1903. The first church was a simple log structure built in 1895; the present large church in the country southeast of Stockholm was built between 1917 and 1921. A cairn commemorating New Stockholm as a Saskatchewan historical site was erected in 1959, but the church was not officially designated a provincial heritage site until the late 1980s. The Swedish settlement included the surrounding rural districts of Excel (school named in 1903 after a school district in Minnesota that had been the source of some of the settlers), Freedhome (school named in 1904 after early settlers Eric and Oscar Freed, who built the schoolhouse), Ohlen (rural post office named in 1887 to honour Emmanuel Ohlen, the land agent who was instrumental in establishing the colony; this district was the first to be settled by immigrants from Dorotea and Asele in northern Sweden), Swea (school district established in 1888, named for Svea Stenburg, the wife of a founding trustee), and Scandia (school district near Round Lake). The Swedish Lutheran and mission churches at Ohlen (1896) had hand-sawn lumber roves and joists.[21] At Bird's Point on Round Lake in the Qu'Appelle Valley, at the southernmost extent of the settlement, the beautiful fieldstone home originally of French Count de Cazes was purchased in 1921 by Per and Johanna Stendahl; they raised their nine children there, and the farm is still in the family.[22] By 1971, the Swedish settlement in Fertile Belt RM could not have included more than about 300 people of Scandinavian (primarily Swedish) descent, if those in the nearby town of Esterhazy are included. However, in Stockholm (pop. 323), Scandinavians then comprised only one in ten residents and were outnumbered four to one by Hungarians. In fact, even the neighbouring and far smaller village of Dubuc (pop. 55) to the west has twice as high a proportion of Scandinavians; New Sweden Lutheran congregation was located there between 1905 and 1970.

Another Swedish colony was soon founded nearby in 1889 at Percival, just east of Broadview (pop. 611) and thirty-five kilometres south of Stockholm. At last count (2006), only four residents were left in this community (down from fifteen in 2001). Yet as many as 400 people of Scandinavian origin were found in 1971 in the Percival-Broadview area (but only about one in ten residents of Broadview is Scandinavian), including portions of the rural municipalities of Silverwood, Kingsley, Willowdale, and Elcapo. The historic Percival windmill (ca. 1905–12) was declared a heritage site in 1995. Once no fewer than three Swedish Lutheran congregations were found around Percival: Immanuel (1897–1957), Northwood (by 1914 until 1951), and Logwood (during the 1930s and 1940s). A Swedish Evangelical Lutheran congregation was organized in the Edenland district (toward Kipling) in 1909; the church dated from 1918 and merged with Emmanuel in Percival in 1954. The ELCIC church at Broadview retains many Swedish members. South of Broadview, Swedish Baptist Church was founded in 1922, then changed its name to Highland Baptist Church five years later, presumably to conform to the local Highland School, established in 1897. Nearby, Newborgor School District came into being in 1910; *newborgor* means new beginning in Swedish. Zion Lutheran Church, northwest of Kipling (pop. 973), was built in 1926, and in 1989 it became a heritage site; in Kipling, Christ Lutheran Church (1914) eventually was turned into a museum.

Although Norwegians outnumbered Swedes in most Scandinavian-settled areas in southern Saskatchewan, some rural districts were clearly settled by Swedes. Kirkella, just east of the Saskatchewan-Manitoba border on the Trans-Canada Highway, was founded by Swedes, and the surrounding small Swedish settlement of some 200 people extends across the border around Rotave and Fleming in Saskatchewan, where the Swedish Lutheran Fridheim congregation was organized as early as 1897 (it closed in 1951). In the southeastern region, near Midale, in 1913 Augusta School District honoured Augusta Johnson Larson, the first mother in the district to have a child of school age; born at Karlstad, Sweden, she had come to the district from Wheaton, Minnesota. And the rural telephone company serving Midale and area was named in 1915 after William Floding, a Swede who had come from Cokato, Minnesota, in 1903. The Peterson farm (1916) east of Halbrite (pop. 98) and north of Midale (pop. 462) became a heritage property in 1982, while the Lindblom farm residence (1904) became incorporated into the Souris Valley Antique Association Heritage Park at Midale. Midale retains both ELCIC and LCC congregations with predominantly Scandinavian members. At Goodwater, south of Weyburn, the Bethel congregation served the local Swedish settlers from 1914 to 1939. A small congregation of Swedish Lutherans in the Swanson district between Parkman and Wauchope formed the Evangelical Lutheran Bethania Church of Wauchope and Parkman (1907–52); the pastor travelled widely to serve isolated Swedish congregations at Goodwater and Assiniboia.

In the south-central region, near Assiniboia (pop. 2,305), the post office in the Annieheld district was served in 1914 by Lars Hendrickson, who had settled there with his wife, Anna. The Lake of the Rivers district was served by the Emmanuel congregation (1912–66). And the Bures School District near Ogema (pop. 304) in 1910 was a mixture of Swedes and Norwegians. Gavelin Creek north of McCord (pop. 40) in the Wood Mountain area was homesteaded by Nils John Gavelin in 1909; he had emigrated from Sweden to the New Stockholm Colony in 1891. West of Moose Jaw, the Simrishill School District near Parkbeg was named in 1915 for homesteader and school trustee Alfred Simrose, who, intriguingly, had been born Alf Anderson at Simrishan in southern Sweden but had changed his name while living in Minnesota. There was briefly a Swedish Lutheran congregation, Messiah (1930–31), in Moose Jaw. And in Regina, in 1933, Swedish Lutherans organized the United Evangelical Lutheran congregation, which met during the Depression in rented halls and a basement until 1944, and moved several more times until 1958, when a new church, Central Lutheran, was dedicated.

And, in the southwestern region, a large mixed Swedish and Norwegian settlement developed in the Admiral area, east of Shaunavon. People of Scandinavian origin comprised exactly half of the population in the village of Admiral in 1971, which retained a largely Scandinavian ELCIC congregation; at the time, Admiral had ninety residents but now has just a third that number. Swedish settlement extended westward to the town of Shaunavon (pop. 1,691), which also had a substantial Norwegian element and a Norwegian Lutheran congregation; southward into the Sordahl, Andersonville, and Dahlia districts; and northward to Simmie (where Norwegians concentrated)— in Simmie, Swedish Lutheran settlers formed the Klara congregation (1912–58). In quick succession, several congregations of the Augustana (Swedish Lutheran) Synod were organized in and around Shaunavon: Lebanon Lutheran congregation between Shaunavon and Scotsguard (1910–24); Zion Lutheran in the heart of Grassy Creek RM southeast of Shaunavon (1914–32); Malmo Lutheran congregation at Scotsguard (1914–26); and Salem Lutheran in town in 1916. Perhaps some 600 people of Scandinavian origin lived in this settlement in 1971. Elsewhere in this region, small numbers of Swedes formed short-lived Swedish Lutheran congregations at Abbey (1916–24) and in the Fauna district near Waldeck (Elim, 1916–late 20s); Waldeck was a Swedish Lutheran preaching point from 1911 to 1924.

In central Saskatchewan, a number of small Swedish concentrations can be noted, such as the Fryksende (Swedish church) in the Archive district near Baildon (1905–52). Swedish Lutherans mixed with the predominant Norwegians around Southey and Earl Grey. There was also a Swedish Baptist congregation at Earl Grey.[23] At Govan (pop. 232), where a number of Swedes settled, an early name proposed for the post office was Landstrom, in recognition of Oscar Landstrom, a Swede from Cokato, Minnesota, who had been the first homesteader. His wife, Amanda Sundwall, had the district school named after her and her father, who had also homesteaded there. Some members of the Govan ELCIC church are Scandinavian. It has already been noted that Swedes settled around Colonsay, Viscount, and Young; the latter two communities retain ELCIC congregations that include Scandinavian members. A former Swedish Lutheran congregation in the Young area was Salem (1911–58). Swedes also settled the Forslund district. St. Peter congregation at Meacham lasted from 1908 to 1969.

Many Swedes settled within or adjacent to several predominantly Norwegian settlements, such as at Canwood and Parkside (northwest of Prince Albert), Melfort and the Fairy Glen district (southeast of Prince Albert), Wadena and Hendon, or the Outlook settlement in central Saskatchewan. Canwood was an abbreviated form of "Canadian woods," a name suggested by Ed Bowman, a Swede from Minnesota, and the rural municipality was first known as Thompson RM from 1913 to 1916, after Gust Thompson. The Augustana congregation at Polworth (1935–53) served the Swedish population in the area. Scandia Independent Lutheran Church (1925–49) in the Paddling Lake district near Parkside was predominantly Swedish but included some Norwegians. North of Melfort, Swedes concentrated in certain rural districts: Fairy Glen, Gronlid, Ratner, Hanson (named in 1929 after Pastor Henry Oscar Hanson), Bagley (where Pastor Hanson served as postmaster), Lund (school, 1916), and Beatty/Stoney Creek. ELCIC congregations still functioning at Ratner–Fairy Glen, at Beatty, and farther afield at Tisdale, as well as an LCC congregation at Melfort, have some Swedish members. Around Young, Bethel Lutheran Church and Evangelical Covenant Church (1916) became designated heritage sites respectively in 1994 and 1995. In the Wadena area, the Tornea district was likely named after the Swedish name for the Finnish city of Tornio (suggesting that these settlers were Swedish Finns). Ebenezer congregation served the Wadena area from

1910 to 1925. Scandia Lutheran Church (now a heritage site) southeast of Hendon was constructed in 1914, and Hendon was a Swedish Lutheran preaching point after 1942.

Elsewhere in the province, a few other Swedish settlements merit mention. In the northeastern prairie region, the village and RM of Bjorkdale (village pop. 201) were named after Charles Bjork, who had immigrated from Worberg, Sweden, to settle there in 1904; the nearby small community of Steen after early settler David Steen; and farther southeast the district of Westerlund near Norquay after settler Levi Westerlund in 1908. A Lutheran congregation in the Kamsack area (Immanuel, 1919–42) used Swedish, German, and English in hymn singing. In the east-central region, at Pennock near Saltcoats, a strongly Scottish area, homesteader J. Walfred Anderson was actually a Swede who had lived at Pennock, Minnesota, before settling there in 1902. The Evangelical Lutheran Swedish congregation of Berea was situated at Punnichy (1920–42) and the Bethel Swedish congregation at Kelliher (1910–65). And at Marchwell, southeast of Langenburg, a Swedish Evangelical Church (renamed Bethel Lutheran Church in 1950) was built in 1910–12 and named a heritage site in 1986; originally, services were conducted entirely in Swedish but gradually changed to English as parishioners became less dependent on their native language.[24] Swedish settlers formed the Elim congregation at Theodore (1912–83) and contributed to the First English Evangelical Lutheran Church in Churchbridge (1919–54). In the west-central region, Swedes settled in and around Kindersley (pop. 4,412), which has an ELCIC congregation, and the Scandia district near Major (pop. 81) has already been noted.

According to recent census data (2006), 33,135 Saskatchewan residents claimed Swedish ethnic origin, of whom a very high proportion, 91.5% (30,330) also claimed other ethnic origins, compared with just 8.5% (2,805) claiming only Swedish origin. Most communities in Saskatchewan with a substantial Swedish proportion have been declining, and the few exceptions have increased by very few (and not necessarily Swedish) residents.

DANISH SETTLEMENTS

Recent census data (2006) revealed that 10,445 residents of Saskatchewan claimed that they are of Danish ethnic origin, of whom the vast majority, 88.9% (9,285) also claimed other ethnic origins; only 11.1% (1,160) claimed only Danish origin. Although people of Danish origin now constitute the third most numerous Scandinavian ethnic group in Saskatchewan, most people of Danish origin, unlike people of other Scandinavian origins, concentrated in cities, particularly Saskatoon, where they pioneered the Saskatoon Scandinavian Club. Small numbers or individual families settled among other Scandinavians in several rural settlements or in mixed areas where they were not sufficiently numerous to constitute a settlement of their own.

The impetus for establishing Danish settlements came largely from Dansk Folkesamfund, started in 1887 by Pastor F.L. Grundtvig, who had been the pastor of a Danish Lutheran church in Clinton, Iowa; he was the son of Bishop N.F.S. Grundtvig, a well-known church leader and hymn writer in Denmark. This organization intended to preserve the cultural heritage of Danish immigrants in North America. In 1894, Dansk Folkesamfund sponsored a Danish settlement called Danvang in Texas, and in 1905 another settlement, Askov, in Minnesota, then negotiated with the Canadian Pacific

Railway for similar settlements to be established in Western Canada. One such settlement was Dalum, centred on the Bethlehem Lutheran congregation in central Alberta, formed in 1918. Meanwhile, only a single, small, specifically Danish settlement came into existence in Saskatchewan: the Redvers (pop. 878) area in the southeastern region, where Danish families settled around 1910 southwest of town and formed the Dannevirke Danish Lutheran congregation in 1923 and completed building their church two years later (in 1973, the church was moved into town and is now an ELCIC congregation). In the old stone Hearts of Oak schoolhouse, some sixteen kilometres northwest of Redvers, adult Danes who settled there during the 1920s took English lessons, and Lutheran services were held during the summer months; in keeping with Danish tradition, evergreen branches were hung over the entrance for special events, and Christmas concerts were held in the schoolhouse.[25] However, in 1971, the town of Redvers was little more than 10% Scandinavian, as was the surrounding Antler RM; altogether there could not have been more than 200 people of Scandinavian origin (mostly Danes) in this area.

Two other rural locales where Danes settled were Dannebrog farm near Zelma, southeast of Saskatoon, where C.G. Henrickson settled in 1929, and Wingard (ferry, 1895; post office, 1888) northwest of Duck Lake, where Andreas Emil Lauritz "Nels" Peterson from Copenhagen homesteaded in 1882. Wingard was a somewhat anglicized version of his original Danish/German *Weingarten*. The local church there, of which he was an active member, was St. Cyprian's Anglican.

ICELANDIC SETTLEMENTS

In 1875–76, some 1,200 Icelanders immigrated to Western Canada to establish the New Iceland Colony along the west shore of Lake Winnipeg in Manitoba; they became the first *Westur Islendingurs* (Western Icelanders). New Iceland consisted of a series of adjoining settlements (*bygd[t]*or *byggd* in Icelandic) along the lakeshore: from south to north, Vidirnesbygd (Gimli, Vidir, Husavik), Arnesbygd (Arnes, Valhalla), Hnausabygd (Hnausa), Isafoldarbygd (Grassy Narrows), and Mikleyjarbygd (Hecla). Up the Icelandic River were Islendingafljotsbygd (Riverton), Geysirbygd (Geysir), Ardals-og-Framnesbygdir (Arborg and Framnes), and Vidirbygd (Vidir). The Icelandic settlers declared their colony an independent republic in 1878, with its own constitution, laws, and government, and Icelandic as the only official language. It lasted almost a decade before the Canadian government abolished it in 1887.

In the meantime, Icelandic settlers continued to move westward, eventually establishing a series of colonies across the prairies as far west as Markerville, Alberta. Icelanders arrived in Saskatchewan not only from these earlier settlements in Manitoba and North Dakota but also as immigrants directly from Iceland. Soon a series of Icelandic settlements became virtual stepping stones across the prairies into Saskatchewan and beyond. First some of the New Iceland settlers moved south into North Dakota, where they established the Pembina settlement in 1878 (around Gardar, Mountain, Hensel, Hallson, Akra, Cavalier, Svold, etc.). Two years later the Baldur settlement was established in southwestern Manitoba, in the Tiger Hills; the Frikirkju (Free Church) was founded in 1884 and the Frelsis (Liberty) congregation in the Grund district in 1895, and the small settlement included the Bru and Hekla districts. A Sidabotafelagid (Reform League) assured "moral uplift"—it opposed smoking, drinking, and swearing.[26] In 1885–87, thirty-five Icelandic families settled around Shellmouth, right on the Saskatchewan border about twenty kilometres east of the Churchbridge settlement that was developing at the same time. Icelanders settled around the Shoal Lakes in the Interlake region of Manitoba in 1887 (including Markland, Vestfold, Otto, and Lundar); the Narrows of Lake Manitoba from 1889 to 1912 (Reykjavik, Siglunes, Vogar, Hayland and Gudmundson Road, Dog Lake and Sigurdson Road, Isberg Point and Sveistrup Road, Silver Bay, Moosehorn, Steep Rock, etc.); around Pipestone, thirty-five kilometres east of the Saskatchewan border, in the small Laufas settlement in 1892; and around Langruth on the west shore of Lake Manitoba from 1894 (when some of the Churchbridge settlers, driven back into Manitoba by drought in Saskatchewan, resettled the Big Point district) to 1900 (when some of the North Dakota settlers moved into the Marshland district).

The earliest and largest Icelandic settlement in Saskatchewan had its beginnings in 1882 when the first settlers homesteaded near Fishing Lake in the central region. Called Vatnabyggd—lakes settlement—it grew in the region around Foam Lake, Fishing Lake, Little Quill Lake, and Big Quill Lake particularly after 1891. The three main towns in the region—Wynyard, Foam Lake, and Wadena—form a triangle around the settlement: Wynyard to the west, Foam Lake to the east, and Wadena to the north. The settlement began around Foam Lake, then spread westward; soon it had expanded to include the communities of Tuffnell (where Fountain School dates from 1895 and Fountain Post Office from 1907) to the east of Foam Lake; Fishing Lake to the north; Leslie, Elfros (possibly from Icelandic *elfarosee*—valley of roses), and Mozart (an unlikely name for an Icelandic community, but the post office there was originally called Laxdal in 1907 after Thorstein Laxdal, the first postmaster) between Foam Lake and Wynyard (where the original post office in 1905 was called Sleipner after Norse mythology); and Kandahar (an even more unlikely name!) and Dafoe west of Wynyard. Yet Icelanders, preferring the family farm, settled heavily in many rural districts around these communities. Around Foam Lake, they settled the districts of Bertdale (post office, 1906), Bildfell (one of the earliest Icelandic cemeteries), Marshall (settled by Norwegians; a Lutheran cemetery there dates from 1909), Inge Bay (where Ingemandur E. Inge and Steinum Jonsdottir originally homesteaded in 1892), and West-Sidel (Westside). Toward Fishing Lake, they settled the districts of Kristnes (literally meaning Christ's promontory; rural post office, 1905) and Osland (school, 1921). Toward Wadena, the Tornea district was settled by Swedish Finns. South of Leslie and Elfros, Icelanders concentrated in the districts of Old Holar, Walhalla (school, 1908, named after Norse mythology), Mount Hecla (school district named in 1906 after a volcano in Iceland that erupted, leading to the increased emigration of Icelanders to Canada), Eddleston (post office, 1909), and Haglof (rural post office named in 1907 for four brothers from Minnesota). To the east of Wynyard, Icelanders settled the Halldorson Spring district (named after settlers Jonathan and Thomas Halldorson), Hoseasson and Nupdal Lakes (named after early homesteaders), Gardar (school, 1906, named after Gardar, North Dakota, where some of the Icelandic settlers in this district had most recently originated), Little Quill, Vatnasofnudar (the lake district congregation from 1907 to 1937), and Grandy (school district named in 1906 for settlers Einar and Katrin Grandy, who had arrived from Washington state). To the south of Wynyard and Big Quill Lake, they settled

Harvard and Nordra (schools, 1908), Mountain (where the school was named in 1906 after Mountain, North Dakota), and Magnusson Creek (where Magnus Magnusson homesteaded), while Norwegians homesteaded in the Aarnes district (a Lutheran cemetery dates from 1906).

Icelandic communities became cultural centres with bands, choirs, and libraries. *Felagsheimilum* (community halls) played especially important roles, as did country *skolum* (schools). *Heimhusum* (home meetings) were held, while travelling preachers often visited to serve religious needs. Each year was filled with celebrations, including *Thorrablot* in spring, the first day of summer on June 17, and Iceland Independence Day on August 2. These Icelandic pioneers were strongly dedicated to the traditional Icelandic emphasis on *myndlistar* (the arts), *bokmennta* (literature), education, and *fjölskylda* (family life), which they brought to Canada.

This is by far the largest Icelandic settlement in Saskatchewan, with an estimated Scandinavian (mostly Icelandic) population numbering about 1,700 in 1971 in the towns and incorporated villages and the surrounding rural municipalities of Big Quill, Elfros, Foam Lake, and Sasman. None of the three main towns was predominantly Scandinavian; in all three towns, people of British or Ukrainian origin outnumbered people of Icelandic and other Scandinavian origins: in Wynyard, 18.3% of the residents were Scandinavian, 14.4% in Foam Lake, and 18.6% in Wadena. Nor did Scandinavians predominate in the incorporated villages of Elfros (38.8%) and Leslie (just 7.1%), though Mozart was largely Icelandic. Today Wynyard has 1,744 residents, Wadena 1,315, Foam Lake 1,123, Elfros 110, while smaller communities have all but disappeared: Mozart has only thirty-four residents, Leslie twenty, Kandahar twenty-five, Tuffnell ten, and Dafoe ten. Apart from Kandahar, which actually gained ten residents between 2001 and 2006, recent trends indicate that all of these communities—even the larger towns—have been losing population. The most dramatic decline has been in Dafoe, which had 408 residents in 1941, when a military base was located there, but the base closed in 1954, and by 1971 only a tenth of that number—forty-one residents—remained. Many of the original Icelandic Lutheran churches in the settlement have closed over time: the Lake District congregation in the Grandy district (1907–37), the Augustine Icelandic congregation at Kandahar (1909–60), Leslie (1909–54), the Prairie congregation and Sunny World congregation at Mozart (1907–37), Immanuel at Wynyard (1911–49), Kristnes (1906–21), and around the Quill Lakes Hallgrims (1914–35), Sion (1917–31), and Sletter (1916–27), while the Icelandic Lutheran congregation at Elfros, founded in 1916, merged with the United Church congregation to form the Union Church in 1935.

In 1998, the Vatnabyggd Icelandic Club of Saskatoon (founded in 1981 "to foster and promote Icelandic cultural heritage and harmony and cooperation between all cultural groups") unveiled a memorial to Icelandic pioneers of Saskatchewan. The memorial, in a park in Elfros, includes a bronze statue of a young Icelandic couple, information on the first Icelanders to settle in the Vatnabyggd (Lakes) settlement, murals of Iceland in the 1880s, the voyage to Canada, and Vatnabyggd then and now. The memorial has received visitors such as the president of Iceland, the Icelandic ambassador to Canada, and touring Icelandic artists and musicians. In recognition of the Icelandic pioneer settlers, trails in the Foam Lake marsh have been named Vatnabyggd and given Icelandic names for local birds and animals.[27]

Meanwhile, a second Icelandic settlement was developing in Saskatchewan, the Thingvalla-Logberg Colony just outside Churchbridge, in the east-central region, in 1886. Thingvalla (named after the plain in Iceland where the first *älthing*—parliament—met) was immediately east of Churchbridge, while Logberg (the *lögberg* was the speaker's platform in the *älthing*) was several kilometres north. Farther north were Pennock, Rothbury, and Minerva Schools. In 1892, both Thingvalla and Logberg became rural post offices. Thingvalla once included a Lutheran congregation, the older and newer Thingvalla Schools, a cemetery, and a hall on Einarsvatn (Einar's Lake). Logberg included an older and a newer school and Concordia Lutheran Church; the Concordia congregation was initially formed in 1901, and the church was built four years later; it was closed in 1953. The Thingvalla congregation, formed in 1888, joined the Concordia congregation in 1963 and the next year the Peace German Lutheran congregation; the Concordia church building was moved into town in 1967, so all that remains in the country now is the cemetery. The Luters congregation in the Calder area was very short lived: 1891–94. Today both ELCIC and LCC congregations still function in Churchbridge. In 1971, fewer than 10% of the residents of Churchbridge (pop. 704 and declining) were Scandinavian; there were an estimated 200 Scandinavians (mostly Icelanders) in the immediate area in Churchbridge RM.

A third settlement, Holar-byggd (Icelandic for hills settlement), soon developed about forty kilometres to the south, on the edge of the Qu'Appelle Valley (which the Icelanders called Vatnsdalur, meaning water valley), near Tantallon, in 1887. Holar School was built in 1894 and doubled as a church; it was moved onto Holar Hill in 1901. It became a community hall, while still functioning as a church, in 1919 and was an active meeting place for dances, picnics, community meetings, and sports. In 1985, it was moved into Tantallon, where it has served as the village office, information centre, and heritage site. The settlement's name originated in the Holar homestead of Sigurdur Anderson. The Icelanders added the Vallar-byggd (meaning flat prairie settlement) to the north of Tantallon; it became a school district in 1904. Isafoldar—the Dongola district west of Spy Hill—contained an Icelandic congregation from 1903 to 1938. Today Icelandic and other Scandinavian farms are still scattered throughout these districts (e.g., Olafson, Olson, Arnason, Magnusson, Einarson, Ingaldson, Swanson, Johnson, Bergstrom). Relatively few Scandinavians live in the neighbouring villages, though a Norwegian Lutheran congregation came into existence in Spy Hill (pop. 201); fewer than 100 people of Icelandic origin remained in this small settlement by 1971, in Tantallon (pop. 105) and Spy Hill RM. Both communities have been losing population.

According to recent (2006) census data, people of Icelandic origin in Saskatchewan numbered 6,445, of whom the overwhelming majority, 89.3% (5,755), also claimed other ethnic origins, compared with just 10.7% (690) claiming only Icelandic origin. However, some of these latter people might be descended from people claiming other Scandinavian origins, such as in the Wadena area, where Icelanders have likely mixed to some extent with Swedes, or around Spy Hill, where Norwegians also settled, and of course in the cities, where Icelanders have shared the Scandinavian Club with other Scandinavian people.

FINNISH SETTLEMENTS

Finnish immigrants began to arrive in Canada as early as 1825, working on large-scale construction projects such as canal and railway building. Many of the early immigrants came via the United States, arriving in increasing numbers during the 1880s to work on railway lines, in coal and nickel mines, in forestry, and eventually in farming. However, during the period of "America fever" lasting until about 1920, only about one in ten emigrating Finns went directly to Canada; this was to change during the 1920s, with the tightening of US immigration regulations, and more Finnish emigrants left directly for Canada—an estimated 30,000 during this one decade. Yet those who ventured out west soon encountered both the Depression and the drought, so a considerable number returned to Finland and some to Russia. At least another wave of 20,000 immigrated to Canada between the end of the Second World War and the mid-1960s, by which time, though, the bulk of Finnish immigration to Canada had occurred: between 1901 and 1931, some 40,000 Finns entered Canada, including those who came via the United States, compared with only about half as many during the next several decades. During the two world wars, the number of immigrants from Finland dropped drastically, reaching none at all in 1941–42, when Canada declared war on Finland, which was then allied to Nazi Germany. Given these vagaries in the immigration of Finns to Canada, especially directly from Finland, the population of ethnic Finns in Canada increased rapidly from just 2,502 in 1901 to 15,497 in 1911, 21,494 in 1921, and 43,885 in 1931, then stabilized at 41,683 in 1941 and 43,745 in 1951, after which it increased to 59,436 in 1961 and 59,215 in 1971.[28] By 1971, however, estimates by Finnish Canadian scholars considered the total population of Canadians who were wholly or partially of Finnish origin, plus many Swedish-speaking Finns who might have identified themselves as Swedish Canadians, to be in the 70,000 to 110,000 range. This estimation was perhaps not much of an exaggeration, for official census data in 1971 still counted ethnicity through the paternal lineage only, when many Finnish Canadian women were becoming intermarried; moreover, Swedish-speaking Finns constituted approximately 7% of the total population of Finland and were concentrated along western and southern coastal areas that produced numerous emigrants. By 1971, almost two-thirds of Canadians claiming Finnish ethnic origin through the male lineage were living in Ontario (primarily in Toronto and northern Ontario, around Thunder Bay and Sudbury); Finnish Canadians in British Columbia also far outnumbered those in the Prairie Provinces. Only about one in ten Finnish Canadians (counted in the census) was living then on the prairies, just 1,730 in Saskatchewan.[29] However, with the change in Canadian census data after 1981 to count both single and ethnic origin, through either parent or both parents, recent census data (2006) indicated that 3,960 people in Saskatchewan claimed Finnish ethnic origin, of whom 21.1% (840) claimed to be completely Finnish and 78.9% (3,125) partly Finnish. A particularly interesting feature of Saskatchewan Finns is that they have been predominantly rural, unlike Finns in the neighbouring provinces and unlike other Scandinavian ethnic groups. Using the former census data, 62.1% of Finns in Saskatchewan in 1971 were still rural. Moreover, the Finnish settlements that developed in Saskatchewan were among the earliest and best-defined agrarian Finnish settlements in Canada.

In Saskatchewan, three isolated rural areas can be discerned where Finns have concentrated. The small but cohesive New Finland Colony was founded southwest of

Tantallon and northeast of Whitewood by a small number of "Church Finns" affiliated with the Suomi (Finnish) Lutheran Synod in 1887.[30] Numerous Finns have settled there over several decades: the first settler was Jeremiah Kautonen, who immigrated from Kauhawa, Finland, in 1887 and homesteaded in 1889; his friend John Lautamus from Kauhawa joined him the following year, and the Lautamus family arrived later that year. Although the parkland was heavily wooded with poplar, berry, and willow bushes, and rough, with ravines, sloughs, and creeks, it was fertile land. In 1891, Mat Mustama walked the more than thirty kilometres from Whitewood with his wife and young son, carrying a bundle of clothing, and John Kangas arrived in mid-winter from Copper Cliff, Ontario. He built his cabin with just a hand axe, covering it with sod blocks to keep out the bitter cold. The next year Isaac Polvi arrived by wagon from Michigan with his wife and son. Jacob Myllymaki, from Whitefish, Ontario, and Solomon Petays arrived in 1893. Soon more settlers arrived in the growing Finnish settlement, equipped with axes, saws, bedding, spinning wheels, and a few precious dishes. They gradually cleared the bush; single-room log and sod cabins were built, with birchbark roofs and log floors. Imported grocery boxes doubled as rudimentary furniture. Soon these Finns had erected *saunas* near their homes. The settlers had to be largely self-sufficient. They hunted and traded with the Native people. Clothing was mostly homemade, including skin breeches, vests and jackets for the men, and dresses, shawls, and headscarves for the women. Farmland was broken with oxen and wooden implements; wheat was sown and cut by hand. It took a full day to reach neighbouring towns by sleigh during the winter, and cordwood was exchanged for supplies; the singing voices of the drivers would ring through the frigid air.

Between 1888 and 1900, forty-five couples or families and nineteen single homesteaders arrived in the settlement, from 1901 to 1910 another twenty-five couples or families and twenty-seven single persons, and from 1911 to 1920 nine families or couples and thirteen single persons; from 1920 to 1933, the settlers dwindled to just nine families or couples and four single persons. The vast majority came from Vaasa province, but others came from throughout Finland. Coastal Finland has always been primarily Swedish speaking, and Swedish Finns comprised a substantial proportion of settlers, as their surnames revealed (Anderson, Burkman, Dorma, Flykti, Hagberg, Hemming, Hilberg, Holma, Jaakobson, Johanson, Johnson, Linden, Nordland, Peterson, Sandberg, Venberg).

In the heart of the New Finland Colony were the school (1896–1961), community hall, St. John's Lutheran Church and cemeteries (the main Lutheran church, now affiliated with the ELCIC, was organized in 1893 and built in 1907), and post office (1896–1921). To the northeast were Nurmi Oja School (1905–58) and Apostolic Lutheran Church (built in 1921, previously an *esikoisuus*—first-bornism—congregation and after 1975 affiliated with the Association of American Laestadian Congregations). To the east were Convent Creek School (1925–61), Finnish National Evangelical Lutheran Church (*Kansallis Seurakunta*, also known locally as the *kivikurkku*—the stone church—from the 1920s through the 1940s), and Polvi's store. Farther east were Carnoustie School, Post Office (1895–1935), and cemetery. To the southeast was Woodleigh School. To the southwest were Deerwood School (1898–1962), Clayridge Post Office (1949–69), and Full Gospel Church (since 1963). To the west were Forest Farm School and Kangas's store. And to the northwest were Grove Park School (1899–1966) and Post Office (1899–1963). Eventually, the settlement included not only churches, schools (the first classes were held in a private home in 1893), and post offices but also general stores, a blacksmith, a sawmill, a community recreation club, skating and curling rinks, and baseball diamonds. The New Finland Temperance Society was formed in 1911, and it erected a large hall in 1914. In 1971, the number of people who claimed Scandinavian and other ethnic origins (Finns do not necessarily count themselves as Scandinavian) in the nearby town of Whitewood and the rural municipalities of Willowdale and Rocanville was only about 500, so Finns remaining in the area could not have exceeded several hundred at most.

In 1910, more people of Finnish ethnic origin arrived from earlier Canadian and American colonies to settle in a second backcountry district, Rock Point, about forty kilometres southwest of Outlook in central Saskatchewan.[31] Some 200 Finnish families settled there, some direct from Finland but most from earlier Finnish settlements in Ontario and the Great Lakes states. Contact among Finnish settlements, notably including New Finland in Saskatchewan, became increasingly common, as did marriages. The early years of settlement were hard: homesteaders were plagued by prairie fires, insects, and a flu epidemic. Land was originally broken by oxen. People of Finnish origin became concentrated in the former Finland School District (1913–41), Rock Point School District (1916), Big Valley, King George, and Coteau Hills School Districts, along Pavo (more likely originally Paavo in Finnish) Road, and extending toward Macrorie (pop. 78), Dunblane (now just a small hamlet), Birsay (pop. 53), Lucky Lake (pop. 295), and Dinsmore (pop. 269). The central community of Rock Point (just a rural locality today) once had a general store, post office, service station, community hall, and Pentecostal church. This larger settlement was long divided between the fundamentalist Laestadian sect, concentrated to the east in the East Finn district (Coteau RM), where the Laestadian church west of Dunblane was constructed in 1969, and the socialist "Red Finns," concentrated in the West Finn district (King George RM) to the west, while the community of Rock Point was situated in the centre of the settlement. It has been estimated that perhaps two-thirds of the Finns in the settlement (130 families) were "Church Finns" (mostly Laestadians and Pentecostals but including some Scandinavian Lutherans), while the others (seventy families) were "Red Finns." Repression of communists in Saskatchewan during the 1930s led to the emigration of some of these leftists to Karelia in the Soviet Union.[32] Finns in the Rock Point district held socials to support the Finnish Relief Fund in 1939.

Today an estimated 300–400 Finns remain in this settlement (eighty-one families in 1980 with forty-eight surnames), yet one resident suggested that more than 1,000 Finns and their descendants have lived in the Rock Point settlement at one time or another. Altogether, in 1971, little more than 800 people in the surrounding communities (Macrorie, Dunblane, Birsay, Beechy, Lucky Lake, Conquest) and the rural municipalities of Coteau, King George, and Fertile Valley claimed Scandinavian and other ethnic origins. Dunblane had been a railway terminus and later a division point in 1908; by the 1920s, it had over 200 residents, and over 500 during the 1940s, but severe rural decline eventually led to it being disorganized as a village in 1975, when just a post office was left. Despite rural depopulation, these descendants still retain a strong sense of Finnish identity, evidenced in many folk traditions. A well-known local character was Tom Sukanen (1873–1943), an eccentric bachelor who constructed a small ship on his farm near Macrorie in which he intended to sail down the nearby South Saskatchewan River all the way back to Finland; his ship was eventually ensconced in the Prairie Pioneer Museum near Moose Jaw in the 1970s.

Finns from this latter settlement gradually began to obtain summer cottage properties in the Turtle Lake area, northwest of North Battleford.[33] Following settlers Jeremiah Kahtava, from Finland and Michigan, who settled there in 1912, Bill and Felix Kivimaa (after whom Kivimaa Bay was named), who arrived from Alavieska in northwestern Finland in 1929, and Jakko Niskala, who arrived that year from the large Finnish settlement around Thunder Bay, Ontario, some Finns eventually settled there on a more permanent basis, many working as commercial fishermen on the lake. Now there might be as many as 300–400 Finns and Scandinavians in the area, in resort colonies around the lakes, and in the nearby communities of Turtleford (pop. 461) and Mervin (pop. 228). Kivimaa–Moonlight Bay resort community, organized by Waino Kykkanen in the early 1950s, has Finnish street names: Kivimaa, Kykkanen, Kahtava, Mattila. The two main Finnish settlements in Saskatchewan have both been losing population, whereas Turtle Lake has been growing—but as a resort with a concomitant proportionate decrease in the Finnish population.

Mention should also be made of several other Finnish-settled areas. The Nummela district, in Grassy Creek RM southeast of Shaunavon in southwestern Saskatchewan, had a post office in 1911 (misspelled Nummola) and a community hall in 1913 (designated a heritage site in 1985); in Finnish, *nummela* means on the meadow, and there is a community in Finland west of Helsinki with this name, also a common Finnish surname. In the east-central region, a country hall dating from 1935 was the social centre of the Banner district north of Melville; the hall was next to Runeberg School, named in 1911 most likely for Johan Ludvig Runeberg, a famous Swedish Finn poet during the nineteenth century. In an isolated Finnish settlement near Invermay, the Finnish Lutheran Church lasted from 1913 to 1944. Already mentioned was a concentration of Swedish Finns in the Tornea district southeast of Wadena.

SCANDINAVIAN/FINNISH ETHNIC IDENTITY AND LANGUAGE

Although there is much evidence that the Nordic groups in Saskatchewan rapidly assimilated into general Canadian society, a tradition-oriented attitude often prevailed within Scandinavian and especially Finnish bloc settlements. One Saskatchewan historian, writing in 1924, commented that, in the case of the Swedish settlement around New Stockholm, "it looks rather as if the Swedes are assimilating us."[34] This could hardly be viewed as exceptional, at least in the early years of settlement, considering that a high proportion of Scandinavians and Finns, like other ethnic groups, settled in fairly well-defined bloc settlements. Moreover, by 1926, a considerable proportion of them still had not adopted Canadian citizenship (even though many of them came after first settling in the United States): 58% of the foreign-born Danes, 25% of the Swedes, 19% of the Norwegians, and 11% of the Icelanders.[35] Preservation of a Scandinavian or Finnish identity was never regarded as incompatible with Canadian citizenship. While Scandinavian Canadians were noted for their contribution during the two world wars, we must remember that neither were they from countries hostile to Britain and Canada (as was the case for immigrants from Germany or Austria-Hungary)—though Finland was technically an ally of Germany for several years during the Second World War, Sweden was neutral, and Denmark and Norway were occupied by German forces—nor were they pacifists (as were the Mennonites, Hutterites, and Doukhobors). Thus, their contributions to the Canadian cause and the Scandinavian one were not incompatible. For example, during the Second World War, Frank Eliason raised $34,000 to aid Norwegian and Finnish war victims, and he was decorated for his services by King Haakon of Norway.[36] Nor did the British Canadian population in Saskatchewan tend to view Scandinavian immigrants as "unassimilable." In fact, even the Ku Klux Klan, which drew some support from Scandinavian settlers, suggested that "trained" Scandinavian immigrants should be allowed to settle on the land.[37]

Yet decades of de-emphasizing Scandinavian identity, particularly in the school system, but also in the local prairie community (where people of Scandinavian origin seldom predominated) and through intermarriage, brought about significant differences among generations in attitudes toward ethnic identity. An extensive survey of ethnic identity changes among generations, conducted by the author in the ethnic bloc settlements in the north-central region from 1969 to 1972, included interviews with eighty-six Scandinavian families in the primarily Norwegian settlements around Birch Hills and Shellbrook.[38] Among these Scandinavian respondents, 16.3% strongly favoured the retention of Scandinavian identity, 58.1% were more or less in favour, and 25.6% expressed indifference; no case of actual opposition was found. However, it was also found that almost three-quarters of the respondents (74.4%) believed that there had been a major loss of emphasis on ethnicity from generation to generation, while the remaining quarter (25.6%) noted a minor loss. All of the first (immigrant) generation stressed their ethnic identity, compared with 79.4% of the second generation and 61.9% of the third generation. Still, it was interesting to find that a majority of the third generation respondents continued to take an interest in their Scandinavian ethnicity.

Scandinavian Canadians have tended to believe that it is possible to maintain a general interest in the "Scandinavian connection" without maintaining an ability to speak a Scandinavian language. The proportion of the Scandinavian-origin population in Saskatchewan claiming an ability to speak a Scandinavian language declined from 59% in 1941 to 40% in 1951 to 28% in 1961 and to 20% in 1971; by 1971, hardly 1% actually used such a language as the primary language spoken in the home. Many, if not most, of the original Scandinavian settlers in the province had formerly lived in the United States (for periods of time ranging from a few years to a couple of generations), so a considerable proportion had probably already considered English to be their primary language before immigrating to Canada. If the 1950s comprised a decisive decade of linguistic change among Scandinavian-origin people in Saskatchewan, ethnic language loss during that decade was actually occurring more rapidly among the Scandinavian-origin rural farm population (from 43% in 1951 to 30% in 1961) than among the rural non-farm (36% to 32%) or urban (29% to 24%) population. Yet in 1971 a higher proportion of Scandinavian-origin rural population (23% for rural farm and 25% for rural non-farm) than urban population (17%) could still speak a Scandinavian language. According to the survey data, a far higher proportion of older people than younger people retained this ability (67% of the sixty-five and older group compared with 38% of the forty-five–sixty-four group, 16% of the thirty-five–forty-four group, 6.5% of the twenty–thirty-four group, 3.9% of the nine–nineteen group, and 2.1% of the one–nine group). Nonetheless, the survey data indicated that a very high proportion (89.5%) of respondents interviewed within the selected bloc settlements at the time claimed at least some familiarity with a Scandinavian language, though relatively few (37.2%) were actually using this language. To be more specific, a quarter (25.6%) of the respondents preferred to use their Scandinavian language both at home and in the community; 11.6% preferred this language at home but English in the community; a little over half (52.3%) preferred English in both contexts yet were familiar with a Scandinavian language; and relatively few (10.5%) could speak only English. The most interesting finding, though, was that there had been a drastic decline in the proportion preferring to speak a Scandinavian language (primarily or exclusively) with each succeeding generation: from 92.3% in the first generation to 55.9% in the second and just 2.6% in the third.

Of course, these survey findings in primarily Norwegian bloc settlements in one particular region were not necessarily representative of the Scandinavian-origin population as a whole in Saskatchewan. Sharp distinctions could be drawn between people of Scandinavian origin resident in urban areas and those still living within relatively homogeneous rural bloc settlements, also between people completely of Scandinavian origin and those of mixed parentage; moreover, differences exist among the various Nordic ethnic groups and likely even among the settlements of a particular Scandinavian or Finnish ethnic group. For example, within the extensive Scandinavian (primarily Norwegian) settlement around Outlook and Hanley, Norwegian was rarely spoken at home, even among the older generation in homogeneous families, even though this generation could speak Norwegian fluently, claiming that they had "no trouble at all" when visiting Norway (which many of them often did, almost annually, though the older generation tended to speak archaic local dialects that have increasingly been replaced by *Nynorsk*—standardized new Norwegian). Norwegian conversation in the community was limited to only the occasional expression. The second generation was less familiar with the language, the third hardly at all; however, whole families would often visit relatives in Norway, which doubtless served to maintain familiarity with the language.

Differences exist between the Scandinavian and Finnish groups in their propensity to maintain fluency in the traditional ethnic language. A major contrast can be drawn between the Scandinavian groups proper, on the one hand, and the Finnish group, on the other. There is little contrast among the four Scandinavian groups. Of 36,000 people of Norwegian descent living in Saskatchewan in 1971, 6,800 (18.9%) claimed that they spoke Norwegian as their mother tongue, compared with 3,400 (23.5%) of 15,000 Swedes who were speaking Swedish, 1,300 (24.6%) of about 5,000 Danes speaking Danish, and 840 (27.1%) of some 3,000 Icelanders speaking Icelandic. In contrast, 745 (43.2%) of the 1,700 Finns could speak Finnish.[39] Thus, despite their relatively smaller numbers, a far higher proportion of people of Finnish origin used their mother tongue than people of Scandinavian origins in the province. These differences were even more pronounced in Canada as a whole: 61% of Finnish Canadians still considered Finnish as their mother tongue and could speak it, compared with only a quarter of Scandinavian Canadians who could still speak a Scandinavian language. Even more striking was the fact that at the time 31% of Finnish Canadians continued to use Finnish as a primary language at home, compared with just 2% of Scandinavian Canadians speaking a Scandinavian language. Yet in Saskatchewan the rate of language decline seemed to be happening faster among Finns than among Scandinavians: in the decade before 1971, the proportion of Finns in the province speaking Finnish dropped from 60.2% to 43.2%. And, with another generation since then, perhaps fewer than one in five people in the province claiming Finnish ethnicity can speak Finnish and proportionately fewer still a Scandinavian language; in other words, few third- or fourth-generation residents claiming Finnish origin, and fewer claiming Scandinavian origin, can still speak Finnish or a Scandinavian language.

Finnish is not a Scandinavian language; rather, it is related to Finno-Ugric languages within the Ural-Altaic family. Yet Swedish influence on Finland lasted for almost half a millennium, from 1323 to 1809; Swedish sovereignty over Finland resulted in a Swedish aristocracy as well as farmers and fishermen in Finland. Approximately 7% of the total population of Finland speaks Swedish as their first home language; moreover, many Swedes intermarried with Finns, so it became common for a Finnish speaker to have a Swedish surname, and most Swedes and Finns shared the Lutheran religion. Most communities along the western and southern coasts of Finland (from which many people emigrated to Canada) were predominantly Swedish speaking. At the same time, Finnish emigrants tended to possess a strong sense of national identity and referred to people who did not speak Finnish or were not of Finnish descent as *kielinen*, meaning of that language. Older immigrants in Canada were apt to tell the younger generation that "Even poor Finnish is better than English."[40] Yet Finnish and Scandinavian immigrants tended to be devoted to education, and they were quick to acquire at least a working knowledge of English. It is striking that in Saskatchewan people of Scandinavian ethnicity were far quicker to adopt English as their home language than certain other ethnic groups, such as Ukrainians, French, conservative Mennonites and of course Hutterites, and even far less numerous groups such as Chinese and Greeks. Nonetheless, among Finns within a compact bloc settlement such as Rock Point, far more use of the Finnish language was prevalent: in a 1981 study, it was found that almost all of the Finnish-origin adults in the settlement could communicate in Finnish, but among the younger generation intermarriage with non-Finns was becoming increasingly prevalent, and in a mixed family it was unlikely that Finnish would be retained as a preferred language at home.[41]

RELIGION

Although many of the Lutheran parishes in rural Saskatchewan can be classified as ethnic parishes of a general denomination today, for several decades they were all in ethnic sub-denominations patterned after national churches in Scandinavia and Germany. During this early period, the ethnic nature of each sub-denomination was evident. Where Lutherans of various Scandinavian origins settled in one area, Norwegians, Swedes, and Danes each organized their own congregations.[42] Scandinavians organized Trinity Lutheran congregation in Saskatoon in 1919 (it changed its name to Zion the following year), and Swedish members withdrew in 1929 to form their own Augustana congregation, thus consolidating Zion as a predominantly Norwegian congregation. During the early years of settlement, Icelanders had their own *kirkjufelag* (synod), which conducted the *messusvar* (liturgy) in the Icelandic language. Backed by affiliated bodies in the mother countries or bloc settlements in the American Midwest, the Scandinavian Lutheran churches tended to support bloc settlement isolationism, ethnic traditionalism, and religious conservatism.[43]

These sub-denominations have been consolidated into more general Lutheran organizations since the 1940s.[44] But at the individual congregation level, many Lutheran churches, especially those in rural areas, remain virtual ethnic parishes. Even within the large Evangelical Lutheran Church of Canada, until recent years, pastors serving parishes where most of the congregation were of Scandinavian origin tended to be of Scandinavian origin themselves.[45] Services in all parishes, however, are invariably conducted in English, though on occasion they might be conducted in a Scandinavian language. And this church's junior college at Outlook long remained mindful of its Norwegian heritage, flying the Norwegian flag on occasion and celebrating a traditional Norwegian holiday.

On the other hand, an increasing proportion of people of Scandinavian origin are not Lutherans but converts to various evangelical sects. In fact, the proportion of Scandinavian/Finnish people in Saskatchewan who are Lutherans has steadily declined: from over two-thirds (67.1%) back in 1941 to little over half (56.2%) by 1951, less than half (45.3%) by 1961, and only four in ten (40.4%) by 1971. Even in solidly Scandinavian settlements, Lutherans have long been less numerous than people of Scandinavian origin. For example, in Canwood, Scandinavians made up 42.0% of the community in 1961, while Lutherans constituted only 29.8% in 1951; Parkside was 48.0% Scandinavian yet 23.1% Lutheran; Weldon was 50.0% Scandinavian yet 42.6% Lutheran.[46]

The 1972 survey data clearly indicated generational differences in emphasis on ethnicity and preferred language use, but such differences were not as noticeable when religion was considered. A very high proportion (87.2%) of respondents reported attending Lutheran church services "as regularly as possible" (usually every Sunday) compared with just 8.1% who attended "sometimes" or "usually but not always" and just 4.7% who attended "rarely"; not a single respondent reported "never" attending. By generation, 69.2% of the first reported regular attendance compared with 82.4% of the second and an astonishing 97.4% of the third. However, this can be partly explained by the strong expectation among younger respondents that they were expected to attend church regularly.

As noted earlier, the Rock Point settlement became divided between religious "Church Finns" and socialist "Red Finns."[47] Of some 200 families in the early settlement, perhaps two-thirds were Church Finns, most of whom belonged to the fundamentalist Laestadian Apostolic sect, a controversial derivation from Finnish Lutheranism, while some Church Finns attended Scandinavian Lutheran churches in nearby communities, the Elim Finnish Pentecostal Church in the community of Rock Point, or the "Swedish" Adventist Church near Macrorie. This was a rather unique subdivision, for back in Finland the vast majority were at least nominal Lutherans. Although the Finnish Evangelical Lutheran Church (Suomi Synod) was established in the early years of settlement among Finns in North America, its influence was lessened by the Laestadian movement and other churches. Clearly, the Lutheran Church held a stronger position over the Laestadians and Pentecostals in the New Finland settlement, with a large congregation served during the early years by Finnish pastors (however, since merging with several largely Scandinavian synods into a consolidated Evangelical Lutheran Church of Canada, the congregation has more recently been served by non-Finnish pastors).

The Laestadian movement had developed in Sweden and Finland during the nineteenth century as a protest against what Laestadians perceived to be the secularization of the Lutheran Church (it levied taxes, and confirmation was compulsory); Laestadians strove to return to a stricter interpretation of the Bible and a simpler basic religious lifestyle. In the Finnish diaspora, this movement took two directions. The *esikoiset* claimed to be the original apostolics; their lifestyle discouraged excessive pictures on the wall, dancing, and eventually television and encouraged simple and modest dress. Laestadians greeted one another with *jumalan turva* (God's peace) and referred to themselves as *jumalan lapset* (God's children). With increased religious freedom in North America, Laestadians tended to thrive in immigrant communities; their conservatism was combined with a strong sense of community and in turn strengthened ethnic ties. Intermarriage outside the Finnish community was uncommon; Finnish was used, together with English, in services; yet the church rather than the community halls was the centre of Laestadian community life.

CUSTOMS

Scandinavian-origin people in Saskatchewan tend to be familiar with a wide variety of Scandinavian folk traditions, particularly foods but also performing arts, décor, and clothing. In the solidly Norwegian rural districts, many types of typically Norwegian baking and other traditional foods (e.g., *lutefisk* and meatballs) are occasionally prepared, such as at Christmas. There is a wide assortment of traditional baking and sweets, including *lefse, krumkake, kransekake, rosettes,* buttermilk pie, sour cream cake/pie, Norwegian macaroons and oatmeal cookies, *vianabrod, berlinerkrans, fattigeman, sandkaker, blötkake* (sponge cake), "Bergen doughnuts," and so on. Traditional meat, fish, and vegetable dishes include *lutefisk* (fish fermented in lye), meatballs, fish balls, *faar i kaal* (mutton and cabbage), *kumla* (potato dumplings), *pytt i pande* (egg and meat), and *spekeskinke* (smoked ham). Soups and porridges are varied, including *rømmegrøt* and *fløtegrøt* (cream porridge), *fruktsuppe* (fruit soup), *fisksuppe* (fish chowder), and *lopskaus* (potato and ham porridge). Smorgasbords were popular, as they still are in Scandinavia (literally, *smørbrød* means open-faced sandwich, often topped with *reke*, shrimp). Popular cheeses are *gjetost* (goat cheese) and *gammelost* (aged cheese). Such traditional foods are prepared primarily by older women, though it is not that uncommon to find second- and even third-generation women preparing them. It should be stressed, however, that many of these foods are prepared only on special occasions back in Scandinavia; consequently, they become ever rarer in Scandinavian homes in Canada. Some traditional Scandinavian foods (e.g., *flatbrød*, flatbread) have become common in mixed communities and are not necessarily recognized as Scandinavian; Lutheran Ladies' Aids regularly serve Scandinavian-style baking or *smorgasbords* (simply equated with "pot luck" suppers). Among Finns, roast pork and rice pudding have long been traditional Christmas dishes. More uniquely Finnish is *kaalikaaryleet* (cabbage rolls) and *fiili* (fermented milk congealed to form a traditional dessert). At least among older-generation Norwegian immigrants, it would be discourteous to end a meal without thanks for the meal (in Norwegian, *mange takk for mat(e)/mjøl*).

As for other customs, Scandinavian folk dancing and music can be seen or heard at ethnic gatherings such as the annual *Islendingadagurinn* or Icelandic Day in Gimli, Manitoba, and a smaller version near Foam Lake, Saskatchewan, and especially at annual multicultural festivals in Saskatoon and Regina. Interior home décor cannot be underestimated. Although less common than in homes in Scandinavia, one can find miniature Scandinavian flags, embroidery and tapestries, tablerunners, and artifacts in Scandinavian Canadian homes in Saskatchewan. Although some weaving might still be practised, most of this décor is brought or imported directly from Scandinavia, as is traditional clothing or complete folk dress (e.g., a woman's *bunad* and jewellery representing a particular region in Norway). In Scandinavia, full folk costume is worn only on special occasions such as national days, baptisms, weddings, confirmations, and family gatherings (usually by older women, hardly ever by men). In Canada, such full dress is restricted to ethnic gatherings, folk performances, and festivals. Finally, visits "home" to Scandinavia still seem to be common; families might "return" every two or three years, sometimes every year, or exchange visits with relatives in Scandinavia.

Finns have been well known for their *saunas* (steam baths), used by whole families and even visiting neighbours. They have also taken pride in their *sisu* (stubbornness or grit), which could explain their common propensity for hard work, industriousness, self-reliance, and restraint in social relations. Finns have tended to have a strong sense of community (despite their religious and political differences). With the exception, perhaps, of most Laestadians, community halls played a significant role—especially during the earlier years of settlement—in Finnish community life represented in active sports, music, dances, and plays. So the eventual closing of the halls by the 1960s created a vacuum in Finnish community life in many respects.[48] Special occasions were celebrated not only by Finns but also by Scandinavians, and both inherited a rich legacy of folk tales.

Many community activities in rural districts, however, were either typical of any rural community or linked to the Lutheran Church (or other largely Scandinavian or Finnish churches) and did not necessarily assume an ethnic character. A common practice in Scandinavia was to celebrate seasonal and national days; to some extent, this practice has been preserved among Scandinavians in Saskatchewan. For example, Norwegians celebrate *syttende Mai* (May 17, the national day) and *midtsommernat* (mid-summer night), similarly Swedes and Finns *Juhannus midsommar* and Icelanders *sumardaginn fyrsta* (the first day of summer). In the Icelandic community of Mozart each year, the Viljinn Ladies' Aid would present a concert, poetry reading (in Icelandic, of course), play, song, or dance in the community hall under a banner proclaiming "happy summer" in Icelandic.[49] The Saskatoon Scandinavian Club held dinners to celebrate these events. As with other ethnic groups, Christmas remains an occasion for ethnic traditions. An annual *Norsk Julegudstjeneste* (Norwegian Christmas candlelight service) is still held at Zion Lutherske Kirke (Zion Lutheran Church) in Saskatoon, with all hymns sung in Norwegian, a procession of children (from Norskola, the Norwegian-language school of the Norwegian Cultural Society of Saskatoon) wearing traditional dress, and a light supper of Norwegian dishes and baking.

INSTITUTIONS

When the Martin government outlawed foreign-language teaching during school hours in 1919, there were few schools in Scandinavian settlements in Saskatchewan to which the legislation could apply.[50] Three reasons can be singled out as accounting for the relative lack of interest in teaching Scandinavian languages. First, because of a high standard of education in Scandinavia, immigrants were already literate in their traditional languages and well prepared to adjust to English. Second, many people of Scandinavian origin who settled in Saskatchewan had already settled in the United States long enough to have become familiar with English. Third, like other minorities, Scandinavians were under considerable pressure to conform to the British group.

Scandinavian settlers in Saskatchewan never really made much of an attempt to control the schools or use their languages in the schools, perhaps largely because of their relatively high literacy rate and ready adjustment to English, their interim residence in American states for a sufficient amount of time to allow them to learn English there, and their apparent acceptance of Anglo-conformity.

Scandinavian voluntary associations in Saskatchewan underwent a rapid transformation from an orientation toward the ethnic group to one toward the general society. They still are, for the most part, centred on Lutheran congregations. For example, among Norwegian Lutherans, the Kwende-Forening, a ladies' club, quickly became the Ladies' Aid, and the Ungdoms Forening, a young people's association, became the Young People's Luther League. Other youth groups were directly descended from similar ones in Scandinavia, such as the Little Children of the Reformation, the Lutheran Daughters of the Reformation, and the Dorcas Girls' Society.[51] It has become unusual to hear choirs in these churches sing the occasional song in Norwegian, and services in Norwegian (even partially) are now rarely held.

The Norwegian Lutheran Outlook College of 1911 became the Saskatchewan Lutheran Bible Institute in 1938; the Saskatchewan Norwegian Lutheran Association of 1911 disappeared with church mergers; and the Norwegian Lutheran Church Seminary in Saskatoon of 1937 is now the Lutheran Theological Seminary of the University of Saskatchewan. Moreover, closure of the rural schools, also focal points for Scandinavian activities in bloc settlements, mainly during the 1950s and 1960s, went far in lessening the significance of Scandinavian ethnic identification. When people of Scandinavian origin immigrated to Saskatchewan from their bloc settlements in the American Midwest, they brought with them their associations, notably the Sons of Norway Lodges (since 1906), the *bygdelag* associations of immigrants from the same region in Norway, the Norwegian Singers' Association (since 1891) consisting of *sangforeninger* (choral societies), similar Swedish societies, and the Danish Brotherhood and Sisterhood (since 1882). Although most of these organizations are no longer found in Saskatchewan, a large Scandinavian Club developed in Saskatoon as well as a Norwegian Cultural Society and Sons of Norway Chapter.[52]

Aside from some periodicals imported from Scandinavia itself, such as *Norske Ukeblad*, magazines and newspapers in Scandinavian languages, or pertaining to Scandinavian culture, have found their way into Saskatchewan from Ontario, Manitoba, and particularly Minnesota. The *Hyrden*, a bimonthly Norwegian-language paper of the former Norwegian Lutheran Church in Canada, became the *Shepherd*, the monthly

English-language magazine of the Evangelical Lutheran Church of Canada, and now the *Lutheran*. Also published in English was the *Lur*, the monthly magazine of the Alberta-based Scandinavian Historical Society, and the newsletter of the Saskatoon Scandinavian Club.

As noted, Finns were divided between religious and socialist factions. The socialist movement dates well back into Finnish history—in support of the struggle of *meikäläset* (commoners) against *herrat* (aristocrats), Finns again as emigrants became strong supporters of labour unions, cooperative movements, and occasionally utopian colonies (e.g., Sointula on Malcolm Island off the BC coast). In the Rock Point settlement in Saskatchewan, where Finns with socialist inclinations once comprised about a third of all families, East Finn Hall (1915) and West Finn Hall (1923) became lively community centres; the latter became particularly involved in socialist activities. However, these activities caused concern outside the Finnish community (and inside it, for they were frowned upon in varying degrees by the "Church Finns"). During the First World War, the War Measures Act effectively banned leftist gatherings, especially among ethnic communities. Then, during the 1930s, some disillusioned but inspired radical socialists left the settlement to resettle in Karelia, then a largely Finnish autonomous republic in the Soviet Union. Finally, during the Second World War, in 1942–43, the RCMP closed both the East Finn Hall and the West Finn Hall for suspicious political activities (all people in Canada who had been born in Finland or were naturalized after September 1922 were categorized as "enemy aliens"; in 1941, Finland had joined Nazi Germany to fight Russia, thus becoming a country at war with Canada). To be sure, though, some Finnish halls were not closed, if they had church approval, were conservative, or did not reveal any possibly controversial political connections. They included temperance societies, the Kalevala Lodge, and the Knights of Kalevala. In Saskatchewan, people of Finnish origin have continued to be strong supporters of the Pool, Co-op, National Farmers' Union, CCF, and NDP, its successor.[53]

INTERMARRIAGE

There can be little doubt that increasing intermarriage tends to profoundly affect the ability to maintain ethnic identity and ethno-cultural traditions. By 1971, 80.9% of the Canadian-born family heads claiming Scandinavian ethnicity were married to spouses of other ethnic origins. In 1961, 36.5% of married people claiming Scandinavian origin in Saskatchewan had married within their particular group. However, there has been relatively less intermarriage of Scandinavian Canadians within the rural bloc settlement context of the Prairie Provinces. In the survey conducted in the bloc settlements of the north-central region in 1969–72, 95.8% of the married Scandinavian respondents were endogamous (married to Scandinavian spouses). Opposition to ethnic exogamy (marrying a person of other ethnic origin) was not as significant as opposition to religious exogamy (marrying a non-Lutheran): 52.3% compared with 77.0%. However, religious intermarriage was becoming increasingly acceptable at the time. Over 90% in both the first generation and the second generation believed that ideally one should seek a Scandinavian Lutheran spouse, whereas third-generation respondents thought that marrying someone of the same ethnicity and religion was "more interesting" or "so much the better" but not necessary. Again, such attitudes might have reflected at that time a more conservative orientation within these particular bloc settlements studied than might have been found in other settlements, not to mention among people partially of Scandinavian descent outside these settlements. Perhaps Finns within their ethnic settlements in Saskatchewan have tended to be most conscious of marrying their own kind, but doubtless with migration out of these settlements because of rural depopulation and progressive urbanization intermarriage has become more common.

CONCLUDING THOUGHTS

Tens of thousands of descendants of the original Scandinavian and Finnish settlers in Saskatchewan remain concentrated in specific rural areas, where they have preserved some aspects of Scandinavian ethno-cultural identity. Yet, while there are numerous rural pockets where people of Scandinavian origin predominate, they were seldom concentrated to the extent that they formed a majority of the population in a local town or village. Most Scandinavian immigrants in Saskatchewan (with the possible exception of Icelanders) did not actually settle within well-defined, compact, homogeneous ethnic settlements but in dispersed patterns of rural settlement or in cities or communities with mixed populations. This has doubtless facilitated their intermarriage and has served to lessen their emphasis on Scandinavian languages and traditions and their link with Lutheranism. Nonetheless, it would be misleading to overly stress the decreasing emphasis on Scandinavian identity in Saskatchewan. As a case in point, the large *Norsk Hostfest* held each year in Minot, North Dakota, remains popular with people of Norwegian origin from Saskatchewan.

The principal Finnish settlements in Saskatchewan, New Finland and Rock Point, have both become affected by relative rural isolation, which of course might have enhanced ethnic solidarity but also made rural life harder. "Independent" young people who moved to larger centres and cities have often returned to their extended families still in the settlements. However, the strong ethnic character of the settlements has steadily been reduced by mass media, rural depopulation, intermarriage with non-Finns, and the resulting de-emphasis on the Finnish language and traditions. Be that as it may, the younger generation can still take pride in the *sisu* of their predecessors.[54]

SOURCES

General Sources on Scandinavian Settlements and People in Saskatchewan/Canada
Sources on Scandinavian Canadians in general (which might include information on Saskatchewan) include V.J. Eylands, *Lutherans in Canada* (Winnipeg: Icelandic Lutheran Synod in North America, 1945); V.W. Larsen, "The Challenge of the Lutheran Church in the Rural Areas of Saskatchewan," presented at the Meeting of the Lutheran Ministerial Association, Melville, SK, October 31, 1960; L. Ruus et al., *The Return of the Vikings: Scandinavians in Canada*, Canadian Culture Series No. 7 (Vancouver: Tantalus Research, 1978); and M.A. Jalava, "The Scandinavians as a Source of Settlers for the Dominion of Canada: The First Generation, 1867–1897," in *Scandinavian-Canadian Studies*, ed. E.W. Laine (Ottawa: Association for the Advancement of Scandinavian Studies in Canada, 1983), 3–14.

CHAPTER 8

On Scandinavian settlements in general in Saskatchewan, see A.B. Anderson, "Scandinavian Settlements in Saskatchewan: Migration History and Changing Ethnocultural Identity," in *Scandinavian-Canadian Studies*, vol. 2, ed. G.A. Woods (Ottawa: Association for the Advancement of Scandinavian Studies in Canada, 1986), 89–113; and A.B. Anderson, "Scandinavian Settlements," in *Encyclopedia of Saskatchewan* (Regina: Canadian Plains Research Center, 2005), 836–37.

A great deal of information has been gleaned from local histories of settlements, communities, and rural districts.

Norwegians in Saskatchewan/Canada

For the historical background to Norwegian migration to North America, see A.W. Andersen, *The Norwegian-Americans* (Boston: Twayne Publishers, 1975); I. Semmingsen, *Norway to America: A History of the Migration* (Minneapolis: University of Minnesota Press, 1980); and Universitetsforlaget, *Norwegians to America* (Lommedalen, Norway: Nye Intertykk, 1984).

Sources on Norwegians in Canada (including Saskatchewan) are G. Loken, *From Fjord to Frontier: A History of the Norwegians in Canada* (Toronto: McClelland and Stewart, 1980), and G. Loken, "Norwegians," in *Encyclopedia of Canada's Peoples*, ed. P.R. Magocsi (Toronto: University of Toronto Press, 1999), 1014–19.

On Norwegians specifically in Saskatchewan, see A.B. Anderson, "Norwegian Settlements," in *Encyclopedia of Saskatchewan* (Regina: Canadian Plains Research Center, 2005), 658–59.

Details on the Norwegian settlement in the Hanley-Outlook area have been drawn from Hanley community histories (1955, 1982, 2005), a fiftieth anniversary history of the Hanley Evangelical Lutheran Church (1953), and histories of the Bethlehem (1955), Bohrson (1956), Nary/Saskatchewan River, and other districts.

Swedes in Saskatchewan/Canada

For the historical background to Swedish migration to North America, see H. Runblom and H. Norman, eds., *From Sweden to America: A History of the Migration* (Minneapolis: University of Minnesota Press, 1976).

Swedes in Canada (including Saskatchewan) are described in C.S. Hale, "Swedes," in *Encyclopedia of Canada's Peoples*, ed. P.R. Magocsi (Toronto: University of Toronto Press, 1999), 1218–33.

On Swedes specifically in Saskatchewan, see A.B. Anderson, "Swedish Settlements," in *Encyclopedia of Saskatchewan* (Regina: Canadian Plains Research Center, 2005), 918–19.

A detailed description of the New Stockholm Colony in Saskatchewan is G.M. Halliwell and M.Z.D. Persson, *Three Score Years and Ten: 1886-1956: A History of the Swedish Settlement of Stockholm and District* (Saskatoon: Modern Press, 1986).

Danes in Saskatchewan/Canada

Danes in Canada (including Saskatchewan) are described in F.M. Paulsen, *Danish Settlements on the Canadian Prairies: Folk Traditions, Immigrant Experiences, and Local History* (Ottawa: National Museum of Man, 1974), and C.S. Hale, "Danes," in *Encyclopedia of Canada's Peoples*, ed. P.R. Magocsi (Toronto: University of Toronto Press, 1999), 406–13.

On Danes specifically in Saskatchewan, see A.B. Anderson, "Danish Settlements," in *Encyclopedia of Saskatchewan* (Regina: Canadian Plains Research Center, 2005), 238.

Icelanders in Saskatchewan/Canada

Icelanders in Canada (including Saskatchewan) are described in W. Kristjanson, *The Icelandic People in Manitoba* (Winnipeg: R.W. Kristjanson, 1965, 1990); V.J. Lindal, *The Icelanders of Canada* (Winnipeg: National and Viking, 1967); E. Simundsson, *Icelandic Settlers in America* (Winnipeg: Queenston House, 1981); and A. Brydon, "Icelanders," in *Encyclopedia of Canada's Peoples*, ed. P.R. Magocsi (Toronto: University of Toronto Press, 1999), 685–700.

On Icelanders specifically in Saskatchewan, see V.J. Lindal, *The Saskatchewan Icelanders* (Winnipeg: Columbia Press, 1955), and A.B. Anderson and J. Eyolfson Cadman, "Icelandic Settlements," in *Encyclopedia of Saskatchewan* (Regina: Canadian Plains Research Center, 2005), 476.

Finns in Saskatchewan/Canada

Finns in Canada (including Saskatchewan) are described in C. Ross, *The Finn Factor in American Labor, Culture, and Society* (New York Mills, MN: Parta Printers, 1978); D. Ahola, "The Karelian Fever Episode of the 1930s," *Finnish Americana* 5 (1982–83); *Archival Sources for the Study of Finnish Canadians* (Ottawa: National Archives of Canada, 1989); V. Lindstrom, "Finns," in *Encyclopedia of Canada's Peoples*, ed. P.R. Magocsi (Toronto: University of Toronto Press, 1999), 513–26; and M. Roinila, *Finland-Swedes in Canada: Migration, Settlement, and Ethnic Relations* (Turku, Finland: Institute of Migration, 2000).

On Finns specifically in Saskatchewan, see G. Johnson, "The New Finland Colony," *Saskatchewan History* 15, 2 (1962): 69–72; A.B. Anderson and B. Niskala, "Finnish Settlements in Saskatchewan: Their Development and Perpetuation," in *Finnish Diaspora*, vol. 1, ed. M.G. Karni (Toronto: Multicultural History Society of Ontario, 1981), 155–82; N.M. Schelstraete, ed., with the New Finland Historical and Heritage Society, *Life in the New Finland Woods: A History of New Finland, Saskatchewan* (Edmonton: Ronalds Western Publishing, 1982); L. Warwaruk, *Red Finns on the Coteau* (Saskatoon: Core Communications, 1984); and A.B. Anderson, "Finnish Settlements," in *Encyclopedia of Saskatchewan* (Regina: Canadian Plains Research Center, 2005), 332.

Chapter 9
OTHER SETTLEMENTS AND URBAN MINORITIES

The development of networks of ethnic and ethno-religious bloc settlements across the prairie portion of Saskatchewan (i.e., the southern half of the total land area of the province) by immigrants and settlers who were almost entirely of European ethnic origins has created a vast ethnic diversity. So, too, has the more recent (but sometimes older) settlement of increasing numbers of immigrants who have mostly been of non-European origins in the larger cities. These mainly or exclusively urban ethnic groups have added greatly to the globalization of the Saskatchewan population. This chapter, therefore, explores this process. First recent immigration to Saskatchewan will be described, within a broader Canadian context, and the ways in which newer immigrants are becoming integrated into Canadian society and contributing to multiculturalism. Then each ethnic group or generalized category will be discussed in order of current population size, respectively Chinese, Southeast Asians, Blacks, South Asians, Latin American Hispanics, Middle Eastern groups (all of whom are considered "visible minorities"—i.e., non-European origins), and finally Greeks and Italians (almost exclusively urban European groups that have long been part of the Saskatchewan scene).

RECENT IMMIGRATION AND IMMIGRANT INTEGRATION

Saskatchewan was settled primarily by foreign-born immigrants; excluding the Aboriginal population, by definition all of the remaining residents—a large majority—are either immigrants or the descendants of immigrants. Yet the proportion that immigrants formed of the Saskatchewan population steadily declined over the past century. Back in 1911, almost half of the province's almost half-million residents were immigrants; this proportion had already dropped to one-third by the early 1930s, one-quarter by the early 1940s, and just one-tenth by the mid-1970s. Toward the final decades of the century, the total provincial population had doubled, but in 2001 there were fewer than 50,000 immigrants living in Saskatchewan. This decline has been due to several factors: the natural aging of the population (Saskatchewan now has the highest proportion of seniors of any province in Canada), the fact that the province has not been able to retain many of the most recent immigrants (little more than half of the immigrants who initially arrive in Saskatchewan continue to reside in the province after several years), and, most importantly, the peak period of settlement having occurred during the first couple of decades of the twentieth century.[1] During the past several decades, Saskatchewan has been one of the least attractive destinations for new immigrants: 87% of foreign-born Canadians reside in just three provinces with the largest cities: Ontario, Quebec, and British Columbia. The most recent data reveal that Toronto now receives 32.8% of immigrants, Montreal 16.3%, and Vancouver 13.3%; these three cities still received 62.4% of the 1.2 million immigrants to Canada between 2006 and 2011. The most recent rate of immigration to Canada was the highest in seventy-five years. In fact, by 2030, Statistics Canada predicts as much as 80% of Canada's population growth will rely on immigration. Canada currently receives close to a quarter of a million (approximately 240,000) regular immigrants a year, of whom approximately 156,000 are classified as economic (63% of total arrivals), 56,000 family class (23%), and 28,000 refugees (11%). Between 2006 and 2011, Canada's foreign-born population increased by 13.6%, whereas the rate of increase in Saskatoon and Regina was respectively only 7.6% and 7.4%. Yet Saskatchewan is now receiving a rapidly increasing number of immigrants: 28,000 between 2006 and 2011 (three times as many as arrived during the previous five-year period), representing 42% of total population growth. Moreover, federal government data might be an underestimate. According to provincial data, 31,000 arrived during 2007–11, including 23,000 through the Saskatchewan Immigrant Nominee Program. The federal government currently limits the Saskatchewan intake through this program to 4,500 skilled workers per year (actually more like 12,500 if spouses and children are included); the provincial government is proposing that this be increased to 6,000. Immigrants comprise 18% of the total Canadian population; almost one in five Canadians was born abroad. However, in Saskatchewan, immigrants constitute just 5% (whereas back in 1911 they comprised virtually half of the provincial population).

A controversial issue is how many regular immigrants compared with temporary foreign workers should be admitted. In Canada, 191,000 temporary foreign workers were admitted in a single year (2011), far outnumbering economic immigrants. In 2012, 213,576 were admitted (more than three times as many admitted a decade earlier), 446,847 the previous year if agricultural workers are included. There were more than 2 million such temporary workers in Canada by 2012, representing 13.6% of the total Canadian labour force (but only a tiny proportion of the estimated 640 million global migrants). Temporary workers have been increasing at more than triple the pace of permanent employment: between 2009 and 2012, temporary workers increased 14.2%, permanent employment only 3.8%. By the end of 2012, an estimated 23,000 temporary workers were arriving in Saskatchewan each year. Temporary foreign workers are actively recruited especially by fast-food franchises such as Tim Hortons and Subway. About 4,000 a year come to Saskatchewan from the Philippines.

Between 2001 and 2006, Saskatchewan lost 17,290 residents; 25,380 left the province, but 8,090 immigrants arrived. Analyzing these trends, taking into account interprovincial and international migration, becomes complicated: in the most recent year prior to the 2006 census, for example, 20,510 people actually left Saskatchewan for other provinces or territories, and 13,645 arrived, yielding a net loss of 6,865. During the five years between 2001 and 2006, though, 37,430 left Saskatchewan for Alberta alone, whereas 16,635 arrived here from Alberta—a net loss of 20,795 between just these two provinces and 6,360 in the most recent year. Moreover, the approximately 8,000 immigrants who settled in Saskatchewan during 2001–06 were far outnumbered by the 31,000 who settled in Manitoba.[2] The annual natural population increase (excess of births over deaths) now accounts for only about 6,000 residents of Saskatchewan; during 2012, 7,178 came from other provinces, while 5,892 left. Of 48,155 immigrants (foreign-born population) in Saskatchewan in 2006, 79.0% were living in one of the larger urban centres. In fact, of the 8,095 who immigrated between 2001 and 2006, 85.0% became residents of a larger urban centre: 73.7% settled in Saskatoon compared with less than half that proportion—32.3%—in Regina.[3]

Over time, the origins of immigrants have been changing. Early immigrants were almost entirely from Europe, whereas most recent immigrants come from developing countries in Asia, Latin America, and Africa. Almost six of every ten immigrants to Canada now are from Asia; this was the approximate proportion of European immigrants in 1971—now Europeans comprise just 16.1%. Of those who moved to Canada between 1991 and 2001, and who were still Saskatchewan residents in 2001, 42% were born in Asia. Other countries that are common birthplaces among recent immigrants to the province include the United States (11% of recent immigrants, who of course can be of diverse ethnicities), European countries such as the former Yugoslavia (9%), and South Africa (4%), which has contributed many medical doctors to both urban and rural Saskatchewan. South Asians have become the largest visible minority collectivity in Canada, though Canada gained more than 40,000 Chinese in just one year. The Philippines emerged as the top supplier of immigrants to Canada by 2010; it had been ranked seventh in 1980, then fourth in 1990 and 2000. India was ranked second by 2000 (and Pakistan third) and again in 2010; it had been eighth in 1970, fourth in 1980, fifth in 1990. China is now ranked third; it was ninth in 1970, eighth in 1980 and 1990 (but Hong Kong, then separate, was respectively fifth and then first), and first in 2000 (with the inclusion of Hong Kong). British immigration initially declined and then rebounded somewhat: the United Kingdom was ranked first back in 1970, second in 1980, seventh in 1990, tenth in 2000, but back up to fourth in 2010 (of course, immigrants from the United Kingdom are no longer necessarily British in ethnic terms). In Saskatchewan, the largest numbers of the most recent immigrants have come from China (970), followed by the United States (825), United Kingdom (645), Philippines (505), Sudan (495), India (355), Afghanistan (275), South Africa (250), Iraq (220), and South Korea (220). However, in a particular city, Saskatoon (which receives the largest numbers of new immigrants), the rank order is a bit different: China (500), Sudan (285), United Kingdom (240), India (190), and Philippines (185).[4] European sources have most recently been increasing because of serious economic recession in a number of countries. In better economic times, Eastern European skilled workers became commonplace in

Western European countries, including Ireland. The Economic and Social Research Institute in Ireland estimates that, during the past couple of years (2011–12), almost 1,000 people were leaving every week. During just 2011, 5,200 left Ireland for Canada; a provincial government recruiting drive in Ireland in March 2012 offered 280 skilled workers positions in Saskatchewan. As noted in Chapter 5, Ukrainians have also been recruited by Ukrainian Canadian labour organizations; Poles and Greeks have also arrived. Europe's loss has been Canada's and Saskatchewan's gain.

Despite the relatively low absolute number of immigrants, many of the province's residents are not that far removed from their immigrant roots: among current residents fifteen years of age and older, only 7% were born outside Canada (i.e., first-generation immigrants), but another 22% are second-generation residents (i.e., Canadian born, having at least one of their parents born outside Canada).[5]

Until the Second World War, most of the Saskatchewan population resided in rural areas, so ethnic diversity was more closely associated with rural ethnic bloc settlements than with distinctive urban neighbourhoods. However, with the liberalization of Canada's Immigration Act during the 1960s, immigration from "non-traditional sources" such as East and South Asia increased substantially, and almost all of these recent immigrants settled in cities rather than rural communities. Over a longer period of time, rural to urban migration, including most recently of Aboriginal people, led both to increasing urban ethnic diversity and concomitantly to the development of specific ethnic neighbourhoods, particularly in Saskatoon and Regina. Immigrant "reception areas" are not readily found in either city, though Saskatoon has historically had a Chinatown as well as a concentration of Ukrainians and Poles in a west-side neighbourhood, while in early years Regina had the most ethnic diversity in poorer neighbourhoods just east of the city centre. Yet today visible minorities are found in all neighbourhoods in both cities. Their distribution patterns seem to indicate the relative ease with which newer immigrants settle in neighbourhoods with diverse income levels. Low levels of immigration largely explain the relatively small sizes of visible minority populations in Saskatchewan; only in Saskatoon and Regina do visible minorities (apart from Aboriginals, mostly immigrants and their families) exceed 5% of the total city population.[6]

As ethnic populations age, intermarriage and ethnic mixing become increasingly common. Half of Saskatchewan's residents reported multiple ethnic origins by 2001. This proportion was higher than those in all other provinces and perhaps was highest in Saskatoon and Regina. Of course, most ethnic mixing has been among European-origin ethnic groups. The relative absence of multiple ethnic origins among visible minority immigrant groups can be due largely to the recency of immigration of most of these groups and to some extent a reluctance to cross racial lines.

The Saskatoon Folk Arts Council was formed in 1964; it became the Saskatoon Multicultural Council (SMC) in 1981 and during the following decade the Saskatchewan Intercultural Association (SIA). During the 1980s, the SMC, in collaboration with the City of Saskatoon, developed the three-day Folkfest, in which the various ethno-cultural groups showcase their traditional foods, music, and dances; this highly popular event now draws thousands of visitors. A major concern of the SMC and its successor the SIA has been coordination of efforts to preserve "heritage languages."

The SIA originally established a "multilingual school" consisting of eleven member groups (Chinese Mandarin School, Escuela Hispanica, German Language School, Hellenic School Association, Japanese Language School for Children, Nehiyawatan Parents Group, Norwegian Cultural Society, Pakistani Association, Punjabi School, Saskatoon Chilean Association, and Saskatoon Club Italia). Currently, over 800 students attend classes taught by approximately ninety teachers representing twenty-one ethno-cultural groups. Other activities of the SIA have included performing arts and an Equity and Anti-Racism Committee.

Immigrant integration into Canadian life remains, and is increasingly, an important service in Saskatchewan cities. The Saskatoon Open Door Society (SODS) was founded in 1980, soon after the Regina Open Door Society, to serve the growing needs of refugees (at the time mostly from Vietnam but also from Poland, Bulgaria, Hungary, and Ethiopia). The mission of Open Door, as noted in its brochure, has been "to welcome and assist refugees and immigrants to become informed and effective participants in Canadian society and to involve the community in their hospitable reception and just acceptance." During its first year of operation, SODS settled about 100 government-sponsored refugees. Since then, Open Door has assisted refugees and immigrants from numerous countries in Latin America, Africa, the Middle East, South Asia, East Asia, Southeast Asia, and Europe. SODS, with a staff of over forty (not including board members and many volunteers), now assists over 1,600 clients a year, including more than 200 government-assisted refugees (almost a third of whom in 2002–04 were from Sudan and a quarter from Afghanistan, plus others from Sierra Leone, Colombia, Burma, Iran, Ethiopia, Pakistan, Burundi, Eritrea, Congo, etc.). Staff and volunteers together speak some forty languages. This agency currently offers language training to about 200 immigrants and refugees a year from at least twenty-five countries (not counting casual "drop-ins") or as many as ninety people on a busy day. In January 2008, SODS, in partnership with the SIA, announced Enhanced Language Training and Immigrant Internship Programs, focusing on language training of new immigrants (in Canada for less than ten years) holding university degrees or professional diplomas/certificates with integration into the labour market in mind (especially health professions, trades, business and finance, social sciences, education, public administration, and natural sciences and engineering). Between 400 and 500 people a year are assisted in finding suitable employment. SODS also offers many other programs and services: multicultural child care, youth programs, refugee reception and resettlement, family and parenting programs, men's and women's programs, social and recreational activities, employment services, community outreach and home visits, civic orientation, interpretation services, personal counselling, and so on. SODS and the Regina Open Door Society are part of an extensive network of agencies assisting with immigrant integration, such as the Saskatoon Refugee Coalition, Immigrant Women of Saskatchewan, Global Gathering Place, Saskatchewan Intercultural Association, plus a broad range of health, family, youth, and children services. Doubtless all of these agencies and services have played significant roles in the successful integration of increasingly diverse immigrants into the Saskatchewan population.

The recent increase in immigration to Saskatchewan has affected schools. The number of school children in Saskatoon learning English as an additional language has increased sixfold during the past six years, from 400 to 2,600 by June 2012. Now there are more residents speaking Tagalog (2,360), the principal language of the Philippines, Chinese (1,805), or Urdu (1,410), an official language of Pakistan, at home than French (1,020). About one in every five Canadians now speaks a language other than English, French, or an Aboriginal language at home.

VISIBLE MINORITIES

The misleading term "visible minorities" has long been used in Canada to distinguish ethnic groups of non-European origins from the European-origin ethnic groups that predominate in this country as well as from Aboriginal Canadians. Thus, visible minorities are the "other ethnic groups" in Canada that are neither of European origin nor Aboriginal. The implication is that visible minorities are "visible" insofar as they are racially distinct from White ethnic groups (and from Aboriginals)—bearing in mind, however, that "whiteness" can vary in degree according to popular perceptions and that ultimately "race" is a socially constructed concept.

People of non-European immigrant origins in Saskatchewan have settled mainly in larger cities (Saskatoon and Regina), especially in recent decades, yet there are examples of long-standing non-European immigration to rural Saskatchewan. As café owners, Chinese have long been widely dispersed in rural communities, Lebanese were itinerant traders for decades, and an early Black settlement was established at Eldon near Maidstone in 1909.

According to recent census data, visible minorities comprise only about 3% of the total population of Saskatchewan and approximately 6–7% of the total populations of Saskatoon and Regina; as in Canada, in Saskatchewan visible minorities are concentrated in the larger cities, though relatively few visible minority immigrants have selected Saskatchewan cities compared with the largest cities of Canada. Visible minorities now constitute 16% of the total population of Canada—some 5 million people, more than double the number of just fifteen years ago. Saskatchewan residents of non-European origins (excluding Aboriginals) numbered 27,580 in 2001. Yet, as noted, this relatively small visible minority population in Saskatchewan is extremely diverse. Apart from these specific ethnic origins, 420 residents have listed other visible minority origins, and 640 residents were of either mixed or undifferentiated visible minority origins.[7]

Chinese

The largest numbers of visible minority population were of East Asian origin or ethnicity; moreover, a large majority, 11,100 in 2006, were Chinese (plus thirty-five who claimed to be Taiwanese). Another 785 were Japanese (many likely being descendants of Japanese deported from British Columbia during the Second World War), 745 residents claimed Korean ethnic origin, and smaller numbers were Mongolian or simply undifferentiated Asian.

Although the majority of Chinese in Saskatchewan are relatively recent immigrants, Chinese have long been residents of the province. Chinese settlement commenced in the 1880s with completion of the Canadian Pacific Railway. The earliest Chinese immigrants tended to arrive in Saskatchewan primarily from British Columbia. By 1901, there were still only forty-one Chinese in what would soon become the province of

Saskatchewan. With growing hostility toward the concentration of Chinese on the West Coast at the turn of the century, Chinese immigrants started to move eastward. Moose Jaw soon became one of the largest Chinese communities in Saskatchewan; by 1913, the city contained about 450 Chinese men and only two women, at least thirty-five Chinese laundries, and three Chinese restaurants. But the introduction of larger steam laundries, together with the Depression during the 1930s, drove smaller Chinese laundries out of business, with the result that the Chinese population of the city declined steadily to 320 in 1921 and 260 in 1941. Its lively Chinatown had largely disappeared by the 1940s. The First Presbyterian Church (1883) later became the Chinese United Church and has been preserved as a heritage site since 1984. Other early Chinese communities were in the major cities: Saskatoon, Regina, Swift Current, and the Battlefords. The total Chinese population in Saskatchewan had grown to almost 1,000 by 1911.

In Saskatoon, Chinese numbered just 228 in 1921, but increased to 308 in 1931, by which time the number rivalled that in Moose Jaw. A short-lived concentration of Chinese businesses was established downtown but no longer existed by the late 1930s, except for a few restaurants. The Chinese population in the city declined to 225 in 1951 but grew to 499 in 1961. During the mid-1960s, several Chinese restaurants and other businesses developed in the near west side, and by 1986 this new Chinatown consisted of about twenty Chinese businesses.[8]

A Chinatown did not develop in Regina, partly because of the small number of Chinese residents and partly because of a mutual agreement made among early Chinese settlers that they would avoid competition with one another by not setting up businesses close together. In 1907, there were only four Chinese laundries, two Chinese restaurants, and one Chinese grocery scattered throughout the city centre. The Chinese population numbered only eighty-nine in 1911. By 1914, there were twenty-nine Chinese laundries but only a couple of Chinese grocery stores and restaurants. Chinese laundries declined during the 1930s, and by 1940 only eight were left. In 1941, Regina had only 250 Chinese residents.[9]

Historically, Chinese in Saskatchewan were victimized by racial discrimination. In 1885, the first of a series of federal "head taxes" was imposed on Chinese immigrants: all persons of Chinese origin wishing to enter Canada were obliged to pay a tax of fifty dollars; this tax was doubled in 1901 and then increased to $500 two years later (equivalent at the time to a typical two years of wages). The Chinese in Saskatchewan were disenfranchised in 1908. In Moose Jaw in 1912, a Chinese restaurant owner was arrested after his White waitress filed a formal assault complaint against him; subsequently, the Saskatchewan legislature forbade the employment of White women in restaurants and other businesses kept or managed by Chinese. Any Chinese violating this act would be fined $100. Although the act was repealed in 1918, it was replaced by the Female Employment Act, requiring Chinese businessmen to obtain a special municipal licence before hiring a White female worker. Then in 1923 Parliament passed the Oriental Exclusion Act, effectively preventing Chinese and other East Asians from immigrating. This act remained in force until 1947 and had the effect of prohibiting the reunion of families—since Chinese men could not bring their wives and children to Canada, the male disproportion among Chinese in Canada was very high: sixty men to every woman in Regina, twenty-seven to one in Saskatoon, sixteen to one in

Moose Jaw in 1921.[10] Finally, in 1947, the Chinese in Saskatchewan were permitted to vote. With the repeal of the Oriental Exclusion Act that year, Chinese families could be reunited after an entire generation, so the Chinese population in the province started to increase, from 2,249 in 1941 to 3,660 in 1961. Then, with further liberalization of Canadian immigration processes since 1967, the point system was applied to all prospective immigrants regardless of country of origin. Now that Chinese immigrants could qualify to come to Canada from mainland China and other East Asian and Southeast Asian countries (including Taiwan, Hong Kong, Malaysia, Vietnam, Singapore, the Philippines, and Indonesia), the ethnic Chinese population in Saskatchewan grew at a faster rate: between 1971 and 2001, it doubled from 4,605 to 9,280. Five years later 11,100 Chinese were counted, approximately three-quarters of whom (8,405) claimed only Chinese ethnic origin compared with a quarter (2,695) who claimed more than one ethnic origin.

In 2006, there were 3,550 residents of Saskatoon claiming single Chinese origin plus another 915 claiming to be partly Chinese, for a total of 4,465; in Regina, Chinese numbered 2,085 single origin and 660 multiple origins for a total of 2,745; in Moose Jaw respectively 185 single and 125 multiple for a total of 310. Chinese continued to represent the largest visible minority group in Saskatchewan, accounting for 29% of the total visible minority population (i.e., non-White immigrants and their descendants), yet only 1% of the total Saskatchewan population.

Today Chinese in Saskatchewan constitute a heterogeneous population with diverse cultural, professional, and social backgrounds. Unlike the early Chinese, who were almost exclusively Cantonese who toiled mainly in restaurants and laundries, Chinese in Saskatchewan now represent a broad socio-economic spectrum. Yet traditional involvement in the restaurant business is reflected in between forty and fifty Chinese restaurants in Saskatoon alone. Many Chinese have lived for three generations or more in Saskatchewan, while many are more recent immigrants with their families. Although over time they have concentrated in the larger cities, Chinese cafés and families remain omnipresent in smaller towns and rural communities. The Federation of Saskatoon Chinese-Canadian Organizations represents an attempt to connect the various Chinese organizations that have emerged in the city.

Other East Asian Groups
The Asia-Pacific Pavilion at the annual Folkfest in Saskatoon provides a wide range of East Asian—Chinese, Taiwanese, Japanese, Korean—entertainment, food, displays, and demonstrations. There are few residents of Japanese origin in Saskatoon, yet recently the number of Japanese restaurants has grown and now includes the earlier Samurai, Otowa, and Edo and the newer Sushiro, Fuzion, Yohei, Nagoya, Go for Sushi, among others. And several new Korean restaurants have just opened. One Japanese resident was Haruye Hattori, born in 1913 and died in Saskatoon at the age of ninety-six. Her father, Jukichi Onishi, had shipped to San Francisco in 1895, then after the catastrophic earthquake and fire moved to Mission, British Columbia, where he married Shika Kawasaki, who died in the influenza epidemic of 1918. Haruye married Francis Masao Hattori in 1940, only soon to have their property confiscated, and they were deported to New Denver, in the BC interior, then to work in the beet fields of southern

Alberta, like thousands of other Japanese Canadians during the Second World War. Haruye worked for years as a seamstress. In 1992, following the death of her husband, Haruye moved to Saskatoon, where her son operated a photography studio.

Southeast Asians
People of Southeast Asian origins in Saskatchewan numbered 7,345 in 2006. Most were Filipino (4,160), of whom 67.3% claimed a single ethnic origin and 32.7% more than one ethnic origin. Vietnamese numbered 1,640, of whom 72.0% (1,180) were Vietnamese only and the remaining 28.0% (460) were of mixed ethnic origins. Other Southeast Asians have been estimated to include 630 Laotians, 255 Thais, 180 Indonesians, 160 Cambodians, 150 Burmese, 120 Malaysians, and fifty undifferentiated. One should note, though, that some immigrants from Southeast Asia might have claimed Chinese or, in the case of Malaysia and Singapore, Indian ethnic origin. Southeast Asians in Saskatchewan are almost entirely recent immigrants (and their families, including Canadian-born children) to cities.

Numerous Vietnamese refugees came to settle in Saskatchewan during the late 1970s and early 1980s. The "Boat People" fled their homeland to find a safe haven in Canada after the conclusion of the Vietnam War in 1975. In 2001, 1,870 Saskatchewan residents were wholly or partially of Vietnamese origin, among whom 915 resided in Regina and 770 in Saskatoon. Vietnamese have established community organizations, religious institutions, language and culture schools, as well as an increasing number of restaurants. Both Regina and Saskatoon now have Vietnamese Buddhist temples and associations (e.g., Avalokitesvara Buddhist Temple, Chánh Tâm Temple, and the Union of Vietnamese Buddhist Churches in Canada in Saskatoon), Roman Catholic congregations, senior citizens' associations and other voluntary associations, language and culture schools, and radio programs.[11] The descendants of those refugees are now contributing to the province's workforce in diverse occupations, not the least in the food industry—at last count, there were at least fourteen Vietnamese restaurants in Saskatoon.

There is an active Filipino community in Saskatoon that meets at the Filipino Community Church. The annual Filipino Pavilion at Folkfest showcases performances by the Kumintang Folk Ensemble of Saskatoon and the visiting Folklorico Filipino Canada Ensemble from Toronto and provides a broad variety of traditional Filipino dishes. About 400 Filipino community members participate in *Kalayaan*, the Philippines Independence Day, in Saskatoon every June. Other events organized by the Filipino-Canadian Association of Saskatoon, founded in 1960, include *Maligayang Pasko* at Christmas, a Valentine's Day party, sports events, and so on. Filipino institutions in Saskatoon include a Catholic parish as well as an Alliance church, a Filipino Seniors' Social Club, and a Filipino Heritage School. Filipino immigrants and temporary foreign workers constitute a significant and increasing flow into Canada, with a substantial proportion now becoming fast food workers, domestics and home care workers in addition to the long-standing commitment to nursing.

Although comparatively few in number, other Southeast Asian nationalities are now represented in the variety of restaurants in Saskatoon: the two Keo's Cambodian restaurants, the Burmese Golden Pagoda, and at least three authentic Thai restaurants.

Blacks

An explanation of the origin of settlements founded by Oklahoma Blacks implies delving further back into history. After the American Civil War in 1865, thousands of newly freed Blacks began to move westward from the southern states, in the hope of gaining racial equality, notably into the Indian Territory established by the US government in order to resettle diverse Indian tribes obliged to move out of the way of advancing White settlement. These Blacks now had the chance to obtain their own farmland, and the territory was governed directly by the federal government, supposedly ensuring the protection of civil rights. In fact, an interesting aspect of Blacks moving into the Indian Territory was the development of a mixed race population—an increasing number of Indians came to possess some Black blood, while Blacks not infrequently had some Native American admixture. However, rapidly increasing numbers of Whites also settled in the Indian Territory, with the opening of formerly Indian lands. In 1908, the territory became the state of Oklahoma. The majority of these Whites had also originated in the southern states, inevitably resulting in racist policies of segregation; in 1910, for example, following a state-wide referendum, Blacks lost their right to vote.

Attracted to Western Canada by advertising placed in Oklahoma newspapers for farming settlers, some Oklahoma Blacks who had originally migrated westward within the United States to escape from discrimination and racism now, one or two generations later, felt compelled to move again—this time northward into Canada. In 1910, Black homesteaders settled near Maidstone, Saskatchewan, and soon the Lafayette brothers from Iowa settled near Rosetown, while other Blacks settled in the Battlefords. These few early settlers initially did not garner much attention; however, this would soon change when larger numbers of Black men, women, and children began to arrive on Western Canada's border with the United States. They had been driven north from Oklahoma by both segregation and disenfranchisement and attracted to Western Canada by opportunism. But now, as American Blacks began arriving in Canada in what White Canadians perceived alarmingly as increasing numbers (in actuality there were comparatively few), they were not exactly welcomed; Western Canadian farmers' organizations, women's groups, and boards of trade pressured the federal government to halt the immigration and settlement of Blacks. In response, the issue was debated heatedly in Parliament. The Department of the Interior decided to investigate this migration further and appointed an agent, a doctor from Chicago who himself was Black, who was dispatched to Oklahoma ostensibly to assist in stemming further immigration.[12] So by 1911 the immigration of Oklahoma Blacks had virtually ceased. Meanwhile, in any case, the Laurier government approved an order-in-council prohibiting anyone of African descent from entering Canada.

Most of the thousand Black settlers who had been successful in entering Western Canada during those few years settled in Alberta, particularly at Amber Valley east of Athabasca as well as at Wildwood west of Edmonton. The largest number of Blacks in Saskatchewan settled the Eldon district north of Maidstone, close to the North Saskatchewan River Valley. In 1910, Mattie Mayes, the matriarch of a large extended family, emigrated from Oklahoma to settle there with about forty relatives. Later they were joined by other families, and an extensive settlement was soon established. The following year Shiloh (or Charlow) Baptist Church was built, with hand-hewn log benches, though an official deed for the church and cemetery was not obtained until five years later. This small church with its cemetery would serve as the focal point of the rural community for many years. But when the settlers, known as the "Shiloh people," attempted to create a school district, they encountered many delays and obstructions; the White settlers of the surrounding region refused to send their children to school with Blacks. Thus, a racially segregated school came to exist in Saskatchewan for several years (apart from the many Indian residential schools). Nonetheless, the perseverance and sheer determination of the Black settlers helped them to defy and overcome the racial stereotyping that they encountered from Canadian officials at every level and not the least from their neighbours in Saskatchewan. Possessing limited means, they were able to achieve ownership of their homesteads.

The settlement was abandoned during the 1940s. Forty-eight settlers lie buried there in the churchyard, of whom thirty-nine were listed in a memorial donated in 2002 by the Shiloh Baptist Church and Cemetery Restoration Society in Edmonton. But not Mattie Mayes—she lived past 100 years of age and was finally buried in Edmonton. Twenty-two had been born between 1847 and 1899; they had died and been buried there between 1913 and 1945. But two graves are relatively more recent: 1975 and 1987, so some descendants of early settlers chose to return there to be buried. The church and cemetery were designated a provincial historic site in 1991.

Over time, the Eldon settlement started losing many of its younger people to the cities, which could provide more or better employment. Yet Blacks encountered racial prejudice in the cities, just as they already had in the rural areas, and many were obliged to settle for menial employment, such as railway porters, while the better-paid and more prestigious position of conductor was not available to them for many years.[13] As a result of this discrimination, Blacks from Western Canadian families could be found from coast to coast with roots in the prairie settlements that they founded a century earlier.

One of the more illustrious alumni from this settlement was Reuben Mayes, the grandson of George Harvey Mayes, who farmed just south of the church. In 1980, as a high school student in North Battleford, he led the football team to an undefeated season. He then played for Washington State University, setting a number of records that still stand. As a professional football player for the New Orleans Saints from 1986 to 1990, he was honoured as Rookie of the Year in 1986 and went on to play for the Seattle Seahawks in 1992–93. Later, after earning an MBA, he was appointed the senior director of development for the College of Business and Education at Washington State University in 2005.

Today the almost exclusively urban Black residents of Saskatchewan have originated in diverse countries and cultures. The term "Blacks" is used today to denote people of African descent in Canada, yet this generalized category consists not only of the descendants of African Americans who established rural settlements in Saskatchewan but also generations of Canadian-born descendants of Black former slaves, Loyalists, and Civil War refugees who were brought to Canada via the "Underground Railroad" (organized by a network of abolitionists during the early to mid-nineteenth century), who eventually drifted westward from Ontario and the Atlantic provinces. More recently, since the 1960s, because of the gradual liberalization of Canada's immigration policy, Canada has received a major immigration of Blacks, primarily from the

Caribbean and most recently from Africa. The vast majority of these newer Black immigrants have settled in central Canadian cities, especially Toronto, yet far smaller numbers have settled in Saskatoon and Regina, where Black immigration has continued to increase, though at a much slower rate than for other visible minorities. The Black population in Saskatchewan cities has been further augmented during the past couple of decades with the arrival of substantial numbers of refugees from Somalia, Eritrea, and Sudan. Black landed immigrants in Saskatchewan increased from just 0.2% of total landed immigrants in 1980 to 3.1% in 2001. Moreover, there has been a shift in gender during the 1980s: there were more male than female migrants from Africa, whereas there were more females than males migrating from the Caribbean.[14] By the 1990s, the data changed for female immigrants from Africa, whose number began to surpass that of male immigrants, while the situation for Caribbean-origin immigrants remained unchanged. It is noteworthy that most of the recent Black immigrants have come from the Horn of Africa; in fact, during certain of the past few years, Sudanese constituted the largest proportion of new immigrants and refugees, outnumbering those from any other country.

So the period of the early Black settlements (founded primarily by Oklahoma Blacks) has long since passed into history, at least in Saskatchewan (though the Amber Valley settlement continued in Alberta), and Saskatchewan Blacks today are thoroughly urban and extremely diverse. Any attempt to estimate the total Black population of Saskatchewan is very complicated, but the number must exceed 7,000. In 2006, just an estimated 635 people claimed to be of general Black ethnicity (though others might have claimed American ethnic origin). People actually of immediate African origin totalled 4,515: they included Sudanese (555), Eritreans and Ethiopians (together totalling about 480), and Somalis (290) from the Horn of Africa; Ugandans (50), Kenyans (10), and other East Africans (60); South Africans (545), Zambians (145), and Zimbabweans (80) from southern Africa; Congolese (65), Rwandans and Burundians (60) from central Africa; and Nigerians (430), Ghanaians (160), and Sierra Leonese (30) from west Africa. People of Caribbean origin included Jamaicans (830), Trinidadians (295), Barbadians (240), Guyanese (195), and smaller numbers of Haitians, St. Vincentians, Grenadians, Bahamians, St. Lucians, Martiniquans, Antiguans, and Bermudians, as well as people who have identified themselves in general as of West Indian or Caribbean origin (500). Extremely diverse, the Black population of Saskatchewan does not represent a single ethnic group but many cultures. Blacks have come to Saskatchewan from the United States, the Caribbean, and directly from Africa (note, however, that not all recent immigrants to Saskatchewan from Africa or the Caribbean have been Black—they include, for example, many White doctors from South Africa as well as Indian families from South and East Africa). In the two decades between 1980 and 2001, a total of 3,993 immigrants from Africa arrived in Saskatchewan, compared with just 564 from the Caribbean.[15]

The Afro-Caribbean Pavilion at Folkfest in Saskatoon is one of the largest, most active, and most popular, offering entertainers such as the Saskatoon Caribbean Dancers, the Saskatoon Steelband, the Prince Niah limbo show, and various African dancers and traditional food and drink such as Jamaican beef and veggie patties, jerk and curry chicken with peas and rice, beef and chicken *roti*, *gazzadas* (coconut tarts), mango, pineapple and coconut loaves, island soft drinks, *mauby*, St. Lucian punch, and "Jamaica me crazy" punch. The diversity of the Afro-Caribbean element in the Saskatchewan population is further reflected in the two traditional Ethiopian restaurants, one in Regina and the other in Saskatoon, as well as a new Oromo Ethiopian pavilion in Folkfest.

South Asians

Saskatchewan residents of South Asian origin were estimated to number over 6,000 in 2006, reflecting wide ethno-cultural diversity—they include Sikhs, Indian Hindus, Pakistani and Bangladeshi Moslems, Sri Lankan Tamils (mostly Hindus) and Sinhalese (mostly Buddhists), as well as Christians from throughout the subcontinent. In the census, they were identified generally as East Indian (4,465) or South Asian (175); by country or ethnic group of origin in South Asia, such as Pakistani (470), Sri Lankan, Sinhalese, or Tamil (together 335); by ethnic group or region within India, such as Punjabi, Bengali, or Kashmiri; or perhaps some by country where they had previously settled in the diaspora, such as Guyanese (195), Mauritian (185), Fijian, South African, Kenyan, and so on (though not all people from these countries have been of South Asian ethnicity).

Immigrants of South Asian ethnicity started coming to Saskatchewan in more substantial numbers during the early 1960s. They often came with high levels of education that qualified them for professions such as university professors, doctors, and engineers. They almost entirely became residents of Saskatoon and Regina. Many were immigrants who either had young families or Canadian-born children. Most wives, also well educated, were employed either full or part time in various occupations. Thus, the early South Asian settlers added much human capital value to the province.[16] All were acquainted with and educated in the English language, so they tended to adapt readily to Canadian life; nonetheless, these immigrants have sometimes had to overcome challenges in achieving professional accreditation in Canada. Although a majority initially spoke Hindi, Gujarati, Punjabi, or other South Asian languages at home, English gradually became the prevalent home language in perhaps half of the families; the younger generation, born in Canada, certainly have preferred to speak English. This loss of traditional languages for that generation has become a concern to the South Asian communities, and efforts are being made through language classes offered with the assistance of multicultural associations. Moreover, South Asian dance and cultural classes have helped to preserve an interest in Indian Canadian, Pakistani Canadian, and other South Asian cultures. The communities showcase their arts and cuisine at annual ethno-cultural festivals such as Folkfest in Saskatoon and Mosaic in Regina. Each year the Punjabi Cultural Association of Saskatoon holds Punjabi Mela, a celebration of singing and dancing now drawing more than 1,600 people. The majority of these immigrants soon acquired Canadian citizenship, yet they maintained close ties with and often travelled to visit family members and friends back home and thus retained cultural links for their children. The Shastri Indo-Canadian Institute has been instrumental in providing a lecture series at the two universities in the province and offering opportunities for studies and research in India. Statues of Mahatma Gandhi have been erected in central locations in Saskatoon and Regina.

An increasingly wide variety of Indian and Pakistani restaurants and grocery stores in Saskatoon are offering unique food.

Although fewer and fewer people remain from earlier families, as many retired parents have followed their adult children who have headed away from Saskatchewan to pursue careers, they have been replaced by more recent immigrants who reinforce South Asian culture. The diversity of the present South Asian population of Saskatchewan can hardly be overstated. South Asians in the province have originated not only from South Asia (India, Pakistan, Sri Lanka, Bangladesh, Afghanistan, Nepal, Bhutan) but also from Africa (Uganda, Kenya, Tanzania, South Africa), the Indian Ocean (Mauritius), the Caribbean (Trinidad and Guyana), as well as Britain. Moreover, South Asians are diverse in terms of religion—they can be Hindus, Sikhs, Moslems, or Christians. Hindu temples, Moslem mosques, and Sikh *gurudwaras* have been added to the urban cultural landscape of Saskatchewan. During the 1960s, a small number of Hindu families shared prayer services in homes; in 1977, the Vedanta Society of Saskatoon (later the Hindu Society of Saskatchewan) was established; the construction of a new temple was completed in 1985. The Ahmadiyyah Moslem community in Saskatoon, consisting largely of Pakistanis and other South Asians, has reportedly grown rapidly to over 800 from just 100 during the past five years. A new Ahmadiyyah mosque holding 2,000, to be constructed at a cost of $1.6 million, is anticipated to replace the existing small Dar-Ur-Rehmat (House of Blessing) mosque. The new mosque will feature classrooms, a sports facility, and separate prayer, meal, and meeting halls for men and women. Although South Asian families have increasingly tended to associate primarily with one or another of those religious affiliations, as their numbers have grown, secular cultural associations—including the India-Canada Association of Saskatchewan—as well as multicultural festivals and organizations have transcended these specific religious communities.

A unique addition to the South Asian population of Saskatoon—and to the ethnocultural diversity of Saskatchewan—has been the arrival of some eighty refugees from Bhutan since 2009. They are from the Lhotshampa minority, which has been persecuted by the Bhutan government because of their Hindu religious affiliation when a national policy adopted in 1988 called for "one country, one people." The Lhotshampa had entered Buddhist Bhutan from neighbouring—and predominantly Hindu—Nepal from 1885 through the 1960s. This policy banned the wearing of traditional non-Buddhist clothing and the speaking of minority languages; the Lhotshampa were branded illegal immigrants despite their having been in Bhutan for generations and were to be expelled. With the creation of a refugee crisis, 105,000 fled to refugee camps in Nepal; in 2006, a number of countries sought a longer-term solution for resettlement. The United States took 60,000 and Canada 5,500 over five years; all told, an estimated 75,000 have been resettled to date. The refugees accepted by Canada were widely scattered, settling in twenty-one cities, including Saskatoon, and families were split up.

Latin Americans
Perhaps more than 6,000 residents of Saskatchewan are of Latin American origin. Part of the larger Hispanic community (in the 2006 census, 3,255 residents claimed that they were "Spanish," though it was very unlikely that they all had come from Spain, and only

twenty-five claimed that they were "Hispanic"), they have come from diverse countries of origin. The largest number are of South American origin. Of 985 Chileans, 58.9% (580) claimed only Chilean ethnicity, while the remaining 41.1% (410) Chilean and other ethnic origins. Others of South American origin included Colombians, Aboriginals, Brazilians (who speak Portuguese rather than Spanish), Argentinians, Uruguayans, Venezuelans, Peruvians, Ecuadoreans, Bolivians, and Paraguayans. A substantial number of Latin Americans in Saskatchewan have come from Central America; they include Salvadorans (700), Mexicans (675), and smaller numbers of Guatemalans, Nicaraguans, Costa Ricans, Mayans, and Belizeans. Likely not included in these data on South and Central American ethnic origins were increasing numbers of Mennonites, conversant in Spanish, who have been returning to Saskatchewan from their settlements in Paraguay, Belize, and Mexico. Finally, a few Hispanics have come from the Spanish-speaking Caribbean: Dominicans, Puerto Ricans, and Cubans.

Prior to the influx of Chilean refugees after the 1973 *coup d'état* in Chile, and of Central Americans, especially Salvadorans who fled the civil strife of the 1980s, there were few Hispanics in Saskatchewan. The province's two largest cities received almost all of the Hispanic immigration. To an appreciable extent, Hispanics in Saskatchewan have tended to socialize with people of their own nationalities; however, organizations such as Circulo Hispanico in Saskatoon bring together Hispanics regardless of original nationality. In Saskatoon, the Spanish-language Hispanic Alliance Church is active. The recency of Latin American immigration has had a significant cultural impact in Saskatchewan—supermarkets now offer the ingredients for typical Latin American dishes; restaurants serving Latin American food are becoming more common; Latin American dance classes are popular; Spanish classes have become more available; and the several Hispanic/Latin American/Caribbean pavilions have become among the most popular in the annual multicultural festivals. Finally, along with other ethnic groups, Hispanics have contributed to the internationalization of and specifically a global political consciousness in Saskatchewan, represented in the fair trade movement, human rights concerns, refugee assistance, and other forms of social activism.[17]

After 1973, more than one million Chileans fled their homeland for their very lives and freedom from persecution. Of the several thousand who came to Canada, a few hundred chose to settle in Saskatchewan. According to the 2001 census, the province had 845 Chilean residents, of whom a virtually equal number were living in Saskatoon (290) and Regina (285). The Saskatoon and Regina Chilean Association folklore groups, Mamma Llajta, the Salvador Allende Folklore Group, Raices Chileanas (Chilean Roots), Desde el Sur (From the South), and Espiritu Latino Dancers exemplify performing artists whose singing and dancing enable Chilean and Latin American traditional culture to be enjoyed by Saskatchewan audiences. In sports, Barrabases in Regina and Arauco in Saskatoon are two successful soccer teams at the provincial level in their respective divisions, and both have been comprised primarily of Chileans. The solidarity, cultural, athletic, and educational organizations created by Chilean immigrants in Saskatchewan have helped many of them to re-establish their social and cultural identities, a testament to the resilience of a community whose members overcame the trauma of a military coup at home and quickly adjusted to the realities of a new society, a new language, and a new climate.[18]

Middle Eastern Groups

The National Household Survey (released in May 2013) revealed that, during the past decade, the number of Moslems in Canada increased by at least 62% and is projected to triple to at least 2.8 million within eighteen years. Saskatchewan residents of Middle Eastern origins totalled close to 5,000 in 2006, according to census data. Many are Arab and Moslem and have arrived recently; Moslem residents of Saskatoon are estimated to have increased from 1,000 to 4,000 during the past five years. However, they are not all Arabs: some are Iranians, Afghans, Turks, Armenians, Somalis, even Chinese; in fact, Moslems in Saskatchewan reportedly come from at least seventy countries. Apart from the new Ahmadiyyah mosque (mentioned above), Sunni Moslems in the city are building a new mosque to supplement their existing community centre; the Misbah School will move to the new mosque as soon as it is finished. Moslem celebrations in Saskatoon have been drawing large numbers. More than 2,000 Ahmadiyyah Moslems participated in a Western Canadian gathering in Saskatoon in July 2009. The most recent celebration of Eid al-Fitr (marking the end of Ramadan) drew 5,000 participants in August 2012 and collected $150,000 in donations to the Islamic Association of Saskatchewan. Then in October thousands gathered for three days of feasting known as Eid al-Adha (Feast of the Sacrifice).

Nor are people of Middle Eastern origins necessarily Moslems: many are Chaldean and Antiochean Christians. The parish of St. Vincent of Lerins in Saskatoon, established in 1987, is a member of the Antiochean Orthodox Church, now headquartered in Damascus (but as the name implies originally in Antioch, now in Turkey close to the Syrian border). The present priest was actually raised Mennonite, became Pentecostal, then Orthodox; most of the 100 or so parishioners converted from various denominational backgrounds, including Roman Catholic; relatively few were originally Eastern Orthodox.[19] Chaldean and other Christians from Iraq claim to number some 150 families—representing 800 individuals—in Saskatoon. After the first immigrants reportedly arrived in Saskatoon in 1976, a small congregation was formed, and, with rapidly increasing numbers, in 2009 they purchased the former St. Timothy's Anglican Church, which was then converted into Sacred Heart Chaldean Catholic Church.[20] Some Eastern Orthodox in Saskatoon—including from Middle Eastern countries—not wishing to attend Ukrainian or Greek Orthodox churches have also gravitated to a pan-Orthodox church affiliated with the Orthodox Church of America, which holds services in English.

People of Middle Eastern origins are not completely recent immigrants—Syrians and Lebanese have long lived in Saskatchewan. In striking contrast to more recent immigrants from the Middle East, people of Lebanese/Syrian origin began immigrating to Saskatchewan in the early 1900s, and they tended to live in rural more than urban areas. Several families settled in the southeast region, in or near Radville, Ceylon, Lampman, and North Portal. More significantly, in the southwest region, over forty families and individuals homesteaded or started businesses in and around Swift Current. Some soon moved on to larger centres, or out of Saskatchewan, but many stayed to become an integral part of rural life. These earliest Lebanese/Syrian immigrants sought to leave behind social and economic hardships in their homelands and wanted better lives for themselves and their families. However, their search was hindered by the Canadian government's uninterest in receiving immigrants from the

Middle East. In a 1914 letter, W.D. Scott, the superintendent of immigration, gave his opinion that "None of the races belong to those likely to assimilate with the Canadian people; none of them are of a class whose presence could reasonably be expected to improve the status of the Canadian race, whether considered from a political, social, moral, mental, physical or economic standpoint."[21]

Lebanese, classified as Asians according to the Immigration Act, were required to pay $200 (rather than the usual twenty-five dollars) as a condition of landing in Canada. Yet young men still persisted in coming, often after spending a year or two in the United States, where there was a strong Arab community in Detroit. These initial American contacts provided a chance to work in North America and begin to learn some English. After arriving in Canada, they homesteaded in Saskatchewan, then returned to Lebanon or the United States to find suitable wives and bring their families back with them.

Many of the families that came to Swift Current and surrounding area originated in three small communities in eastern Lebanon—Ain Arab, Bire, and Qaraoun. Lebanese immigrants were divided between Moslems and Eastern Rite Christians; both encountered difficulties maintaining their religious traditions within a rural Saskatchewan context. The Christians relied on infrequent visits from itinerant Orthodox or Eastern Rite Catholic priests; however, the latter tended to be Ukrainian, and Lebanese had not settled near Ukrainian areas; Roman Catholic priests were readily available but not familiar with Eastern Rites. So some immigrants felt obliged to travel to the United States to get married or have babies baptized. Some eventually became Anglicans. And some simply improvised, such as Alex Himour, who, following a visit to Mecca in 1922, organized the congregation of Jamah with himself as *imam*. His house at Rush Lake became a mosque, serving families in the immediate area and others in the Pambrun and Gouverneur districts. Himour travelled throughout the West to perform Islamic religious rites.[22]

In keeping with the tradition of itinerant peddling in Lebanon, Lebanese men did so in Saskatchewan to supplement their incomes. Saleh "Charlie" Gader first carried wares on his back, frequenting farms in the McMahon district, then later travelled by horse and buggy and even learned to speak some German to better serve his Mennonite customers.[23]

Businesses were also established in small towns. The Haddad family operated widespread general stores in Meyronne, McCord, Hazenmore, Eastend, and Morse. Several members of the Salloum family had stores, a bakery, a café, and a pool hall in Aneroid, Vanguard, and other communities. The Kouri family owned a grocery store and meat market in Ponteix for eight decades (1921–2000).

Ameen "King" Ganam, born in Swift Current in 1914, formed a band in Edmonton in the 1940s that regularly performed on radio; he moved to Toronto in 1952, where he had his own radio program and became a regular performer on country and western television shows during the 1950s. Ganam became one of the inaugural inductees into the Canadian Country Music Hall of Fame in 1989. Incidentally, doubtless the most famous Canadian entertainer of Syrian/Lebanese origin is Paul Anka, originally from Ottawa.

Lebanese immigrants continued to arrive in Swift Current and district during the 1950s, initially assisted by established Lebanese families, and during the 1970s, including young women who were to become brides. Although the earlier families had settled in the district two generations previously, in 1982 several families organized classes to teach their children Arabic and created an Islamic Centre. A new city cemetery contains a section reserved for Moslem burials, with plots oriented toward Mecca.

According to the 2006 census, Lebanese and Syrians in Saskatchewan together numbered 1,295, of whom approximately a third (32.8%, or 465) claimed to be only Lebanese or Syrian and two-thirds (67.2%, or 870) also claimed other ethnic origins. Far fewer people were of other Near Eastern origins (e.g., Palestinians, Israelis, Jordanians); 380 were Turkish and a few Cypriot; 1,515 originated primarily in Iraq or Iran (e.g., including 630 Iranians, 610 Iraqis, 160 Assyrians, and 115 Kurds); 435 were from Afghanistan (Afghans plus a few identifying as Pushtuns); 575 were North African (370 Egyptians, 140 Libyans, and fewer Algerians, Moroccans, and Berbers); and 130 from the Caucasus (including Armenians, Azerbaijanis, and Georgians). In addition, 410 people claimed to be simply Arabs, and even more generally another 100 were "West Asian."

GREEKS AND ITALIANS

Greek settlement in Saskatchewan dates back at least to the turn of the century. Influential early pioneers of Greek origin in Saskatoon included Kostas Valaris in 1901, Gus Thanagen, and Gus Golf and his brothers respectively in 1909 and 1910. The first permanent Greek settler in Regina was likely Gus Trihas in 1903, who ran a coffee shop and candy store. However, most early settlers of Greek origin arrived during the 1930s. George Kangles in Regina and the Girgulis family in Saskatoon were particularly responsible for encouraging chain migration from the Peloponnesos region (the southernmost region of mainland Greece)—especially Kastri in Arkadia and later Nafplion in Argolis. "Uncle Bill" Girgulis owned the Elite Café in Saskatoon with his brothers Sam and James; Sam's wife, Cleo, known as "Nouna" (godmother), earned her nickname by participating in many baptisms, and examples of her support of Greek newcomers were numerous.[24] Throughout Canada, the Greek population increased substantially after the Second World War because of crop failures, excessive taxation, escalating inflation, widespread unemployment, hunger, and continuing civil unrest in postwar Greece. In these years, a large proportion of Greek immigrants were single men who initially lived in shared apartments and rooming houses. Once established and employed in Canada, they were joined by women and children whom they sponsored. Greeks tended to develop restaurants in Saskatchewan cities—for example, in Saskatoon the Gem Café established by James Chronos, the Commodore by Steve Leakos, and the Ritz Hotel by William Geatros. There were more than forty Greek-owned restaurants in Saskatoon alone by the 1970s, most operated by relatives and/or immigrants from the same areas in Greece. Although these restaurant businesses were by definition competitive, they were largely established through the strong Greek tradition of mutual help. A close familial and geographical link prevailed in the Greek communities of Saskatoon and Regina. Greek restaurant owners eventually became investors in prime urban real estate, condominiums and apartment buildings, the stock market, and many business ventures. They tended to view the restaurant business as an intermediary step toward improving the financial and social status of the next generation. While the educational level increased with each generation—many second- and third-generation Greek Canadians entered university—efforts were made to preserve Greek cultural heritage in Canada. Greek-language schools had been established in Saskatchewan cities by 1970. These schools served to familiarize the younger generation with Greek history, literature, and drama, to teach non-Greek partners in mixed marriages, and to cement bonds among Greek children.

While Eastern Orthodox churches had long existed in Saskatchewan, specific Greek Orthodox congregations were not established in Regina until 1961 and in Saskatoon until 1964. In Regina, a larger new church (St. Paul's) was constructed in 1976. In Saskatoon, a former German Protestant church was purchased in 1976 through fundraising by the American Hellenic Educational Progressive Association (AHEPA). The first priest of Koimisis Tis Theotokou was Father Kakavalakis, himself an immigrant from Greece, who held a conservative view of the traditional role of the church in the Greek community. He was replaced by a Canadian-educated priest, Father John Nikolaou, who immigrated in 1960; he attempted to maintain age diversification in the parish rather than simply cater to the now elderly immigrants. His wife, Diana, immigrated to Saskatoon in 1958 and married John three years later. In 1966, he was ordained and served congregations in Quebec City and Edmonton before returning to Saskatoon in 1980. Diana was always active in the Greek Orthodox community, teaching Sunday School for more than three decades. Services were completely in ancient Greek originally, yet now they accommodated an increasing demand for contemporary Greek and English. This congregation now consists of about forty families.

A chapter of AHEPA (an organization founded in the United States in the early 1900s) was established in Saskatoon in 1930. A downtown hall during the 1960s included apartments and rooms above it; it was eventually replaced by a modern new hall in a suburban neighbourhood. Through the 1980s, differences between a more traditional church and a more secular and modern AHEPA led to a split in the Greek community, with rival duplication of community services.[25] The church had its Saturday "Greek school" and Sunday School, while AHEPA had its own language school. Both the church-oriented community and AHEPA organized separate pavilions at Folkfest for several years. The Women's Auxiliary of AHEPA (founded in 1938) had its counterpart in the Philoptochos Society (meaning friends of the poor) in the church. The AHEPA junior orders, Sons of Pericles and Maids of Athena, had their counterparts in the international Greek Orthodox Youth Association. Although some more secular Greek Canadians have tended to view as intrusive the church's efforts to become more involved in socio-cultural aspects of the Greek community (some Greek Canadians do not participate in the church), the third generation has become more interested in compromise. By the 1960s, the Saskatoon Greek Society had been founded. Today meetings of Greek community organizations are usually conducted in English. Both Saskatoon and Regina have Greek dancing ensembles, and Regina has a Greek band, Arkadia. Traditional Greek foods are available on a regular basis at the many Greek and Greek-owned restaurants in these cities: typically, *souvlaki, spanakopita, tiropites, dolmades,* "Greek chicken," *yemista, pastichio, keftedes,* and so on as a main course; with *Elliniki salata* or Greek salad; *baklava, loukoumades,* and so on for dessert; and "Greek coffee," *retsina, ouzo,* or *visinatha* to drink. Many of these foods are now familiar to Saskatchewan people not of Greek origin.

A previously high degree of ethnic endogamy was gradually replaced by increasing exogamy; in Saskatchewan, this is to be expected given the relatively small size of the Greek population compared with the populations of many other ethnic groups. An estimated 2,530 people claimed Greek ethnicity in whole or part in 2006, divided almost equally between those claiming to be completely of Greek descent (48.6%, or 1,230) and those claiming to be of Greek and other ethnic origins (51.4%, or 1,300). In addition, a few people claimed Cypriot identity, so they could be Greek or Turkish.

People of Italian origin actually outnumber people of Greek origin in Saskatchewan: 7,565 people claimed Italian ethnicity in 2006, 22.3% (1,690) as a single ethnic origin and 77.7% (5,875) in combination with other ethnic origins; thus, a far higher proportion of Italian Canadians have intermarried than Greek Canadians. Additionally, some people more specifically claimed Sicilian ethnicity. Of people of Italian origin, 2,525 were living in Regina and 2,040 in Saskatoon. However, they seem to have been a lot less active as a cohesive group in Saskatchewan than Greeks, have tended not to have their own churches or organizations, pavilions at multicultural events, and distinctive businesses, though as already mentioned Italian heritage language classes have been offered. In fact, many restaurants in Saskatchewan offering Italian pizza and other pasta dishes have actually been Greek. One small rural settlement of Italian homesteaders developed near Old Wives, in the south-central region. In addition to Greeks and Italians, other Mediterranean ethnic origins in the Saskatchewan population have included 3,255 Spanish (though, as already suggested, most of these "Spanish" are likely Hispanics from Latin America), 1,070 Portuguese, and seventy Maltese.

CONCLUDING THOUGHTS

In sum, these various "other" ethnic groups have added an incredible amount of diversity to the Saskatchewan population. Only the Blacks actually established a well-defined rural bloc settlement, though over time almost all have moved into the cities, where they have been augmented by new arrivals reflecting the cultural diversity of ultimately an African-origin population. Yet both the Chinese and the Lebanese have long histories of settlement in Saskatchewan and not only in urban areas; both of these groups have long been found in rural communities, though most recent Chinese and other East Asian as well as Middle Eastern immigrants have settled in the cities. So, too, do Greeks have a long history in Saskatchewan, albeit virtually entirely urban. And, finally, South Asians, Hispanic Latin Americans, and Southeast Asians have been, with few exceptions, more recent arrivals who have settled in the larger cities.

SOURCES

Recent Immigration and Visible Minorities in Saskatchewan

A recent comprehensive source is R. Loewen and G. Friesen, *Immigrants in Prairie Cities: Ethnic Diversity in Twentieth-Century Canada* (Toronto: University of Toronto Press, 2009). Sources specifically on Saskatchewan have included D. Elliott, "International Immigration"; B.D. Thraves, "Urban Ethnic Diversity"; A.B. Anderson, "Visible Minorities" and "Immigrant Integration"; and R. Pino, "Saskatchewan Intercultural

Association," in *Encyclopedia of Saskatchewan* (Regina: Canadian Plains Research Center, 2005), 976–77, 990, 477, 811; also see B.D. Thraves, "Regina's Ethnic Geography," in *Saskatchewan: Geographic Perspectives*, ed. B.D. Thraves, M.L. Lewry, J.E. Dale, and H. Schlichtmann (Regina: University of Regina and Canadian Plains Research Center, 2007), 318–24.

Chinese
The history of Chinese settlement in Canada has been described in C. Ma, *Chinese Pioneers* (Vancouver: Versatile Publishing, 1979); H. Con et al., eds., *From China to Canada: A History of the Chinese Communities in Canada* (Toronto: McClelland and Stewart, 1982); A.B. Chan, *Gold Mountain: The Chinese in the New World* (Vancouver: New Star Books, 1983); P.S. Li, *The Chinese in Canada* (Toronto: Oxford University Press, 1988); M. Cannon, *China Tide: The Hong Kong Exodus to Canada* (Toronto: HarperCollins, 1989); and P.S. Li, "Chinese," in *Encyclopedia of Canada's Peoples*, ed. P.R. Magocsi (Toronto: University of Toronto Press, 1999), 355–73.

The history of Chinese in Saskatchewan has been described in L. Zong, "Chinese Community," in *Encyclopedia of Saskatchewan* (Regina: Canadian Plains Research Center, 2005), 170–71.

Southeast Asians
The historical background to Southeast Asian and particularly Vietnamese settlement in Canada has been described in B. Grant, *The Boat People* (New York: Penguin Books, 1979); E.L. Tepper, ed., *Southeast Asian Exodus: From Tradition to Resettlement* (Ottawa: Canadian Asian Studies Association, 1980); H. Adelman, *Canada and the Indochinese Refugees* (Regina: L.A. Weigl Educational Associates, 1982); and L-J. Dorais, "Vietnamese," in *Encyclopedia of Canada's Peoples*, ed. P.R. Magocsi (Toronto: University of Toronto Press, 1999), 1312–24. On Filipino settlement in Canada, see A.B. Chan, *From Sunbelt to Snowbelt: Filipinos in Canada* (Calgary: Canadian Ethnic Studies Association, 1998).

The Vietnamese community in Saskatchewan has been described in V-T. Lam, "Vietnamese Community," in *Encyclopedia of Saskatchewan* (Regina: Canadian Plains Research Center, 2005), 988–89.

Blacks
Among comprehensive sources on the history of Blacks in Canada are R.W. Winks, *The Blacks in Canada: A History* (Montreal: McGill-Queen's University Press, 1971), and J. Walker, "African Canadians," in *Encyclopedia of Canada's Peoples*, ed. P.R. Magocsi (Toronto: University of Toronto Press, 1999), 139–76.

Sources specifically on Black settlement in Saskatchewan and Western Canada include C.A. Thompson, *Blacks in Deep Snow: Black Pioneers in Canada* (Don Mills, ON: J.M. Dent and Sons, 1979); R.B. Shepard, "The Little 'White' Schoolhouse: Racism in a Saskatchewan Rural School," *Saskatchewan History*, 39, 3 (1986): 81–93; R.B. Shepard,

Deemed Unsuitable (Toronto: Umbrella Press, 1997); R.B. Shepard, "Blacks: Early Settlements," and P. Elabor-Idemudia, "Blacks: Recent Immigration," in *Encyclopedia of Saskatchewan* (Regina: Canadian Plains Research Center, 2005), 116–17; and R.B. Shepard, "Plain Racism: The Reaction against Oklahoma Black Immigrants in the Canadian Prairies," in *Immigration and Settlement, 1870–1939*, ed. G.P. Marchildon (Regina: Canadian Plains Research Center, 2009), 483–506.

South Asians

General sources on the history of South Asian settlement in Canada include H. Johnston, *The East Indians in Canada* (Ottawa: Canadian Historical Association, 1984); N. Buchignani, D.M. Indra, with R. Srivastiva, *Continuous Journey: A Social History of South Asians in Canada* (Toronto: McClelland and Stewart, 1985); S. Chandrasekhar, ed., *From India to Canada* (La Jolla, CA: Population Review Books, 1986); M. Israel, ed., *The South Asian Diaspora in Canada: Six Essays* (Toronto: Multicultural History Society of Ontario, 1987); H. Johnston, *The Voyage of the* Komagata Maru: *The Sikh Challenge to Canada's Colour Bar* (Vancouver: UBC Press, 1989); and H. Johnston, "Sikhs," in *Encyclopedia of Canada's Peoples*, ed. P.R. Magocsi (Toronto: University of Toronto Press, 1999), 1148–64.

On South Asians in Saskatchewan, see K. Srinivas, "Indo-Canadian Community," in *Encyclopedia of Saskatchewan* (Regina: Canadian Plains Research Center, 2005), 481.

Latin Americans

An overview of Chilean immigration to Canada is provided in H. Diaz, "Chileans," in *Encyclopedia of Canada's Peoples*, ed. P.R. Magocsi (Toronto: University of Toronto Press, 1999), 347–55.

On Chileans in Saskatchewan, see M. Sanchez, "Chilean Community," in *Encyclopedia of Saskatchewan* (Regina: Canadian Plains Research Center, 2005), 169–70.

On Hispanics in Saskatchewan, see R. Pino, "Hispanic Community," in *Encyclopedia of Saskatchewan* (Regina: Canadian Plains Research Center, 2005).

Middle Eastern Groups

General sources on Middle Eastern groups in Canada include B. Abu-Laban, *An Olive Branch on the Family Tree: The Arabs in Canada* (Toronto: McClelland and Stewart, 1980), and E.H. Waugh, B. Abu-Laban, and R.B. Qureshi, eds., *The Muslim Community in North America* (Edmonton: University of Alberta Press, 1983).

An informative American study of a Chaldean immigrant community is M.C. Sengstock, *The Chaldean Americans: Changing Conceptions of Ethnic Identity* (New York: Center for Migration Studies, 1982).

The background to Lebanese immigration in Canada has been described in N.W. Jabbra and J.G. Jabbra, *Voyageurs to a Rocky Shore: The Lebanese and Syrians of Nova Scotia*

(Halifax: Dalhousie University Institute of Public Affairs, 1984); J.G. Jabbra and N.W. Jabbra, *Lebanese* (Tantallon, NS: Four East Publications, 1987); and N.W. Jabbra and J.G. Jabbra, "Lebanese," in *Encyclopedia of Canada's Peoples*, ed. P.R. Magocsi (Toronto: University of Toronto Press, 1999), 919–29.

Lebanese and Syrians in Saskatchewan have been described by G. Johnson, "The Syrians in Western Canada," *Saskatchewan History* 12, 1 (1959): 31–32 and H. Henry, "Lebanese Community," in *Encyclopedia of Saskatchewan* (Regina: Canadian Plains Research Center, 2005), 545.

Greeks and Italians
General sources on Greek Canadians include P.D. Chimbos, *The Canadian Odyssey: The Greek Experience in Canada* (Toronto: McClelland and Stewart, 1980), and P.D. Chimbos, "Greeks," in *Encyclopedia of Canada's Peoples*, ed. P.R. Magocsi (Toronto: University of Toronto Press, 1999), 615–26.

Sources on Greeks in Saskatchewan include *Saskatoon's Greek Community: The Pioneers (1901–1949)* (Saskatoon: Hellenic Greek Orthodox Community of Saskatoon, 1984), and A.B. Anderson, "Greek Community," in *Encyclopedia of Saskatchewan* (Regina: Canadian Plains Research Center, 2005), 415–16.

A comprehensive summary of Italian immigration and settlement in Canada is F. Sturino, "Italians," in *Encyclopedia of Canada's Peoples*, ed. P.R. Magocsi (Toronto: University of Toronto Press, 1999), 787–832.

A small rural Italian settlement is described in S. Bellissimo, "They were Trionfante: The Italian Homesteading Experience in Saskatchewan," M.A. thesis in history, University of Saskatchewan, 2012.

Chapter 10

CONCLUSION: CHANGING TIMES

This final chapter represents an attempt to provide a theoretical framework, beginning with a concise overview of demographic trends in Saskatchewan, then focusing on rural depopulation and urbanization and the effects that these trends have had on ethnic bloc settlements. Next our attention is turned to intermarriage and population mixing in answer to the inevitable question of how "ethnic" are people in Saskatchewan today? Finally, the strength and persistence of ethnic identification are discussed at some length, summarizing changing attitudes toward ethnicity, language trends, religious persistence or change, the preservation of traditions and customs, and the impact on the cultural geography of Saskatchewan. Demographic/ecological factors are also considered. Finally, the chapter returns to a discussion of the changing emphasis in Saskatchewan from policies of forced assimilation to an appreciation of multiculturalism and ethnic diversity.

OVERVIEW OF DEMOGRAPHIC TRENDS IN SASKATCHEWAN

Before discussing specifically the effects that rural depopulation, urbanization, and migration have had on ethnic bloc settlements in Saskatchewan (in the next section), it is useful to review demographic trends in general, commencing with a historical background, then proceeding respectively with discussions of the factors inherent in population change, changing population distribution, migration, and changing population composition.[1]

Prior to the 1870s, the lands that would become incorporated into the province of Saskatchewan were inhabited relatively sparsely by First Nations and during the early nineteenth century by Métis and fur traders. However, by the mid-1870s, the new dominion of Canada sought both European and American immigrants to supplement the inadequate migration of eastern Canadians as farming settlers out West. Canadian politicians began to view Western Canada, with sparsely populated but rich farmland, as ideal for expanding Canadian agriculture, especially wheat farming. In 1870, the dominion government purchased Rupert's Land from the Hudson's Bay Company, then enacted the Dominion Lands Act in 1872. Although the act opened this territory to free homesteading, initially it had a relatively limited effect in attracting settlers. When the Canadian Pacific Railway reached Regina in 1882, homesteaders began to arrive, but it was not until a more aggressive settlement policy was inaugurated in 1896 by Clifford Sifton, Minister of the Interior, that larger numbers of settlers came. In 1896, 16,835 immigrants entered Canada, the following years respectively 21,716, 31,900, and 44,543; the 100,000 mark was surpassed in 1903; and just a couple of years later 146,266 immigrants arrived. All told, Sifton was responsible for bringing well over 1 million immigrants to Canada. As Dafoe later reflected, "By 1900 the Laurier government, going to the [Canadian] people for a renewal of their mandate, could point to the success of the Sifton policy as one of the convincing reasons why they should be returned to office."[2] In the new province of Saskatchewan, in 1907, 15,307 immigrants arrived, representing 12.2% of the total immigration flow into Canada; from 1911 to 1914, more than 40,000 immigrants a year arrived, representing between 10.6% and 13.1% of the total Canadian immigration.[3] Sifton sought to attract immigrants from Central and Eastern Europe as farmers and opened alternate quarter-sections of railway lands in a first phase, creating a checkerboard settlement pattern. As ethnic bloc settlements rapidly proliferated, there was a concomitant increase in ethnic diversity.

This settlement process was well under way when the province of Saskatchewan was created in 1905. Regina, the "Queen City," was the focal point of the new province, the seat of the provincial government. Saskatoon, emerging out of the Temperance Colony and destined to be the location of the larger university, had a population of only 4,500 when it officially became a city in 1906. That year the first census of the new province revealed a population exceeding a quarter of a million, the vast majority (84.4%) of whom were rural. The highest period of population growth in Saskatchewan was from 1901 to 1915: the five-year rates of increase were between 1901 and 1905 (+182.4%), 1906 and 1910 (+91.0%), and 1911 and 1915 (+31.6%). The population continued to increase rapidly through the early 1930s, fed by the largest immigration flow in Canadian history, most of which headed west. The First World War only temporarily interrupted this massive flow. By 1931, the Saskatchewan population already numbered close to 1 million and represented 8.9% of the total Canadian population; in fact, Saskatchewan had the third largest population of any province in Canada (after Ontario and Quebec). The population peaked at 931,547 in 1936 and then declined during the late 1930s and 1940s to 831,728 in 1951 because of the Depression and recurrent drought. The population then slowly began to increase again with the postwar baby boom, but it did not recover fully to the 1936 level until the early 1960s. By that time, however, Saskatchewan contained only about 5% of the Canadian population.

In fact, fluctuations have characterized overall population trends in Saskatchewan during the past several decades. The population reached 955,344 in 1966, declined again to 921,323 in 1976, then increased again, to over 1 million (1,009,613) in 1986, only to be relatively static since then. Data from 2001 showed a population of 978,933, representing just 3.3% of the Canadian population, and five years later the population was closing in on a million (it should be noted, however, that census data produced every five years have counted fewer residents than annual estimates by Statistics Canada and the Saskatchewan Bureau of Statistics—these estimates have counted the Saskatchewan population at just over 1 million every year since 1986). The net population gain between 1981 and 2001 came to only 1.1%. Another way to summarize these trends is to point out that, since 1941, the provincial population declined slightly by 2% to 7% during four five-year census periods; it grew slightly by 2% to 6% during another five five-year periods; and it was essentially static—increasing or declining within plus or minus 2%—during the remaining four five-year periods. In the data for five-year intervals, there have been four periods of substantial population decline: the total provincial population decreased between 1936 and 1940 by -3.8%, between 1941 and 1945 by -7.1%, between 1966 and 1970 by -3.0%, and between 1986 and 1990 by -2.0% (though there were several other intervals when the population was virtually static or decreasing more slowly). With the exception of Newfoundland, Saskatchewan until very recently had the slowest growing population of any province in Canada. The population began to increase again in 2006 with a slight net gain (just 1,691), but in five of the previous six years there was a net loss of population, largely because of substantial out-migration. Then the population reached 1,023,810 by 2008, growing by more than 15,000 a year (the highest annual increase since 1988), yet just 1,093,880 by April 2013, despite increasing by more than 22,000 during 2011 (an annual growth rate of 2.16%, the highest annual increase in nine decades, since 1921). At the current quarterly growth rate, the estimated annual increase could be 16,000. Among the other provinces, only Alberta now has a higher annual rate of increase (however, now the quarterly growth rate in Saskatchewan is a modest 0.4%, adding approximately 4,000 to the population, compared with 0.9% in Alberta, adding 34,000).

Population change is measured in terms of natural increase or decrease, based on offsetting fertility and mortality trends, and controlling for migration. According to demographic transition theory, if the gap between the birth rate and the death rate narrows, then the population trend becomes static (the usual case recently for the general Saskatchewan population); if the birth rate remains high while the death rate starts to decline, then the gap widens, making for rapid population growth (the case currently for the Aboriginal population); conversely, if both the birth rate and the death rate are high, then again population growth is limited (the historical case for the Aboriginal population).

In Saskatchewan, the rate of natural increase has fluctuated since the 1940s, and a recent decreasing trend can be noted, for example from 10.3 per 1,000 in 1985 to 3.3 in 2001. The latest provincial data (based on quarterly trends) reveal that the current natural increase can be estimated as 5,340 a year: 15,008 births offset by 9,668 deaths. Overall birth and death rates have remained relatively stable for more than half a century, so population growth in this province has been largely dependent on positive net migration. Although the Saskatchewan fertility rate is one of the highest in Canada, the absolute number of births is declining.

The "baby boom" of the 1950s through the early 1960s was followed by the "baby bust" of reduced fertility, then the "echo boom" during the late 1970s through the early 1980s, when the many former baby boom babies had now grown up and were reproducing. Specifically, the Saskatchewan birth rate peaked at 27.9 per 1,000 in 1947, declined slightly, then was high again during the baby boom; it declined markedly to 16.2 in 1973 (perhaps primarily because of the increasing cost of living together with more reliable, and accessible contraception), then began increasing again during the echo boom. Couples with children are currently declining proportionately in Regina, whereas non-family households, lone parent families, and couples without children are increasing.

However, some qualifications should be made to these general trends. Ethno-cultural variations in fertility trends can be noted. Some visible minorities, usually recent immigrants from high-fertility countries, tend to have higher birth rates. Aboriginals, Mennonites, and Hutterites have exhibited larger average family size, though in all three cases fertility has been declining (among Aboriginals because of urbanization—fertility rates remain far higher on reserves than in cities, which thus reduces the rate of Aboriginal urbanization).

The Saskatchewan death rate, long in the 7.5–8.5/1,000 range, increased to 9.2 in 2001, perhaps to some extent because the baby boom generation of the 1950s was now reaching retirement age but mostly because of a significant expansion of an older-aged population; because of improving health care, more people are living longer. Of deaths each year, 62% occur among people aged seventy-five and older. During the past several decades, though, the Aboriginal mortality rate has been steadily decreasing while still remaining much higher than that for the non-Aboriginal population for certain causes of death and illnesses.

Population density in Saskatchewan as a whole averages only 1.7 people per square kilometre. Among Canadian provinces, only Newfoundland has a lower density. Yet there are great differences between areas: for example, density is as low as 0.1 in northern areas and less than 1.0 in 257 of 297 rural municipalities, whereas in Saskatoon and Regina the density exceeds 3,000 people per square kilometre in some residential areas, though average population density in the Saskatoon CMA (Census Metropolitan Area) averages 1,326.8 per square kilometre.

As we will see in more detail in the next section, rural Saskatchewan has long experienced depopulation and decline, particularly during the Depression and dust storms of the dirty thirties, when some areas—especially semi-arid areas—lost as much as three-quarters of their population and many smaller communities were turned into virtual ghost towns, in contrast to towns that survived as regional service centres.

There has been a marked shift in population from rural to urban. Back in 1901, 15.6% of the Saskatchewan population were living in urban places; the provincial population was one-third urban by the early 1940s, predominantly urban by the late 1960s, and now almost two-thirds urban, largely Saskatoon and Regina (which together contain 38.3% of the total population). The Saskatoon urban region has consistently experienced more rapid population growth than the Regina urban region ever since 1951, with the fastest growth for any decade since then actually occurring during the 1950s. Saskatoon had passed Regina as the largest city in Saskatchewan by the mid-1980s. Typically, the urban region population tends to increase faster than the city proper; this has been the case in Regina ever since 1981, in Saskatoon just since 1996. Saskatoon proper had a population of 196,811 in 2001, while there were 178,225 residents of Regina proper. This represented a slight increase of 1.6% in Saskatoon during the past five years, whereas

Regina's population declined by 1.2%. The Saskatoon CMA had a population of 225,927 in 2001, an increase of 3.1% since 1996, whereas the Regina CMA had declined by 0.4% to 192,800.

Despite this urbanization, the urban proportion in Saskatchewan is less than those of the neighbouring provinces (80.9% in Alberta and 71.9% in Manitoba) or Canada as a whole (79.7%). In Saskatchewan, the non-urban proportion has been reduced to less than one in five people (19.2%, 187,825 people, excluding 43,274 on reserves).

It was noted in Chapter 2 that urbanization of the Aboriginal population has contributed to provincial urban growth. In 2001, 36.2% (47,070) of the Aboriginal identity population was on reserve, compared with 46.7% (60,840) in urban places, including 26.8% (34,935) who lived in Saskatoon (where they constituted 9.8% of the city population) and Regina (8.7% of the city population). Despite this significant and continuing rural to urban shift, the Aboriginal population remains less urbanized than the general population.

Population change, of course, is not simply a matter of measuring the rate of natural increase/decrease and fertility and mortality trends. Migration serves as a crucial counterpoint to natural increase/decrease. Population growth occurs when in-migration exceeds out-migration. Migration can be international (between other countries and Saskatchewan), interprovincial (between Saskatchewan and other provinces), or intraprovincial (within Saskatchewan).

Saskatchewan once had one of the highest immigration rates in Canada, during the first two decades of the twentieth century. By 1931, immigrants made up more than a third (34.6%) of the province's population, and the rest of the population was seldom more than second or third generation. But then the immigration flow into Saskatchewan was greatly affected negatively by the Depression with low urban employment and recurrent drought making for persistent rural depopulation; Saskatchewan had become an unattractive destination for immigrants. Between 1931 and 1945, the province particularly suffered from the lowest immigration rates to Canada in history. The Canadian immigration rate was increasing again by 1951, but Saskatchewan was no longer a prime destination; moreover, in recent decades, most immigrants to Canada have headed for Toronto, Montreal, and Vancouver—the country's three largest cities. Between 1981 and 2001, Saskatchewan experienced positive net international migration (i.e., more immigrants arriving than emigrants leaving), but the net gain in population was only 30,985. Although 18% of Canadians are foreign born, only 5% of Saskatchewan residents are. In terms of population growth, it has long been problematic that a substantial proportion of immigrants and refugees eventually leave the province; until very recently, Saskatchewan had one of the lowest immigrant retention rates in Canada (57%). The most recent net international migration now exceeds 16,000 a year at the present rate. The foreign-born (immigrant) population of the province has been aging, yet recent immigrants have also been arriving (as noted in the previous chapter). For example, 30.0% of foreign-born people arrived before 1961, 23.8% during the 1990s. Visible minority populations in Saskatchewan, while increasing, remain minimal. Despite new immigration from Asia, Africa, and Latin America, fully half of the immigrants in Saskatchewan and 87.1% of immigrants who arrived before 1961 are of European origin. The preceding chapter discussed how increasing numbers of immigrants and refugees are arriving from Latin America, tropical Africa, the Middle East, South Asia, East Asia, and Southeast Asia. Currently, one-third of government-assisted refugees arrive from Sudan and a quarter from Afghanistan, yet in recent years refugees have also come from Europe: Poland, the former Yugoslavia, and the former Soviet Union. Now almost half of immigrants to Saskatchewan come from Asia, and as noted a majority of immigrants are members of visible minority groups. Almost three-quarters (74%) of recent immigrants live in Saskatoon and Regina. Most recent immigrants are skilled workers, family members, or refugees. Their educational levels are far higher than those of non-immigrant residents—more than a quarter of adults possess a university degree.

As for interprovincial migration, Saskatchewan has long had sustained net migration losses, primarily affected by changing economic conditions. Yet net migration has varied from year to year; some years there were gains rather than losses, but losses have been continuous every year since 1983. The largest annual loss was in 1989–90 (19,928), the largest over a five-year period in 1987–92 (69,721). The net loss of population over two decades from 1981 to 2001 was 120,000, of which 76,690 was to Alberta, 34,358 to British Columbia, and 13,594 to Ontario. There has been a vast movement in recent decades out of Saskatchewan. Between 1981 and 2001, out-migrants totalled 482,676, compared with 357,615 in-migrants. However, analysis of the latest data from Statistics Canada (again based on quarterly trends) reveals a slight net annual loss of about 1,356 from interprovincial migration (with 20,116 leaving and 18,760 arriving). More than 85% of migrants coming from other provinces are from Ontario and Alberta. Alberta has usually been both the major destination (60% of out-migrants) and the major source of interprovincial migrants (half of all in-migrants), though the most recent movement between Saskatchewan and Ontario has resulted in a substantial net gain. Predicting from analysis of quarterly trends, an estimated 8,768 could arrive from Alberta this year (2013) for a net gain of 2,296. A significant proportion of people move to find work, and with a current annual economic growth rate of 2.9% Saskatchewan (now ranked third among provinces but very recently first) is attracting interprovincial as well as international migrants.

Of course, to some extent, those leaving and arriving can be the same people, the coming-and-going syndrome or return migration, such as someone going to Alberta to work and then returning to Saskatchewan. This degree of major out-migration has not been equalled in other provinces. The exodus has been influenced by many factors, especially unemployment or limited employment, farm sales and closures, and leaving to retire in warmer climates (which can also significantly contribute to international emigration). The greatest movement has been between neighbouring provinces, especially between Saskatchewan and its more affluent neighbour Alberta, so distance can be a factor. The relatively limited movement between Saskatchewan and Quebec (far exceeded by movement between Saskatchewan and Ontario) can be partially explained in cultural terms, given the substantial francophone minority in Saskatchewan. Moreover, age of migrants is a consideration. Younger members of the labour force seem most likely to leave: over half (51.5%) of out-migrants between 1981 and 2001 were aged between fifteen and twenty-nine, 84.9% between zero and forty-four. These people constitute a serious economic loss to the province. In a sense, the universities are educating young people to leave, depending on whether occupations for which they have been educated provide adequate employment opportunities in Saskatchewan. This large number of young adult out-migrants certainly has an effect on the most important reproductive cohorts, again affecting population growth. Saskatchewan has one of the highest youth out-migration rates of any province. Older people are less likely to move, except perhaps to retire in a warmer climate.

The third basic type of migration, intraprovincial, or migration within the province, largely assumes the form of urbanization (rural to urban migration) but can also refer to other types of movement, including rural farm to rural non-farm, changing residence within the city (intraurban), or moving from one city to another (interurban). Analyzing these movements can become very complicated. There are distance and temporal factors and even socio-cultural ones. For example, though there has recently been substantial migration of non-Aboriginal people out of mining communities in the far north, the Aboriginal population up north has been growing. Rural depopulation has augmented urban populations to a considerable extent. There has been continuous out-migration from reserves, especially of young adults, because of a lower standard of living, less health care, limited educational opportunities, unemployment and low income, harsh living conditions, and so on. Yet, to some extent, as conditions improve in some reserves, migrants are attracted back to the reserve.

Lower birth rates mean that the main source of population growth has to be migration. But until very recently, Regina as well as other cities in the province have not been attracting substantial numbers of either interprovincial or intraprovincial migrants. Regina actually had the lowest rate of in-migration compared with all other cities in Saskatchewan: considering who moved into each city during the period 1996–2001, we can note that smaller cities (including Lloydminster, Melfort, Yorkton, Swift Current, North Battleford, and Weyburn but not Estevan) all attracted proportionately more migrants (typically in the 20%–30% range) than Saskatoon, Regina, Moose Jaw, or Prince Albert (typically in the 14%–18% range).

Saskatchewan had an exceptionally high male disproportion in the sex ratio throughout the 1940s, ranging from 118.1 in 1901, to a peak of 145.6 in 1906, to 113.2 in 1946. Since then the sex ratio has become more balanced, but still a male disproportion can be noted: 109.4 in 1951 to 100.3 in 1986. Then, more recently, partially because of a higher age-specific mortality rate for males, males still have lower life expectancy; the older the age cohorts, the more females outnumber males.

The dependency ratio, the proportion of the total population aged sixty-five and older (elder dependency) plus fifteen and younger (child dependency), has gradually been declining since the 1960s—it was 56.8 in 2001. Child dependency declined from 69.9 in 1901 to 60.0 in 1961 and then to 33.2 in 2001, whereas elder dependency increased from only 4.4 in 1901 to 16.3 in 1961 and then to 23.6 in 2001. Compared with other provinces, Saskatchewan has high proportions of both elderly and young populations: 29.2% of the provincial population is under the age of twenty, 19.0% over the age of sixty. The median age among the Aboriginal population is currently just 22.6, compared with 40.9 among the non-Aboriginal population. The provincial age structure has been affected by significant out-migration of young adults as well as by rural decline—many smaller communities have an inverted age structure, with very few children yet most adults middle-aged or elderly. There is a "youth bulge" among the Aboriginal population, a disproportionate number of people in younger age cohorts; even in urban areas, almost half of the Aboriginal population is under twenty years of age. A disproportion of the residents under twenty in Saskatoon and Regina is Aboriginal, reflected in inner-city schools where Aboriginal pupils now form a majority. The Aboriginal dependency ratio (74.9) is far higher than that for the general population, and even higher (82.8) on reserves, but lower in Saskatoon and Regina (68.3). The median age on some reserves is under twenty, and all northern reserves have child dependency ratios exceeding half of the total population there. A substantial proportion of the province's natural increase is from the Aboriginal population; moreover, the Canadian Centre for Policy Alternatives estimates that as many as two-thirds of Aboriginal children in Saskatchewan live in poverty as well as one-third of children in immigrant families and a quarter of visible minority children.

The ethno-cultural composition of the Saskatchewan population has changed dramatically over the years. With the settlement process and high immigration between the 1880s and 1920s, much of the prairie area of the province was rapidly converted into ethnic bloc settlements. Increasing intermarriage or exogamy over time has led to an increasing proportion of the population claiming multiple rather than single ethnic origins, though recent immigrants have tended to be more endogamous. Increasing numbers of visible minorities are again adding to the ethnic diversity of Saskatchewan, now in an urban rather than a rural setting. Visible minorities now constitute 2.9% of the Saskatchewan population (compared with 13.4% nationally), far fewer than in the neighbouring provinces. The provincial population declined by 1.4% in the five years between 1996 and 2001, whereas the visible minority population grew by 2.4%, thus accounting for at least some population growth in Saskatchewan. Visible minorities are concentrated in Saskatoon, forming 5.6% of the city population in 2001, and Regina, forming 6.3%; 80.8% (20,290) of the province's visible minority population live in these two cities.

After a rapid diminution of the Aboriginal proportion of the Saskatchewan population for several decades, recently this proportion has been fast increasing. Aboriginal people now form a higher proportion in Saskatchewan (13.5%) than in any other province (except possibly Manitoba). The Aboriginal population increased by 17% in just five years, 1996–2001. With almost half of the Aboriginal population under twenty years of age, continued growth of the population and large-scale movement into the future labour force are assured.

RURAL DEPOPULATION AND URBANIZATION

Let us now examine rural depopulation and urbanization in more detail before considering the effects that these trends have had on ethnic bloc settlements.[4] Since reaching a peak of 138,713 farms in 1941, the number of farms in Saskatchewan steadily declined into the new millennium, to 50,598 farms in 2001. This represented a 63.5% decline in the number of farms. The largest decrease occurred between 1941 and 1951. This trend has continued: the number of farms was reduced by 16.8% from 1991 to 2001, and by 16.6% from 2006 to 2011, by which time there were only 39,952 operating farms left.

Similarly, ever since 1941, across Canada the number of farms has been steadily decreasing, although not as fast as in Saskatchewan: the total number declined by

10.3% during the past five years: 205,730 farms were counted in the 2011 census, 23,643 less than in 2006, while the number of farm operators fell by 33,135 (10.1%) to 293,925. The number of farms has been decreasing in every province (with the possible exception of Nova Scotia); in fact Saskatchewan had the second largest percentage decline (after Manitoba).

This decline in the number of farms has largely been the result of the incorporation of smaller farms into larger farms. In 2001, the average size of farms in Saskatchewan was 519 hectares, almost three times larger than the average farm size (175 hectares) in 1941. The overall increase in average farm size from 1941 to 2001 was 196.57%. Saskatchewan has the largest average size of farms compared with farms in other provinces. In Canada as a whole, average farm size increased by 6.9% during the past five years, from 728 to 778 acres. In Saskatchewan, during the same period, average farm size increased at more than twice that rate, by 15.0%, to more than 1,668 acres (the greatest increase in the country). One of the main forces behind the increase in farm size and the reduction in farm number has been the mechanization of farming, the substitution of capital for labour, and the application of fertilizers, herbicides, insecticides, and other related technologies.

Farmers in Saskatchewan have been more likely to rely on crop production, particularly wheat, than farmers in Manitoba and Alberta, who have tended to have more diversified operations, including livestock production, yet Saskatchewan farmers have been responding to changing market conditions and are engaging in more diversified types of crop and livestock production. Although there are far more smaller than larger farms in Canada, large farms dominate both revenue and profit; farms with annual revenue in excess of $500,000 represent only 11% of farms in Canada but account for 55% of revenue, have higher operating margins and carry larger debt loads, but also have more efficient sales-to-asset ratios and a higher return on equity. Farms with $1 million or more in annual revenue represent the fastest growing agricultural sector in Canada, increasing by 31.2% just since 2006. Such farms still comprise only 4.7% (up from 3.2% five years earlier) of the total number of farms, yet they account for almost half of the total Canadian food production; these 9,602 farms generate 49.1% (up from 42.8%) of total gross farm receipts (which now reach $51 billion).

Among the largest corporate farms in Saskatchewan are Assiniboia Capital Corporation, which calls itself "the largest farmland investment management company in Canada," with more than 100,000 acres (it tripled its landholdings in just two years), and One Earth Farms Corporation, a collaborative First Nation investment enterprise in Saskatchewan and Alberta, aiming to control over 1 million acres (though it was formed just in 2009).

The relative size of the farm population has also declined along with the decrease in the number of farms and farm families resulting from the amalgamation of smaller farms into larger units. In comparison with previous periods when farm families of six or more were relatively common, the farm family of the 1980s, 1990s, and 2000s was more likely to have one or two children. A large number of children were previously desirable as a ready supply of labour on the farm. However, the mechanization of farming (along with more reliable contraceptives and other factors) has reduced the number of children. By 2001, the total farm population in Saskatchewan was just 123,385, comprising only 12.6% of the provincial population and decreasing by about 3.0% a year.

CHAPTER 10

It is a well-worn saying that farming can be a risky business. Take, for example, farming income. Net farm operating incomes decreased in 2010–11 to $44,171 per farm in Canada but just $14,693 in Saskatchewan, barely half the amount just a year earlier according to data from Agriculture Canada, the Statistics Canada Census of Agriculture, and the Agricultural Producers Association of Saskatchewan. Farmers are increasingly participating in off-farm work to supplement the variable and somewhat uncertain incomes derived from farming. Net average farm income (which increased 20% from $37,732 in 2007 to $44,480 in 2008) slightly exceeded non-farm income on Saskatchewan farms for the first time in years, but this figure does not take the costs of farming, such as depreciation of machinery and replacement of worn-out equipment, into consideration. The largest increase in farmer participation in non-farm work occurred in the youngest age group, more than half of whom (56% in 2001) now work part time away from their farms. Between 2002 and 2006, total crop receipts for Saskatchewan farmers averaged $3.32 billion a year, but this amount increased to almost $6 billion by 2008 (an 80% increase). However, Saskatchewan farms' realized net income (net income with depreciation and in-kind income) was expected to decrease an incredible 66% in2011 to $592 million, down from $925 million the previous year (though it had increased in 2008–09 from $1.6 billion to $1.9 billion). Moreover, the National Farmers Union estimates that, for every dollar of net income earned, the average farmer shoulders $23.25 of debt.

Meanwhile, farmland values have been increasing across Canada and in Saskatchewan. In 2008, the average price of farmland in Saskatchewan came to $435 an acre (compared to $772 in Manitoba, $1,392 in Alberta, and $4,593 in Ontario). However, according to Statistics Canada and Farm Credit Canada, the value of Saskatchewan farmland has been increasing by approximately 6.8%–17.6% per year (and nationally by about 7.2%). Yet the most recent data suggest an even faster increase, reaching an estimated average of 20.2% in 2011 (compared with 9.0% in Alberta and 3.8% in Manitoba), with wide fluctuations by season and depending on the quality and use of the land. For example, the highest-quality grain-producing land in Saskatchewan currently averages approximately $1,200–$1,800 an acre, increasing by about 20% a year (compared with $2,000–$4,500 in Alberta, increasing by about 25%).

Like the majority of modern industrialized areas, Saskatchewan has witnessed an increasing concentration of its population in larger urban centres, with a corresponding decrease of the population in smaller rural towns, villages, and the countryside. Urbanization of the population has transformed a basically rural province into an urbanized one dominated by a few larger cities. For much of its history, Saskatchewan was considered a rural agricultural province, but now the majority of the provincial population is urban. Typically, a larger proportion of the Saskatchewan population was classified as rural than was evident for the total Canadian population during those early years. This was largely because of the greater involvement in and dependence of the Saskatchewan labour force on farming and extractive activities compared with the residents of other Canadian provinces.

Over one-third of the total Saskatchewan population lives in either Saskatoon or Regina. Of the 978,933 people living in Saskatchewan in 2001, 196,811 lived in Saskatoon and 178,225 in Regina. Moreover, Saskatoon is continuing to grow faster than Regina: the former experienced a 1.6% increase in its population from 1996 to 2001, while the latter had a loss of 1.2% of its population during the same five-year span. Of ten smaller regional centres, seven experienced declines in their populations from 1996 to 2001 (the three centres that increased their populations were Lloydminster, Humboldt, and Estevan).

Urbanization in Saskatchewan and other provinces has meant more than increasing concentrations of population in larger centres—it has also meant the increasing concentration of businesses, services (education, health), and opportunities and the relative decline or closure of their counterparts in rural areas and trade centres. With the closure of grain elevators, businesses, schools, hospitals, and other services, the rural population is required to travel greater distances for these services. The changing relative sizes of rural and urban populations are largely the results of migration from rural to urban areas for employment, education, and other opportunities and the displacement of people in farming as a result of mechanization and other technological developments.

The aging of the Canadian and Saskatchewan populations is particularly evident in the farm operator population in Saskatchewan. In 2001, the average age of farm operators in the province was almost fifty-one. Concurrently, the percentage of farm operators in the young adult age group (under thirty-five years of age) decreased by 7.7% from 1991 to 2001, while the percentages in the two older age groups increased during the ten-year period: in 1991, 20.0% of Saskatchewan farmers were under thirty-five, 44.0% were thirty-five to fifty-four, and 35.4% were older than fifty-five; ten years later these proportions were respectively 12.3%, 51.1%, and 36.7%. Currently (in 2012), 48.3% of all Canadian farmers are fifty-five years or older (the highest proportion ever), compared with 40.7% in 2006 and 32.1% in 1991, while the proportion under thirty-five has fallen to 8.2% from 9.1% in 2006 and 19.9% in 1991. The relative stability in the older age group is possibly the result of operators continuing to farm beyond the normally accepted retirement age of sixty-five. This might be because of the lack of younger operators willing or able to purchase farm operations. Increases in the capital investments in farming have made it increasingly difficult for younger people to become established in farming unless by inheritance. Other reasons that discourage younger people from taking up farming are the attractions of higher and more regular incomes, regular hours, paid vacations, and other benefits associated with non-farm occupations most likely located in urban centres.

EFFECTS OF RURAL DEPOPULATION ON ETHNIC BLOC SETTLEMENTS

The decrease in the number of farmers in all age groups and the dramatic decline of those in the younger age group introduce some serious questions about the farmer of the future and the future of farming. Throughout Saskatchewan, intensive rural settlement has been transformed into extensive rural depopulation, while physical and social isolation, and lack of—or resistance to—mobility have been replaced by steadily increasing physical and social mobility. Rural focal points (e.g., one-room country schoolhouses, churches, community halls, post offices, general stores, and most recently grain elevators) have disappeared. The younger generation often might not even be familiar with local district names. The effects of these changes on bloc settlement segregation, and thus on ethnic and religious identification, have been marked.

During the early years of rural settlement, settlers—most of them immigrants—revealed a strong preference for rural as opposed to urban life; they tended to emphasize neighbourliness and healthy living.[5] Farm size generally was small, frequently limited to a single quarter (160 acres), so rural settlement was fairly intensive, with farms close to each other. Resistance to assimilatory tendencies advocated by the provincial government and the Anglo-Canadian population was enhanced by spatial as well as social isolation, so that de facto segregation corresponded with intensive settlement and close-knit community life.

However, this situation was soon to change. With the arrival of prolonged drought and the Depression in 1929, the prices for increasingly meagre crops dropped drastically, affecting all ancillary businesses in rural communities. With severe drought continuing through 1937, topsoil drifted, many farm families were driven from their ruined farms, and those who remained often became dependent on relief payments while their taxes went unpaid, their idle machinery rusted, and they were forced to surrender their farms to the banks. The exodus was particularly evident in the southern regions; most left Saskatchewan, but some who abandoned their farms moved north to take up farming again in areas less affected by drought or into cities. Then, just when an economic recovery began to a modest extent in 1939, young men were sent off to war in Europe.[6]

By the 1960s, the populations of many areas still had not regained their levels of three decades earlier. Rural decline was widespread and pronounced, double that of the province as a whole during the 1936–51 period. For example, even in the relatively prosperous north-central prairie region, only a single rural municipality out of thirty-five revealed a population increase in excess of 10%; all of the other rural municipalities were either declining or essentially static. Moreover, during the 1950s, populations in many rural municipalities continued to decrease, while most of the remainder remained static; only a couple increased. And, during the early 1960s, only four rural municipalities were clearly increasing. Generally, there was a consistent and often rapid decline of the rural farm population throughout this region, though that population did increase in certain farming areas, around a few significant towns and villages, and on First Nations reserves. By 1951, some 1,800 farms, more than a quarter of the total number of farms in Division 16, had been abandoned, yet only 300 of these abandonments or "withdrawals" were by young farmers, suggesting that most occurred because of the retirement of older farmers along with the expansion of larger farms at the expense of smaller ones. In fact, many smaller farms were incorporated into larger ones, so original farmhouses became derelict while the farmland continued to be used; moreover, with the aging of numerous farmers, there was an increasingly prevalent tendency to "move into town" while the farms continued to be used, perhaps by younger family members.[7] Nor was the north-central region the hardest hit; it was more typical, located in the heart of the prairie portion of Saskatchewan, but other regions, notably in southwestern Saskatchewan, were more affected by drought and financial circumstances. In fact, in poorer regions, as many as three-quarters of the original population left their farms during those difficult years.

While the rural farm population steadily continued to decrease, the rural non-farm population was generally more stable or slowly increased, and the populations of certain area service centres classified as "urban" (in Saskatchewan, an urban community is defined as having a population within incorporated boundaries of at least 1,000) eventually tended to increase more substantially. A fairly safe generalization is that, the smaller the community, the faster the population decrease. Even the population stability or population increase in larger communities has, in quite a few cases, turned out to be only temporary, when much of this increase occurred because of older farmers retiring in the countryside and moving into larger communities. The younger generation has been moving away not only from the farms but also from the local communities. One study in 1966 found that in Division 16, for every nine persons who left the rural parts of municipalities, only one was retained by a growing local trade centre; among young adults, the proportion was negligible, whereas among older adults, the centres accounted for a quarter to a third of rural migrants.[8] Numerous communities in Saskatchewan might seem stable now or exhibit modest growth, but in the not-too-distant future they might experience substantial decline because of a lack of replenishment of the community population by young people; these communities now have an age structure in which there is a strong disproportion of middle-aged to elderly residents. With increased physical mobility, local businesses have shut down. It is noteworthy, though, that in Saskatchewan the census distinction between rural farm, rural non-farm, and urban population can become blurred because an increasing number of farmers now live off farms in villages, towns, and occasionally even cities.

Rural depopulation can be partially explained by farming families' disillusionment with the challenges of modern-day farming. The difficulty of farming on such an extensive scale today cannot be overemphasized. The sophisticated prairie farmer must be something of an agronomist (knowing which crops are best suited to various types of soil and land, also exactly when to seed and harvest), a capitalist (a shrewd dealer in loans and investments), a mechanic (capable of maintaining and repairing tens of thousands of dollars worth of agricultural machinery), a political economist (familiar with international trade and market fluctuations), a meteorologist (understanding the vagaries of weather), a veterinarian (able to care for diverse livestock), a plant pathologist (treating crop diseases), a biochemist (comprehending herbicides, fungicides, pesticides, not to mention the risks of genetically modified foods). ... Saskatchewan farmers have become increasingly challenged and often depressed by the high cost of good farmland, relatively poor world markets, what they might perceive as the federal government's encouragement of summerfallow and diversification rather than beneficial international trade, and not the least the dwindling of active small community life. Although farmers are obliged to invest in very expensive machinery, in some years their actual net income might not seem to make it all worthwhile. Changes have been made to better control the environment since the dirty thirties, but in some areas the physical environment continues to pose great challenges and does not offer much of an inducement to stay in farming. In much of the Saskatchewan prairies, soil capability ranges from moderate to severe limitations (including insufficient water-holding capacity, periodic inundation, erosion, stones, and hills). Moreover, the Saskatchewan climate can often be prohibitive.

Yet a number of noteworthy initiatives serve to resist rural depopulation. Diversification of farming from too heavy a dependence on grain crops (especially wheat) to mixed farming with livestock and vegetable crops has proven beneficial. As noted, part-time farming supplemented by other sources of income (especially in rural areas closest to larger urban centres or extractive industries) has promoted the financial stability of farm families. This has been augmented by the development of local community industries, businesses, and cooperatives, including small-scale manufacturing, food processing, sawmills, mining, automotive dealers, agricultural machine repair shops and distributors, grid road construction and maintenance, banking, restaurants, craft shops, diverse home-based businesses, and so on.

Nonetheless, the larger forces of physical and social mobility have corresponded closely with rural depopulation. The physical mobility of rural residents has markedly increased with improvements in road transportation. Since the 1950s, virtually all major highways in the province have been converted from gravel to pavement, with the inevitable result that the residents of innumerable small communities have easier and faster access to stores, services, and facilities in larger centres; however, this mobility has also contributed to the closure of many local community businesses, institutions, and services.

In the extensive survey conducted within bloc settlements in the north-central region in 1968–72, it was learned that "permanent" physical mobility (out of the local community) ranged from a quarter to half of the families interviewed in various ethno-religious groups down to none at all among Hutterites (who by definition all reside in colonies). There had been physical mobility, in the sense of leaving the local community on a long-term basis, in almost every third family interviewed; the proportion was half or almost half among Doukhobors, Poles, Ukrainian Orthodox, and Mennonites. But considerable variation was found among these groups in attitudes to physical mobility. All of the Hutterites were strongly opposed. Over half (54.0%) of the French were non-commital or indifferent, with quite a few (28.3%) strongly or generally in favour. Many (66.3%) of the German Catholics were in favour, with the remainder either indifferent (22.7%) or opposed (11.1%). Similarly, the largest number (47.2%) of Mennonites were in favour, with the remainder indifferent (30.7%) or opposed (22.1%). The largest proportion of Ukrainian Orthodox were opposed (44.6%), compared with 34.9% in favour and 20.5% indifferent. A majority of Ukrainian Catholics were opposed (62.9%), most of the rest indifferent (29.2%), very few in favour (7.8%). The Poles were divided between those opposed (53.3%) and those in favour (46.7%). Conversely, a majority of Doukhobors were in favour (60.0%), most of the remainder opposed (35.0%), very few indifferent (5.0%). And the Scandinavians were the most evenly divided among opposed (32.9%), in favour (34.0%), and indifferent (33.1%).

But to what extent have physical mobility and rural depopulation actually affected the preservation of ethnic or ethno-religious identities? Sociologists have emphasized that improved transportation and increased physical mobility inevitably promote economic and social integration and urbanization, thereby having a pronounced effect on rural ethnic identification. Dawson and Younge described the Saskatchewan situation in similar terms as early as 1940.[9] Greer has suggested that urbanization should refer not simply to a changing rural-urban proportion but also to what he calls the "increasing scale of society" or what we would prefer to call the "delocalization" of rural society. By this he means that changing technology is forcing formerly relatively isolated rural areas into a network of functional interdependence, so that a former emphasis on ethnic particularism is replaced by a societal structure emphasizing economic function and characterized by social stratification indifferent, if not antithetical, to considerations of ethnicity. Thus, within a particular rural locality, individuals increasingly fail to regard local groups such as their ethnic group or community as primary reference groups. In other words, socio-economic changes have tended to bring ethnic enclaves from a small-scale social organization into a larger social system. This continuing increase in scale in turn causes other bases of differentiation in society to change or disappear. As ethnic or rural origins become progressively less crucial within the larger social system, what Greer views as regional variations also become less important than they once were in organizational autonomy characteristic of smaller-scale society. And, as "nation-spanning organizational networks" increase and interdependence becomes more intensive, the local group loses its distinctive organizational and cultural form. When the local area is exposed to large-scale organizational networks and mass media, the result is acculturation to the normative structure of the larger society.[10] This theory has rather obvious historical applicability to Saskatchewan, insofar as ethno-religious bloc settlements have gradually become less isolated and more interdependent within a national social system dominated by conformity to Anglo-Canadian values enforced through the residential school system imposed on Aboriginal people, the rapid elimination of small country schools and community halls that had been the focal points of local ethnic community life, opposition to non-White immigration, and discriminatory measures enacted against non-White communities.

During and since the 1950s, innumerable rural focal points—country schoolhouses, churches, community halls, post offices, general stores, and most recently grain elevators—have disappeared in Saskatchewan. Localities or rural districts and unincorporated hamlets were named after these focal points (or vice versa). Today, however, there is little evidence of them; many of the younger generation still on farms might not even have heard of them. These focal points, once the centres of highly localized rural districts, have become the victims not only of rural decline but also of a purposive "delocalization" or consolidation process that has had a profound effect on the identification of bloc settlements.

Mainly during the 1950s and early 1960s, and sometimes earlier or later, hundreds of one-room country schoolhouses throughout Saskatchewan were closed in favour of larger schools in selected communities serving far broader areas. For example, within the small French settlement around St-Denis, Canoe Lake School was shut down in 1950, Lamartine in 1955, Trojan and Grierson in 1959, Dinelle and Casavant in 1960, and Glenmour in 1961. In the five new school districts in the southern part of Division 15, in north-central Saskatchewan, by 1968–69 there were only six single-teacher country schoolhouses left (at Kaminka near Tway, Willow Ridge and Dixon near Humboldt, Banner near Muenster, Dana, and One Arrow Reserve near Batoche). Another eight schools were very small, with two to five teachers (at Meskanaw, St. Henry near Marysburg, St. Gregor, Fulda, Vonda public and separate, St-Denis, and Peterson). Fourteen schools had six to ten teachers, twelve had eleven to fifteen, eight had sixteen to twenty, and six had more than twenty.[11] Some of these schools had long connections with particular ethno-religious groups (e.g., the German Catholic-oriented Monastery School and

St. Peter's College at Muenster, St. Augustine's and St. Dominic's Schools at Humboldt, Sacred Heart School at Watson, and Ursuline Academy at Bruno; the French-oriented Prud'homme, Vonda separate, St-Denis, Domrémy, and St-Louis Schools and Collège Notre-Dame at St-Louis; and the Mennonite Rosthern Junior College). But with the eradication of small country schools, ethnic/religious group control of education was dealt a heavy blow.

So, too, have numerous small ethnic churches disappeared from rural Saskatchewan. Take as an example the Lutheran churches. Lutherans erected churches almost side by side to serve nationality groups as similar as Norwegian and Swedish Canadians. In 1960, forty-five communities in Saskatchewan had from two to six Lutheran churches each. Over 80% of the approximately 300 Lutheran congregations in the province were in rural areas. They were served by about 100 pastors, so most pastors served several congregations.[12] Smaller congregations in the countryside felt the shortage of clergy most acutely. In the early years of settlement, because of the tendency of Scandinavian and Finnish, and perhaps to a lesser extent German, settlers to concentrate in rural areas rather than in towns and villages, numerous small country churches were built as the centres of rural districts so that they would be easily accessible by horse and buggy and later slow-moving vehicles, as were country schoolhouses. However, with rural depopulation, what were already small congregations became even smaller, and with the delocalization process in full swing these country churches soon found themselves the centres of localized communities that in many respects no longer really existed. A shortage of pastors, together with the consolidation of congregations through the merging of nationality churches into broader conferences and synods, combined with rural depopulation to force the closure of one small country church after another throughout Saskatchewan.

Take as another example the similar closure of Roman Catholic churches in the countryside. Again, rural depopulation combined with a shortage of clergy to force the closure of most country churches that had been local district centres of active community life within bloc settlements. In the extensive German Catholic settlement between Leader and Maple Creek, most of the rural churches are now closed (some have even been removed, as noted in Chapter 4), including Sts. Peter and Paul at Blumenfeld (once the "mother church" of the colony) and the academy for young women at Prelate.

Take as a further example the Ukrainian Catholic churches in the Redberry bloc settlement. During a sample period of only four years, 1964–68, there was a steady decline in membership in the Krydor congregation: from 185 registered members (fifty-two families and twenty singles) in 1964 to 150 members (forty-four families and eighteen singles) in 1968; thus, this congregation was losing members during the 1960s at a rate of more than eight a year—at such a rate, there would be no one left in less than two decades. The Blaine Lake congregation was decreasing even faster: in the same period, from 145 (thirty-eight families and ten singles) to 102 (thirty-three families and six singles). The small country church at Orolow lost almost half of its members: from 110 (twenty-six families and three singles) to sixty (fifteen families and two singles). The church at Uhriniw did lose exactly half of its members: from eighty (twenty families and no singles) to forty (eleven families and a couple of singles). Krydor, Blaine Lake, and Orolow were holding services twice a month in 1969, Uhriniw just once a month during summer only. Other country churches at Sich, Great Deer, and Alticane were already virtually abandoned.[13] The priest serving these churches knew of very few families in which a son planned to take over the family farm. Yet a movement developed in the settlement to try to preserve the country churches. Sts. Peter and Paul at Albertown, one of the more active congregations, once packed every Sunday, now has at best a couple of dozen participants. Built in 1927, the church still has no power, and the only source of heat during the long winter is a pot-bellied stove. But the congregation lovingly cares for the church, its hand-made pews, its gold-leaf icons and cherubs decorating the traditional tongue-in-groove ceiling. Services are now held twice a month only during summer between Easter and October, and the church has an active women's group, an annual family feast day, and *moleben* (cemetery commemorative service). Although efforts are made to involve children and youth in church activities, almost all youth eventually leave for the cities. Some congregants with roots in farms in this district live far away, such as in the town of Blaine Lake or farther away in Saskatoon, and participate only once a year on the feast day. St. John the Baptist at Alticane was in jeopardy of closure by the eparchy in 2000; the dwindling congregation is attempting to persuade church authorities to permit them to keep the church open provided that the congregation can maintain the building, but today only one scheduled service is held a year on the feast day.[14] Similarly, the Welechko/Velychko church has been designated a heritage site and holds only one service a year.

Holy Trinity Ukrainian Orthodox congregation near Smuts now consists entirely of members living in Saskatoon (but having roots in the district); by 1991, it had reportedly declined to just ten members (though much larger numbers were attending special services). The church is in excellent condition, completely renovated for its seventy-fifth anniversary in 2000. Scheduled services—including the "blessing of the baskets" and an annual memorial service—are held only twice a year around Easter. The priest, based in Wakaw, now serves thirteen congregations scattered as far away as Melfort, Nipawin, and Meacham (he travels as much as thousands of kilometres a year, not only for scheduled services but also for weddings, baptisms, funerals, and hospital and nursing home visits).[15]

To complete the delocalization process, many community halls, once popular especially among Ukrainians and Finns, have been left deserted or used only on rare special occasions; dances and social gatherings have largely become distant memories of the older generation. Innumerable country post offices have closed in the interest of consolidation; now rural post offices are limited to selected towns and villages. So many country and community general stores have closed as to leave country crossroads barren and to turn numerous small communities into virtual ghost towns. Grain elevators, long the "sentinels of the prairies," have largely been destroyed; once they were markers of communities that could be seen for long distances, but now communities are almost invisible until you are close to them. Already by the early 1970s, many branch rail lines were either abandoned or scheduled for imminent abandonment, and 144 railway stations—also markers of communities—were scheduled for closure and removal.[16]

Consolidation of farm ownership does not necessarily affect the solidarity of a bloc settlement, nor do physical mobility and rural depopulation necessarily affect ethnic or ethno-religious identity, yet social changes and community reorganization resulting from population change have had major effects. A continuum of social change can often parallel a continuum from conservative to liberal social collectivities. For example, among the Anabaptist groups, it has been suggested that even the Hutterites will succumb to some extent, albeit slowly, to urbanization and mass cultural influences; already they have adjusted technologically, unlike the Old Order Amish and the most conservative Mennonites. But the latter in Saskatchewan have abandoned most of their communal villages, sold their poor small farms to larger-scale farmers from more liberal Mennonite factions, and ignored the traditional discouragement of living in town to settle in Swift Current, Hague, and Warman. Increasing numbers of Mennonites now commute into Saskatoon. Some settled in Martensville, the closest community within the Mennonite bloc settlement to Saskatoon, which grew rapidly during the 1960s and 1970s initially as a virtual Mennonite suburb of the city.[17] By 1970, almost two-thirds of General Conference Mennonites in the province were classified as urban, and 41% of them were residents of Saskatoon.[18] And, with construction of a new route of the main highway between Saskatoon and Prince Albert through the heart of the Old Colony, conservative Mennonites lost much of their one-time isolation, and the eventual merging of Mennonite sectarian distinctions became more likely, as did a new identity de-emphasizing traditionalism.

Sociologists have paid frequent attention to social mobility raising the status of immigrants and their descendants, thereby contributing to assimilation. However, in examining rural ethnic and ethno-religious bloc settlements, the relationship between physical and social mobility and ethnic identity change should not be misconstrued. It is possible, after all, to have physical mobility without social mobility or identity change; for example, farm operators might live in urban centres yet maintain ties to rural communities and be active participants in ethnic communities—in fact, many ethnic institutions are primarily urban based. Similarly, it is possible to witness identity change without physical or social mobility, or economic integration without social integration, without affecting social segregation or cultural pluralism. However, in general (with some exceptions), physical mobility has been closely related to social mobility and identity change, especially for the younger generation. Typically, many younger people have asked why they should speak a traditional mother tongue and maintain their group's traditions when they do not want to take over the family farm but get "a better job" in a city, where ethnic identity matters less. In the 1968–72 survey, asked whether "any of your sons or daughters now have professional occupations requiring more education than you have had," respondents revealed that they were generally either in favour of social mobility or rather indifferent to it (except for Hutterites, who were all opposed). Yet respondents who were most conservative about identity also tended to be the most concerned about both physical and social mobility, and they were most likely the eldest respondents.

INTERMARRIAGE AND POPULATION MIXING

Given the degree of ethnic and religious homogeneity in ethnic bloc settlements in Saskatchewan, on the whole there has probably been relatively limited intermarriage among people still residing within these settlements yet considerably more among those who have left them. In the extensive study of ethnic identity change conducted in the north-central region in 1968–72, it was learned that Slavic groups had relatively higher rates of intermarriage: 30.0% of Doukhobor respondents, 26.7% of Polish, and respectively 9.7% and 9.6% of Ukrainian Catholics and Orthodox; German Catholic and French respondents had lower rates (7.9% and 6.5%), Scandinavian and Mennonite respondents very low rates (3.5% and 2.0%); by definition, no Hutterites were intermarried. However, in this study, an appropriate distinction was made between ethnic intermarriage and religious intermarriage as well as intermarriage between similar as opposed to different ethnic and religious groups. Thus, Ukrainians, Poles, and Russians were considered to be fairly similar ethnic groups, and Ukrainian Orthodox, Ukrainian Catholics (Eastern Rite), and Polish Catholics (Western Rite) similar religious groups, as were Russian Doukhobors and Russian Baptists ("Stundists") or Mennonites and German Lutherans.

In general, with certain qualifications, ethnic intermarriage tends to occur between identical or similar religious groups (e.g., French, German, Polish, and Hungarian Roman Catholics) as well as between similar ethnic groups (e.g., Ukrainians, Poles, and Russians); religious intermarriage tends to occur between identical or similar ethnic groups as well as between similar religious groups (e.g., Ukrainian Orthodox and Ukrainian Catholics, or Doukhobors and Russian Baptists, but not necessarily Mennonites and German Lutherans and never Mennonites and Hutterites—though some lapsed Hutterites—*Prairieleut*—redefine themselves as Mennonites). It was found in this survey that there was no case of intermarriage between similar ethnic groups only, also none between people belonging to different ethnic groups but similar religions. Evidently, all of the French respondents and most of the German Catholic respondents who had intermarried did so outside their ethnic group but not outside their Roman Catholic religion. The few Mennonites who had intermarried married spouses from completely different ethnic and religious groups; no instance of marriage between Mennonites and German Lutherans was found. The Ukrainian Orthodox who had intermarried did so for the most part with Ukrainian Catholics and Polish Catholics, though several cases of marriages to spouses from completely different groups were noted. Half of the Ukrainian Catholic respondents were married to spouses from completely different groups; the remainder were married to people of Ukrainian origin but completely different religious affiliation, to Doukhobors, and to Ukrainian Orthodox and Polish Catholics. Virtually all of the intermarried Polish Catholics had Ukrainian Orthodox or Ukrainian Catholic spouses. Although Doukhobors revealed a fairly high rate of intermarriage, two-thirds of those intermarried had married Russian Baptists, and the remaining third had married people claiming Russian origin but not Doukhobor or Russian Baptist religious affiliation. The few Scandinavians who had intermarried were divided three ways, one-third married to German Lutherans, one-third to non-Lutherans of Scandinavian origin, and one-third to people who were neither Lutheran nor Scandinavian. Bear in mind, though, that at the time ethnicity was specified only through the paternal lineage; in cases in which the respondent's parents themselves were intermarried (in either ethnic or religious terms or both), a respondent might not necessarily have been entirely of one ethnicity.

Asked whether they were opposed to ethnic intermarriage (ethnic exogamy) or religious intermarriage (religious exogamy), not surprisingly all of the Hutterites were strongly opposed to both; most interestingly, almost all of the other groups studied were more opposed to religious than ethnic intermarriage. But significant differences were found among the groups: all of the Hutterites, 81.2% of the French, 77.9% of the Scandinavians, 73.4% of the Polish Catholics, 69.5% of the German Catholics, 69.3% of the Mennonites, 68.8% of the Ukrainian Catholics, but only 43.4% of the Ukrainian Orthodox and 35.0% of the Doukhobors expressed their opposition to religious intermarriage. Yet opposition to ethnic intermarriage was generally far less: 56.5% of the Mennonites, 52.3% of the Scandinavians, 45.6% of the French, and strikingly only 10.0% of the German Catholics; moderately less for the Ukrainians—61.7% of Catholics and 41.0% of Orthodox; a higher proportion of Doukhobors expressed concern over ethnic intermarriage (45.0%) than religious intermarriage (35.0%).

Although it might seem complicated to explain the findings from this informative survey conducted more than four decades ago in this one region, nonetheless generalizations can be drawn concerning the rate and effect of intermarriage within bloc settlements throughout the province. A number of factors hinder intermarriage, while other factors encourage it.[19] Both ethnic and religious intermarriage might be lessened because of settlement in blocs limiting contact with people who are ethnically and religiously different; reinforcement of ethnic and religious differences among groups; minimization of primary group contacts among different groups; and conservative family attitudes. Ethnic intermarriage in particular can be lessened by the traditional attempts of ethnic groups to maintain in-group solidarity or integrity through endogamy and prohibition or discouragement of intermarriage (especially among Hutterites, who still retain well-defined socialization processes, dating procedures, and partially arranged marriages in strict compliance with group traditions, as well as among conservative Mennonites, expected to marry members of their own sects or, failing that, at least other Mennonites, and among the most conservative Doukhobors); group prejudices and intergroup conflicts; and fear of assimilation and possibly dilution of what group members consider to be their cultural heritage. Religious intermarriage has been hindered by religious values (especially among Hutterites and other conservative groups or subdivisions); official discouragement of mixed marriages by a particular church (e.g., Roman Catholic; even marriage between Catholics of Western and Eastern Rites—e.g., Poles and Ukrainians—used to be discouraged); and a fear of weakening religious beliefs and corresponding family structures and values (e.g., Roman Catholic).

On the other hand, certain factors have encouraged both ethnic and religious intermarriage: generational differences, with the younger generation rebelling against previous conventions and what they might conceive as meaningless or unimportant traditions, against parental authority, and against a former emphasis on arranged marriage rather than romantic love; an ethnic or religious group finding itself outnumbered in the local setting; social disorganization (whereby less attention is paid to group values); and urbanization and mobility (which tend to promote more opportunities for contact among people of different ethnic origins or religious affiliations). However, intermarriage has been minimal among people still living within bloc settlements. This can simply be because of demographic considerations. For example, someone of Ukrainian descent living within the vast Ukrainian settlements in east-central

Saskatchewan might be more likely to marry another Ukrainian than someone of different ethnicity and religious affiliation, whereas someone of French descent in a relatively small francophone settlement isolated from other such settlements might have some difficulty finding a French spouse. Ethnic intermarriage in particular has been encouraged by repudiation by individuals of an emphasis on ethnic identification and a corresponding decrease in intragroup solidarity; weak endogamous attitudes; and a decline of membership in ethnic associations and congregations. Finally, religious intermarriage has been encouraged by a decline of religious authority or more generally by secularization.

Is intermarriage—or more specifically intermarriage between completely different ethnic and religious groups—increasing in the rural bloc settlements of Saskatchewan? Some sociologists, commenting generally, have suggested that "intermarriage is not likely to become commonplace as long as a substantial proportion of a group still lives in segregated colonies" yet that "intermarriage is even increasing in rural areas remote from urbanization influences."[20] In all likelihood, both of these contrasting opinions can apply to the bloc settlements in Saskatchewan, though intermarriage between different rather than similar groups still seems limited. It is hard, of course, to generalize when the rate of intermarriage fluctuates from one ethno-religious group to another and even from one local community to another. Yet one can conclude that in general ethnic intermarriage seems to occur before religious intermarriage. For example, the rate of ethnic intermarriage was higher than that of religious intermarriage among French and German Catholics in the 1968–72 study, just as a far higher proportion of respondents in these groups opposed religious than ethnic intermarriage. Intermarriage, moreover, tends to be cumulative; the proportion of intermarriages in one generation is likely to increase with each succeeding generation.

Doubtless some intermarriage did occur at an early date in Saskatchewan bloc settlements. As early as 1918, intermarriage was described as "a daily occurrence," and in 1931 the intermarriage of "Russian" Mennonites and Ukrainians was noted in the area east of Rosthern.[21] Nonetheless, according to statistical data in 1921, a far higher proportion of men and women of Northern European origin (43.4% of Dutch origin, 34.5% of Danish, 22.6% of Norwegian, 21.5% of Swedish, and 16.8% of German, with the rate for women slightly higher than that for men) had married people of British origin than had men and women of Eastern European origin (just 4.4% of Russian origin, 3.6% of Polish, 1.3% of Austro-Hungarian, 0.7% of Ukrainian, and 0.5% of Galician, with the rate for women generally slightly lower).[22] However, by 1961, the national rates for ethnic endogamy did not reveal such a clear distinction between Northern and Eastern European groups (at the time, 54.5% of Dutch, 52.0% of Germans, and 31.2% of Scandinavians were married to spouses of their own ethnic groups, compared with 61.8% of Ukrainians, 49.0% of Poles, and 47.7% of Russians).[23] However, the survey conducted in 1968–72 in Saskatchewan seems to have indicated that the rates for intermarriage were far lower within the bloc settlement context (though admittedly many young people leave these settlements to later become intermarried and live in cities).

What effect does intermarriage tend to have on ethnic identification? Sociologists have associated intermarriage with rapid assimilation and acculturation, alienation from the individual's own group, adoption of the larger society's standards regarding mate selection, and entry into voluntary associations and institutions of the larger society.[24] This might be true in urban areas; however, given the relative slowness of intermarriage within the rural bloc settlement context (in the 1968–72 study, just 1.5% of the total sample had married completely outside both their ethnic and their religious groups, if those married to similar groups were not counted), intermarriage in these settlements has had little to do with assimilation—in that study, most of the relatively few intermarriages (6.9% of the total sample) were between similar ethnic and/or religious groups. Of course, these data do not include people who had left the settlements and were living elsewhere, a higher proportion of whom were likely intermarried. In that study, even reverse assimilation through intermarriage was occasionally noted, such as a British-origin man in Debden and a woman in Bellevue who had become primarily French-speaking like their spouses since French was then the common language of these communities and a German Catholic woman in the St. Julien area who was learning and often using the Ukrainian language of her husband. Nonetheless, the prevalent generalization that can be made, in either urban or rural areas, is that intermarriage—especially between very different groups—in all likelihood serves to lessen ethnic identification, though there have been exceptions, families raising their children to be proud of both their ethnic or religious heritages, headed by parents who continue to be active participants in their own ethnic cultures and traditional religious affiliations.

THE STRENGTH AND PERSISTENCE OF ETHNIC IDENTIFICATION

Most of the prairie area of Saskatchewan was rapidly incorporated into ethnic bloc settlements that revealed remarkable ethnic diversity. Moreover, a large proportion of the rural population continues to reside within settlements that reflect their particular ethnic origins. But how "ethnic" are all of these people today? The answer is necessarily complicated.

Ethnic or ethno-religious bloc settlements are still today, or hitherto have been, significant or functional forms of social organization as regional variations of ethnicity within the Canadian context, yet this significance is changing and should not be viewed as static. If group settlements have been changing, why, where, how, and when has this change been occurring? Within a particular region or area, have different groups exhibited different rates of ethnic identity change? Have bloc settlements established by a particular group differed? Have communities within these settlements differed? Bloc settlements can persist or be in a gradual process of dissolution; moreover, while settlements might persist in demographic terms, rural ethnic identities might be reinterpreted. Although it is possible to discern factors that contribute to persistence or dissolution, considerable variation can be noted in comparing the settlements of particular ethnic groups.

Specifically, which people in which communities within which settlements of which ethnic groups are still "segregated," reflect "multiculturalism," "pluralism," or "accommodation," or are becoming "assimilated"? However, describing just how and why ethnic identity tends to change in the bloc settlements is no simple task; rather, it involves a complicated interrelating of factors. In general, assimilation can be viewed as a reorientation of ethnic group members from an orientation primarily toward the ethnic group to one primarily toward the general (Canadian) society. More specifically, assimilation refers to identity change. But what exactly is changing? Which factors comprise identity? Sociologists as well as other social scientists have tended to focus on a number of factors that together or separately can define ethnic identification: physical appearance (which might be less relevant for European-origin groups than in distinguishing among broad racial categories, real or imagined, which through the process of racialization can be given more social than scientific significance), group or outside emphasis on ethnicity (represented in ethnic "origins"), familiarity with and use of a unique traditional language (mother tongue), a specific religious affiliation historically associated with a particular group, and a traditional group culture (which can include unique customs, folkways, values and associated practices, foods, folk music and dance, arts, etc.). So ethnicity can be quite complicated to define; suffice it to say that certain factors can be regarded as vital to the identification of one group, while others are more salient for another group.[25] In Saskatchewan, certain ethnic groups have regarded the preservation of an ability to communicate in a traditional mother tongue to be the essence of group identification, whereas others do not place such an emphasis on language or might from the beginning largely share the prevalent English language (e.g., groups as diverse as Scots and American-origin Blacks). Some groups are defined as ethno-religious groups (notably Hutterites, Doukhobors, and traditionally Mennonites, though this term can also be applied in a looser sense to German Catholics, Ukrainian Orthodox, etc.). Moreover, certain groups have clearly retained strong and easily identifiable cultures for generations while some have not in Saskatchewan; some groups devote much time and effort to maintaining their cultural traditions, while other groups seem to be less organized. There is considerable variation among ethnic cultures in terms of their relative strength.

In the 1968–72 study of changing ethnic identification conducted in the bloc settlements of north-central Saskatchewan, significant differences among groups were observed. In the total sample of 1,000 respondents, 25.5% thought that it was imperative to preserve identity under any circumstances; 42.6% were in favour of preservation yet somewhat resigned to loss; 24.6% seemed indifferent; and 7.3% were opposed. Hutterites were predictably the most conservative. A high proportion of Polish Catholics felt strongly in favour of preservation, as did many Ukrainians. Most of the Mennonites, Scandinavians, French, and Doukhobors were in favour yet resigned to loss. The German Catholics were divided, with one-third resigned, one-third indifferent, and one-third opposed. Again, when asked their opinions on the loss of ethnic identification among their youth, all of the Hutterites reported that there had been little or no loss; one-third of the French and Ukrainian Catholics thought that there had been little of no loss, and most of the rest of the respondents in these groups noted only a minor loss; and almost half of the German Catholics and three-quarters of the Scandinavians suggested a major loss.

The extent to which a reorientation of group members has been apparent in intermarriage across ethnic or religious lines was examined earlier in this chapter. In sum, the pattern of ethnic settlement in Saskatchewan has effectively reduced the opportunity for intermarriage between ethnic or religious groups, though attitudes toward such intermarriage have progressively become more open; moreover, with urbanization, interethnic contacts have been increasing. Religious intermarriage has long tended to be more evident than ethnic or especially racial intermarriage. Thus, German Catholics, for example, have intermarried with Polish, Hungarian, French, and other Catholics. Yet people of relatively similar ethnic origins have also tended to mix—for example, Ukrainians with Poles or Russians or people of various British, Scandinavian, or German origins. A steadily increasing proportion of Saskatchewan residents now claims more than a single ethnic origin. It is likely that, as the population becomes more mixed, emphasis on ethnic identity will decrease. Locally, it is becoming increasingly common, especially in mixed communities (e.g., between two ethnic settlements), to find people of one particular ethnic origin with spouses of a different ethnic origin, hence people with surnames indicative of one ethnicity who might speak the language of a different ethnicity.

Today it is questionable, of course, to what extent people within bloc settlements still retain traditional languages. Language retention, however, tends to be highly variable, depending on which ethnic group is considered. The *Fransaskois* community has tended to strongly emphasize the ability to speak French; to be truly *Fransaskois* has implied being francophone, reinforced by official language status in Canada, schools and broadcasts in French, and meetings of provincial organizations such as the ACFC (now the ACF) conducted in French. Yet less than half of the French-origin population still speaks French, and a decreasing number of formerly francophone parishes still offer services primarily, much less exclusively, in French. Eastern European ethnic groups have tended to retain their traditional languages from generation to generation more than people of German or Scandinavian origins, for various reasons, including better-defined bloc settlements, strong ethnic cultures, and the degree of perceived social difference from other Saskatchewan people. People of Scandinavian origins have tended not to use Scandinavian languages very often or to resist intermarriage with the larger population of British origins. The one-time emphasis on German culture in Saskatchewan was dealt a harsh blow during two world wars with Germany, making for a sharp decrease in the ability to speak German by the second or third generation. Yet, to some extent, this trend has been reversed with the immigration of German immigrants to the cities in postwar years, and there has been a re-emphasis on German language and culture through the Saskatchewan German Council. In general, language retention rates tend to be highest among recent immigrants, who are almost exclusively urban residents. In the rural population, familiarity with traditional languages has inexorably declined from first to second to third generation, though at very different rates for specific ethnic groups; the only group not affected by this generalization has been the Hutterites.

In the 1968–72 study, significant group differences in traditional language retention were observed. All of the Hutterites used their unique German dialect frequently. The highest proportion for any ethnic group speaking only their mother tongue was found among the French (9.9%); 78.2% were still using French quite often, and almost all (99.0%) could speak French. Among German Catholics, none spoke only German, 29.0% were still using German, yet still a high proportion (93.2%) were at least somewhat familiar with some German. Mennonites were rather more conservative, with a few elderly respondents (1.6%) speaking just German, 68.9% continuing to use their

Low German dialect fairly often, and 97.2% still able to speak German. A considerable proportion of older Ukrainian Orthodox (6.0%) and Ukrainian Catholics (3.2%) spoke only Ukrainian; many Ukrainian Orthodox (62.6%) and Catholics (68.8%) were still using Ukrainian fairly often, and all of the Orthodox and a high proportion (98.7%) of the Catholics were familiar with Ukrainian. Similarly, among Polish Catholics, 6.7% spoke just Polish, 86.7% were often speaking Polish, while all were familiar with Polish. As for Doukhobors, 5.0% (elderly) were speaking only Russian, 70.0% were speaking Russian often, and 95.0% could speak at least some Russian. Respondents of Scandinavian origin differed markedly in language use: none spoke only a Scandinavian language, 37.2% were still speaking such a language at least fairly often (most likely because of return family visits to Scandinavia), and a surprisingly high proportion (89.5%) were familiar to some extent with a Scandinavian language.

These data, now four decades old, reveal that at the time ethnic language familiarity was still prevalent in these bloc settlements, yet substantial differences among groups were noted in actual language use. Hutterites preferred to speak their German dialect at home, in the colony, and outside it among themselves, but all could speak English. The highest proportion of French (48.0%) preferred to speak French both at home and in the local community yet were bilingual; significant proportions, though, were speaking French at home yet preferred mostly English beyond the home (20.3%) or spoke mainly English both at home and beyond (20.8%). This was also the case for Mennonites, a slight majority of whom (52.5%) were bilingual and preferred *Plattdeutsch* both at home and outside it, while significant numbers were bilingual, preferring German at home but mostly English in the community 14.8%) or English both at home and outside it (28.3%). Ukrainians tended to be more mixed in their language preferences: a higher proportion of Catholics (44.2%) than Orthodox (33.7%) were bilingual and preferred primarily Ukrainian both at home and outside it; roughly the same proportions of Orthodox and Catholics (respectively 22.9% and 21.4%) preferred mostly Ukrainian at home but English in the community; more Orthodox (37.3%) than Catholics (29.9%) preferred English both at home and outside it. Polish Catholics differed in that a third (33.3%) preferred Polish both at home and beyond it; almost half (46.7%) Polish at home but English in the community; and a relatively smaller proportion (13.3%) English rather than Polish both at home and outside it. Similarly, the largest number of Doukhobors (40.0%) preferred to speak Russian at home but English outside it, compared with a quarter who preferred Russian both at home and in the community and another quarter who preferred English both at home and beyond it. The largest number of German Catholics (64.2%) were bilingual yet preferred to speak English both at home and outside it; smaller proportions preferred German at home and out of it (13.7%), spoke German at home but English in the community (15.3%), or could only speak English (6.8%). Similarly, Scandinavian respondents largely favoured speaking English both at home and outside it (52.3%); smaller proportions preferred a Scandinavian language both at home and in the community (25.6%), spoke such a language at home but English outside it (11.6%), or were not at all familiar with their traditional mother tongues (10.5%). In the total sample of 1,000 respondents, 3.6% could only speak their mother tongues, 38.5% preferred that language both at home and in the community, 18.3% spoke a traditional language at home but English in the community, 36.2% were bilingual yet preferred English both at home and outside it, and just 3.4% were only familiar with English. Of course, these findings are highly subject to interpretation. There were in all groups studied except Hutterites marked differences in the degree of claimed familiarity with a traditional mother tongue, moreover between younger and older respondents. So, in the forty years since that detailed survey was conducted in all groups studied (again with the notable exception of Hutterites), it is highly probable that traditional language use has declined, though to a different extent depending on the group (and even the local community). Nonetheless, these interesting data reveal the relative strength of traditional mother tongues among various ethnic groups in the bloc settlements of at least one region in Saskatchewan back in the late 1960s and early 1970s.

Changes over time, and among generations, of personal names can be related to language change as a part of ethnic identity change. As linguistic assimilation occurs, personal names tend to undergo change and therefore become progressively less reliable indicators of ethnic identity. Name changing might not necessarily be a deliberate attempt to obscure one's ethnic origin; rather, it might be a practical attempt to alleviate the embarrassment of people of other ethnic origins not being able to pronounce a name typical of a particular ethnic group. Given names tend to change before family surnames. Yet either type of name can be altered without being converted entirely into, or exchanged for, an English name; the name can be shortened for convenience, or the spelling can be changed for easy phonetic pronunciation by English speakers. There has been very little changing of surnames in the rural bloc settlement context. Yet significant differences exist among ethnic groups with reference to changing given names. For example, in the north-central region, a generation ago, among the francophone farmers in the Duck Lake–St-Louis settlement (most of whom were relatively older generation), typical French first names were common (Pierre, René, Emile, Yvonne, Marcel, Antoine, Gaston, Napoleon, André, Jean, François, etc.). Among the German Catholic farmers in St. Peter's Colony, German given names at the time were still numerous (Johannes, Bernard, Ernst, Alois, Reinhold, Otto, Herman, Gottlied, Anton, etc.). Hungarian farmers scattered in settlements around Wakaw still bore Hungarian given names (Nandor, Gaza, Ezydor, Bela, Ferencz, Istvan, Mihal/Myhaly, Emre/Emeric, Sandor, Janos, etc.). Among the Mennonite farmers in the Saskatchewan Valley settlement, German given names were still common (Waldemar, Karl, Helmuth, Konrad, Ludwig, Klaus, Werner, Ernst, etc.). Biblical names were also common, whether used in the German language (Johannes, Jakob, Abram, etc.) or as English versions (John, Jacob, Abe, Isaac, Peter, etc.). Occasional Latin given names were also used by both German Catholics (Aurelius, Marcellus) and Mennonites (Cornelius). Among the Ukrainian and Polish farmers in the Redberry settlement, use of traditional Slavic names seemed to be lessening, though numerous varieties were still noted (Wasyl, Dmytro, Orest, Jaroslav, Bohdan, Slawko, Taras, Metro, etc.). But there was increasing use of English translations of popular saints' names (Steve, Peter, John, Mike, Paul, Nick, etc.). Doukhobor farmers tended to adopt the same few saints' names translated into English; few retained Russian given names (Malasha, Sergius, Kuzma)—even in the older generation, English translations of common Russian saints' names were far more frequent (particularly Sam, John, and Peter). Although family names among Norwegians were retained, first names tended to become anglicized often by the second generation and certainly by the third, though occasionally typical Norwegian given names were still used. But numerous first- and many second-generation farmers in the Hanley-Outlook and Birch Hills settlements had distinctly Norwegian given names (including Ole, Olaf, Trygve, Einar, Nils, Karsten, Arne, Lumen, Lars, Sven, Helmar/Hilmer, Kristian, Jens, Joar, Bjorn, Knut, Torger, Ingval[d], Aagot, Axel, Ivar/Iver, Halvor, Sivert, Sigurd, Torbjorn, Karl, Magne, Gunnar, Oskar, Arvid, Gudrun, Jorgen, Thor, etc.). In the first generation, and sometimes in the second, their wives also bore typical Norwegian names (Ragna, Bronla, Olava, Olina, Guni, Karen, Petra, Magda, Gida, Olga, Britha, Matilda, etc.). But with another generation or two, use of traditional first names typifying each ethnic group in the settlements has changed substantially; in most groups, the younger farmers, and especially their children, now have common English names, though there remains prevalent use of saints' names (often as nicknames) among Slavic people and biblical names among Mennonites, while among francophones French names remain predominant.

Religious affiliation is often closely related to ethnic identification. Although there is a subjective element in ethnicity (the degree to which the member of an ethnic group chooses to emphasize and preserve his or her ethnic identity), ethnicity is primarily objectively defined, whereas religion is primarily subjectively defined. An individual might be objectively classified in a certain ethnic category on the basis of specific criteria, and ethnic identity is inherited, whereas he or she can choose to accept, reject, or change a religious affiliation. But if language is usually (but not always) a key factor in ethnic identification, so too is religion. In fact, religious affiliation is often so closely associated with ethnic identification that groups that have founded bloc settlements on the prairies might often not be defined simply as ethnic groups but more specifically as ethno-religious groups. When ethnic identification is entirely concomitant with religious identification, we have ethno-religious groups in a strict sense, such as Doukhobors, Hutterites, and historically Mennonites (though contemporary Mennonites, especially in urban areas, are becoming less defined as German origin); virtually all of the members of such a group also share a particular (perhaps compound) ethnic origin—for example, to be Doukhobor implies Russian origin, and to leave a Hutterite colony permanently implies that one is no longer Hutterite. Yet groups can also be considered to be ethno-religious in a more general sense: Scandinavians, Ukrainians, Poles, and French are ethnic groups, but traditionally the vast majority of members of each group share a particular religious affiliation—thus, Scandinavians are Lutherans, Ukrainians are Ukrainian Orthodox or Catholic, and Poles and French are Roman Catholic.

Many of the functions of religion are oriented toward the preservation of ethnic identity, as sociologists have explained. Religion has contributed to a sense of identity in an age of depersonalization; it has been a nationalistic force and has assumed the role of protector of ethnic identity; it has promoted social integration; it has attempted to validate customs and values; it has inculcated values through socialization; it has affirmed the dignity of ethnic group members who might be considered by non-members to have low status; it has tended to be a pillar of conservatism; and it has often encouraged conscious social isolation from outsiders.[26] Half a century ago one prominent social psychologist commented pointedly that

> The chief reason why religion becomes the focus of prejudice is that it usually stands for more than faith. ... It is the pivot of the cultural tradition of a group. ... The clergy of a church may and often do become defenders of a culture. ... In defending the absolutes of their faith, they tend to defend their in-group as a whole, finding in the absolutes of their faith justification for the secular practices of their in-group. Not infrequently they justify and sweeten ethnic prejudices with religious sanctions. ... Piety may thus be a convenient mask for prejudices which intrinsically have nothing to do with religion. ... Whereas ... conflicts between religions may occasionally occur, most of what is called religious bigotry is in fact the result of a confusion between ethnocentric self-interest and religion, with the latter called upon to rationalize and justify the former. ... In its institutional organization, therefore, religion is divisive. ... The divisions that exist make it easy to contaminate the universalistic creeds of religion with irrelevant considerations of ... national origin, cultural differences, and race.[27]

On that final point, it is relevant to recognize that a religious denomination or sect can be primarily universalistic or ethnocentric in its orientation; it can be a universal or folk religion. In Saskatchewan, a distinction can be drawn among ethnic parishes of general inter- or transethnic denominations (French, Polish, Hungarian, or German Catholic parishes; various Scandinavian or German Lutheran congregations; etc.), autonomous ethnic sub-denominations (exemplified in Ukrainian Catholics), and independent ethnic or nationality denominations (Ukrainian or Greek Orthodox etc.). A further distinction can be drawn between juridical and non-juridical ethnic parishes, the former being parishes officially designated as serving the interests of a particular ethnic group, the latter unofficially or coincidentally doing so (congregation members share the same ethnicity). In addition to these distinctions, certain religious organizations represent divisions of formerly united denominations, while others are inclusive of a variety of sects and subdivisions, and still others are related to various similar churches and sects that are offshoots from the parent organization.[28] To a considerable extent, the proliferation of church schisms and sectarianism can best be explained by variations in values and practices even within an ethnically homogeneous society rather than simply by theological influences. For example, Mennonites represent one branch of Anabaptism, Hutterites another. Mennonites in Saskatchewan became divided into relatively conservative Old Colony Mennonites, *Bergthaler* and *Sommerfelder*, Church of God in Christ (Holdeman Mennonites), and Conservative Mennonites; more middle-of-the-road Mennonite Brethren churches (including *Krimmer*, Evangelical, and *Bruderthaler* Mennonite Brethren); and more liberal General Conference Mennonites (including the original *Rosenort Gemeinde*). Moreover, many people of Mennonite origin have joined evangelical churches that often have pastors of Mennonite origin: in the Saskatchewan Valley settlement, Alliance Churches in Rosthern and Martensville; the Baptist Church in Martensville; Apostolic Church of the Living God in Duck Lake; Evangelical Free Community Church in Osler; Martensville Mission Church; Evangelical Missionary Church in Rosthern; Evangelical Bible Churches in Dalmeny, Langham, and Waldheim; Gospel Churches in Hague, Hepburn, and Warman; Osler

CONCLUSION: CHANGING TIMES

Mission Chapel; Living Faith Pentecostal Church in Rosthern, Christian Life Pentecostal Church in Warman. ...

Religion can either cause or result from social change. To some extent over time, there has been a movement away from any form of religious belief, in other words a general secularization. Another form of religious change is conversion from traditional religious affiliations. In Saskatchewan, both secularization and conversion of ethnic groups might have been related to forces such as assimilation in schools, migration and mobility, intermarriage, and the preoccupation of once more ethnic-oriented religious groups with secular concerns.[29] But to what extent have ethnic groups in this province been moving away from their traditional religious affiliations? It is instructive to compare data for 1941 and 1961.[30] In these two decades, there was little change in the proportion of French-origin population who were Roman Catholics: 86.4% in 1941 and 83.7% in 1961. Or German-origin population who were Catholics: 42.0% and 40.3%; but there was a slight increase in Mennonites (5.2% to 7.4%) and a more pronounced decline in Lutherans (31.9% to 25.0%); altogether the proportion of Germans claiming to be Catholics, Mennonites, and Lutherans declined from 79.1% to 72.7%. Among Ukrainians, there was a major decline in adherence to traditional religious affiliations—less so for Ukrainian Orthodox (36.6% to 30.0%) than Ukrainian Catholics (55.7%, including those attending Roman Catholic churches, down to 38.0%); thus, in just twenty years, the proportion of Ukrainians who were Orthodox and Catholics fell sharply from 92.3% to 68.0%. A significant decline in the propensity of people of Polish origin to be Roman Catholics can also be observed (from 79.9% to 65.2%). Relatively little change was apparent for Russians who were Doukhobors or members of other Protestant churches such as Baptist: 46.0% to 42.1%. When more than two-thirds (67.1%) of people of Scandinavian origins were Lutherans in 1941, twenty years later fewer than half (45.3%) were. What seems so striking in these data is that, to a greater or lesser extent, even more than half a century ago, every one of these ethnic groups revealed a decline in adherence to the traditional religious affiliation.

The study conducted in the bloc settlements of north-central Saskatchewan during 1968–72 revealed major differences among the ethno-religious groups studied in frequency of attendance at ethnic-oriented parishes: all of the Hutterites attended regularly, compared with 93.7% of the German Catholics, 91.1% of the French Catholics, 87.2% of the Scandinavian Lutherans, 86.1% of the Mennonites, 81.8% of the Ukrainian Catholics, 69.9% of the Ukrainian Orthodox, 55.0% of the Doukhobors, and 53.3% of the Polish Catholics. Among the Ukrainian Orthodox, 18.1% reported that they attended sometimes/usually and 10.8% rarely; among the Doukhobors, 20.0% attended sometimes/usually, 10.0% rarely, and 15.0% never; and among the Polish Catholics, a third attended sometimes/usually and 13.3% rarely. These data were subject to some interpretation, however: in the smallest and most isolated churches, services were held less and less frequently, thereby limiting the opportunities to attend on a more regular basis. But this in itself is indicative of social change.

Will religion persist when an emphasis on ethnicity has declined? Or can religion, or at least an adherence to a traditional affiliation, be lost even when ethnicity persists? The foregoing analysis of intermarriage suggested that intermarrying across ethnic lines seemed to occur more often than across religious lines, perhaps implying that religion is more important to people than ethnicity. Group settlements based on traditional religious beliefs have tended to survive the forces of assimilation more effectively than group settlements that were essentially ethnic in character, especially when religion served to reinforce ethnic separateness.[31] However, this does not necessarily preclude the possibility of a decline of religious and/or ethnic emphases in the bloc settlements—in other words, of these settlements, or certain types of them, becoming progressively less ethnic or religious in a traditional sense.

Although language and religious beliefs can be considered important aspects of an ethnic group's culture, the sum of the customs of similar individuals in a group or minority has been more specifically defined as their culture or subculture.[32] In turn, customs can be equated with various folkways contributing to the uniqueness of each ethnic or ethno-religious group's identity. Depending on the particular ethnic group, these customs can consist of a wide variety of traditional practices, perhaps including performing arts (folk music, singing, and dancing), traditional clothing, foods (cooking and eating traditional foods unique to the group), crafts and arts (traditional woodcarving, embroidery, and other handicrafts and arts), furniture (homemade furniture with traditional designs), norms and values (pacifism and group prohibition of smoking, drinking, dancing, and immodest dress), home décor, village layout and community organization, traditional farming practices and tools, recreational activities, ceremonies and social gatherings, family practices (behaviour at meals, deference to elders, family authority structure), and so on. To repeat, some groups continue to exhibit rich and diverse ethnic cultures, others less so. Yet, with respect to social change, even those groups having many sorts of traditions have often struggled to maintain them: for example, how many Ukrainians in Ukrainian settlements continue to prepare Ukrainian foods, make *kylymy* (woven rugs or mats), decorate *pysanka* (Easter eggs), celebrate special occasions, practise woodcarving, join Ukrainian choirs and dance troupes, or decorate their homes in a traditional manner? Obviously, many still do—many traditional practices that typify most ethnic groups in the province have been noted in detail, not only longer-settled groups rooted in their own bloc settlements but also more recent urban minorities—but the question is whether there has been any lessening of such practices with each new generation.

Whatever might have been the ability to maintain ethnic traditions and promote knowledge of and interest in the history of ethnic settlements in Saskatchewan, the influence that these settlements have had on the cultural geography of Saskatchewan can hardly go unnoticed. Although it is unfortunate that many rural churches have been closed, abandoned, or even removed over the years, together with country schoolhouses and community halls that were once the very foci of community life, Saskatchewan still retains numerous examples of striking ethnic architecture such as the many onion-domed Ukrainian churches that dot the countryside. Even patterns of settlement might occasionally have tended to be unique to specific ethnic groups, such as the *strassendorf* line villages of Mennonites (and formerly of Doukhobors), the *rang* or riverlot pattern of settlement that characterized the Batoche and St-Laurent-Grandin Métis settlement, and the orderly arrangement of buildings in Hutterite colonies.

DEMOGRAPHIC-ECOLOGICAL CONSIDERATIONS

The strength of ethnic culture and identification can depend to some extent on the demographic strength of particular ethnic groups. Does a specific ethnic group form a significant part of the population of Canada or Saskatchewan? Does the population of a particular local community consist completely of one ethnic group, two or three, or more? How do demographic-ecological conditions such as vital statistics (age, generation, gender, occupation, and education), community differences (in terms of size, homogeneity, and location), and community decline and mobility (rural depopulation and physical mobility, social mobility, and delocalization or the eradication of rural focal points) relate to identity change?

Again, some pertinent conclusions can be drawn from the detailed study in 1968–72 of changing ethnic identity in the bloc settlements of north-central Saskatchewan. Age differences among respondents in the ethno-religious groups studied were significant, with the obvious exception of the Hutterites. In virtually all of the other groups, the older the respondents, the stronger the emphasis on ethnic identity preservation, and the differences were striking: in all groups except German Catholics, more than 90% of respondents aged seventy and older favoured ethnic identity preservation (69.5% of older German Catholics did), whereas among middle-aged (thirty to forty-nine) and senior adult (fifty to sixty-nine) respondents the range was mostly between three-quarters and all (but only respectively 36.5% and 20.5% of German Catholics in these two age categories), among young adults in their twenties close to or just over half of French, Mennonite, and Ukrainian respondents (but all Hutterites and very few, just 6.7%, of German Catholics), and among teenagers wide variation (all of the Hutterites, 45.0% of Ukrainian Catholics, 35.7% of Mennonites, 28.6% of Ukrainian Orthodox, and none of Doukhobors, Scandinavians, or German Catholics). Similarly, with the obvious exception of Hutterites, the older the respondent, the greater the likelihood of speaking a traditional mother tongue and of being opposed to or concerned about both ethnic and religious intermarriage.

Taking generational differences into account, all first-generation (immigrant) Hutterites, Ukrainians, Poles, and Doukhobors favoured identity preservation, as did a strong majority of Mennonites (95.3%), French (87.5%), and German Catholics (73.0%). Of the second generation (first Canadian born), all of the Hutterites and approximately between 80% and 90% of all other groups (but only 34.6% of German Catholics) favoured identity preservation. The third generation, however, was very mixed, ranging from all of the Hutterites to 60%–69% of Ukrainian Orthodox, Mennonites, Scandinavians, and Doukhobors, just over half of Ukrainian Catholics, but only about one in ten German Catholics. Again, with the exception of the Hutterites, the immigrants were far more likely than the third generation to speak a traditional mother tongue, attend an ethnic parish on a regular basis, and express their opposition to both ethnic and religious intermarriage.

An initial hypothesis that a higher proportion of females would support ethnic identity preservation was substantiated to a limited extent among German Catholics, Mennonites, Ukrainians, and Scandinavians; however, Poles and Doukhobors to some extent countered this hypothesis, while Hutterites and French were equally divided. With the exception of German Catholics, full-time farmers tended to be consistently among the more conservative respondents. In general, the higher the level of education attained, the less the emphasis placed on ethnic identification, except for university-educated informants; this was likely because the "professional" supporters of ethnicity (clergy, teachers, participants in ethnic voluntary associations) tended to have a university education.

That study also revealed some differences among communities in attitudes toward identity preservation. French, Mennonite, and Ukrainian communities tended to be divided fairly equally between those that were very conservative and those that were generally conservative; very few were found not to be conservative. On the other hand, just a few German Catholic communities were classified as conservative; by far the largest number were not conservative. A single Scandinavian community was deemed to be very conservative, while several others were generally conservative. Interestingly, no correlation was found between the size of each community and the strength of ethnic identification; nor was a correlation found between the degree of ethnic homogeneity of the community and the strength of ethnic identification—however, in situations in which the community was divided between two ethnic groups, ethnic and religious consciousness and rivalry tended to become more intense. For example, in one community divided equally to the last person between French and Ukrainians, the French residents tended to favour shopping at the "French store," Ukrainians at the "Ukrainian store." A roadside crucifix once erected by the French was removed by the Ukrainians. The sign on a new rural municipality office was in Canada's two official languages, but the Ukrainians argued that this unreasonably favoured the French, so Ukrainian was added to the sign. When a local pub owner who was French put up a bilingual banner announcing the opening of his renovated pub, Ukrainians pulled it down. Even more dramatic was a case in which rivalry between Ukrainian Catholics and Orthodox in one community led to the clandestine removal of the second church![33] Such incidents surely were the exception rather than the rule; ethnic groups in Saskatchewan soon learned to live together in shared communities and rural areas where settlements overlapped.

Finally, did community location have anything to do with ethnic identity preservation? The relative degree of accessibility versus marginality of particular rural communities could have played a role, if we can hypothesize that the more isolated communities and areas were the most likely to retain strong ethnic identification.[34] Accessibility has been closely related to physical mobility; with improved access to larger towns and cities, the long-standing isolation of many small communities has lessened or ended, with the inevitable result of increased population mixing (not the least of young people in consolidated schools now serving larger areas originally settled by a variety of ethno-religious groups). But likely more influential has been the omnipresent penetration of television (primarily in English) affecting interests, styles, parochialism, home values, and expectations.

ASSIMILATION AND MULTICULTURALISM
The bloc settlements of Saskatchewan have changed, over the course of more than a century, from relative segregation (somewhat imposed, somewhat voluntary) to assimilation (originally enforced through Anglo-conformity, then later occurring through

increased contact among groups as well as conformity to national Canadian expectations) and finally to multiculturalism (as a national and provincial policy and a fact of contemporary life).

Clearly, during the early years of settlement, Canadian identity was largely considered to be British identity, despite rapidly increasing evidence to the contrary. At that time, ethnic stereotyping by the British-origin population was prevalent, as were ethnocentrism (a feeling that one's particular ethnic group and race are superior to other ones) and xenophobia (fear and mistrust of "strangers").[35] "Anglo-conformity" has been described as a broad term "which may be used to cover a variety of viewpoints about assimilation and immigration. All have as a central assumption the desirability of maintaining English institutions, the English language, and English-oriented cultural patterns as dominant and standard [in Canadian life]."[36] Yet Smith has argued that "even a charter group like the British enjoyed few advantages when it came to settlement. ... The virtues of race and empire, the cornerstones of British values to the passionate minority who proclaimed them, were never widely endorsed."[37] In the Canadian Prairies, there has been a gradual shift from a primary emphasis on Anglo-conformity to a liberal policy acknowledging and emphasizing cultural pluralism. But just how and why these pro-British attitudes gradually became inculcated into a broader nationalism emphasizing a synthetic Canadian identity is a good question; even as late as the 1960s, Canada was still being defined officially as bilingual and bicultural, shared by British and French Canadians, "*les deux races fondatrices du Canada*," who were called "charter groups," the founders of Confederation (apparently, the many First Nations and other Aboriginal groups, not to mention Canadians of other ethnic origins, were not consulted). Yet the official Canadian and Saskatchewan policies on immigration and ethnic diversity and settlement have actually wavered between assimilation and multiculturalism for decades. As late as 1949 (if not even more recently), the federal government's willingness to grant landed immigrant status was still largely dependent on assimilability to Anglo-conformity; although Canada never officially had the rigid quota system of the United States, it certainly long had a hierarchy of preferences governing who exactly would settle Canada. Yet back in 1931 the Saskatchewan Royal Commission on Immigration and Settlement seemed to cautiously acknowledge a pluralist viewpoint: "Assimilation ... is at bottom a problem in adaptation. This, however, is not a one-sided process. It is just as important that we should adapt ourselves to what is best in what the newcomers bring from their homelands, as that they should adapt themselves to what is worthwhile in our economic and cultural life."[38]

English Canadians frequently dictated their doctrine of Anglo-conformity in Saskatchewan. The remarks of one exuberant writer from Wakaw in 1932 should suffice as an illustration of the direction of assimilation toward the British group rather than a Canadian identity:

> This district, settled by the pioneers of many tongues and races, has contributed no little part toward the establishment of a social organization built upon British principles in this small corner of a vast new land. Our individual pioneer, be he ... Hungarian ... Ukrainian ... French ... Pole ... German ...

has contributed to the growth of this British social organization. ... Here's to the worth of our pioneers! ... Here's to the memory of pioneers! You gave of your youth and your worthwhile years to the white-hot iron, which with branding sears the mark of Great Britain's glory![39]

J. Hawkes, a Saskatchewan historian writing in 1924, was less enthusiastic: in his opinion, European immigrants

never really become British, and have no interest in the country outside their material interests; they occupy land, and receive wages, which should by rights belong to our people; and it is a piece of folly to encourage foreign immigration when there is a surplus population in the British Isles of our own race who could profitably occupy the land, and provide the labour necessary for our development.[40]

The central problem, in the eyes of the British Canadian authorities, was how to go about melding such a diversity of cultural heritages into the Canadian nation. Even the prime minister at the time, Sir John A. Macdonald, commented that "A British subject I was born and a British subject I will die."[41] (Many of his fellow Scots today would have a different view, being Scottish nationalists.) As one historian has written,

In a world where the sun never set on the British Empire, where Britannia ruled the waves and kept the lesser breeds from warring with each other, it was self-evident to every British subject that being British was the best thing in the world to be. It was, *ergo*, taken for granted that the "foreigners", having been given the chance to "become British", would rush to do so with all prudent haste. Complete assimilation would happen, presumably, by some divinely sparked process of osmosis, despite the fact that the newcomers were hived away in ethnic blocs, almost totally out of contact with other blocs or the Anglo-Saxon population.[42]

American sociologist Milton Gordon has suggested that in the United States "Anglo-conformity never really reached the point of structural assimilation, due to the resistance of immigrants; moreover, while it is impossible for cultural pluralism to exist without the existence of separate sub-societies, it is possible for such sub-societies to continue their existence even while the cultural differences between them become progressively reduced and even in great part eliminated."[43] What, then, has been the reaction of ethnic groups in the bloc settlements of Saskatchewan to assimilation in the form of Anglo-conformity? Which aspects of their cultures have been lost and which retained?

Saskatchewan's ethno-religious groups on the whole were still segregated in rural bloc settlements during the 1920s and 1930s. Hawkes wrote that the European immigrant "undoubtedly clings to his own nationality, his own religion, and his own customs. ... It is too much to expect him to become a full-fledged Canadian in feeling or in aspiration. ... It is just as impossible to turn a mature Pole into a Canadian, as it would be to turn a Canadian into a Pole. ..."[44] Of course, by Canadian was actually meant *British* Canadian. And C.H. Young wrote that

> It is necessary to labour the point that blocs of this size permeated with the atmosphere of the Old World and composed of members knit together by the common recollection of neighbourly association in the past, are inimical to the assimilation of these people. ... If the question of assimilation is largely one of contact between immigrants and native-born, these bloc settlements prevent contact with the native-born.[45]

However, during the same period, at least some assimilation was already becoming evident. Hawkes observed that "communalism was breaking down," that there was a "great deal of intermarriage between immigrants and the English-speaking folk," and that "the immigrant in general was anxious to see his children educated and Canadianized."[46] Similarly, Young wrote that, though

> we are wont to think of the colonies where these people live as closed districts in which the solidarity of the people is reinforced by their remoteness from others of different racial stocks and by their lack of contacts with them, nonetheless they do at times meet others and by virtue of such contact, their customs, attitudes and standard of living are unquestionably modified, and this to a remarkable extent.[47]

And, according to V.J. Lysenko, "the transformation which the solid bloc community has undergone in the past thirty years is being duplicated in every Ukrainian community in the country. The old fear, prejudice, ignorance are being swept away in an irresistible tide of change."[48]

Assimilation, defined in a more contemporary sense as a weakening of the distinctiveness of ethnic cultures, has been retarded by a number of factors: differences of ethnic minorities from each other and from the majority (or "host population")—especially different languages, religious beliefs and practices, and cultures; an attitude emphasizing traditionalism, especially when transformed into ethnic and religious nationalism, ethnocentrism, or any form of resistance movement; social distance of the minority from the majority, as evidenced in the perceived low status of the minority; spatial isolation and segregation, effectively reducing opportunities for contact between the minority and others; the very strength of ethnic subsystems, serving to lessen minority integration into the general social structure; and, finally, perpetuation of closeness of immigrants to their countries of origin as well as continuing replenishment of ethnic settlements and urban quarters with new arrivals.

But, conversely, assimilation has been enhanced by other factors: economic integration; physical and social mobility; improved transportation; a demographic redistribution within bloc settlements—ethnic population decline or replacement of the priority of one ethnic group in an area with another (which can particularly affect the viability of smaller settlements); similarity of minority institutions to those of the general society; identity change through secularization, religious conversion, and intermarriage; intergenerational changes stimulated by educational policies; the lessening of parochialism, especially through the mass media; and, as we have seen, the entire delocalization process.[49]

Assimilation has usually been implied as an inexorable unidirectional process. Yet there is some evidence of a return to a re-emphasis on ethnicity and a renewed interest in ethnic traditional culture after some assimilation. Most importantly, in recent decades, and to some extent even earlier, assimilation has been countered by a Canadian emphasis on integration without a diminution of ethnic cultures, an emphasis on ethnic pluralism within a policy of multiculturalism. The distinctive identities of ethnic minorities tend to persist only as long as they remain positively valued as useful. Pluralism has been highly valued and defended by many minority spokespeople, particularly Ukrainian Canadians. According to Paul Yuzyk in 1967, Canadian domestic policy has not subscribed to "a dead uniformity of culture or behaviour—not a fusion of souls in a dead jelly of oneness as dreary as the caked mud of a dried-up slough," the product of the proverbial "melting-pot." Rather, it has encouraged citizens and ethnic groups to "be themselves" and "bring their gifts of different cultures to the common Canadian treasury, which constantly enriches our Canadian heritage." Although Yuzyk suggested that "the supreme loyalty of each citizen and each ethnic group must of course be to Canada," he also cautioned that "ancestry should not be denied, discouraged, or suppressed, but rather should be regarded with pride, which is a positive force." Ukrainian and other advocates of multiculturalism were stimulated by Canadian public figures such as Lord Tweedsmuir (John Buchan), the one-time governor general of Canada, who advised them in a speech at Fraserwood, Manitoba, in 1939 that "You will all be better Canadians for being also good Ukrainians," and Dr. Watson Kirkconnell, a former president of Acadia University, who commented that "There is nothing so shallow and sterile as the man who denies his own ancestry."[50] Even as early as 1909, J.S. Woodsworth seemed to depart from the emphasis on the need to become British by emphasizing a new Canadian identity:

> Within the past decade, Canada has risen from the status of a colony to that of a nation. A national consciousness has developed—that is, a nation has been born. A few years ago Canadian-born children described themselves as English, Irish, Scotch, or French. ... Today our children boast themselves Canadians, and the latest arrivals from Austria and Russia help to swell the chorus, The Maple Leaf Forever. There has not been sufficient time to develop a fixed Canadian type, but there is a certain indefinite *something* that at once writes us and distinguishes us from all the world besides. Our hearts all thrill in response to the magical phrase, This Canada of Ours. We are Canadians.[51]

And Robert England, who provided a lot of fascinating detail on Central and Eastern European settlement on the prairies, observed that "every immigrant settler in Canada carried a memory of past culture."[52]

Indeed, Canadian identity has come a long way in the past 100 years from being "a certain indefinite something." Since multiculturalism became official Canadian policy in 1971 under the Trudeau government, ethnic pluralism has received official recognition at the federal level as well as provincial levels, and being Canadian has been essentially redefined as nothing less than the sum of the immense ethnic diversity found in this country and particularly Saskatchewan.

CONCLUDING THOUGHTS

Surely the answer to the question of whether ethnic groups in Saskatchewan—particularly those concentrated within rural bloc settlements—are successfully preserving their unique identities, or whether they are becoming assimilated to a general Canadian identity, must be affirmative. On the one hand, hundreds of thousands of Saskatchewan people continue to live within well-defined, historic ethnic bloc settlements. Many of them still speak their traditional languages, adhere to traditional religious affiliations, practise a wide variety of customs, and marry within their own ethnic and religious groups.

On the other hand, though, over the years and generations, many people have left these settlements for the cities or left the province entirely. Hundreds of small rural communities and surrounding districts have lost population and their one-time prosperity. Over time, an emphasis on ethnic identity might have declined for some groups and certain settlements. A policy of Anglo-conformity and two world wars have taken their toll. Dozens of rural communities have been conscientiously and unconscionably destroyed (as evidenced in almost all of the Communal Doukhobor and many Old Colony Mennonite villages). Intermarriage across ethnic and religious lines has steadily eroded ethnic solidarity, yet perhaps with continuing intermarriage all of these ethnic/religious groups could be viewed as strands woven into the complex tapestry that is the Saskatchewan population today.

Indeed, the story of the ethnic settlements of Saskatchewan has not been without its trials, challenges, difficulties, naïveté, and short-sighted or specifically discriminatory policies. However, a great legacy of this history remains: the magnificent contributions that these settlers and immigrants have made in "taming the land," developing hundreds of communities, building pervasive ethnic-inspired architecture, and—most importantly—learning to all live together in this province with its incredible ethnocultural diversity. These are accomplishments for which the people of Saskatchewan can justifiably be proud.

SOURCES

Population Trends

For general overviews of population trends in Saskatchewan, see A.B. Anderson, "Population Trends," in *Encyclopedia of Saskatchewan* (Regina: Canadian Plains Research Center, 2005), 705–08, and B.D. Thraves, "Change and Diversity in Saskatchewan's Population," in *Saskatchewan: Geographic Perspectives*, ed. B.D. Thraves, M.L. Lewry, J.E. Dale, and H. Schlichtmann (Regina: University of Regina and Canadian Plains Research Center, 2007), 201–26.

On the role that immigration has played, also see D. Elliott, "International Immigration," in *Encyclopedia of Saskatchewan* (Regina: Canadian Plains Research Center, 2005), 483.

Rural population trends have been described in D.H. Hay, "Rural Population," in *Encyclopedia of Saskatchewan* (Regina: Canadian Plains Research Center, 2005), 787–89, and M. Lewry, "Rural Settlement Patterns," in *Encyclopedia of Saskatchewan* (Regina: Canadian Plains Research Center, 2005), 789.

Selected rural communities in Saskatchewan that have virtually disappeared have been described in Frank Moore, *Saskatchewan Ghost Towns* (Regina: First Impressions, 1982).

Specific Trends in Bloc Settlements
Historical trends in farming in Saskatchewan have been described in D. Owram, "Uncertain Promise: The Prairie Farmer and the Post-War Era," M. Fedyk, "The Dream Still Lives: Promised Land Narratives during the Saskatchewan Golden Jubilee," and B. Fairbairn, "From Farm to Community: Co-Operatives in Alberta and Saskatchewan, 1905–2005," in *The Prairie West as Promised Land*, ed. R.D. Francis and C. Kitzan (Calgary: University of Calgary Press, 2007), 335–54, 379–404, 405–32; and A. Newman, "Relief Administration in Saskatoon during the Depression," in *Pages from the Past: Essays on Saskatchewan History*, ed. D.H. Bocking (Saskatoon: Western Producer Prairie Books, 1979), 239–58.

On generational differences in ethnic identification, intermarriage, and so on, see A.B. Anderson, "Generation Differences in Ethnic Identity Retention in Rural Saskatchewan," *Prairie Forum* 7, 2 (1982): 71–95.

On language use among ethnic groups, see A.B. Anderson, "Linguistic Trends among Saskatchewan Ethnic Groups," in *Ethnic Canadians: Culture and Education*, ed. M.L. Kovacs (Regina: Canadian Plains Research Center, 1978), 63–86.

On intermarriage, see A.B. Anderson, "Intermarriage in Ethnic Bloc Settlements in Saskatchewan," paper presented at the Annual Meeting of the Western Association of Sociology and Anthropology, Banff, December 1974.

The debate over education (covered in several chapters) has been discussed in detail in M.R. Lupul, *The Roman Catholic Church and the North-West School Question: A Study in Church-State Relations in Western Canada, 1875–1905* (Toronto: University of Toronto Press, 1974), and A.B. Anderson, "Ethnicity and Language in Saskatchewan Schools," paper presented at the Symposium on Ethnicity on the Great Plains, Center for Great Plains Studies, University of Nebraska, Lincoln, April 1978.

NOTES

Chapter 1: Introduction

1. This discussion is derived largely from A.B. Anderson, "Assimilation in the Bloc Settlements of North-Central Saskatchewan: A Comparative Study of Identity Change among Seven Ethno-Religious Groups in a Canadian Prairie Region" (Ph.D. diss., University of Saskatchewan, 1972), 8–9.

2. An interesting discussion of the emergence of distinct identities in the Prairie West is provided by T. Binnema, "A Feudal Chain of Vassalage: Limited Identities in the Prairie West, 1870–1896," in *Immigration and Settlement, 1870–1939*, ed. G.P. Marchildon, History of the Prairie West Series (Regina: Canadian Plains Research Center and University of Regina, 2009), 157–79.

3. Anderson, "Assimilation in the Bloc Settlements of North-Central Saskatchewan," 37–38.

4. B. Berry, *Race and Ethnic Relations* (Boston: Houghton-Mifflin, 1958), 94; cited in ibid., 38.

5. R. England, *The Central European Immigrant in Canada* (Toronto: Macmillan, 1929), 15–20.

6. The Sifton settlement policy is described particularly in J.W. Dafoe, *Clifford Sifton in Relation to His Times* (Toronto: Macmillan, 1931); D. Hall, "Clifford Sifton's Vision of the Prairie West," in *The Prairie West as Promised Land*, ed. R.D. Francis and C. Kitzan (Calgary: University of Calgary Press, 2007), 77–100; D.J. Hall, "Clifford Sifton and Canadian Indian Administration, 1896–1905," in Marchildon, *Immigration and Settlement, 1870–1939*, 183–211; and J.C. Lehr, J. Everitt, and S. Evans., "The Making of the Prairie Landscape," *Prairie Forum* 33, 1 (2008); reprinted in Marchildon, *Immigration and Settlement, 1870–1939*, 13–56.

7. See B.G. Smillie, ed., *Visions of the New Jerusalem: Religious Settlement on the Prairies* (Edmonton: NeWest Press, 1983); P. Berton, *The Promised Land: Settling the West, 1896–1914* (Toronto: McClelland and Stewart, 1984); D. Owram, "The Promise of the West as Settlement Frontier," in Francis and Kitzan, *The Prairie West as Promised Land*, 3–28; and R.D. Francis, "The Kingdom of God on the Prairies: J.S. Woodsworth's Vision of the Prairie West as Promised Land," in Francis and Kitzan, *The Prairie West as Promised Land*, 225–41.

8. Illustration in J.H. Gray, *Boom Time: Peopling the Canadian Prairies* (Saskatoon: Western Producer Prairie Books, 1979), 41.

9. Dafoe, *Clifford Sifton in Relation to His Times*, 140–41. American settlement in Saskatchewan at the time is described in R.W. Widdis, *With Scarcely a Ripple: Anglo-American Migration into the*

United States and Western Canada, 1880–1920 (Montreal: McGill-Queen's University Press, 1998); and R. Widdis, "American-Resident Migration to Western Canada at the Turn of the Twentieth Century," in Marchildon, *Immigration and Settlement, 1870–1939*, 347–71.

10 Gray, *Boom Time*, 52.

11 *Report of the Saskatchewan Royal Commission on Immigration and Settlement*, 1930, 42–43.

12 E. Eager, "The Conservatism of the Saskatchewan Electorate," in *Politics in Saskatchewan*, ed. N. Ward and D. Spafford (Lindsay, ON: Longmans of Canada and John Dyell, 1968), 5; C.E.S. Franks, "The Legislation and Responsible Government," in Ward and Spafford, *Politics in Saskatchewan*, 23.

13 Cited in J. Bruce, *Last Best West* (Toronto: Fitzhenry and Whiteside, 1976), 20.

14 D. Smith, "Instilling British Values in the Prairie Provinces," *Prairie Forum* 6, 2 (1981): 136.

15 Briefs submitted to the Saskatchewan Royal Commission on Immigration and Settlement.

16 Cited in Anderson, "Assimilation in the Bloc Settlements of North-Central Saskatchewan," 197–98.

17 Cited in ibid., 26.

18 Dafoe, *Clifford Sifton in Relation to His Times*, 323.

19 See, for example, C. Martin, *"Dominion Lands" Policy* (Toronto: McClelland and Stewart, 1973); B. Waiser, "'Land I Can Own': Settling in the Promised Land," in Francis and Kitzan, *The Prairie West as Promised Land*, 155–74; and Lehr et al., "The Making of the Prairie Landscape."

20 Anderson, "Assimilation in the Bloc Settlements of North-Central Saskatchewan," 45–46.

21 Gray, *Boom Time*, 52.

22 See, for example, Lehr et al., "The Making of the Prairie Landscape."

23 The role that women played in the settlement process has been described by Waiser, "'Land I Can Own'"; C.A. Cavanaugh, "'No Place for a Woman': Engendering Western Canadian Settlement," in Francis and Kitzan, *The Prairie West as Promised Land*, 261–90; and R. Warne, "Land of the Second Chance: Nellie McClung's Vision of the Prairie West as Promised Land," in Francis and Kitzan, *The Prairie West as Promised Land*, 199–224.

24 P.L. McCormick, "Transportation and Settlement: Problems in the Expansion of the Frontier of Saskatchewan and Assiniboia in 1904," in Marchildon, *Immigration and Settlement, 1870–1939*, 81–102.

25 Anderson, "Assimilation in the Bloc Settlements of North-Central Saskatchewan," 176–88; England, *The Central European Immigrant in Canada*, 22–38; B.S. Osborne and S.E. Wurtele, "The Other Railway: Canadian National's Department of Colonization and Agriculture," in Marchildon, *Immigration and Settlement, 1870–1939*, 103–28.

26 Osborne and Wurtele, "The Other Railway."

27 Anderson, "Assimilation in the Bloc Settlements of North-Central Saskatchewan," 42.

28 C.A. Price, "Immigration and Group Settlement," in *The Cultural Integration of Immigrants*, ed. W.D. Borrie (Paris: UNESCO, 1959), 270–72.

29 Anderson, "Assimilation in the Bloc Settlements of North-Central Saskatchewan," 43; C.A. Dawson, *Group Settlement: Ethnic Communities in Western Canada* (Toronto: Macmillan, 1936), 378–80; C.A. Dawson and E.R. Younge, *Pioneering in the Prairie Provinces: The Social Side of the Settlement Process* (Toronto: Macmillan, 1940), 12–16.

30 Saskatchewan Royal Commission on Immigration and Settlement, 193.

31 O. Handlin, *Race and Nationality in American Life* (Garden City, NY: Doubleday, 1957), 90; cited in Anderson, "Assimilation in the Bloc Settlements of North-Central Saskatchewan," 43.

32 Price, "Immigration and Group Settlement," 273–77; cited in Anderson, "Assimilation in the Bloc Settlements of North-Central Saskatchewan," 43–44.

33 Gray, *Boom Time*, 108.

34 Anderson, "Assimilation in the Bloc Settlements of North-Central Saskatchewan," 4.

35 T.L. Smith's definition of "settlement" in *Dictionary of Sociology*, ed. H.P. Fairchild (n.p.: Littlefield, Adams, 1962).

36 T.L. Smith's definition of "group settlement" in Fairchild, *Dictionary of Sociology*.

37 Price, "Immigration and Group Settlement," 270–72.

38 A.B. Anderson, "Ethnic Bloc Settlements, 1850s–1990s," in *Atlas of Saskatchewan*, ed. K. Fung (Saskatoon: University of Saskatchewan, 1999), 85–87.

39 N. Ward, "The Contemporary Scene," in Ward and Spafford, *Politics in Saskatchewan*, 280; G.E. Britnell, *The Wheat Economy* (Toronto: University of Toronto Press, 1939), 15–16.

40 See, for example, Dawson, *Group Settlement*; Dawson and Younge, *Pioneering in the Prairie Provinces*; and England, *The Central European Immigrant in Canada*, 11–12.

Chapter 2: Aboriginal Reserves and Settlements

1 Data on reserve populations from Indian Affairs and Northern Development, Registered Indian Population by Sex and Residence, 2007, Ottawa, 2008.

2 See H. Buckley, *From Wooden Plows to Welfare: Why Indian Policy Failed in the Prairie Provinces* (Montreal: McGill-Queen's University Press, 1992); S. Carter, "Demonstrated Success: The File Hills Farm Colony," in *Immigration and Settlement, 1870–1939*, ed. G.P. Marchildon (Regina: Canadian Plains Research Center, 2009), 235–63; and S. Carter, "'We Must Farm to Enable Us to Live': The Plains Cree and Agriculture to 1900," in *The Prairie West as Promised Land*, ed. R.D. Francis and C. Kitzan (Calgary: University of Calgary Press, 2007), 103–26.

3 Cited in M. Fieguth and D. Christensen, *Historic Saskatchewan* (Toronto: Oxford University Press, 1986). A particularly useful account is provided in C.F. Turner, *Across the Medicine Line: The Epic Confrontation between Sitting Bull and the North-West Mounted Police* (Toronto: McClelland and Stewart, 1973).

4 Data from Statistics Canada report on Aboriginal population released January 2008, based on the 2006 census.

Chapter 3: British Settlements

1 J. Bruce, *The Last Best West* (Toronto: Fitzhenry and Whiteside, 1976), 8.

2 J.W. Dafoe, *Clifford Sifton in Relation to His Times* (Toronto: Macmillan, 1931), 138.

3 J.H. Gray, *Boom Time: Peopling the Canadian Prairies* (Saskatoon: Western Producer Prairie Books, 1979), 45–46.

4 M. Lalonde and E. LaClare, *Discover Saskatchewan: A Guide to Historic Sites* (Regina: Canadian Plains Research Center, 1998), 55–56; K. Ondaatje, *Small Churches of Canada* (Toronto: Lester and Orpen Dennys, 1982), 169; J. DeVisser and H. Kalman, *Pioneer Churches* (Toronto: McClelland and Stewart, 1976), 14; M. Fieguth and D. Christensen, *Historic Saskatchewan* (Toronto: Oxford University Press, 1986), 60.

5 Lalonde and LaClare, *Discover Saskatchewan*, 53.

6. C. MacDonald, "Pioneer Church Life in Saskatchewan," *Saskatchewan History* (winter 1960), reprinted in *Pages from the Past: Essays on Saskatchewan History*, ed. D.H. Bocking (Saskatoon: Western Producer Prairie Books, 1979), 120–38.
7. B. Barry, *Geographic Names of Saskatchewan* (Regina: People Places Publishing, 2005), 125.
8. M. Hryniuk and F. Korvemaker, *Legacy of Stone: Saskatchewan's Stone Buildings* (Regina: Coteau Books, 2008), 24.
9. G. Johnson, "The Harmony Industrial Association: A Pioneer Co-Operative," in Bocking, ed., *Pages from the Past*, 80.
10. Lalonde and LaClare, *Discover Saskatchewan*, 55.
11. Barry, *Geographic Names of Saskatchewan*, 411.
12. Hryniuk and Korvemaker, *Legacy of Stone*, 116–19.
13. K. Foster, "The Barr Colonists: Their Arrival and Impact on the Canadian North-West," *Saskatchewan History* 35, 3 (1982): 81; H. Stoffel, "The Barr Colony," in *Encyclopedia of Saskatchewan* (Regina: Canadian Plains Research Center, 2005), 92.
14. Foster, "The Barr Colonists," 81, 84.
15. I.M. Barr, *British Settlements in North-Western Canada on Free Lands*, Barr File, Public Archives of Canada, 23, cited in ibid., 82.
16. Foster, "The Barr Colonists," 83.
17. Ibid., 83–84.
18. Ibid., 91.
19. *Evening News and Evening Mail*, March 31, 1903, cited in ibid., 81.
20. *The Herald*, March 11, 1903, cited in Foster, "The Barr Colonists," 84.
21. *Manitoba Free Press*, in *Saskatoon Phenix*, April 10, 1903, cited in Foster, "The Barr Colonists," 85.
22. Foster, "The Barr Colonists," 94.
23. G. Langley to J.O. Smith, July 31, 1903, Barr File, cited in ibid., 94.
24. *Saskatoon Phenix*, April 24, 1903, *The Herald*, April 22, 1903, cited in Foster, "The Barr Colonists," 89–90.
25. *Regina Leader*, June 18, 1903, cited in Foster, "The Barr Colonists," 96–97.
26. *Manchester Guardian*, August 16, 1904, cited in Foster, "The Barr Colonists," 97.
27. Dafoe, *Clifford Sifton in Relation to His Times*, 322–23.
28. Barr File, untitled circular, March 1903, cited in Foster, "The Barr Colonists," 82–83.
29. *Canadian Churchman*, July 2, 1925, cited in C. Kitzan, "Preaching Purity in the Promised Land: Bishop Lloyd and the Immigration Debate," in *The Prairie West as Promised Land*, ed. R.D. Francis and C. Kitzan (Calgary: University of Calgary Press, 2007), 291.
30. *Regina Leader*, May 7, 1903, cited in Foster, "The Barr Colonists," 90.
31. *The Herald*, November 12, 1902, and unidentified newspaper, March 15, 1904, cited in Foster, "The Barr Colonists," 83, 97.
32. Barr, *British Settlements in North-Western Canada on Free Lands*, 18, cited in Foster, "The Barr Colonists," 89.
33. Sifton in London, February 18, 1903; *The Herald*, February 25, 1903; *Manchester Guardian*, August 16, 1904, cited in Foster, "The Barr Colonists," 83–84, 97.
34. Foster, "The Barr Colonists," 96, 99.

35 Barry, *Geographic Names of Saskatchewan*, 26.

36 Ibid., 397–98; D. McLennan, *Our Towns: Saskatchewan Communities from Abbey to Zenon Park* (Regina: Canadian Plains Research Center, 2008), 372–73.

37 Hryniuk and Korvemaker, *Legacy of Stone*, 70–73, 126–29.

38 Ibid., 152–55, 160–63, 168–71, 176–79, 184–87, 200–03.

39 "Advice to English Emigrants in 1912," *Saskatchewan History* 32, 1 (1979): 35 (abridged from "Settling on Canada's Free Land," by an anonymous homesteader, for the Minister of the Interior, 1912).

40 D. Smith, "Instilling British Values in the Prairie Provinces," *Prairie Forum* 6, 2 (1981): 129; reprinted in *Immigration and Settlement, 1870–1939*, ed. G.P. Marchildon, History of the Prairie West Series (Regina: Canadian Plains Research Center and University of Regina, 2009), 441–56.

41 Ibid., 131.

42 MacDonald, "Pioneer Church Life in Saskatchewan," 7.

43 Smith, "Instilling British Values in the Prairie Provinces," 132–33.

44 Data from Dominion Bureau of Statistics through the 1950s and Statistics Canada since the 1960s.

45 *Globe and Mail*, February 10, 2010.

46 H. Hamilton, *An Economic History of Scotland* (Oxford: Clarendon Press, 1963), 11, cited in K. Stuart, "The Scottish Crofter Colony, Saltcoats, 1889–1904," *Saskatchewan History* 24, 2 (1971): 41.

47 R.H. Campbell, *Scotland since 1707* (Bristol: Western Printing Services, 1965), 293–94; Hamilton, *An Economic History of Scotland*, 381, cited in Stuart, "The Scottish Crofter Colony, Saltcoats, 1889–1904," 41.

48 A.R. Turner, "Scottish Settlement of the West," in W.S. Reid, ed., *The Scottish Tradition in Canada* (Toronto: McClelland and Stewart, 1976), 82.

49 Bruce, *The Last Best West*, rear cover photograph.

50 Hryniuk and Korvemaker, *Legacy of Stone*, 188–91.

51 Ibid., 164–67.

52 MacDonald, "Pioneer Church Life in Saskatchewan," 13.

53 Hryniuk and Korvemaker, *Legacy of Stone*, 50–53, 104–11.

54 "Report on Crofter Settlement Near Saltcoats with General Remarks on Aided Colonization," July 3, 1989, 5, cited in Stuart, "The Scottish Crofter Colony, Saltcoats, 1889–1904," 43.

55 W. Norton, *Help Us to a Better Land: Crofter Colonies in the Prairie West* (Regina: Canadian Plains Research Center, 1994).

56 Stuart, "The Scottish Crofter Colony, Saltcoats, 1889–1904," 42.

57 "Report of Her Majesty's Commissioners to Carry Out a Scheme of Colonization in the Dominion of Canada of Crofters and Cottars from the Western Highlands and Islands of Scotland," Vol. II, 1890, cited in Stuart, "The Scottish Crofter Colony, Saltcoats, 1889–1904," 43; ibid., 48.

58 Reverend I. Macdonald to H.H. Smith, June 29, 1889, cited in Stuart, "The Scottish Crofter Colony, Saltcoats, 1889–1904," 44.

59 Stuart, "The Scottish Crofter Colony, Saltcoats, 1889–1904," 43, 45.

60 H.H. Smith to Reverend I. Macdonald, July 3, 1889, 6–7, and A.M. Burgess to Honourable E. Dewdney, July 18, 1889, cited in Stuart, "The Scottish Crofter Colony, Saltcoats, 1889–1904," 45, 47.

61 A.F. Eden to H.H. Smith, February 11, 1890, cited in Stuart, "The Scottish Crofter Colony, Saltcoats, 1889–1904," 45.

62 Stuart, "The Scottish Crofter Colony, Saltcoats, 1889–1904," 46.

63 Norton, *Help Us to a Better Land*; Stuart, "The Scottish Crofter Colony, Saltcoats, 1889–1904," 42.

64 Stuart, "The Scottish Crofter Colony, Saltcoats, 1889–1904," 46–47.

65 Ibid., 48–50.

66 E.C. Morgan, "The Bell Farm," in Bocking, ed., *Pages from the Past*, 45–63; Hryniuk and Korvemaker, *Legacy of Stone*, 14–17.

67 Lalonde and LaClare, *Discover Saskatchewan*, 41–42.

68 Hryniuk and Korvemaker, *Legacy of Stone*, xiii, 6–9.

69 Ibid., 2, 18–21.

70 MacDonald, "Pioneer Church Life in Saskatchewan," 7.

71 Cited in Hryniuk and Korvemaker, *Legacy of Stone*, 30–33.

72 Ibid., 58–61, 92–95.

73 MacDonald, "Pioneer Church Life in Saskatchewan," 2.

74 Hryniuk and Korvemaker, *Legacy of Stone*, 1, 10–13, 42–45, 66–69.

75 Ibid., 144–47.

76 Ibid., 34–37, 62–65.

77 The Aird district west of Elrose was named by John MacDonald after his local school on the island of Lewis in the Outer Hebrides; in Lewis/Eilean Leodhais, the Gaelic language is still prevalent, and *àirde* is a common prefix in place names.

78 MacDonald, "Pioneer Church Life in Saskatchewan," 18.

79 I. McFadyen, *Our Legacy: The Govan-Walter Story* (Regina: Your Nickel's Worth Publishing, 2009).

80 Hryniuk and Korvemaker, *Legacy of Stone*, xv, 148–51.

81 J.C. Lehr, "The Geographical Background to Church Union in Canada," in Marchildon, ed., *Immigration and Settlement, 1870–1939*, 543–56.

82 Gray, *Boom Time*, 110.

83 Clifford Sifton in *Maclean's Magazine*, April 1, 1922, cited in Dafoe, *Clifford Sifton in Relation to His Times*, 139–40.

84 J. Coughlin, *The Irish Colony of Saskatchewan* (Scarborough, ON: Lochleven Publishers, 1995).

85 MacDonald, "Pioneer Church Life in Saskatchewan," 4.

86 Ibid., 9.

87 M. Cottrell, "The Irish in Saskatchewan, 1850–1930," in Marchildon, ed., *Immigration and Settlement, 1870–1939*, 507–42. Also see P. Kyba, "Ballots and Burning Crosses: The Election of 1929," in *Politics in Saskatchewan*, ed. N. War and D. Spafford (Lindsay, ON: Longmans of Canada and John Dyell, 1968), 105–23; J. Sher, *White Hoods: Canada's Ku Klux Klan* (Vancouver: New Star Books, 1983).

88 Cottrell, "The Irish in Saskatchewan, 1850–1930," 510.

89 G. Johnson, "The Patagonia Welsh," *Saskatchewan History* 16, 3 (1963): 90; L.H. Thomas, "From the Pampas to the Prairies: The Welsh Migration of 1902," *Saskatchewan History* 24, 1 (1971): 1–3; reprinted in Bocking, ed., *Pages from the Past*, 90–101.

90 Thomas, "From the Pampas to the Prairies," 4, 7.

91 Johnson, "The Patagonia Welsh," 90–91; Thomas, "From the Pampas to the Prairies," 2–4, 7.

92 Personal correspondence between David Williams in Patagonia and the author, September 11, 2001; Johnson, "The Patagonia Welsh," 91; Thomas, "From the Pampas to the Prairies," 3; R. Perry, *Patagonia: Windswept Land of the South* (New York: Dodd, Mead, ca. 1973), 68.

93 Johnson, "The Patagonia Welsh," 90; Thomas, "From the Pampas to the Prairies," 2, 3, 7.

94 Johnson, "The Patagonia Welsh," 91; Thomas, "From the Pampas to the Prairies," 4–5.

95 Johnson, "The Patagonia Welsh," 91; Thomas, "From the Pampas to the Prairies," 3, 8.

96 Johnson, "The Patagonia Welsh," 92; Thomas, "From the Pampas to the Prairies," 10.

97 Johnson, "The Patagonia Welsh," 92; W. Davies, "Welsh Settlement," in *Encyclopedia of Saskatchewan* (Regina: Canadian Plains Research Center, 2005), 1006.

98 Johnson, "The Patagonia Welsh," 93–94; Thomas, "From the Pampas to the Prairies," 11–12.

99 MacDonald, "Pioneer Church Life in Saskatchewan," 10.

100 Davies, "Welsh Settlement."

101 Smith, "Instilling British Values in the Prairie Provinces," 129.

Chapter 4: Germanic Settlements

1 G.L. Maron, *The Germans in Canada* (Winnipeg: Der Nordwesten, 1911), 6–7; C.A. Dawson, *Group Settlement: Ethnic Communities in Western Canada* (Toronto: Macmillan, 1936), 275–79.

2 Maron, *The Germans in Canada*, 13–17, 35.

3 A.B. Anderson, *German Settlements in Saskatchewan* (Saskatoon: Saskatchewan German Council, 2005), 5.

4 G. Grams, "Immigration and Return Migration of German Nationals, Saskatchewan, 1919 to 1939," in *Immigration and Settlement, 1870–1939*, ed. G.P. Marchildon, History of the Prairie West Series (Regina: Canadian Plains Research Center and University of Regina, 2009), 414–15, 424.

5 A. Giesinger, *From Catherine to Kruschev: The Story of Russia's Germans* (Winnipeg: Marian Press, 1974), 364.

6 Grams, "Immigration and Return Migration," 413.

7 Ibid., 423.

8 Data derived from the Census of Canada for various years.

9 M. Lalonde and E. LaClare, *Discover Saskatchewan: A Guide to Historic Sites* (Regina: Canadian Plains Research Center, 1998), 54.

10 Personal correspondence with Father Eric Melby, Ottawa, great-grandson of Dominic Deschner, March 24, 2010.

11 Anderson, *German Settlements in Saskatchewan*, 7.

12 A.B. Anderson, "Abbot Bruno (George) Doerfler," in *Dictionary of Canadian Biography*, vol. 14 (Toronto: University of Toronto Press, 1995), 1–4.

13 Reverend J. Weber, *St. Peter's Abbey, 1903–1921* (Muenster, SK: St. Peter's Abbey, 1949); Reverend P. Windschiegl, *Fifty Golden Years, 1903–1953* (Muenster, SK: St. Peter's Abbey, 1953); Dawson, *Group Settlement*, 279–88; cited in A.B. Anderson, "Assimilation in the Bloc Settlements of North-Central Saskatchewan" (Ph.D. diss., University of Saskatchewan, 1972), 64.

14 W.C. Sherman, *Prairie Mosaic: An Ethnic Atlas of North Dakota* (Fargo: North Dakota Institute for Regional Studies, 1983), 15.

15 Data on the expansion and growth of the colony between 1902 and 1907 come from Windschiegl, *Fifty Golden Years, 1903–1953*, 19, 33–35, and from other sources cited in Anderson, "Assimilation in the Bloc Settlements of North-Central Saskatchewan," 65.

16 C. MacDonald, "Pioneer Church Life in Saskatchewan," *Saskatchewan History* 13, 1 (1960): 1–18.

17 J. Cadham, *The Prairie Does Flourish* (Humboldt, SK: Sisters of St. Elizabeth, 2010).

18 Grams, "Immigration and Return Migration," 417.

19 Based on detailed demographic data from the 1971 census of incorporated communities and rural municipalities (also see Anderson, "Assimilation in the Bloc Settlements of North-Central Saskatchewan," 69).

20 Anderson, *German Settlements in Saskatchewan*, 10.

21 Ibid.; Lalonde and LaClare, *Discover Saskatchewan*, 79.

22 H. Lehmann, *The German Canadians, 1750–1937: Immigration, Settlement, and Culture*, trans. G.P. Bassler (St. John's: Jesperson Press, 1986), 204–12, 266.

23 *Canada Lutheran*, January 1991, 15.

24 L.K. Munholland, *Pulpits of the Past* (Strasbourg, SK: Three West Two South Books, 2004).

25 Information on church closures gathered by the author; see Anderson *German Settlements in Saskatchewan*, 12.

26 Ibid., 14.

27 *The Shepherd*, October 1984, 28.

28 M. Hryniuk and F. Korvemaker, *Legacy of Stone: Saskatchewan's Stone Buildings* (Regina: Coteau Books, 2008), 196–99, 226.

29 MacDonald, "Pioneer Church Life in Saskatchewan," 13.

30 B. Barry, *Geographic Names of Saskatchewan* (Regina: People Places Publishing, 2005), 194.

31 L.K. Munholland, *Bread to Share*, 2 vols. (Strasbourg, SK: Three West Two South Books, 2006).

32 Described in detail in G. Johnson, "The Germania Mutual Fire Insurance Company of Langenburg," *Saskatchewan History* 14, 1 (1961): 27–29.

33 Munholland, *Bread to Share*.

34 Ibid.

35 MacDonald, "Pioneer Church Life in Saskatchewan," 11.

36 Ibid., 17.

37 Hryniuk and Korvemaker, *Legacy of Stone*, 82–85.

38 Ibid., 122–23.

39 "Memoirs of a Pioneer Pastor," *Canadian Lutheran*, May 1989, 16–28.

40 "In Memoriam for Dr. Henry Kroeger, 1889–1984," *The Shepherd*, December 1984, 25.

41 Based on data from Census of Canada, 1971; see Anderson, *German Settlements in Saskatchewan*, 12.

42 Grams, "Immigration and Return Migration," 429–31.

43 A. Amstatter, *Tomslake: History of the Sudeten Germans in Canada* (Saanichton, BC: Hancock House, 1978); R. Schilling, *Sudeten in Saskatchewan: A Way to Be Free* (St. Walburg, SK: Sudeten German Club, with the Saskatchewan German Council, 1989).

44 Barry, *Geographic Names of Saskatchewan*, 248.

45 *Saskatchewan Genealogical Society Bulletin* 9, 3 (1978): 117–20.

46. D. McLennan, *Our Towns: Saskatchewan Communities from Abbey to Zenon Park* (Regina: Canadian Plains Research Center, 2008), 141.

47. Anderson, *German Settlements in Saskatchewan*, 12.

48. Saskatoon *Star-Phoenix*, September 8, 1979.

49. *Davidson Leader*, April 18, 2011.

50. *The Shepherd*, August 1982.

51. Details on Bergheim from a church brochure and historical plaque on site.

52. Information provided by C. Flath, author's archives, 1987.

53. M. Fieguth and D. Christensen, *Historic Saskatchewan* (Toronto: Oxford University Press, 1986), 64.

54. J.J. Friesen, *Building Communities: The Changing Face of Manitoba Mennonites* (Winnipeg: CMU Press, 2007), 29.

55. Ibid., 29–33.

56. Estimates from F.H. Epp, *Mennonites in Canada, 1782–1920: The History of a Separate People* (Toronto: Macmillan of Canada, 1974; and F.H. Epp, *Mennonites in Canada, 1920–1940: A People's Struggle for Survival* (Toronto: Macmillan of Canada, 1982).

57. This detailed information on the *Prairieleut* has been drawn from R. Janzen, *Prairie People: Forgotten Anabaptists* (Hanover, NH: University Press of New England, 1999), 122–24.

58. Epp, *Mennonites in Canada, 1782–1920*; Archives of Saskatchewan, cited in A.B. Anderson "Assimilation in the Bloc Settlements of North-Central Saskatchewan" (Ph.D. diss., University of Saskatchewan, 1972), 72.

59. Archives of Saskatchewan, cited in Anderson, "Assimilation in the Bloc Settlements of North-Central Saskatchewan," 73.

60. Data from City of Saskatoon and Statistics Canada, 2008.

61. L. Driedger, *At the Forks: Mennonites in Winnipeg* (Kitchener: Pandora Press, 2010).

62. Anderson, *German Settlements in Saskatchewan*, 22.

63. Ibid., 22–23.

64. MacDonald, "Pioneer Church Life in Saskatchewan," 1, 17.

65. Saskatchewan Association of Architects, *Historic Architecture of Saskatchewan* (Regina: Architects and Focus Publishing, 1987), 40, 44, 48; Hryniuk and Korvemaker, *Legacy of Stone*, 5.

66. Barry, *Geographic Names of Saskatchewan*, 207.

67. Details of the Nordheim Mennonite Congregation in the Hanley-Dundurn area are from *Nordheimer Mennonite Church of Saskatchewan, 1925–1975* (Saskatoon: Heese House of Printing, 1975).

68. Data compiled from Mennonite yearbooks; Epp, *Mennonites in Canada, 1782–1920* and *Mennonites in Canada, 1920–1940*; T.D. Regehr, *Mennonites in Canada, 1939–1970* (Toronto: University of Toronto Press, 1996); B. Barry, *Ukrainian People Places* (Regina: Centax Books, 2001), 80; M.L. Reimer, *One Quilt — Many Pieces: A Guide to Mennonite Groups in Canada*, 4th ed. (Waterloo: Herald Press, 2008).

69. Historical data derived primarily from J.A. Hostetler, *Hutterite Society* (Baltimore: Johns Hopkins University Press, 1974); see also Anderson, *German Settlements in Saskatchewan*, 24.

70. See Janzen, *Prairie People*.

71. Reimer, *One Quilt — Many Pieces*.

72. Anderson, "Assimilation in the Bloc Settlements of North-Central Saskatchewan."

73 Ibid., 127.

74 Ibid., 128.

75 Ibid., 229.

76 Ibid., 141–43.

77 Ibid., 144–48.

78 Ibid., 230.

79 P.S. Gross, *The Hutterite Way* (Saskatoon: Freeman, 1965), 91–108; cited in Anderson, "Assimilation in the Bloc Settlements of North-Central Saskatchewan," 146.

80 Details on Mennonite dialects from H. Voth, "Mennonites: Languages and Geographic Locations," 1970, author's archives; and L. Driedger, "A Sect in Modern Society: A Case Study of the Old Colony Mennonites of Saskatchewan" (MA thesis, University of Chicago, 1955), 82–85, cited in Anderson, "Assimilation in the Bloc Settlements of North-Central Saskatchewan," 146–47.

81 Driedger, "A Sect in Modern Society," 109, cited in Anderson, "Assimilation in the Bloc Settlements of North-Central Saskatchewan," 147.

82 Driedger, "A Sect in Modern Society," 82–85; C.H. Smith, *The Story of the Mennonites* (Newton, KS: Mennonite Publication Office, 1957), 643; F.H. Epp, *Mennonite Exodus* (Altona, MB: D.W. Friesen and Sons, 1962), 207–08, all cited in Anderson, "Assimilation in the Bloc Settlements of North-Central Saskatchewan," 147–48.

83 Anderson, "Assimilation in the Bloc Settlements of North-Central Saskatchewan," 168, 231.

84 Ibid., 337–40.

85 Ibid., 232.

86 L. Buchanan, "Mennonite Folklore and Folklife: Old Colony Life in the Rosthern Settlement," 1983, author's archives.

87 K.A. McLeod, "Politics, Schools, and the French Language, 1881–1931," in *Politics in Saskatchewan*, ed. N. Ward and D. Spafford (Lindsay, ON: Longmans of Canada and John Dyell, 1968), 128–30, cited in Anderson, "Assimilation in the Bloc Settlements of North-Central Saskatchewan," 290.

88 Archives of Saskatchewan, cited in Anderson, "Assimilation in the Bloc Settlements of North-Central Saskatchewan," 290.

89 Archives of Saskatchewan; C.A. Dawson, *Group Settlement: Ethnic Communities in Western Canada* (Toronto: Macmillan, 1936), 318–24, 330–32; C.A. Dawson and E.R. Younge, *Pioneering in the Prairie Provinces: The Social Side of the Settlement Process* (Toronto: Macmillan, 1940), 169–70, all cited in Anderson, "Assimilation in the Bloc Settlements of North-Central Saskatchewan," 291.

90 Archives of Saskatchewan, cited in Anderson, "Assimilation in the Bloc Settlements of North-Central Saskatchewan," 292.

91 Ibid.

92 Driedger, "A Sect in Modern Society," 68–73, 89–90; R. England, *The Central European Immigrant in Canada* (Toronto: Macmillan, 1929), 39; Smith, *The Story of the Mennonites*, 644–48; Dawson, *Group Settlement*, 155–59, 168–71, all cited in Anderson, "Assimilation in the Bloc Settlements of North-Central Saskatchewan," 293.

93 Driedger, "A Sect in Modern Society," 68–73; Smith, *The Story of the Mennonites*, 644–48; J.T.M. Anderson, *The Education of the New Canadian* (Toronto: J.M. Dent, 1918), 65, 74–76; Archives of Saskatchewan, all cited in Anderson, "Assimilation in the Bloc Settlements of North-Central Saskatchewan," 293–94.

94 Archives of Saskatchewan, cited in Anderson, "Assimilation in the Bloc Settlements of North-Central Saskatchewan," 294.

95 Ibid.

96 Driedger, "A Sect in Modern Society," 68–73, 89–90; Smith, *The Story of the Mennonites*, 644–48; Epp, *Mennonite Exodus*, 95–97; Archives of Saskatchewan, all cited in Anderson, "Assimilation in the Bloc Settlements of North-Central Saskatchewan," 294–95.

97 Archives of Saskatchewan, cited in Anderson, "Assimilation in the Bloc Settlements of North-Central Saskatchewan," 295–96.

98 Ibid., 296.

99 Grams, "Immigration and Return Migration," 413.

100 R. Loewen, *Diaspora in the Countryside* (Toronto: University of Toronto Press, 2006).

101 See W. Schroeder and H.T. Huebert, *Mennonite Historical Atlas* (Winnipeg: Springfield Publishers, 1990); D. Polachic, "Mennonite Migration Comes Full Circle," *Saskatoon Sun*, March 30, 2008.

102 B. McKinstry, *Bridges: A Book of Legacies for Saskatchewan People of German-Speaking Backgrounds* (Saskatoon: Saskatchewan German Council, 2006).

Chapter 5: Ukrainian and Polish Settlement

1 J.W. Dafoe, *Clifford Sifton in Relation to His Times* (Toronto: Macmillan, 1931), 141–42.

2 Ibid., 317; *Report of the Saskatchewan Royal Commission on Immigration and Settlement* (Regina: King's Publisher, 1930), 187–88; W. Darcovich, *Ukrainians in Canada: The Struggle to Retain Their Identity* (Ottawa: Ukrainian Self-Reliance Association, 1967), 2–3; T. Skwarok, OSBM, *The Ukrainian Settlers in Canada and Their Schools, 1891–1921* (Edmonton: Basilian Press, 1959), 1–12, cited in A.B. Anderson, "Assimilation in the Bloc Settlements of North-Central Saskatchewan: A Comparative Study of Identity Change among Seven Ethno-Religious Groups in a Canadian Prairie Region" (Ph.D. diss., University of Saskatchewan, 1972), 78; J. DeVisser and H. Kalman, *Pioneer Churches* (Toronto: McClelland and Stewart, 1976), 154.

3 Skwarok, *The Ukrainian Settlers in Canada and Their Schools*, 1–7, cited in Anderson, "Assimilation in the Bloc Settlements of North-Central Saskatchewan," 79.

4 C.H. Young, *The Ukrainian Canadians: A Study in Assimilation* (Toronto: Thomas Nelson and Sons, 1931), 72–75, cited in Anderson, "Assimilation in the Bloc Settlements of North-Central Saskatchewan," 79.

5 Young, *The Ukrainian Canadians*, 76–77; M.A. Sherbinin, *The Galicians Dwelling in Canada and Their Origin*, Historical and Scientific Society of Manitoba, Transaction No. 71 (Winnipeg: Manitoba Free Press, 1906), 12, cited in Anderson, "Assimilation in the Bloc Settlements of North-Central Saskatchewan," 79.

6 Young, *The Ukrainian Canadians*, 295–98; J.T.M. Anderson, *The Education of the New Canadian* (Toronto: J.M. Dent, 1918), 54–56, 60–61; Skwarok, *The Ukrainian Settlers in Canada and Their Schools*, 12–21.

7 J.H. Gray, *Boom Time: Peopling the Canadian Prairies* (Saskatoon: Western Producer Prairie Books, 1979), 65–67.

8 Edited by the author from the original in the Ukrainian Canadian Archives and Museum, Edmonton, translated by M.B. Kohut in November 1979.

9 A.M. Baran, *Ukrainian Catholic Churches of Saskatchewan* (Saskatoon: Modern Press, 1977).

10 C. MacDonald, "Pioneer Church Life in Saskatchewan," *Saskatchewan History* 13 (1960): 13.

11 K. Ondaatje, *Small Churches of Canada* (Toronto: Lester and Orpen Dennys, 1982), 28–29; DeVisser and Kalman, *Pioneer Churches*, 172.

12 V.J. Kaye, *Early Ukrainian Settlements in Canada, 1895–1900* (Toronto: University of Toronto Press, 1964), 300–17; Young, *The Ukrainian Canadians*, 75, cited in Anderson, "Assimilation in the Bloc Settlements of North-Central Saskatchewan," 80.

13 Archives of Saskatchewan, cited in Anderson, "Assimilation in the Bloc Settlements of North-Central Saskatchewan," 81.

14 DeVisser and Kalman, *Pioneer Churches*, 157–58.

15 Ondaatje, *Small Churches of Canada*, 28–29.

16 Government of Saskatchewan, 1909, 1914; H.J. Boam, *The Prairie Provinces of Canada* (1914), 188–89, cited in Anderson, "Assimilation in the Bloc Settlements of North-Central Saskatchewan," 81.

17 For example, according to the Rosthern Board of Trade, Stefan Rogozinsky immigrated in 1900 with assets of seventy-five dollars, yet by 1911 he had six quarters of productive farmland producing 10,000 bushels a year; similarly, Anton Hrabshak immigrated with $125, and by 1911 he had five quarters producing between 8,000 and 10,000 bushels a year. Cited in Anderson, "Assimilation in the Bloc Settlements of North-Central Saskatchewan," 81–82.

18 Archives of Saskatchewan; Hafford History Committee, *Hafford and District Golden Jubilee* (1963), cited in Anderson, "Assimilation in the Bloc Settlements of North-Central Saskatchewan," 82–85.

19 Archives of Saskatchewan; Young, *The Ukrainian Canadians*, 65, cited in Anderson, "Assimilation in the Bloc Settlements of North-Central Saskatchewan," 88.

20 Anderson, "Assimilation in the Bloc Settlements of North-Central Saskatchewan," 131.

21 Ibid., 132; A.B. Anderson, "Ukrainian Identity Change in Rural Saskatchewan," in *Ukrainians in American and Canadian Society: Contributions to the Sociology of Ethnic Groups*, ed. W.W. Isajiw (Cambridge, MA: Harvard Ukrainian Research Institute, Harvard University; New York: Ukrainian Center for Social Research, 1976), 113.

22 Anderson, "Assimilation in the Bloc Settlements of North-Central Saskatchewan," 132.

23 Young, *The Ukrainian Canadians*, 29, 74, 152–53, 275, cited in ibid., 133.

24 Young, *The Ukrainian Canadians*, 151–52, 172–75; V. Lysenko, *Men in Sheepskin Coats: A Study in Assimilation* (Toronto: Ryerson, 1947), 286, cited in Anderson, "Assimilation in the Bloc Settlements of North-Central Saskatchewan," 133–34.

25 Young, *The Ukrainian Canadians*, 172–75, cited in Anderson, "Assimilation in the Bloc Settlements of North-Central Saskatchewan," 134.

26 R.E. Park, *Race and Culture* (Glencoe, IL: Free Press, 1950), 368, cited in Anderson, "Assimilation in the Bloc Settlements of North-Central Saskatchewan," 134.

27 Archives of Saskatchewan; *Regina Daily Post*, July 10, 1919, cited in Anderson, "Assimilation in the Bloc Settlements of North-Central Saskatchewan," 134.

28 J. Hawkes, *The Story of Saskatchewan and Its People* (Regina: S.T. Clark, 1924), 689, 731–34, cited in Anderson, "Assimilation in the Bloc Settlements of North-Central Saskatchewan," 134.

29 *Winnipeg Tribune*, May 27, 1897, cited in Kaye, *Early Ukrainian Settlements in Canada, 1895–1900*, 282.

30 Lysenko, *Men in Sheepskin Coats*, 98–100; Young, *The Ukrainian Canadians*, 289, cited in Anderson, "Assimilation in the Bloc Settlements of North-Central Saskatchewan," 134.

31 J.F.C. Wright, *Saskatchewan: The History of a Province* (Toronto: McClelland and Stewart, 1955), 169–70, 210–11, cited in Anderson, "Assimilation in the Bloc Settlements of North-Central Saskatchewan," 134–35.

32 N.F. Black, *History of Saskatchewan and the North-West Territories* (Regina: Saskatchewan Historical, 1913), 740; Young, *The Ukrainian Canadians*, 28, cited in Anderson, "Assimilation in the Bloc Settlements of North-Central Saskatchewan," 135.

33 *Report of the Saskatchewan Royal Commission on Immigration and Settlement* (Regina: King's Publisher, 1930), 78, cited in Anderson, "Assimilation in the Bloc Settlements of North-Central Saskatchewan," 135.

34 S. Lieberson, *Ethnic Patterns in American Cities* (Glencoe, NY: Macmillan, 1963), 139, 141, 145, cited in Anderson, "Assimilation in the Bloc Settlements of North-Central Saskatchewan," 135.

35 Young, *The Ukrainian Canadians*, 250; Hawkes, *The Story of Saskatchewan and Its People*, 731–34, cited in Anderson, "Assimilation in the Bloc Settlements of North-Central Saskatchewan," 135.

36 Archives of Saskatchewan; *Regina Leader Post*, May 8, 1920, cited in Anderson, "Assimilation in the Bloc Settlements of North-Central Saskatchewan," 135.

37 Ukrainian Canadian Culture Group, *Canadians on the March: Canada United* (1944), cited in Anderson, "Assimilation in the Bloc Settlements of North-Central Saskatchewan," 135–36.

38 Anderson, "Assimilation in the Bloc Settlements of North-Central Saskatchewan," 126–31, 224–33; Anderson, "Ukrainian Identity Change in Rural Saskatchewan."

39 R. England, *The Central European Immigrant in Canada* (Toronto: Macmillan, 1929), 55–56, 60, 76–77; Young, *The Ukrainian Canadians*, 179, 186–90, cited in Anderson, "Assimilation in the Bloc Settlements of North-Central Saskatchewan," 149.

40 Archives of Saskatchewan, cited in Anderson, "Assimilation in the Bloc Settlements of North-Central Saskatchewan," 149–50.

41 Lysenko, *Men in Sheepskin Coats*, 245–46; Sherbinin, *The Galicians Dwelling in Canada and Their Origin*, 3–4, cited in Anderson, "Assimilation in the Bloc Settlements of North-Central Saskatchewan," 150.

42 A. Milnor, "The New Politics and Ethnic Revolt, 1928–1938," in *Politics in Saskatchewan*, ed. N. Ward and D. Spafford (Lindsay, ON: Longmans of Canada and John Dyell, 1968), 172; Young, *The Ukrainian Canadians*, 172, cited in Anderson, "Assimilation in the Bloc Settlements of North-Central Saskatchewan," 150.

43 Anderson, "Assimilation in the Bloc Settlements of North-Central Saskatchewan," 139–45, 226, 230.

44 Ibid., 151–53.

45 The Ukrainians of Galicia were largely Ukrainian (Eastern Rite) Catholics after 1595, whereas the Carpatho-Russian Orthodox Greek Catholic Church did not unite with Rome until the seventeenth century. The Ukrainians of the Ukraine proper (i.e., what is today eastern Ukraine) and Bukovina remained Russian Orthodox; a specifically Ukrainian Orthodox Church was not organized in Ukraine until 1925 with the birth of the Autocephalous Ukrainian Synodal Church. A number of Western Rite dioceses also existed within the Russian Empire.

46 See E. Tremblay, CSsR, *Le Père Delaere et l'Eglise Ukrainienne du Canada* (Berthierville, QC: l'Imprimerie Bernard, 1960).

47 In its first couple of years, the Greek Independent Church had 20,000–30,000 adherents gained from Russian Orthodox and Ukrainian Catholics. This church was sponsored by the Presbyterian Church, but its priests were ordained and trained by Russian Orthodox priests. Services were held in the Ukrainian vernacular, as distinguished from the Old Church Slavonic of the Russian Orthodox Church, and followed traditional Orthodox ritual, very popular in a time of extensive Latinization of Ukrainians. But when the link with Presbyterian Protestantism became more obvious in 1912, numerous church members, fearing assimilation, left the church.

48 O.S. Trosky, *The Ukrainian Greek Orthodox Church in Canada* (Winnipeg: Bulman Brothers, 1968), 17–37.

49 DeVisser and Kalman, *Pioneer Churches*, 173.

50 Young, *The Ukrainian Canadians*, 143.

51 Y.W. Lozowchuk, "Religious Conflict in a Community" (1966), author's archives.

52 Reverend M. Schudlo, booklets published by *Redeemer's Voice* in 1951 and 1962; Young, *The Ukrainian Canadians*, 134–36, 143.

53 K. Yaganiski, "A Case Study of Sts. Peter and Paul Ukrainian Catholic Church, Rosthern, Sask." (1990), author's archives.

54 G. Krajci, "A Study of the Ukrainian Catholic Parish in Foam Lake, Sask." (1990), author's archives.

55 Archives of Saskatchewan; Hawkes, *The Story of Saskatchewan and Its People*, 731–34, cited in Anderson, "Assimilation in the Bloc Settlements of North-Central Saskatchewan," 173.

56 M. Fieguth and D. Christensen, *Historic Saskatchewan* (Toronto: Oxford University Press, 1986), 28–32.

57 J. Lehr, "The Log Buildings of Ukrainian Settlers in Western Canada," *Prairie Forum* 5, 2 (1980): 183–96.

58 J. Bruce, *The Last Best West* (Toronto: Fitzhenry and Whiteside, 1976), 107.

59 P. Durant, "Learning about Polish and Ukrainian Culture," *Folklore* (fall 2010): 14–18. See also Lysenko, *Men in Sheepskin Coats*, 206, 217–27, 239, 246–47; England, *The Central European Immigrant in Canada*, 57; and Anderson, *The Education of the New Canadian*, 62.

60 Saskatoon *StarPhoenix*, January 6, 2009.

61 Saskatoon *StarPhoenix*, December 22, 2008.

62 Trosky, *The Ukrainian Greek Orthodox Church in Canada*, 58; Skwarok, *The Ukrainian Settlers in Canada and Their Schools*, 19; K.A. McLeod, "Politics, Schools, and the French Language, 1881–1931," in Ward and Spafford, eds., *Politics in Saskatchewan*, 128–30.

63 Skwarok, *The Ukrainian Settlers in Canada and Their Schools*, 117–18; Archives of Saskatchewan, cited in Anderson, "Assimilation in the Bloc Settlements of North-Central Saskatchewan," 297.

64 The foregoing information is drawn from Archives of Saskatchewan, cited in Anderson, "Assimilation in the Bloc Settlements of North-Central Saskatchewan," 298–99; Young, *The Ukrainian Canadians*, 186, 189–90; Skwarok, *The Ukrainian Settlers in Canada and Their Schools*.

65 Photograph in H. Robertson, *The Salt of the Earth* (Toronto: James Lorimer and Company, 1974), 135.

66 H.W. Foght, *Saskatchewan School Survey* (1918), 151–52, cited in England, *The Central European Immigrant in Canada*, 108–12; Young, *The Ukrainian Canadians*, 186–87; Anderson, *The Education of the New Canadian*, 56–58; Archives of Saskatchewan, cited in Anderson, "Assimilation in the Bloc Settlements of North-Central Saskatchewan," 299–300.

67 Archives of Saskatchewan, cited in Anderson, "Assimilation in the Bloc Settlements of North-Central Saskatchewan," 300–01.

68 Trosky, *The Ukrainian Greek Orthodox Church in Canada*, 80–82; Archives of Saskatchewan, cited in Anderson, "Assimilation in the Bloc Settlements of North-Central Saskatchewan," 301.

69 V. Buyniak, "Ukrainian Language Teaching," in *Encyclopedia of Saskatchewan* (Regina: Canadian Plains Research Center, 2005), 964.

70 Lysenko, *Men in Sheepskin Coats*, 206–12, 227, 286.

71 Trosky, *The Ukrainian Greek Orthodox Church in Canada*, 70–80; Young, *The Ukrainian Canadians*, 151–52; C.A. Dawson, *Group Settlement: Ethnic Communities in Western Canada* (Toronto: Macmillan, 1936), 76–77.

72 Royal Commission on Bilingualism and Biculturalism, *Report of the Royal Commission on Bilingualism and Biculturalism* (Ottawa: Information Canada, 1967), cited in Anderson, "Assimilation in the Bloc Settlements of North-Central Saskatchewan," 308.

73 Archives of Saskatchewan, cited in Anderson, "Assimilation in the Bloc Settlements of North-Central Saskatchewan," 254; England, *The Central European Immigrant in Canada*, 11–12.

74 L. Kasperski, "Polish Settlements," in *Encyclopedia of Saskatchewan* (Regina: Canadian Plains Research Center, 2005), 696–97.

75 G. Wolffe, "A Survey of Three Families from Queen of Peace Church" (1988), author's archives; information also from D. Polachic, "Faithful Families Mark Smuts-Area Church Centenary," Saskatoon *StarPhoenix*, July 3, 2004.

76 M. Smolinski, "Our Lady of Czestochowa Parish: Keeping More than the Faith" (1992), author's archives.

77 M. Kruchak, "Ukrainian Immigrants See Future in Saskatchewan," Saskatoon *StarPhoenix*, December 31, 2007; L. Simcoe, "Support System Strong for Ukrainians in City," Saskatoon *StarPhoenix*, August 25, 2008.

Chapter 6: *The Settlements of Other Eastern European Groups*

1 K.J. Tarasoff, *A Pictorial History of the Doukhobors* (Saskatoon: Modern Press, 1969), 41 etc.; C.A. Dawson, *Group Settlement: Ethnic Communities in Western Canada* (Toronto: Macmillan, 1936), 1–7.

2 S. Holt, *Terror in the Name of God* (Toronto: McClelland and Stewart, 1964), 27; A. Maude, *The Doukhobors: A Peculiar People* (New York: Funk and Wagnalls, 1904), 53, 179; Dawson, *Group Settlement*, 7–11.

3 J.W. Dafoe, *Clifford Sifton in Relation to His Times* (Toronto: Macmillan, 1931), 143.

4 V. Vereshagin's report on the Prince Albert/Saskatchewan Colony, fall 1900, cited in Maude, *The Doukhobors*, 206.

5 Saskatchewan Association of Architects, *Historic Architecture of Saskatchewan* (Regina: Focus Publishing, 1987), 118–21.

6 Data compiled from C.J. Tracie, *"Toil and Peaceful Life": Doukhobor Village Settlement in Saskatchewan, 1899–1918* (Regina: Canadian Plains Research Center, 1996).

7 Details from Dawson, *Group Settlement*, 26–46; Holt, *Terror in the Name of God*, 27; Tarasoff, *A Pictorial History of the Doukhobors*; and Tracie, *"Toil and Peaceful Life."*

8 Clifford Sifton, letter, November 1901, cited in Dafoe, *Clifford Sifton in Relation to His Times*, 142.

9 For details on homestead entries, see Tracie, *"Toil and Peaceful Life."*

10 G. Woodcock and I. Avakumovic, *The Doukhobors* (Toronto: McClelland and Stewart, 1968), 240.

11 N.F. Black, *History of Saskatchewan and the North West Territories* (Regina: Saskatchewan Historical, 1913), 729 etc.

12 Dawson, *Group Settlement*, 26–46; Holt, *Terror in the Name of God*, 47–48; Tracie, *"Toil and Peaceful Life"*; K.J. Tarasoff, "Doukhobor Settlements," in *Encyclopedia of Saskatchewan* (Regina: Canadian Plains Research Center, 2005), 254–56.

13 Tarasoff, "Doukhobor Settlements."

14 Holt, *Terror in the Name of God*, 50; Tracie, "Toil and Peaceful Life," 104; Tarasoff, "Doukobor Settlements."

15 The Doukhobor Dugout House historic site at Oospenia claims that between 200 and 300 people lived there.

16 The foregoing data were compiled from Tracie, "Toil and Peaceful Life."

17 Woodcock and Avakumovic, *The Doukhobors*, 242.

18 Holt, *Terror in the Name of God*, 48; Maude, *The Doukhobors*, 203; Tarasoff, *A Pictorial History of the Doukhobors*, 65.

19 B. Barry, *People Places: Saskatchewan and Its Names* (Regina: Canadian Plains Research Center, 1997), 85; B. Barry, *Geographic Names of Saskatchewan* (Regina: People Places Publishing, 2005).

20 Maude, *The Doukhobors*, 183, 203, 257; Woodcock and Avakumovic, *The Doukhobors*, 285–86; Holt, *Terror in the Name of God*, 85–88, 142.

21 Dawson, *Group Settlement*, 18–19, 79–91; Tarasoff, *A Pictorial History of the Doukhobors*, 21–28.

22 Population estimates are based on 1961 census data.

23 Population data based on 1971 census data; also see Tarasoff, "Doukobor Settlements."

24 A.B. Anderson, "Assimilation in the Bloc Settlements of North-Central Saskatchewan: A Comparative Study of Identity Change among Seven Ethno-Religious Groups in a Canadian Prairie Region" (Ph.D. diss., University of Saskatchewan, 1972).

25 M. Lalonde and E. LaClare, *Discover Saskatchewan: A Guide to Historic Sites* (Regina: Canadian Plains Research Center, 1998), 94.

26 "Historical Blaine Lake" (provincial anniversary community study, 1955), author's archives.

27 Archives of Saskatchewan, cited in Anderson, "Assimilation in the Bloc Settlements of North-Central Saskatchewan," 299.

28 Saskatoon *StarPhoenix*, August 12, 2010.

29 See G. Dojcsak, "The Mysterious Count Esterhazy," *Saskatchewan History* 26, 2 (1973): 63–72, and M. Vajcner, "Paul Esterhazy," in *Encyclopedia of Saskatchewan* (Regina: Canadian Plains Research Center, 2005).

30 M. Hryniuk and F. Korvemaker, *Legacy of Stone: Saskatchewan's Stone Buildings* (Regina: Coteau Books, 2008), 156–59.

31 Barry, *People Places*, 76.

32 Saskatoon *StarPhoenix*, January 25, 2005.

33 See R. Blumstock, ed., *Bekevar: Working Papers on a Canadian Prairie Community* (Ottawa: National Museum, 1979), and M.L. Kovacs, *Peace and Strife* (Kipling, SK: Kipling District Historical Society, 1980).

34 See St. Laszlo Historical Committee, *With Faith and Hope: St. Laszlo — Our Heritage* (North Battleford: Turner-Warwick Printers, 1979).

35 Lalonde and LaClare, *Discover Saskatchewan*, 112.

36 G.J. Patterson, "Ethnicity and Religious Affiliation in Romanian Communities in Saskatchewan," Central and East European Studies Association of Canada, 1978.

37 Ibid.

38 Romanian traditions are described in detail in G. Johnson, "The Romanians in Western Canada," *Saskatchewan History* 14, 2 (1961): 64–70; interview with priest from Patterson, 1978.

39 The region known as Subcarpathian Ruthenia, long included within the Austro-Hungarian Empire, was mostly part of the new country of Czechoslovakia from 1920 to 1938. However,

Slovaks were outnumbered by Ruthenians (Ukrainians), while Magyars (Hungarians) and Romanians constituted substantial minorities. Hungary regained control first of the southern frontier areas of Uzhorod/Ungvar and Mukachevo/Munkacs in 1938, then of the entire region the following year, but in 1945 most of the region was incorporated into the Ukraine Soviet Socialist Republic (except for the southernmost frontier area inclusive of Sihot/Sighetul/Maramarossziget, retained by Romania).

40 Saskatoon *Star-Phoenix*, November 15, 1975.

41 A. Feldman, "Jewish Rural Settlements," in *Encyclopedia of Saskatchewan* (Regina: Canadian Plains Research Center, 2005), 491–92.

42 H. Robertson, *Salt of the Earth* (Toronto: James Lorimer, 1974), 34.

43 Photograph in ibid., 35.

44 M. Fieguth and D. Christensen, *Historic Saskatchewan* (Toronto: Oxford University Press, 1986), 67.

45 K. Ondaatje, *Small Churches of Canada* (Toronto: Lester and Orpen Dennys, 1982), 136.

Chapter 7: French Settlements

1 M. Fieguth and D. Christensen, *Historic Saskatchewan* (Toronto: Oxford University Press, 1986), 21.

2 Information on the history of Lebret compiled primarily from M. Lalonde and E. LaClare, *Discover Saskatchewan: A Guide to Historic Sites* (Regina: Canadian Plains Research Center, 1998), 38–39, and M. Hryniuk and F. Korvemaker, *Legacy of Stone: Saskatchewan's Stone Buildings* (Regina: Coteau Books, 2008), 180–83.

3 See *"Their Dreams ... Our Memories": A History of Duck Lake and District*, 2 vols. (Altona, MB: Friesen Printers, 1988).

4 These details on the St-Laurent settlement have been drawn from E.H. Oliver, "Economic Conditions of Saskatchewan, 1870-1881," *Transactions of the Royal Society of Canada*, 3rd series, 28, section 2 (1933): 20–29; Reverend J. LeChevalier, *St-Laurent-de-Grandin* (Vannes, France: Lafolye and J. de Lamarzelle, 1930); M. Giraud, *Le Métis Canadien* (Paris: Université de Paris, 1945), 1047, 1138–52; D. Frémont, *Les Français dans l'Ouest Canadien* (1959; reprinted, St-Boniface, MB: Les Editions du Blé, 1980), 111; Fieguth and Christensen, *Historic Saskatchewan*, 45; J.F.C. Wright, *Saskatchewan: The History of a Province* (Toronto: McClelland and Stewart, 1955), 47–53; G.F.G. Stanley, "French and English in Western Canada," in *Canadian Dualism/La dualité canadienne*, ed. M. Wade (Toronto: University of Toronto Press, 1960), 17–25; J.K. Howard, *The Strange Empire of Louis Riel* (Toronto: Swan Publishing, 1970); and J.H. Archer, *Footprints in Time* (Toronto: House of Grant, 1965), 44 et seq.

5 Louis Riel to Sir John A. Macdonald, September 4, 1882, Canada Sessional Papers No. 116, 1885; Wright, *Saskatchewan*, 80–82.

6 Details from the Batoche National Historic Site guidebook and *I Remember: A History of St. Louis and Surrounding Areas* (Altona, MB: Friesen Printers, 1980).

7 Hryniuk and Korvemaker, *Legacy of Stone*, 38–41.

8 D.P. Payment, *The Free People — Li gens libre* (Calgary: University of Calgary Press, 2009).

9 For details on the role and attitudes of the French Catholic clergy and hierarchy during the North-West Resistance, and on Riel's view of his cause as a religio-ethnic movement, see Giraud, *Le Métis Canadien*, 1190–96, 1201–06; Wright, *Saskatchewan*, 87; N.F. Black, *History of Saskatchewan and the North West Territories* (Regina: Saskatchewan Historical, 1913), Chapters 28–29; and A-H.

de Trémaudan, *Histoire de la Nation Métisse dans l'Ouest Canadien* (1935; reprinted, St-Boniface, MB: Editions des Plaines, 1984), 411–14, 421–31. For details on the Métis exodus from the settlement, see Giraud, *Le Métis Canadien*, 1263–64, 1283. For details on the destitution of the Métis at the time and to the 1930s, see Giraud, *Le Métis Canadien*, 1220, 1224, 1279–80; Black, *History of Saskatchewan and the North West Territories*, Chapter 27; and Métis Conference Proceedings, Regina, July 30, 1946, 25, 38–40. For details on the identity crisis facing the Métis following the resistance, see Wright, *Saskatchewan*, 52, and Giraud, *Le Métis Canadien*, 1223, 1253–54, 1270, 1279–80, 1282.

10 D. Fremont, *Les Français dans l'Ouest Canadien* (Winnipeg: Les Editions de la Liberté, 1959), 112.

11 Many of these details on the history of Bellevue have been drawn from Père Denis Dubuc, *Généalogie des familles de la Paroisse St-Isidore-de-Bellevue, Saskatchewan, 1902–1970* (1970), and *Souvenirs, 1902–2002, St-Isidore-de-Bellevue* (2002), abridged in *Lectures du milieu Bellevue*.

12 "Their Dreams ... Our Memories."

13 C. MacDonald, "Pioneer Church Life in Saskatchewan," *Saskatchewan History* (winter 1960): 1, 10.

14 Details from *St-Brieux, 1904–1929: Reminiscences d'un Pionnier* (1929); *Cinquantenaire de la Paroisse de St-Brieux, Saskatchewan, 1904–1954* (1954); as well as other local sources.

15 MacDonald, "Pioneer Church Life in Saskatchewan," 6, 18.

16 *Hier et aujourd'hui/Yesterday and Today: Zenon Park 1910–1983* (1983).

17 These details are from F. Moore, *Saskatchewan Ghost Towns* (1982), 5.

18 Cited in Hryniuk and Korvemaker, *Legacy of Stone*, 54–57, 192–95.

19 Ibid., 74–77.

20 M. Guitard, "La Rolanderie," *Saskatchewan History* 30, 3 (1977): 110–14.

21 Laurier Gagnon, "L'église de Ste-Marthe," *Revue historique* 13, 1 (2002).

22 *Jubilé Souvenir, 1906–1956* (Forget, SK: Académie St-Joseph, 1956).

23 See Reverend Mother St. Stephen, "Father Gravel, Missionary-Colonizer," *Saskatchewan History* 12, 3 (1959): 107–09; also see J.W. Dafoe, *Clifford Sifton in Relation to His Times* (Toronto: Macmillan, 1931), 141.

24 Lalonde and LaClare, *Discover Saskatchewan*, 24–26.

25 An extensive discussion of these processes is found in B.R. Hamilton, "Francophone Settlement in the Gravelbourg Bloc Settlement and Francophone and Métis Settlement in the Willow Bunch Bloc Settlement in Southwestern Saskatchewan, 1870–1926" (MA thesis, University of Regina, 2007).

26 Adrien Chabot, "On s'garoche à Ferland," *L'eau vive*, août 15–21, 1979.

27 R. Lacoursière-Stringer, *Histoire de Ponteix/History of Ponteix* (Steinbach, MB: Derksen Printers, 1981).

28 Eastend History Society, *Range Riders and Sodbusters: Eastend, South Fork, and Districts* (North Battleford: Turner-Warwick Printers, 1984).

29 See Laurier Gareau, "La Paroisse St-Jean-Baptiste de Regina: Si seulement ... ," *Revue historique* 15, 2 (2004): 11–12.

30 This section is revised and updated from A.B. Anderson, "Profil demographique des Canadiens-français de la Saskatchewan: 1885–1985," in *Héritage et avenir des francophones de l'Ouest*, les Actes du Cinquième Colloque du Centre d'Etudes Franco-Canadiennes de l'Ouest Tenu au Collège St. Thomas More, Université de la Saskatchewan, octobre 1985, 175–77.

31 Revised and updated from ibid., 177–79.

32   Revised and updated from ibid., 179–83.

33   These data come from Statistics Canada, 2001; and the *Atlas de la francophonie: Saskatchewan* website, 2008.

34   K. McLeod, "Politics, Schools, and the French Language, 1881–1931," in *Politics in Saskatchewan*, ed. N. Ward and D. Spafford (Lindsay, ON: Longmans of Canada and John Dyell, 1968), 124; C.A. Dawson and E.R. Younge, *Pioneering in the Prairie Provinces: The Social Side of the Settlement Process* (Toronto: Macmillan, 1940) 168–69; Stanley, "French and English in Western Canada," 331.

35   McLeod, "Politics, Schools, and the French Language, 1881–1931," 125–31.

36   M.R. Lupul, *The Roman Catholic Church and the North-West School Question: A Study in Church-State Relations in Western Canada, 1875–1905* (Toronto: University of Toronto Press, 1974).

37   Archives of Saskatchewan, cited in A.B. Anderson, "Assimilation in the Bloc Settlements of North-Central Saskatchewan: A Comparative Study of Identity Change among Seven Ethno-Religious Groups in a Canadian Prairie Region" (Ph.D. diss., University of Saskatchewan, 1972), 283–84; R. Huel, "The French Canadians and the Language Question in 1918," *Saskatchewan History* 23, 1 (1970): 1; McLeod, "Politics, Schools, and the French Language, 1881–1931," 134.

38   Huel, "The French Canadians and the Language Question in 1918," 1–4; McLeod, "Politics, Schools, and the French Language, 1881–1931," 135.

39   Huel, "The French Canadians and the Language Question in 1918," 14; Archives of Saskatchewan, cited in Anderson, "Assimilation in the Bloc Settlements of North-Central Saskatchewan," 284–85.

40   Huel, "The French Canadians and the Language Question in 1918," 4–7, 9, 13; McLeod, "Politics, Schools, and the French Language, 1881–1931," 138–42; Archives of Saskatchewan, cited in Anderson, "Assimilation in the Bloc Settlements of North-Central Saskatchewan," 285.

41   Huel, "The French Canadians and the Language Question in 1918," 6–15; Archives of Saskatchewan, cited in Anderson, "Assimilation in the Bloc Settlements of North-Central Saskatchewan," 285–86.

42   Archives of Saskatchewan, cited in Anderson, "Assimilation in the Bloc Settlements of North-Central Saskatchewan," 286.

43   Ibid., 287; Huel, "The French Canadians and the Language Question in 1918," 13–14.

44   Archives of Saskatchewan, cited in Anderson, "Assimilation in the Bloc Settlements of North-Central Saskatchewan," 287–88; Huel, "The French Canadians and the Language Question in 1918," 11–14.

45   Archives of Saskatchewan, cited in Anderson, "Assimilation in the Bloc Settlements of North-Central Saskatchewan," 288.

46   Ibid., 288–89; McLeod,"Politics, Schools, and the French Language, 1881–1931," 143–44.

47   McLeod, "Politics, Schools, and the French Language, 1881–1931," 144–47.

48   Stanley, "French and English in Western Canada," 338; K.W. Taylor, "A Comparative Study of Images Associated with Biculturalism" (MA thesis, University of Saskatchewan, 1966), 122–23.

49   Saskatoon *Star-Phoenix*, May 20, 1977.

50   Saskatoon *Star-Phoenix*, May 26, 1977.

51   Saskatoon *Star-Phoenix*, June 14, 1977.

52   Saskatoon *Star-Phoenix*, August 29, 1977; September 6, 1977; September 24, 1979.

53   Saskatoon *Star-Phoenix*, January 19 and 22, 1981; *Maclean's*, March 7, 1988.

54   Saskatoon *StarPhoenix*, January 24, 2008.

55   Saskatoon *StarPhoenix*, April 26 and 28, 1990.

56 See A. Dubé, *La voix du peuple* (Regina: Société Historique de la Saskatchewan, 1994).

57 Stanley, "French and English in Western Canada," 334–35.

58 F. Scott and M. Oliver, eds., *Quebec States Her Case* (Toronto: Macmillan of Canada 1964), 2.

59 F.R. Beaulieu, "Revendiquer la télévision française en Saskatchewan," *Revue historique* 15, 2 (2004): 1–10.

60 W.B. Denis, "From Minority to Citizenship: The Challenges of Diversity in Saskatchewan's Francophone Community," and Y. Bouchamma, "The Challenges that Francophone Minority Schools Face in Integrating Immigrant Students," in *Immigration and Diversity in Francophone Minority Communities*, ed. C. Belkhodja, special issue of *Canadian Issues/Thèmes canadiens* (spring 2008): 42–44, 109–12.

Chapter 8: Nordic Settlements

1 J.P. Johansen, "Immigrant Settlements and Social Organization in South Dakota," Bulletin No. 313, Department of Rural Sociology, Agricultural Experimental Station, South Dakota State College of Agriculture and Mechanic Arts, Brookings, SD, June 1937, 8–22.

2 Annual Report of the Canadian Department of the Interior for 1895.

3 N.F. Black, *History of Saskatchewan and the North West Territories* (Regina: Saskatchewan Historical, 1913), 725.

4 Calculated from 1971 census data.

5 Calculated from 2006 census data.

6 P. Myrvold, "Norwegian Colonization in Canada," paper presented at the Norse Convention, Swift Current, SK, July 10–12, 1929.

7 Data compiled from L.K. Munholland, *Pulpits of the Past* (Strasbourg, SK: Three West Two South Books, 2004).

8 See A.B. Anderson, "Scandinavian Settlements in Saskatchewan: Migration History and Changing Ethnocultural Identity," in *Scandinavian-Canadian Studies*, vol. 2, ed. G.A. Woods (Ottawa: Association for the Advancement of Scandinavian Studies in Canada, 1986), 89–113.

9 F. Moore, *Saskatchewan Ghost Towns* (1982), 24.

10 *Saskatchewan Genealogical Society Bulletin* 9, 3 (1978): 121–22.

11 L.K. Munholland, *Bread to Share*, 2 vols. (Strasbourg, SK: Three West Two South Books, 2006).

12 D. McLennan, *Our Towns: Saskatchewan Communities from Abbey to Zenon Park* (Regina: Canadian Plains Research Center, 2008), 339–40.

13 Munholland, *Bread to Share*.

14 C. MacDonald, "Pioneer Church Life in Saskatchewan," *Saskatchewan History* (winter 1960): 16.

15 Myrvold, "Norwegian Colonization in Canada."

16 Ibid.

17 B. Barry, *Geographic Names of Saskatchewan* (Regina: People Places Publishing, 2005), 248.

18 Ibid.

19 Munholland, *Bread to Share*.

20 MacDonald, "Pioneer Church Life in Saskatchewan," 9, 18.

21 Ibid., 11.

22. M. Hryniuk and F. Korvemaker, *Legacy of Stone: Saskatchewan's Stone Buildings* (Regina: Coteau Books, 2008), 77.

23. See MacDonald, "Pioneer Church Life in Saskatchewan," 7.

24. M. Lalonde and E. LaClare, *Discover Saskatchewan: A Guide to Historic Sites* (Regina: Canadian Plains Research Center, 1998), 127.

25. Hryniuk and Korvemaker, *Legacy of Stone*, 130–33.

26. W. Kristjanson, *The Icelandic People in Manitoba* (1965; reprinted, Winnipeg: R.W. Kristjanson, 1990), 332–33.

27. A.B. Anderson and J. Eyolfson Cadman, "Icelandic Settlements," in *Encyclopedia of Saskatchewan* (Regina: Canadian Plains Research Center, 2005), 476.

28. The foregoing data are from A.B. Anderson and B. Niskala, "Finnish Settlements in Saskatchewan: Their Development and Perpetuation," in *Finnish Diaspora*, vol. 1, ed. M.G. Karni (Toronto: Multicultural History Society of Ontario, 1981), 157–58.

29. Ibid., 158–59.

30. Details on this settlement have been drawn from ibid., 159–61, and N.M. Schelstraete, ed., with the New Finland Historical and Heritage Society, *Life in the New Finland Woods: A History of New Finland, Saskatchewan* (Edmonton: Ronalds Western Printing, 1982).

31. Details on this settlement have been drawn from Anderson and Niskala, "Finnish Settlements in Saskatchewan," 162–63.

32. Described in L. Warwaruk, *Red Finns on the Coteau* (Saskatoon: Core Communications, 1984).

33. Details on this settlement have been drawn from Anderson and Niskala, "Finnish Settlements in Saskatchewan," 161–62, and other sources.

34. J. Hawkes, *The Story of Saskatchewan and Its People*, vol. 2 (Regina: S.T. Clarke, 1924), 686, 707.

35. *Report of the Saskatchewan Royal Commission on Immigration and Settlement* (Regina: King's Publisher, 1930), 78.

36. Saskatchewan Diamond Jubilee and Centennial Corporation, *The Saskatchewanians* (Regina: n.p., 1967).

37. Brief submitted to the Saskatchewan Royal Commission, 1930.

38. A.B. Anderson, "Assimilation in the Bloc Settlements of North-Central Saskatchewan: A Comparative Study of Identity Change among Seven Ethno-Religious Groups in a Canadian Prairie Region" (Ph.D. diss., University of Saskatchewan, 1972).

39. Data derived from the 1971 census.

40. Anderson and Niskala, "Finnish Settlements in Saskatchewan," 171–72.

41. Ibid., 173–74.

42. Reverend W.A. Mehlenbacher, "The Lutheran Church in Canada," undated brochure in author's archives, cited in Anderson, "Assimilation in the Bloc Settlements of North-Central Saskatchewan," 164–65; Reverend I. Rasmussen, in the *Lur*, Scandinavian Historical Society (spring 1971): 4; O. Bruun, in the *Lur* (September 1970): 2; V.J. Eylands, *Lutherans in Canada* (Winnipeg: Icelandic Lutheran Synod in North America, 1945).

43. W.E. Mann, *Sect, Cult, and Church in Alberta* (Toronto: University of Toronto Press, 1955), 49–53; A. Ricke, *Geschichlicher Uberblick des Zwanzigjahren Bestehens des Kanada Disticts der Evangelisch-Lutherischen Synode von Ohio und Anderen Staaten* (Regina: Evangelical Lutheran Synod, 1928), cited in G.E. Britnell, *The Wheat Economy* (Toronto: University of Toronto Press, 1939), 188–90.

44. Mehlenbacher, "The Lutheran Church in Canada."

45 Based on information from the *Shepherd*, the publication of the Evangelical Lutheran Church of Canada, during past decades.

46 Anderson, "Scandinavian Settlements in Saskatchewan," 101–02.

47 This discussion is derived from Anderson and Niskala, "Finnish Settlements in Saskatchewan," 163–68.

48 These details on Finnish customs come from ibid., 175–77.

49 O. Asgeirsson Struthers, review of *The Saskatchewan Icelanders*, by V.J. Lindal, *Saskatchewan History* 9, 2 (1956): 76–78.

50 A couple of years earlier it was reported that no instance of a Scandinavian language being taught during the final school hour was known in the Kinistino Inspectorate, while in the Humboldt Inspectorate only five schools were probably using Norwegian and two more possibly using it. Archives of Saskatchewan, cited in Anderson, "Assimilation in the Bloc Settlements of North-Central Saskatchewan," 301–02; K. McLeod, "Politics, Schools, and the French Language," in *Politics in Saskatchewan*, ed. N. Ward and D. Spafford (Lindsay, ON: Longmans of Canada and John Dyell, 1968), 128–30.

51 Anderson, "Scandinavian Settlements in Saskatchewan," 104.

52 Ibid., 105.

53 The foregoing discussion is from Anderson and Niskala, "Finnish Settlements in Saskatchewan," 168–72; also see Warwaruk, *Red Finns on the Coteau*.

54 Anderson and Niskala, "Finnish Settlements in Saskatchewan," 177–80.

Chapter 9: Other Settlements and Urban Minorities

1 D. Elliott, "International Immigration," in *Encyclopedia of Saskatchewan* (Regina: Canadian Plains Research Center, 2005), 483.

2 Compiled from Statistics Canada data, reported in the *Globe and Mail*, December 5, 2007, and the *Saskatoon StarPhoenix*, December 5 and 6, 2007.

3 *Saskatoon StarPhoenix*, December 5, 2007.

4 Ibid. See also Elliott, "International Immigration."

5 Elliott, "International Immigration."

6 B.D. Thraves, "Urban Ethnic Diversity," in *Encyclopedia of Saskatchewan* (Regina: Canadian Plains Research Center, 2005), 976–77; Statistics Canada data, reported in the *Globe and Mail*, April 3, 2008.

7 Data are from Statistics Canada; see A.B. Anderson, "Visible Minorities," in *Encyclopedia of Saskatchewan* (Regina: Canadian Plains Research Center, 2005), 990.

8 Details from L. Zong, "Chinese Community," in *Encyclopedia of Saskatchewan* (Regina: Canadian Plains Research Center, 2005), 170–71.

9 Ibid.

10 Ibid.

11 For details, see V-T. Lam, "Vietnamese Community," in *Encyclopedia of Saskatchewan* (Regina: Canadian Plains Research Center, 2005), 988–89.

12 R.B. Shepard, "Blacks: Early Settlements," in *Encyclopedia of Saskatchewan* (Regina: Canadian Plains Research Center, 2005), 116.

13 Ibid.

14 P. Elabor-Idemudia, "Blacks: Recent Immigration," in *Encyclopedia of Saskatchewan* (Regina: Canadian Plains Research Center, 2005), 116–17.

15 Ibid.

16 K. Srinivas, "Indo-Canadian Community," in *Encyclopedia of Saskatchewan* (Regina: Canadian Plains Research Center, 2005), 481.

17 R. Pino, "Hispanic Community," in *Encyclopedia of Saskatchewan* (Regina: Canadian Plains Research Center, 2005), 443–44.

18 M. Sanchez, "Chilean Community," in *Encyclopedia of Saskatchewan* (Regina: Canadian Plains Research Center, 2005), 169–70.

19 *Saskatoon StarPhoenix*, August 18, 2007.

20 *Saskatoon StarPhoenix*, March 25, 2008.

21 Cited in H. Henry, "Lebanese Community," in *Encyclopedia of Saskatchewan* (Regina: Canadian Plains Research Center, 2005), 545.

22 Ibid.

23 Ibid.

24 See *Saskatoon's Greek Community: The Pioneers (1901–1949)* (Saskatoon: Hellenic Greek Orthodox Community of Saskatoon, 1984), and A.B. Anderson, "Greek Community," in *Encyclopedia of Saskatchewan* (Regina: Canadian Plains Research Center, 2005), 415–16.

25 This division has been detailed in J. Brand, "Black Shiner to Entrepreneur: A General View of the Development of the Greek Community in Saskatoon" (1980); A.R. Poisson, "The Greek Community of Saskatoon" (1990); and S. Spanos, "An Overview of the Greek Community in Saskatoon: Past and Present" (1990), in the author's archives.

Chapter 10: Conclusion: Changing Times

1 This section has been revised from A.B. Anderson, "Population Trends," in *Encyclopedia of Saskatchewan* (Regina: Canadian Plains Research Center, 2005), 705–08; see also B.D. Thraves, "Change and Diversity in Saskatchewan's Population," in *Saskatchewan: Geographic Perspectives*, ed. B.D. Thraves, M.L. Lewry, J.E. Dale, and H. Schlichtmann (Regina: University of Regina and Canadian Plains Research Center, 2007), 206–26.

2 J.W. Dafoe, *Clifford Sifton in Relation to His Times* (Toronto: Macmillan, 1931), 144, 316–17.

3 Data from Immigrant Arrivals in Saskatchewan, Canadian Department of the Interior.

4 Much of this section is based on D.H. Hay, "Rural Population," in *Encyclopedia of Saskatchewan* (Regina: Canadian Plains Research Center, 2005), 787–89, and data from the 2011 Census of Agriculture, Statistics Canada.

5 See, for example, N. Ward and D. Spafford, eds., *Politics in Saskatchewan* (Lindsay, ON: Longmans of Canada and John Dyell, 1968), 280, and G.E. Britnell, *The Wheat Economy* (Toronto: University of Toronto Press, 1939), 15–16.

6 J.H. Archer, *Footprints in Time* (Toronto: House of Grant, 1965), 98.

7 C.A. Dawson, *Group Settlement: Ethnic Communities in Western Canada* (Toronto: Macmillan, 1936), 307–14; ARDA, *Research Project: A Resources Inventory of Census Division 16 in Saskatchewan* (Saskatoon: Canadian Centre for Community Studies, 1966), 47–48, 72–77, 135, cited in A.B. Anderson, "Assimilation in the Bloc Settlements of North-Central Saskatchewan: A Comparative Study of Identity Change among Seven Ethno-Religious Groups in a Canadian Prairie Region" (Ph.D. diss., University of Saskatchewan, 1972), 254.

8   ARDA, *Research Project*, 72–77, 139–40, 150.

9   C.A. Dawson and E.R. Younge, *Pioneering in the Prairie Provinces: The Social Side of the Settlement Process* (Toronto: Macmillan, 1940), 39–40.

10 S. Greer, *The Emerging City* (Glencoe, IL: Free Press, 1964), 41, 45, 72–75.

11 Data are from the Saskatoon School Board, cited in Anderson, "Assimilation in the Bloc Settlements of North-Central Saskatchewan," 269–70.

12 These data on Lutheran churches in rural Saskatchewan are from V.W. Larsen, "The Challenge of the Lutheran Church in the Rural Areas of Saskatchewan," paper presented at a meeting of the Lutheran Ministerial Association, October 31, 1960.

13 These data are from parish records.

14 D. Polachic, "The Little Church in Peril," *Western People*, September 28, 2000, 4–5.

15 D. Polachic, "Congregation Few in Number, Great in Resolve," Saskatoon *StarPhoenix*, July 29, 2000; D. Polachic, "Have Church, Will Travel," *Western People*, October 5, 2000, 8–9.

16 *Atlas of Saskatchewan* (Saskatoon: University of Saskatchewan, 1969), 20; Saskatoon *StarPhoenix*, May 12, 1971.

17 E.J. Abramson, "The Development of a Satellite Community," paper presented at the Eighth International Congress of Anthropological and Ethnological Sciences, Tokyo and Kyoto, 1968.

18 L. Harder, *Fact Book of Congregational Membership* (Newton, KS: General Conference Mennonite Church, 1971).

19 See Anderson, "Assimilation in the Bloc Settlements of North-Central Saskatchewan," 340–41.

20 T. Shibutani and K.M. Kwan, *Ethnic Stratification: A Comparative Approach* (New York: Macmillan, 1965), 531; A. Locke and B.J. Stern, eds., *When People Meet: A Study in Race and Culture Contacts* (New York: Hinds, Hayden, and Eldridge, 1946), 414, cited in Anderson, "Assimilation in the Bloc Settlements of North-Central Saskatchewan," 343.

21 J.T.M. Anderson, *The Education of the New Canadian* (Toronto: J.M. Dent, 1918), 62; C.H. Young, *The Ukrainian Canadians: A Study in Assimilation* (Toronto: Thomas Nelson and Sons, 1931), 158.

22 *Report of the Saskatchewan Royal Commission on Immigration and Settlement* (Regina: King's Publisher, 1930).

23 W. Darcovich, *Ukrainians in Canada: The Struggle to Retain Their Identity* (Ottawa: Ukrainian Self-Reliance Association, 1967).

24 See Shibutani and Kwan, *Ethnic Stratification*, 515, 554–56; A.I. Gordon, *Intermarriage: Interfaith, Interracial, Interethnic* (Boston: Beacon Press, 1964), 64, 80; R.E. Park, *Race and Culture* (Glencoe, IL: Free Press, 1950), 51, cited in Anderson, "Assimilation in the Bloc Settlements of North-Central Saskatchewan," 340–43.

25 A.B. Anderson and J.S. Frideres, *Ethnicity in Canada: Theoretical Perspectives* (Toronto: Butterworths, 1981).

26 Anderson and Frideres, *Ethnicity in Canada*, 41–42.

27 G.W. Allport, *The Nature of Prejudice* (New York: Doubleday, 1954), 415–18.

28 Anderson and Frideres, *Ethnicity in Canada*, 41–42.

29 Ibid., 42.

30 Anderson, "Assimilation in the Bloc Settlements of North-Central Saskatchewan," 167.

31 C.A. Price, "Immigration and Group Settlement," in *The Cultural Integration of Immigrants*, ed. W.D. Borrie (Paris: UNESCO, 1959), 285–86, cited in Anderson, "Assimilation in the Bloc Settlements of North-Central Saskatchewan," 168.

32 Anderson and Frideres, *Ethnicity in Canada*, 42.

33 These incidents were gathered through research in the Archives of Saskatchewan together with personal interviews and observations by the author.

34 This was extensively studied in the north-central region in 1968–72; see Anderson, "Assimilation in the Bloc Settlements of North-Central Saskatchewan," 251–53.

35 Ethnocentrism and xenophobia are extensively described in Anderson and Frideres, *Ethnicity in Canada*; also see Anderson, "Assimilation in the Bloc Settlements of North-Central Saskatchewan," 192.

36 M.M. Gordon, *Assimilation in American Life: The Role of Race, Religion, and National Origins* (New York: Oxford University Press, 1964), 85, 88, 98, 104, cited in Anderson, "Assimilation in the Bloc Settlements of North-Central Saskatchewan," 195.

37 D. Smith, "Instilling British Values in the Prairie Provinces," *Prairie Forum* 6, 2 (1981): 129–30.

38 *Report of the Saskatchewan Royal Commission on Immigration and Settlement*, 199.

39 B.M. Frith, *A Short History of the Wakaw District* (1932).

40 J. Hawkes, *The Story of Saskatchewan and Its People* (Regina: S.T. Clarke, 1924), 678.

41 J.H. Gray, *Boom Time: Peopling the Canadian Prairies* (Saskatoon: Western Producer Prairie Books, 1979), 108.

42 Ibid.

43 Gordon, *Assimilation in American Life*, 110–11, 114, 151, 157–58.

44 Hawkes, *The Story of Saskatchewan and Its People*, 681.

45 Young, *The Ukrainian Canadians*, 76.

46 Hawkes, *The Story of Saskatchewan and Its People*, 685–86.

47 Young, *The Ukrainian Canadians*, 68.

48 V. Lysenko, *Men in Sheepskin Coats: A Study in Assimilation* (Toronto: Ryerson, 1947), 237.

49 Anderson, "Assimilation in the Bloc Settlements of North-Central Saskatchewan," 198–99; Anderson and Frideres, *Ethnicity in Canada*.

50 P. Yuzyk, *Ukrainian Canadians: Their Place and Role in Canadian Life* (Toronto: Ukrainian Business and Professional Federation, 1967), 84–87.

51 J.S. Woodsworth, *Strangers within Our Gates* (1909; reprinted, Toronto: University of Toronto Press, 1972).

52 R. England, "Ethnic Settlers in Western Canada: Reminiscences of a Pioneer," republished in *Canadian Ethnic Studies* 8, 2 (1976): 19.

SELECTED BIBLIOGRAPHY

This selected bibliography focuses on primary sources on ethnic settlements in Saskatchewan. Other sources (including many local histories and general sources on Aboriginal peoples, ethnic group histories in Canada, historical background prior to immigration, and Western Canadian history) are listed following each relevant chapter.

Note: *Specific chapters in selected edited books, as well as specific entries in encyclopedias, are also indicated in sources by topic after each chapter.*

Aberdeen Historical Society. *Aberdeen*. Edmonton: Friesen Printers, 1982.

Amstatter, A. *Tomslake: History of the Sudeten Germans in Canada*. Saanichton, BC: Hancock House, 1978.

Anderson, A.B. "Assimilation in the Bloc Settlements of North-Central Saskatchewan: A Comparative Study of Identity Change among Seven Ethno-Religious Groups in a Canadian Prairie Region." PhD diss., University of Saskatchewan, 1972.

———. "Intermarriage in Ethnic Bloc Settlements in Saskatchewan." Paper presented at the Annual Meeting of the Western Association of Sociology and Anthropology, Banff, December 1974.

———. "Ukrainian Identity Change in Rural Saskatchewan." In *Ukrainians in American and Canadian Society: Contributions to the Sociology of Ethnic Groups*, edited by W.W. Isajiw, 93–121. Cambridge, MA: Harvard Ukrainian Research Institute, Harvard University; New York: Ukrainian Centre for Social Research, 1976.

———. "Ethnic Identity in Saskatchewan Bloc Settlements: A Sociological Appraisal." In *The Settlement of the West*, edited by H. Palmer, 187–225. Calgary: University of Calgary Press, 1977.

———. "Linguistic Trends among Saskatchewan Ethnic Groups." In *Ethnic Canadians: Culture and Education*, edited by M.L. Kovacs, 63–86. Regina: Canadian Plains Research Center, 1978.

———. "Ethnicity and Language in Saskatchewan Schools." Paper presented at the Symposium on Ethnicity on the Great Plains, Center for Great Plains Studies, University of Nebraska, Lincoln, April 1978.

———. "Ukrainian Ethnicity: Generations and Change in Rural Saskatchewan." In *Two Nations, Many Cultures: Ethnic Groups in Canada*, edited by J.L. Elliott, 250–69. Scarborough, ON: Prentice-Hall Canada, 1979.

——. "French Ethnicity in North-Central Saskatchewan." In *Two Nations, Many Cultures: Ethnic Groups in Canada*, edited by J.L. Elliott, 262–69. Scarborough, ON: Prentice-Hall Canada, 1979.

——. "German Migration from Romania to the Prairies." Paper presented at the Meeting of the Central and East European Studies Association of Canada, Université du Québec à Montréal, June 1980.

——. "Generation Differences in Ethnic Identity Retention in Rural Saskatchewan." In *Ethnic Studies and Research in the Prairies*, edited by A.B. Anderson. Special issue of *Prairie Forum* 7, 2 (1982): 171–95.

——. "German Settlements in Saskatchewan." In *Roots and Realities among Central and Eastern Europeans*, edited by M.L. Kovacs, 175–227. Edmonton: University of Alberta Press, 1983.

——. *French Settlements in Saskatchewan* and *Ethnic Identity Retention in Francophone Communities in Saskatchewan*. Research Unit for French-Canadian Studies, University of Saskatchewan, Report Nos. 5 and 6, 1985.

——. "Profil demographique des Canadiens-Français de la Saskatchewan: 1885–1985." In *Héritage et avenir des francophones de l'Ouest*, 175–95. Les Actes du Cinquième Colloque du Centre d'Etudes Franco-Canadiennes de l'Ouest Tenu au Collège St. Thomas More, Université de la Saskatchewan, octobre 1985.

——. "Scandinavian Settlements in Saskatchewan: Migration History and Changing Ethno-cultural Identity." In *Scandinavian-Canadian Studies*, vol. 2, edited by G.A. Woods, 89–113. Ottawa: Association for the Advancement of Scandinavian Studies in Canada, 1986.

——. *Guide des sources bibliographiques des communautés francophones de la Saskatchewan/ Guide to Bibliographic Sources on Francophone Communities in Saskatchewan*. Research Unit for French-Canadian Studies, University of Saskatchewan, Report No. 13, 1987.

——. *German, Mennonite, and Hutterite Communities in Saskatchewan: An Inventory of Sources*. Saskatoon: Saskatchewan German Council, 1989.

——. *German Settlements in Saskatchewan*. 2nd ed. Saskatoon: Saskatchewan German Council, 2005.

——. "Abbot Bruno (George) Doerfler." In *Dictionary of Canadian Biography*, vol. 14, 1–4. Toronto: University of Toronto Press, 1995.

——. "Ethnic Bloc Settlements, 1850s–1990s." In *Atlas of Saskatchewan*, 56–58. Saskatoon: University of Saskatchewan, 1999.

——. *Home in the City: Urban Aboriginal Housing and Living Conditions*. Toronto: University of Toronto Press, 2013.

Anderson, A.B., and L. Driedger. "The Mennonite Family: Culture and Kin in Rural Saskatchewan." In *Canadian Families: Ethnic Variations*, edited by K. Ishwaran, 161–80. Scarborough, ON: McGraw-Hill-Ryerson, 1980.

Anderson, A.B., and B. Niskala. "Finnish Settlements in Saskatchewan: Their Development and Perpetuation." In *Finnish Diaspora*, vol. 1, edited by M.G. Karni, 155–82. Toronto: Multicultural History Society of Ontario, 1981.

Anderson, J.T.M. *The Education of the New Canadian*. Toronto: J.M. Dent, 1918.

Anwender, B. "Zichydorf Colony: A Brief History." *Saskatchewan Genealogical Society Bulletin* 27, 3 (1996): 103–05.

l'Association catholique franco-canadienne de la Saskatchewan. *L'album-souvenir cinquantenaire de l'ACFC: 1912–1962*. Saskatoon: ACFC, 1962.

Baran, A.M. *Ukrainian Catholic Churches of Saskatchewan*. Saskatoon: Modern Press, 1977.

SELECTED BIBLIOGRAPHY

Barkwell, L.J. *Veterans and Families of the 1885 Northwest Resistance*. Saskatoon: Gabriel Dumont Institute, 2011.

Barry, B. *People Places: Saskatchewan and Its Names*. Regina: Canadian Plains Research Center, 1997.

———. *Ukrainian People Places*. Regina: People Places Publishing, 2001.

———. *Geographic Names of Saskatchewan*. Regina: People Places Publishing, 2005.

Becker, A. "St. Joseph's Colony, Balgonie." *Saskatchewan History* 20, 1 (1966): 1–18.

———. "The Germans from Russia in Saskatchewan and Alberta." In *German-Canadian Yearbook*, vol. 3, 108–19. Toronto: Historical Society of Mecklenburg, 1976.

Bennett, J.W. *Hutterian Brethren: The Agricultural Economy and Social Organization of a Communal People*. Stanford, CA: Stanford University Press, 1967.

Berton, P. *The Promised Land: Settling the West, 1896–1914*. Toronto: McClelland and Stewart, 1984.

Betcherman, L.R. *The Swastika and the Maple Leaf: Fascist Movements in Canada in the Thirties*. Toronto: Fitzhenry and Whiteside, 1975.

Blumstock, R., ed. *Bekevar: Working Papers on a Canadian Prairie Community*. Ottawa: National Museum, 1979.

*Bocking, D.H., ed. *Pages from the Past: Essays on Saskatchewan History*. Saskatoon: Western Producer Prairie Books, 1979.

Bruce, J. *Last Best West*. Toronto: Fitzhenry and Whiteside, 1976.

Carlson, M. "The Swabian Germans at Wakaw: The Portable People Who Found a Permanent Home." 1988. Author's archives.

Chabot, Reverend A. *Histoire du Diocèse de Gravelbourg, 1930–1980*. Willow Bunch, SK: 1981.

Comité du livre historique. *Echo des pionniers: Histoire de Debden et district, 1912–1985*. Altona, MB: Friesen Printers, 1985.

Coughlin, J. *The Irish Colony of Saskatchewan*. Scarborough, ON: Lochleven Publishers, 1995.

Dafoe, J.W. *Clifford Sifton in Relation to His Times*. Toronto: Macmillan, 1931.

Dawson, C.A. *Group Settlement: Ethnic Communities in Western Canada*. Toronto: Macmillan, 1936.

Dawson, C.A., and E.R. Younge. *Pioneering in the Prairie Provinces: The Social Side of the Settlement Process*. Toronto: Macmillan, 1940.

de Trémaudan, A-M. *Histoire de la Nation Métisse dans l'Ouest Canadien*. 1936; reprinted, St-Boniface, MB: Editions des Plaines, 1984.

Denis, W. "Politics of Language." In *Race and Ethnic Relations in Canada*, edited by P. Li, 148–85. Toronto: Oxford University Press, 1990.

———. "La gestion scolaire fransaskoise." In *A la mesure du pays*, edited by J-G. Quenneville, 11–30. Saskatoon: CEFCO, 1990.

Denis, W., and P. Li. "The Politics of Language Loss: A Francophone Case from Western Canada." *Journal of Education Policy* 3, 4 (1988): 351–70.

Diocèse de Gravelbourg. *Croquis historiques des paroisses du Diocèse de Gravelbourg, Saskatchewan*. Gravelbourg, SK: Diocèse de Gravelbourg, 1956.

Doell, L. *The Bergthaler Mennonite Church of Saskatchewan, 1892–1975*. Winnipeg: CMBC Publications, 1987.

Dojcsak, D.V. "The Mysterious Count Esterhazy." *Saskatchewan History* 26, 2 (1973): 63–72.

SELECTED BIBLIOGRAPHY

Driedger, L. "A Sect in Modern Society: A Case Study of the Old Colony Mennonites of Saskatchewan." MA thesis, University of Chicago, 1955.

———. *Mennonite Identity in Conflict*. Lewiston, NY: Edwin Mellen Press, 1988.

Driedger, W. *Jakob Out of the Village*. Regina: Your Nickel's Worth Publishing, 2007.

Dubuc, Père D. *Généologie des familles de la Paroisse de St-Isidore-de-Bellevue, Saskatchewan, 1902–1970*.

Ducharme, Abbé R. *Servir et non etre servi: Un Fransaskois se raconte*. Regina: Les Editions de la Nouvelle Plume, 2005.

Duck Lake History Committee. *"Their Dreams... Our Memories": A History of Duck Lake and District*. Altona, MB: Friesen Printers, 1988.

*Encyclopedia of Saskatchewan. Regina: Canadian Plains Research Center, 2005.

England, R. *The Central European Immigrant in Canada*. Toronto: Macmillan, 1929.

Epp, F.H. *Mennonite Exodus*. Altona, MB: D.W. Friesen and Sons, 1962.

———. *Mennonites in Canada, 1782–1920: The History of a Separate People*. Toronto: Macmillan of Canada, 1974.

———. *Mennonites in Canada, 1920–1940: A People's Struggle for Survival*. Toronto: Macmillan of Canada, 1982.

"Father Bruno's Narrative, 'Across the Boundary.'" Reprinted in *Saskatchewan History* 9, 2 (1956): 26–31, 70–74.

Feldman, A. "Were Jewish Farmers Failures? The Case of Township 2-15-W2nd." *Saskatchewan History* 55, 1 (2003): 21–30.

Fieguth, M., and D. Christensen. *Historic Saskatchewan*. Toronto: Oxford University Press, 1986.

*Francis, R.D., and C. Kitzan, eds. *The Prairie West as Promised Land*. Calgary: University of Calgary Press, 2007.

Frémont, D. *Les Français dans l'Ouest Canadien*. 1959; reprinted, St-Boniface, MB: Les Editions du Blé, 1980.

Friesen, J.J. *Building Communities: The Changing Face of Manitoba Mennonites*. Winnipeg: CMU Press, 2007.

Friesen, T. *Pushing through Barriers: A Canadian Mennonite Story*. Dawson Creek, BC: Peace PhotoGraphics, 2011.

Froeschle, H. "German Immigration into Canada." In *German-Canadian Yearbook*, vol. 6 (1981), 16–27.

Giraud, M. *Le Métis canadien*. Paris: Institut d'ethnologie, Université de Paris, 1945.

Grams, G. *German Emigration to Canada and the Support of Its Deutschtum during the Weimar Republic*. Frankfurt: Peter Lang, 2001.

Gray, J.H. *Boom Time: Peopling the Canadian Prairies*. Saskatoon: Western Producer Prairie Books, 1979.

Guenther, J.G. *"Men of Steele": Lifestyle of a Unique Sect: Saskatchewan Valley Mennonite Settlers and Their Descendants*. 1981.

Gutkin, H. *Journey into Our Heritage: The Story of the Jewish People in the Canadian West*. Toronto: Lester and Orpen Dennys, 1980.

Halliwell, G.M., and M.Z.D. Persson. *Three Score Years and Ten: 1886–1956: A History of the Swedish Settlement of Stockholm and District*. Saskatoon: Modern Press, 1986.

SELECTED BIBLIOGRAPHY

Hamilton, B.R. "Francophone Settlement in the Gravelbourg Bloc Settlement and Francophone and Métis Settlement in the Willow Bunch Bloc Settlement in Southwestern Saskatchewan, 1870–1926." MA thesis, University of Regina, 2007. [Partially published as B.R. Hamilton, "Francophone Settlement in the Gravelbourg Area," in *Saskatchewan: Geographic Perspectives*, ed. B.D. Thraves, M.L. Lewry, J.E. Dale, and H. Schlichtmann (Regina: University of Regina and Canadian Plains Research Center, 2008), 146–52.]

Harbuz, M. *Ukrainian Pioneer Days in Early Years, 1898–1916, in Alvena and District, Saskatchewan*. North Battleford: Appel Printing, ca. 1978.

Hawkes, J. *The Story of Saskatchewan and Its People*. Regina: S.T. Clarke, 1924.

Holst, W.A. "Ethnic Identity and Mission in a Canadian Lutheran Context." In *German-Canadian Yearbook*, vol. 5 (1979), 20–24.

Hryniuk, M., and F. Korvemaker. *Legacy of Stone: Saskatchewan's Stone Buildings*. Regina: Coteau Books, 2008.

Jackson, M. "Les Franco-Canadiens de la Saskatchewan." *Revue d'études canadiennes/Journal of Canadian Studies* 7, 3 (1972): 1–20.

Jaenen, C.J. *Promoters, Planters, and Pioneers: The Course and Context of Belgian Settlement in Western Canada*. Calgary: University of Calgary Press, 2011.

Janzen, R. *The Prairie People: Forgotten Anabaptists*. Hanover, NH: University Press of New England, 1999.

Jeffery, C. *Arriving 1909–1919*. Edmonton: Roadie Books, 2011.

Johnson, G. "The Syrians in Western Canada." *Saskatchewan History* 12, 1 (1959): 31–32.

———. "Swabian Folk Ways." *Saskatchewan History* 13, 2 (1960): 73–75.

———. "The Romanians in Western Canada." *Saskatchewan History* 14, 2 (1961): 64–70.

———. "The New Finland Colony." *Saskatchewan History* 15, 2 (1962): 69–72.

———. "The Patagonia Welsh." *Saskatchewan History* 16, 3 (1963): 90–94.

Kaye, V.J. *Early Ukrainian Settlements in Canada, 1895–1900*. Toronto: University of Toronto Press, 1964.

Kirkby, M.A. *I Am Hutterite*. Prince Albert: Polka Dot Press, 2007.

Klippenstein, L., and J.G. Toews. *Mennonite Memories: Settling in Western Canada*. Winnipeg: Centennial Publications, 1977.

Kovacs, M.L. *Esterhazy and Early Hungarian Immigration to Canada*. Regina: Canadian Plains Research Center, 1974.

———. *Peace and Strife*. Kipling, SK: Kipling District Historical Society, 1980.

Lacoursière-Stringer, R. *Histoire de/History of Ponteix*. Steinbach, MB: Derksen Printers, 1981.

Lapointe, R., and L. Tessier. *Histoire des Franco-Canadiens de la Saskatchewan*. Regina: Société historique de la Saskatchewan, 1986.

LeChevallier, Reverend J. *St-Laurent-de-Grandin: A Mission and Shrine in the Northwest of America*. Vannes, France: Lafolye and J. de Lamarzelle, 1930.

Lehmann, H. *The German Canadians, 1750–1937: Immigration, Settlement, and Culture*. Translated by G.P. Bassler. St. John's: Jesperson Press, 1986.

Lehr, J.C., J. Everitt, and S. Evans. "The Making of the Prairie Landscape." *Prairie Forum* 33, 1 (2008): 1–38.

Léonard, C.J. *Mémoire des noms de lieux d'origine et d'influence françaises en Saskatchewan*. Québec: Editions GID, 2010.

SELECTED BIBLIOGRAPHY

Leonoff, C.E. *The Architecture of Jewish Settlements in the Prairies*. Winnipeg: Jewish Historical Society of Western Canada, 1975.

——. *Wapella Farm Settlement*. Winnipeg: Historical and Scientific Society of Manitoba and Jewish Historical Society of Western Canada, 1975.

Lindal, V.J. *The Saskatchewan Icelanders*. Winnipeg: Columbia Press, 1955.

——. *The Icelanders of Canada*. Winnipeg: National and Viking, 1967.

Loewen, R. *Diaspora in the Countryside: Two Mennonite Communities and Mid-Twentieth-Century Rural Disjuncture*. Toronto: University of Toronto Press, 2006.

Loewen, R., and G. Friesen. *Immigrants in Prairie Cities: Ethnic Diversity in Twentieth-Century Canada*. Toronto: University of Toronto Press, 2009.

Lohrenz, G. *The Mennonites of Western Canada*. 1974.

Lupul, M.R. *The Roman Catholic Church and the North-West School Question: A Study in Church-State Relations in Western Canada, 1875–1905*. Toronto: University of Toronto Press, 1974.

Lysenko, V. *Men in Sheepskin Coats: A Study in Assimilation*. Toronto: Ryerson, 1947.

MacLennan, G. "A Contribution to the Ethnohistory of Saskatchewan's Patagonian Welsh Settlement." *Canadian Ethnic Studies* 7, 2 (1975).

*Magocsi, P.R., ed. *Encyclopedia of Canada's Peoples*. Toronto: University of Toronto Press, 1999.

Marcotte, G.M. "Being French-Canadian in Zenon Park, St-Isidore-de-Bellevue, and Marcelin, Saskatchewan." MA thesis, University of Saskatchewan, 1994.

Martin, C. *"Dominion Lands" Policy*. Toronto: McClelland and Stewart, 1973.

*Marchildon, G.P., ed. *Immigration and Settlement, 1870–1939*. History of the Prairie West Series. Regina: Canadian Plains Research Center and University of Regina, 2009.

McKinstry, B. *Bridges: A Book of Legacies for Saskatchewan People of German-Speaking Backgrounds*. Saskatoon: Saskatchewan German Council, 2005.

McLennan, D. *Our Towns: Saskatchewan Communities from Abbey to Zenon Park*. Regina: Canadian Plains Research Center, 2008.

Moore, F. *Saskatchewan Ghost Towns*. Regina: First Impressions, 1982.

Munholland, L.K. *Pulpits of the Past* and *Bread to Share*. Strasbourg, SK: Three West Two South Books, 2004, 2006.

Neufeld, T.R. "Jewish Colonization in the Northwest Territories." MA thesis, University of Saskatchewan, 1982.

Nordheimer Mennonite Church of Saskatchewan, 1925–1975.

Norton, W. *Help Us to a Better Land: Crofter Colonies in the Prairie West*. Regina: Canadian Plains Research Center, 1994.

Paroisse de St-Brieux. *Reminiscenses d'un pionnier: St-Brieux jubilé d'argent, 1904–1929*, and *Cinquantenaire de la Paroisse de St-Brieux, Saskatchewan, 1904–1954*.

Patterson, G.J. "Ethnicity and Religious Affiliation in Romanian Communities in Saskatchewan." Central and East European Studies Association of Canada, 1978. [Later included in *The Romanians of Saskatchewan: Four Generations of Adaptation* (Ottawa: National Museum of Man).]

Paulsen, F.M. *Danish Settlements on the Canadian Prairies: Folk Traditions, Immigrant Experiences, and Local History*. Ottawa: National Museum of Man, 1974.

Payment, D.P. "*Les gens libres — Otipemisiwak*": *Batoche, Saskatchewan, 1870–1930*. Ottawa: Environment Canada, 1990.

——. *The Free People — Li gens libre*. Calgary: University of Calgary Press, 2009.

Pidskalny, K. *Saskatchewan's Ukrainian Legacy*. Saskatoon: Saskatchewan Ukrainian Historical Society, 2006.

Rasporich, A.W. *For a Better Life: A History of the Croatians in Canada*. Toronto: McClelland and Stewart, 1982.

Regehr, T.D. *Mennonites in Canada, 1939–1970: A People Transformed*. Toronto: University of Toronto Press, 1996.

Report of the Saskatchewan Royal Commission on Immigration and Settlement. Regina: King's Publisher, 1930.

Riegert, P.W. *2005 Memories: A History of the Hamburg School District No. 2005, Laird, Saskatchewan*. 1979.

Rivard, R., and C. Littlejohn. *The History of the Métis of Willow Bunch*. 2003.

Robertson, H. *Salt of the Earth: The Story of the Homesteaders in Western Canada*. Toronto: James Lorimer, 1974.

Rondeau, Abbé C. *La Montagne de Bois: Willow Bunch, Saskatchewan*. Québec: Imprimerie l'Action Sociale, 1923.

Rosthern Superintendency. *A Historical Review of Rosthern Superintendency*. 1967.

Russell, E.T. *What's in a Name? The Story behind Saskatchewan Place Names*. Saskatoon: Western Producer Prairie Books, 1973, 1997.

St-Isidore-de-Bellevue. *Souvenirs, 1902–2002*. 2002.

St. Laszlo Historical Committee. *With Faith and Hope: St. Laszlo — Our Heritage*. North Battleford: Turner-Warwick Printers, 1979.

St. Louis Local History Committee. *"I Remember": A History of St. Louis and Surrounding Areas*. Altona, MB: Friesen Printers, 1980.

St. Peter's Abbacy and College. *A Journey of Faith: St. Peter's Abbacy: 1921–1926*. Muenster, SK: Muenster Diocese, 1996.

Saskatchewan Association of Architects. *Historic Architecture of Saskatchewan*. Regina: Focus Publishing, 1987.

Schilling, R. *Gabriel's Children*. Saskatoon: Saskatoon Métis Society, 1983.

———. *Sudeten in Saskatchewan: A Way to Be Free*. St. Walburg, SK: Sudeten German Club with the Saskatchewan German Council, 1989.

Schroeder, W., and H.T. Huebert. *Mennonite Historical Atlas*. Winnipeg: Springfield Publishers, 1990.

Schulte, Father W., OMI, with Oblate priests of the colony. *St. Joseph's Colony: 1905–1930*. Translated by L. Schneider and T. Schneider. Regina: Order of Mary Immaculate, 1930.

Shepard, R.B. "The Little 'White' Schoolhouse: Racism in a Saskatchewan Rural School." *Saskatchewan History* 39, 3 (1986): 81–93.

———. *Deemed Unsuitable*. Toronto: Umbrella Press, 1997.

Sherbinin, M.A. *The Galicians Dwelling in Canada and Their Origin*. Historical and Scientific Society of Manitoba, Transaction No. 71. Winnipeg: Manitoba Free Press, 1906.

Sisters Faithful Companions of Jesus. *Journeying through a Century: Sister Pioneers, 1883–1983*. Edmonton: Technical Graphics, 1983.

Skwarok, J., OSBM. *The Ukrainian Settlers in Canada and Their Schools, 1891–1921*. Edmonton: Basilian Press, 1959.

*Smillie, B.G., ed. *Visions of the New Jerusalem: Religious Settlement on the Prairies*. Edmonton: NeWest Press, 1983.

SELECTED BIBLIOGRAPHY

Stanley, G.F.G. "French and English in Western Canada." In *Canadian Dualism/La dualité canadienne*, edited by M. Wade, 311–50. Toronto: University of Toronto Press, 1960.

Stefanow, M. "A Study of Intermarriage of Ukrainians in Saskatchewan." MA thesis, University of Saskatchewan, 1962.

Stevenson, W.I. "Welsh Settlement in Southwest Saskatchewan." MA thesis, Simon Fraser University, 1974.

Taft, M. "The St. Laurent Pilgrimage: A Religious Ritual of Faith and Healing." In *Discovering Saskatchewan Folklore*, 83–111. Edmonton: NeWest Press, 1983.

*Thernstrom, S., ed. *Harvard Encyclopedia of American Ethnic Groups*. Cambridge, MA: Harvard University Press, 1980.

Thomas, L.H. "Welsh Settlement in Saskatchewan, 1902–1914." *Western Historical Quarterly* 4, 4 (1973).

Thompson, C.A. *Blacks in Deep Snow: Black Pioneers in Canada*. Don Mills, ON: J.M. Dent and Sons, 1979.

*Thraves, B.D., M.L. Lewry, J.E. Dale, and H. Schlichtmann, eds. *Saskatchewan: Geographic Perspectives*. Regina: University of Regina and Canadian Plains Research Center, 2007.

Tischler, K. "The German Canadians in Saskatchewan with Particular Reference to the Language Problem, 1900–1930." MA thesis, University of Saskatchewan, 1978.

———. "The Efforts of the Germans in Saskatchewan to Retain Their Language before 1914." In *German-Canadian Yearbook*, vol. 6 (1981), 42–61.

Tracie, C.J. *"Toil and Peaceful Life": Doukhobor Village Settlement in Saskatchewan, 1899–1918*. Regina: Canadian Plains Research Center, 1996.

Tremblay, E., CSsR. *Le Père Delaere et l'Eglise Ukrainienne du Canada*. Berthierville, QC: l'Imprimerie Bernard, 1960.

Turner, A.R. "Scottish Settlement of the West." In *The Scottish Tradition in Canada*, edited by W.S. Reid, 76–92. Toronto: McClelland and Stewart, 1976.

Usiskin, M. *Uncle Mike's Edenbridge: Memoirs of a Jewish Pioneer Family*. Winnipeg: Peguis, 1983.

Wagner, J. "*Heim ins Reich*: The Story of Loon River's Nazis." *Saskatchewan History* 29, 2 (1976): 41–50.

———. "The Deutscher Bund Canada in Saskatchewan." *Saskatchewan History* 31, 2 (1978): 41–50.

———. *Brothers beyond the Sea: National Socialism in Canada*. Waterloo, ON: Wilfrid Laurier University Press, 1981.

Ward, N., and D. Spafford, eds. *Politics in Saskatchewan*. Lindsay, ON: Longmans of Canada and John Dyell, 1968.

Warwaruk, L. *Red Finns on the Coteau*. Saskatoon: Core Communications, 1984.

White, C.O. "The German Catholic Parochial Schools of Saskatchewan's St. Peter's Colony, 1903–34: Their Teachers, Curriculum, and Quality of Instruction." *Prairie Forum* 24, 1 (1999).

Widdis, R.W. *With Scarcely a Ripple: Anglo-Canadian Migration into the United States and Western Canada, 1880–1920*. Montreal: McGill-Queen's University Press, 1998.

Windschiegl, Reverend P., OSB. *Fifty Golden Years, 1903–1953*. Muenster, SK: St. Peter's Abbey, 1953.

Woodsworth, J.S. *Strangers within Our Gates*. Toronto: Young People's Forward Movement Department of the Methodist Church, 1909; reprinted, University of Toronto Press, 1972.

Young, C.H. *The Ukrainian Canadians: A Study in Assimilation*. Toronto: Thomas Nelson and Sons, 1931.

INDEX

Note: This index focuses on place names and ethnic groups. Churches and schools may be found using the place name. People may be found using associated place name or ethnic group. Names beginning with *St.* or *St-* are filed as though spelled *Saint*.

A

Aarnes, 333
Aaskana, 55
Abbey, 93, 130, 329
Aberdeen, 116, 117, 118, 119, 120, 121, 144
Abernethy, 46, 60–61, 274
Aboriginal peoples, 1–2, 22–42
  businesses, 39–40, 381
  culture and customs, 39–40
  education, 26, 35, 37–38, 39
  ethnic identity, 33–34
  historic sites, 23, 27, 28, 32, 39
  historical background, 1–2, 23–25, 36–37
  information sources, 40–42
  language use, 25, 39
  locations, overview, 25
  organizations and institutions, 37, 38, 39–40, 249
  poverty, 37–39, 380
  reserves: territory consolidation, 1–2, 10; urban reserves, 27, 36
  terminology, 22–23
  territory, 10, 23–25
  treaties, 24–25, 26–27, 28
  urbanization, 36–40, 376–77, 380
  See also Assiniboine/ Nakota; Chipewyan/ Dene; Cree/ Nehiyawewin; Métis; Michif language; Saulteaux/ Nahkawiniwak; Sioux/ Dakota and Lakota
Aboriginal peoples, demographics
  age structure, 35, 37, 379–80
  birth rates, 34, 375, 376
  death rates, 34–35, 375, 376
  education levels, 35, 37
  life expectancy rates, 35
  lone-parent families, 39
  migration and mobility, 37
  out-migration, 379
  overview, 33–35
  population: Canadian rank, 34; dependency ratio, 380; growth rate, 34, 375, 380; off-reserve population, 22–23, 34, 377, 379; on-reserve population, 34, 36, 377, 379, 380, 384; proportion, 34
  poverty rates, 38
  prisoners, 38
  unemployment, 35–36, 38
  urban areas, 34, 36–39, 377
Acadians, 9, 252, 287
Adair, 62
Adamiwka, 170
Admiral, 316, 328–29
Adventists
  settlers: Germans, 77, 82, 83, 95, 96, 101, 110, 126; Nordic peoples, 342–43
Afghans, 352, 366, 367, 378
African Americans, 359–61
  See also Blacks
Africans. *See* Blacks
Ahtahkakoop Cree, 28

444

INDEX

Akerlund Lake, 317
Alameda area, 106
Albanians, 235
Alberta
  demographics:
    interprovincial migration, 352, 378; population growth, 375; population urban proportion, 377
  farms, 381, 382
  historic sites, 360
  settlers, German: Catholics, 82, 91, 92–94; Dutch, 131; Hutterites, 129, 130; Mennonites, 125, 145; population, 79
  settlers, other: Aboriginals, 26, 381; Blacks, 359–60, 361; Danes, 331; Doukhobors, 214; French, 261; Icelanders, 331; Jews, 230, 232; Romanians, 222; Ukrainians, 156, 160, 170, 177, 182
  See also Lloydminster
Alberton/Albertown, 13, 175, 201, 264, 389
Albertville, 259, 260, 291–92
Albion, 50
Aldag, 111
Aldenburg, 109
Aldina, 264
Aldrich, 315
Algrove, 325
Alida, 271–72
Allan, 112
Allenbach, 92
Alma, 272
Alsace/New Elsass, 15, 82–83, 96–98, 99
Alsask, 111, 125, 232
Alticane, 13, 175, 201, 389
Alton, 88
Altona, 117, 144
Alva, 59
Alvena, 172, 173, 174, 192, 193, 199
Alvena Farms, 171, 189
American Lutheran Church (ALC), 93, 95, 106
Amiens, 114
Anabaptists
  conservative communities, 139, 390
  historical background, 115, 128
  sectarianism, 400
  social change and, 390
  See also Hutterites; Mennonites
Anderson Bay, 59
Anderson Lake, 59
Andersonville, 329
Andreasheim, 84
Anerley, 319
Aneroid, 281
Anglo-conformity. *See* British cultural dominance
Annaheim, 86, 88, 89
Annak, 162
Annenthal, 94
Antelope Creek, 314
Antler, 272, 331
Antoniwka, 162
Arabs, 367
Arbana, 93
Arborfield, 261, 262, 263
Arbury, 97
Arbuthnot, 276
Archangelskoe, 208
Archerwill, 201, 324, 325
Archive, 329
Arcola, 62, 63, 105
Ardath, 125, 319, 320
Ardill, 109, 314
Ardine, 57
Arelee, 210, 215
Argonne, 251
Argyle, 62, 63
Arleux, 266
Arlington, 283
Arm River, 130
Arm River Valley, 61
Armorin, 276
Arnold, 111
Aroma Lake, 92
Arran, 65, 168, 208, 214
Artland, 111
arts. *See* culture and customs
Ashford, 317
Asians
  demographics, 352, 355, 378
  See also Chinese; Japanese; Koreans; South Asians; Southeast Asians
Asimakaniseekan Askiy urban reserve, 27, 36
Asor, 92
Asquith, 51
Assemblée communautaire fransakoise (ACF), 286, 288, 300
  See also Association catholique franco-canadienne (ACFC)
assimilation, 404–9
  anglicized names, 187–88, 212, 318, 398–99
  bloc settlements and, 402, 406–9
  citizenship adoption, 157, 183–84, 338
  conflict and ethnic identity, 189, 404
  definitions: assimilation, 394–95, 407; ethnocentrism, 405; xenophobia, 405
  ethnic nationalism, 181
  factors to increase or decrease, 181, 384, 407–8
  government policies, 405–6, 408–9
  homesteading requirements and, 183–84
  linguistic assimilation, 135
  multiculturalism and, 405–9
  names, personal, 398–99
  national Canadian expectations, 404–5
  national consciousness, 181
  religion and, 229–30, 402
  research (1968–72), 132–36, 140, 184
  Royal Commission on, 5–6, 405
  social mobility and, 390
  See also British cultural dominance; ethnic identity; nationalism
Assiniboia, 63, 109, 110, 179, 223, 225, 277, 278, 328

445

INDEX

Assiniboine/Nakota,
    24–25, 27, 29–31
Association catholique
    franco-canadienne
    (ACFC)
    conseil-régional, 253, 262,
        265, 279, 284, 285, 286
    history, 254–55,
        293–94, 300
Assomption-de-la-Vierge, 276
Assyrians, 366, 367
Athlone, 68
Atlas, 316
Attica, 113
Atwater, 72, 326
Aussant, 276
Austenson, 320
Austenville, 316
Austrians, 81
Austro-Hungarians
    colonizers, 4
    ethnic identity, 181
    historical background,
        107, 108, 181, 183, 426n39
    intermarriage, 393
    WWI, 203
    See also Bukovina, as
        origin of settlers;
        Galicia, as origin of
        settlers; Ruthenia, as
        origin of settlers
Auvergne, 280, 281
Avonhurst, 101
Avonlea, 65, 109, 110, 320
Aylesbury, 98
Aysgarth, 163

B

Baber, 102
Baden, 94
Bagley, 324, 329
Baie-Gaumond, 276
Baildon, 130
Bainesville, 114
Balcarres, 46, 60, 61, 179
Baldwinton, 111
Balgonie, 63, 83, 85
Ballinora, 68
Balmoral, 212
Balrobie, 60
Banat, as origin of settlers
settlers: Germans, 78,
    80, 84, 86, 97, 98, 105,
    108; Romanians, 222,
    226; Swabians, 108
Bangor, 69, 71–72, 73
Bankend, 168, 169
Banner, 88
Bansgrund, 312
Bapaume, 321
Baptists, German. *See*
    Germans, Protestant
Baptists, Russian, 176, 210,
    215, 216, 217, 391
Barbadians, 361
Barish Lake, 231
Barr Colony, 15, 47–51, 73
Barra, 59
Barrier Valley, 261, 326
Barthel-Loon River, 105
Barvas, 57, 165
Basin Lake, 220
Basques, 287
Bastness, 323
Bateman, 110
Batoche, 54–55
Battle of Batoche,
    55–56, 246–47
    culture and organizations,
        33, 249–50
    historical background,
        15, 240, 244–48, 251
    national historic sites,
        55–56, 246–47, 249
    parishes and missions,
        244–45, 254
    riverlots, 33, 246
    school-language issue, 293
    Scots, 54–55
Battle River, 263
Battlefords area
    demographics, 379
    historic sites, 285
    historical background,
        239–40
    settlers: Aboriginals,
        28, 29, 30, 36; Blacks,
        359, 360; Chinese,
        356; French, 262–63,
        284–86; Germans, 147;
        Métis, 36; Norwegians,
        318; Poles, 202; Scots,
65; Ukrainians,
    174–75, 180, 199
Battrum, 316
Bavelaw, 57
Bay Trail, 88
Bayard, 109, 278
Bayne, 221, 257
Bazentin, 267
Beacon Hill, 104
Bear Stream/Doroshenko, 162
Beardy's Reserve, 27
Bearhead Creek, 208
Beatty/Stoney Creek, 329
Beaubier, 275, 312
Beauchamp, 86, 258, 282
Beausite, 264
Beauval, 26, 241
Beauvallon, 266
Beaver Creek, 315, 323
Beaver Dale, 126, 164
Beaver Flat, 314
Beaver Hills, 161, 163,
    165, 168, 189
Beaver River, 102, 104, 114
Beaver Valley, 111
Beaverbrook, 105
Beblo, 162
Béchard, 274
Beckenham, 164, 169, 201
Bedfordville-Church Hill, 165
Beechy, 123, 130, 317, 337
Bégin, 259, 260
Bekevar, 220
Belanger, 283
Belbutte, 124, 267
Belgians
    colonizers, 4, 250, 253, 272
    diversity, 283
    ethnic identity, 287
    family names, 132
    historical background,
        286, 288
    language use: Flemish,
        131–32, 286, 287;
        Walloon, 132, 287
    locations, 132, 251, 253,
        254–56, 259, 268–69,
        271–75, 280, 282, 285
    population, 131, 286, 287
Bell Farm, Qu'Appelle
    Valley, 60
Bell Rock, 320

446

INDEX

Belle Plaine, 130
Bellegarde, 271–72, 280
Belleville, 270
Bellevue, 252–53, 255, 292, 295, 299, 394
Bellevue, Château, 269
Belmont, 89
Benbecula, 57
Bench, 129
Benedictines (Order of St. Benedict), 85, 87, 88, 141
Bengough, 109, 110
Benson, 105
Berard Beach, 257
Beresford, 103
Beresina, 99
Bereziw, 175
Bergfield, 106
Bergheim, 113–14
Bergthal, 117, 144
Bergthaler Mennonites. *See* Chortitzer Mennonite Conference
Bern, 94
Bernadette, 266
Bernard, 317
Bertdale, 332
Bessarabia, as origin of settlers
  historical background, 78, 222
  settlers: Germans, 78, 80, 93, 99, 101, 103; Jews, 231; Swabian dialect, 102, 108
Bethania area, 316, 320
Bethany, 316
Bethel, 124, 316
Bethlehem, 320
Bethune, 61, 98
Beynes, 269
Bhutanese, 363
Bienfait, 106, 179
Big Beaver, 313–14
Big Four, 315
Big Island Lake Reserve, 28
Big Muddy Badlands, 313
Big Quill, 169, 333
Big Quill Lake, 332
Big River, 28, 114, 265, 266
Big Rose, 130
Biggar, 91, 179
Bigstone, 324
Bildfell, 332

Billimun, 110
Bilya-Velechka/Welechko, 175
Birch Hills, 114, 311, 318, 321–24, 339, 399
Birch Narrows First Nation, 32
Bird's Point, 269, 327
Birmingham, 165, 326
Birsay, 65, 337
Bisednoe, 209
Bjelde Creek, 317
Bjorkdale, 261, 330
Black Lake First Nation, 32
Blackfoot peoples, 23–24
Blackley, 114
Blacks, 359–62
  African Americans, 359–61
  Africans, 288, 360–61
  anti-Black sentiment, 359
  culture and customs, 361–62
  demographics, 361
  information sources, 370–71
  locations, 359–62
  settlement patterns, 8, 18, 361, 369
  terminology, 360–61
Blackwood, 60
Bladworth, 229, 319
Blagodarovka, 208
Blagosklonoe, 209
Blagovishennie, 209
Blaine Lake
  population, 176, 215, 388
  settlers: Doukhobors, 176, 207, 213–17; French, 264; Mennonites, 216; Ukrainians, 174, 175, 176, 388
Blair Athol, 61
Blakely, 61
bloc settlements, 2–18
  Anglos preferred, 4–6, 8–9, 405–6
  anti-immigration sentiment, 5–6
  area: expansion, 11, 16; overlap, 10–12; size/extent, 7, 11–12, 16
  assimilation and, 402, 406–9
  benefits, 7, 8, 407
  colonizers, 2–5, 7–8

definitions: bloc settlement, 10–11; colony, 9; enclave, 9; group settlement, 10; rural areas, 10; settlement, 9–10
government policies, 3–6
historical overview, 2–3, 15–17, 373–75, 380, 406–7
historical periods, 6, 15–17
homogeneity, 11
information sources, 18–21
intermarriage, 392–94
naturalization toward citizenship, 157, 183–84, 211
overview, 2–12
religion and, 402
scattered settlers, 14, 18
types: chain migration, 8, 16; colonization schemes, 2–5, 7–8; gravitation to common background, 8; organized, 2, 8, 16; territory consolidation (Aboriginals), 2
utopian visions, 4
See also homesteading
Blue Hill, 314
Blue Jay, 126
Blue Spruce, 113
Blumenfeld, 92, 93, 94, 388
Blumenheim, 115–16, 117, 118, 121
Blumenhof, 116, 117, 122
Blumenort, 122
Blumenthal, 118, 121
Bobulynci, 166, 167
Bodanofka, 210
Bode, 122
Bodmin, 266
Bodnari, 171, 172
Bogdanovka, 208
Boghumdanoe, 208
Bohdan, 175
Bohrson, 320
Bois-Lagassé, 276
Bon Accord, 165
Bond, 325
Bone Creek, 129
Bonne Eau, 248
Bonne-Madone
  historic sites, 257

447

population, 255
research (1968–72), 291–92
school-language issue, 293, 295
settlers: French, 257–58, 291–92, 295; Ukrainians, 295
Bonneauville, 278
Bonnie Brae, 61
Bonnie Hill, 323
Bonvouloir, 276
Borden, 120, 124
Borshchiv, 171, 172
Borszczow, 167, 171, 201
Bosnians, 230
Boucher Colony, 245
Boudreault, 266
Bourassa, 274–75
Bourgogne, 280–81
Bournemouth, 124
Boutin, 266, 295
Box Elder, 129, 320
Boyne, 68
Braaten, 323
Braemar, 60
Brena, 162
Bresaylor, 248
Brewer, 201
Bridgeford, 51
Bridok, 162
Briercrest, 315
Brightholm, 64
Brightsand, 104, 227
Brithdir, 72
British
 colonizers, 7–8
 demographics: population, 17, 43–44, 54; population history, 53–54
 diversity, 73–74
 ethnic identity, 43–44, 54, 408–9
 historical background, 15–16, 44
 intermarriage, 393
 new immigrants, 352
 settlement patterns, 8, 44, 73
 terminology, 17, 43–44
 See also English; English language; Irish; Scots; Welsh

British cultural dominance
 Anglo-conformity defined, 405
 cultural pluralism and, 405–6
 delocalization and, 387
 education and, 44, 52
 immigration preferences for Anglos, 4–6, 8–9, 405–6
 media and, 404
 organizations and institutions: Orange Order, 5–6, 68, 111, 183–84, 294, 296; religion, 53
 overview, 52–53, 73–74, 404–9
 pro-British sentiment, 68, 293–94, 405–6
 rural school consolidation and, 387–88
 school-language issue, 292–99
British Columbia
 interprovincial migration, 378
 settlers: Chinese, 355–56; Doukhobors, 212, 213, 214, 216; Finns, 335; Germans, 105; Japanese, 335, 357–58; Mennonites, 122, 145; new immigrants, 351
Brittania, 49–50
Broadacres, 90, 91
Broadview, 62, 179, 269, 327
Brock, 273
Broderick, 227, 319
Bromhead, 106, 312
Bronfmans, 231
Bronsch Road, 114
Brook Hill, 212
Brooking, 127
Brooksby, 177
Brora, 61
Brownlee, 129
Bruderfeld, 118, 119, 123, 144
Bruderthaler (Evangelical) Mennonites, 119, 124, 126, 144, 400

See also Mennonites, religion
Brunendahl, 100
Bruno, 86, 87, 88, 146, 171, 172, 388
Bryn Mawr, 72
Bryntirion, 72
Buchach, 167
Buchanan, 65, 165–66, 201, 203, 214, 325, 326
Buckland, 178, 260
Buda, 220
Buddhists, 358, 362
Budd's Point Reserve, 28
Buffalo Gap, 109
Buffalo Head, 93, 94
Buffalo Narrows, 241
Buffalo River Dene First Nation, 32
Bukovina, as origin of settlers
 dialects, 160
 ethnic identity, 13
 historical background, 78, 80, 181–82
 religion, 179, 182, 188, 423n45
 settlers: Germans, 80, 84, 97, 103, 109; Hungarians, 221, 223; Romanians, 222, 225, 226; Ukrainians, 161, 163, 165, 168, 177, 179, 181, 188, 190, 194
 urbanization, 179
Bukowina, 171, 173, 220
Bulgarians, 78, 234–35
Bulyea, 96, 98, 321
Bunker Hill, 88
Burgis, 162
Burmese, 358
Burnham, 51
Burnside, 61
Burr, 320
Burstall, 93, 94, 95
Burundians, 361
Busch, 111
Butte, 123, 129
Butte-de-Cheval-Caillé/ Pinto Butte, 278, 281
Butte-Paradis/Paradise Hill, 104, 267–68
Butte-St-Pierre, 267–68
Byrtnyky, 167

448

C

Cabana, 267
Cabri, 93, 131, 316
Cactus Lake, 90, 91–92, 179
Cadillac, 281
Cairnbank Farms, 57
Calder, 59, 60, 161, 334
Calling River, 27
Calvary Shrine, 200
Calvin, 67
Cambodians, 358
Cambria, 72
Camholt, 112
Campbell, 61
Campbelltown, 59
Cana, 59, 60, 201, 219–20, 326
Canadian National
   Railway (CNR)
   historical background,
      4, 7–8
   lines, 164–65
   naming of stations, 112
   See also railways
Canadian Pacific
   Railway (CPR)
   colonizers, 156, 218, 227
   historical background,
      4, 7–8
   lines: Foam Lake branch,
      168; Regina, 374; Soo
      line, 7, 106, 107, 200,
      311–13; Yorkton and
      Saskatoon, 163
   See also railways
Candiac, 160, 178–79, 200, 273
Cando, 317
Cannington Manor,
   15, 45, 47, 269
Canoe Lake, 267
Canoe Lake First Nation, 26
Canora, 161–63
   CNR lines, 165
   demographics, 162–63
   settlers: Doukhobors,
      214; Germans, 100;
      Hungarians, 222;
      Jews, 234; Poles, 201;
      Romanians, 222,
      224, 225; Ukrainians,
      161–63, 165, 199

Cantal, 271–72
Canvasback, 88
Canwood, 267, 322, 329, 342
Capasin, 124, 266
Capeland, 122
Cardiff, 72
Cardigan, 72
Cardross, 63
Carievale, 63
Carlea, 61
Carlsberg, 107
Carlton, 254, 255
Carlton House (National
   Historic Site), 240
Carlton Trail, 240, 245, 267
Carlton Trail Siding, 259–60
Carlyle, 62, 67, 105
Carmel, 86, 87, 88, 89
Carmichael, 129
Carnagh, 68
Carnarvon, 72
Carnduff, 62, 63, 67, 127
Carnoustie, 57
Carpenter, 171, 174
Carragana, 113
Carribbean origin, 361
Carrignan, 276
Carrot River, 113, 126, 127, 167
Carrot River Cree, 28
Carry-the-Kettle
   Reserve, 29, 30
Carson, 118
Catholics. *See* French:
   religion (Roman
   Catholic); German
   Catholics; Poles: religion
   (Roman Catholic);
   Ukrainians, religion
Cathrinthal, 84
Caucasus peoples, 367
Cavalier, 263
Cavell/Coblenz, 224
Cecil, 178
Cedoux, 200, 273
Ceepee, 210
census. *See* demographics
Central Americans
   See also Latin Americans
Central Americans,
   demographics, 364
Central Butte, 123
Ceylon, 109, 110, 315

Chamberlain, 98
Chamberland, 261
Chambéry, 283
Champlain, 258
Chapelle, 271
Charlottenburg, 97
Château Bellevue, 269
Château Richelieu, 269
Chaucer, 161
Chekhiv, 167
Chelan, 167, 323
Chelton, 88
Chemin Gobeil, 259
Chemin Lessard, 263
Chemin L'Heureux, 263
Cheremosz, 167
Chester, 62, 179
Chicken/Black Lake
   Reserve, 32
Chileans, 354, 364, 371
   See also Latin Americans
Chimney Coulee, 242
Chinese, 355–57
   demographics, 352,
      355–56, 357
   heritage sites, 356
   historical background,
      355–57
   information sources, 370
   language use, 354, 355
   locations, 353, 356–57
   new immigrants, 352
   settlement patterns,
      14, 18, 355–56, 369
Chipewyan/Dene, 23,
   24, 25, 26, 32
Chitek Lake Cree, 28
Chorney Beach, 166
Chorolofka, 209
Chortitz, 118, 122, 123
Chortitzer Mennonite
   Conference
   (Sommerfelder/
   Bergthaler), 116–17, 120,
   126, 127–28, 137, 145, 400
   See also Mennonites,
   religion
Christ Church Settlement, 47
Christiana, 326
Church Missionary
   Society (CMS), 26
Churchbridge, 60, 99, 330, 334

INDEX

churches. *See* religion
Churchill Lake, 32
citizenship
   assimilation and,
      183–84, 362
   citizenship adoption
      by groups, 183, 338
   Doukhobor refusals, 211
   homesteading
      requirements, 6,
      157, 183–84, 211
   nationality and, 13
   Nordic peoples, 338
   rates by ethnic identity, 183
   See also ethnic identity
Clare, 62
Clarkboro, 117
Claustre, 283
Clavet, 113
Claybank, 109
Clayridge, 336
Clayton, 167, 168
Claytonville/Husiatyn, 178
Clear Springs, 124, 130, 144
Clearwater River Dene, 32
Climax, 227, 315
Cloarec, 259
Clonfert, 68
Clonmel, 59
clothing. *See* culture
   and customs
Cluffield, 325
CNR. *See* Canadian National
   Railway (CNR)
Coal Valley, 111
Coan Park, 215
Coblenz, 92
Cochery, 268
Cochin, 262, 263
Coderre, 279
Codette, 177, 325
Coleville, 90, 91
Colonie des Laplantes, 284
Colonsay, 61, 125, 329
Colwyn, 72
communities and districts
   focal points, 12–13,
      16, 387–89
   identification of, 12–13
   overview, 12–13
   place name historical
      backgrounds, 12

population estimates, 14
See also rural areas
Compass, 124
Concordia, 120, 124, 175
Congolese, 361
Congress, 109, 110, 314
Connaught, 66, 262
Connell Creek, 113
Conquest, 319, 337
Conseil scolaire fransaskois
   (CSF), 299, 301
Consul, 111
Cookson, 322
Coronach, 109, 110, 277, 278
Cosine Lake, 90
Cosmopolitan, 320
Cote First Nation, 29
Cote Saulteaux, 29,
   162–63, 214
Coteau, 291–92, 337
Coulée-Gallienne, 283
Couleé-Gregoire, 283
Couléeville, 270
Courcellette, 281
Court, 317
Courval, 279
Cowessess First Nation, 27, 29
CPR. *See* Canadian Pacific
   Railway (CPR)
Craik, 61, 321
Cramersburg, 131
Crane Lake Valley, 316
Cree/Nehiyawewin, 25–28
   Assiniboine
      relations, 29, 30
   Battle of Frenchman's
      Butte, 247
   groups: Plains Cree, 25,
      26–27, 28; Swampy Cree,
      24, 26, 28, 29; Woods,
      Western Woodland,
      or Northern Cree,
      24–25, 26, 28, 32
   historic sites, 26, 28
   language: Cree-Michif,
      25, 241, 242; dialects,
      25, 28; school-language
      issue, 292–93; use, 33, 39
   Oji-Cree mixing,
      25, 27, 29, 39
   reserves, 25, 27–28;
      urban, 27

terminology, 25–26
   See also Aboriginal peoples
Creighton, 127
Crescent View, 320
Crest/Blue Spruce, 113
Crimea, 111
Crimeans, 90, 93, 94, 110
Croatians and Yugoslavs,
   228–30
   culture and customs, 229
   demographics, 229, 230
   ethnic group mixing,
      227, 320
   farms, 229–30
   heritage sites, 229
   historical background,
      16, 228–29
   information sources, 237
   language use, 229
   locations, 228–29, 319, 320
   religion, 229
   settlement patterns,
      11, 228, 229, 234
   urbanization, 229–30
   See also Yugoslavs
Crooked Lake, 89, 161,
   162–63, 189, 220
Crystal Creek/Rivière-
   de-Saules, 263
Crystal Springs, 258
Cudworth
   population, 88, 174
   settlers: Germans, 86,
      87, 88, 89, 173; Poles,
      200; Ukrainians,
      171, 172, 173–74, 177
culture and customs
   Anglo-conformity, 405–6
   cultural pluralism, 405–6
   defined, 402
   ethnic identity
      and, 395, 402
   religion and, 399–400
   research (1968–72),
      136, 191–92
   social change, 402
   See also assimilation;
      British cultural
      dominance; ethnic
      identity; Saskatoon:
      culture and customs,

INDEX

Folkfest; *and specific ethnic groups*
Cumberland House, 239, 248
Cumberland House Reserve, 27, 28, 242
Cupar, 60, 97, 98, 221, 223
customs, folk. *See* culture and customs
Cut Knife, 262
Cymri, 72
Cymric, 72
Cypress, 129
Cypress Hills, 27, 30, 129
Cypress Lake, 315
Cyprus, 208
Czechs and Slovaks, 226–28
   colonizers, 218–19, 226–27
   culture and customs, 227, 228
   demographics, 228
   ethnic group mixing, 227
   ethnic identity, 228
   heritage sites, 227
   historical background, 15–16, 105, 426n39
   information sources, 236
   intermarriage, 227
   locations, 218, 226–28
   organizations, 228
   origins of settlers, 218, 226–27
   religion, 227
   settlement patterns, 11, 227–28, 234
Czernawka, 161

D

Dafoe, 112, 332, 333
Dahinda, 223
Dahlia, 316, 329
Dahlton, 324, 325
Daisy Meadow, 124
Dakota. *See* Sioux/Dakota and Lakota
Dalmeny, 118, 119, 121, 143, 147, 176, 317, 400
Damour, 264
Dana, 86, 88, 89, 171, 172, 174, 176, 387
Danbury, 168
Dandonneau, 274
Danes, 330–31
   citizenship adoption, 338
   colonizers, 4, 330–31
   culture and customs, 330–31
   demographics: population, 310, 330, 331
   ethnic group mixing, 341
   ethnic identity, 310, 330, 338
   historical background, 16, 310, 330–31, 338–39
   information sources, 349
   intermarriage, 393
   language use, 331, 340
   locations, 322, 330–31
   organizations, 345
   religious affiliations, 311, 341
   settlement patterns, 310
   See also Nordic peoples
Dankin, 111
Danube Swabians, 97, 102, 107–9, 150
   See also Germans
Danzig, 116
Daphne, 87, 88, 324
Darmody, 315
Davidson, 61, 227
Davin, 52, 84, 85
Davyroyd, 107
Day Star Cree, 27
Daylesford, 88
Dead Moose Lake, 88
Debden, 265–67, 291–92, 295, 302
Deborah, 231
Deer Forks, 93
Deer Ridge, 322
Delena, 171
Delisle, 111, 266, 268
Delmas, 262, 263
Delorme, 263
Demaine, 317
demographics
   census data: Aboriginal terminology, 33–34; male lineage (before 1971), 13, 287; multiple ethnic origins (after 1971), 13–14, 287, 353, 380, 396; rural farm, rural non-farm, and urban distinctions, 385; sampling, 14, 50; use of 1971 data, 13–14
demographic transition theory, 375
dependency ratios, 379
migration factors, 377
population change factors, 375, 377
demographics, population
   birth rates, 375–76, 379, 381
   Canadian trends: foreign-born, 377; urban areas, 377; visible minorities, 380
   comparisons with other provinces: growth rates, 375; population density, 376
   death rates, 375–76
   density, 376
   farm operations, 381–85
   foreign-born immigrants, 377
   information sources, 409–10
   interprovincial migration, 352
   new immigrants, 351
   out-migration, 352, 375, 377, 378–79
   overview, 350–51, 373–80
   population change factors, 375, 377
   rate of growth/decline, 351, 375, 380
   rate of natural increase, 352, 375
   sex ratios, 379
   urban, 382–83
demographics, trends, 373–80
   age structure: dependency ratio, 379; median age, 174, 379; seniors, 351
   historical background, 373–75, 377, 379, 380
   homes with overcrowding, 39
   information sources, 409–10
   intermarriage, 380
   labour force: income, 36, 38; unemployment rate, 36, 38
   out-migration, 352, 375, 377, 378–79
   poverty rates, 38

See also depopulation
and delocalization;
farms and farm
operators; immigration,
recent; urban areas;
visible minorities
Dene/Chipewyan, 23,
24, 25, 26, 32
Dennington, 67
Denzil, 90, 91
depopulation and
delocalization,
16–17, 383–90
age structure, 385
assimilation and, 407
delocalization, 16–17,
386–87, 388
delocalization
defined, 1, 386–87
demographic
history, 376–77
Depression and reduced
immigration, 377
focal point closures,
12–13, 16, 387–90
historical background,
376–77, 383–86
physical mobility
and, 383, 386
population size and
rate of decrease, 385
research (1968–72):
physical mobility, 386
rural non-farm
population, 384–85
See also rural areas
Derganagh, 68
Deutscher Bund (German
Alliance), 91, 94, 98,
100, 103–6, 109, 112
Didsbury Stock Farm, 45
Diehl's Creek, 116
Dilke, 52, 96, 98, 321
Dinsmore, 129, 337
Dirt Hills, 223
Dixon, 88
Dnieper, 127, 161, 162
Dniester, 161, 162
Dnipro, 161
Dobraniwka, 170
Dobronoutz, 166
Dobrowody, 166, 201

Dobruja, as origin of settlers,
78, 80, 100–101, 222–23
Dodsland, 90, 91
Dollard, 282–83
Dominion, 194–95
Domrémy, 251–52, 253,
255, 295, 302, 388
Donegal, 92
Donnellyville, 68
Donovan, 111
Donwell, 162
Doonside, 57
Dorintosh, 124
Doroshenko/Bear Stream, 162
Douglaston, 62
Doukhobor Dugout
House (National
Historic Site), 217
Doukhobors, 207–18
anti-Doukhobor
sentiment, 49, 183, 211
architecture: prayer
homes, 209, 216, 217;
village homes, 210, 213
assimilation, 401
colonizers, 208
culture and customs,
217–18
demographics:
depopulation, 212–13;
population, 207, 208,
210, 212, 214–15
education, 212
ethnic group mixing, 208,
216–17, 218, 224, 391
ethnic identity: ethno-
religious groups,
399; preservation,
215, 395, 403–4
heritage and historic
sites, 216, 217, 426n15
historical background,
15, 207–8, 211, 213
information sources, 235
intermarriage, 191, 215,
216, 217, 224, 391–92
language use, 215–16,
217, 397–98, 401
locations, 51, 162, 176,
207–10, 212–17
migration and mobility:
physical mobility,

386; prohibition
on immigration,
120; settlements in
BC, 212–14, 216
names, 212, 398
religion: beliefs and
values, 207, 210–11, 213;
church attendance,
216, 401; sects, 212,
213–14; transethnic
churches, 216–17
research (1968–72),
215–16, 386, 391–92, 395,
397–98, 401, 403–4
settlement patterns:
communal villages,
208, 209, 212, 234;
homesteads, 208,
210–13; line villages,
209, 210, 212, 402;
mixed villages, 208,
209–10; scattering, 210
social protests, 209,
211–12, 213
urbanization, 217
Dovedale, 227
Downey Lake, 93, 129
Drahomanow, 171
Drake, 125
Drinkwater, 315
Drobot, 163
Dubuc, 326, 327
Duck Lake/Lac-aux-
Canards, 253–55
education, 253–54
historic sites, 247
historical background, 244
population, 178, 255
religion, 244, 300
research (1968–72), 291–92
settlement, 244, 251–55, 261
settlers, French:
assimilation, 291–92;
family names, 398;
language use, 253–54, 255;
media, 255, 302; school-
language issue, 293
settlers, Métis: conflict,
56, 240, 246; culture
and customs, 247;
settlements, 244–45

settlers, other: Aboriginals, 27; Belgians, 253; French, 253; Mennonites, 120, 400; Swiss, 253; Ukrainians and Poles, 178, 247
Duck Mountain, 209
Duff, 46, 103, 104
Dumas, 269–70
Dummer, 127
Dunafoldvar, 220–21
Dunblane, 337
Dundee, 61
Dundurn, 61, 113, 125, 126, 227, 320
Dungannon, 67
Dungloe, 68
Dunkeld, 72
Dunleath, 57, 59, 68
Dutch, 131–32
  colonizers, 4, 7, 131
  information sources, 154
  intermarriage, 393
  language use, 131, 132, 134, 287
  Mennonites, 18, 131
  population, 131–32
  settlement patterns, 77
Duval, 96, 98
Dydland, 326
Dysart, 60, 97, 98, 179, 221, 222, 223, 225

E

Eagle Creek, 130, 209–10, 214–15, 217, 317
Ear Hill, 91
Earl Grey, 96, 97, 98, 329
Earview, 129
East Asians. *See* Chinese; Japanese; Koreans
East Finn, 337
East Indians, 362
  See also South Asians
East London, 46
Eastend, 283
Easter Lily, 99
Eastern Europeans
  ethnic identity and language use, 396
  historical overview, 373–74
  information sources, 148–49, 160, 206
  intermarriage, 391–92, 393
  names, 399
  terminology, 18
  See also Croatians and Yugoslavs; Czechs and Slovaks; Doukhobors; Hungarians; Jews; Poles; Romanians; Ukrainians
Eatonia, 111, 130
Ebenau, 111
Ebenezer, 100, 144
Ebenfeld, 116
Edam, 131–32, 263
Eddleston, 332
Edelane, 96
Eden Valley, 319
Edenberg, 119
Edenbridge Colony, 232
Edenburg, 118, 121, 143
Edenland, 107, 327
Edenwold, 10, 83, 101, 147
Edfield, 325
Edgeley, 51
Edmore, 169
education
  English-language schools, early, 142–43
  ethnic groups and education levels: Aboriginals, 35, 37; ethnic identity and, 404; new immigrants, 378; social mobility approval, 390
  information sources, 307
  language rights, 297–99
  legislation: (1896–1919), 140–41, 194–95, 293, 295; (1930–1979), 296–98
  out-migration and, 378–79
  private schools, 142, 144
  religious emblems ban, 141, 296
  research (1968–72), 390
  rural school consolidation: and delocalization, 387–88; impact on ethnic groups, 145, 296, 387–88
  school district historical backgrounds, 12
  school-language issue, 140–43, 292–99, 307
  school trustee language qualifications; 294, 296
  schools as focal points, 12, 16, 387–88
  See also British cultural dominance
Effromovo, 208
Egyptians, 367
Eigenfeld, 91, 116
Eigenheim, 113, 116, 125
Eildon Vale, 61
Einar's Lake, 334
Elberfeld, 116
Elbow, 123, 126, 319, 320
Elcapo, 62, 327
Eldersley, 325
Eldon, 50, 359–60
Eldred, 266
Elfros, 169, 332, 333
Elk, 91
Ellisboro, 51, 62
Elm Springs, 223
Elrose, 111
Embury, 144
Emerald, 169, 203
Emilbourg, 259
Endeavour/Rusally, 127, 167, 175, 325
Englefeld, 86, 88
English, 44–54
  architecture: Gothic and Tudor buildings, 45; "soddie" home, 52; stone churches, 52
  child migration, 53
  colonizers, 45, 46–47, 51, 53
  demographics: depopulation, 50, 51–52, 53; population, 53–54; population proportion, 50, 53–54
  ethnic group mixing, 45
  ethnic identity, 54
  farming, 44–45, 48–49, 50–51
  historic and heritage sites, 45, 47, 49, 50, 52
  historical background, 15–16, 44–45
  information sources, 74–75

locations, 45–52; Barr
    Colony, 15, 47–51, 73;
    Cannington Manor,
    15, 45, 47, 269
place names, 51
Quakers, 47, 208, 216, 218
religion, 53–54
settlement patterns, 51, 73
terminology, 17, 44
See also British cultural
    dominance
English language
    anglicized names, 187–88,
        212, 318, 398–99
    official language status, 293
    research (1968–72) on
        bilingualism, 396–98
    school-language
        issue, 292–99
    See also British cultural
        dominance; language use
English River First Nation, 32
Enniskillen, 66, 67
Ens, 88, 220
Ensz, 111
Environ, 210
Epinard, 282
Erin, 68
Erinferry, 66, 68
Eritreans, 361
Erlösser, 102
Ermine, 72
Ernewein, 106
Erwood, 127, 168
Esk, 112
Esperance, 200
Esterhazy, 11, 218–19,
    226–28, 234
Estevan
    demographics, 379, 383
    settlers: Belgians, 275;
        Germans, 106, 147; Jews,
        231, 234; Norwegians,
        311, 312; Ukrainians, 179
    Soo rail line, 106, 311
Eston, 111, 317
Estonians, 235
Estuary, 93, 94, 95, 130
Ethiopians, 361
ethnic bloc settlements.
    See bloc settlements
ethnic identity, 394–402

age differences and, 403–4
bloc settlements and, 8
census data: ethnic
    identity, 13–14; ethnic
    origin, 44; male
    lineage (before 1971),
    13; multiple origins
    (after 1971), 13–14, 287,
    353, 380, 396; regional
    identities, 13; sampling,
    14; sampling (20%), 50
communities:
    homogeneity, 14, 404;
    population estimates, 14;
    rivalries, 404; size, 404
conflict and, 189, 404
culture and customs, 402
defined: ethnic identity,
    399; ethnicity, 14; ethno-
    religious groups, 399;
    objective definition, 399
delocalization and
    depopulation, 386–87
education level and, 404
ethno-religious
    groups, 399
factors: culture and
    customs, 395; language,
    395–99; physical
    appearance, 395;
    religion, 395, 399–401
gender and, 403–4
intermarriage and,
    395–96, 401–2
media and, 404
mobility and, 404
name changes, 187–88,
    212, 318, 398–99
organizations and, 197
preservation of, 403–4
research (1968–72), 133,
    140, 184, 215–16, 291–92,
    386, 395, 401, 403–4
variability, 13–14
See also assimilation;
    bloc settlements;
    citizenship; culture
    and customs; language
    use; multiculturalism;
    religion; *and specific
    ethnic groups*
Europeans

new immigrants,
    352–53, 377–78
See also Belgians; French;
    Germans; Nordic
    peoples; Swiss
Evangelical Lutheran Church
    in Canada (ELCIC),
    95, 312–13, 316, 322,
    324, 325, 327, 328, 329,
    330, 331, 334, 336
Evangelical Lutheran Church
    of Canada (ELCC),
    95, 114, 342, 343, 346
Evangelical Mennonite
    Brethren (EMB), 119,
    122–23, 126, 127, 128
See also Mennonites,
    religion
Evangelical Mennonite
    Mission Conference
    (EMMC), 117,
    122–23, 126, 128
See also Mennonites,
    religion
Evesham, 91
Excel, 278, 327
Excelsior, 122
exogamy. *See* intermarriage
    and population mixing
Expanse, 314
Eyebrow, 123
Eyre, 232

F

Fairholme, 124
Fairlight, 107
Fairy Glen, 323, 329
Fairy Hill, 97
Faresfield, 123
Farmington, 320
farms and farm
    operators, 380–83
    Aboriginal
        corporations, 381
    architecture: fieldstone
        farmhouses,
        63; Mennonite
        buildings, 125; stone
        farmhouses, 101, 268
    demographic trends:
        average size, 381, 384;

corporate farms, 381; family size, 381; farm operators, 381, 383; income, 382, 383, 386; land values, 382, 385; number of, 380–81; number of farms, 380; population, 381–82, 384–85; size, 380, 384
diversified operations, 381, 385–86
ethnic identity preservation, 403–4
historical background, 380–86
lifestyle difficulties, 385–86
migration: rural farm to rural non-farm, 379; rural to urban, 383–86; south to north, 384
physical mobility, 386
research (1968–72), 403–4
social change factors, 389–90
See also depopulation and delocalization
Fedoruk, 162
Fedyak, 163
females and males. See gender
Fenton, 323
Fenwood, 103, 104, 165
Ferguslea, 62
Ferland, 278–79, 280, 289
Fertile, 272
Fertile Belt, 72, 219, 327
Fertile Valley, 319, 320, 337
Festubert, 279
Fielding, 124
Fife Lake, 277, 279
File Hills, 27, 29, 30, 165
Filipinos, 351, 352, 355, 358, 370
See also Southeast Asians
Fillmore, 179, 200
Findlater, 61, 179
Finns
citizenship adoption, 338
colonizers, 4
culture and customs, 336, 337–38, 343–44
demographics: depopulation, 337, 388, 389; population, 335, 337

education, 341
ethnic identity, 310, 335, 337, 341, 347
historical background, 15–16, 310, 335, 338–39, 341, 346
information sources, 349
intermarriage, 335, 341, 347
language use, 340–41
locations, 335–38, 341–43, 346–47
organizations, 337
place names, 338
population, 310
religion, 311, 337, 341–43, 388
settlement patterns, 310, 335, 338, 388
socialist factions, 337, 342, 346
See also Nordic peoples; Swedish Finns
Fir Mountain, 279
First Nations. See Aboriginal peoples
First Osvoborsdennie, 208
First World War
anti-German sentiment, 78, 81, 108, 141, 144
anti-immigration sentiment, 5, 53
conscientious objectors, 119, 144, 213
"enemy aliens," 80, 144, 203, 346
impact on immigration, 374
pro-British sentiment, 52–53, 294
settlers: Belgians, 132; Doukhobors, 213; Finns, 346; Germans, 80, 87, 103, 141; Hutterites, 119, 129; Mennonites, 119, 129, 144; Nordic peoples, 338–39; Ukrainians, 183, 203
Fish Creek, 170–76
population, 174
research (1968–72), 184
riverlots, 246
school-language issue, 293
settlers, other: Métis, 200, 246–47; Poles, 185, 200, 246, 247

settlers, Ukrainian: depopulation, 199; education, 194, 195, 196; ethnic identity, 184, 187; language use, 185–87, 194, 196; religion, 184, 188–89; settlement, 170–76, 178, 194
Fishing Lake, 332
Fishing Lake First Nation, 29, 213
Fiske, 112, 125
Flaata Creek, 314
Flat Valley, 104
Fleming, 127, 328
Flemish settlers, 131–32, 286–87
Flett's Springs, 221, 258, 323
Flintoft, 223, 225
Flower Valley, 99
Flowing Well, 110, 111, 123
Flying Dust Cree, 28
Foam Lake
CPR line, 168
place names, 66, 68
population, 164, 333
settlers: Icelanders, 66, 332–33, 334; Irish, 68; Mennonites, 126; Norwegians, 325; Ukrainians, 164, 169, 170, 191, 333
focal points. See depopulation and delocalization
Folgoët, 258
folk customs. See culture and customs
Folkfest, Saskatoon. See Saskatoon: culture and customs, Folkfest
Fond-du-Lac First nation, 32
Forest Glen, 106
Forgaard, 322
Forgan, 317
Forget, 132, 272–73
Forslund, 329
Fort-à-la-Corne, 238
Fort Carlton, 240
Fort-Espérance, 239, 242
Fort-la-Jonquière, 238
Fort Pelly, 325
Fort Pitt, 130, 240
Fort-Providence, 239

INDEX

Fort Qu'Appelle, 52, 54, 224, 225, 242
Fort Walsh, 242
Forward, 313
Fosston, 166, 167, 201, 203, 324, 325
Fosterton, 316
Fosti, 163
Fournierville, 279
Fox Valley, 93, 94, 95
Foxford, 178
Francis, 85, 274
Franko, 162
Frankslake, 101
Fransfeld, 84, 97
Freedhome, 327
French, 238–308
  anti-French sentiment, 296, 298
  architecture: aristocratic homes, 269; stone farmhouses, 268
  assimilation, 291–92
  businesses, 253, 259–60, 262, 265, 269, 300
  colonizers, 250–51, 270–71, 273, 275
  culture and customs: arts, 252–53, 262, 265, 273, 276–77, 281; ethnic identity and, 288; museums, 258–59, 265, 281, 282; organizations, 300–302
  demographics: place of origin, 286–87; population history, 53, 286–87, 288–89; population proportion, 289; urban population, 284–86, 289
  demographics, depopulation: locations, 255, 259, 262, 272–73, 283; regions and rates, 289; trends, 289–90, 303
  diversity, 283, 288
  education: school consolidation, 387–88; school-language issue, 292–99, 307
  ethnic group mixing, 45, 250, 254, 257, 269, 283
  ethnic identity, 11, 289, 291–92, 303, 395
  ethnic identity preservation, 403–4
  Fransaskois defined, 288, 396
  heritage and historic sites, 255, 256, 257, 259, 261, 264, 269, 274, 275, 276, 285
  historical background: fur trade, 238–40, 286; Métis settlements, 240–50; French settlements (1890–1910), 15–16, 250–84
  information sources, 305–8
  intermarriage: ethnic identity and, 289; Métis and French, 277; trends, 303, 391–92, 403–4
  locations: central, 251; Duck Lake–St-Louis, 251–55; north-central, 255–60, 290, 291, 294–95; northeast, 250, 260–62; northern, 251–55; northwest, 262–68, 291; south-central, 250, 275–79; southeast, 250, 268–75; southwest, 250, 280–84, 289; St-Hubert/La Rolanderie, 45, 268–70
  media, 301–2
  organizations, 251, 252–53, 262, 265–66, 276–77, 285, 300–302
  origin, overview, 286–87
  origin, from Europe: bloc settlements, 270–73, 286–87, 289; St-Hubert/La Rolanderie, 45, 268–70
  origin, from Quebec, 286–87; bloc settlements, 250–51, 261, 265, 275; fur trade, 239–40
  origin, from United States, 261, 265, 275, 286–87
  physical mobility, 386
  religion (Roman Catholic): adherence to, 401; attendance, 401; clergy as colonizers, 250; organizations, 300; trends, 292
  research (1968–72), 291–92, 386, 391–92, 395, 401, 403–4
  settlement patterns, 8, 11, 250–51, 286
  urbanization, 289, 291, 303
  See also French language; Métis, francophone
French language
  bilingualism, 258, 283, 290–91
  bloc settlements, 272, 286
  court system use, 298
  demographics: global population, 288; patterns of use, 290–92, 396–98; population proportion, 279, 290, 396; rural vs. urban, 290–91
  ethnic identity and, 395, 396
  Fransaskois defined, 288, 396
  historical background, 238, 292–93
  names: family names, 258, 261, 264, 268, 269, 270; personal, 398–99; place names, 240, 241, 264, 275, 303, 307
  new immigrants, 288, 299, 303
  organizations, 300–302
  research (1968–72), 396–98
  retention, 396
  rights, 293–94, 297
  school-language issue, 292–99
  trends, 289–92, 303
  urban areas, 284–86, 355
  See also French; language use
Frenchman Butte, 267–68
Frenchman River Valley, 283
Frenchman's Flats, 248
Frenchville, 282

456

Freudenthal, 97
Freyling Lake, 88
Friedensfeld, 116
Friedland, 118, 143
Friends Colony, 47
Friesen, 129
Friesen Creek, 116
Frobisher, 106
Frog Lake, 247, 267
Frog Portage Reserve, 28
Frohlich, 94, 98
Frontier, 315
Fulda, 387
fur trade, 54, 238–40
   See also Hudson's Bay Company (HBC)
Furness, 50
Fusilier, 91, 317

G

Gabriel Dumont Institute, 33, 249
Gabriel's Crossing, 245
Gagnier, 276
Galicia, as origin of settlers
   anti-Galician sentiment, 211
   citizenship adoption, 183
   ethnic identity, 13, 181–82
   historical background, 78, 80, 181–82, 194, 199, 203
   intermarriage, 393
   population proportion, 183
   religion, 178, 181–82, 188, 423n45
   settlers: Czechs, 227; Germans, 80, 92, 101, 102–3, 106, 107; Poles, 182, 199, 200–201; Ukrainians, 160, 161, 163, 164, 165, 168, 170, 174, 176, 177, 178, 179, 194
Galician Lake, 175
Gap, 274
Gardar, 332
Garden Plain, 129
Garden River, 177–78
   research (1968–72), 184, 186–87, 199
   settlers, other: French, 260; Poles, 177–78, 186, 199, 202
   settlers, Ukrainian: education, 194; ethnic identity, 184, 199; language use, 184–87, 194; religion, 189; settlement, 177–78, 198; urbanization, 180
Gardepuis Crossing, 245
Garrick, 113
Garry, 164, 220
Garthland, 120, 121
Gascoigne, 94
Gauthier, 275, 276
gender
   Aboriginals: Bill C-31, 34; female leadership, 30
   ethnic identity preservation and, 403–4
   homesteading by women, 7
   imbalances: Blacks, 361; Chinese, 356–57
   male lineage in census data, 13, 287
   mortality rates, 379
   sex ratio in population, 379
General Conference Mennonites, 119–20, 122–27, 136, 144, 390, 400
   See also Mennonites, religion
George Gordon Cree, 26, 27, 29
Georgina, 111
Gerald, 219, 227
Gergovia, 282
German Hill, 99
Germans, 77–154
   anti- and pro-German sentiment, 78–81, 87, 108, 141, 144
   architecture: adobe churches, 101; stone farmhouses, 101
   colonizers, 4, 78, 80, 96, 99
   culture and customs: celebrations, 97, 114; museums, 103; revival, 146–47; Swabian traditions, 108–9
   Danube Swabians, 97, 102, 107–9, 150
   demographics: depopulation, 88–89, 91–92, 95, 103; population, 17, 77, 81; population history, 77, 80; population proportion, 79
   diversity, 79–80, 146
   education: school consolidation, 387–88; school-language issue, 140–44
   ethnic identity, 146–47; nationalism, 78; trends, 81
   ethnic identity, nationalism: Deutscher Bund, 91, 94, 98, 100, 103–6, 109, 112; exodus to Germany, 104–5
   heritage and historic sites, 105
   historical background: Danube Swabians, 107–8; "enemy aliens," 80–81, 144; immigration prohibition, 80–81; overview, 77–83; religious affiliations, 77–78, 82; settlements, 15–16; Sudentenland arrivals, 105
   information sources, 148–54
   intermarriage, 100, 391–93
   language use, 396–98; demographics, 79, 291; ethnic identity and, 396; history, 78–79, 291, 396; prohibition on publications, 87; religious instruction, 113; Swabian dialect, 108–9; trends, 81, 396
   locations overview, 82–83
   names, 83, 115–16
   new immigrants, 81, 147
   organizations and institutions, 80, 147, 154
   research (1968–72), 396–98
   settlement patterns: mixed origins, 80, 82; organized type, 8; religious affiliations, 77, 80, 82; scattered, 95
   Soo rail line, 106, 107
   urbanization, 108, 147
   See also Dutch; German Catholics; German

Protestants; Hutterites; Mennonites
German Catholics
architecture: communal village, 83
colonizers, 8, 85, 89
cultural pride, 140
culture and customs: art, 86, 90; celebrations, 109; folk traditions, 136; museums, 90, 92
demographics: depopulation, 88–89, 91–92, 95, 103–4, 110–11, 388; population, 85, 86, 88, 90, 91, 94, 103–4
diversity, 80, 98
education: control of schools, 140–41; school consolidation, 387–88; school-language issue, 140–41
ethnic group mixing (Lutherans), 84, 87–88, 90–91, 93–94
ethnic identity, 133, 140, 395
ethnic identity preservation, 403–4
heritage and historic sites, 83, 84, 85, 86, 87, 92, 102, 106, 110
historical background, 77–78, 82, 83, 92
information sources, 148–54
intermarriage, 136, 391–92, 393, 396
language use, 91, 133–34, 135, 396–98
locations overview, 82–83
locations by colony: Katharinental Colony, 82; Kronau-Rastadt Colony, 82, 84–85, 93, 94, 95; Odessa settlement, 84–85; Prelate Colony, 82, 92–95; St. Elizabeth Colony, 108, 110; St. Joseph's Colony (1886–), 82, 83–85; St. Joseph's Colony (1905–), 89–92, 111; St. Paul's Colony, 84, 91, 114, 321; St. Peter's Colony (1894–), 84
locations by region: central, 112–13; east-central, 113; north-central, 113–14; northeast, 113; northwest, 114; south-central, 107–10; southeast, 105–7; southwest, 110–11; west-central, 111–12
names, 398
nationalism, 91
organizations, 80
physical mobility, 386
religion: adherence to, 401; church attendance, 135, 401; church closures, 388
research (1968–72), 132–36, 386, 391–93, 395, 396–98, 401, 403–4
settlement patterns: bloc, heterogeneous, 80; bloc, homogeneous, 8, 77, 80, 82; communal village *(dorf)*, 84; religious affiliations, 80
See also Germans; St. Peter's Colony (1902– ; German Catholic)
German Protestants
Adventists: locations, 83, 95, 96, 101, 110, 126; settlement patterns, 77, 82
architecture, 101
Baptists: historical background, 99–101; locations, 83, 86, 94, 96–97, 98, 99–101, 103, 114, 216; population, 104; settlement patterns, 77, 80, 82, 95
colonizers, 8, 96
culture and customs: celebrations, 114; museums, 104
demographics: depopulation, 98, 110–11; population, 98, 99, 100, 401
heritage and historic sites, 96, 97, 114
historical background, 77–78, 115
information sources, 148–54
intermarriage, 391
locations overview, 82–83
locations by colony: Beaver River, 104; Edenwold, 100–101; Hohenlohe, 99, 100; Loon River, 104–5; Melville area, 102–4; New Elsass, 96–98, 99; Prelate (Catholic), 93–94; Saskatchewan Valley area, 121; St. Joseph's, 90–91; St. Peter's (Catholic), 87–88; St. Walburg, 104–5; Volga, 99–100
locations by region: central, 112–13; east-central, 113; north-central, 113–14; northeast, 113; northwest, 104–5, 114; south-central, 107–10, 121; southeast, 105–7; southwest, 93–94, 110–11; west-central, 111–12
locations overview, 82–83
Lutherans: affiliations, 95–96, 400; church attendance, 342; demographics, 401; locations overview, 83; settlement patterns, 77, 80
mixed settlements: Catholics, 87–88, 93–94, 98, 102–5; Mennonites, 112
nationalism, 104–5
organizations, 319, 345
research (1968–72), 401
settlement patterns, 8, 95, 120; bloc, homogeneous, 77; religious affiliations, 80
See also Germans
Gerrond, 55

Gestingthorpe, 51
Ghanaians, 361
Gibbs, 96, 98
Gillies, 212
Gillis Blakely Heritage Museum Site, 61
Gilnockie, 65
Gilroy, 123
Girvin, 61
Gjosund Road, 320
Gladmar, 106, 312
Gladue Lake Reserve, 28
Glasgow, 59
Glaslyn, 114, 175, 192
Glasnevin, 63
Glen Bain, 65
Glen Elder, 168
Glen Ewen, 62
Glen Kerr, 63
Glen Mary, 65, 322, 323
Glen McPherson, 65
Glen Murray, 60
Glen Valley, 61
Glenbain, 110, 111
Glenbrae, 61
Glenbush, 124
Glengariff, 68
Glenside, 61, 227, 319
Glentworth, 179, 279
Glidden, 111, 125, 130
Glocca Morra, 68
Glyndwr, 71
Goldburg, 228
Golden Jubilee area, 161
Golden Prairie, 93, 94, 95, 101
Golden View, 130
Gollier, 276
Good Lake, 166, 214
Good Spirit Lake Annex, 209–10, 213, 214
Goodeve, 103, 165, 201
Goodhue, 326
Gooding, 111
Goodsoil, 104–5
Goodwater, 313, 328
Goodwin House, 248–49
Gooliaff, 213
Goose Lake, 317
Gorilloe, 209
Gorlitz, 100, 162
Gouldtown, 122, 123
Gouverneur, 281

Govan, 98, 329
Grace, 109
Grainland, 107
Gramlich, 92
Grand Trunk Pacific Railway, 7, 71
Grand Valley, 114
Grandy, 332, 333
Grant, 175, 257, 316
Grassy Creek, 111, 329, 338
Gravelbourg
　language use, 289, 292, 299
　media, 276, 301–2
　settlers, 16, 109, 275–77, 280
Graydahl, 316
Grayson, 72, 102, 103, 104, 200
Great Bend, 209–10, 215
Great Deer, 120, 124, 389
Greeks, 367–69
　culture and customs, 368
　demographics, 369
　historical background, 367
　information sources, 372
　intermarriage, 369
　language use, 368
　religion, 368
　urban locations, 367–68
Green Canyon, 175
Green Lake/Lac-Vert, 239, 241, 248, 260, 267
Green Leaf, 130
Green Prairie, 123
Green Valley, 320
Greenfarm, 123
Greenville, 62
Gregherd, 97, 98
Grenfell, 106, 179
Griffin, 200
Grismerville, 111
Grizzly Bear's Head First Nation, 30
Gromovoe, 208
Gronlid, 177, 232, 329
Gros Ventre people, 23–24, 29
Grosswerder, 90, 91
group settlements. *See* bloc settlements
Gruenfeldt, 118, 121, 137, 138
Gruenthal, 116, 117, 118, 121, 144
Grunert, 100
Grunfeld, 123
Guernsey, 113, 125, 128, 172

Gull Lake, 111
Gutenberg, 92
Guyanese, 361, 362
Gypsies, 235

H

Hafford
　ethnic relations, 189
　population, 176
　settlers, other: French, 176, 189, 201, 264; Poles, 176, 185, 189, 201
　settlers, Ukrainian: culture and customs, 193; education, 195; farm size, 198; historical background, 174–75; home construction, 192; language use, 176, 185; population proportion, 176; religion, 175–76, 189
Hagen, 321, 322–23
Haglof, 332
Hague, 116, 117, 120, 121, 128, 137, 144, 390, 400
Halbrite, 63, 313
Halbstadt, 118
Halcro, 55–56, 64, 65
Halcyonia, 124
Halech, 165
Halicz, 168
Halldorson Spring, 332
Hallonquist, 111
Halycry, 167
Hamburg, 116
Hampton, 162
Hamre, 320
Hamton, 100
Handel, 90, 91
Hanley, 318–20
　colonizers, 227, 322
　information sources, 348
　language use, 340, 399
　population, 319
　settlement patterns, 11
　settlers: Croatians, 228; Mennonites, 124–26; Nordic peoples, 11; Norwegians, 311, 315, 318–20, 322, 340, 342, 345, 399; Scots, 61

INDEX

Hanson, 329
Happy Valley, 266
Happyland, 94
Haralowka, 216
Hardy, 109
Harmonia, 47, 210, 216
Harris, 111, 125, 268
Hart, 314
Hat Creek, 88
Hatchet Lake First Nation, 32
Hatton, Alberta, 93, 94, 95, 101
Hauge, 312
Haultain, 113
Haven, 130
Hawarden, 72, 227, 319, 320
Hawkshaw, 321
Hay Lands Cree, 27
Hazel Dell, 167, 325, 326
Hazel Lake/Sheremata Farm, 171
Hazelwood, 220
Hazlet-Sanford area, 316
Headlands, 103
Heart's Hill, 90, 91
Heiberg, 313
Heidelberg, 116
Heil Lake, 102
Heiland, 92
Hendon, 324, 325, 329, 330
Henke, 111
Henribourg, 260
Henrietta, 210
Henry, 102
Henty, 210
Hepburn, 117, 118, 121, 144, 400
Herbert, 68, 122–23, 314
Herman, 94
Herschel, 125, 317
Herzel, 165, 231
Hesseldale, 114
Hessians, 77–78
Heuboden, 117
Heward, 52
Hidatsa people, 23
High Tor, 167, 201
Hill, 111
Hill Farm, 102
Hillcrest, 130
Hillside, 104
Hillsvale, 130
Hinchcliff, 325
Hindus, 362–63

Hirsch, 106, 222, 231, 312
Hispanics. *See* Latin Americans
Hitchcock, 106
Hlebedardoe, 208
Hnatiw Lake, 170
Hochfeld, 118, 120, 142
Hochstadt, 118
Hodgeville, 110, 111, 129, 179
Hoey, 251–52, 255
Hoffenthal, 99
Hoffer Colony, 222, 232
Hoffman, 89
Hoffman Coulee, 106
Hoffningsort, 116
Hoffnung, 94, 111
Hoffnungsfeld, 116, 120, 124, 144
Hogg Colony, 46
Hohelinden, 94
Hohenlohe, 83, 99, 100, 113
Holar, 168
Holar-byggd, 334
Holar Hill, 334
Holdeman Mennonites, 117, 127, 128, 400
  See also Mennonites, religion
Holdfast, 96, 98, 243, 321
Holland. *See* Dutch
Hollow, 111
Homestead, 100
homesteading
  demographics, 374
  Doukhobor policies, 208, 210–13
  historical background, 3–9, 210–11, 374
  historical period, 6
  homesteading system: allotment improvements, 6–7; allotment size, 6–7; citizenship, 6, 157, 183–84, 211; English language use, 184; fees, 6, 208; female ownership, 7; legal requirements, 6–7; oaths, 208, 211, 213
  legislation, 6–7, 210, 374
  national historic sites, 60–61

  Royal Commission on, 5–6, 405
  settlement stories, 157–59
  See also bloc settlements; Sifton, Clifford
Honey Bank, 168
Honeymoon, 178, 259
Hong Kong, 352, 357, 370
Hoodoo, 89, 221, 258
Hoosier, 317
Hopehill, 57
Horelofka, 209
Horfield, 314
Horizon, 109, 110
Horodenka, 171, 175
Horosziwci/War End, 163
Horse Lake, 120, 121
Horseshoe Lake, 321
Horsham, 94, 95
Hory, 171
Hoseasson Lake, 332
Hovdestad, 316
Hryhoriv, 167
Hubbard, 103, 165, 201
Hudson Bay, 118, 127, 167, 261
Hudson's Bay Company (HBC), 54, 239–40, 242–44, 246
Hull, 89
Humboldt
  demographics, 383
  school consolidation, 387–88
  settlers: Germans, 85, 86–88, 136, 140–41, 146–47, 388; Irish, 67; Norwegians, 320, 432n50; Ukrainians, 172
Hungarians, 218–22
  citizenship adoption, 183
  colonizers, 218–19, 220, 221–22
  culture and customs, 109, 220, 222
  demographics: depopulation, 219, 220, 221; population, 219–20, 221, 222, 226; population in Canada, 222; population proportion, 183, 221

460

INDEX

ethnic group mixing, 218, 219, 220, 221, 223, 227, 258
ethnic identity, 18, 222, 226
German Catholics, 110
heritage and historic sites, 110, 220
historical background, 15–16, 218, 426n39
information sources, 235–36
intermarriage, 221, 391, 393, 396
language use, 195, 220
locations, 108, 110, 173, 218–22, 226, 227, 258, 327, 398
names, 398
new immigrants, 222
religion, 110, 219, 220, 400
settlement patterns, 8, 11, 234
See also Austro-Hungarians
Huron, 130
Husiatyn/Claytonville, 178
Hutterites, 128–30
agriculture, 130, 138
anti-Hutterite sentiment, 129, 130, 183
assimilation, 133–35
culture and customs: celebrations, 139–40; clothing, 130, 137, 139; food, 130, 137–38; home life, 136, 139–40
demographics: birth rates, 376; population, 129
education, 130, 135, 138, 142, 145–46
ethnic identity, 133, 391, 395, 399, 403–4
historical background, 9, 16, 77, 78, 115, 120, 128–29
information sources, 153–54
intermarriage, 135, 391–92
language use, 130, 133–35, 396, 397–98
legislation on, 120, 130
Mennonites (Old Colony), comparison, 136–40, 142
physical mobility, 386
Prairieleut (non-communal), 119, 127, 129, 140, 391

religion: Anabaptist movement, 128–29; beliefs, 136, 139; church attendance, 401; divisions, 129–30; pacificism, 139
research (1968–72), 133–35, 140, 386, 390, 391–92, 395, 396, 397–98, 401, 403–4
settlement colonies, 16, 129–30, 137
settlement patterns, 8, 16, 77, 80, 129–30
social change, 138, 390, 392
social control, 139
Hyas, 127, 168, 208, 325

I

Ibsen, 313
Icelanders, 331–34
citizenship adoption, 338
culture and customs, 333, 344
demographics: depopulation, 170, 333, 334; population, 310, 333, 334
ethnic group mixing, 112, 333, 334
ethnic identity, 310, 334, 338
heritage sites, 334
historical background, 15, 310, 331–32
information sources, 349
language use, 340, 342
locations, 66, 170, 325, 332–34, 344
religion, 310–11, 333, 342
settlement patterns, 310, 347
See also Nordic peoples
identity, ethnic. *See* ethnic identity
Iduna, 321
Ile-à-la-Crosse, 26, 32, 241, 242, 243–44, 248
Ile Bernier, 263
Ile Blais, 263
Iles Caplette, 263
Iles Michaud, 263
Illerbrun, 111
Imhoff, 147
Immanuel, 144

immigration, early
Anglos preferred, 4–6, 8–9, 405–6
historical overview, 15–17, 373–75, 377, 380
population history, 350–51
See also bloc settlements; British cultural dominance; homesteading; refugees; *and specific ethnic groups*
immigration, recent
demographics: birth rates, 376; child poverty rates, 380; country of origin, 352–53; economic arrivals, 351; family class, 351; immigration rate, 351; population proportion, 351; refugees, 351; retention rates, 351; visible minorities, 355
ethnic groups: Blacks, 360–61; francophones, 284, 288, 299, 303; Germans, 81, 147; Poles, 203; Romanians, 226; Ukrainians, 199, 203
first- and second-generation immigrants, 353
immigration system: Anglo-conformity, 405–6; non-traditional sources of immigrants, 353; point system, 357
integration services, 354
intermarriage, 380
new immigrants: language retention, 396; population, 352, 377–78
overview, 351–52, 377–78
programs: nominee program, 351; temporary foreign workers, 351
urban locations: in Canada, 199, 351, 352, 361, 377; Regina, 147, 351, 352, 378; Saskatoon, 147, 351, 352, 378
See also migration and mobility; refugees;

INDEX

visible minorities; *and specific ethnic groups*
Imperial, 98
Inchkeith, 57
Indian Head, 60–61, 106
Indians, 352
See also South Asians
Indonesians, 358
Inge Bay, 332
Ingebright, 93
Insinger, 163–64
Instow, 111, 316
intermarriage and population mixing, 390–94
　assimilation and, 393–94
　bloc settlements, 392–94, 407
　demographics, 353, 380
　ethnic identity: and conflict, 189, 404; male lineage in census data, 13, 287; mixed populations and, 395–96; multiple origins in census data, 13–14, 287, 353, 380, 396; preservation, 403–4
　ethnic intermarriage, 391–93, 396, 401–2
　generational differences, 392–93, 403–4
　historical background, 393
　language use, 394
　new immigrants, 380
　racial intermarriage, 396
　religious intermarriage, 391–93, 396, 401–2
　research (1968–72), 135–36, 191, 390–94
　urban areas, 394
Inuit, 23, 33
Inveay, 166
Invercauld, 60
Invergordon, 195, 221, 258, 323
Invermay, 64, 166, 201, 325, 326, 338
Invernairn, 61
Inverness, 61
Iona, 57
Iowa, as origin of settlers
　settlers: Dutch, 131; Germans, 86; Norwegians, 318

Iranians, 366, 367
Iraqis, 352, 365, 366, 367
Irish, 66–69
　culture and customs, 68–69
　demographics: depopulation, 67; new immigrants, 353; population, 43, 54, 69
　ethnic identity, 43–44, 54, 69
　family names, 67
　historic sites, 68
　historical background, 15, 43, 66–67
　information sources, 75–76
　locations, 66–69
　organizations: Orange Order, 5–6, 68, 111, 183–84, 294, 296
　place names, 66, 68
　religion, 67–68
　settlement patterns, 9, 66, 73
　terminology, 17, 43
　See also British; British cultural dominance; English language
Irish Colony, 66–67
Iron Spring, 88
Irvine, Alberta, 93, 94
Isafoldar, 334
Isbister, 55, 241
Isham-Tyner area, 317
Island Lake First Nation, 28
Italians, 369, 372
Ituna
　CNR line, 164–65
　settlers: Poles, 201, 203; Ukrainians, 165, 177, 189, 203

J

Jackfish Lake, 262–63
Jamaicans, 361
James Smith, 27
Janow Corners, 178
Jans Bay, 26
Jansen, 112, 125
Jansen Lake, 320
Japanese, 354, 355, 357–58

Jarema, 161
Jaroslaw, 164
Jasmin, 165, 274
Jeanne d'Arc, 283
Jedburgh, 64, 65, 164, 201
Jew Lake, 230
Jews, 230–34
　anti-Semitism, 230, 233
　assimilation, 233–34
　colonizers, 230–31
　culture and customs, 231, 233–34
　demographics: depopulation, 231, 232–33, 234; population, 226, 234
　ethnic identity, 18, 226, 234
　farms, 232–33
　government relations, 230
　heritage and historic sites, 231, 232
　historical background, 15–16, 78, 230
　information sources, 237
　language use, 232, 233
　locations, 222, 230–34
　organizations, 233–34
　religion, 233
　Romanian Jews, 222, 231
　settlement patterns, 8, 230, 232, 234
　urbanization, 231, 233–34
Joffre, 273
Johannesthal, 116
Johnsborough, 93, 95
Jolie-Prairie, 266
Joseph Bighead/Big Island Lake Reserve, 28
Josephsburg, 106
Josephstal, 84, 93, 95
Jumbo Butte, 283

K

Kahkewistahaw First Nation, 27, 29
Kalmakovo, 209
Kalyna, 178
Kaminka, 171, 195, 208
Kamsack
　language use, 330
　settlers: Doukhobors,

INDEX

162, 207, 208, 209, 214;
   Hungarians, 222; Métis,
   240; Saulteaux, 29;
   Ukrainians, 162–63
Kandahar, 112, 320, 332, 333
Kansas, as origin of settlers
   settlers: Croatians, 229;
   Germans, 86, 93, 96, 98;
   Mennonites, 117, 118,
   119, 120, 125, 127, 136
Kaplychka, 162
Kaposvar Colony, 218–19
Kapustina, 209
Karilowa, 210
Karl Lake–Olson Lake, 312
Karlsruhe, 99
Karmelheim, 90
Kars, 208
Kassel, 94
Katepwa Beach, 47
Katharinental, 84
Kawacatoose Cree, 27, 29
Kayville, 109, 223
Keatley, 175
Keeseekoose First Nation, 29
Kegworth, 62
Kelfield, 91
Kelliher, 165, 330
Kelross, 221, 223
Kelso, 57
Kelstern, 110, 123
Kelvington, 127, 167, 201,
   261, 325, 326
Kenaschuk, 163
Kenaston, 227, 228–29
Kendal, 83, 84, 85
Kenlis, 60
Kenmare, 144
Kennedy, 57, 270
Kennel, 96
Kenyans, 361
Keppel, 64
Kerguelen, 258
Kermaria, 258
Kerrobert, 90, 91, 125
Kersor, 92
Kessock, 59
Ketchen, 167, 325
Key Reserve, 29
Keys, 168, 214
Keystown, 64
Khedive, 110

Kidron-Gull Lake, 122
Killaly, 103, 104, 200
Kilmenny, 114
Kilronan, 68
Kilshannig, 68
Kinbrae, 59, 99
Kincardine, 61
Kincora, 68
Kincorth, 316
Kindersley, 52, 125, 330
King Colony, 58, 59
King George, 124, 337
Kingsley, 62, 220, 270, 327
Kinistin First Nation, 29
Kinistino, 234, 323, 324
Kintyre, 61
Kipling, 107, 179, 220, 328
Kirkella, 328
Kisbey, 67
Kitzman, 100
Kivimaa-Moonlight
   Bay resort, 338
Kleczkowski, 175, 201
Klein (Little) Sudetenland, 105
Kloppenburg, 88
Klosterdorf, 84
Kobzar, 168
Koemstedt, 92
Koenigsberg, 103
Kohleschmidt Creek, 116
Kokesch, 92
Kolin, 226–27, 228
Kolo Blokhiv, 170
Kolo Bodnariv, 172
Kolo-Havrylyukiv, 171
Kolo Kaminskykh, 170, 172
Kolo Lazaruk, 168
Kolo Pidkowich, 169
Kolo Pidskal'noho, 171, 172
Kolo Shevchuka/Kolo
   Kozakevychiv, 163
Kolo Solomyanoho, 171
Kolo Vasyliev/Wasyliw, 166
Kolo Yurchyshyn, 177
Kolomyria, 171
Kolstad, 320
Kopperud, 311, 312
Korbel, 88
Koreans, 352, 355, 357
Kosovars, 230
Kossuth, 220
Kotzko, 171

Kovalivka, 166, 168
Kowalowka, 166, 168, 201
Kramer, 111
Krasne, 163, 168, 169, 175, 201
Krassna, 92, 94, 95
Krim, 117
Krimmer Mennonite
   Brethren (KMB), 119,
   123, 127, 129, 144, 400
   See also Mennonites,
   religion
Krimmerfeld, 93
Krist, 92
Kristnes, 332, 333
Krivoisheim, 175
Kronau, 84, 85, 98
Kronsberg, 97
Kronsfeld, 93, 94
Kronsthal, 118
Krupp, 94
Krydor, 174, 175, 176–77,
   201, 388
Ku Klux Klan, 5, 68,
   243, 296, 339
Kuest, 94
Kulikiw, 166
Kulykiv, 166
Kuprowski, 163
Kurchakiv, 161
Kurds, 367
Kuroki, 166, 201, 325
Kvitka, 164
Kyjiw/Kiev, 171
Kyle, 317
Kylemore, 65, 213, 214, 325
Kyrilovo, 209
Kyziv-Tiaziv, 166

L

La Fourche, 282
La Loche, 32, 241
La Maison-de-Terre, 283
La Petite Ville, 243, 244
La Plaine/Leckford, 254
La Prairie-Ronde, 31, 244, 248
La Rolanderie/St-Hubert,
   45, 268–70
Lac-Adelard, 264
Lac-aux-Canards/Duck
   Lake. *See* Duck Lake/
   Lac-aux-Canards

INDEX

Lac-Bassin, 257
Lac-Bergot, 258
Lac-Bérubé, 266
Lac-Bonneau, 278
Lac-Boyer, 284
Lac-Breynat, 241
Lac-Casavant, 264
Lac-Chapleau, 273
Lac-Cheval, 254
Lac-de-Charles, 259
Lac-de-Maronds, 279
Lac-Delaine, 258
Lac-Delaronde, 241
Lac-des-Noisettes/Nut Lake, 29, 260
Lac-des-Prairies. *See* Meadow Lake/Lac-des-Prairies
Lac-Dezou, 258
Lac-Dormouse, 258
Lac-Doucet, 266
Lac-Driscol, 282
Lac-Dubois, 257
Lac-Eauclair, 267
Lac-Fafard, 267
Lac-Filion, 266
Lac-Frenette, 266
Lac-Gagné, 266
Lac-Hélène, 263
Lac-Ignace, 258
Lac-Kleczkowski, 273
Lac-la-Pèche, 264
Lac La Ronge First Nation, 26
Lac-Labatte, 278
Lac-Lavallée, 241
Lac-Lavigne, 263
Lac-Léon, 283
Lac-Leroy, 258
Lac-Levasseur, 263
Lac-Lezard, 257
Lac-Louis, 257
Lac-Lucien, 257
Lac-Marguerite, 273
Lac-Marneau, 260
Lac-Martin, 264
Lac-Morin, 266
Lac-Mudie, 267
Lac-Natal, 264
Lac-Olivier, 257
Lac-Pelletier, 111, 281–82, 316
Lac-Perran, 266
Lac-Poisson-Blanc, 267
Lac-Rivard, 278

Lac-Royal, 264
Lac-Savard, 266
Lac-Theriau, 241
Lac-Venne, 257
Lac-Vert/Green Lake, 239, 241, 248, 260, 267
Lac-Voisin, 241
Lac-Qui Parle, 312
Lacs-Orléans, 283
Lacombe, 258
Lacordaire, 278
Lady Lake, 326
Laflèche, 275–76, 277
Laird, 117, 118, 121
Lajord, 129, 274, 313
Lake Alma, 106, 312
Lake Athabasca Reserve, 32
Lake Diefenbaker, 111
Lake Johnston, 314
Lake Lenore, 86, 87, 88, 89, 221, 258
Lake of the Rivers, 278
Lake Park, 323
Lake Valley, 314
Lakeburg, 118
Lakeview, 130, 167, 214, 326
Lakota. *See* Sioux/Dakota and Lakota
Lamoyle, 114
Lampard, 125
Lampman, 105, 106
Lancer, 93, 94, 95
Landau, 105
Landestreu, 99
Landis, 90, 91
Landshut, 99
Landstrom, 329
Lang, 63, 106, 313
Langbank, 57
Langenau, 100
Langenburg, 99
Langenhoff, 88
Langham
  commuters, 121, 147
  demographics, 121, 215
  settlers: Doukhobors, 209–10, 214, 215; German Lutherans, 121; Hutterites, 119, 127, 129, 140; Mennonites, 119–21, 144, 400; Norwegians, 311, 317, 318

Langley, 175
language use
  age differences and, 403
  English language use, 355
  ethnic identity and, 395, 396–98
  ethnic identity preservation, 403–4
  heritage language revival, 353–54
  intermarriage and, 396
  names, personal: anglicized, 187–88, 212, 318, 398–99; and ethnic identity, 187–88, 398–99
  non-English language use, 355
  research (1968–72), 133–34, 186–87, 199, 291–92, 339–40, 396–98, 403–4
  school-language issue, 140–43, 292–99, 307
  trends, 353–54, 398–99, 403–4
  See also education; English language; French language; Michif language; *and specific ethnic groups*
Lanigan, 67, 112, 125
Lanigan Farms, 172
Laniwci, 171, 172, 189
Laotians, 358
Laporte, 111, 317
Larisa, 168
Larsen, 320
Lashburn, 50, 65, 111, 125
Last Mountain Lake, 54, 61, 96, 98, 321
Latin America, as origin of settlers
  settlers: Germans, 81; Mennonites, 118, 120, 128, 144–45; Patigonian Welsh, 69–72
Latin Americans, 363–64
  Chileans, 354, 364, 371
  demographics, 363–64
  information sources, 371
  Mennonite returnees, 145, 364
  Patigonian Welsh, 69–72

population, 363–64, 369
urban locations, 364
Latvians, 232, 235
Laura, 111
Laurier, 274
Laurier, Sir Wilfrid,
    government
    immigration policies,
    4, 359, 374
    See also Sifton, Clifford
Lautier, 278
Laventure, 266
Lawson, 123, 314
Laxdal, 332
Layco, 317
LCA. *See* Lutheran Church
    of America (LCA)
LCC. *See* Lutheran Church
    Canada (LCC)
Leader, 82, 92–95, 388
Lean Man First Nation, 30
Leask, 114, 130, 229, 264, 322
Lebanese and Syrians, 365–67
    language use, 367
    population, 367
    settlement patterns,
    14, 18, 365–67
Lebret, 242–43, 274
Leckford/La Plaine, 254
Leech Lake Cree, 26, 27
Lefort, 276
Leibel, 92
Leinan, 316
Leipzig, 90, 91, 92
Lemberg, 83, 102, 103, 104, 200
Lemsford, 93, 95
Leney, 51–52
Lennard, 223
Lenore, 88
Leofeld, 85
Leofnard, 88
Leoville, 132, 265, 266,
    267, 291–92, 295
Lepine, 171, 173, 257
Leross, 165, 221
Leroy, 67, 86, 88, 112
Les Cypres, 283
Leslie, 332, 333
Lestock, 221
Libedevo, 208
Liberty, 96, 98, 321
Libyans, 367

Lichtfeld, 123
Liebenthal, 93
Lillestrom-Orland, 314
Lilly, 143, 144
Limerick, 66, 68, 314
Linacre, 94
Lintlaw, 167, 201, 325
Lipton, 46, 97, 98, 222,
    223, 227, 231
Lisieux, 277, 278
Lithuanians, 232, 235
Little Black Bear Cree, 27
Little Bone Cree, 27
Little Manitou Lake, 113
Little Moose Lake, 220, 258
Little Norway, 320
Little Pine Reserve, 28
Little Quill Lake, 332
Little Woody, 277, 278
Livingston, 168, 214
Llanvair, 72
Llanwenarth, 72
Llewelyn, 71
Lloyd George, 72
Lloydminster
    demographics:
        in-migration, 379;
        population, 36, 50, 383
    historical background,
        48–50, 72
    settlers: Aboriginals, 36;
        British (Barr colony), 15,
        47–51, 73; Germans, 147
Lockwood, 98
Lodi, 167
Logberg, 334
Loiselle Creek, 260
Lomond, 179
Lone Pine, 220
Long Creek, 242, 313
Long Lodge Reserve, 29–30
Longnor, 72
Loon Creek, 97
Loon Lake, 83, 104, 227
Loon River, 102, 104–5, 114
Loraine, 278
Loreburn, 319, 320
Lorenzo, 124
L'Orignal, 270
Lorraine, 275
Lost Lake, 175
Lost River, 127, 319, 320

Lothian, 58, 59, 61
Love, 113
Loverna area, 317
Loyal, 59
Lubomeernoe, 208
Lubovnoe, 208
Lucky Lake, 123, 337
Lucky Man First Nation, 28
Luella, 109
Lumsden, 61, 65, 234
Lund, 329
Lunner, 320–21
Lurgan, 68
Luseland, 90, 91
Lutherans
    church attendance, 342, 401
    depopulation and
        church closures, 388
    German Catholic mixing,
        84, 87–88, 90–91, 93–94
    German Lutherans:
        affiliations, 95–96, 400;
        locations overview, 83;
        settlement patterns, 77, 80
    Laestadian movement, 343
    Nordic Lutherans, 310–13,
        318, 321, 341–43
    organizations and
        institutions, 319, 345
    research (1968–72), 401
    See also American
        Lutheran Church (ALC);
        Evangelical Lutheran
        Church in Canada
        (ELCIC); Evangelical
        Lutheran Church
        of Canada (ELCC);
        Lutheran Church Canada
        (LCC); Lutheran Church
        of America (LCA)
Lutheran Church Canada
    (LCC), 313, 320, 324,
    328, 329, 334
Lutheran Church of America
    (LCA), 95, 106, 113,
    114, 310, 318, 321
Luxembourg, 4, 81, 104,
    264, 286, 287
Luzan, 208
Lysenko, 163

M

Macdonald, Sir John A., on British, 406
MacDougall, 59
MacDowall, 55, 178
Macedonians, 230
Macklin, 90, 91
MacLeod, 57
MacNutt, 59, 99, 223, 225
Macoun, 63, 106, 313
Macrorie, 111, 319, 337, 338, 342
Madelon, 283
Madraga Farm, 171
Maeshowe, 65
Magyar, 221
Maidstone, 50, 125, 359–60
Main Centre, 122, 123, 129
Maine, as origin of settlers French, 259, 265
Maisonneuve, 278
Major, 90, 91, 125, 330
Makaroff Lake, 210
Makwa, 267
Makwa Lake Reserve, 28
Malaysians, 358
Malden, 144
males and females. *See* gender
Maloneck, 168
Maltese, 369
Malyk Lake, 163
Mamornitz, 163
Manitoba
  demographics: interprovincial migration, 352; new immigrants, 352; urban population, 377
  farms, 381, 382
  new immigrants, 352
  settlers, Aboriginal: demographics, 34, 380; Métis, 23, 33, 54–55; Sioux/Dakota and Lakota, 30–31; territory, 25–26, 29, 30, 32
  settlers, British: child migration, 53; colonizers, 46; English, 44, 46; origin of settlers, terminology, 44; Scots, 54–55, 59; Welsh, 70
  settlers, Eastern European: Czechs and Slovaks, 226; Doukhobors, 210; Hungarians, 218, 226; Jews, 230, 233; Poles, 202; Romanians, 223–24; Ukrainians, 156, 160, 168, 169, 170, 172, 177
  settlers, French: Belgians, 272; demographics, 286, 292; official bilingualism, 298; settlers, 250, 251, 253, 255, 260, 261, 268, 269, 270, 271, 280, 282, 285, 286, 292
  settlers, German: Dutch, 131; Hutterites, 129; Lutherans, 95; Mennonites, 115, 116–20, 122, 127–28, 144–45; population, 79
  settlers, Nordic: Icelanders, 331–32, 344; Swedes, 328
  See also Red River settlement, Manitoba
Manitou Lake, 172
Mankota, 110, 279
Mannheim, 98
Manor, 45, 132
Maple Creek, 82, 92–95, 129, 179, 388
Marcelin, 243, 263–65, 291–92, 302
Marchantgrove, 266
Marchwell, 99, 330
Margo, 113, 166, 325
Mariahilf colony, 83, 102
Mariavolgy, 221
Marie Hill, 278
Marienthal, 106
Marieval, 242, 243, 274
Markinch, 60, 98
Marne, 257
Marquette, 276
Marquis, 61
Marriott, 111, 227
Marsden, 317
Marshall, 50, 317, 332
Martensville
  commuters, 121, 147, 390

Mennonites, 117, 121, 138, 390, 400
  population, 121
Martheton, 270
Martin, 57
Martin's Lake, 264
Marx, 111
Maryfield, 57, 313
Maryland, 108
Marysburg, 86, 87, 88, 147, 387
Masefield area, 111, 282
Mattes, 265, 266
Matyasfold, 220–21
Mauritians, 288, 362
Maxim, 312
Maxstone, 277
Maybridge area, 168
Mayerling, 84
Mayfair, 124, 175, 176
Mazenod, 109, 110, 275, 277
Mazeppa, 162
McCargar, 61
McCord, 279, 328
McCraney, 61, 229, 319
McDonald Hills, 60
McKay, 57
McKim, 59
McLean, 63
McLeod, 46, 65, 104
McMahon, 65, 122, 123
McTaggart, 63
McVey Camp, 208
Meacham, 171, 172–73, 174, 189, 329
Meadow Lake/Lac-des-Prairies
  population, 241, 267
  settlers: French and Métis, 241, 262, 267; Mennonites, 124; Romanian, 224; Ukrainian, 179
Meadow Lake Reserve, 28
Meath Park, 66, 177, 178
Medicine Hat, Alberta, 82, 92, 94
Medstead, 124
Meeting Lake, 122–23, 124
Melaval, 276
Melfort
  in-migration, 379
  population, 323

466

INDEX

settlers: Jews, 232, 234; Nordic peoples, 319, 323, 324, 329; Poles, 202; Scots, 64; Ukrainians, 177, 389
Melness, 61
Melnychuk, 163
Melville
   CNR line, 103, 164–65
   settlers: Germans, 83, 102–4, 147; Hungarians, 219–20; Mennonites, 113; Norwegians, 326; Poles, 169, 201; Ukrainians, 164–65, 169, 189
men and women. *See* gender
Menard, 272, 273
Mendham, 93, 94, 95
Mennon, 118
Mennonite Brethren, 118, 120, 122, 124, 125, 128, 136, 144, 400
   See also Mennonites, religion
Mennonite Church Canada (MCC), 116, 127
   See also Mennonites, religion
Mennonite Church Saskatchewan, 127
   See also Mennonites, religion
Mennonites, 115–28
   anti-Mennonite sentiment, 120, 144, 183
   architecture: farm buildings, 125
   assimilation, 133–35
   colonizers, 8, 116, 117, 119–20
   culture and customs: celebrations, 125, 126, 136, 140; clothing, 137, 139; food, 136, 137–38; home life, 136, 139–40; museums, 116
   demographics: birth rates, 376; depopulation, 118, 123, 127; population, 104, 117, 120, 122, 123, 127–28; population in Canada, 120, 122
   education: language use, 118, 126, 138, 143–44; limited education, 138, 142; Old Colony schools, 141–43; school consolidation, 145, 387–88; school-language issue, 140–44
   ethnic group mixing: Lutherans, 121, 123, 124
   ethnic identity: age differences and, 403–4; Dutch origin, 18; ethno-religious groups, 399; preservation, 395, 399, 403–4
   farms, 125, 138
   heritage sites, 122, 123, 147
   historical background: "enemy aliens" in WWI, 144; exodus to Latin America, 118, 120, 122, 128, 144–45, 364; overview, 115, 118, 128–29; prohibitions (1919), 120; settlements, 16
   information sources, 149, 150–53
   intermarriage, 135–36, 391–92
   language use, 115–16, 133–35, 142, 396–98
   locations: Saskatchewan Valley, 116–22, 132–37, 142–43, 147, 398, 400; Swift Current-Vermilion Hills, 122–23
   names, 115–16, 126, 398–99
   organizations, 116, 126, 127–28, 147–48
   pacificism, 119, 133, 139, 144, 218
   physical mobility, 386
   research (1968–72), 132–36, 140, 386, 391–92, 395, 396–98, 401, 403–4
   settlement patterns: bloc, 8, 77, 116, 136; line villages, 117–18, 136–37; mixed religious groups, 82; scattering, 124; villages, 136–37
   social change, 138, 390
   social control, 139, 142, 143
   urbanization, 122, 147–48, 218, 390
Mennonites, religion
   Bruderthaler (Evangelical), 119, 124, 126, 144, 400
   Chortitzer Mennonite Conference *(Sommerfelder/ Bergthaler)*, 116–17, 120, 126, 127–28, 137, 145, 400
   Evangelical Mennonite Brethren (EMB), 119, 122–23, 126, 127, 128
   Evangelical Mennonite Mission Conference (EMMC), 117, 122–23, 126, 128
   General Conference Mennonites, 119–20, 122–27, 136, 144, 400
   historical overview, 117, 119–20, 127–28, 390, 400
   Holdeman Mennonites, 117, 128, 400
   Krimmer Mennonite Brethren (KMB), 119, 123, 127, 129, 144, 400
   membership numbers, 127–28
   Mennonite Brethren, 118, 120, 122, 124, 125, 128, 136, 144, 400
   Mennonite Church Canada (MCC), 116, 127, 128
   Old Colony *(Reinländer, Furstenländer)*: beliefs, 116, 139; comparison with Hutterites, 136–40; culture, 134, 137–40; education, 138, 141–43, 145; exodus, 120, 128; language use, 134–35, 142; line villages, 117–18, 136–37; locations, 117–18, 122, 127; membership numbers, 127; mobility, 390; religious services, 135
   religion: beliefs, 116, 117, 118, 136, 139; church attendance, 135, 401
   research (1968–72), 401
   See also Mennonites

Meota, 263
Merle, 260
Merry Home, 212
Mervin, 104, 338
Meskanaw, 220, 258, 387
Métis, 32–33
  culture and customs, 33, 54
  demographics: Bill C-31 population, 34; language use, 241; population, 17, 33–34; population growth rate, 34; unemployment rates, 36; urban population, 36
  ethnic group mixing, 250
  ethnic identity, 32–33, 34
  exodus from Red River settlement, 241, 243–44, 247–48
  historical background, 15–16, 32–33
  information sources, 304–5
  language use: anglophones, 241, 287–88; demographics, 241; literacy rates, 35; multilingual, 33–34
  names, 54, 55
  Scottish Métis, 33, 54–56, 241, 287
  settlement patterns: riverlots, 33, 55, 243, 246; scrip lands, 247–48; territory consolidation, 1–2
  terminology: halfbreed and Métis, 241; historical Métis, 23, 32
  urbanization, 249
  See also Batoche; Métis, francophone; Michif language; North-West Resistance (1984–85); Red River Resistance (1869–70); Red River settlement, Manitoba
Métis, francophone, 32–33, 241–50
  architecture: homes, 245, 248–49; missions, 243
  culture and customs, 244, 247, 249–50

  demographics: population, 17, 241, 287–88
  ethnic group mixing, 246, 248
  ethnic identity, 249–50
  exodus from Red River settlement, 241, 243–44, 247–48
  heritage sites, 241, 242, 243, 246–47
  historical background, 54–55, 240–41
  information sources, 304–5
  language use, 241, 243, 286, 287; French-Michif, 25, 241
  locations: mentioned, 31, 241–45, 248–50, 252, 274, 281–82; St-Laurent settlement, 244–48, 251
  names, 55, 241, 248
  Scottish Métis, 33, 55–56, 241, 287
  settlement patterns: riverlots, 33, 55, 243, 246; scattering, 247–48; scrip lands, 247–48; winter camps, 242, 244
  urbanization, 249
  See also Métis
Métis Nation of Saskatchewan (MNS), 33, 34, 249
Mexicans, 364
  See also Latin Americans
Meyronne, 275, 277, 314
Michaelovo, 208
Michif language
  dialects: Chippewa-Michif, 25; Cree-Michif, 25, 241, 242; French-Michif, 25, 241
  historical background, 32–33
  language use, 33, 249, 287–88
  terminology, 18
Michigan
  settlers: Belgians, 272; French, 264, 280, 281; Germans, 98; Romanians, 224

Midale, 106, 313, 328
Middle Eastern peoples, 365–67
  See also Lebanese and Syrians
Middle Lake, 87, 88
Mierau, 119
migration and mobility
  assimilation and, 407
  depopulation and, 383–86, 390
  ethnic identity and, 386–87, 390
  ethnic identity preservation and, 404
  interprovincial migration: age of migrants, 378–80; destinations, 378; factors, 378–79; out-migration, 378–79; return migration, 378
  intraprovincial migration factors, 379
  migration: comparisons with other provinces, 377, 378; immigration rates, 377; out-migration, 352, 375, 377, 378–79
  physical mobility: ethnic identity and, 386–87, 404; social change factors and, 390
  population growth and, 379
  research (1968–72): physical mobility, 386
  See also depopulation and delocalization
Mikado, 162, 201
Milden, 227, 319
Milestone, 106, 313
Millard Lake, 266
Milly, 279
Ministikwan Reserve, 28
Minnesota, as origin of settlers
  settlers: Czechs and Slovaks, 227; French, 288; Germans, 78, 85, 86, 87; Mennonites, 118, 119–20; Nordic peoples, 309, 332, 345; Norwegians,

INDEX

309, 311, 312, 313, 314, 316, 318, 320, 324, 325, 326; Québécois, 9, 252, 259; Sioux, 30; Swabians, 108; Swedes, 327, 329, 330
Minnesota Settlement, 320
Minoahchak Cree, 27
Minton, 106, 312
Miry Creek, 131
mobility. *See* migration and mobility
Model Farm, 168, 169, 201
Moffat, 62, 63
Mohyla-Swiatoho Mychaila, 162
Moisayovo, 209
Moldenhauer family, 112
Moleski, 165
Moline, 267
Mona, 103
Mongolians, 355
Monrose, 61
Mont Nebo, 321
Montana
    settlers: Aboriginals, 29, 30; Dutch, 131; French, 259; Métis, 56, 248; Norwegians, 311, 313, 315
Montcalm, 278
Montefiore Jewish Colony, 232
Montenegrins, 230
Montmartre, 178, 179, 200, 273, 280
Montreal Lake First Nation, 26
Montreal, Quebec, new immigrants, 351
Montrose, 315, 319
Monvoisin, 279
Moon Hills, 224, 264
Moose Jaw
    demographics: in-migration, 379
    settlers: Chinese, 356–57; Dutch, 131; French, 285; Germans, 106, 107; Hutterites, 130; Jews, 234; Nordic peoples, 315, 328; Romanians, 225; Ukrainians, 180; Welsh, 72
    Soo rail line, 7, 106
Moose Mountain
    settlers: Aboriginals, 24, 27, 29, 30, 31; Assiniboine, 29–30; French, 270
Moose Valley, 322
Moose Woods, 31, 244
Moosomin, 46, 47, 57, 107, 230, 269
Moosomin First Nation, 28
Moravia, as origin of settlers
    settlers: Hutterites, 9, 78, 128; Mennonites, 126
Morneau, 266
Morning Glory, 99
Morris, 320
Morse, 123, 132
Mortlach, 314
Moscow, 122
Moslems, 363, 365, 366, 367
Mosquito First Nation, 30
Moss Lake, 201
Mossbank, 63, 109, 110, 314
Mostetz, 99, 161
Motherwell Homestead, 60–61
Moulin, 264
Mount Hecla, 332
Mount Nebo, 248
Mourey, 254
Mozart, 332, 333, 344
Mt. Carmel shrine, 89
Muchowsko, 167
Muenster, 85, 86, 87, 88, 141, 387–88
Mullingar, 68, 124
multiculturalism
    assimilation and, 405–9
    Canadian identity and, 408–9
    government policies, 230, 405–6, 408–9
    melting pot or mosaic, 2–3, 9, 408
    organizations, 353–54
    religion and, 230
    Royal Commission (1930), 5–6, 405
    See also assimilation; culture and customs
Munchen, 84
Murraydale, 65
Muscowpetung Cree, 27, 29
music. *See* culture and customs
Muskeg Lake Cree First Nation, 27–28, 264
Muskeg River Reserve, 28
Muskiki Lake, 221
Muskiki Springs, 88
Muskoday Reserve, 27
Muskowekwan Cree, 27, 29
Mutrie, 273, 296

N

Na-Prymovin, 171
Nadeauville, 283–84
Nadon, 263
Nahkawiniwak. *See* Saulteaux/Nahkawiniwak
Naicam, 87, 88, 324
Najersda, 209
Nakota. *See* Assiniboine/Nakota
Napoleon, 267
Nary, 319
National Doukhobor Heritage Village, 217
National Historic Sites, 52, 55–56, 60, 217, 240, 246–47, 249
nationalism
    assimilation and, 408
    associations and, 197
    Canadian identity and, 405–6, 408–9
    ethnic identity and, 181–83, 399, 408–9
    ethnic identity and conflict, 189, 404
    language and, 185
    multiculturalism and, 405–8
    religion and, 181–82, 399
    settlers: German, 91, 104; Ukrainians, 181–83, 185, 189, 196; Welsh, 69
Nauka, 175
Nebraska
    settlers: Germans, 86; Mennonites, 118, 119
Nehiyawewin. *See* Cree/Nehiyawewin
Neidpath, 314
Neigel Plains, 94
Nekaneet Cree Reserve, 27

INDEX

Nerada Creek area, 227
Nesdoly Lake, 175, 210, 216
Neshem, 323
Ness, 263
Netherlands. *See* Dutch
Netherton, 326
Netterville, 67
Neu Elsass/Alsace, 15, 82–83, 96–98, 99, 112
Neu Kronsfeld, 94
Neuanlage, 116, 117, 118, 120, 121, 142
Neudorf, 83, 102, 103, 104
Neuheim, 94
Neuhoffnung, 111, 144
Neuhorst, 117, 118, 121, 138
Neuve-Chapelle, 270
Neville, 123
New Finland, 335–37, 343, 347
New Gorilloe, 209
New Holstein, 84
New Home, 118, 144
new immigrants. *See* immigration, recent
New Jerusalem, 230, 232
New Moisayovo, 209
New Munster, 96
New Osgoode, 72
New Ottawa, 51
New Spring Creek, 129
New Stockholm Colony, 327, 328, 338
New Sweden, 327
New Thunderchild Reserve, 28
New Tulcea/Neu Tulscha, 100
New Wolf Creek, 129
New Yaroslav, 161
Newfield, 127
Newfoundland, demographics, 375, 376
Nichlava, 170
Nickoliaevka, 208
Nigerians, 361
Nipawin, 113, 127, 177
Njaa's Hill, 323
Nobleville, 260
Nokomis, 64, 98, 125
Nolin, 263
non-European ethnic groups. *See* visible minorities
Nora, 166, 167, 324–25

Nordal, 321
Nordalen, 312
Norden, 323
Nordic peoples, 309–49
  assimilation, 338–39, 341
  colonizers, 4, 7
  culture and customs, 343–44
  demographics: population, 17, 170, 310, 322
  depopulation and church closures, 388
  education, 345–46
  ethnic identity, 310, 339–40, 342, 395, 396
  ethnic identity preservation, 403–4
  historical background, 309–11, 338–39
  information sources, 347–48
  intermarriage, 339, 346–47, 391–92, 393, 396
  language use, 339–41, 342, 345, 396, 397–98
  media, 345–46
  organizations, 345–46
  origin of settlers, 309–10
  physical mobility, 386
  religion, 310–11, 341–43, 401
  research (1968–72), 339–40, 346–47, 386, 395, 397–98, 401, 403–4
  settlement patterns, 8, 338, 340
  terminology, 18
  urbanization, 339–40
  See also Danes; Finns; Icelanders; Norwegians; Swedes; Swedish Finns
Nordland, 316
Nordra, 333
Norge, 314
Norquay, 167, 168, 201, 325
North Africans, 367
North Atlantic Trading Company, 4
North Battleford. *See* Battlefords area
North (Doukhobor) Colony, 208, 210, 214

North Dakota, as origin of settlers
  settlers: Aboriginals, 29, 31; Belgians, 272, 275, 279; French, 259, 261, 280; Germans, 78, 85, 86, 90, 96, 98, 101, 112, 129; Hutterites, 129, 140; Nordic peoples, 309, 315–16, 317, 318, 331, 332, 347
North Portal, 66
North Qu'Appelle, 274
North Star Pottery, 89
North West Company (NWC), 54, 239
North-West Resistance (1984–85)
  Dakota support, 31
  historical background, 240, 246–48, 250, 427n9
  Scottish Métis support, 55–56
North-West Territories
  districts created from, 286
  language use, 286
  population, 241, 286
  school-language issue, 292–93
Northern Beauty, 104
Northern Cree. *See* Cree/Nehiyawewin
Northway, 258, 323
Norwegian Grove, 324
Norwegian Lutheran Church of America, 318, 321
Norwegians, 311–26
  assimilation, 338
  colonizers, 4, 8
  culture and customs, 320, 321, 323–24, 342, 343–44, 347
  demographics: depopulation, 311, 315–16, 388; population, 310, 311, 322, 326, 340; population proportion, 310, 313, 315, 319, 322, 323, 324, 325, 326
  education, 319, 344, 345, 432n50
  ethnic group mixing, 320, 321, 325, 327,

470

328–29, 341, 388
ethnic identity, 310,
  315, 338, 339
heritage and historic sites,
  312, 313, 314, 315, 319,
  321, 322–23, 324, 325
historical background,
  16, 310, 311–12, 315, 339
information sources, 348
intermarriage, 311, 393
language use, 312, 340, 344,
  345, 398–99, 432n50
locations: Birch Hills,
  322–24; central, 320–24;
  east-central, 170,
  320–24, 326; far north,
  326; northeast, 324–26;
  Outlook-Hanley, 315,
  318–20, 322, 340, 342,
  399; Shellbrook, 321–22;
  Soo rail line, 311–13;
  south-central region,
  313–15; southeast, 311–13;
  southwest, 315–17, 328–29;
  west-central, 317–18
locations mentioned, 112,
  170, 321–24, 328–29,
  332–34, 339–40, 344
media, 345
names, 318, 398–99
organizations, 345
religious affiliations:
  Lutherans, 310–13,
  318, 341–42; overview,
  341–42, 345; rural
  depopulation, 311, 388
research (1968–72), 339–40
settlement patterns, 11,
  310, 313, 314, 320, 326
urban areas, 345
See also Nordic peoples
Nova Scotia,
  demographics, 381
Nova Slavenska, 209
Novo Troitzkoe, 209
Novoe Golubovo, 209
Nummela, 338
Nupdal Lake, 332
Nut Lake Reserve, 29, 260
Nut Mountain, 113, 325
Nutana, 45
Nystrom Lake, 325

O

Oakshela, 106–7
Oakville, 109
Ocean Man First Nation,
  27, 29, 30
Ochapowace Cree, 27
Odel, 320
Odessa, 84, 85
Ogafeld, 118
Ogema, 63, 85, 109, 110, 315, 328
Ohlen, 327
Oji-Cree mixing, 25, 27, 29, 39
  See also Cree/Nehiyawewin;
  Saulteaux (Ojibwa)/
  Nahkawiniwak
Ojibwa. See Saulteaux
  (Ojibwa)/Nahkawiniwak
Okanese Cree, 27, 29
Okemasis Reserve, 27
Okla, 167, 325
Oklahoma, as origin of settlers
  settlers: Blacks, 359–61;
  Croatians, 229;
  Mennonites, 118, 120, 125
Okno, 163
Old Colony Mennonites. See
  Mennonites, religion
Old Holar, 332
Old Post, 278
Old Wives Lake, 314
Oleksince/Oleksyntsi, 201
Oleskow, 161
Olga, 315
Olha, 161
Ollenburger, 92
O'Malley, 68
Omand, 258
One Arrow Reserve, 27, 387
Onion Lake, 268
Onion Lake Reserve, 28
Ontario
  Aboriginal territory, 26
  demographics:
    interprovincial migration,
    378; new immigrants,
    351; populations, 374
  farms, 382
  new immigrants, 199,
    222, 351, 361, 377
  settlers, British: child
    migration scheme, 53;
    demographics, 69, 72;
    English, 44, 45, 46–47, 51;
    fieldstone farmhouses, 61,
    63; Irish, 67, 68, 69; place
    names, 51, 64; Scots, 51,
    61, 64, 66; terminology,
    44; Welsh, 72
  settlers, other: Blacks,
    360–61; Finns, 335–38;
    French, 250, 261, 280,
    286–87; Hungarians, 222;
    Jews, 233; Mennonites,
    125, 127, 128, 136, 145;
    Ukrainians, 198, 199
Oobezhdennie, 209
Oospennie/Oospenia, 208,
  209, 212, 217, 426n15
Ootishennie, 209
Opawakoscikan urban
  reserve, 36
Orange Order, 5–6, 68, 111,
  183–84, 294, 296
Orangeville, 67
Orcadia, 65
Ordale area, 321
Orel, 175
Orkney, 60, 65, 111, 164, 220
Orlovsky, 208
Ormeaux, 266
Ormiston, 109
Ormside, 201
Orolow, 175, 201, 388
Ortopan, 229
Oscar Lake, 175
Osin, 168
Osland, 332
Osler, 116–21, 137–38, 144, 400
Ossa, 105
Osterwick, 118
Osvoborsdennie, 208
Otradnoe, 209
Ottawa, 212
Otthon, 11, 201, 219–20
Oukrania, 174–75
Oungre, 106, 231, 312
Outlook-Hanley, 65, 315,
  318–20, 322, 340,
  342, 345, 399
  See also Hanley
Outram, 312
Oxarat, 283
Oxbow, 63, 67, 106
Ozeranko, 171
Ozeriany, 169, 171

INDEX

P

Paddockwood, 178, 322
Pakistanis, 352, 354, 355, 362–63
  See also South Asians
Pakrofka, 210
Pakrov, 162
Pambrun, 281
Pangman, 109, 110
Paniowci, 168
Pappenfus Lake, 88
Paradise Hill/Butte-Paradis, 104, 267–68
Park, 92
Park Valley, 266
Parkbeg, 328
Parkerview, 164
Parkman, 328
Parkside, 321, 322, 329, 342
Parkview, 126
Parry, 127
Pasariofka, 209
Pascal, 92, 266
Paseika, 168
Pasqua Cree, 27, 29
Paswegin, 113
Patience Lake, 114
Patuanak, 32
Paul Lies, 313
Pavlovo, 208
Paynton, 50
Pazeraevka, 209
Peace, 102, 106
Peaceful Cove, 208
Pearl, 175
Pechet, 274
Peebles, 62, 107
Peepeekisis Cree, 27, 30
Peerless, 104
Pelican Lake First Nation, 28
Pella-Neville, 122
Pelletier, 276
Pelly, 127, 168, 208, 214
Peltier Crossing, 242
Pembroke, 144
Pennant, 130, 316
Pennock, 330
Penzance, 96, 98, 321
Percival, 327
Perehodnoe, 208
Périgord, 260–61
Petaigan, 127
Petain, 284
Peter Ballantyne Cree First Nation, 26
Peter Pond Lake, 32
Peterson, 86, 88, 171, 172, 257, 387
Petit-Nord, 276, 284
Petrofka, 208, 209–10, 212–13, 216
Pheasant Forks, 46
Pheasant Rump First Nation, 29–30
Philippines. *See* Filipinos
Phippen, 91
physical mobility, 386–87
  See also migration and mobility
Piapot Cree, 27, 30, 316
Piché, 259, 276
Pickthall, 109
Pierceland, 104, 124, 223
Pike Lake area, 317
Pilger, 87, 88
Pilon, 258
Pine Bluff Reserve, 28
Pinehouse, 26, 32
Pinkefalva Colony, 221–22
Pinkham, 317
Pinto Butte/Butte-de-Cheval-Caillé, 278, 281
Pinto Creek, 277, 314
Pipestone, 268, 332
Pitt, 171
Plain View, 164, 165, 326
Plains Cree. *See* Cree/Nehiyawewin
Plateau, 283
Pleasant Point, 125, 126
Pleasantdale, 261, 324, 326
Plenty, 317
Plessis, 279
Plumi Moos Hill, 122
Plunkett, 221–22
Pocrovskoe, 208
Podillia, 168
Podole, 178
Poelcapelle, 168
Pohorlowtz, 163
Point-Lemire, 282
Pokrovka, 209
Poles, 199–203
  assimilation, 183
  colonizers, 8
  demographics:
    population, 169, 177, 178, 183, 202, 203–4
  education, 195
  ethnic group mixing, 176, 182, 200, 324
  ethnic identity, 187, 202, 203–4, 395
  ethnic identity preservation, 403–4
  heritage sites, 200, 201
  historical background, 15–16, 199
  information sources, 206
  intermarriage, 191, 199, 200–201, 203–4, 391–92, 393
  language use, 185, 195, 199, 201, 202, 397–98
  literacy, 185
  locations, 163, 164, 165, 166, 167, 168, 169, 173, 176, 177, 179, 201–2, 324
  migration and mobility, 386
  new immigrants, 203, 353
  physical mobility, 386
  religion (Roman Catholic):
    adherence to, 401;
    historical background, 181–82, 188–91, 199;
    intermarriage, 199–201;
    sectarian divisions, 181–82, 202–3
  research (1968–72), 386, 391–92, 395, 397–98, 401, 403–4
  settlement patterns, 8, 200
  Soo rail line, 200
  urbanization, 202
Poltawa, 171
Polworth, 329
Ponass Lake, 166–67, 203, 261, 325, 326
Ponteix, 16, 129, 280–81, 366
Pontoville, 94
Pontrilas, 72
Poor Man Cree, 27
Poplar Grove, 325
Poplar Valley, 278

472

INDEX

population. *See* demographics, population
population mixing. *See* intermarriage and population mixing
Porcupine, 167
Portreeve, 93, 94
Portuguese, 369
Postnikoff Creek, 210
Poulin, 276
Poundmaker First Nation, 28
Prairie Butte, 29
Prairie Pioneer Museum, Moose Jaw, 338
Prairie River, 167
Prairie Rose, 67, 125
Prairieleut. *See* Hutterites
Pré-Ste-Marie, 260
Preeceville, 167, 227, 325, 326
Prelate, 82, 92, 93, 94, 95, 388
Prestfoss, 323
Pretty Lake, 171
Primate, 90, 91, 92
Primitive Methodist Colony, 46
Prince, 114, 263
Prince Albert
  demographics: in-migration, 379; population, 178
  heritage and historic sites, 64, 285
  historical background, 55, 239
  new immigrants, 379
  settlers, French: historical background, 239, 251; language use, 285, 292; media, 285, 302; organizations, 285; population, 255, 260, 284; religion, 285, 300
  settlers, other: Aboriginals, 36, 37; Germans, 114, 147; Jews, 234; Mennonites, 390; Métis, 36, 54–55, 241, 249; Norwegians, 322; Poles, 178, 202; Scots, 54, 55; Ukrainians, 178, 180, 199
Product, 112
Proswita, 175, 194

Prud'homme
  population, 173, 174, 257
  research (1968–72), 291–92
  school consolidation, 388
  settlers, French: assimilation, 291–92; heritage sites, 172, 255; historical background, 174, 255–57, 266; language use, 174; origin of settlers, 255; place names, 255; school-language issue, 295, 297
  settlers, other: Hungarians, 221; Poles, 174, 200; Ukrainians, 171, 172, 173, 174, 257, 295
Prussia, 93, 115, 116
Punjabis, 362
  See also South Asians
Punnichy, 97, 169, 221, 330
Pysklyvetz, 175

Q

Quakers, 47, 208, 216, 218
Qu'Appelle Valley/Val-Qu'Appelle
  settlers: Aboriginals, 27, 29–31; British, 47, 52, 58, 60–61; French, 242–43, 269, 274, 327; Icelanders, 334; Métis, 242–43, 274; Romanians, 224–25; Scots, 60–61; Swedes, 327
  See also Fort Qu'Appelle
Quebec
  Acadians, 9, 252, 287
  British child migration, 53
  demographics, 286–87, 288
  francophone settlers: colonizers, 250, 259, 273, 275, 279; fur trade, 239–40; overview, 286–87, 378; settlements, 250–53, 259–61, 263–65, 275, 278–80, 282–83
  interprovincial migration, 378
  Jews, 233
  language qualifications of teachers, 295–96

  new immigrants, 351
Quebec district, 273
Queen Maud, 323
Quill Lakes, 130, 189, 201, 325, 333
Quimper, 281
Quinton, 97, 98, 221

R

Rabbit Lake, 124
Radant, 97
Radimno, 164
Radionovka, 208
Radisson, 114, 175, 176
Radouga Creek, 210
Radville, 109, 274, 275, 315
railways
  depopulation and closures, 12, 389
  historical background, 4, 7–8
  place names, 12, 51
  See also Canadian National Railway (CNR); Canadian Pacific Railway (CPR); Grand Trunk Pacific Railway
Rainbow, 320
Rak, 171
Ralph, 313
Rama, 166, 201, 203
Ranger, 267
Rastadt, 84, 93, 94, 95
Rastel, 267
Rathmullen, 111
Ratner, 329
Rausch Creek, 110
Ravenhead, 175
Raymore, 97, 98, 221
Razbegallovo/Troitska, 209
Readlyn, 315
Reciprocity, 272
Red Deer Hill, 55
Red Earth Cree, 28
Red Pheasant First Nation, 28
Red River Resistance (1869–70), 243, 246
Red River settlement, Manitoba
  demographics: out-migration, 241,

243–44, 247–48;
population, 241
Métis terminology, 241
riverlot system, 33, 243
winter sheltering
camps, 242
Redberry, 174–77
research (1968–72), 184
settlers, other: French,
264; Poles, 201, 398
settlers, Ukrainian:
communities, 13;
education, 194, 195;
ethnic identity, 184,
187; language use, 187,
194, 195; names, 398;
religion, 175, 184, 189,
388; settlement, 174–77;
urbanization, 180
Redberry Lake, 174–75
Redberry Park/Grant, 175
Redfield, 175, 201
Redvers, 271–72
refugees
new immigrants, 351
settlement services, 354
settlers: Aboriginals,
30–31; Africans, 361, 378;
Bhutanese, 363; Blacks,
359, 360; Germans,
81, 105; Hungarians,
222; Latin Americans,
364; Russian Jews,
230–31; Russians, 120,
208; Ukrainians, 203;
Vietnamese, 358
Regina
anti-immigrant
sentiment, 5
CPR rail line, 374
culture and customs:
ethnic neighbourhoods,
108, 353; folk festival
(Mosaic), 301, 362
demographics:
Aboriginals, 36–39,
377, 380; CMA growth,
376–77, 382–83;
households, 376;
in-migration, 379;
multiple ethnic origins,
353; new immigrants, 351,
352, 353, 378; population,
376–77, 382–83;
Saskatoon comparison,
376–77, 382–83; visible
minorities, 353, 355, 380
historical background, 374
immigrant services, 354
intermarriage, 353
new immigrants,
352, 353, 378
settlers, Aboriginal:
demographics, 36–39,
377, 380; education, 35,
37–38, 39; institutions,
37, 38, 39, 249; language
use, 39; Métis, 36,
249; migration, 37;
poverty, 38–39
settlers, French: language
use, 284–85; media,
302; population, 284;
school-language issue,
293, 299, 301–2
settlers, German: Danube
Swabians, 107–8;
ethnic neighborhoods,
108; Hutterites, 130;
Lutherans, 107; new
immigrants, 147;
organizations, 147
settlers, other: Jews, 231,
233, 234; Nordic peoples,
315, 344; Poles, 202;
Romanians, 222–26;
Scots, 66; Serbians,
229; Swedish, 328;
Ukrainians, 179–80,
196, 199; Welsh, 72
settlers, visible minorities:
Blacks, 361–62; Chileans,
364; Chinese, 353,
356–57; Greeks, 367–68;
Hispanics, 364; Italians,
369; Latin Americans,
364; South Asians,
362; Vietnamese, 358
Regway, 106
Reimche, 127
Reimer, 103
Reims, 275
Reinfeld, 117

Reinländer (Old Colony). *See*
Mennonites, religion
religion
assimilation and,
229–30, 402
bloc settlements and, 402
church attendance, 401
church closures, 388–89
churches as rural focal
points, 12, 16, 387, 388–89
defined subjectively, 399
ethnic group
mixing, 229–30
ethnic identity and,
395, 399–401
interethnic churches,
224–25
intermarriage, 401–2
merging of nationality
churches, 388
multiculturalism and, 230
nationalism and,
181–82, 399
religious affiliation,
399–401
research (1968–72): church
attendance, 135, 190, 401
sectarianism, 400
social change and, 401
transethnic
denominations, 400
*See also specific
ethnic groups*
Rempel Lake, 116
Renfrew, 144
Renown, 98, 321
Rensby, 319
research (1968–72)
areas of study: culture
and customs, 136,
191–92; education
levels, 390; ethnic
identity preservation,
133, 140, 184, 215–16,
291–92, 386, 395, 403–4;
intermarriage, 135–36,
191, 390–94; language
use, 133–34, 186, 199,
291–92, 339–40, 396–98,
403–4; physical mobility,
386; religion (church

INDEX

attendance), 135, 190, 401; social mobility, 390
locations: Albertville, 291–92; Birch Hills, 339; Bonne-Madone, 291–92; Coteau, 291–92; Debden-Leoville, 291–92; Duck Lake, 291–92; Fish Creek-Yellow Creek, 184; Garden River, 184, 199; Marcelin, 291–92; Meeting Lake Mennonites, 132; north-central region, 215–16, 291, 339, 386, 391, 401; north-western region, 291; Prud'homme, 291–92; Redberry, 184; Riverview Hutterite Colony, 133–34; Saskatchewan Valley Mennonites, 132–33; Shellbrook, 339; St-Brieux, 291–92; St. Peter's German Catholic Colony, 132–33
reserves, First Nations. See Aboriginal peoples
Revenue, 90, 91, 92
Reward, 90, 91, 92
Reynaud, 257, 258
Rhein, 100
Rheinfeld, 117, 122
Rheinland, 118, 122, 142, 145
Rhondda, 72
Rhyl, 72
Richard, 175, 176, 264
Richelieu, Château, 269
Richlea, 317
Richmound, 92, 94, 95, 316
Rideauville, 284
Riduonovo, 208
Riel-Dana, 171
Riel, Louis, 55–56, 243, 246–47, 249
River Park, 118, 143, 144
Riverbend, 130
Riverhill, 212
Riverlot, 116, 254
Riversdale, 45
Riverside, 163
Riverview Hutterite Colony, 130, 133–35
Rivière-de-Saules/Crystal Creek, 263

Rivière-la-Vieille/Wood River, 275, 276, 277
Rivière-Rouge. See Red River settlement, Manitoba
Robsart, 315
Rocanville, 57, 270, 337
Roche Plain, 282
Rock Point, 337–38, 341, 342, 346, 347
Rock Valley, 88
Rockglen, 109, 110, 277, 278
Rockhaven, 91
Roka, 222
Rokeby, 59
Rolling Prairie, 316
Roman Catholics. See French: religion (Roman Catholic); German Catholics; Poles: religion (Roman Catholic); Ukrainians, religion: Roman Catholics
Romance, 86, 88, 89
Romanians, 222–26
 citizenship adoption, 183
 culture and customs, 226
 demographics: depopulation, 223; population, 221, 223, 226; population proportion, 79, 183
 ethnic identity, 18, 183, 226
 heritage sites, 223
 historical background, 16, 78, 426n39
 information sources, 236
 intermarriage, 224, 225, 226
 Jews, 222, 231
 language use, 223, 225, 226
 locations, 11, 66, 108, 221–26, 279
 new immigrants, 226
 organizations, 225–26
 religion, 222–25, 279
 settlement patterns, 11, 170, 234
 urban settlers, 222–26
Roscommon, 68
Rose Hill, 323
Rose Valley, 91, 130, 167, 170, 201, 324, 325
Roseberry, 175

Rosebud, 109
Rosedale, 229, 319, 320
Roseland, 144
Rosenberg, 101
Rosenfeld, 94, 118
Rosengart, 117
Rosenort, 116
Rosenthal, 92, 94
Rosetown, 111, 130, 359
Rosewood, 102
Rosthern
 historical background, 116
 language use, 143–44
 population, 121, 173
 settlers, Mennonite: education, 116, 143–44, 388; museums, 116; population, 120, 121; religion, 120, 121, 400–401; settlement patterns, 116, 117, 118, 121, 124
 settlers, other: French, 255; Germans, 113, 121
 settlers, Ukrainian: language use, 144, 198; religion, 171–72, 190; settlement patterns, 170, 173, 178
Rotave, 328
Rothbury, 99
Rothermere, 222
Rouleau, 106
Round Lake/Bird's Point, 269, 327
Royal Commission on Immigration, 5–6, 405
Royer, 276, 280
Rudy, 229, 319, 320
Rue Grimard, 266
Ruisseau-Charette, 263
Ruisseau-Chasse, 270
Ruisseau-Christopher, 259
Ruisseau-Denniel, 282
Ruisseau-Gavelin, 276
Ruisseau-Girard, 278
Ruisseau-La Berge, 276, 279
Ruisseau-Laville, 276
Ruisseau-Loiselle, 260
Ruisseau-Morin, 267
Ruisseau-Nolin, 267
Ruisseau-Seguin, 245
Ruisseau-Tetrault, 279

INDEX

Runnymede, 100, 161
rural areas
   definitions: hamlet,
     12; rural area, 10;
     town, 12; village, 12
   delocalization of focal
     points, 387–89
   historical background,
     380–86
   identification of, 12–13
   intraprovincial
     migration, 379
   place name historical
     backgrounds, 12, 387
   See also bloc settlements;
     depopulation and
     delocalization; farms
Rus, 194–95
Rusally/Endeavour,
   127, 167, 175, 325
Rush Lake, 122, 123
Ruskin, 129
Russian Baptists, 176, 210,
   215, 216, 217, 391
Russian Doukhobors.
   See Doukhobors
Russians
   Black Sea Germans, 78
   colonizers, 4
   demographics: citizenship
     adoption, 183;
     population, 166, 183, 215
   ethnic identity, 215
   ethnic settlements, 77–78
   historical background,
     77–78
   information sources,
     148–49
   intermarriage, 215, 393
   language use, 186
   Mennonites, 116, 118, 120
Ruthenia (district), 171
Ruthenia, as origin of settlers,
   13, 181–83, 426n39
Rwandans, 361

S

Saar, 84
Sacristan, 258
Sagathun, 93, 94, 316
St-Alexis, 278
St. Alphege, 92
St-Alphonse, 257
St-André, 258
St. Andrew, 55, 57
St. Benedict, 85, 87, 88, 221
St-Boniface, 302
St. Boswells, 110–11
St-Brieux, 87, 221,
   258–59, 291–92
St-Charles, 279
St. David's, 71
St. Demetrius, 171, 172
St-Denis settlement,
   256–57, 297, 387–88
St. Elia/Toporiwtzi, 161
St. Elias, 162, 167
St. Elizabeth colony,
   108, 110, 111
St. Elizabeth, Sisters of, 87
St-Florent mission,
   242–43, 274
St-Front, 260–61
St. Gregor, 88, 387
St. Henry, 88
St-Hilaire, 257, 283
St-Hippolyte, 263
St-Hubert/La Rolanderie,
   45, 268–70
St-Isidore-de-Bellevue,
   252, 292
   See also Bellevue
St. Johannes, 84
St. John the Baptist, 179
St. Joseph's Colony
   (1886–), 83–85
St. Joseph's Colony (1905–),
   82, 89–92, 111
St. Julien, 171, 172, 173, 192, 193
St. Laszlo Colony, 220–21
St-Laurent settlement,
   32–33, 244–48, 250,
   251, 253, 254, 283
St-Léon at Sergent, 267
St-Louis settlement, 241,
   246, 251, 255, 258,
   291–92, 323, 388, 398
St. Lucia, 92
St. Mark's Anglican
   Church, 28
St. Mary, 84
St. Michael, 162, 263
St. Nicholas, 162, 177
St-Olivier, 275
St-Pascal, 267
St. Paul's colony, 84, 114
St. Peter's College, 87
St. Peter's Colony (1894–), 84
St. Peter's Colony (1902– ;
   German Catholic), 85–89
   assimilation, 132–33
   culture and customs,
     136, 146–47
   demographics, 86, 88
   ethnic group mixing
     (Lutherans), 87–88
   ethnic identity, 87, 133
   historical background,
     15, 84
   information sources, 149
   intermarriage, 136
   language use, 86,
     87, 133–34, 135
   names, 398
   overview, 85–89
   religion, 135
   research (1968–72), 132–36
   school-language
     issue, 140–41
   settlement patterns, 83, 84
St. Philips, 162, 168, 214
St-Quentin, 257
St. Ursula Academy, 87
St-Victor, 23, 277–78, 302, 314
St. Volodymyr, 161, 168
St. Walburg, 83, 102,
   104–5, 114, 147, 227
Ste-Colette, 275
Ste-Marguerite, 268
Ste-Marthe-Rocanville, 270
Sakamayak, 241
Sakimay Cree, 27, 29
Salem, 118, 144
Saline Creek, 321
Saloun, 60
Saltcoats
   settlers: Scots, 58, 59, 60,
     65, 330; Ukrainians,
     161; Welsh, 71
Salvador, 90, 91, 92
Salvadorans, 364
   See also Latin Americans
Sambor, 97
Samburg, 177, 178, 193
Sanctuary, 130

476

INDEX

Sand Hills, 130, 319
Sand Lake, 129, 212
Sandal, 267–68
Saron, 323
Saskatchewan
   Aboriginal term, 22
   historical overview,
      25, 286, 373–74
Saskatchewan (Doukhobor)
   Colony, 209–10,
      212, 213, 214
Saskatchewan Landing, 248
Saskatchewan Royal
   Commission on
   Immigration and
   Settlement, 5–6, 405
Saskatchewan Valley
   Mennonites, 116–22
   assimilation, 132–35
   depopulation, 121–22
   historical background,
      116–17
   intermarriage, 135–36
   language use, 133–35
   line villages, 117–18, 136–37
   names, 398
   Old Colony conservatism,
      117–18, 142
   population and area, 121
   religion, 116–18, 119–20, 400
   research (1968–72), 132–36
   school-language
      issue, 142–43
   urbanization, 122, 147
   See also Mennonites
Saskatoon
   culture and customs: ethnic
      neighbourhoods, 353;
      folk festival (Folkfest),
      66, 68, 147, 184, 222, 301,
      353, 357, 358, 361, 362, 368;
      organizations, 353–54
   demographics: CMA
      growth, 376–77,
      382–83; in-migration,
      379; migration, 376;
      new immigrants,
      351, 352, 353, 355, 378;
      population, 46, 374,
      376–77, 382; population
      change, 382–83; Regina
      comparison, 376–77,
      382–83; vacancy rate,
      39; visible minorities,
      353, 355, 380
   education: English as
      additional language,
      354–55; school-language
      issue, 296–99
   historic sites, 45
   historical background,
      45–46, 48, 353, 374
   immigrant services, 354
   intermarriage, 353
   language use, 353–55
   mobility: commuters, 121,
      390; CPR rail lines, 163–65
   new immigrants, 352,
      353, 358, 363, 365, 378
   settlers, Aboriginal: culture
      and customs, 23, 39;
      demographics, 36–39, 377,
      380; education, 35, 37–38;
      institutions, 37, 38, 39;
      language use, 39; Métis,
      36, 248, 249; migration,
      37; poverty, 37, 38–39;
      urban reserves, 27, 36
   settlers, British: Barr
      colonists, 48; Irish, 68–69;
      new immigrants, 352;
      Quakers, 218; Scots, 66,
      69; Temperance Colony,
      15, 31, 45; Welsh, 72
   settlers, Eastern European:
      Croatians, 229–30;
      Doukhobors, 215,
      218; Hungarians, 222;
      Jews, 233–34; Poles,
      202; Romanians, 225;
      Slovenians, 229–30
   settlers, French: culture,
      284, 301–2; demographics,
      284, 292; education, 284;
      language use, 284, 292;
      population, 284; school-
      language issue, 296–99
   settlers, German: Dutch,
      132; eduation, 141;
      Hutterites, 130; Lutherans,
      114; Mennonites, 121,
      122, 138, 218, 390; new
      immigrants, 147;
      organizations, 147;
      population, 122
   settlers, Nordic, 341–42,
      344, 345, 346; Danes,
      330; Icelanders, 333;
      Norwegians, 344, 345
   settlers, Ukrainian:
      culture, 180, 184, 197–98;
      demographics, 199;
      history, 180; language
      use, 196; religion, 166,
      173, 180, 197–98, 389
   settlers, visible minorities:
      Bhutanese, 363; Blacks,
      361–62; Chileans,
      364; Chinese, 353, 354,
      356–57; Greeks, 367–68;
      Hispanics, 364; Italians,
      369; Latin Americans,
      364; South Asians,
      362–63; Southeast Asians,
      358; Vietnamese, 358
Sasman, 166, 214, 326, 333
Saulteaux (Ojibwa)/
   Nahkawiniwak
   historical background,
      24–25, 27, 29, 240
   language use, 25, 39
   "Oji-Cree" mixing,
      25, 27, 29, 39
   overview, 29
   territory, 24, 25, 27, 30, 31
Saulteaux Reserve, 29
Sawiuk, 164
Scalat, 161
Scandia, 327
Scandinavians. *See*
   Nordic peoples
Sceptre, 93, 94, 95
Schantzenfeld, 122
Schell, 98, 105
Schmidt, 94
Schmidtsburg, 118
Schmidtz farm, 107
Schmidtz Lake, 88
Schneider, 106
Schoenfeld, 122
Schoenwiese, 117, 118
Schonfeld, 118
schools. *See* education
Schroeder, 94
Schuck, 90

INDEX

Schuler, 88
Schuler, Alberta, 93, 94, 101
Schultz, 94
Schutt, 109
Scots, 54–66
   architecture: churches, 57, 60, 62–63; homes, 57, 60–61, 62; stonemasonry, 57, 60, 62, 63, 65
   colonizers, 54, 57–58, 61
   culture and customs, 66
   demographics: population, 54, 65
   ethnic identity, 43, 54
   farms, 55, 60
   heritage and historic sites, 60, 61, 62, 63, 65
   historical background, 54–57, 58–60
   information sources, 75
   language use: Gaelic, 56, 60
   locations, 51, 54–65, 241
   Métis, 33, 54–56, 241, 287
   names: personal, 54–55, 57, 60, 61–62; place, 55, 61, 63, 64–65
   organizations, 66
   religion, 53, 57, 65–66
   settlement patterns, 65, 73
   See also British cultural dominance; English language
Scotsguard, 316, 329
Scott, 90, 91
Scottsburgh, 111
Scottville, 114
Scout Lake, 109, 110, 314
Scrip, 325
Seaforth, 61
Second Osvoborsdennie, 208
Second World War
   anti-German sentiment, 108
   conscription, 145
   settlers: Finns, 346; Germans, 81; Japanese, 355; Mennonites, 124, 145; Nordic peoples, 338–39; Ukrainians, 203
Sederstrom, 316
Sedley, 85, 274

Seifert, 92
Seitz, 84
Selz, 92, 94
Semans, 98
Serath, 97, 98
Serbians, 229, 230
settlements, bloc. *See* bloc settlements
Shackleton, 93, 95
Shamrock, 68, 314
Shannon, 68
Shaunavon, 111, 283, 315, 316, 329
Sheho, 126, 163, 164, 177, 192, 325
Shekinah Retreat Centre, 121
Shell Lake, 114, 322
Shell River, 266
Shell Valley, 223
Shellbrook, 321–22, 339
Sheremata Farm/ Hazel Lake, 171
Shesheep Cree, 27
Shield, 212
Shipman, 178
Shoal Lake Cree, 28
Sibel Plains, 84
Sich, 175, 389
Siczynsky, 171
Sierra Leonese, 361
Sifton, Clifford
   on British settlers, 49, 50, 66
   ethnic group immigration policies: Doukhobors, 208, 210–11; French, 275; Ukrainians, 155–56, 183
   immigration policies, 3–5, 374
   See also homesteading
Sikhs, 362–63
   See also South Asians
Silberfeld, 116, 118
Silton, 96, 98
Silver Grove, 321
Silverwood, 57, 220, 270, 327
Simeonovo, 208
Simmie, 65, 111, 129, 316, 329
Simpson, 321
Singapore, 357, 358
Sinhalese, 362
   See also South Asians

Sinnett, 66–67, 89
Sintaluta, 273
Sion, 333
Sioux/Dakota and Lakota, 30–32
   historical background, 24, 25, 29, 30–31
   information sources, 42
   languages, 25, 30
Sisley, 50
Sisseton Sioux, 30–31
Sjollie, 88
Sjovold Creek, 320
Skala, 171
Skjerdal Park, 312
Skudesnes, 319, 320
Slager, 132
Slavenska, 208
Slavic groups. *See* Eastern Europeans
Slavnoe, 209
Slavyanka, 209
Slawa, 175
Sletter, 333
Sliding Hills, 161, 162–63, 189, 214
Slovaks. *See* Czechs and Slovaks
Slovenians, 229, 230
Smales, 228
Smeaton, 178
Smiley, 130
Smuts, 171, 173, 192, 198–99, 389
Smyrennie, 209
Snake Plain First Nation, 27
Snake/Shoshone people, 23
Snarum, 320
Sniatyn, 171, 173
Snowbird, 116
Snowden, 113
Sochawski, 163
social change
   continuum, 390
   culture and customs, 402
   delocalization and, 387–90
   religion and, 401
   research (1968–72), 390
   social mobility and, 390
   See also assimilation; intermarriage and population mixing;

migration and physical mobility
Sokal, 171, 172, 175
Sokhalom, 219
Solmond, 88
Solverson Creek, 314
Somalis, 361
Sommerfelder Mennonites. *See* Chortitzer Mennonite Conference
Sonnenfeld Colony, 231–32
Soo rail line (CPR), 7, 106, 107, 200, 311–13
Sopoff, 168
Sordahl, 329
Souchez, 242
Souris Valley/Val-Souris, 179, 274–75
South Africans, 332, 352, 361
South Americans. *See* Latin Americans
South Asians, 362–63
   culture and customs, 362
   demographics, 362
   information sources, 371
   language use, 362
   new immigrants, 352
   religions, 363
   urban locations, 362–63
South Battleford. *See* Battlefords area
South Colony, 208–9
South Dakota, as origin of settlers
   settlers: French, 283; Germans, 78, 86, 90, 96, 115, 127, 129; Hutterites, 129, 140; Norwegians, 309, 311, 318
South Fork, 283
South Koreans. *See* Koreans
South Qu'Appelle, 274
South Russia (Ukraine), as origin of settlers
   historical background, 78–80, 115
   information sources, 148–49
   settlers: Doukhobors, 207; Germans, 78, 83, 84, 90, 96, 98, 101, 116; Hutterites, 128; Mennonites, 16, 77, 115, 116, 117–18, 122, 134
South Tyrol, 128
South Valley, 323
Southeast Asians, 358
   information sources, 370
   population, 358
   See also Filipinos
Southey, 97, 98, 320, 329
Sovereign, 130
Spalding, 86, 87, 88, 258, 261, 324, 326
Spanish language, 364
Sparling's Coulee, 68
Spaskoe, 209
Spasofka, 212
Speers, 51, 114, 124, 175, 176
Speier, 84
Spenst, 122
Speyer, 93, 94, 95
Spiritwood, 175, 266–67
Spokoene Zaleev, 208
Spooner, 113
Spring Creek, 129, 319, 320
Spring Lake, 129
Spring Valley, 109, 110
Springfield, 118, 122, 130
Springside, 100, 164
Springwater, 91, 125, 130
Spruce Home, 259, 322
Spy Hill, 334
Spyridge, 91
Sri Lankans, 362
   See also South Asians
Stadnyk, 163
Stahl, 94
Stalwart, 98
Standard Hill, 111–12
Standing Buffalo Reserve, 31–32
Stanley, 46, 165
Stanley Mission, 26
Stanyslavtsi/Stanisloff, 169
Star Blanket Cree, 27
Star City, 130, 323, 325
Stawchan/Stavchany, 161
Steele, 144
Steelman, 105
Steinreich, 118
Stenen, 168, 201, 325
Stobard, 253
Stockholm, 219, 327
Stone, 111
Stonehenge, 278
Stoneside, 316
Stoney Creek, 49, 329
Stoney Lake, 120, 121
Stoneys (Alberta), 29
Stoneys (Battleford), 30
Stony Creek, 208
Stony Hill, 116
Stony Lake Reserve, 32
Stony Rapids Reserve, 32
Stornoway, 59–60, 100, 161, 201
Storthoaks, 271–72, 280
Stoughton, 52, 67, 105, 106, 273
Stove Creek, 167
Stradaevka, 208
Strand, 326
Strasbourg, 15, 96, 98
Strawberry Valley, 114
Stringer, 50
Strong, 320
Strong Pine, 178
Strongfield, 227, 319, 320
Struthers Lake, 258
Stryj, 99, 165
Stuckel, 88
Stump Lake, 266, 322
Stundists. *See* Russian Baptists
Sturgeon Lake Reserve, 28, 259
Sturgeon Weir, 26
Sturgis, 167, 168, 201, 325, 326
Sudanese, 352, 361, 378
Sudetenland Germans, 105, 147, 227
Sudom, 108, 109
Suedflus, 117, 118
Summerberry, 51, 107
Sunlight, 89
Sunny Brae, 326
Sunny Valley, 318, 320
Sunnydale, 130
Sunrise, 320
Superb, 91, 125
Surprise Valley, 315
Survivance, 279
Sutton, 277
Svoboda, 171
Swabians, Danube, 97, 102, 107–9, 150
Swampy Cree. *See* Cree/Nehiyawewin
Swan Plain, 167, 168

Swan River Valley, 208, 209
Swanson, 319
Swarthmore, 47
Swea, 327
Swedes, 327–30
   assimilation, 338
   colonizers, 4
   culture and customs, 344, 345
   demographics: depopulation, 388; population, 219, 310, 330
   ethnic group mixing, 219, 310, 327, 328, 329, 334, 341, 388
   ethnic identity, 310, 335, 338
   heritage and historic sites, 327, 328, 329, 330
   historical background, 15–16, 78, 310, 336, 339
   information sources, 348–49
   intermarriage, 341, 393
   language use, 330, 340
   locations, 97, 219, 320–22, 324, 327–30, 332, 334, 338, 341–42
   religion, 310, 327, 341–43, 388
   settlement patterns, 11, 310, 313
   urbanization, 310
   See also Nordic peoples; Swedish Finns
Swedish Finns
   education, 341
   ethnic identity, 341
   historical background, 336, 341
   intermarriage, 341
   language use, 335, 336, 338, 340–42
   locations, 329, 332, 338
   names, 336
   population, 335, 336
   religion, 341
   See also Nordic peoples
Sweetgrass First Nation, 28
Swift Current
   demographics: in-migration, 379; population, 123

settlers: Chinese, 256; French, 286; Germans, 147; Hutterites, 129; Irish, 68; Jews, 234; Lebanese/Syrians, 365, 366; Mennonites, 16, 83, 122–24, 128, 136–37, 147, 390; Norwegians, 316; Ukrainians, 179
Swiss
   colonizers, 4, 250
   historical background, 286, 287, 288
   locations, 107, 253, 268, 276
   population, 81, 287
Swystun Bay, 175
Syke's Farm, 122
Syrians. *See* Lebanese and Syrians
Szekelyfold, 221, 223

T

Tabor, 227
Tadei Lake, 116
Tadmore, 167
Taiwanese, 355, 357
Talle-de-Saules/Willow Bunch, 16, 242, 266, 277–78, 302, 314
Tallman, 210, 264
Tambofka village, 210, 212, 215
Tamils, 362
   See also South Asians
Tantallon, 47, 334, 336
Taras, 177
Tarnopol, 171, 173, 174, 193, 200
Techomeernoe, 208
Techomeerovka, 208
Tecumseh, 273
Temesvar, 222
Temperance Colony, 15, 31, 45
Terpennie, 208, 209
Tessier, 111, 268
Thackery, 91
Thais, 358
Theodore, 163, 164, 192, 330
Theresa, 279
Thickwood Hills, 28, 124
Thiel-Krentz, 89
Thingvalla-Logberg Colony, 334

Thistledale, 124
Thompson Valley, 316
Thorndale, 91
Three Lakes, 221, 258
Thunder Creek, 179
Thunder Hill Colony, 208, 210, 214
Thunderchild Reserve, 28
Tiefengrund, 116, 121
Tiger Hills, 323
Tilly, 258
Tiny, 166, 201
Tipperary, 61
Tisdale, 234, 325, 329
Titanic, 251, 254, 255
Togo, 100
Tollefson's Hill, 321
Tolstoy, Leo, 208
Tomboscoe, 208
Tomman Lake, 175
Tompkins, 129, 316
Toporiwtzi/St. Elia, 161
Toporoutz/Toporivtsi/Chaucer, 161
Torch River, 178
Torhovytsia/Torhowycia, 171
Torkelson farm, 312
Tornea, 329, 332, 338
Torondal, 97, 108
Toronto, Ontario
   new immigrants, 222, 351, 361
Torquay, 106, 312
Torsk, 161
Totzke, 88
Touchwood, 221, 223
Touchwood Hills, 27, 29, 165, 221, 242, 243
Trafalgar, 50
Tramping Lake, 89, 90, 91
Transylvania, as origin of settlers
   settlers: Germans, 78, 107; Hutterites, 9, 128–29, 146; Romanians, 222, 225, 226
Trepannia, 171
Tribune, 106, 179, 312
Trinidadians, 361
Trinity/Troitzkaja, 209, 212, 216
Troitska/Razbegallovo, 209

Troitzkaja/Trinity, 209, 212, 216
Troitzkoe, 208
Trojan, 171
Troodeloobevoe, 208
Trossachs, 63
Truax, 109, 127
Trusdennie, 208
Tuffnell, 163, 164, 169, 332, 333
Tugaske, 123
Tulcea/Tulscha, New, 100
Tullymet, 60, 165
Tummel, 59
Tunstall, 94
Turks, 367
Turnhill, 123
Turnor Lake, 32
Turtle Lake area, 114, 338
Turtle River, 132, 263
Turtleford, 338
Tway, 171, 172, 174, 192, 257, 387
Twin Lakes, 114
Twin Valley, 278
Tynder, 111

U

Ugandans, 361
Uhriniw, 175, 388–89
Ukraine. *See* South Russia (Ukraine), as origin of settlers
Ukrainians, 155–99
  anti-Ukrainian sentiment, 156, 183, 195, 203
  architecture: churches, 156, 162, 169, 172–73, 190, 193; homes, 192
  colonizers, 8, 155–56, 203
  culture and customs: alphabet, 181; clothing and crafts, 192–93, 195; food and entertainment, 184–85, 192, 193; holidays, 169; museums, 193, 197–98
  demographics: arrivals, 156; depopulation, 164, 168, 174, 176–77, 179, 198–99; new immigrants, 353; population, 169, 186, 190, 203–4; population trends, 170, 199
  diversity, 160
  education, 171, 194–97, 295; school-language issue, 171, 194–96, 295
  ethnic group mixing, 169–70, 173–74, 176, 179, 181, 182, 195
  ethnic identity: census data, 186–88; citizenship adoption, 183; development of, 181; and language use, 396–98, 404; nationalism, 181, 182–83, 189, 195, 196, 197; preservation, 181–85, 395, 399, 403–4; regional origin identities, 13, 181–82; trends, 203–4
  heritage and historic sites, 161, 162, 163, 167, 169, 172, 173, 176
  historical background: "enemy aliens" in WWI, 203; overview, 155–57, 181–83; religion, 181–82, 188–91; settlements, 15–16
  information sources, 160, 204–6
  intermarriage, 187, 190, 191, 203–4, 391–92
  language use: anglicization, 187–88; dialects, 160, 186, 187, 199; diversity, 160; and ethnic identity, 396–98; literacy support, 185–86; school-language issue, 171, 194–96, 295; trends, 186–87, 202, 397
  locations: east-central, 161–70; Fish Creek, 170–74; Garden River, 177–78; north-central, 170–74; Redberry, 174–77; southern, 178–79; Willow Creek, 177; Yellow Creek, 170–74; Yorkton and Canora, 161–70
  media, 198
  names: anglicization, 187–88, 398–99; personal names, 168, 187–88; place names, 194
  new immigrants, 199, 203
  organizations, 184–85, 194–98
  physical mobility, 386
  research (1968–72), 184–87, 190–92, 199, 386, 391–92, 395, 397–98, 403–4
  settlement patterns: bloc settlements, 156–57, 169–70; chain migration, 8; expansion, 11, 170, 173, 174; religious affiliations, 188, 203
  settlement stories, 157–59
  urbanization, 179–80, 184–85, 199, 203–4
  See also Galicia, as origin of settlers; South Russia (Ukraine)
Ukrainians, religion
  culture and customs, 191–93, 196–98
  demographic trends, 189–90
  depopulation and church closures, 388–89
  ethnic identity, 395, 403–4
  historical background, 181–82, 188–91
  intermarriage, 190, 191, 199, 391–92
  language use, 196–97, 397–98
  organizations and associations, 196–97
  Protestant relations, 189
  research (1968–72), 184, 190–92, 395, 397–98, 401, 403–4
  rivalries, 188–89, 404
  Roman Catholics (Western Rites): intermarriage, 199; Polish and Ukrainian affiliations, 181–82, 202–3; rivalries, 189, 195
  settlement by affiliation, 188
  shared church buildings, 189
  Ukrainian Catholics: church attendance, 190–91, 401; ethnic

identity, 160, 184;
  intermarriage, 391–92
Ukrainian Orthodox
  (Eastern Rites): church
  attendance, 190–91, 401;
  church closures, 389;
  ethnic identity, 160,
  184; locations, 188–89;
  organizations, 197
Ulmer, 102
Ulrich, 90
Uneeda, 321
United Kingdom. *See* British
United States
  Anglo-conformity, 405–6
  land survey system, 7
  "melting-pot" attitudes,
    2–3, 9, 408
  new immigrants from, 352
  preferred status for
    immigrants from, 4–5
United States, as origin
  of settlers
  settlers: Aboriginals,
    29, 31; Bhutanese,
    363; Blacks, 359–61;
    British, 44; Dutch, 131;
    Finns, 335; French,
    261, 265, 275, 286–87;
    Germans, 78, 79, 92, 96,
    110, 113; Hungarians,
    219; Hutterites, 129;
    Jews, 233; Lebanese,
    366; Mennonites, 116,
    122; Nordic peoples,
    309, 318, 338, 339, 345;
    Romanians, 224, 225;
    Scots, 61–62; Ukrainians,
    155; Welsh, 69
  See also specific states
Unity, 90, 91
urban areas
  definitions: city, 12; urban
    community, 385
  demographics:
    intraprovincial
    migration, 376–77,
    379; non-urban
    proportion, 377;
    population, 12, 382–83
  intermarriage, 394
  new immigrants, 353

overview, 382–83
poverty, 38, 380
visible minorities, 353, 380
See also Regina; Saskatoon
Ursulines (Order of St.
  Ursula), 83, 84, 87,
  93, 103, 146, 388
Usborne, 67
Usherville, 167
Uspenska, 162
Uxbridge, 283
Uzelman, 92

V

Val-Marie, 280, 282
Val-Qu'Appelle. *See*
  Qu'Appelle Valley/
  Val-Qu'Appelle
Val-Souris/Souris River
  Valley, 274–75
Valbrand, 322
Valence, 276
Vallar-byggd, 334
Vallée-Ste-Claire, 281–82
Valley Centre, 130
Valley Plain, 64
Valroy, 283
Vancouver, British Columbia
  settlers: Doukhobors, 214;
    Mennonites, 122; new
    immigrants, 351, 377
Vandura, 270
Vanguard, 110, 129,
  280–81, 316
Vanscoy, 317
Vatnabyggd, 332
Vatnasofnudar, 332
Vawn, 263
Veillardville, 260–61
Venice, 144
Vera, 208
Verboska, 161
Verchères, 261
Veregin, 208, 209, 210,
  212, 214, 217
Verenczanka, 161
Verndale, 87, 88
Verovka, 208
Verulam, 92
Verwood, 109, 277, 314
Vesna, 168

Vibank, 84, 85
Viceroy, 314
Victoire, 266
Vidora, 315–16
Vier Lake, 88–89
Vietnamese, 358
Viking, 323
Villefranche, 278
Villeroy, 275
Vindictive, 276
Violette, 274
Virtue, 144
Viscount, 113, 222, 320, 329
visible minorities
  demographics: birth rates,
    376; child poverty, 380;
    European/non-European
    origin, 377–78; growth
    rate, 380; population
    proportion, 355, 380;
    urban areas, 353, 355, 380
  diversity, 355
  terminology, 18, 355
  See also Blacks; Chinese;
    Greeks; Italians;
    Japanese; Koreans; Latin
    Americans; Middle
    Eastern peoples; South
    Asians; Southeast Asians
Vladimir, 171
Vogel, 110
Volga Germans, 83,
  99–100, 110, 112, 113
Volhynia, as origin of settlers
  dialects, 108, 160
  settlers: Czechs, 227;
    Germans, 78, 80, 92,
    99, 100, 102, 106, 107,
    114; Mennonites, 117,
    121; Ukrainians, 160,
    161, 168, 182, 188
Voll, 111
Vonda
  heritage sites, 256
  historical background,
    198, 256
  language use, 185, 387
  population, 174, 198, 257
  school consolidation,
    387–88
  school-language issue,
    293, 295, 297

settlers: Belgians, 256;
    French, 171, 256–57, 293,
    295, 297, 387; Poles, 171,
    185; Ukrainians, 171,
    172, 174, 183, 185, 198
Voskrisennie, 208
Vosnisennie, 208
Vossen Lake, 88
Voszennie, 208
Vozvyshenie, 208

W

Wabash, 105
Wadena
    CNR line, 165
    population, 333
    settlers: Icelanders, 170,
        332, 334; Nordic peoples,
        170, 324, 325, 329–30, 333,
        334; Poles, 201; Russians,
        214; Ukrainians,
        166–67, 168, 170
Wahpeton First Nation, 30–32
Waitville, 323
Wakaw
    population, 88, 173, 174, 221
    settlement patterns,
        11, 173–74
    settlers: British, 195, 405–6;
        Danube Swabians,
        108; Germans, 88, 195;
        Hungarians, 108, 195,
        220, 221, 398; Poles,
        173; Ukrainians,
        171–73, 189, 195, 389
Wakaw Lake, 171, 174
Walawa, 163
Waldeck, 122, 123, 129, 329
Waldheim
    demographics, 121
    language use, 144
    settlers: Germans,
        121; Hutterites, 129;
        Mennonites, 117, 118,
        119, 121, 144, 400
Waldron, 71, 103, 104, 326
Waldsee, 88
Waler, 326
Wales. See Welsh
Walhalla, 332
Wallace, 60, 161

Wallard, 281
Wallenstein, 97
Walloon, 132, 287
Walpole, 57
Walter Scott, 124
Walz, 92
Wanuskewin Heritage
    Park, 23, 39
Wapella, 46, 52, 57, 65, 107, 231
War End/Horosziwci, 163
Warington, 92
Warman
    population, 121
    settlers: German Lutherans,
        121; Mennonites, 116,
        117, 118, 119, 120, 144,
        147, 390, 400–401
Waseca, 50, 125
Wasileff, 163
Wasyl Kurish homestead, 175
Wasyliw, 166
Waterbury, 114
Waterhen Lake Reserve, 28
Waterhen Marsh, 258
Waterloo, 125
Watrous, 112, 125, 320
Watson, 86, 88, 168, 169, 388
Wauchope, 132, 271–72, 328
Waverley, 279
Wawken, 57, 220, 270
Wawota, 107, 270
Webb, 129
Weekes, 168
Weicker Lake, 109
Weirdale, 177, 178
Weissenburg, 102
Weldon, 323, 324, 342
Welechko/Bilya-Velechka, 175
Wellington, 179, 200
Welsh, 69–73
    demographics:
        population, 54, 72
        ethnic identity, 43, 54, 72–73
        historical background,
            15, 69, 70–71
        information sources, 76
        language use, 70, 71
        locations, 69, 71–73
        names, 71, 72
        Patigonian colony, 69–72
        religion, 71–72

settlement patterns,
    69, 72–73
See also British
    cultural dominance;
    English language
Welwyn, 57
Wergeland, 325
West Bench, 129
West Bend, 168, 169
West Finn, 337
West Indian origin, 361
West Prairie, 316
West-Sidel, 332
Westbrook, 163
Westerheim, 94, 314
Westerlund, 330
Western Woodland Cree. See
    Cree/Nehiyawewin
Westlea, 60
Wexford, 68
Weyburn
    in-migration, 379
    settlers: Belgians, 132, 275;
        British, 51; Germans, 106;
        Jews, 234; Ukrainians
        and Poles, 179, 200
    Soo rail line, 200, 311
Wheatheart, 114
Wheatland, 130
Wheatwyn, 97
Whiska Creek, 281
White Bear, 317
White Bear Reserve,
    27, 29, 30, 31
White City, 85
White Eagle, 104
White Star area, 259–60
White Valley, 283
Whitebeech, 168
Whitebeech Creek, 208
Whiteberry, 175, 264
Whitecap First Nation,
    30, 31–32
Whitehawk, 325
Whitesand, 162, 325
Whitesand-Pakrov, 162
Whitesand River, 209
Whitewood, 52, 63, 107,
    221, 268–70, 336, 337
Whitkow, 13, 175, 176, 199
Wilcox, 63, 315
Wilfred, 88

Wilkie, 90, 91
Willmar, 105
Willmont, 86, 88, 89
Willow Bunch Lake, 63
Willow Bunch/Talle-de-Saules, 16, 242, 266, 277–78, 302, 314
Willow Cree Reserve, 27
Willow Creek, 177, 323
Willow Park, 130
Willowbrook, 164
Willowdale, 270, 327, 337
Wilton, 50
Wimmer, 88, 168, 169
Windermere, 323
Windthorst, 107
Wingard, 120, 121, 331
Winona, 317
Wirral, 50
Wisconsin, as origin of settlers
　settlers: Dutch, 132; French, 259; Germans, 86; Norwegians, 315, 318
Wise Creek, 281, 316
Wishart, 126, 168, 169, 201, 203
Witchekan, 266
Witchekan Lake Cree, 28
Wolendale, 315
Wolia, 175
Wolkowetz, 163
Wollerman, 92
Wolna, 166
Wolseley, 51, 62, 83, 273
Wolverine, 67, 171, 172, 222
Wolverine Lake, 323
women and men. *See* gender
Wood End Post, 242
Wood Hill, 114
Wood Mountain area
　settlers: Aboriginals, 27, 30–31; French, 278–79; Métis, 242, 243; Norwegians and Swedes, 313, 314, 328; Romanians, 223, 225, 279
Wood Mountain Reserve, 30–31, 32
Wood River/Rivière-la-Vieille, 275, 276, 277
Woodley, 105
Woodrow, 123, 127, 277

Woods Cree. *See* Cree/Nehiyawewin
Wordsworth, 105
World War I. *See* First World War
World War II. *See* Second World War
Wrench Lake, 120
Wroxton, 161, 195
Wurtzburg, 129, 144
Wyle, 283
Wymark, 122–23
Wynyard, 66, 125, 126, 169, 170, 234, 332, 333
Wysla, 162

Y

Yarbo, 219, 227
Yellow Creek, 170–74
　depopulation, 174
　research (1968–72), 184
　settlers, other: British, 171; Hungarians, 221; Poles, 171
　settlers, Ukrainian, 170–74; demographics, 173; education, 171, 194, 195; ethnic identity, 184; language use, 171, 185–87, 194; religion, 172, 173, 174, 184; settlement, 171–74
Yellow Grass, 106
Yellow Quill First Nation, 29
Yorkton
　CPR lines, 163
　demographics: in-migration, 379; population, 161, 169
　historical background, 46–47, 51
　settlers, other: Aboriginals, 36; British, 46–47; Doukhobors, 51, 209, 217; Dutch, 131; Germans, 100, 188; Hungarians, 220; Jews, 234; Poles, 161, 169; Romanians, 222
　settlers, Ukrainian: colonizers, 51; language use, 188; population, 161, 169, 199; religion, 180, 225; settlement patterns, 100, 164
Young, 112, 320, 329
Yugoslavs
　information sources, 237
　locations, 229
　new immigrants, 352, 378
　population, 230, 234
　settlement patterns, 234
　See also Croatians and Yugoslavs

Z

Zalischyky, 168, 171, 196
Zambians, 361
Zamok, 178
Zangwill, 112, 232
Zaporozhe, 174
Zazula, 166
Zehner, 101
Zelma, 112, 331
Zeneta, 219
Zenon Park/Zénon-Parc, 261–62, 302
Zentner, 111
Zhoda, 162
Zichydorf, 107–8
Zid, 227
Ziegler Coulee, 111
Zimbabweans, 361
Zimmer, 92
Zoller Lake, 92
Zoria, 175
Zorn, 99
Zorra, 59
Zypchen, 175

About the Author

ALAN ANDERSON is Professor Emeritus in the Department of Sociology and Research Fellow in Ethnic and Indigenous Studies in the Department of Political Studies, University of Saskatchewan, and was a Research Fellow of the Canadian Plains Research Center, University of Regina. He has been president of the Canadian Ethnic Studies Association and vice-president of the Central and East European Studies Association of Canada, and an associate editor of *Canadian Studies in Population*. The author of many publications on Saskatchewan ethnic groups and settlements, spanning four decades, he authored the ethnic settlements section of the *Atlas of Saskatchewan* (1999) and was the contributing editor for population and settlements in the *Encyclopedia of Saskatchewan* (2005).